DATE DUE			

VIKING REPRINT EDITIONS

Antonina Vallentin

Mirabeau

TRANSLATED BY E. W. DICKES

AUGUSTUS M. KELLEY • PUBLISHERS
CLIFTON 1973

First Published 1948
(New York: The Viking Press, Inc.)
Copyright 1948 by The Viking Press, Inc.

RE-ISSUED 1973 BY

AUGUSTUS M. KELLEY · PUBLISHERS

Clifton New Jersey 07012

By Arrangement with THE VIKING PRESS

Library of Congress Cataloging in Publication Data

Vallentin, Antonina, 1893-1957.
   Mirabeau.

   (Viking reprint editions)
   A translation of the author's works: Mirabeau avant
la Révolution and Mirabeau dans la Révolution.
   Reprint of the ed. published by Viking Press,
New York.
   Bibliography: p.
   1. Mirabeau, Honoré Gabriel Riquetti, comte de,
1749-1791.   I.   Title.
DC146.M7V2715   944.04'1'0924 [B]   70-122070
ISBN 0-678-03173-8

PRINTED IN THE UNITED STATES OF AMERICA
by SENTRY PRESS, NEW YORK, N. Y. 10013

Contents

List of Illustrations

(Illustrations follow page 306)

Mirabeau at the time of the French Revolution

L'Ami des Hommes, Mirabeau's father

Le Bailli, Mirabeau's uncle

Sophie de Monnier

Costumes of the Three Orders of the States General, 1789

Mirabeau presiding at the Jacobin Club

Louis XVI and Marie Antoinette on a Paris street during the Revolution

The National Assembly taking the "Oath of the Tennis Court"

The Storming of the Bastille

Mirabeau's funeral

>> <<<<<<<<<<<<<<<<<<<<<<<<<<<<<<<<<<<<<<<<<<<

Book One

Before the Revolution

The Tempestuous Race

"I HAVE often said that if this eldest boy had not come into the world at a place where there were no visitors, I should have believed him to be a bastard."

From his earliest years Gabriel de Mirabeau's life was overshadowed by his father's malevolence. All that was perverse in the Comte de Mirabeau, all his extravagance in revolt, his reckless pursuit of his aims in precocious self-confidence, the sullen obduracy that took pleasure in providing justification for the mistrust that surrounded him, all this may be traced back to that poisoned source in his childhood. The father's bitterness reproached young Mirabeau, almost from birth, as *un enfant mal né*—a low-class child. His first uncertain steps in life were made under the critical eyes of his father, who could not see in him the physical and moral imprint of what he called "the tempestuous race."

2

Family pride was the master passion of Victor, Marquis de Mirabeau. From his youth his aim had been to make the Provençal family one of the great houses of France. His one purpose was to work for its future glory; he did not hesitate to heighten its past lustre—even at the cost of some distortions of the truth.

The Riqueti family possessed no record of its ancestry before the sixteenth century; at all events, none that was credibly documented. A certain Jehan Riquety, also called Riquet, came one day from Digne to establish himself at Marseille. He claimed to be of Italian descent, and to be a noble. According to the family traditions he had the pride that could put up a fierce and spirited defence against any who belittled his avocation. He seems to have given a sharp reply to a bishop's chaff:

"As for being a trader (which is no disgrace to anyone, since our kings have even asked the nobility to take an interest in the commerce

3

of this city), I am or was a seller of law and order as Monseigneur is a seller of holy water."

He had also the firmness in action that could establish his authority in difficult times. He was elected chief consul of Marseille, and repressed a rising organized by the Protestants, saving the city for King Charles IX, who rewarded him by the grant of extensive landed properties. This first known ancestor very soon showed himself a worthy founder of a distinguished house. He allied himself by marriage with one of the great families of Provence, the Glandèves.

Jehan or Jean Riqueti succeeded so well that it was he who endowed the house with the title with which it was to pass into history. He bought the castle of Mirabeau. From it he took the name which until then had been borne by the Barras family, becoming the Seigneur de Mirabeau. But the old nobility were on the watch for encroachments upon their rights. They claimed that as a commoner Jean Riqueti, on becoming the holder of estates of the nobility, must pay the dues for frank fees. During the proceedings brought against him he alleged that he possessed titles of nobility inherited from Italian ancestors, but he seems to have been ill-informed about them, for he produced no details of his family or of the place of its origin. Witnesses deposed, however, that they had often been told by their elders that people named Riqueti, from Italy, had lived in the town of La Seyne, and their evidence induced the commissioners to decide in his favor.

The Italian ancestors whom the grandsons of Jean Riqueti succeeded in tracing were, according to them, the Ariqueti family of Florence. Strictly conscientious genealogists later charged the family with falsifying a document brought forward in support of its claims, changing the name Arigucci into Ariqueti. Out of a more or less engineered confusion there emerged a remote ancestor Pierre Ariqueti, described by those who first discovered him as a Guelph noble. Victor de Mirabeau turned him into a Ghibelline.

Always spurred on by his pride of nobility, he tried to bring precision into the vagueness of the family origins. "From time to time," he wrote in his memoirs, "I brought from Florence all the books cited, and extracts from public documents." But his love for his house got the better of his conscientiousness as historian. He omitted to bring supporting evidence, but he declared with plenty of assurance that when the Guelphs triumphed "the whole family of the *Gibelin* Arrighetti was expelled from Florence." Relying on a record of the marriage of Catherine de Fossis to one of the first Riquetis whom he succeeded in tracing in France, he added the further detail that the first Arrighetti who established himself in France, in the thirteenth century, "had espoused that Sibylle de Fos, of the house of the counts of Provence, whose talents and beauty were sung by so many troubadours."

When Victor de Mirabeau wrote of his family he indulged in romance for lack of self-knowledge. He thought he saw himself in his ancestors—they figured as political outlaws, proud and indomitable, taking the road to exile. "It has been proved," he wrote, "that the Arrighettis arrived in Provence with the titles and the spirit of the nobility of their day." In his search through documents of that early time he discovered that a Signorina Arrighetti (or Arigucci, according to the genealogists) had espoused a Medici, and he declared on one occasion, in the presence of a hundred persons assembled in the residence of the governor of his province, that "in all the history of the house of Mirabeau there has only been a single misalliance—with the Medicis."

3

But if this Italian descent and the remote aristocratic origin are more or less open to doubt, there is no doubt about the prosperity of the first known Riqueti. Jean Riqueti founded at Marseille a firm that dealt in coral. He also started the manufacture of scarlet cloth. Altogether, he did "very good business."

But the Riquetis were not content with just looking for lucrative business. They strengthened their family by brilliant marriages, by alliances with the most illustrious Provençal families. While exuberance came to them from the Glandèves, hot-headed arrogance was an inheritance from the Pontèves. The marquis accumulated and treasured the records of the fits of haughtiness of Anne de Pontèves, wife of Thomas de Riqueti, a grandson of Jean. In her there survived the purest spirit of feudalism, in an age whose slackness she deplored. "You men," she wrote to her nephew, "are diminutives of men. We, in our time, carried pistols in our belts, and we knew how to use them." Anne de Pontèves could make just as good use of her tongue as of a firearm; and no less deeply implanted than her family pride was her sense of being a woman of virtue. One day at church, at the holy water basin, she met a lady of unfortunate reputation and pushed her aside, giving her a resounding box on the ear. "Here," she exclaimed, "as in the army, the baggage comes last."

Her descendants were to inherit her hastiness and her capacity for caustic comment.

4

Over the difficult childhood of Mirabeau there hung, magnificent and overpowering, the memory of the man who had become a legend in his lifetime, the child's redoubtable grandfather. Jean-Antoine de Mirabeau was typical of the over-proclaimed hero. On the strength of that reputation he permitted himself any sort of extravagance. He was a born soldier, combining reckless bravery in action with the gift of leadership, constancy in misfortune and calmness in the face of peril with the most exacting demands on his troops and on himself. The most critical day in his life, the day that was his title to glory, was that of the engagement at Cassano. He had been ordered to stop the Imperial troops at a bridge. He gave the order to his soldiers to lie flat on the ground. He alone stood, a man of enormous height, contemptuously offering an absurdly easy target. A shot broke his right arm; he bandaged it with a handkerchief, seized an axe with his left arm, and faced the oncomers. A second shot went through his throat. With the jugular vein and the nerves of the neck severed, he collapsed. The regiment, terrified, took to flight. The whole army of Prince Eugène, cavalry and infantry, passed over him. When the bodies of the dead on the bridge were picked up, his tallness, and the sumptuous clothes it was his habit to wear in action, attracted notice. He was still breathing. Prince Eugène had him brought into the camp of the Duc de Vendôme. His body was one mass of wounds, his head half off his shoulders. A celebrated surgeon was moved at the sight of that tenacious vitality in a mutilated body. He worked hard to save him. Jean-Antoine de Mirabeau came back to life, covered with scars, his neck held in place by a silver collar which his cravat could not entirely cover. He had the feeling of having returned from the beyond. He spoke of the engagement at Cassano as a ghost might, as "that day when I was killed."

He was deeply pious, with an ecstatic faith that could seek to compel a miracle. One day, when one of his woods was on fire, he had the Holy Sacrament carried past the fire, and swore that he had seen the flames recoil. But his sense of duty was stronger even than his religious feeling. In the course of his campaigns in Italy, he learned one day that deserters from his regiment had taken refuge in a monastery. The monks claimed the right of asylum for the men and barred his way. He had the doors broken open. The abbot stood on the threshold, in his priestly robes, swinging the Sacrament in front of the intruder. Colonel de Mirabeau shouted to his major in his stentorian voice, "Dauphin, send for the regimental chaplain to come and take God out of the hands of this ass."

Jean-Antoine de Mirabeau was formidable in his impatience with human stupidity. Gabriel de Mirabeau was to inherit this trait; he used to say: "Nothing tries the patience like stupidity, but nothing is more stupid than that impatience." At the same time he liked to repeat his grandfather's maxim that "patience is the virtue of cuckolds and donkeys."

Jean-Antoine carried this offensive independence even into the insipid atmosphere of Versailles. The Duc de Vendôme had taken to court this valiant soldier who, with all his exploits and his mutilations, had never got beyond the rank of colonel. But there was nothing of the petitioner about Jean-Antoine de Mirabeau. He grumbled in the face of the stupefied Louis XIV: "If on leaving the colours I had come to fool about at court, I should have got my promotion and fewer wounds." Vendôme hurriedly took him away from the royal presence. "I ought to have known you by now. Henceforth I shall present you to the enemy, but never again to the king."

The eccentricities of Jean-Antoine de Mirabeau had endowed the family with a peculiar notoriety. "Thanks to him and to my great uncle," wrote Victor de Mirabeau, "when I entered the world our name was of no less repute for marked peculiarities than that of Roquelaure for witticisms, with the difference that this repute was of the sort that inspires respect and warns off rogues."

5

Tall and maimed, with a rigid neck, he was a dead man resuscitated. His peasants called him *"Col d'argent"*—Silverneck. His right arm was in a sling. He had always been impetuous, and after his encounter with death he became a man of fixed convictions and prejudices. He was forty-two years old, taking the waters at Digne, when he met a young girl, Françoise de Castellane Norante, only twenty-three years old. She was a tall, magnificent blonde, with clear blue eyes and a brilliant complexion. Jean Mirabeau proposed to her without the knowledge of her parents. He wanted her without a dowry, for herself, but also free of all restrictions, for himself alone. Françoise de Castellane could yield to none but a man who demanded everything, even the impossible, from her. "He wanted her not only to have no dowry," writes his son, ". . . but not even to bring her underclothing, and to be dressed only in clothes, which he had had made for her; and Mme. de Castellane, her mother, was never to set foot in her daughter's home. . . . He intended to be master in his own house."

Jean-Antoine de Mirabeau did, in fact, like a bird of prey, carry off his young and beautiful wife to his cliff-top Provençal castle. Parisian scandal-mongers spread the story that he had shut her up in his château until she had given him three male children. In reality this unequal marriage had every appearance of being a happy one. They had seven children, six boys and a girl. Only three boys survived. Age did not soften Silverneck's obstinate rigidity. He declared on his deathbed: "All my life, when I have said *no*, I have meant *no*."

Jean-Antoine died at seventy. "It was my mother who kept him alive," his son wrote. Always exacting, severe, methodical, this virtuous and passionately austere woman energetically imposed on her family the law of her own conscience. She long preserved her clearness and strength of mind and her indomitable vitality. She was seventy-five years old when her youngest son wrote: "She expresses herself with an energy that makes the half-men of these times tremble."

The children of Jean-Antoine were born and grew up in an atmosphere of terror. If the surroundings the tall old man liked were heroic, they were also glacial. Sensitiveness was a weakness, tenderness a shortcoming; indeed, more than a shortcoming, a piece of bad taste. The two first children of Jean-Antoine died at an early age. The parents shut themselves up in their home with their violent grief. They did not show themselves until they had succeeded in regaining composure. No visitor ever found them other than haughty—of magnificent and inhuman serenity.

Victor de Mirabeau, Gabriel's father, was born in 1715, the third of their children. He withstood the test of contact with that redoubtable father. The father's worship of his son was equalled only by the fear he inspired in him. This heir so long looked forward to, this son who survived, the son, moreover, of a man on the verge of the fifties, had no knowledge whatever of his father's secret passion for him, his secret tenderness. Jean-Antoine never ceased to behave as a hero and a Stoic, even in front of a young child. If a scolding was due it had to be written to the boy by his mother. As a grown man the Marquis de Mirabeau wrote: "I had become so used to being frightened by these letters that all through my life I have never been able to open a note from my mother without palpitation of the heart."

The result of this education was, in the marquis' own words, "a distortion of conduct that became second nature to me." The excessively harsh constraint exasperated a youth of spirit. But if Victor de Mirabeau revolted against his parents' austerity, he did so with a bad conscience. He adored his father, he had a passionate love for his mother, he never dreamed of rebelling against their interventions in his life, and still less of escaping from the powerful hold their example had over him. His veneration of them weighed on him more heavily than their severity. Throughout his life he tried to conform to an impossible model. His chaotic character struggled in a mould too vast for it, and too inflexible. As a son of the hero of Cassano, he was attached at thirteen to the regiment of Duras, which his father had long commanded. But he had not the stuff of a soldier in him, and the routine of the profession exasperated the youth in his eagerness for self-expression. His father sent him to Paris to be formed in an academy. But Victor merely took advantage of the pleasures of the capital. He fell in love with an actress. The stern father insisted that this banal liaison be broken off. Meanwhile he cut off supplies: "He left me six months without a sou." In the end the young lover gave way.

The death of his father left him at twenty-two heir to the name and fortune. He was now master of his own fate. As a captain in his father's regiment he went through the war of 1734 and several subsequent campaigns. But he realized that he would never gain distinction in the army, and he wanted above all else to gain distinction. "I am devoured by ambition," he wrote to his friend Vauvenargues when he was twenty-three years old, "but in a strange manner; it is not for honours that I am ambitious, nor for money, nor for favours, but for a name and to be somebody." He felt his natural impetuosity to be a defect. Naturally discursive and garrulous, he took as his model the stoical attitude which he had admired in his childhood. Impressionable but very self-centred, a man of sudden impulses and of violent antipathies, he thought himself inaccessible to the influence of others. He was as self-willed as he was weak, and merely obstinate where he imagined that he was being logical. His aspirations went beyond his natural capacity. His dreams of greatness envisioned immense projects, but he frittered away his energy on meticulous preparations. His brother, the Bailli de Mirabeau, once wrote to him, with the clear vision of deep affection: "You were made to be at the head of a great machine and you have only been at the head of a little one, which you have tried to work like a big one."

With his misjudgment of his character he deceived himself as to his true vocation. He abandoned the profession of arms with the rank of a mere captain and tried to establish influence at Versailles, where a maternal uncle presented him to the king, the queen, and the dauphin. But he did not get on very well in court circles.

His "innate exuberance" revealed itself in desultory literary work. He wrote comedies and tragedies, in prose and in verse, which were no more than an outlet for the effervescence of his verbosity. Montesquieu, who met him when he was in garrison at Bordeaux, said of him, with his Gascon accent: "What energy in that head, and what a pity it can produce nothing but fuss."

One day, when writing to a woman friend for whom he had a deep regard, he exposed in a sentence the secret of his failures: "Providence did not make me the sort that could ever be of use."

6

The good genius of the Marquis de Mirabeau was his younger brother, the one who was known by his judicial title of "Bailli de Mirabeau." The magistrate's nature was as harmonious as his brother's was discordant. Of all the children of Jean-Antoine, he was the best-looking, the most like his mother. He had inherited from the beautiful Françoise de Castellane her fair hair, her limpid blue eyes that looked people straight in the face, her clear skin and bright complexion; and he had his father's stature and robust health. But he resembled his father above all in being cast in a simple mould. He also inherited his father's gift of command and his proud self-assurance and contempt for human follies and weaknesses.

The dreadful constraint of his childhood had driven him, too, to every sort of excess. When he went into the navy—at twelve and a half, straight from the home environment—he went wild at once, like a spring released. His special failing was drunkenness, which made him quarrelsome and irascible. For three or four years, said his elder brother later, he was not out of prison four days in the year. The moment he came out he ran to the brandy bottle and then fell upon anyone in his path, until he was knocked down and carried back to prison.

But suddenly, as though in those years of folly he had exhausted his surplus energy and liberated himself from the torments of his imagination, he "brought himself up short." The poison was eliminated, and he regained his fundamental balance, the governing quality which in his individual style he called "aquanimity." He had the impassiveness to which his brother aspired in vain; he was as sparing in gestures and in words as the marquis was talkative and excitable. As he grew older his self-command assumed the appearance of haughtiness.

Handsome though he was, women played only a small part in his life. The excesses of his youth left him destitute of passion. He was a Knight of Malta from childhood, but took his vows only very late in life, after leaving it to his elder brother to decide whether he should marry or not. His whole life was governed by this deference to his brother.

His lack of imagination made this self-effacement easy for him. "I am only the shirt, you are the skin," he said. His nephew said of him later, "This good man has no fault except his invisible weakness for his brother."

7

Many mothers spoil their youngest child; Françoise de Mirabeau was stricter with her third son than with the two elder ones. It was as though she distrusted his gracefulness and his good looks. Alexandre-Louis' features were over-refined—a little nose slightly rounded, a mouth like the Cupid's bow of an eighteenth-century pastel. His rather effeminate exterior masked a good deal of turbulence. His quick impulses were accompanied by extreme obstinacy and persistence in error.

This he proved by the great sentimental adventure of his life. During a campaign in which he did his duty bravely as a soldier, he happened to meet one of the actresses whom Marshal de Saxe was in the habit of bringing with him for a day's amusement or a night's pleasure. What for one of the young debauchees among his brother-officers would have been at most an expensive pastime became in him a passion. He offered marriage to Mlle. de Navarre, thus hitting his family in its tenderest spot, pride of race. This misalliance produced a scandal even in a society whose morals were loose. His mother, deeply wounded, was implacable; his eldest brother spoke of the "dunghill" he had brought into the family, and used all his influence to get the bridal pair arrested; they had taken refuge in the Papal territory at Avignon. The young woman, who was in childbed, was seized with such terror at the entry of the myrmidons of the law that she died a few days later. Alexandre-Louis was disowned by all his relatives. He was "that Avignon scamp." His career seemed ruined. But he was a Mirabeau. And he was superlatively endowed with one of the family characteristics, an astonishing resilience.

One day the Margrave of Bayreuth and his wife, the witty sister of Frederick II, came to Avignon. They were delighted with the brilliance and charm of the Comte de Mirabeau. They took him with them to Italy, and then to Germany, where he made for himself a new career in the petty court of Bayreuth. He did so with brilliant success. He was appointed grand chamberlain and privy counsellor to the margrave. The day came when he returned to France charged with an important negotiation. His protectress had unlimited confidence in his capacities. At a grave moment when Frederick II was in a desperate situation, alone in face of a coalition of powerful enemies, she recommended her protégé for the purpose of secret negotiations. At that moment the King of Prussia knew that his destiny was at stake. He was ready to kill himself rather than fall into the hands of his enemies. He snatched at any plan that might offer safety. "Do please send this M. de Mirabeau to France," he wrote to his sister. He knew that at that French court favours cost money, and was ready to offer "up to five hundred thousand crowns to the Favourite for peace." Count Alexandre-Louis moved cautiously. For the first time a Mirabeau appeared on the scene of international politics, as a negotiator between Prussia and France. His mission was doomed from the outset to failure. There is no mercy for those whom fortune abandons: a few days later came the victory of Rossbach.

The grand chamberlain of the court of Bayreuth, Frederick the Great's envoy, was no longer a "scamp." When his brothers spoke of him now, they called him "Germanicus." The count returned once more to France as the margrave's envoy to Choiseul. This time his mission was an entire success. Françoise de Mirabeau pardoned him when he redeemed his youthful folly by a rational and brilliant marriage. The Gräfin von Kunsberg, of good family and with a good dowry from the margrave, was a daughter-in-law to her taste.

When Alexandre-Louis, reconciled with his family, his rebellions redeemed by his honours, died, his family welcomed his widow, a pale, fair-haired, self-effacing young woman. Until her death some ten years later she remained in the marquis' home.

8

"The pleasures of the senses, my dear friend, have become the executioner of my imagination." So wrote the Marquis de Mirabeau, at the age of twenty-five, to Vauvenargues. He could not find occupation for this imagination that tormented him. The château of Mirabeau bored him. Unsatisfied self-esteem, unoccupied imagination, and a thirst for pleasures that dared not proclaim itself, made him desert Provence and establish himself in Paris.

Here he associated with men much older than he, men not of his sort, whose admiration flattered him and confirmed him in his impulsive ways. One of his friends was the Marquis de Saint-Georges, married and father of a family, gay, pleasant, dabbling in everything, in science and in business, a man who, according to Vauvenargues, was "too accomplished." Victor de Mirabeau bought the property of Bignon, near Nemours, at a high price, although, he said, the land was "in a state of enormous deterioration," and the manor house was "neither finished nor furnished." He bought also, with the help of his friend Saint-Georges, a dwelling in Paris, in the rue Bergère, "a carcass of a house," where three years later, although the marquis had spent on it more than a hundred thousand livres, the rain came through the roof. His younger brother anxiously watched these essays in an ambitious building up of the future. They shook even his blind confidence, and he declared later: "Your fine plans often seemed to me to be founded on Seine fogs."

9

"I shall pay very dearly for my follies and for changing my way of life," the young marquis wrote one day to Vauvenargues. Prodded by his bad conscience, and desiring to perpetuate his race, of which he was proud, the Marquis de Mirabeau decided to marry. He had name and fortune (it had been sixteen thousand livres a year before he had launched out into his adventurous speculations) and a good appearance. He could reasonably expect to make an excellent marriage. But his boundless self-esteem gave way for a time to profound discouragement. He realized that he had sacrificed some prestige by leaving the service, and that his family had a reputation for extravagance and wildness. In his haste to be married, he was prepared to be content with an ordinary match. He was twenty-eight years old and felt that he had waited too long.

He had few relations in Paris, but Saint-Georges, never at a loss in the giving of advice, knew a M. de Vassan, whom he considered a man "of no help for any good purpose." But Mme. de Vassan was the only daughter of the Marquis de Salveboeuf, a notable of Périgord, with an estimated income of thirty thousand livres a year. The only daughter and future heir of the Vassans had "great expectations." This was enough to send the Marquis de Mirabeau straight off to the Limousin, to marry a girl he had never met.

Marie-Geneviève de Vassan was seventeen years old. Her brother-in-law, who detested her, said of her later that "without having any of the charms of her sex," she had "all its vices and ours as well." Nobody ever called her pretty. A portrait of her, no doubt flattering like most of the pastels of the period, shows fairly regular features with nothing striking about them except an expression of sensuality.

Her father seems to have been, at the most, insignificant. Her mother had, according to the marquis, "a bifurcated spirit: a good woman at bottom, but the most worrisome, worried, worrying woman in the world; she has the misfortune to be so wrong-headed that nothing comes into her head in the way it would into anybody else's."

In such surroundings the daughter had received, according to the marquis, "the most pestilential and immodest education." In point of fact she does not seem to have had any at all. Her letters reveal an ignorance of spelling rare even for the women of that period; they are the letters of an illiterate. She had not a trace of good breeding. She spoke with a strong Limousin accent. She was not in the least fitted to be the head of a great house. She was gay and lively. She was very talkative and would say whatever came into her head. She was constitutionally active and passionate to excess.

For the Marquis de Mirabeau the marriage with Mlle. de Vassan was an "ordinary deal." It was even a poor deal, since the lady brought a dowry of no more than four thousand livres a year, a sum barely sufficient for her personal expenditure. But for Marie-Geneviève de Vassan it was a brilliant marriage. It had been arranged by third parties, but for her it was a love match. At the first sight of her fiancé she fell passionately in love with him. The marquis spoke to her at a later date of "the turbulent attachment with which you exasperated me for ten years." He reproached her also with having been "so conjugal." But at the moment of her marriage, the man tormented by sensuality, the executioner of his imagination, and the young wife with senses still unsatiated, were in the same state of furious fleshly excitement. They were one day to hate each other as only those can hate who have been intimately, furiously, united by desire.

If Marie-Geneviève de Vassan had married a country gentleman of placid and robust temperament, she might have surmounted his innate indifference and become a normal mother of a family. "She was quite easily led," her son wrote of her later, "but her husband set out to subjugate her"—and all he did was to scare her. She became confirmed in her shortcomings. She found herself from the first in a thoroughly hostile atmosphere. The old Marquise de Mirabeau would have received as an intruder any woman who competed with her for the love of that adored son. Since she had not been consulted as to his choice, she may also have felt a secret resentment. Moreover, she discovered in her daughter-in-law a nature diametrically opposed to her own—in essential characteristics as well as in way of living, in expression, and in the girl's habits of negligence and slovenliness.

At seventeen the young woman was full of goodwill. She tried to adapt herself to this husband whom she adored. She wanted to learn, but her untutored mind quickly tired at any effort: "She wanted to read, but never in her life could she open a serious book or even a true one without going to sleep." She wanted to occupy herself, but, as is the way of women with an eternally roving imagination, she was never able to make a job of anything. "As for needlework, she started a thousand little trifles, got them dirty, let them drag on. . . ." She persisted, nevertheless, in her zeal to become domesticated, but her fits of activity found little favour with those who were watching her with no goodwill. Her husband later drew a picture of her devoting herself to some humble domestic task, hemming napkins or dusters, "with her foot twisted, her legs crossed and covered by petticoats all askew, with dressing-jackets thrown on anyhow, her head right down to her knees."

Discouraged by constant nagging, the young woman fell back into her old indifference. "Men, women, work people, traders, loungers, men-servants, anyone and everyone went into her room, whether she was in bed or not. They saw her dishevelled, bare-breasted, running after a tippet or a handkerchief, with her room all in disorder." Such was the portrait which the marquis traced pitilessly for his daughter by way of warning, and he added this terrible phrase:—"the distinctive mark of prostitutes."

But in spite of the profound difference in their characters, in spite of the friction of everyday life, in spite even of resentment or of contempt, husband and wife remained united for a long time through the excitation of their senses, which threw them into each other's arms, sometimes ashamed, but always brought together by the same persistent desire.

And there was another powerful bond between them. Marie-Geneviève was soon a mother. She was full of pride at having accomplished her destiny as a woman. She wore her successive pregnancies with ostentation, "showing a belly before the time, making much of fecundity," her husband said later in his malevolent indictment. Insatiably amorous, she was both a passionate and a listless mother of eleven children, born in eleven years of marriage.

10

The first child was a son. The young couple were overjoyed. He was "a most hopeful child." But when scarcely more than three years old, he died suddenly. And a strange death. Son of this father who all through his life was incessantly putting ink to paper, he drank some ink and was poisoned.

The second child was a daughter. Marie de Mirabeau was very like her father. She grew up with a majestic figure, and with big eyes, bulging like his, but bright and tender. She was a high-spirited child with an excess of energy which degenerated into a mental affliction. In the end Marie de Mirabeau dragged out her life between fits of insanity and intervals of lucidity.

Of the eleven children only five survived. Among these, the second daughter, Caroline, was the very type of a normal healthy child. She had the good sense of children in sound health, who readily make the best of things and know better than to cry for the moon. "A big girl," her father wrote, "quite well built and solid as a carpenter's tool, a sweet girl, good-natured, gay, the heartiest laughter in France; intelligent, though she may seem simple and childish; with a splendid memory, cross-grained sometimes, undecided, soft, dreamy."

11

After a short spell in the Périgord, where the young couple went in order, as the marquis put it, to eat up one of his estates, he decided in 1746 to settle in Paris. The old Marquise de Mirabeau went with them. Her son did not want to be separated from her. The marquis had had to sell at a considerable loss his house in the rue Bergère, which was too big and ruinously expensive. He then bought a more modest house in the rue des Saints-Pères.

He was especially attached to his estate at Bignon. It was "a little vegetable basket so quaintly mixed with trees, coppices, sheets of water, and plantations, that one might well say that all the birds of the district had agreed to meet there." The house was a rambling single-story building in Renaissance style. Nine windows along the façade looked out on the park across a moat full of water. A little bridge crossed the moat, leading to the main entrance.

The house was dilapidated and the lands waste. The marquis went to work on an ambitious scale. An army of masons, carpenters, and joiners invaded the property. Spending heavily for a poor return, he still prided himself on his practical good sense. "Everything in my place is for use and nothing for ornament." What pleased him above all was his role of *grand seigneur*, watching with paternal benevolence over the welfare of his subjects. The whole population lived on him, counting on him for employment.

In 1749 there was famine in the country, bringing a whole succession of maladies in its train. The marquis felt entirely equal to the situation, as dispenser of benefactions. His wife, too, spent herself in the care of the humble. "She shows her innate courage in tending the most hideous ulcers," wrote the marquis. This was the more meritorious since she was expecting her fifth child.

The marquis was passionately anxious for an heir. The Duc de Nivernois, one of his oldest friends, gave him a secret recipe for engendering male children. A great-great-nephew of Mazarin, a peer of France by birth, a grandee of Spain and a prince of the Holy Roman Empire, a rare wit, a musician, a painter, and a poet, a minister of state and three times an ambassador, Nivernois was one of those in whom the age was gently dying.

At a later date a revolutionary lampoon drew his portrait under the name of Mytis; it may have been inspired by Gabriel de Mirabeau himself. "There are men who have acquired a certain reputation, nobody knows how; who are given employment, nobody knows why. Mytis is one of these. Born with the sort of intelligence that is of no use for anything, he has achieved just nothing."

The marquis awaited anxiously the arrival of one who should perpetuate his race. The birth was particularly difficult. The wait for delivery was long. The child's head, according to the family, was "of more than natural size." The mother's life was in danger. At last the door opened. There was the soothing gesture of bearers of bad news. The father long remembered the mournful sound of the preliminary caution—"Don't be alarmed."

The child who had been born with such difficulty on March 9, 1749, had a twisted ankle; he was also tongue-tied, and it was feared that he would be dumb. But he was robust. His head was enormous, and he had two teeth already formed in his mouth, sign, perhaps, of a furious appetite for life. He was given the names Honoré Gabriel.

In April 1749 the marquis, overflowing with gratitude for the recipe his friend had sent him, wrote to the Duc de Nivernois: "You know now that I have a son who owes his existence to you." Above the cradle of Mirabeau hung, graceful and perfumed, the silhouette of Nivernois, perfect representative of a regime which the child was one day to help overthrow.

The village of Bignon shared the father's joy at the birth of a son. "From a sort of superstition due to the birth of the first one having been fêted, I had forbidden any sort of village festivities," the marquis wrote to the Duc de Nivernois; "but the peasants assembled from neighbouring parishes and bore witness to a joy I had not asked of them."

For wet-nurse the baby had a sturdy *maréchale*—a first-class woman —said the marquis, one who had borne a whole brood of her own. A vigorous woman of the people nurtured this child full of vigour.

His father trembled no longer for the boy's life. He was reassured by his robust health. He knew also that his son was to be free from any physical defect. He was still full of the joy of paternity when in February of the following year he wrote to his brother: "I have nothing to tell you of my enormous son, save that he thumps his wet-nurse, who pays him back properly. They pummel one another in competition. A pretty pair of them."

৯ II ৶

The Friend of Mankind

"FROM the time of those pitiable misunderstandings that roused the people in 1750," wrote the marquis to his brother, "and gave rise to the building of the road from the Porte Maillot to Saint-Denis by which the king has since gone from Versailles to Compiègne without passing through Paris, it has seemed to me that I see sprouting the seeds of unrest. The very name of the road, the Chemin de la Révolte, is a subject for speculation."

This letter, written toward the end of 1754, was addressed to Guadeloupe, where the bailli had been established for a year as governor, "or rather," he said, "half bishop, half intendant, half, or even completely, president." Across the ocean that separated them, the brothers shared the same apprehension for the present and fear for the future which reflected the spasms of terror that were passing through the minds of all those occupied with public affairs.

For the bailli, the general corruption, the contempt for the virtues and admiration for clever rogues, was the great evil of society. "We are wasting our time in vain laments while the machine, with every spring corroded, threatens to fly to pieces and become once more *quem Graeci dixere chaos.*" From Guadeloupe he was better able to judge the international situation. "Those with the slightest vision are saying here," he wrote to his brother, "that in less than forty years the New World will have shaken off the yoke of the old one and will be treating with it on equal terms. The English colonies will be the first, for already New England submits to England scarcely more than did Carthage to Tyre."

At that distant post the vices of internal administration were also clear to him and confirmed him in his opinions: "I have long calculated that the worst of masters is gold, the worst of all slaveries that to wealth." His uprightness made of the bailli a democrat without knowing it. He was disgusted with the treatment the whites inflicted on the Negroes. "The lowest section of white humanity has a higher opinion of itself here than a peer of France in Paris. Making sugar, beating Negroes, producing bastards, and getting drunk—such is the main business of the creoles." In that distant country he was the incarnation of all the dignity of France. He was also justice incarnate. "People are quite astonished that I am not ready to let a man be killed here with less ceremony than a dog anywhere else." In his disgust he exclaimed: "A slave, slave though he be, ought to be considered a man, and for my part I think I ought also to consider him a brother. . . . It is not only true that the Negroes are the most unfortunate of all men; actually they are the most miserable of all living beings."

The marquis was disturbed at the bailli's uncompromising attitude and begged him to moderate it: "I adjure you, dear brother, grease the axles of your carriage, or we shall be overturned. In God's name, go a little more softly." But the bailli burst out indignantly: "Would you rather I were an honest man, even if I broke my neck, or do you want me to make a fortune of which I shall be ashamed all my life and in terror on my deathbed?"

But he scarcely dreamed of touching the regime that authorized or tolerated the abuses he denounced. For him the one remedy for all evils was a return to the virtues of the past, a step backward, not forward to the uncertain future of a social upheaval.

His brother, on the contrary, had the faculty, valuable in times of transition, of judging the currents and the forces at work and foreseeing coming events. His agitation drove him to leave the beaten track. In 1750, a year after the birth of his son, the Marquis de Mirabeau anonymously published a work on the utility of provincial assemblies. With the publication of this first book he found his true path. In modern terms, he was a born sociologist. He was without creative genius, but he possessed great gifts as a publicist. He had the flair of a modern journalist, the journalist's faculty of being in the midst of events but aloof from them. In the disturbed period to come he was to play an important part.

The first question of social policy with which he dealt might seem of secondary importance, but it touched on an essential principle of the structure of the state, that of administrative autonomy. A quarter of a century later autonomy was demanded by Turgot, and it was subsequently advocated by Necker. A current that had gained strength in the interval imposed on the king in 1787 the creation of provincial assemblies. In 1788 the marquis wrote to his brother with regard to these assemblies: "I look on them as in a sort of way their father; I can see that in general they are fulfilling what I expected of them."

2

"Your nephew is as ugly as Satan's," wrote the marquis to his brother. At three years of age the child caught smallpox. At that period inoculation was resisted by the doctors as very dangerous; from the point of view of religion it was attacked as an act of rebellion against the divine will. In this home dominated by the marquis' pious mother, who in his words was "the entire and unshakable enemy of everything new," the child was not inoculated. Worse still, his mother, who "has lots of recipes," applied fomentations to his swollen face; she used a salve that accentuated the marks of the malady and scored the little face with deep scars.

The child was incessantly told how ugly he was. Something in his soul revolted, and a premature self-consciousness fought against his elders' verdict. "My son, whose body grows, whose prattle increases, and whose face grows incredibly ugly," wrote the marquis to a woman friend, "is moreover ugly by choice and predilection; and, in addition, interminably oratorical. His mother made him a sort of anti-declaration as from his future wife; he replied that he hoped that she would not gauge him *by his face;* his mother said innocently: 'Where do you want her to look at you,' and everybody laughed. He retorted: 'What's underneath will help what's up top'; and we all roared, quite apart from the fact that there is something to think about in this sally from an infant."

But it was not only the ugliness of his eldest boy that disturbed the marquis. The child was the innocent victim of conjugal disharmony. The marquis grew more and more impatient with his wife's shortcomings, and his impatience was increased by his own faults. The marquise accused him later of having had a long liaison with a person she named, a liaison dating back to the year of his son's birth. The marquis visited on the child his disappointment and his rancour against his wife. The whole cause of his resentment is contained in this phrase in one of his letters to the bailli: "He is the very image of his odious [maternal] grandfather." In the face of a little child, two hereditary currents—two races, his father said—carried on a fight of which the issue was his family's love for him. His paternal grandmother, looking at him with a glance sharpened by her hatred of her daughter-in-law, agreed that he was "entirely a Vassan."

The marquis exchanged long letters with the bailli, but in a whole year he mentioned his son only a few times. The bailli protested: "You tell me nothing about your son." The marquis found himself obliged—apparently with reluctance—to concede the child a precocious intelligence. "Your nephew is big and strong," he wrote to the bailli. "His knowledge is the talk of all Paris; and yet," he added at once, "it amounts to little as yet; few faults, apart from a mechanical aping, if it were permitted, but little sensitiveness; he is sand that holds nothing; but he is only five years old."

When Gabriel was three years old a daughter was born; when he was five a second son. With the birth of this second boy the marquis' pride of race was satisfied. He considered that "after eleven children one may stop." The plainness of little Gabriel was emphasized by the beauty of the other children. His younger sister Louise was a delightful little girl; she was to become remarkably beautiful. In addition to her beauty she had a grace that ravished her father: "In intelligence and judgment she is unique in her day."

But it was little Boniface who supplanted his elder brother in the affections of the whole family. The marquis found him "wholly Mirabeau." His grandmother, too, discovered in him from the day of his birth all the qualities and all the defects of his race. From then on the elder brother lived in the shadow of the marked preference for the last-born.

As is natural in a child with a very lively imagination, the boundaries between dream and reality, truth and fancy, were vaguely defined in little Gabriel. But an innocent childish "story" was a crime in the eyes of the marquis. Worse still, it was a Vassan trait. He exclaimed to his brother when Gabriel was seven: "I must repudiate any claim of that individual to the character of our race; but, good Lord! were it his pet lie, he shall abjure it, or I shall know how to annul it with disgrace." Mirabeau wrote later to his father: "I may say that from my childhood and my first steps in the world I received few marks of your goodwill; that you treated me rigorously before I could possibly deserve ill of you." In fact the marquis searched for faults in his son as if he wanted an excuse for that absurd rigour; he drew up very early an indictment against him, as though to satisfy a secret rancour. There are signs of physical repugnance in his condemnation of the child. He painted him pitilessly in a letter to a friend: "He is cross-grained, fantastic, fiery, awkward, with a drift to evil before he knows of it or is capable of it."

3

"Everywhere, without any exception, coercive methods are the likeliest to have on men the contrary effect to that at which they aim," declared the marquis. But in practice he contradicted his theory to an extent of which he could hardly have been conscious. He subjected his son to a rigid discipline. "Yet," wrote Mirabeau later to his father, "you should have seen very quickly that that method excited my natural fieriness instead of allaying it; that it was just as easy to touch me as to irritate me; that the former method achieved its object and the latter drove me in the opposite direction."

The childhood of Gabriel de Mirabeau was weighed down by the formidable tutelage of a former lawyer of the *parlement* named Poisson, a man of integrity but no imagination, whom the marquis engaged grudgingly at a salary of twelve hundred livres a year. Poisson acquitted himself of the task assigned to him with all the conscientiousness of an inflexible character, never softening an iron discipline. The marquis, with the idealized figure of his father before his eyes, was obsessed by memories of his own rigorous education. He had forgotten the unfortunate results of that constraint, his own moral lapses and those of the bailli, and the belated revolt of Alexandre-Louis. This discipline seemed to him still more necessary for a child whom he distrusted. "He keeps us busy," wrote the marquis, "but we are watching him, and he is in excellent hands."

Poisson prepared to mould the son in the idealized image and in accordance with the requirements of this father whom the marquis revered. The result of this vigilance was noted by the marquis himself. "Monsieur le Comte is never out of his succession of punishments, and

indeed he gets them and deserves them thoroughly." The child was
then only seven years old. The marquis went on: "I am one more instrument for Poisson, for when he has promised remission I make it possible for him to fail to give it without breaking his word, and I keep
a tight hand." The bailli tried to restrain his brother's "maternal inclination to pedantry. That sort of thing irritates men who are made
and mars men in the making." But he preached in vain.

The child himself complained that he was being badly treated. He
tried to persuade his father that excessive severity and excessive strict-
ness were not quite suitable for him. He brought to bear all the resources
of his precocious eloquence. "He argued very well at times," his father
admitted later. But these arguments had no effect on an ill-will of which
the child did not know the source.

His father could not but recognize in him "an intelligence, a memory,
a capacity that are striking, breath-taking, alarming." He recognized
also in him "a high spirit beneath his boy's jacket, a strange instinct of
pride, noble in spite of everything." It might almost be said that these
were the very qualities that frightened him.

Rebuffed on all sides, struggling in a narrow circle of incomprehensi-
ble restrictions, the child, by turns, revolted against this oppression and
tried to disarm his father by his docility. But all he did was to exasperate
him. "He is of an utterly unheard-of type of baseness," exclaimed the
marquis in a letter to his brother, "absolutely commonplace and of the
quality of the rough and muddied caterpillar that will never be a
chrysalis."

Gabriel de Mirabeau was to retain throughout his life traces of the
terror of that childhood. Nothing could put right certain tendencies
distorted by its constraints.

When Poisson fell ill, the marquis was reduced to despair at the idea
of having to undertake the sole responsibility for his elder son, then only
eight years old. He wrote to the bailli, thoroughly scared: "Poisson
will die and I shall go on dragging my son along without knowing what
river to throw him into."

4

"The author writes like Montaigne and thinks like Montesquieu," remarked the encyclopaedic journal of Bouillon in July 1757. The Marquis
de Mirabeau had become famous overnight with the publication in 1756
of the great work of his life, *L'Ami des hommes*. He had achieved the
ambition which many authors pursue in vain: he had said aloud what

many people were thinking, or imagined, after they had read his book,
that they had been thinking. He had spoken at a moment particularly
favourable for securing a hearing. The awareness of man that marked
the eighteenth century was in the book. Men were half-way to a new
social order. Individuals and classes no longer lived in social isolation,
though the theory of the equality of all men still waited for acceptance.
The very title of the book was a sign of an epoch of transition. As often
occurs with happy inspirations, it went beyond the author's own
thought. It lived an almost independent life. It was on everyone's lips;
the shopkeepers of Paris, always in search of novelties, used it as a sign
for their shops. At forty, the Marquis de Mirabeau had acquired a name.
More still, he had bartered away a surname for it; he had attained that
supreme sort of celebrity that consists in being identified with one's
work. Thenceforth he was *l'ami des hommes*, the Friend of Mankind.

The sales of his book were exceptional for the period. "The publishers
themselves admit that they have made eighty-six thousand livres out
of it," the marquis reported. This success with the public, this hubbub,
was remarkable in the case of a book that was simply what its sub-title
called it—a treatise on population. Any specialist would have made it
a dry book. The marquis, fortunately for himself, was just an amateur.
He made no attempt to fit his subject into any doctrine or to subordinate it to any school. He had said what seemed to him to want
saying, and had said it in his own way with the assurance and the air of
finality natural to amateurs, who imagine that they have no predecessors
and who explain their discoveries with a persuasive warmth and a captivating audacity.

In this easy and picturesque style the marquis compared the state to
a tree: "The roots are agriculture, the trunk is the population, the
branches are industry, the leaves are commerce and the arts; it is from
its roots that the tree draws the nourishing sap, . . . and it is to the
roots that a remedy must be applied if the tree is not to perish." One
of the great evils of the country, according to the marquis, was the
flight from the land: "We desert the villages for the towns, the towns
for the cities, the cities for the capital, and this is what a whole nation
tends to do if the government is not careful to give it a contrary pro-
pensity." Another cause of the decay of agriculture was the concentration of estates in the hands of one person, but the Marquis de Mirabeau had no scruple about dissociating theory and practice, and perhaps he did so in good faith. While he himself was busy adding to his
property, the Friend of Mankind wrote with fine courage and a particularly happy turn of phrase that "the big pike depopulate the pool,

the big owners stamp out the little ones." He was still more daring when he attacked the abuse of wealth; his condemnation voiced the muttered popular wrath: "A nation in which wealth has undisputed pre-eminence is an assembly of open or disguised thieves, of civilized brigands, of whom some are in full pursuit and others lying in wait."

To the abuse of wealth was joined a contempt for poverty which discouraged work on the land. Carried away by his feelings—he says himself that he wrote his book under the spur of emotion—he asked those filled with the pride of class to show genuine respect to the water-carrier, "and to put up with contacts with a beggar of infectious odour in rags that bear reproachful witness to an unadmitted brotherhood." To this aristocrat lying in wait for great ideas, labour was the true dignity of man. Respect for labour was fundamental in society; he even considered it as a guarantee of all the civic liberties: "As for tolerance, I think it is more likely to destroy false cults than to authorize them, and the liberty of the press has no danger in a country in which labour serves to maintain public order." Pursuing his thoughts to the end, he said: "The man who lives on interest is an idler at play, and the greater part of the evils of society are due to him."

In order to assure full scope to labour on the land, the Friend of Mankind demanded freedom of trade both at home and abroad: "Europe will never be at peace if we do not work for fraternity among us all, both in the Old World and the New."

Anticipations of ideas of later times illuminate the work. In order to combat depopulation, he claimed consideration for abandoned babies: "They are not at all what they are called, the children of debauchery; debauchery does not produce abandoned children. It is poverty, misfortune, or debility that bring you their offspring." He demanded a number of institutions for the unmarried mother, and "on leaving, if she is necessitous, let her receive ten silver crowns as the price of the present she has made to the state."

His book was a sort of sounding-board for all the strings on which the spirit of the time was playing. Alongside "unadmitted brotherhood" he demanded equity, "a feeling of respect for every right. If force runs counter to the sense of equity, it becomes tyranny."

One day Gabriel de Mirabeau, commenting on that passage in his father's book, exclaimed: "I say, and I shall contend to all the powers of the earth, that slaves are as blameworthy as their tyrants, and I do not know whether Liberty has more complaint to make of those who have the insolence to invade her or of the imbecility of those who do not know how to defend her."

5

Dr. Quesnay, chief consulting physician to the king, was attached to the person of Mme. de Pompadour. He cut a strange figure in that court environment. He had started life on the land, on a little property worked by his mother. At eleven years of age he was still unable to read. But he made up for the lost time and became a brilliant student. He had decided to become a surgeon, but his eager and inquiring intelligence was interested in all things. He went deeply into mathematical studies. He drew, and he studied engraving with a celebrated master of his day. Everything pointed to the career of a cultivated amateur, immersed in the sciences and arts on the fringe of his profession. He was one of those original spirits who are the glory and the scandal of small towns.

As chance would have it, in refuting a treatise on bleeding that was famous at the time, he attracted the attention of an eminent Paris surgeon, who persuaded him to leave his provincial town and settle in the capital, and who secured for him the post of permanent secretary of the Academy of Surgery, then just founded. Quesnay then bought the post of principal physician to the king.

Chance came once more to his aid. He happened to be present when a friend of Mme. de Pompadour had an epileptic fit, and he tended her with authority combined with discretion. His patient's grateful enthusiasm won for him the support of her powerful friend. Thereafter Quesnay was quartered at Versailles, in the mezzanine of the residence of Mme. de Pompadour.

Quesnay was deeply concerned with the subject of personal liberty, which he said was the foundation of human existence. Also, he had not forgotten the lessons he had gathered from his labour on the land. He applied himself to the formulation of certain fundamental laws of nature, and to the erection in conformity with them of a system of government and administration. He and his disciples took the name of Physiocrats. They established certain natural and imprescriptible rights of man.

After reading *L'Ami des hommes*, Quesnay, who "never left his post, day or night," asked the Marquis de Mirabeau for an interview. It was stormy, the clash of two temperaments and two prides. The little doctor with the simian face, "bitter in disputes, implacable in resistance, armed with sarcasms and disdain," first made on Mirabeau the impression of a madman. But, shaken in spite of himself, the marquis went back to see him the same evening. Quesnay proved to him "that he was swimming in an ocean of uncertainties," and placed before him a system. At a later date the marquis wrote to Jean-Jacques Rousseau: "The principles of my science are not mine at all; I was more than forty years old when I adopted them, and to do that I had to make my vanity jump the hurdle of the disavowal of the work to which I owe my celebrity and my public name, and to bend my head before the man who was the most antipathetic to my innate exuberance."

Quesnay thus gained one of the first and one of the most fanatical of his disciples. The Friend of Mankind gained a programme. He also gained an object in life, which was thenceforward to prevent him from dispersing his energies, was to stimulate his enthusiasm, and was to conquer his fits of impatience and lassitude.

From then on the Marquis de Mirabeau was a frequent visitor to the mezzanine of the Pompadour's palace. He, too, worked at "stirring up a world of citizens."

6

The Marquis de Mirabeau pursued his ambition to turn "a house of Provence into a house of France."

His father-in-law died, and the marquise received a share of his fortune. The marquis soon sold one of his estates in the Périgord. He had found in the property left by his father-in-law a concession for a lead mine and imagining himself to be a great entrepreneur, saw himself at the head of an important industrial concern. He recruited friends among the high aristocracy for the formation of a company. Frequent appeals for capital proved necessary, but after many years the mine still yielded nothing but "good hopes."

The marquis learned one day that the Rohan family was prepared to sell the duchy of Roquelaure. Borrowing four hundred and fifty thousand francs, he bought it without seeing it. Once the purchase had been made, he learned from local people that he had paid a hundred thousand livres more than the value of the property. Some years later he was glad to get rid of it by reselling the duchy to the king at a loss.

Always on the look-out for risky aggrandizements and costly improvements, he struggled incessantly in "a tissue of poignant anxieties." To these financial difficulties was added the friction of everyday life, which became worse as time went on. The disagreements between husband and wife grew more and more acute. The Marquise de Mirabeau felt that her husband was slipping away from her, and lost what little self-control she had ever had. Violent scenes came one after another, followed by long periods of estrangement during which the two communicated only through a third party. The house had the tense and suffocating air of a centre of discord.

The new intellectual interest, in which his wife could take little part, and his recent celebrity, finally detached him from her. The continuance of his race was assured. He now dreamed of separation. He tried to make one of their periods of estrangement irreparable.

But habits are more tenacious than feelings. Their life together continued to unite under the same roof a dry and imperious old woman, an impatient and exasperated man, a woman with over-excited senses whom her husband was forsaking, and an impetuous, expansive, confiding child, who suffered in this hate-filled atmosphere. Mirabeau later told a friend that his family was "that of Atreus and Thyestes: the division between father and mother, forming two enemy sections among their children, habituated them early to constraint and dissimulation."

7

The Seven Years' War brought terrible suffering to the country. The state finances were heavily burdened; and a series of defeats showed the disorganized state of the army and the weakness of the navy. The English had landed in Brittany. The bailli was appointed inspector of the coast-guard militia.

His charge of coastal inspection showed him the weakness of the French defences. "The frightful dilapidation here fills me with shame as a Frenchman. . . ." But no less fatal than the incompetence of those in charge of coastal defence were the risky improvisations for attack. The bailli saw at Le Havre the preparations for a landing in England— three hundred flat-bottomed boats with which it was proposed to cross the Channel. His common sense asked: "How are troops, baggage, sick, wounded, water, provisions to be got on to them?" All that these very costly preparations did, in fact, was to draw upon the port a violent bombardment from the English fleet. Next day the three hundred boats that were to have attempted the crossing were sunk, burnt, or captured by the English.

Louisbourg and L'Ile Royale, the key to Canada, fell into the hands of the English. Guadeloupe was taken, two great naval battles were lost; the navy was almost destroyed, the army defeated, demoralized, leaderless. But the bailli, who had foreseen the reverses the country would suffer, and who knew their causes, retained all his confidence in the indestructible forces of France: "Nothing is lost. I know the enormous loss we are suffering, but I know our resources, and all I am afraid of is Versailles. There are two paths before us. The easier one will bring everybody to Paris; . . . the other, rough, hard, and difficult, will lead us to the splendour that is our due. We have to choose."

The Marquis de Mirabeau was filled with the same anxiety over public affairs, greater even than his financial preoccupations and the worry of his private life.

He was greatly attached at this time to the Comtesse de Rochefort, mistress of the Duc de Nivernois, and daughter of Marshal de Brancas.

Widowed at an early age and without children, also without fortune, she lived in a suite of rooms in the Luxembourg which the king had granted her in consideration of the services rendered by her father. She was without ambition and in poor health, but she gathered round her without effort people of distinction.

In the salon of the Comtesse de Rochefort the Marquis de Mirabeau enjoyed a privileged situation. In this authoritarian and peremptory man she had discovered an element of childishness that demanded consolation and above all flattery. She called him "my big Merlou," like a cat. She put all her influence at his service, and induced the Duc de Nivernois to do all the things for which the marquis was constantly asking. She praised all that was best in him. At the time when he was plunging into the risks of his literary career, she wrote to him: "It seems to me that it is the character of chivalry that is dominant in you. In Bayard's time you would have redressed wrongs sword in hand, and in the age of philosophy the same urge has made you take up the pen."

8

Taxation weighed heavily on the impoverished country. Besides direct taxes, there were indirect levies, which increased the prices of the most essential foodstuffs, and external and internal customs duties. The burden was increased by the way in which the taxes were collected. The state had farmed out its revenues, delivering over the country to some thirty business men who, with their army of thirty thousand agents, set out to draw the maximum profit from their lease. The collectors of the *fermiers généraux*, the farmers general of taxes, dropped like locusts on the land, respecting neither persons nor property. They ransacked cellars and demanded payment of excise on all they found. They went into the dining-rooms and tasted the salt: if it was of good quality they declared it to be contraband, for the farmed salt was mixed with grit. In this way they extracted millions from the poorest people, increasing their misery and sowing hatred against the state. Thirty years later the *fermiers généraux* were to be among the first victims of the popular wrath.

The end of their lease was approaching. This was the moment for exposing abuses, for showing the government the gravity of the situation and placing before it, as a remedy for all the evils, a just and equitable system of taxation.

Quesnay urged the Marquis de Mirabeau to launch this campaign. The marquis was well aware of the audacity of the enterprise. He wrote to his brother: "I am sticking to my subject, and here is the picture I shall put before them. This picture entails inescapably so many physical, palpable, present, and terrible truths for our vampires that it will be a prodigy of public spirit to have ventured so far, and of good luck if all goes as peaceably as in the past. In any case, I am taking the risks, from a feeling based on principles above petty transient considerations."

The Friend of Mankind struck a shrewd blow. His *Théorie d'Impôt*, published in December 1760, came like a fanfare of revolution. It was addressed to Louis XV, in a style which Louis XVI was to hear nearly thirty years later: "Your Majesty has twenty million men. . . . Their services are to be had only for money, and there is no money with which to pay for their services." The marquis did not deal gently with the exploiters. He showed the profit they were drawing from the impoverishment of the country. On the sale of tobacco alone, thirty-one millions went into their pockets. Of the indirect taxes collected at the cost of such great privations, only a small part was received by the state: of six hundred millions collected, only two hundred and fifty were paid to the Treasury.

It was a terrible indictment. But though the blow struck by the marquis was courageous, it achieved nothing at all. It was not the act of a realist. At that moment of national distress, the king could not do without the farmers general. They had made immense profits, but they had advanced considerable sums to the state. As creditors they held the government at their mercy. Only utopians like Quesnay and his disciples could have chosen so unsuitable a moment for demanding their suppression.

From the same domain of pure theory came the system of taxation proposed by the marquis, following the doctrine of the Physiocrats. The most natural, just, and advantageous tax would be levied on the income drawn from the land, after deducting all expenses. This was what the

Physiocrats called the "net product," the principal point in their system. The marquis daringly proclaimed that the king had no right to impose taxation on his subjects without their collaboration and their consent.

In spite of its unexciting title, the work caused a sensation. "It is a tempest," wrote Mme. d'Epinay to Voltaire, and she added, shrewdly summing up the qualities and defects of the book, which were also those of the man: "Everything in it is confused, obscure, and there are passages that are brilliant and overwhelming; miscalculations, sound ideas, eloquence, rubbish, bold to the point of temerity [anybody else would perhaps have said to the point of insolence, and perhaps quite rightly]. . . . For the rest, a striking and a true picture of our misfortunes, with a slight sketch of rather doubtful remedies."

The publication shocked public opinion. The farmers general were indignant, and financial circles were alarmed. They were powerful, and demanded that steps be taken against the author. "Marmontel, banker to the court," wrote the marquis, who was aware of what was under way, "has declared that if there is not an outcry against me his credit will drop." The marquis had foreseen that he was running big risks. Yet he seems to have been surprised when he was arrested by the king's command. He was committed to the château of Vincennes.

The arrest of *l'ami des hommes* greatly perturbed not only his friends but even those who were indifferent or hostile to him. Even Voltaire, who had ridiculed the Economists and against whom the Marquis de Mirabeau had retaliated with such epithets as "that villainous Voltaire," and "a base-hearted madman with a bright mind but a pusillanimous soul," expressed his sympathy.

Quesnay was in despair. He had led a disciple and friend into danger. He pleaded for him with Mme. de Pompadour. He found her well disposed toward the marquis. But just when Quesnay was making his urgent appeal, the lieutenant of police appeared. Mme. de Pompadour asked the lieutenant what he thought of the book. As a good courtier, he replied that the marquis might have said a great deal of what he wanted to say "in more restrained language." He quoted the violent phrases of the opening. She was horrified. "What? Is that in it, Doctor?" she asked indignantly of Quesnay, who beat a retreat. "Those are the first lines," he said, "and I agree that they are imprudent." Timidly he pointed out that the work was dictated by the patriotism that was "vanishing from men's hearts." The entry of the king put an end to the conversation. Mme. de Pompadour managed to get in a word in favour of the marquis. "The king is very angry," she told her maid later, "but I tried to calm him."

The marquis himself wrote to Mme. de Pompadour. His brother, most desperate of all, rushed to see her. But the favourite did not want to mortgage her credit too heavily and refused to see him. Powerful influences were at work round her. The bailli, stirred in his deepest feeling, his love for his brother, wrote to the prisoner at Vincennes: "You are greatly mistaken if you think the lady you wrote to is favourable or even neutral. You may be sure that she is your worst enemy."

The furor caused by the marquis' arrest merely contributed to the success of his book. This "sublime work," as the Physiocrats called it, ran into eighteen editions.

The marquis' detention lasted barely a week. On leaving Vincennes he obtained permission to return to his estates at Bignon, where he was to remain until further orders. Fame pursued the marquis in his pleasant exile. "Letters are coming here in packets," he boasted to his brother.

His son later mocked at this attitude of "martyr to the public weal." "The Economists," he wrote, "count that gentle and brief detention among the historic sufferings of their sect as oriental fanatics revere the Hegira of their Prophet."

9

The marquis' mother, his brother, and his sons had remained in Paris with Poisson in charge. But husband and wife were not alone at Bignon. "One of our lady friends," wrote the marquis to the Comtesse de Rochefort, "has agreed to share our journey, and in my opinion she is one of the persons of her sex who do it most honour through the breadth and solidity of her mind and the goodness of her heart."

The "lady friend" was Mme. de Pailly, who was to dominate the rest of the marquis' life. She was the ruling passion of an excitable and passionate man, the controlling influence over a character both impressionable and resistant to influence, which was moved equally by a spirit of opposition and by firmly rooted prepossessions and prejudices. He had had the experience of sentimental affection, of ephemeral liaisons, and of a long attachment through the senses; he was forty-six years old when he first made the acquaintance of love.

Mme. de Pailly was of the stuff of royal mistresses, of the morganatic wives of elderly sovereigns. The Marquis de Mirabeau happened to be the only man of mark who crossed her path. She was thirty years old when he was exiled to Bignon, and had little hope that she would capture a man who could do more for her. She made sure that he did not escape. He could give her what she wanted above all—entry into society and the pleasure of exercising her domination.

Born Marie de Malvieux, at Berne, of a Protestant family of French origin, daughter of a captain of one of the Swiss companies in the French service, she had talents and ambitions above her birth. Her status permitted her no more than a modest marriage. She was primarily intellectual, and sought in marriage neither love nor the satisfaction of the senses. At an early age she married a man thirty years her senior. M. de Pailly, a Swiss officer, was not merely to give her his name. She had the talent to keep always on the right side of her husband. Though the two were almost always separated, she succeeded in keeping up a semblance of affectionate conjugal relations, a façade behind which she pursued all that was adventurous in her life. She had the still greater talent of maintaining friendly relations with her sisters-in-law, four spinsters who lived at Lausanne with their brother. Her supreme tact was revealed by the welcome they gave her when she went to see them, and still more by the fact that they made her their heir although her liaison had become public. Marie de Pailly had a genius for wheedling the respectable.

She was pretty, with a well-fed, pasty beauty. She had sufficient taste to dress always in black. Dark clothes disguised her ample proportions and set off her complexion. They also gave her the air of austerity which she deliberately assumed, as though to overcome her equivocal position. Her friends called her the black hen, or, a nickname the marquis adopted, the black cat—which expressed still better her feline mixture of languor and aggressiveness. She had developed a personality that corresponded to her expansive physique, that of a healthy and well-balanced vivacious woman.

Mme. de Pailly knew the social value of good humour. She was always lively in a salon, always full of high spirits, exuberant, witty, bringing out the contrast between her pose of *grande dame* with her austere clothing and her frank gaiety.

But in more intimate relations Marie de Pailly wore a very different expression. She was tortured, fitful, desperate in her complaints against the world. She was tormented by an inherited Protestant rigidity, and still more by her sense of her equivocal social position; smiling in front of the world, she made her lover pay for the fact that he was unable to give her respectability. Hers was not a great passion hurling defiance at society: she was an ambitious woman still troubled by lower middle-class scruples.

When the marquis was over seventy and she herself nearly sixty, though she was living with him, she insisted on being housed under a separate roof.

The marquis, so impatient with his family, so ready to exaggerate their defects, so annoyed at anyone's loss of good humour or failure to keep up with expectations, bore the scenes made by Mme. de Pailly with infinite patience. "She does herself a lot of harm and does no good to those who love her," he once sighed; but he added magnanimously: "Natural defects should never suffer reproach."

The marquis succeeded entirely in imposing her on his friends. He tried to impose her also on his family. The most difficult task was the reconciliation of his mother, a pious Catholic, to the Protestant Mme. de Pailly. This devoted and respectful son, who gave way to his mother in all the small things in life, who let himself gradually but steadily be won over by her antipathies and repugnances, took no notice at all of her vehement protests against the presence of Mme. de Pailly.

There were violent scenes between the two women. Mme. de Pailly went off, leaving the marquis to go after her and beg her to return. In the end she was clever enough and persistent enough to win over the old marquise.

The bailli was fascinated by her at their first meeting, like all those to whom she showed her company face. "I admire the ideas of Mme. de Pailly; in spite of my humdrum judgment I have distinguished in her an intelligence as sound and as subtle as has ever been born on the Helvetic hills." Later he realized the baleful part she was playing in his brother's life. "Women can do nothing but intrigue, especially women of intelligence, the most dangerous of all animals; the one in whom you are placing too much confidence is like the rest. Every woman in her position wants to govern absolutely; whatever may stand in the way of her empire or share it she cordially hates."

"He is jealous without knowing it," the marquis said one day of the bailli in comment on his remonstrances. It was the only shadow that ever troubled the friendship of the two brothers.

But the influence most laden with unfortunate consequences was that which Marie de Pailly exercised over the relations between the marquis and his children. What she wanted to do was to subjugate them completely, as she had enslaved their father. She did not forgive those of the children whom she failed to dominate. Her one thought was to destroy them in the eyes of their father. With her acute susceptibility, she demanded of them the more marked attentions because of her equivocal position. Herself an intruder in their home, she demanded that they should legitimize her relations with their father by the recognition of her rights. Through them she persecuted the legitimate wife whose place she had usurped.

From the moment when she welcomed her to Bignon, the Marquise de Mirabeau had no doubt of the important part which Mme. de Pailly was to assume in her husband's life. The marquis wrote at the time to his brother: "Mme. de Pailly shows me, as well as Mme. de Mirabeau, to whom her brightness is as welcome as to me, the utmost friendship through the calm and the pleasure she brings here." With her natural indolence, Marie-Geneviève de Mirabeau allowed this stranger to assume more and more control over her husband. The visit seems to have been preceded by an exchange of letters. Letters, no doubt, of warm and comprehensive admiration. In the isolation of Bignon the exchange of ideas with a pretty woman took on other accents. Nobody troubled the two, least of all the young marquise. The winter evenings were long in the country. "My wife goes to sleep, and we chat for another hour, Mme. de Pailly and I." While the marquise slept the uneasy sleep of an unsatisfied woman, a dangerous game was transformed under her closed eyes into passion.

Mme. de Pailly did not stay long. She did the cleverest thing she could do at the moment—she went away to be missed and wanted. Each time she went away she left the marquis with the same feeling of an insupportable void. He could no longer endure Bignon. He urged his brother and his mother to work for permission to be granted to him to return to Paris. He threatened to return without permission. The bailli soon discerned the cause of his brother's impatience: "I know you have special reasons for not liking to be where you are." As a sensible man he tried to bring him to reason and to remind him of his responsibilities. But no arguing was of any use against the hold of passion over this man of mature age. The family worked for the marquis' return, and the pretext of sickness of the old marquise brought him permission to go to Paris for a certain time. It was, in fact, the end of his glorious exile. L'ami des hommes had given place to an impatient lover whose one thought now was to unite his destiny with that of Marie de Pailly.

10

The Marquise de Mirabeau had gone in the spring to rejoin her mother in the Limousin. "Mamma very much wants to see you; you cannot refuse her this satisfaction. . . . Come quickly, do," she wrote her husband. The marquis hastened to reply to her appeal, but his only purpose was to obtain her consent to the plan of separation which he had discussed with her four years earlier. She was no more prepared to agree now than then. This marriage, disunited though it was, could not be dissolved by a friendly arrangement.

The marquis sought a pretext for separation from his wife and found a scandal that justified him. The marquise had given her lover, an officer, a certificate of her full satisfaction, and had signed it with her name. The officer must have boasted of his achievement. Mme. de Mirabeau had not even taken the precaution to choose as her lover a man of honour. "A certain horribly scandalous certificate" fell into the hands of the marquis.

The Marquise de Mirabeau made a mess of her defence, alleging a jest on a social occasion. "Set out your complaints, Monsieur," she wrote to her husband, "establish them. I will set out mine in reply, and if I have any faults they are entirely caused by yours. The way you have treated me has changed my heart in regard to you: it is wounded and will never heal." The poverty of the reasoning and the style of this letter, with its defective spelling, revealed clearly a semi-irresponsible mind and possibly a sick one.

"You do not deign to reply to me about my return to Paris, Monsieur, where I consider that my honour is attacked by all the noise and scandal spread about my conduct, which others may have regarded as what it is—easiness and good heart." But this attitude of offended dignity did not last long. Thrown into a panic by her own lapses, in her fear of her husband she gave way on every point. "You want me to stop here? Very well, I consent." She showed neither remorse nor regrets; she did not even mourn her children: "I am sacrificing my friends, my family, who, although absent, will love me, at least I think I may say so." On condition of obtaining a sufficient allowance, she promised "never to return to Paris, since that journey is so objectionable."

Her poor unhinged brain could not realize the indignity of this conduct nor the final nature of her renunciation. She added to her long letter the pitiful sentence: "Perhaps in my absence you will like me better and will do me justice, which is my due in every respect."

A guilty mother had effaced herself under the threat of a scandal. The children of the Marquis de Mirabeau—the elder boy was barely fourteen and the younger an invalid threatened with phthisis; the daughters were being brought up at a convent—the children knew only that there was a stranger in their home. At times they heard bits of conversations that made them blush for their mother.

Gabriel de Mirabeau retained from this terrible experience of his childhood a distrust of all the women he loved, a jealousy never free from suspicion, and, worse still, a contempt for all women. As his heritage from the tempestuous race and from the sexual irresponsibility of his mother, a fever in his blood was to devour him all his life. He was to lack the subconscious restraint born of respect for woman, the instinctive reaction of every son able to esteem his mother. His senses were aroused at an early age. He boasted later that at the age of thirteen he had taken advantage of his tutor's daughter. A precocious adolescent had breathed an atmosphere poisoned by the mutual wrongs of his parents, and this was his reaction.

The Marquise de Mirabeau thus deprived herself of the right to be concerned with the future of her children. In that same stormy year her eldest daughter, Marie, decided to take the veil. Her brother said later of her that she "certainly had plenty of mental energy: she was thought to be mad because her senses, which were as ill-suited as could be for convent life, had inflamed her. I think a husband would have made of her a woman capable of playing a great part." The mother's heart took alarm at this decision. "I have an absolute duty," she wrote to the marquis. "I wish to see my daughter before she becomes a nun."

The marquis refused to allow the interview. She could not even claim to feel the anguish of a mother. She continued to lead a disordered life. She quarreled with her mother. Her passion for gaming increased, and she ran into debt. Always incapable of resisting her impulses, she compromised herself with a guardsman. Three years after the breach, the marquis applied for a *lettre de cachet* for her.

Mme. de Pailly supervised the application of the most rigorous measures; she watched over the safety of the compromising documents that placed the marquise at the mercy of her husband, and she let no one approach these pathetic and precious securities.

II

"The elder of my boys," wrote the marquis at this time, "seems to me, so far at least, to have the making of nothing but an incurable maniac, on top of all his vile qualities. I see in him an animal nature, and I do not think it will ever be possible to make anything of him."

The marquis thought he could see nothing in the boy but the faults of his mother. He tightened the reins. He tried on Gabriel a programme of education to remedy the "cross-grained spirit" from which he thought came "the strange passions and the vices of this child." He confided him to a geometrician charged with "watching over him and correcting him," and then to a fencing-master, who was to "smarten him up." He took note of their ideas as confirmation of his own conviction that the boy was incorrigible. The self-confidence of a boy still quite young was in danger of being destroyed. It may be that it was saved only by a reaction to the very excess of the father's severity and the violence of his condemnation.

Writing later of the paths followed by the marquis' children, Gabriel de Mirabeau accused his father of having "disfigured, mutilated, lost," them all by his harshness, his prejudices, and his hatred.

❥ III ❦

Mr. Hurricane

G ABRIEL DE MIRABEAU had no longer the right even to use his name. The marquis rid himself of this inconvenient son by boarding him out with a former captain of cavalry at Versailles. The black sheep, so as not to dishonour the family, bore the name of an important property of his mother's in the Limousin—Pierre Buffière.

M. de Sigrais was capable of applying military discipline to a turbulent boy, but as a member of the Académie des Inscriptions et Belles-Lettres, he was also able to recognize a bright intelligence. Mme. de Sigrais, formerly chief lady-in-waiting to the dauphine, had no children. The couple seemed well chosen for watching over the boy.

The new tutor was delighted at first with his pupil. But rarely has a father made such violent efforts to destroy any possible good opinion of his child. He complained to the bailli that Sigrais, with his "noble and almost romantic mind," was applying too soft a regime "to the invasive and devouring nature of that rascal. He is captured, he is fascinated, he is full of praise for that memory that absorbs everything, without taking the trouble to realize that sand, too, takes every imprint, and that it is not enough to gain knowledge, it has to be retained and taken care of; he magnifies his goodness of heart, which is nothing but flabby and commonplace familiarity toward the lower classes, which puts them at ease and which he joins to an instinct of baseness; he praises his parrot mind. I am sick of all this, and shall see about it."

A few months later he wrote with satisfaction to the bailli: "The Sigrais, that excellent couple, have signified to me by the mouth of the husband, with tears in his eyes, that he would be the jailer of M. de Pierre Buffière as long as I wished, but that he despaired of ever being of any use to him." The Sigrais' experiment, begun under such good auspices, had ended in failure. The marquis explained it by the boy's "inexplicable mental kink."

Gabriel de Mirabeau gave another explanation of his removal—a satire he had written against Mme. de Pailly, which brought down upon him new thunders of paternal wrath. Nobody did so much writing up of the tumultuous relations between father and son as the two parties themselves. The boy was as yet too young to be able to dissimulate his hatred of Mme. de Pailly and to be cautious with so powerful a person.

The marquis transferred him to the care of the Abbé Choquard. "This man," said the marquis, "is unbending and enforces punishments in case of need. Now that I have made and carried through this last effort, if there is no improvement, and I have no hope of it, I shall send him right out of the country." Perhaps that was the very solution he hoped for.

The Abbé Choquard's college was a fashionable and stern military school for boys of good family, and was attended by many foreigners of distinction. Physical drill and even manœuvres, in the Prussian style, played an important part in the school routine. This severe discipline had little success with a boy accustomed to constraint. After a few months the marquis registered with satisfaction another failure. He sent his faithful factotum Garçon to fetch his son, planning to send him to a reformatory.

But Pierre Buffière had not wasted his time at the boarding school. This time he had come in contact, perhaps for the first time, with boys of intelligence and spirit. In this first contact there was already manifested his masterful quality, his seductive charm. His schoolfellows, he relates, rebelled and drew up a petition which they sent by deputation to his father, demanding that he be sent back.

With this declaration in his favour Gabriel de Mirabeau's adolescence started. The step taken by his comrades surprised his father. But it taught him only to be wary in future of this power of his son, of which he had had no knowledge until then.

Gabriel remained three years with the Abbé Choquard. His father

soon noted that the abbé had "more than half tamed and reformed
M. Pierre Buffière." His schoolfellows' good opinion undoubtedly did
much for the spiritual development of a gifted but recalcitrant pupil.
With Poisson he had learnt nothing but Latin. Now he revealed a special
gift for modern languages. His father declared that "his mind is a
succession of glimmers and sparks, incapable of steady work and consistent reasoning." But his mathematics master was surprised by his
ability. In two years Gabriel mastered differential and integral calculus.
The mathematics master was interested in his pupil; he lent him books,
and heard him exclaim, after reading Locke's *Essay on the Human
Understanding*, "That's the book I need."

Another of his talents attracted the attention of his masters. The
great orator was early revealed by his gift of recitation. At a public
examination he was the one assigned by the Abbé Choquard to deliver
a speech in honour of mathematics. Pierre Buffière was no longer the
pupil tolerated because of a petition. He was a brilliant pupil, a subject
of pride, and was shown in public. In his third year at the boarding
school he delivered a speech of his own composition, a eulogy of the
Prince de Condé, whom he compared to Scipio Africanus.

Thanks to his success, his father permitted him to use his own name
again. The journals of the time devoted some flattering remarks to this
brilliant pupil: "We see that this young eaglet is already flying in the
wake of his illustrious father," wrote the editor of the *Recueil de
Bachaumont* in January 1767, and he added: "The son has more neatness and elegance in his style, and his speech is very well written."

The marquis had every reason to be content. Strangers had discovered
the father's gifts in his son. His pride might have been satisfied. But
another feeling seems to have been born in his agitated soul, a feeling
that found full expression only in later years. Gabriel later told a woman
friend: "All my misfortunes owe their origin to my having offended
my father, to whom I once said with a youngster's indiscreet openness
these trenchant and too well-founded words, which, to my misfortune,
he has never forgotten: 'Alas, if you had but self-esteem, would not my
successes be also yours?'" The marquis no longer found his son stupid
—he found him dangerous.

The father's great complaint against him was that he tried to keep
in touch with his mother. He cut off all his correspondence. Gabriel's
grandmother, the Marquise de Vassan, complained in vain of getting
no news of him. But one day the marquis learned that the boy's mother,
who "uses all she has and all she has not to debauch the rotten part
of the family," had secretly sent money to "that ne'er-do-well."

He never forgave Gabriel for being the son of his mother. He made him pay for it with all the ferocious tenacity of hatred of which he was capable. He wrote one day to the bailli: "The twenty years I lived with that woman were twenty years of renal colic. Ah, well! at the time of my worst trials I said to Mme. de Pailly: 'It's nothing. My true cross is her son who is growing up.'"

2

In the year during which the rupture with his wife occurred, the year in which his eldest daughter took the veil, the marquis' second daughter, Caroline, was married to the Marquis du Saillant, a young man of very good family. But the young man's parents had demanded a big dowry, eighty thousand livres. "It would be murderous to refuse so good a match," said the marquis, and he made up the sum by borrowing.

It proved a happy marriage, without shocks or shadows. Caroline always had a baby coming; she devoted herself to her vocation as mother to the extent of losing all feminine daintiness. She had been a robust and healthy girl; she became a strong, stout woman, "slack and ungainly" in carriage. Her ready good-nature, her affectionate effusiveness, were at everyone's service. She "always had her arm round someone's neck." She was not without culture. She knew Latin, and she could draw and could play on the harpsichord. But she was active above all in amusing others. According to her father she had "an enormous repertoire of light and comic songs." There was an element of vulgarity in that prematurely broadened figure, in her freedom of speech, in her taste for the "spicy."

There was nothing of the rebel in her: she took things as they came, and was easygoing to the length of seeming to have some end in view. She was the only one of the marquis' children who found grace in the eyes of Mme. de Pailly. Caroline took her part, and by her friendship gave a show of justification to the intruder's presence. She was her father's faithful ally. In the tormented existence of the family she represented the triumph of common sense, the stability of a well-balanced mind.

The other pole of this stability was the bailli. The marquis' second success was the career he induced his brother to take up. He settled his brother in the same year in which he settled his daughter, arranging his life for him, a little against the brother's inclination. At the moment when the marquis was settling things for him, the bailli was thinking of getting married. He was paying court to a woman, in his brusque way, hampered by timidity. He dreamed of having a family of his own. But the elder brother turned him in a direction that required the renunciation of his dreams. He opted for the Order of Malta.

A great financial difficulty presented itself. A General of Galleys had to expend up to a hundred and fifty thousand livres. The bailli's share of the paternal inheritance represented only about a third of this. But the marquis borrowed for his brother as he had borrowed for his daughter. The modest patrimony of Mme. de Pailly was also used. The marquis did things in grand style: the bailli was set up sumptuously. His fine, manly presence was enhanced by the laced garments his brother had provided. On his arrival at Malta he found unlimited credit placed at his disposal. It was a place where gold had to be scattered lavishly. With his modest standards, the bailli was frightened by all this expenditure. "I am looking after that," the marquis reassured him. "When," he added, prophesying a good deal better than he knew, "when you are a *grand seigneur*, and I still a poor devil, you will come to the aid of the family."

In Malta the bailli began by making a great impression, and went on to inspire confidence. "My white hair has been very useful, it is liked in high quarters." He spent two years learning his duties as General of Galleys. He established his authority; his rather gruff uprightness carried the day in an environment seething with rival ambitions. At first there fell to him a modest commandery, but soon he received the richest in Provence. The marquis had not been mistaken. The younger brother became a *grand seigneur;* his commandery was farmed out at thirty-nine thousand livres per annum. But he won much more in Malta: he won general esteem, and could have aspired to the highest posts. His brother, however, recalled him to France. Forty knights of different nations called on him begging him to put off his departure. He could have looked forward to succession to the office of Grand Master. "I replied to them that I owed everything to you, that to me your desires were commands, and that I was waiting to hear from you."

The Marquis de Mirabeau was waiting to install the bailli in the paternal domain which he himself had abandoned, the château of Mirabeau. The bailli resigned himself to this with a sigh. "Feeling that I had some chance of getting to the top, I passed a sleepless night, on the eve of my embarkation, between my great desire to satisfy you and, on the other hand, some promptings of ambition. You won."

3

The old Marquise de Mirabeau was nearly eighty-two. She was as dry and unbending as ever, imperious, apparently clear-headed. Strangers spoke of her astonishing mental power. But suddenly she was seized by acute dementia. It was not a gentle, senile imbecility, a pitiful decay, but a frenzy that seized hold of that dried-up body and that cold brain. "Her mania is all harshness and aversion." The resentments of a whole life were assailing a heart that had sheltered behind a deceptive serenity. All that she had repressed as an over-prudish girl and an austere woman rose up in waves of horror from the hidden depths of her being. Baron von Gleichen, formerly Danish ambassador at Paris, had known her before she lost her reason: he noted her case with the interest of a collector of human curiosities. "This woman, so virtuous, so prudish, who had taken offence at the very suggestion of an equivocal expression, vomited words that would have shocked a grenadier, words which one would have imagined must be totally unknown to her." She was a frightful spectacle, this old woman who tore off all her clothes, who had to be made to lie down on straw and to be kept there by force. She would not allow anyone to come near her. Her rage was redoubled at the sight of a woman. Only an old man-servant "could do anything with her, because she had fallen in love with him," says Gleichen. But she was always ready to see the son she had so loved all her life. "She always recognized me and cherished me to her last moment," wrote the marquis.

She lived another three years in insanity. Before losing her reason she had made her will, bequeathing the whole of her fortune to her second grandson, the only one who had found grace in her eyes as "entirely a Mirabeau."

4

In the Allée des Chartreux the crowd stood three-deep. It was waiting for a great man to whom it wanted to put questions—the Marquis de Mirabeau, who passed this way twice a week, attended by his faithful followers. He had published a work expounding Quesnay's whole theory. This was the *Philosophie Rurale*, with its formidable subtitle, *General political economy of agriculture reduced to the immutable order of the physical and moral laws that assure the prosperity of empires.*

He was, as he himself said, one of the leaders of "a very famous sort of sect." The Physiocrats became more and more fashionable. They had their publication, *Les Ephémérides,* of which the marquis was one of the principal inspirers. The salons of Paris displayed a strange interest in this literature.

For those who were responsible for the well-being of their subjects, Quesnay's theory was seductive because it subordinated moral demands to material improvement. The marquis one day defended it in his drastic way: "I warn those who may accuse me of subordinating the moral too much to the physical element that anybody mad with hunger would eat his father, and that it is no good at all to talk to people about moral virtue before physical needs have been appeased." He referred also to the principle which the Physiocrats called interested justice: "What needs to be done today is to make the personal physical interest of each man become the bond between men and the motive element in all their relations."

Since the Physiocrats admitted a "legal despotism," conforming with the laws of the natural order, their doctrine found favour even among absolute sovereigns. Catherine the Great brought one of their disciples to St. Petersburg. Leopold, Grand Duke of Tuscany and later Emperor of Austria, sent representatives to consult the marquis. The Margrave of Baden came to Paris to see him. The son of the dauphin's tutor asked in his father's name that a publication of the Physiocrats' should be dedicated to the future Louis XVI, but the marquis refused with the pride of an independent savant: "I said that princes must acquire merit with us by deeds or at least by sentiments manifested. I even declared that I should abandon and disavow *Les Ephémérides* the moment they displayed the colours of a court."

A few years later the King of Sweden, Gustavus III, who had met the marquis when journeying incognito in France, sent him the cross of a Grand Commander of the Order of Vasa, which he had just founded, writing in his own hand: "The title which all humanity conferred on you long ago is far above anything kings can do for your glory. I have nevertheless been eager to pay at least a part of the tribute which all nations owe you." He asked at the same time for "the continuation of the useful lessons to which you have devoted your efforts and your rare knowledge," undertaking to profit by these lessons. This letter from an enlightened sovereign to *l'ami des hommes* was written on the eve of Gustavus III's *coup d'état* against the senate of his country. Encouraged by such sensational conversions, the Marquis de Mirabeau was ambitious for others.

Jean-Jacques Rousseau, then a refugee in England, was in the throes of great difficulties, real and imaginary. A quarrel with Hume, envenomed by the insinuations of his entourage, was transformed in the exile's brain into a subtle plot. He placed his quarrel before the whole world. The Marquis de Mirabeau intervened in his own way, profiting by his role of Friend of Mankind. He did not know Rousseau personally, but with his aristocratic haughtiness he judged him "the only professional writer of our time whom I know to be estimable." Rousseau thanked him for this flattering homage and assured him that the marquis' works were the only ones, apart from two treatises on botany, which he had brought away with him to England.

In reply the marquis addressed a long letter to Rousseau, of the sort that could be written only to an old friend on whom one has some call by dint of having lavished devotion on him. "If I had been Mr. Hume," he wrote, plunging into the thick of the quarrel, "I should have replied to you: Believe me, I pray you, that nothing but your imagination, heated from an inextinguishable source, could have produced all this fine story of machinations." But although he scolded him, he showed comprehension for this ailing, galled soul. He divined the anguished perplexity of an exile not knowing where to find shelter from persecution. "I wish you would give me the pleasure of accepting the hospitality of one or more of my bits of ground; for I have all sorts to offer you." His offer found Rousseau particularly responsive to a friendly gesture. "It is worthy of the *ami des hommes* to console the afflicted," he replied with emotion. "I did not expect that it would be you who made advances, and this at the very moment when I am universally abandoned; but generosity can do nothing by halves."

The marquis possessed at Fleury-sous-Meudon a pretty country house where the author of *Emile*—a man for whose arrest a warrant had been issued—could take refuge under an assumed name. Rousseau hastened to take advantage of this asylum. In the little country house the two couples, of such different calibre, met—the Marquis de Mirabeau with Mme. de Pailly, and Rousseau with Thérèse Levasseur. For the marquis the meeting might have been a turning-point. It might have launched him in the direction of the new order of which he vaguely sensed the approach. But all he sought was an adept for this new science which he professed, this panacea for the ills of the age. His hospitable gesture had not been disinterested. A meeting heavy with significance quickly turned into a passing episode. After a fortnight Rousseau rejoined the Prince de Conti. The sensational conversion did not take place: Physiocracy could not enrol so celebrated a disciple as this.

The marquis had done his best. He had made Rousseau read his *Philosophie Rurale;* he had sent him the outline of the doctrine made by a brilliant disciple of Quesnay. "Illustrious friend of mankind and of me," Rousseau wrote to him, "I prostrate myself at your feet to implore you to have pity on my estate and my misfortunes and to leave my poor dying head in peace. Love me always, but don't send me any more books." And to ward off any attempts on the part of his enterprising host, he added a sentence that put an end to their relations: "Nobody is sincerely converted at my age."

Was it during this visit that young Gabriel made the acquaintance of his father's guest? He only remarked one day that he had met Rousseau, and that the meeting had left an ineffaceable impression. He retained throughout his life an ardent enthusiasm for Rousseau, whose life and works he once summed up in one of those phrases which he pronounced with the secret desire that they should be applied to himself: "He wrested a thousand times more from his passions than they could steal from him."

5

The Marquis de Mirabeau chose for his son "the roughest and the strictest of military schools." Gabriel was soon to prove that he liked his profession and was interested in it, though the precautions taken by his father might have given him a horror of it.

The regiment of Berri Cavalerie, stationed at Saintes, was commanded by the Marquis de Lambert, whose severity was of the most formidable sort, the severity of a young man, peremptory, exacting, and unrelieved by any lessons of experience. "Feared like the provost marshal," as the marquis put it, he was implacable in the punishment of every breach of discipline. Gabriel spent part of his first year of service in the regimental prison.

To this excessively close surveillance was added the boredom of a little town. Saintes, like all small provincial towns, lived a shuttered, narrow life of idle, peering curiosity. Any young man in such a place would seek distraction, and the only ones to be had were gaming and women. He gambled, and ran into debt because he had no money —little debts of a few dozen louis, which made his father exclaim, to all appearance with ferocious satisfaction: "There he shows himself well moulded in the pattern of his maternal race, which would eat up twenty heritages and a dozen kingdoms if it could get hold of them."

Everything that Gabriel did had excessive repercussions. "I can do nothing right," he complained one day to his mother. "My slightest slips have more fearful results than the worst ones of other fellows." Tormented by the sensuality of which he had a double heritage, he sought appeasement of the senses and satisfaction of his feeling of what was due to him in a liaison with a young woman of the people. He had plenty of imagination and sufficient guilelessness to transform this attachment into a great passion, and a moment's indulgence into an eternal obligation. He promised to marry his young mistress. His adventure created a scandal in the little town. The young man's heated imagination made him believe that his colonel was his rival and see evidence of vengeance in the rigours of the service.

To get out of the complications in which he had involved himself, he adopted the wild expedient of flight to Paris. He begged the Duc de Nivernois to intervene in his favour with his father. He complained of receiving such "deadly affronts" from his colonel that "I have seen a whole town commenting on my patience, regarding it as unworthy."

The marquis seems to have forgotten his own youthful love affairs and money troubles. He seized his opportunity at once, now that his son had put himself in the wrong. He had not yet had time to verify the young man's statements; yet "I felt my father's soul reproaching me for having had any hope of that wretch." In point of fact his decision had already been made, the *lettre de cachet*, by his own admission, was in readiness. Already, almost two years earlier, in December 1766, he had confided to Saillant his plan to send his son "to the *nord*, and to adopt measures calculated to remove that pest." The punishment was ready well before the offence. The young man was consigned to the Nivernois mansion, placed in the charge of his brother-in-law, and surrounded by detectives.

The bailli, too, seems to have forgotten his own youthful excesses and the fact that, according to his brother, "for three or four years he was not out of prison four days in the year," and he proposed even more draconic measures for his nephew. "See whether that wretch's excesses deserve his exclusion forever from society, and, if so, the best thing of all is to send him to the Dutch colonies. You are sure then of never seeing on the horizon again an unfortunate born to be the sorrow of his parents and the shame of his race."

"These things are easier to plan than to carry out," replied the marquis. Gabriel had spoken the truth in declaring that the whole town had taken his part. When the marquis had him taken back to Saintes by Saillant, the colonel did not venture to deal severely with him. He told the marquis that his son had "divided the town and the whole region between reason and himself."

The colonel would have been ready to come to terms, but the marquis was on the watch. Through the Comte de Choiseul, he succeeded in getting his son arrested and taken, under the name of Pierre Buffière, to the Ile de Ré. His father had given him, as he put it, "a good recommendation" to the governor of the island, the Bailli d'Aulan. He had described him as "headstrong, cross-grained, and a liar by instinct."

The Bailli d'Aulan, known for his severity, gave his prisoner a grim reception. If the prisoner found the circle of a little town too narrow for him, now his youthful impetuosity was confined within the walls of a citadel. The injustice of this excessive punishment destroyed such sense of proportion as Gabriel still had left. His one thought was to elude supervision. The financial restrictions which his father imposed on him were so harsh that his one thought now was to get money by any and every means. "At the age of twenty," he wrote later accusingly to the marquis, "I had not had the smallest sum of money in my control—at least so far as it came from you." He had not inherited a sense of economy from either of his parents and had no sense of the value of money. The oppression that had weighed on him since childhood had not fundamentally injured his character, but the tight control during the years of his hot-headed youth had developed in him an incurable prodigality. He himself declared that he was never able to count. He ran into debt with airy irresponsibility, as if he had a steady income.

The citadel regime allowed him occasional outings in the neighbourhood. These moments of liberty were the more precious to him for their rarity, and he profited by them regardless of consequences. He borrowed money from anyone who would lend it, and it was especially the common people who were easily moved by his destitution, the sergeants and even the privates of the garrison. The paternal spy always at his heels described him to the marquis in the course of these short escapades, "cursing, fighting, wounding, and vomiting a wickedness such as never was."

While the father's discontent—deliberately kept up—grew, the Bailli d'Aulan had time to revise his prejudiced first impressions. Little by little he discovered in the young man his serious side and his capacity for improvement, and he no longer saw anything more in his bad behaviour than the boiling over of an ill-directed temperament. The marquis exclaimed in exasperation: "He is bewitching the Bailli d'Aulan himself—who, against my orders, is giving him liberty to walk about in the citadel—and my friends, and everybody."

The Bailli d'Aulan, "bewitched," urged Gabriel's father to revoke the *lettre de cachet.* He advised him to put the young man on probation. "I know quite well," complained the marquis, "that once he is let out he will get himself shut up forever within three months; but still, I cannot keep M. Pierre Buffière caged up much longer."

The marquis, most reluctantly following the advice of the Bailli d'Aulan, put his son on probation. Upon his release Gabriel learned of the fate he had escaped. Many years later he still remembered the horror with which he had been filled: "After releasing me you admitted, in one of your letters, that you had been on the point of sending me to the Dutch colonies at the time of my detention in the Ile de Ré. That statement made a deep impression on me and had a prodigious influence on the rest of my life. What had I done, at eighteen years of age, that you should have had such an idea, one that makes me tremble to this day?—to bury me alive in my tomb!"

6

On top of all the vices with which the father charged his son, he imputed cowardice to him. He made him take part in the Corsican expedition, which was in preparation in the spring of 1769, to suppress an insurrection that threatened French rule in the island. The young sub-lieutenant was seconded to the Lorraine legion, whose colonel had been recommended to the marquis as "the man who was needed, as well as that service, to curb his hot-headedness, which threatens to swallow everything and which will be swallowed only by virtue of plenty of sword-play, if he has the virtue to face it."

The marquis had warned all the young sub-lieutenant's superiors against him, and had been promised that "he will be hanged at the public expense if he is not worthy of his father."

But the wild rebel of Saintes revealed himself in Corsica as a remarkable young officer. He explained it by the confidence shown in him by his commanding officer, the Baron de Viomenil. "A Lambert was capable of sending me to perdition," Gabriel wrote later, "a Viomenil could get anything out of me." The confidence shown in him brought out his best qualities and incited him to surpass himself in order the better to justify it. He retained infinite gratitude toward this commanding officer, who had believed in him at a time when his father wanted to deprive him of his name and his country. He was sure, and his colonel agreed, that he had found his true vocation. He threw himself into his duties with the tireless ardour of his nature.

The short campaign and his interest in his profession did not exhaust his great curiosity about men and things. It was the first time he had been out of France, and he was greatly interested in the customs, the institutions, the economic and social conditions, and the psychology of the people of the country he was traversing, and also in its past. And on his way through this fragrant and beautiful island, Gabriel de Mirabeau, at barely twenty years of age, revealed a sturdy independence of mind.

He was one of an army that had come to repress a movement of insubordination. He knew nothing as yet of the magical and irresistible appeal of liberty. Twenty years later, as a member of the National Assembly, he publicly expressed his regret that his "early youth had been soiled by participation in the conquest of Corsica." But his fresh vision, roving over an unknown country, detected already in the traces of the ancient Genoese domination, in the ruins of an oppression overcome, the proud past of this little island. He tried to learn more of it, set himself to learn everything. He associated with intelligent Corsicans, who were at pains to supply him with all the information he was so eager to accumulate. He had not yet completed any personal achievement, and he felt already that there was material here for a solid work. No research daunted him, no detail, however dry it might seem to a young imagination, escaped him. He conceived the ambitious plan of writing a history of Corsica. He set himself to describe it "step by step," he relates, "seeing everything with my own eyes, and supplying all the political, economic, and historical details possible."

At the end of the campaign his chiefs certified that he had "shown distinguished valour and intelligence." His father, who had considered that he had emerged entirely from the maternal stock, was obliged to recognize in him a grandson of the hero of Cassano. The young man burned with eagerness to show himself a worthy descendant of Jean-Antoine.

From the Corsican campaign Gabriel brought away great hopes and a fine faith in his destiny. If he could secure a reconciliation with his father, a brilliant career would open before him. He needed only the aid of favourable circumstances for his future to be free from troubles.

7

"A burning sky, a climate of extremes, a wild aspect, arid walks, rocks, birds of prey, devouring rivers, torrents either dried up or overflowing, and strong, hard, free, and restless men"—thus had the Marquis de

Mirabeau described to Jean-Jacques Rousseau his native Provence. The château of Mirabeau stood upon a precipitous rock, between two deep gorges, its walls of tawny yellow blending with the rocks burnt by a pitiless sun. The countryside beneath the castle, with its rounded hills and its steep-sided valleys, resembled undulating floods of lava suddenly petrified. In its deepest hollows sparkled the irregular ribbon of the Durance. The rough majesty of the country was matched by the castle, a great rectangular mass flanked by towers, which looked more like a citadel than a seignorial dwelling. It was a feudal castle of the sort to please the bailli, who considered that a house without towers was fit only to be "the dwelling of a rich burgess." He installed himself there on his return from Malta, with no further personal ambition, placing himself and his fortune at the service of his family, firmly anchored to his conservative convictions and his prejudices, and strangely amenable to his brother's injunctions.

One evening in May 1770, when the bailli was at Aix, a soldier brought him a letter. It was from "M. de Pierre Buffière," asking his uncle for the favour of an hour's interview. The bailli knew nothing of his nephew beyond his father's complaints. He knew only of his misdeeds, and had not learnt to regard him in any but an unfavourable light. He prepared to give him a cool reception. But Gabriel was not to be intimidated, as the bailli soon discovered.

For the first time Gabriel found himself acknowledged to have a family resemblance. To the marquis he was always "entirely a Vassan." But the bailli, who scrutinized him at first severely and then fondly, found him plain, but revealing beneath the pockmarks "intelligence, grace, nobility," and with a "singular resemblance to his youngest uncle, the dead Comte Alexandre-Louis, in attitude and gesture and expression." The marquis at once discounted this favourable impression. "You have seen him at his best, for he is seductive when he is in the mood to be."

Gabriel had to fight hard against his father, who used his hold over the bailli to influence him against his son. "Be careful," he wrote. "Your goodness carries you on faster than my letters can reach you to persuade you that before long you will be hissing at the effigy of which you are trying to make a man." The marquis' letters fought inch by inch against the young man's advance. The bailli himself ventured only timidly to ask his brother to permit Gabriel to join him at Mirabeau. The marquis gave grudging assent.

Gabriel was not even taken into the family château. He was lodged with the Abbé Castagny, the marquis' former agent. The bailli and the abbé watched him with a keenness heightened by the father's injunctions. The bailli assured the marquis that he was not in the least blind, that he saw Gabriel's defects; he reproached him, for example, for the nasal speech which the young man, with his imitative gift, had copied from his superiors. As for the abbé, he approached Gabriel with his peasant's suspicion. "You know the level-headed Abbé Castagny," wrote the bailli to his brother. But the two men were unable to resist the onslaught of their young visitor's prodigious vitality. Gabriel was at an advantage with an audience whose concealed goodwill he detected. The abbé, the bailli wrote, "opens his eyes and then weeps with joy. As for me, this child opens my heart." They agreed in finding in him "a little vivacity and fire, but not a word that does not indicate uprightness of heart, elevation of soul, and a powerful mind, all perhaps a little exuberant."

This good opinion disturbed the marquis, who continually insisted: "Be cautious, keep on guard against his gilded beak. There is nobody to beat him at eating out of your hand." "That head," the bailli replied, "is a mill of thoughts and ideas, of which many are very novel. You will find, as I have done, that the furnace is very hot; but, dear brother, let us recall his age, and the explosive that is in our blood." He added, a little provoked by his brother's attitude, "It is a good thing that we should have an opportunity of getting to know him, for while he is perfectly able to see reason, he will listen to nothing else, and finds it torture to have to submit to all other human restraints."

He, too, was astonished at the work his nephew had done during the campaign, and he wrote enthusiastically to his brother, at the risk of wounding his self-esteem. "He has just been reading to me, during our walk this morning, the preface to a history of Corsica. I assure you that at twenty-two you had not done so much, and as for me, I could not have done a hundredth part of it at forty. I found in it clear principles dictated by a head full of elevation, of fire, of nerve and genius, and by a firm, strong, good heart."

The marquis was maddened by these reports. He complained to his daughter Caroline. "The romantic element that perfumes that worthless fellow from top to bottom has gone to his uncle's head, good head though it is; he has been absorbed, it is his own word. . . . The fellow has been working his big marionettes." He added: "He may win over his uncle, but he will not win his father back so cheaply."

The bailli discussed the young man's future with him. With his seaman's soul he praised the advantages of his own service. Impressionable and eager to please, Gabriel quickly adopted his uncle's ideas and even ran ahead of them. "He said to me," the bailli wrote, "that if he had to wait indefinitely for employment on land, he would prefer the navy." But the marquis cut short these projects. "I do not want romantic dreams and planetary voyages and unfruitful amusements." He himself had deserted his estate, but he wanted to tie his son to it. This apostle of the return to the land ordered his son to "compile for the agriculture of the Limousin and the Périgord the same particulars that he had collected in Corsica, with the economic standard which he must have acquired since."

Gabriel, who was incapable of remaining idle, had gone to work without waiting for these paternal instructions. "M. le Comte Pierre Buffière is working like a galley slave at getting the lands of Mirabeau into his head," the bailli reported. "The young fellow is shaping well. He lets nothing distract him or interfere with his work. I have never seen a bohemian who was less afraid of sun and wind, rain or hail." His robust health defied the elements; his alert brain, interested in everything, seemed able to absorb everything. "It is work and success in it that give pleasure," the marquis commented sententiously. "What is wrong everywhere in France is the resistance to work." The bailli replied that his son was "writing volumes: the most prolific and the most rapid of writers; neither you nor I can compare with him. I assure you that, except that in a week he has used up my stock of paper for half a year, I am very content with him."

The bailli fought indefatigably for the soul of this father who obstinately refused to yield. This bachelor who had never had children or a home, this man of simple and fixed ideas, showed a rare accuracy of judgment, a wealth of comprehension, in the interpretation of the complicated soul of a young man with extraordinary gifts. He saw the childish side of this youth who had grown up too quickly, with his overstrong body and his insatiable appetite. After Gabriel had been some weeks at the château of Mirabeau the bailli wrote to the marquis: "I am still studying Pierre Buffière, and I affirm that he has a good heart; for the rest, he is young for his age. It is a strange contrast, his childishness combined with reflections and thoughts and writings that seem to come from Locke; all in all, it is a head that wants a lot to browse on."

Before his candid blue eyes there had risen a vision of his nephew's glorious destiny. "I repeat, either he is the cleverest humbug in the world, or he will be the greatest man in Europe, general on land or sea, or minister or chancellor or pope, or whatever he wants to be."

8

"With all the glory of the most brilliant youth, the most eloquent black eyes, the freshness of Hebe, she had that air of nobility that is no longer to be found except in antique statues, and the most beautiful figure I have ever seen."

Gabriel de Mirabeau remembered all his life the dazzling picture of his youngest sister as he met her in the château of Mirabeau. They were virtually strangers, for he had left the château when still a child. As a little girl she had given promise, according to her father, of becoming "the rarest creature of her time." She showed a precocious ripeness of mind. One day, when her father paid her a compliment on her intelligence, she replied calmly: "I think, Papa, that the mind is like the hand: whether it is pretty or plain, it is made for use and not for show." At an early age she became aware of her exceptional beauty and her personal worth. She had the ambition to use these possessions in her life in order to bring to full realization her brilliant destiny as a woman. One day, when she seemed entirely absorbed in some child's game, she heard her father and mother discussing the future of their children; breaking into the discussion, she said: "Don't worry about me, I shall be all right."

Everything presaged the exceptional destiny which she awaited as her due. But the moment came when Mme. de Pailly intervened in the life of the marquis. Unlike her sisters, Louise had been brought up at home until she was eleven. The marquis had deluded himself for a moment with the idea that he would find his mistress a better guide for his daughter than her own mother. "The black lady," he wrote at the time to the Comtesse de Rochefort, "would be the most useful and the best duenna in the world." But the "black lady" took offence at the first hint of it and punished the marquis for it. She was so sure of her power over him that she did not hesitate to impose on him a painful renunciation. In the monstrous egoism of his elderly passion, the marquis sacrificed his daughter to her. "I have been forced to promise her," he confessed to the Comtesse de Rochefort, "that I shall see this child only once a year, and then only for a single day, until she is married, and not write to her at all. With great difficulty I secured peace at that price." After seeing discord installed in her home, Louise de Mirabeau found herself sent away from it by a stranger.

The marquis took thought very early for getting her married, fearing that open war with his wife would make a marriage more difficult. But he was not ready to make any sacrifice of pride for the sake of his daughter's happiness. The young Comte d'Orsay, "a well set-up young man, gentle, a good fellow, eighteen years old," and very rich into the bargain, had fallen in love with Louise after seeing her at the convent. But his father, who, moreover, was dead, had been a farmer general of taxes. "My forefathers never allied themselves with publicans," said the marquis disdainfully. The next proposal made to the marquis was by "a young lawyer, rolling in ingots." But he refused again, "in view of my regular habit of being approached humbly by gentlemen of that profession." Louise, very sure of herself, declared for her part: "I don't know what is the use of wealth, but if it is a necessary thing I feel that I have the gift of attracting it in the house I shall enter."

Mme. de Pailly also looked early for a husband for Louise, busying herself more actively than the marquis. The bailli, too, took part in the search, with all the clumsiness of a bachelor. He found in Provence a young man of good family, great possessions, and great expectations. The marquis was pleased to learn that his father was over seventy years of age, but he did not trouble to find out that his future son-in-law was in danger of suffering from impoverished blood and inadequate education. He was not able to obtain from his mother-in-law the addition to the dowry which she had granted to Caroline. But the bailli promised to supply out of income the thirty thousand livres which the family of the young Marquis de Cabris demanded.

Suddenly the Marquis de Mirabeau learned through a friend a fact that was common knowledge in Provence: for a considerable part of his life the old Marquis de Cabris had been mentally unsound, and such cases were frequent in the family. One of the daughters was insane and lived in the family château in the care of a nurse. But the bailli reassured him at once: Mademoiselle de Cabris' "accident" had had "absolutely personal" causes. "The young man offers the best of hopes both in body and mind."

This was enough for the marquis. He did not trouble to see his future son-in-law himself. He refused to allow his daughter to make the acquaintance of the man with whom she was to be united. The Cabris family urged that the two young people meet before the marriage was settled. "My daughter will certainly not go on a journey to meet a husband," the marquis declared loftily. "They have only to find out what she is like, and it is my opinion that so far as the physical matter is concerned the conjugal amalgam is not a difficult thing at twenty years of age, when the two united come together without prejudice."

Bound by his promise to Mme. de Pailly, he permitted this child, whose strength of character he knew, no freedom of choice. "My daughter will leave the convent only to be married at Bignon, which is four leagues away."

Louise was romantic, and excited by her education at the convent and her ignorance of the world. Her capricious and self-willed nature called for a husband with strength of mind and sureness and decision of character. "I have not the slightest doubt," wrote her brother later, "that a man of honour and good sense, in love with her, would have been able to check her impetuosity and keep her from straying." Her temperament, combining intelligence with passion, called for a lover who would capture her senses. In addition to conjugal happiness, Louise's beauty and intelligence demanded a wide stage to enable her to shine, and her ambition presaged an important role for her; frustrated, she would hurl defiance at all the social conventions. But her destiny presented itself in the form of a young man with the morose and listless character of an old one.

The marriage took place on the day following the arrival of the bridegroom with his Provençal family. Louise de Cabris, a woman overflowing with vitality, was tied for life to a man who succumbed later to acute insanity.

When her brother met her she had been married only a few months. She was still enjoying her status of a young married woman, with the new conditions of existence and the independence she had never known. A "magic of seduction" radiated from her. She had the desire to please which, according to her father, was "the sublimity of worthless hearts." Involved in a common reprobation, brother and sister were natural allies.

Strangers to each other and yet so closely related, so different and so alike, they felt drawn to each other by a force more disturbing than the bonds of blood. It was at the sight of her regained brother that Louise realized how her life had been spoilt. Until then she had evaded —through self-esteem as much as through loyalty—the admission that she had nothing in common with the husband who had been given to her. She still tried to persuade herself that she might find at his side a mild conjugal happiness. She was expecting motherhood, and this joy in fulfilment helped to disguise her disappointment. But the meeting with her brother swept away the laborious scaffolding of her illusions. She found in him a part of herself that had been denied effective existence. Her latent romantic imagination was fired by the story of his amorous troubles. She offered to be an intermediary between him and the girl at Saintes. She was to be at his side in the future in his passionate adventures, her ardour increasing with their madness.

Under the burning sky of a Provençal summer, brother and sister dreamed of an impossible love. They dreamed of it with such intensity that they imagined that they had experienced it. A lively interest, a great curiosity, a close communion of feelings and thoughts, a wild mutual admiration, took the appearance of a passion, skirted the abyss of incestuous love. Later, at a time of great disturbance and morbid excitement, Gabriel de Mirabeau mistook the dream for reality.

After their separation, Louise wrote to him: "You have done me a lot of harm, dear friend; did you suspect it?" Thereafter she said to herself: "I should love my husband if he were like my brother." She returned unhappily to her lamentable existence: "I felt empty of soul when you had gone." From then on Louise consciously nursed her grievance against those who had been responsible for her destiny. In that summer of 1770 she tasted all the joys of the bailli's hospitality: she felt a sincere affection for him. Later she came openly into conflict with him. "It was my uncle," she said, "who arranged my marriage." She vowed implacable hatred of the man whom she called "the author of my sufferings, the destroyer of my existence."

9

In August 1770 Gabriel de Mirabeau rejoined his father at the château d'Aigueperse in the Limousin. The bailli urged his brother again and again to give his son a good reception. Knowing his weakness, he warned him: "It may be that you will not find him very strong in the field of the Economist. But, with all due deference, I could wish that you would receive him as a man for whom I have gone bail; and that you would unbend a little, without giving yourself away, and find out what he is aiming at; that he might feel that you are his friend and are greatly interested in him."

"I received him kindly and even affectionately," the marquis replied. After his brother's favourable report he found Gabriel "a Mirabeau entirely, that is to say, a very troublesome individual, a man of intelligence to begin with, and of merit, out of a job." His son's admission to favour was conditional: "I shall examine him for myself and through others, reducing or increasing the tests." It was even subject to threats: "If I should happen to see him in peril or on the wrong path, I should ask him to await maturity in a less dangerous country." He was obliged to recognize that "military service is still good for him, even necessary; he needs plenty of exercise, for what the devil is to be done with this full-blooded intellectual exuberance?"

The bailli was delighted with this qualified mildness. "Go on taking M. le Comte de la Bourrasque [Count Squall] in good part; he needs to find you good-humoured, and, to tell the truth, he deserves to. But is it not true that he is two men at the same time?"

At the beginning of September Mme. de Vassan died. Gabriel was sent to take his mother to the dying woman. It was the first time he saw death at close quarters. The spectacle greatly upset him. Years later he still remembered the painful emotion he had felt at his grandmother's death struggle.

"The death of Mme. de Vassan has driven her daughter stark mad," wrote the marquis. Yet at that very moment when the poor woman was distraught with grief, he proposed that he should be given a free hand in administering her mother's estate, though a great part of it was jointly inherited. He gave vent in front of his son to all his rage and his contempt for his wife. The bailli tried in vain to recall him to a sense of the most elementary decency: "You will realize that one cannot speak to a son about his mother in a certain tone." Gabriel was tossed between two violent hatreds. When his father sent him to negotiate with his mother, she poured out all her resentment to him. Amid a flood of vociferous abuse she recited all her grievances, real or imaginary, revealing to a young man of twenty-two an abyss of depravity.

She accused her husband of having twice tried to poison her in order to bring on a miscarriage. She claimed that he had three times infected her with a shameful disease. She charged him with having associated with courtesans and with her own servants. In her unrestrained violence she said anything, true or false. She further accused her husband of having squandered her fortune, and charged him with sordid avarice and shabby covetousness. Her son was appalled at this fury, which turned also against him as his father's messenger. "Your nephew is making a good start there with the thorns of domestic life," the marquis wrote to the bailli.

Gabriel knew how important it was for him to succeed in his mission. He may have suspected that his father was keeping on good terms with him only to this end. In spite of her excessive violence, he was moved by his mother's distress; he felt full of pity for her. He had himself had experience of his father's harshness. But in his own interest he was obliged to urge her to show moderation, and to induce her to confide her property to the man she hated.

In the course of a stormy ·interview he even risked pronouncing the word "conciliation." At this his mother lost all control of herself. She saw in her son her worst enemy. In a paroxysm of rage she seized a pistol and fired at him. But her hand shook. He came away alive, but ill.

But if his overture had deeply wounded his mother, her hatred brought him the goodwill of Mme. de Pailly. He had realized that he could get nothing from his father without the support of his father's mistress; and, after conquering his uncle and his sister, he tried to win her over. He found in her, as he wrote to his brother-in-law, "the spirit of five hundred thousand demons or angels." He was at pains to bring her over to his side. He succeeded entirely. "I am being killed with kindness," he wrote, and added, speaking of his father: "For the time being, his heart is entirely reconquered."

The marquis himself wrote: "I see that my son now merits my trust." He went on at once to account for his change of attitude: "The immense soul of Mme. de Pailly thinks a great deal of him."

10

"A fearful famine has beset our unhappy country," wrote the marquis. "The comte has proposed to me to buy eighty or a hundred quintals of rice and to start works for these poor people. Gabriel has orders and has started like a man; he works with them, eats at the head of their enormous table, lives on the same fare, cheers them, supports them." This was Gabriel de Mirabeau's debut in social work.

The marquis returned to Paris, leaving his son in the Limousin to go through his apprenticeship as a landowner. Gabriel did not spare himself on this new task. Through a severe winter he was on horseback, when needed, at four in the morning, going along roads full of hollows or covered with glazed frost, up steep mountainsides.

In this province, one of the most rugged in France, "the people are rather wild, enterprising, even fierce in quarrels against those who vex them"—so one reads in the journal *Les Ephémérides*. It was in an environment so refractory to all new ideas and to conciliation that Mirabeau took the risk of a great experiment—the setting up of a *tribunal de prud'hommes* a conciliation tribunal of men of experience and integrity. He sent a notice to all the curés, asking them to facilitate the election in their parish of "a father of a family, of mature age and esteemed."

"Our first task has been done and well done," wrote the marquis to the bailli, "and the young spark is back again. The fellow has been on his mettle. He has just founded a court of *prud'hommes*, a thing I thought almost impossible; he has shown adroitness, subtlety, broadness, energy, has got the curés to work and secured everybody's cordial support."

The marquis contented himself with sending Poisson to attend the opening of the conciliation tribunal, and to write a speech for his son to read on the occasion. Poisson spun a pompous discourse to the peasants; Gabriel contented himself with reading his father's message and adding a very few words. "God knows," the *ami des hommes* reports him as saying, "if ever I regarded a poor labourer otherwise than as my equal, even my master, if suddenly it should please Providence to shuffle our lots."

These phrases, warmly spoken by Gabriel de Mirabeau, deeply moved his audience. He saw tears come into the eyes of simple, sturdy men. The marquis was delighted with the description Poisson gave of the ceremony. "I have been very pleased with my son's speech, and the more so since brevity was not what we used to be afraid of in him." He was pleased, too, with the practical result of the tribunal. More than a hundred cases were submitted to its arbitration in the course of the first year. Summing up his account of his son's experiment, the marquis concluded: "He is a demon for achieving the impossible."

The marquis had sworn that none of his sons "should see Paris before he is twenty-five, because of its inevitable unsettling influence, the first step to the gallows." But he was so pleased with Gabriel that about the middle of February 1771 he sent for him. The successes he achieved there were a new surprise for his father. "So now he is going the round of calls," the marquis wrote to the bailli, "and God knows how hard he is working to acquit himself well. You may be sure he will clear me of any suspicion of wanting to make him a philosopher, especially as he is as ingratiating as I was awkward."

He called with his son on the Comtesse de Rochefort, and there he found the brother-in-law of the Duc de Nivernois, the Comte de Maurepas, a very powerful minister. Introduced at court, Gabriel "astonished even those who have gone the pace at Versailles." The marquis described his son's brilliant debut with a pride that was touched with envy. "Your nephew is at Versailles three times a week. He never pushes himself forward and yet goes everywhere and gathers invitations to everything. Everybody adopts him, the Guéménées, the Carignans, the Noailles, and lots of others."

The marquis was nearer to identifying himself with his son than he ever had been, or ever was again, in his life. He declared with pride:

"For five hundred years the Mirabeaus have always been put up with though they were never like the rest; and this one will be put up with, I can promise you; and he will not bring down the name."

But if he recognized the exceptional quality of his son, if he realized that it was necessary to direct that great natural force toward an end—"We must find occupation for M. l'Ouragan" [Mr. Hurricane] —he refused to let him follow his vocation and adopt the career of his choice. He spoke with contempt of "that superannuated profession, as out of fashion as tourneys." He wrote to the bailli: "*La guerre!* does he imagine that I have the money to provide battles for him like Arlequin and Scaramouche?"

There he revealed his main motive. He did not want to spend money on his son. At his chief's request Gabriel was promoted to captain; he was attached to a corps of dragoons. But this advance merely corresponded roughly to the actual situation of officers of the reserve; it did not call for his presence with the corps more than three or four times a year. In order to go on active service he would have had to purchase a company. There was one vacant in the Lorraine legion, but the marquis said that he had not the necessary funds. Gabriel was left with an uncertain future, with all his inexhaustible energies. The marquis went on asking himself: "What sphere is big enough for him?" He did not allow him to print his history of Corsica, of which he had spoken in such flattering terms; he refused in spite of the entreaties of the friend who had helped Gabriel to compile the work, and, said his disappointed son, "in spite of the demand from all Corsica."

In the spring the marquis was recovering from an illness, and the whole family was reunited at Bignon. His son organized a grand festival for his father's convalescence. He had the *Te Deum* chanted at High Mass, to which the whole village went in procession, and for the evening he prepared a big illumination at Bignon, with fireworks, and a banquet for the whole parish in the courtyard. Half flattered, half reluctant, the marquis admitted: "I have found the trick rather trying, but it shows good nature."

II

Two irreconcilable characters clashed, two enterprising personalities revealed their sharp corners, in their daily contact. There were no longer any helpful influences at work. Had Mme. de Pailly been insufficiently conquered, or was she in danger of being conquered too thoroughly? Had she taken offence at the rejection of advances, as

Mirabeau insinuated later? Did some obscure drama pursue its course that summer at Bignon, or was it simply that mutual incompatibility grew beyond endurance?

The peaceful existence at Bignon did not offer occupation enough for Gabriel. Idleness increased his natural exuberance. His father's friendliness quickly disappeared. All the old hostility was revealed anew in the complaints the marquis poured out to the Comtesse de Rochefort. "Warned and dissuaded from my own opinions," he set down his son as "a scribbler, a fritterer," and he thought only of how to get rid of him. At the beginning of that year Mme. de Pailly had been expecting great things from him; at the end she had so prejudiced the marquis against him that he was ready to condemn whatever he did. The amity between father and son had lasted only a few months—a brief calm in the tempest of their relations.

"In the matter of madmen," he wrote toward the end of the year to the bailli, "I have sent the elixir of my race in that category to Mirabeau to inquire into certain popular stupidities for which my foresters were responsible the moment my back was turned."

The young man who had succeeded so brilliantly in the Limousin was doomed to failure from the outset on the new mission. The rights of the people and the seigneurs in the use and exploitation of the forests had been clearly defined by an arrangement that dated back two centuries. The redoubtable Jean-Antoine had ignored them, imposing service on his vassals in the communes of Mirabeau and Beaumont, and threatening to drown in the Durance the lawyers who brought their "fatal cleverness" to the support of the just claims of the people. Times had changed since the reign of Silverneck, but the Friend of Mankind apparently had not realized it. He preached comprehension for the poorest of the disinherited, but in practice he proved that he had inherited his father's feudal outlook. He had, however, neither the energy nor the prestige of his father. He contented himself with resorting to a trick. He induced a seignorial judge to annul the arrangement in dispute. The communes of Mirabeau and Beaumont entered an appeal against the judgment. The marquis ordered his judge to pay no attention to the appeal, to give full effect to his ruling, and sent his son to watch over its execution.

Gabriel de Mirabeau found the communes seething with unrest. They were advised by lawyers who were no longer to be intimidated, notaries like Gastaud at Mirabeau and advocates from Aix like Boyer at Beaumont. Before long men of this stamp were to be the most active in the ranks of the Third Estate, and to send their representatives to the National Assembly

Gabriel had received orders from his father to crush the rebellion as his grandfather had crushed a similar one. "I had sent him," the marquis wrote to the Comtesse de Rochefort, "to strike fear into the insolent vassals." It was the young man's debut at Mirabeau—the bailli was away—in the role of feudal lord. He spoke, according to Gastaud, in a "high and mighty" tone; he told the assembled inhabitants that they were "abusing his father's kindness." He found his audience glum and hostile. Next day only a few came to the meeting called. He saw that he had taken the wrong line. "He had summoned these republicans," the Abbé Castagny, who had accompanied him to Beaumont, wrote to the marquis, "but he was unable to get them all to come. . . . He harangued those who did come with a power, a gentleness, and a dignity that brought tears to my eyes."

His eloquence was not fruitless. "The people began to be touched." But Boyer was looking on, with all the hostility of a man of the Third Estate to the feudal lord. He knew the instability of the crowd. He thought he could carry them with him by addressing the young seigneur in insolent terms. "He would have roused them," the abbé reported, "but for the patience and calmness of M. le Comte, who astonished me so much the more, knowing him so well, since, priest and an old man though I am, I might not have been capable of it." For the second time Gabriel de Mirabeau had almost won his case. But Boyer rose again with a threat: "If you give in I shall have nothing more to do with you; I shall leave you to be devoured little by little." The peasants recoiled from the prospect of being deprived of all legal advice.

Gabriel de Mirabeau had had his first experience of a discussion in public. He had had a bad case to defend, but he did not yet know that. He, too, felt himself a descendant of Jean-Antoine. He had insistent orders from his father which he had to carry out at all costs. But though he was too young to have definitely formed opinions and to hold them with assurance, and though he went to work under the spell of a fanatically upheld tradition, he had on the other hand a self-mastery astonishing in a young man of his age and temperament.

On Twelfth Night the villages were celebrating, with bonfires blazing in the village squares. Gabriel de Mirabeau was at Beaumont with some young nobles of the neighbourhood. Boyer passed by him without saluting. The young count, infuriated, knocked off Boyer's hat with his stick. Boyer declared that he had not seen him, but he added, according to Gastaud, "that he owed him nothing, that he did not recognize him yet as a seigneur, and that he had but to knock off his hat once more and he would see a pretty game." The young count replied violently, and Boyer made a violent gesture. A tumult started. The inhabitants took Boyer's part. The most excited among them ran for arms. The nobles with Mirabeau went in search of the magistrate. He came on the scene and arrested Boyer. An act of aggression against the young seigneur was a capital crime. There was revolt in the village, and danger of bloodshed.

In the wildly excited crowd one man alone kept cool. He was the most quick-tempered and impetuous of all. But at twenty-two Gabriel de Mirabeau was already a grown man. His lucid brain acted quickly and foresaw all that might ensue. He had what is the most difficult of all things to acquire, especially for a nature like his, complete self-control. He was capable, too, of foregoing the satisfaction of wounded pride. Everything happened in the twinkling of an eye. Still shaken by terrible wrath, but strangely calm, he imposed silence. And in that tense silence he declared that Boyer had not touched him.

Years later he recalled the incident to his father: "I venture to say that I acted there with a wisdom beyond my age, though I was being urged on by pretty violent advisers. One of your relatives said to a number of people round him that he would never have believed that there was such lethargic blood in the veins of a Mirabeau. *You* know," he added, "whether my moderation was attributable to the slowness of my blood. If I had not stopped the *lieutenant criminel* by a formal declaration in public, Boyer would have been condemned to be hanged."

But Gabriel's great effort at moderation had no effect on the issue of the conflict between the marquis and his vassals. The *Chambre des Eaux et Forêts* declared the sentence of the seignorial judge to be "null and void, and an infringement of the rights of the court," and condemned the marquis to pay the costs in the case.

Gabriel had worked day and night in vain to win an impossible case. He thought that at least he would please his father by this proof of his moderation. But the marquis had made up his mind in advance to blame his son for any failure. He wrote: "If you succeed in profiting by the incident, you will give yourself the reputation of having been moderate from your first appearance in the province, and that is pretty odd."

Years later Gabriel recalled that strange criticism. "It was a hard thing to say. It discouraged me, it ruined me!" The old terror of his father took hold of him once more. "My imagination, still agitated by the

thought of Sumatra, weighed on my heart." He realized how dependent he was on the capricious spite of the marquis. "I saw that I should
always be in the wrong, because I was disliked."

12

"I know of nobody but the Empress of Russia for whom this man
would make a suitable match," said the Marquis de Mirabeau of his
son in one of the rare moments in which he judged him at his true
worth. But just as he did nothing to find an occupation for him, he
does not seem to have devoted a thought to finding him the solace
and security of a home. Gabriel's whole future depended on the choice
of a life's companion. But he was only twenty-two. At the château of
Mirabeau the bailli had talked to him about a rich heiress at Aix; he had
listened with his thoughts elsewhere, for at that time he had a passion
for his profession and thought the way was open for him to a brilliant
career. Thereafter, however, he was dangerously unoccupied. He had
no financial resources. His father had punished him by stopping his
allowance, and his dependence weighed painfully on him. There remained only one expedient, the riskiest of all—to marry a fortune.

Emilie de Marignane was the richest heiress in Provence, perhaps one
of the richest in the kingdom. In that little town of Aix, "as big as a
snuff-box," in the marquis' phrase, the talk was all of the suitors to her
hand and fortune. Their chances were discussed as at a race meeting or
round a gaming-table. In this young heiress the society of her day saw
a replica of itself, with its tastes and aspirations, its irresponsibilities and
its weaknesses. Emilie de Marignane had all the precarious and unpredictable character of her time. The exclusive circle, dominant in the
town and its province, in which she spent her whole life was a reduced
but faithful image of contemporary France.

Her paternal grandmother, who ruled the family circle, and who
was called La Renarelle, lived, in what for her was a provincial retirement, on the memories of her brilliant past. When very young she had
been left to herself while her husband was far away at the wars. She
had gone to Paris for consolation, and there she had lived with Mlle.
de Nantes, the daughter of Louis XIV and Mme. de Montespan, who
was called Mme. la Duchesse. Young, brilliant, entirely without scruples
in a circle that had none, related to great families on whose members
she modelled herself, living at the Palais-Bourbon, she had made many
friends, won the favour of Mme. de Pompadour, and acquired a certain
influence. Her eldest son, who inherited the titles of Marquis de

Marignane, Seigneur de Vitrolles, Gignac, Saint-Victoret, and other places, and Governor of the Iles d'Or and of the fortresses of Portcros and of the Levant, was his nominal father's heir only in name. All society, and so all its hangers-on, knew him to be the son of the Marquis de Vence. The old marquise, for that matter, continued after her husband's death to live at Aix in intimacy with her old lover, a little matter that offended nobody.

This son had, in the picturesque phrase of the Marquis de Mirabeau, "an element of the noble that dangles like the abbess's psalter, for want of knowing where to lay hold of it, being entirely characterless." The Marquis de Marignane, amiable through indifference, pleasant through indolence, easy to live with through his horror of any disturbance, had the misfortune to marry a restless, sensual, jealous woman, in need of a constant outlet for her love. Her temperamental femininity was irritated by the barriers of his charming egoism, and she turned into a bitter woman weighed down with imaginary grievances. She ended by destroying her own happiness through her insistence on being the author of her husband's. After the birth of Emilie, the Marquis de Marignane had patience for a few more years, waiting for a male heir. But even the desire for posterity paled before his need for tranquillity. He separated from his wife and took refuge in the calm affection of a mistress. Thereafter he lived sheltered from all vexations, with only one trouble left: a little girl whom he would have to look after. Her mother, haunted by the fear of growing old, seems to have visited her spoilt happiness on the child, solacing her wounded heart by maltreating Emilie. The little girl was taken away from her mother to live with her paternal grandmother. The great lover of days gone by, the woman who had shone at the Palais-Bourbon, had become a miserly old grumbler who, according to the bailli, scolded her granddaughter "all day long." To complete this education, two aunts jealously watched the child—the marquis' two sisters, who would inherit his immense fortune if the little girl died without issue.

The young girl, constantly rebuffed and reprimanded, thought only of the one means of escape that remained to her. She was rather common in appearance, with irregular features, a small coarse nose, dull eyes and a swarthy complexion, and one shoulder slightly higher than the other. But her fortune made up for her physical shortcomings.

The education the girl received only accentuated her impatience for the enjoyment of life. She was pleasure-loving, had no intellectual resources, and was interested in nothing outside her small feminine sphere. This intellectual and emotional lethargy was confirmed in her by the amiable ideal of egoism which was constantly before her eyes. She was naturally imitative, a shallow water that mirrored any image presented to her. The sensuality she had inherited from her mother was partly counterbalanced by the fear of strong emotions inherited from her father. Instead of outstanding qualities, she had been endowed by nature with charms greatly appreciated by society. She had a remarkable faculty of assimilation, a certain keenness of observation, and a talent for mimicry that was the delight of her circle. She also possessed a good dose of common sense, which, if developed and encouraged, might to a certain extent have made up for her lack of strength of character and of intellectual culture.

It was her misfortune and Mirabeau's that two such beings, in whom nothing could induce mutual understanding or even love, should have been brought together. Emilie de Marignane was eighteen years old. She had no aspiration outside the society that met at the château of Tourves, the home of the Comte de Valbelle, a group that had assumed the name of "the Court of Love." The amiable host of that sumptuous château was a great friend of the Marquis de Marignane. All the affection of which the indifferent soul of Emilie's father was capable was lavished on this friend. The comte represented an ideal which the marquis strove to attain, so far as he was capable of any sustained aspiration.

The Comte de Valbelle was the most perfect type of that age. A contemporary said of him that "if anyone wants to give foreigners an impression of an amiable Frenchman, he should present the Comte de Valbelle to them." Sole heir to a great name, with immense revenues, distinguished, of perfect breeding, he was ageing with a particular fragrance that increased as he grew older. His memories of bygone passionate liaisons with celebrated actresses made him interesting to the mistresses of his ripe age; women remained attached to him, even those whom he abandoned nursing a jealous affection for him. He was two years older than the Marquis de Marignane. Emilie was ready to marry a man so admired by her father and by her circle of friends as soon as he sought her hand. But a cabal of mistresses past and present prevented the marriage. The Comte de Valbelle was not the man to fight for a young girl. He contented himself thereafter with watching paternally over her happiness.

There were many aspirants to her hand, among them the young Marquis de Gramont, "handsome as Cupid" and as rich as Croesus. There was a cousin of Emilie, heir to one of the greatest fortunes and the greatest positions in Provence, who seemed to be ahead of all others.

The bailli had been dreaming of marrying this girl to Gabriel ever since Gabriel's return from Corsica. But Louise de Cabris had made inquiries and had written to her brother: "I warn you—as a friend—that Mlle. de Marignane is promised to the son of the Marquis d'Albertas. You have gone about it too late." In the struggle, however, between the government and the *parlements* (the provincial high courts of justice), President d'Albertas and his son had made themselves unpopular in the good society of Aix, which was closely connected with the members of the dismissed *parlements*, by accepting posts in the new one. And the excellent match of yesterday was outlawed.

But at once another candidate appeared, one who enjoyed the high protection of Valbelle—the Marquis de La Valette. Emilie was betrothed to him when Gabriel de Mirabeau returned to Provence. A cousin who lived near Beaumont, a woman of spirit, married to a husband who was much older than she and whose health had been broken by debauchery, carried Gabriel off to Aix and encouraged him to try his luck. She had a personal interest in establishing in the neighbourhood this seductive cousin, and had no fear of the rivalry of a woman like Emilie de Marignane.

In his state of mind at that time Gabriel saw his best opportunity in a rich marriage, and he readily yielded to the energy of his pretty cousin, Mme. de Limaye-Coriolis. But when he asked the Marquis de Marignane for his daughter's hand, he was rejected. The day had already been fixed for the signing of the articles of marriage with La Valette.

The Marquis de Mirabeau learned of his son's failure. He had never had any tenderness for the unlucky, and wrote chaffingly that all his son's enterprises "are worthy of each other: he has lost a fortune by his own fault." It was enough to spur on a sensitive young man. "I was nettled," Gabriel confessed, "and I set out to undo a marriage almost completed."

The beginning of the decisive step in his life was the outcome of boyish *amour-propre*. "I was told that the place was invincible and unassailable," Gabriel wrote to Mme. du Saillant, "and I agree; except, of course, that I know of nothing that is invincible and very little that is unassailable."

He began—according to the marquis—by setting out to "captivate all the females, ascendant, descendant, and on the level," of the family. He had a great power over women of experience, who could see in his young undisciplined ardour the strength of the mature man. In his efforts at allurement for his own ends, he won one of the fine and precious friendships of his life.

The wife of the Comte de Vence (he was in fact the half-brother of the Marquis de Marignane) was one of those *grandes dames* who gave the century all its distinction. She was of illustrious birth, had a fabulous fortune (a dowry of five hundred thousand livres), possessed "the prettiest face in the world" according to Mirabeau, and was "one of the wisest, the wittiest, and the best informed women in the kingdom and perhaps in Europe." She had daughters to marry off when Mirabeau made her acquaintance. One of them, Julie, fell in love with him "in a beautiful and purely spiritual passion." The girl was like a porcelain figurine that had suddenly been brought to life—a scintillating life. This tiny person had wit and grace, prettiness and a forceful temperament. But her mother contented herself with saying to Mirabeau: "Monsieur le Comte, when she is married, do as you both see fit, but leave her to get married." The comtesse had arranged a brilliant marriage for her daughter with the son of the Marquis de la Tourrette. The fiancé was as handsome as Gabriel was plain. But Julie found him too stupid. Her mother reasoned with her on the strength of her own experience: "My daughter, I would have you get into your head that it is possible to count for something and yet not be a prodigy of intelligence. You swear by two men—your father and the Comte de Mirabeau. Patience, patience, my daughter: if all men are not so seductive it makes for peace."

The graceful figurine so well initiated into life made a prudent marriage. Her mother, though so much older than Gabriel, remained the faithful and understanding friend, the safe and precious confidante, of this young man, who devoted to her a passionate admiration and as profound an esteem as he was ever to feel for any woman in his life.

The appreciation shown by the Comtesse de Vence soon had its effect on Emilie. With her habit of reflecting the opinions of others, she gradually allowed herself to be won over. In the brief moments during which Gabriel de Mirabeau made passionate court to her, she even seemed ready to love him. But to awaken a deep passion in a heart so undecided as that of Emilie would have been too long-drawn-out a labour. Gabriel de Mirabeau decided on a bold course.

A rumour suddenly spread through the town of Aix that a carriage was standing at night near the house in which Emilie de Marignane lived, and that this carriage belonged to the young Comte de Mirabeau. A bribed chambermaid was in the secret. But scandal did not work quickly enough or effectively enough in this sceptical society, indulgent for whatever amused it. One fine morning, in this street in the centre of the city, the ostlers heard themselves hailed from the window of the house inhabited by the dowager marquise and her granddaughter by a man in shirtsleeves, collarless, who was intent on being heard and above all on being seen. The noise even brought the Marquis de Marignane to see what was up. "Mlle. de Marignane was thoroughly compromised. I loved her, I thought I was loved, I resolved to make a job of it," said Mirabeau later. He really thought he loved the young girl who had yielded to his unceremonious pursuit. But thereafter he never ceased to suspect her of being too ready to yield to others. He had, indeed, awakened her senses too abruptly. She remained an easy prey to temptation.

The "females, ascendant, descendant, and on the level," intervened to appease the indignation of the Marquis de Marignane, the fury of the suitor nonsuited, and above all that of his powerful protector. "The Court of Love was a little worse than enraged," wrote Gabriel de Mirabeau. "Well, well! I had the effrontery to shoulder the whole lot of them."

13

The marriage was celebrated at Aix with all the customary pomp. The festivities lasted more than a week. Everyone who bore a great name in Provence took part. All Aix talked long of their magnificence.

Before the signing of the marriage contract Mirabeau acknowledged frankly to the Marquis de Marignane that he had debts running into a thousand louis, and that he wanted to pay them before launching out into fresh expenditure. He suggested that the marriage be celebrated at the château of Marignane to avoid heavy expense. On this occasion the indolent marquis revealed a rare energy. The amiable epicurean showed a fund of vindictive meanness. He had accepted this son-in-law against his will, and he acted toward him in the style of an irritated tradesman. Emilie de Marignane was a brilliant match. The fortune of which she was the sole heir represented half a million livres, but for the moment these were but the hopes held out by a distant future. The Marquis de Marignane had promised the Marquis de la Valette four thousand livres a year. Gabriel de Mirabeau received only three thousand. It was the marquis' way of showing his resentment. Apart from her trousseau of linen and lace, the richest heiress of the province was provided only with a single taffeta dress. It was for her bridegroom to dress her, and to dress their servants, it was for the bridegroom to meet the expenses of the marriage and the customary presents to those who had loaded the bride with gifts.

The Marquis de Mirabeau was secretly very flattered by this magnificent marriage, but he refused to give his son the slightest financial aid. He refused to pay his debts. He contented himself with doubling the allowance which the Marquis de Marignane had given the young couple. "Since Marignane diminished by a thousand francs what he had agreed to for La Valette, there was no need for me to do the handsome," he wrote to the bailli.

Still more remarkable, he refrained from going to see his future daughter-in-law. He did not take the trouble to be present at the marriage. Was it Mme. de Pailly who held him back, not being able to go with him? Mme. du Saillant, in servile imitation of her father's attitude, also stayed away. But the bailli, too, was absent. Of the Mirabeau family only the Cabris couple were present. The Marquise de Mirabeau, who had not been consulted at all, refused to contribute to Gabriel's allowance.

The young couple rode to the château of Mirabeau, which was to shelter their new happiness. The peasants acclaimed their young seigneurs with joy. They lined the route of the carriages, waving torches. Behind the row of lights the dark mass of the château rose menacingly, more like a fortress than a love-nest. The young husband's heart overflowed with a pride and excitement that concealed from him his disquiet and a dull irritation.

≱ IV ≰

A Melodious Monkey

"WE ARE running after order, and I hope we shall catch it," wrote Emilie to her father-in-law some months after her marriage. Neither she nor Gabriel had any aptitude for re-establishing their financial situation after the absurdly extravagant expenditure on their marriage. Mirabeau had had to pledge to usurers the whole of his allowance for the following year. There was nobody to look after the preparation of the future residence of these two inexperienced young people. They were received by a forbidding old castle infested with bugs. Their bedroom, which had belonged to the unbridled Anne de Pontèves, Gabriel's great-grandmother, was in a deplorable state.

Mirabeau realized the position he was in. He had carried off a brilliant heiress, a girl spoilt by luxury, and was offering her these austere and uncomfortable quarters. He was ashamed of them. He spent recklessly in order to make up for the bad impression Emilie had gained on entering the château. The bailli complained later of this extravagance: "The madness that led him to panel and gild for his wife the only room that could suit me, and to raise the ceiling, has greatly upset me, for I shall never have the courage to inhabit a room that resembles the salon of the Duc de Nivernois." The room was still unfinished when the work had swallowed twenty thousand livres.

In this marriage there was another hidden defect. Mirabeau had taken his wife as a man takes a girl of loose character; he had conquered her by sensual intoxication. Their relations continued on that level. He talked cynically of his masculine prowess. It might even seem that from fear of cooling their conjugal ardour he forced the note of sexual brutality that accounted for Emilie's first surrender. Later, when she reproached him for being too passionate, he replied: "You knew that passion before our marriage; and remember, your husband has never been so imperious with you as when he was your lover." He may have felt from the first a doubt of the value of his exploit, a doubt that broke the exaltation of his triumph and destroyed his peace of mind from the outset of their new life. Naturally very quick-tempered, he gave vent to his anger more often than ever. Furious quarrels broke out between the two young people, followed by equally passionate reconciliations. His brutality and violence were fed by an unavowed contempt.

Emilie's circle, cynical and dissolute but refined and polished to excess, got on Gabriel's nerves, while he in turn was regarded as an interloper. The visits to the château of Marignane and to the Comte de Valbelle produced scenes of strange violence. The Court of Love, said Emilie later, was scandalized at "the furious behaviour which the Comte de Mirabeau had a way of mixing with the tenderest protestations."

When, one day, the Marquis de Mirabeau saw through his daughter-in-law's character, he defined her feminine temperament in very few words: "What she likes are strong scents, spicy stories, and monkey tricks." The atmosphere of Emilie's circle influenced the young man of twenty-three in spite of the hostility to him. He drank too much on one of his visits and provoked a quarrel; but when later he was reproached for his drunkenness he had an easy reply. "Many others," he said ironically, "were just as far gone. M. de Marignane will remember." He was influenced by the immorality that was practised like a society game in which licentiousness was cultivated as an accomplishment; there was nothing to arm him against the insidious hold of these things. He was ready to deceive Emilie at the first opportunity, just as from the first he had doubts of her fidelity.

But he regretted his outbursts and was keen to win over the young woman of whom he was jealous without having very much love for her. He knew her to be frivolous, and he showered presents on her. He always wanted to adorn with dresses and jewels the women he desired, through a reflex of tenderness and perhaps also through an unconscious masculine contempt that led him to wish to pay for the pleasure given him. In his generosity to Emilie there was the further element of the sensitiveness of a young man suspected of having made a marriage of more brilliance than he had had reason to expect. "I gave her the most exquisite presents," he said later. "I doubled and tripled her diamonds, and she constantly found charming dresses that had been made without her knowledge." In the course of six months the bill from a seller of trinkets alone amounted to eighteen hundred livres; Emilie's clothes cost in the same period some twenty-three thousand livres.

There was a strident and forced note in their ostentatious luxury. The young Seigneur de Mirabeau bought himself a gig and horses; he bought books, an expense which for him was always a necessity. He had a carriage road to the château cut through the rock. He was full of big plans, reasonable plans, which his thorough study of the estate suggested to him. "With thirty thousand francs," wrote a farmer to the Marquis de Mirabeau, "Monsieur le Comte will carry out all the clearing, yielding a big return, and will harness the Durance property." But the marquis refused the necessary credits.

Mirabeau then procured money for big works by methods that multiplied the expense tenfold. An army of workers invaded the château. The servants gave food and drink to everyone who came. There was even ready at all times in the courtyard a mash for all the hounds of the region.

In this imposing château two children were playing at being great and important personages. Emilie had no more sense of realities than her husband. The Marquis de Mirabeau, who did not often go so far as to absolve his son from his responsibilities, said of him one day: "If he had had a wife with any sense, or even one who was not spoilt, she could have made what she liked of him." But at the time when the two launched out on their mad adventure, the marquis made not the slightest effort to see how they were arranging their existence.

Nobody went to see what their heedlessness was costing. Later on the bailli bitterly repented not having done so: "I am sure that if after the marriage I had settled in Provence I should have prevented a lot of harm and served my family better than if I had become pope."

2

In October 1773 their son Victor was born. There was at last a male heir; his birth delighted the marquis, with his pride of race. Fatherhood quickly aroused all the seriousness of the turbulent young man, suddenly investing him with a new dignity. His feeling toward the coming child had nothing of the aristocratic pride in the perpetuation of a name. He was imbued with the spirit of the age, the sense of responsibility toward the beings whom one brought into the world. His child was still unborn when he plunged into a thorough study of all the questions of infant hygiene. His ideas were revolutionary for the age. He would not let old wives do as they chose, would not tolerate the child's body being confined by tight clothing. "Why is it," he asked, "that your swaddled children have the exclusive privilege of being hunchbacked, lame, anchylosed, deformed, rachitic?" He decided to habituate the child early to fresh air and to changes of temperature. He laid down a whole system of close supervision of the child's health. "Above all, cleanliness is the life of children," he said one day. He knew the appropriate harmless remedies for every malady; one of his medical attendants was astonished one day at his knowledge. But his great maxim remained: "Let nature have her way: she knows more about it than we do."

He was in one of his rare moments of happiness. But the thoughtlessness in which he had lived until then was having its effects. He was struggling desperately in inescapable difficulties. "To repair one breach means making ten others. It is incredible with what rapidity the net tightens."

He sought in vain for help. There was nothing to hope for from his father: he turned to his mother. But the marquise did not respond. The creditors of the young couple became more and more threatening. The Marquis de Marignane persuaded the young couple to install themselves at Aix with Emilie's grandmother. There were still ways and means of arranging everything. The Marquis de Marignane was ready to advance sixty thousand livres on Emilie's dowry, but wanted the Marquis de Mirabeau, who alone was authorized to deal with the dowry, to acknowledge receipt of the sum. The marquis refused. He was ready for his part to give eighteen thousand livres, a totally inadequate sum. Later his son reproached him bitterly: "I cannot conceive the right to leave a drowning man to perish when one is able to save him."

While his son was thus drifting to destruction, the marquis addressed to the young couple the biting and peremptory missives in the writing of which he was so skillful. Gabriel took refuge behind his wife. He dictated for her signature a reply to a letter which she pretended to have kept secret from her husband: "I know you and respect you too much to fear that you want to impoverish me; but it would indeed be impoverishing me to diminish my good opinion of my husband."

The son of Emilie de Mirabeau was a pledge of survival for a great family pride. But the young father could not even be present at the child's birth. He had fled from the château of Mirabeau and from Aix before his creditors. Desperately in debt as he was, he still had to pay the costs of medical attendance, of the outfit for the confinement, and of the layette for the newborn baby, and he was obliged to ask Emilie, scarcely more than a day after the child was born, to pawn all her diamonds. The money-lender with whom they were pawned "managed so well," Emilie complained, "that everybody knows here that our diamonds have been pawned." This was in a poor little desolate letter which the young wife, scarcely out of childbed, wrote to her absent husband. Of her mad adventure there remained only the troubles of everyday life, a grudge against her own people, a wounded self-esteem, and resentment against her husband. Her disillusioned lament ended with the passionate appeal: "Come back quickly, for I greatly need your presence."

Perhaps a great love could have resisted these rough shocks of reality, the vexation of the continual reproaches from her family, the financial difficulties never before experienced by a spoilt child, and the thousand irritating troubles of daily life of which Mirabeau himself said later: "I know well that it is not elephants that are a torment, but flies."

But Emilie's cry from the heart was not a cry of love. It was rather an instinct of defence that had made her call her husband to her side.

Emilie's dreary youth had left one sweet and tender memory, that of her first girlish love. The Chevalier de Gassaud was too poor, his family, that of a respectable lawyer, was of insufficient rank, for him to be able to range himself among the candidates for Emilie's hand. But if he had neither title nor fortune, the young fellow, of the same age as Emilie, had in his favour the grace of a tall and slender youth, engaging manners, and tenderness. This young man, considered inoffensive by the easygoing father, was a constant visitor in the house of the Marquis de Marignane. At the time when Emilie was staying there after the birth of her child, the young musketeer was also there, spending his leave. He was using a room which was separated from hers only by a dressing-room. He was thoughtful and tender to the friend of his early youth. He was as steady and well-balanced as Gabriel de Mirabeau was impetuous and unpredictable. His handsome face formed a striking contrast to the aggressive ugliness of her husband. He was as restful as the other was tiring for a young woman whom nothing had prepared for the troubles of life.

There was nothing to protect Emilie from the memories of the past and the sweetness of this young man's presence in the hour of her trial. The moral outlook of her circle was indulgent. And she could not be held back by the sense of duty which might have been aroused by a husband whose fidelity was beyond suspicion. "Our morals are not so pure as to authorize us to regard as infamous anyone who is suspected or even convicted of adultery," exclaimed Mirabeau later in his own defence.

Also Emilie was distrustful of his relations with his cousin, the Marquise de Limaye-Coriolis; she felt that they were too constant and too tender. His cousin had all that Emilie lacked, radiant beauty, a brilliant complexion, a triumphant carriage that revealed her feline litheness and her exceptional vigour. "Strong as a Turk and agile as a Basque," as the bailli put it, she had all the adroitness and all the audacity of a woman who was sure of herself. Her husband was on the verge of the fifties, exhausted and eaten away by a shameful malady that was to carry him off a few years later. His fortune was as broken as his health, and he was soon to be arrested for debt.

The Marquise de Limaye-Coriolis gave birth to a child of whom the bailli said some years later that "that brat" was very like his nephew. But the adventure had yet other consequences. The Marquis de Limaye-Coriolis may have been a blind or complacent husband, but he was above all a dissolute man pitilessly pursued by his creditors. He did not content himself with lavishing advice on his young cousin on the way to get money by running more and more into debt, or with putting him into touch with usurers: he profited by his financial trouble to save himself. By his marriage Mirabeau had inspired confidence in usurers with whom Limaye-Coriolis had already exhausted his credit. "They offered me," said Gabriel later, "much more than I asked for." Later, when the time came for settling his debts, the examination of the rates charged by the usurers and of their exaggerated valuations enabled his total indebtedness to be reduced to about one-third. Moreover, Mirabeau was a minor. An adult was needed to answer for his debts. Limaye did this without his knowledge. "It was not from stupidity by any means that M. de Limaye went surety for me. It was from a much less noble motive," wrote Mirabeau later to the bailli. The money-lender Beaucaire, said Mirabeau, had demanded this surety, preventing the annulment of a minor's debts, as condition for a new loan to Limaye. Limaye bought Mirabeau's silence by referring to his own wife's misconduct. A shady money deal was thus entangled with the faults of passion. Limaye's threats produced a quarrel between the lovers, and Mme. de Limaye went over to the ranks of Mirabeau's violent enemies.

3

"It would be better, dear brother, for our peace of mind at the moment to lock up this bad son of a bad mother," wrote the marquis to the bailli toward the end of 1773. Alarming news had reached the marquis. Tenants on the Mirabeau estate, stewards, obscure enemies set in motion by jealousy, sent him word that his son was cutting down trees, selling furniture, unravelling tapestry to extract its gold. The marquis took not the slightest trouble to check these accusations. "He was scarcely married," the bailli wrote later to the marquis, "when means were sought to destroy him. He gave plenty of opportunity, no doubt; but very full advantage was taken of it. He neither cut down nor sold timber of yours, nor sold furniture."

Another of his enemies, the Marquis d'Albertas, chief justice of Provence, whose son Mirabeau had cut out with Emilie, wrote to the marquis: "I feel it my duty as a good parent and an old friend to warn you of the dangers to which a hot-headed young man, left to his own devices, is exposing himself: he is light-heartedly ruining himself." The Marquis de Marignane roused himself from his lethargy to warn him: "Since my last letter, few days have passed without bringing me news of some new debt or some jewel sold or pawned. Monsieur, your son is himself beginning to be frightened. I have seen a letter written to M. Raspaud [a notary of Aix] in which he informs him that neither you nor I will take any step to come to terms with his creditors, and that rather than be at their mercy he is quite ready to beg you to apply for a *lettre de cachet* confining him in the Château d'If or any other château you may be pleased to choose."

This was the cry of despair of a young man prone to extreme language. Mirabeau did not himself imagine that he could be taken at his word, for his father-in-law went on: "He will regard as a very great mercy the royal warrant you propose to secure, requiring him to reside in the château of Mirabeau."

Gabriel de Mirabeau did not realize how greatly his unruliness weighed on his father-in-law, or that his father, perhaps informed by one of his spies of renewed relations between Gabriel and his mother, wanted nothing better than to get him shut up "for our peace of mind at the moment."

But the marquis did not yet venture to resort to this extreme step. Excited by lying reports, he contented himself with applying for a royal warrant exiling his son to Manosque. He showed no pity in the prohibitions with which he accompanied this order of exile. The young family was not to have the right to take away anything other than personal effects. The marquis was indignant when Emilie carried off the books on which her husband set most store. From a dissipated existence they passed at once to privation, for a rigorous limit was set not only on the sum they could spend, but on the bread and meat they and their servants could have.

On their arrival at Manosque, with their baby only a few months old, they were unable at first to find quarters and were taken in by friends. These friends were the Gassaud family, the parents of Emilie's former suitor. His father, his mother, his three sisters, and an uncle who was an infantry officer, formed this family circle, good people, highly respected in the little town. Mirabeau did not want to burden them for long; he sought quarters appropriate to his modest resources.

The marquis, though incensed against his son, continued his affectionate correspondence with Emilie. It was from a letter of his father's to his wife that Mirabeau learned that proceedings for the attachment of his effects had been started against him. "This blow was terrible for me," he wrote later. "I formed a very humiliating idea of the procedure." The young couple were allowed one-third of their income: the rest was seized by the creditors. A thousand crowns was to serve for their maintenance and that of their child, and their servants—a chambermaid, a cook, and a lackey. If no arrangement was arrived at, this situation of semi-destitution might be prolonged indefinitely. Mirabeau's debts amounted to a hundred and eighty-eight thousand livres, but the greater part of this, a hundred and thirty-six thousand livres, consisted of bills of exchange signed by him which actually corresponded to no more than fifty thousand livres in money and goods received. Later, in exculpation, Mirabeau quoted the case of the lieutenant-general of Marseille "who had received thirty-two thousand livres and owed more than a hundred and twenty thousand," and he added: "That is the frightful story of the wild young men to whose number I blush to have added."

The marquis considered that this humiliation would be salutary. He insidiously undermined the precarious harmony between husband and wife, flattering Emilie at Gabriel's expense. He did not hesitate to write to the young woman at a time when she was undergoing a severe trial that her husband was "without shame, without truth, and without religion," adding: "It is at this time especially, my daughter, when public and private animadversions seem to be poured together upon his head, that in forgetting his hot-headedness your sweet and wise affection, together with the interest M. de Gassaud, with his coolness, his prudence, and his friendship, takes in his condition, should endeavour to disperse the callus that pride and craziness have formed on that heart, which, at bottom, is not bad."

4

Emilie de Mirabeau was pregnant once more. But this new maternity no longer excited the naïve pride of her husband. He was the more distrustful and suspicious because of his own sins. He questioned Emilie's servants. He opened her letters. The relations between husband and wife became tense. Emilie accused him of trying by his suspicions to divert those which she herself had with regard to his relations with his beautiful cousin.

One day Mirabeau got hold of a letter written to his wife by young Gassaud, who had returned to his garrison after spending a period of leave in his father's house. The letter left no doubt about their relations. Gabriel, who had deceived and was still to deceive so many husbands, strongly resented being deceived himself. He fell into the condition of silent rage that is more terrible than shouts of anger. He showed the tell-tale letter to his wife. Emilie threw herself at her husband's feet and implored his forgiveness. The old parents were told what had happened. They feared for their son's life. The father, revolted by this betrayal under his own roof, implored Mirabeau on his knees to spare the wretch's life. The weeping mother bathed his hands in tears. The

young man of twenty-five looked with embarrassment at these white
heads bowed at his feet. In spite of his anger his natural generosity was
awakened, his rather facile good-heartedness was moved. He would
not demand satisfaction from the only son of his old friends. He contented himself with writing a pompous letter "to the vile seducer" and
forgave his wife. Before Emilie's eyes he threw the compromising letter into the fire.

But though he may have imagined that his generosity would bring
him a complete hold over the heart of a guilty and repentant young
woman, all he did was to terrorize her for the moment. She wrote a letter to her lover, in a poverty of style that shows that it was her own
work, but undoubtedly under her husband's eyes, in which she emphasized "the personal moderation he has shown in all this," and said that
"all association between us is ended."

Mirabeau forgave his wife, but he retained his distrust. He burned
the lover's letter, but he demanded from him the return of the letter
breaking off relations, and he kept it. In the margin of this letter he wrote
the significant phrase: *"Mirabeau fils ne varietur."* Too young and too
impulsive to keep his painful secret to himself, he took the Comtesse de
Vence into his confidence. She replied with a letter that revealed her
generous comprehension. "The more unpardonable is your wife's mis-
deed, the greater your merit in pardoning it. From birth she has had
before her nothing but bad examples. Your attitude toward her has
been admirable so far. But reflect for a moment on the lack of equality
that prejudice has established between the husband and his wife, who
often does nothing more than follow the example he has given her."

But the woman with long experience and the too hot-headed young
man both made the same psychological mistake: both were too inclined
to judge Emilie by their own reactions. Neither the comtesse nor Mirabeau calculated how insupportable is the burden of gratitude. Her husband's generosity was a trouble to Emilie: it was too great, it was in-
comprehensible. In self-exculpation she went in search of her husband's
misdeeds. Annoyed at his taking the Comtesse de Vence into his confidence, she commented insidiously on the relations between her husband and his elderly friend. She felt a need to besmirch everything, to
poison the generosity that crushed her. One day in her anger she insulted his mother and sister, and he boxed her ears. It was the only blow
that he admitted having given her, and he claimed that she had
"thoroughly deserved it, for a husband is not to be told that his mother
and sister are whores."

Other violent scenes followed. Mirabeau's fine gesture had been in vain. The storm had passed, but had left all the tension in the air.

Emilie took refuge at Marignane. She paraded her trouble among her friends, exciting pity by her complaints and her visible fear of her husband. She was urged to leave a man who was treating her brutally. The emotional disturbance, followed by a severe chill, brought on a miscarriage. In her illness she seemed more pitiable than ever, and her husband more to blame. The Marquis de Mirabeau, knowing nothing of what had happened, continued to flatter his daughter-in-law and to abuse his own son. "I agree to see only past insanity, I should even agree to future hope; but at my age it is impossible to heal a natural distaste which I have always had for certain actions and for their consequences." And he added this appalling piece of callousness in a father's mouth: "If he does not change it would be better that he should die."

5

After the birth of her daughter Pauline, who was to be her only child, the appearance of conjugal calm which Louise de Cabris had wanted to keep up collapsed. A friend of her husband's from childhood, a young musketeer, a gentleman by birth but without fortune, handsome, combative, ardent, Jausserandy-Briançon, Seigneur de Verdache, was at the time her recognized lover. Her husband, for his part, found consolation in debauchery. As a young man he had been too much under the surveillance of elderly parents and had been too austerely brought up; with a weak character and an unbridled imagination, he had discovered love too late to be adequate for the unappeased eroticism of his wife. Gabriel de Mirabeau had indicated in vain to his sister remedies that could restore masculine vigour to this young degenerate. But what marriage could not give him, Jean-Paul de Cabris found in erotic literature and in coarse pleasures. He compromised his health, and Louise accused him of having infected her. He publicly paraded a mistress, his barber's wife, as though in revenge for a secret humiliation.

In the feeble and tormented mind of this weakling there germinated a plan of vengeance. He wrote or adapted licentious verses "in honour of the ladies of Grasse." With the craftiness of the semi-insane he had them printed in secret, and he put them up himself on the doors of all the great houses. Suspicion quickly fastened upon him, and the whole town was in an uproar. Criminal proceedings were started. Employees of Cabris, accused of having distributed the documents, were thrown into prison and tortured. With the loyalty she always showed in times of difficulty, Louise hurried to Paris to beg her father to intercede with ministers and to save her husband from the consequences of his catastrophic jest. But the marquis refused to use up his credit in order to get Louise out of this tight corner. He knew that she helped her mother with advice and also with Cabris' money. Instead of winning her over by an act of generosity, he alienated her yet more by making promises of help which he had not the slightest intention of keeping. The bailli, too, refused all aid, and in addition went back on his promise to supplement her dowry, fearing that she would profit by it only to support the Marquise de Mirabeau in her proceedings against her husband.

Louise returned in indignation from her fruitless visit to Paris. She felt abandoned by her family. She brought into play all her personal seduction, her ingenuity and her skill in intrigue, as well as twenty thousand crowns, to suppress the judicial proceedings. But her wretched idiot of a husband, who had taken refuge from the storm in the family château with his mistress, showed his gratitude to his wife by sending her a proposal for a divorce by agreement. At the same time he suborned the servants to get evidence against Louise, whom he accused of trying to poison him. He based his accusation on a letter he had stolen, in which Mirabeau had advised his sister to administer aphrodisiacs to her husband. Mirabeau knew the difficult situation in which his sister was struggling. Exiled at Manosque, himself overwhelmed by his own distressing conjugal drama, he could do little to help her.

But one day, in an impulsive step, he took the risk of breaking his ban. Moved by absurd generosity, he surreptitiously left Manosque and galloped on horseback along the roads of Provence. He was out to help the man he hated most, the friend who had deceived him, his wife's lover. Young Gassaud was engaged to the daughter of the Marquis de Tourrettes, and something had happened, something entirely unconnected with Mirabeau's conjugal drama, that threatened to wreck this advantageous marriage. The handsome musketeer's family was greatly troubled by it, and Mirabeau had the impression that he was suspected of having carried out a mean revenge. The suspicion, he says, tore his heart. Overwhelmed as he was, and no longer quite realizing what he was doing, he raced to the château of Tourrettes to plead the cause of his rival. "I urged, I prayed, I implored," he wrote. He played his generous part until he had won. "The negotiation was renewed and succeeded." One motive of his quixotic gesture may have been his distrust of Emilie and a desire to remove from her a young man who was too attractive.

His mission accomplished, he was reluctant to return at once to exile at Manosque. He pushed on to the château of Vence in order to open his heart to his wise friend. The Comtesse de Vence lectured him severely for his rashness. But in his state of mind Mirabeau was not responsive to counsels of prudence. In his anxiety to see his sister once more, he went on to Grasse.

The proceedings in the matter of the placards had been stopped, but agitation continued in the little town. Slander was abroad at the expense of his sister, and he, too, was involved. A certain Baron de Villeneuve-Mouans was among Louise's bitterest enemies, and extended his malevolence to her brother. "My whole family was being attacked in my person," said Mirabeau later. "The effort was made to brand my name by an accusation as absurd as it was infamous."

His sister received him with overflowing joy but with the discretion that his escapade demanded. Mirabeau took up his quarters on the outskirts of Grasse and avoided the town. But next day Louise went early to see him, in male riding attire, accompanied by her inseparable lover. It was a hot August day. They went to the estate of a woman friend near Grasse. Lunch was generously accompanied with wines; the sun was hot; Louise's vivacity was in no way diminished by her personal troubles. Under the sapphire sky and under the spell of the lovely Louise, Mirabeau forgot his cares and his precarious situation. By an unlucky chance the Baron de Villeneuve-Mouans appeared at that moment, from the neighbouring property, which belonged to him and to which he came from time to time to see to work in progress.

Mirabeau quickly reacted. In the existing circumstances he resented the appearance of the baron as a provocation. He jumped up, threw himself upon the baron, seized the walking-stick he was carrying, and broke it over his back, raining blows on him and shouting at him like one possessed. The baron was fifty years old, fat, flabby, and short of breath. Mirabeau and Louise knew him between themselves as "Gras-fondu"—melted fat. He fell beneath the assault of the young man. The hill sloped abruptly, and the two big bodies rolled over one another, Mirabeau hitting out at the older man all the time. Louise, leaning on her elbows on one of the little boundary walls, went into fits of laughter.

But the episode quickly became less amusing. The punishment inflicted on the baron in no way ran counter to the code of honour of a society that was fond of taking justice into its own hands, a society whose impulsive acts were considered to be proofs of a rich blood. The Mirabeaus were proud of being hard hitters. "What is there so extraordinary," wrote the bailli, "in the great-nephew of our uncles and the grandson of our parents giving himself the trouble to brush an insolent self-styled gentleman's coat with a stick, the person in question having his coat at the time on his back? I am not so sure I shouldn't have done the same myself." Even the phlegmatic Marquis de Marignane, while blaming his son-in-law for breaking the ban, wrote: "I admit that the great faults are on the side of your adversary." But the Marquis de Mirabeau was "very irritated"; he observed with justice that Gabriel had done his sister more harm by making a disturbance than if he had passed over the matter in silence. This new act of rashness only confirmed him in his conviction that his son was incurable.

The Baron de Villeneuve-Mouans emerged with nothing worse than a few bruises and scratches, but the code of honour required that he should demand armed satisfaction from Mirabeau. *Gras-fondu*, however, contented himself with lodging a complaint and starting criminal proceedings for lying-in-wait and attempted assassination.

From the court of justice to which he had remitted his honour, the beaten baron obtained a decree of arrest. Mirabeau's escape from confinement made things worse. Only his father could protect him—a father whose lack of indulgence he knew. He decided—it was a difficult decision for him—to send Emilie to plead his cause with his father. He felt that the thanks she owed him ought to make her "his advocate" in this affair, "the most essential of his life." He did not dream that in doing this he was offering Emilie a means of escape. When they parted at the end of that August of 1774, they separated forever.

6

It was an important period in the life of the marquis. "Here is Economism at the height of success," wrote Emilie on arrival at Bignon. The intendant Turgot, who was one of the leaders of the Economists, had entered the government. He already had great renown as an economist and administrator. Louis XVI, a young king, timid, hesitant, with the best will in the world but few means of giving effect to it, had the good judgment to support this old reformer against all the influences he was obstructing and all the routine he was upsetting.

Turgot brought Dupont back from Poland, where he had been tutor to the children of Prince Czartoryski, and appointed him to a high post in the ministry. The marquis had himself expected to play an important part: "The public frequently mentioned him for the ministry," reported Emilie. But he consoled himself with the thought of being the head of a school that was triumphing at the moment; if he lingered at Bignon longer than usual, it was from coquetry; he affected to be taking refuge from all the "new proselytes this would bring him."

His son's terrible troubles did nothing to reduce the marquis' egoistic self-satisfaction, his good humour, which steered clear of all unpleasing emotions, and his self-assurance as a man who considered that he was always right. He welcomed his daughter-in-law with open arms. She arrived at Bignon in the state of mind of an escaped prisoner. She radiated good humour and *joie de vivre*. The "melodious monkey," as he called her, was of the very sort to please the marquis. She was flattering and caressing when she felt that she was admired. Above all, she was shrewd and sly enough to. seize the facts of a situation and to adapt herself perfectly to them. She made friends at once with Caroline, who was charmed by her spirit. She was on the best of terms with M. du Saillant. Most important of all was her conquest of Mme. de Pailly. The "black puss" was suffering, during that fine autumn, from one of her crises of melancholy. The marquis, who could not endure any but smiling faces about him, showed infinite patience with the moody fits of his *amie*. He was particularly grateful to the two young women, who did their best to amuse her, singing ballads for her and telling her stories; "the jests and absurdities they invent are beyond words," reported the delighted marquis. But the real secret joy that brought Emilie all his sympathy was his discovery that, far from being her husband's "advocate," she was scarcely his ally. He told the Marquis de Marignane about this with a sort of malevolent satisfaction. "If there are any who imagined Madame your daughter to be blind on the subject of her husband, they are greatly deceived."

It is not surprising that, delighted as he was with his daughter-in-law, he loaded her with attentions and caresses. "He spends all day kissing me, from the top of my head to my chin," Emilie told her husband. According to her reports everybody was well disposed to the unfortunate young man who was waiting for news of his fate. "Mme. de Pailly is really very interested in you." As for Saillant, "to do him justice, I must say that he is one of your most zealous advocates." Even of his father she said: "He has repeated several times to me that you were the child for whom he had the greatest weakness; he only complained of your head while praising your heart." She summed up: "In truth, I firmly believe that they all love you more than you imagine."

In these conditions she ought to have succeeded in her efforts and saved her husband from prison. But her efforts were less than half-hearted. With a more or less conscious hypocrisy, she allowed a man consumed with anxiety to entertain a false and short-lived sense of security.

While she was relaxing at Bignon and recovering her old jauntiness, Mirabeau, anxiously awaiting the imminent decision as to his fate, started his first work, *L'Essai sur le despotisme*. Mirabeau later described it himself as "the premature fruit of his youth," and greatly regretted "having mutilated so fine a subject." Since his circumstances at the time were far from favourable for any large-scale work, he contented himself with outlining his convictions. Under the spell of Rousseau, from which no enlightened mind of his age escaped, he believed man to be naturally good. But he believed that "the desire and the instinct for despotism are part of human nature."

Mirabeau laid down the revolutionary axiom that the struggle against despotism is a man's first duty, setting it above loyalty to his country. "Where the mother country gives nothing, nothing is owed to it, for duties are reciprocal. A man of feeling will soon leave a country in which despotism has been established. If he cannot do so he will soon be degraded. In justice, of course, there can be no such thing as treason in a despotic state, because the slave cannot be either creditor or debtor. It is impossible to infringe laws and regulations under a government of which the essence is that it has none."

With the courage of isolation he claimed the right of revolt for all victims of despotism: "Duty, interest, and honour call for resistance to the arbitrary orders of the monarch, and even for his deprivation of power, the abuse of which may bring the destruction of liberty if there is no other means of saving it."

At a time when his affairs were in the utmost confusion, Mirabeau discovered his vocation in life.

7

"All my efforts have been of no avail, my dear friend, and I have been unable to save you from the blow that overwhelms me," Emilie wrote to him after having lulled him with vague assurances. She explained that the ministers, who had learned of his leaving Manosque even before his father did, wanted to send him to Pierre Encise and to fix the period of detention. "It was only by asking that he himself should administer your punishment that your father secured the Château d'If, and gave this the air of a paternal punishment, so that it will rest with him to release you when he wishes."

Emilie knew that, failing miracles, her husband's detention would be prolonged and perhaps for life. She knew that this "paternal punishment" would be more terrible than any that the judicial system could have inflicted on him, for it was arbitrary and dictated by an obscure and never appeased resentment. She knew that in order to shorten the period of detention it would be necessary to negotiate with the creditors to begin with, and she could see that nothing was being done. Everything in the young woman's attitude, in these days of terrible suffering for her husband, was lying and hypocritical. "You know, my good friend, that I am always very ready to follow you or to seek you out wherever you may be, and with great joy, I assure you." She repeated her promise: "The moment you want me you have but to speak and I shall fly to you." She knew perfectly well that she would do nothing of the sort. But she still made an effort to humour him, perhaps less from pity than from fear of the disclosures he could make. She took up the attitude of an afflicted wife in deep distress. "I shed tears whenever I am alone or when anyone speaks of you."

Nobody at Bignon saw any sign in her of sadness or affliction. In the family circle no one gave a thought to the unfortunate man. The marquis was in especially good humour and jested with the young women. "I told them yesterday morning," he wrote to the Comtesse de Rochefort, "that I have only one thing to ask in the world, but hope that will last to the end, and that is to have laughter around me; if not I shall go alone and settle on the banks of the Loire, where the people laugh naturally."

Just when the Marquis de Mirabeau was making these gay remarks, an officer was at Manosque arresting his elder son. He did not allow him to take anything with him. Escorted by two troopers, without any of the attentions customary for gentlemen withdrawn from the reach of justice by a *lettre de cachet*, just like a common pickpocket, Gabriel de Mirabeau was taken from Manosque to the Château d'If. He was taken from the side of his sick child, whom he never saw again.

8

"From the Château d'If may God preserve us," the marquis had written once on a pleasant journey. On this "desolate rock" there were some thirty prisoners, of whom Mirabeau found that "only one, from the dregs of the people, was a scoundrel," and that scarcely half a dozen "might pass for ne'er-do-wells. But," he added, "the others were going straight in that direction; . . . one single diseased person infects all the rest." He saw madmen who would never leave the state prisons or the asylums. In examining their cases he found that many of them had fallen into madness through "excessively bad treatment and from the endurance or the horror of solitude." He was convinced that "a gentle and healthy regime and some exercise would restore their sanity." He thought of a monk whom he had known at Manosque and who had devoted himself to the task of restoring to society those who were not incurable. "Six lunatics had come into his hands while I was in touch with him and watching his work; three of them had had to be kept chained up: all of them left him as good and peaceful citizens."

This world of victims and waifs was now Mirabeau's world; he was cut off from all communication with the world outside. The marquis permitted him to exchange letters only with his wife, whose indifference entirely reassured the father. He was forbidden to receive direct news of his son. Emilie, who was supposed to send him news, was less concerned than he for the health of a baby whom she abandoned to the care of strangers.

"I have no news at all of my poor child. Alas, my friend! now that you no longer send me news, it comes very rarely"—so she complained in a letter to the prisoner. But the separation from her husband and child mattered little to her. The whirl of the pleasures of Paris had taken hold of her flighty mind. She told the captive of the Paris fashions, of new headdresses "of astonishing height, and on top of them hats beyond description, plumes, surmounting these twenty-five-inch headdresses, such as you have seen on the ceremonial hats of the king and princes." She wrote to him of the Italian comedy, of visits, of receptions given by the marquis. She told him especially that she had no time to sacrifice to correspondence: "I have not had a single little instant free since I have been here. . . . You must absolutely excuse me for these beginnings, I have not time to turn round. . . . I am caught by some workwomen who never get finished; at another time it is the Mass, for they celebrate all the saints of the calendar here; then there is shopping, and getting my hair done, and so the time goes." She told him also that she had got fatter, that she was having her teeth cleaned and filed and her mouth embellished, and that she had had her hair piled up on top. She did her best to keep up an insipid flow of society talk with a man cut off from the world.

It is from her replies that one is able to guess Mirabeau's state of mind, for with few exceptions his letters are lost, perhaps destroyed by Emilie.

At the outset he showed great self-mastery. "I have been struck, my friend," Emilie was good enough to write, "by the patience with which you accept your sad position. Nobody has more strength of mind than you in misfortune." But as the weeks and months passed, this patience wore out; the frightful solitude weighed on an essentially sociable man. "Try," she advised him, "to curb your imagination, which in you is a blade that is continually wearing away the scabbard at both ends, as they say."

Mirabeau's letters seem to have been an incessant appeal to his wife to join him. He recalled old memories and tried to reawaken her senses, a difficult task from a distance. But when he reminded her of pleasures they had had together in the past she replied with a simper: "As for other naughtinesses, I beg you to believe, Monsieur le Comte, that at present I am a maiden too chaste to listen to them." When he was tormented with jealousy, she assured him that "my senses are as if buried." To his more and more pressing requests she opposed futile arguments, tearful protestations, fallacious excuses. Years later, Mirabeau said of her: "It is her perfidy more than her faithlessness that I abhor."

He fell ill, and complained of haemorrhage, but Emilie took the news calmly, giving him a vague promise that she would come to look after him if he were really ill.

Though Mirabeau's complaints failed to touch the hearts of his family, his sufferings moved his jailers. Commandant d'Allègre wrote to his father: "The whole province is aware, Monsieur le Marquis, that you have made the liberation of Monsieur le Comte de Mirabeau dependent on the report I give you of his good conduct." He sent him the most unmistakable testimony: "The prisoner has never given the slightest cause for complaint either to me or to anyone; he has at all times behaved perfectly; he has endured with all possible moderation the quarrels I have sometimes started with him in order to test his temper."

But the marquis had no desire for any testimony in his son's favour. He believed, or affected to, that the commandant had been "seduced, corrupted, deceived."

Even the lieutenant of Provence intervened in vain with the marquis, pointing out that it was impossible "to keep eternally on this rock a turbulent father of a family."

Yet there was one consolation for this young man tormented by privation. "There was only one woman at the Château d'If who had the face of a woman. I was twenty-six years old. It was a shocking crime to have led her to suspect that I thought her pretty," said Mirabeau later. The canteen attendant at the Château d'If, the woman in question, had a jealous and brutal husband. The young woman, fearing for her life, fled, taking with her a few clothes. The deceived husband meditated vengeance. A little later he sent a letter to the Comtesse de Mirabeau, accusing his wife of having stolen all the family savings and Mirabeau of having been an accomplice in the theft and the instrument of his "total ruin." Later he was called to give evidence before a tribunal and had to retract. When Mirabeau left the Château d'If, the commandant bore witness that he took with him "the esteem and friendship of everyone in the place."

But before the little scandal had broken out, an evil wind brought Mirabeau's brother, the Chevalier Boniface, to the Château d'If. This favourite son of the marquis was returning from Malta with his health ruined. "They are very angry with him because he has been throwing away money on guzzling and women and is thirteen hundred livres in debt," Emilie wrote. The chevalier had inherited his father's self-indulgent concentration on the gay side of life. For him everything was a jest.

Boniface brought away from his visit only the rumours about the liaison with the canteen attendant. He was not vicious, but he loved gossip and scandal. Between visits to the doctors necessitated by his troublesome malady, he entertained his family with the picturesque story of the conjugal misadventures of the canteen manager. Emilie wrote her husband that she knew what had happened "in the greatest detail. Well, Monsieur, just as suits you best."

Mirabeau allowed himself to be duped no longer. He called on his wife once more to join him. Emilie, running short of arguments, at last let him know that her father had ordered her to remain where she was. Mirabeau burst into fury at this proof of her duplicity. "Your father may know nothing of moral and social laws; that does not surprise me— he has little intelligence, his heart is a weathercock, and his opinion is never his own. But even if it was not common knowledge that a father no longer has rights of jurisdiction over a married daughter without her husband's knowledge and connivance . . . your heart ought to have told you . . . that any advice that prevented you from coming to render to me the duties of conjugal affection was cowardly, perfidious, and contemptible, and any authority that tried to impose it was a tyrannical usurpation."

This letter had a postscript. Before sending it off, Mirabeau must have received news that added further to his rage, for he added: "You are a monster. You have shown my letters to my father. I do not want to crush you, though I ought to, but my heart bleeds at the idea of sacrificing what it has so loved. But I do not intend to be, and I shall not be, your dupe any longer. Carry your infamy where you like. Carry further than you have done, if you can, your perfidious duplicity. Farewell forever!"

This appeal would have shaken anyone but Emilie; but she contented herself with saying that she had shown to his father only "the things which you intended I should." To his great shout of wrath she replied with a thin feminine babble that reduced everything to her own paltry measure. She called him a "spoil sport" for his postscript. She had taken a long time to reply, yet expressed surprise that meanwhile she had had no further news from him. In the postscript to her letter she showed clearly how little she realized what she had done: "No letters from you. Do you think it's right to break with me over a simple suspicion?"

A long silence followed this unequal dialogue. The intimate conjugal "thee" and "thou" did not survive it. No further inopportune tenderness or complaints came from the prisoner to disturb the life of pleasure the young woman was living at Paris. Mirabeau broke the silence under the torment of jealousy, more tenacious than his love: "The coronation is bringing to Paris you know whom. I had asked to be set free for a short time, but was unable to get permission for this. I cannot and must not, and I do not want, to put you at the mercy of a danger that will find you too weak. So, make some pretext, and since you do not feel you can return to Provence, a return which would bring you my eternal gratitude and love and esteem and confidence, go into a convent and do not leave it. I conjure you by your son, by yourself, whom I have always loved and love still, not to force me by any disobedience to make you realize the extent of my rights."

Mirabeau threatened in vain. He tried in vain to move her: "My hand trembles in writing these lines, my heart is torn . . . ." Emilie contented herself with assuring him that she had seen the Chevalier de Gassaud only "twice, on the pretext that he was ill as he said." She went on: "If I had been able to carry out the orders you gave me, then, believe me, I should not have failed to do so; but as we were just leaving for Bignon, and our trunks were packed, I felt that the others would think me mad if I suggested such a thing."

9

One day in May 1775, early in the morning, the Marquise de Mirabeau, whom the marquis had not seen for fifteen years, burst into his Paris house and demanded that they live together again. Accompanied by two notaries, she took note of the marquis' refusal and at once made an application for a legal separation. After the death of her mother, she had demanded from her husband an increase in her allowance under an arrangement that had been agreed to earlier. But the marquis refused, alleging that he had been deceived by the Marquise de Vassan, who had bequeathed to her daughter as her exclusive property lands bringing in eight thousand livres.

Sordid money questions were mixed up with grievances which the years had exacerbated—years during which an erring and humiliated wife had incessantly meditated vengeance. Another woman was installed in her home, and she had always before her eyes the picture of this woman's luxury being paid for by her money, while she herself was struggling painfully with her gambling debts, her creditors, and the shady personages hanging round her. Her nature was almost as passionate as at twenty years of age, and with the same unfortunate results.

Two years earlier the marquise had made an appearance in Paris in a first attempt to start separation proceedings, but she had been dissuaded by one of the ministers, a relative of hers, and had been intimidated by the bailli. When she reappeared this time she had large sums at her disposal, the source of which puzzled the marquis. He learned that Louise de Cabris had advanced them to her mother against a promise to bequeath to her the part of her dowry of which she felt herself defrauded. This disloyalty was a terrible blow to him. He never forgave her.

His wife's move placed the marquis in a cruel dilemma. There could be no question for him of the resumption of their life together, but he was equally unable to agree to "the maddest of separations," for a legal separation would entail a separation of properties, and he had so administered her properties that their restoration would have meant his ruin. Vulnerable himself through his liaison with Mme. de Pailly, and dreading a scandal, he did not dare to use against his wife the weapons he held. "All this needs only that we should hold our noses and go peacefully on our way until she has been nonsuited," he wrote to his brother. But he was not to have any more peace. This was only the prelude to long and disastrous proceedings which were to destroy not only his peace, but his fame and his fortune. The marquise was not nonsuited in her first application in separation. The struggle continued furiously.

The arrival of the Marquise de Mirabeau in Paris had a disastrous repercussion on the fate of her son. It was then that the marquis revealed the secret fear that was one of the main motives for his rigorous treatment of Gabriel. To the bailli's naïve proposal that the marquis resign his wardenship of an ungrateful son, the marquis replied that he wanted to keep his son confined for fear that, if he were free, he would come to Paris to aid his mother.

10

"I have had my son transferred from the Château d'If to the Château de Joux, on the frontier of Franche-Comté, where he will be less restricted," wrote the marquis. But Mirabeau wrote: "I have left a prison which was made more endurable by the consideration with which I was treated, to come to the most mournful and the coldest country in Europe. . . ."

Just when his son was in this pitiable situation, the marquis acquired a sumptuous house in Paris, l'Hôtel de la Reine Marguerite, in the rue de Seine, as if to prove to himself that he still had the free disposal of the family fortune. His real motive for transferring his son to the fortress of Joux was not that he should be less restricted, but that he should be yet farther away from his mother and his sister, who had succeeded in getting letters through to him at the Château d'If.

Mirabeau had once more to apply all his personal seductiveness in order to secure tolerable conditions of life. He was the only prisoner in this dismal place, "brightened up by a few invalids."

The commandant of the fortress of Joux and of the town of Pontarlier, M. de Saint-Mauris, an old soldier of distinguished family, was fond of repeating that he was not resigned to playing the part of a jailer. Mirabeau soon obtained permission to take rooms at Pontarlier, the little neighbouring town, to take his meals at the inn, and to go about the country, on condition that he returned to the fortress every evening, a condition that was not rigorously observed. After a few months his material situation improved. But he felt all the more the burden of his unprofitable existence. He assuaged the stirrings of his senses by a few passing adventures, and his spiritual hunger by a work he was preparing—at the request of the commandant himself—on the salt marshes of Franche-Comté. But these expedients were not enough to fill the great gap between his immense energies and his petty existence.

In this spring of 1775 an underground agitation was spreading through the country. Interested circles were combating in every possible way the reforms of Turgot, the suppression of forced labour and of the trade guilds, and especially freedom of trade in grain. They did not hesitate to engineer a rise in prices. The people began to protest. A riot broke out in Paris. A crowd gathered at the markets and pillaged the bakers' shops. The government had to bring in the military. Public and government alike believed that there was an organized plot.

The bailli wrote at this time to his brother: "I should not be in the least surprised if this is the wickedness or the stupidity of those who dare to teach the populace the secret of its strength. I do not know from what source the confidence is drawn that it will be possible to arrest the fermentation of men's minds; but if I am not deceived, such riots have always preceded revolutions."

Mirabeau, so far away from everything, himself felt that something was stirring in this static society, that a great change was under way. "The times are regenerating, and today ambition is permitted," he wrote to the bailli. It was a desperate appeal to his uncle, of whom he knew that at one time he had appreciated his true worth. He wrote to him in his characteristic way, as if he were pleading his cause by word of mouth: "Do you believe, permit me to venture to ask you, do you believe that the emulation that inspires me is absolutely sterile, and that at twenty-six years of age your nephew is capable of nothing good? . . . Save me from the terrible fermentation from which I am suffering, and which might destroy the effect which reflection and the ordeal of misfortune have produced on me." The whole tragedy of his wasted and perverted life was contained in this simple phrase: "There are men who have to have occupation."

His appeal was in vain. The bailli, on his arrival in Provence, had heard the echoes of all the indiscretions his nephew had committed, and he wrote to the marquis: "As for your madman, I have done with that fellow!" And to Gabriel he replied brutally: "What you are pleased to call your flightiness, Monsieur le Comte, leaves you the option only between fortress and prison."

Rebuffed on all sides, more and more tormented, and also more and more drawn by the great appeal of life, Mirabeau took a desperate step. He made a last appeal to his wife. He wrote her a long letter in which he implored her to flee with him to Switzerland, where he could find means of earning a living through literary work. This letter, which Emilie showed to nobody, was in its writer's opinion "the strongest, the most pressing, the most sparkling with spontaneous eloquence inspired by the cause, to induce her to share my lot."

Meanwhile Emilie's grandmother had died, leaving her sixty thousand livres as an increase of her dowry. But Mirabeau knew nothing about this as yet.

Pending his wife's reply, Mirabeau retired into the fortress of Joux and remained in confinement there, like a man awaiting sentence.

The reply that came, after long delay, was short and sharp. "I admit that the proposal you made to me so embarrassed me that I did not know what to reply, being unable to comply with it. . . . I should think I was doing you an irreparable wrong if I joined with you in a step that would give you the air of a fugitive and would embroil you with your father more than ever. . . . I venture to tell you, Monsieur, that you are by no means reduced to that extremity."

It was the voice of reason, replying from the mouth of a woman who no longer loved him, who had forgotten even the time of their mutual passion. "I made a mistake," Mirabeau said later, "in looking for fruit on a tree that bore nothing but flowers."

ঌ V ঌ

"'Twas With You That Love Began"

THERE WAS nothing of the heroine of romance about Sophie de Monnier. She was tall and robust, with a body that seemed an embarrassment to her. She kept her head slightly bent, and carried one shoulder higher than the other as if she wanted to disguise her native vigour. In themselves her features were commonplace and little short of common. She had full and even fat cheeks and an upturned nose; her lips were thick, her chin short and firm; her black hair, loaded with powder and worn in a puffed-out coiffure, was crisp and rebellious. But in spite of her irregular features she created an impression of beauty. A white smooth forehead, high and powerful, saved her face from insignificance; a dazzling complexion and a clear, glossy skin adorned her with the brilliance of her twenty years.

Mentally as well as physically her contradictions saved her from mediocrity. She herself said that she was very ignorant. Her writing was unformed, her spelling particularly defective, her style common-place, at all events until she appropriated that of her model. But she had an extraordinary memory, which enabled her to assimilate information rapidly and lastingly, and which gave firmness even to newly acquired notions. She had always been very fond of reading, indeed of serious study, though haphazard and unmethodical in her choice of books. Her great charm lay in her perfect naturalness. Now naïve, now subtle, she was never anything but frank.

She had a great fund of innate goodness and a gay temperament; she was easy to live with. Her friends and her lover never tired of praising her sweetness. A great faculty of adaptation and a desire to give pleasure to those whom she loved were reinforced by an instinctive tenderness. This big, robust, healthy woman was in no way disturbed by her senses; her lover never ceased to reproach her for the tepidness of her physical reactions, but "her heart," said Mirabeau one day, "is a volcano." She was a woman of exclusive loyalty in love. Outside one single attachment she felt not merely indifference, but violent aversion.

She was a disconcerting young woman, and from the very beginning of her life her apparent submissiveness deceived those on whom her future depended. Her father, Richard de Ruffey, president of the *Chambre des Comptes*, or Exchequer Court, at Dijon, prided himself on his literary tastes and his artistic knowledge. He took his role of Maecenas of Dijon very seriously, carried on a regular correspondence with Voltaire, and gathered round himself a group of savants, such as Buffon, and writers who were later to enter the Academy of Dijon. In spite of her natural intelligence and vivacity, his wife lived intimidated in the shadow of her redoubtable husband.

M. de Ruffey tried to satisfy his vanity even at the expense of the marriage of his younger daughter. When Buffon's wife died, Sophie's father tried to marry her to him, though she was but fifteen years old. Buffon, however, was inconsolable at the loss of his wife; he was over sixty, and was unattracted by the plan.

Sophie's dowry was modest and her father's pretensions great; her mother blindly served her husband's ambition. Their daughter was only seventeen when her parents decided on a marriage that seemed to them to be particularly advantageous. M. de Monnier was very rich; he possessed extensive estates and several châteaux; he was a marquis; he held an important post in the magistracy as first president of the *Chambre des Comptes* at Dôle. But he, too, was a sexagenarian widower. On learning of this marriage Voltaire wrote with his mordant irony to M. de Ruffey: "I did not know that M. de Monnier was a marriageable young man. My compliments to him; I think he is very fortunate to espouse Mademoiselle your daughter. I wish the two of them all possible prosperity!"

These ambitious parents had given their daughter to a mean and timid man who was a mass of prejudices and combined extreme credulity with exaggerated suspiciousness. Rich as he was, this old man remained stingy and close-fisted even with the magnificent young girl he had married. But the hardest blow for Sophie was the discovery of the motive that had led M. de Monnier into this marriage.

The Marquis de Monnier had a daughter by his first marriage, who had fallen in love at nineteen with a musketeer who bore a significant name, Le Boeuf de Valdahon. Her father had opposed this marriage with all the determination of a naturally weak man who had suddenly been crossed. The two young people had hoped to force his hand by a scandal. The girl found means of introducing the musketeer at night into the alcove in which her mother, who kept watch on her, was asleep in a twin bed. But even scandal could not bend the Marquis de Monnier. He prosecuted his daughter's lover for seduction and rape of a minor; he deposited in evidence the breeches that had been left beside Mlle. de Monnier's bed. The girl was condemned to forget her unhappy adventure in a convent. For the sake of peace, she swore to think no more of this marriage. But at the convent she waited patiently until she came of age, and the moment she did she informed her father of her intention to marry M. de Valdahon. "His daughter made him acquire the habit of being taken in, and made him acquire it so thoroughly that he will go on being taken in for the rest of his life," said Sophie later in contempt. The Marquis de Monnier took fresh legal proceedings, but the young couple, who had on their side both the sentimental people and the mockers, won the case. The father's only thought now was of how to disinherit them. He got married out of rage and spite. Sophie, herself essentially generous and impressionable, was deeply wounded at the discovery.

In this marriage, with its absurd disparity of ages, there was no love even in the form of affection or of gratitude. The marquis had wanted especially to punish his disobedient daughter by giving himself an heir. Physical love revealed itself to an inexperienced young girl in the form of the vain and pitiful efforts of an old man. Her first lover found her still a virgin. She was predestined to a series of small adventures or to one great passion.

Sophie seems to have turned first to small adventures. A young man with whom she flirted awakened her imagination. He was a young artillery officer who thought he saw in her an easy prey. He was enterprising and hard up. Sophie, too trustful by nature, wrote him affectionate letters and sent him her portrait. She even gave him money—her husband's money. She addressed him with the intimate "thou." She was not yet his mistress, but any chance might have thrown her into his arms. The man's conceit advertised her already as his mistress in the little town, where Sophie, in her own words, had not a single woman friend, "but twenty spies and a hundred critics." Her husband, "double-dealing by nature, pretended to feel safe to save his face." But Sophie was well aware that the moment anybody chose to tell him stories of imprudence on his wife's part, "he will come down like a clap of thunder." And "he does not know what forgiveness is."

She was menaced before she had committed an irreparable wrong. She had not known happiness, and she was in process of destroying her peace.

2

Shortly after Mirabeau's arrival, the Marquise de Monnier visited the fortress. M. de Saint-Mauris was one of the young woman's admirers. Gabriel and Sophie met. She was so young that she seemed a child to him. She may have been scarcely pretty enough to put him on his guard. The coronation festivities in July, celebrated with great solemnity at Pontarlier, brought frequent meetings between the two young people. Commandant de Saint-Mauris played an important part in the festivities. He was regarded as a wit in the little town. "He wanted me as a witness of his glory, and I owed it to his vanity that I was permitted to go to Pontarlier," wrote his prisoner. Mirabeau was hungry for excitement and for pleasure. There was nothing to prompt him to caution in an ordinary adventure with a young and fresh provincial girl. He was attracted by the passionate response he found in Sophie. When M. and Mme. de Monnier went away for the holidays, the prisoner returned to the fortress, to carry on there a bitter solitary struggle.

Their tragic association began as soon as Sophie returned. Mirabeau had seen many women yield easily to him. His Herculean figure, his fire, his irresistible persuasiveness, the very boldness that had in it a good deal of contempt for women, quickly won them over. But Sophie resisted him because she loved him.

Sophie's love was born of a passionate admiration, boundless and exclusive. It was all contained in a few very simple little words, in this cry from the heart: "Who is there like Gabriel?" She loved even his faults, of which she was fully aware; she loved him in his anger, his jealousy, his excessive susceptibility, and in his changes of humour that tormented her. She loved even his pockmarks. "I have a certain liking for markings," she wrote one day to him. She loved him so much as to find him physically handsome and morally perfect. "When will you learn," she said to him, "that everything about you is lovely, handsome, charming, especially in my eyes, for love would beautify you, but you have no need of that."

Mirabeau, who had enjoyed many women and loved them but little, asked himself later what was the secret of Sophie's power over him: "Whence comes this extreme ascendancy, which I do not like, because it might be taken for despotism by anyone who did not know me?" And he answered: "From her infinite affection."

But Sophie did not yet yield to the man she loved. He was piqued: "You have given me your heart and you refuse me your favours!" She was held back by the consideration she owed to the man whose name she bore and whose fortune she shared; she was held back also by the promptings of modesty, and perhaps also by an instinctive fear of what that final abandonment might mean for her. But Mirabeau argued against her scruples with his seducer's eloquence: "Modesty no more consists in refusing everything to one's lover than sobriety commands that one should starve oneself to death."

Sophie hesitated, but not for long. In the terrible solitude of the fortress of Vincennes, Mirabeau recalled the intoxication of her first surrender. "Your head resting on my arms, your lovely neck, your alabaster breast . . . delivered up to my ardent desires, my hand, my happy hand daring to wander. Your beautiful eyes closed . . . you palpitated, trembled. You were drunk with voluptuous sensations and tormented by modesty. My desires consumed me, I expired, was reborn. . . . I lifted you in my arms . . . the floor escaped from my feet. . . ." His love for Sophie was a furious desire for the flesh. Under the date December 13, 1775, he noted in his diary in capital letters: "*Je fus heureux.*"

3

Neufchâtel was a small enclave under Prussian sovereignty in the midst of the Swiss cantons. A special traffic was carried on there with the same skill with which other industries were carried on in the trading cantons around it—the traffic in free thought. Everything that the censorship suppressed in France was printed there, to return to France by the smugglers' paths of the Jura. The French government was well aware of this traffic, but sometimes it preferred to close its eyes to it.

To this asylum of free speech Mirabeau made his way at the beginning of the winter. He had left, by agreement with the commandant, to look after the publication in Switzerland of his work on the salt marshes of Franche-Comté. In this technical work the author of the *Essay on Despotism* revealed himself in a few remarks: "The French have always boasted that the Inquisition never took root among them. But they devote little thought to public affairs. There is room for a work drawing a parallel between the sacerdotal and the fiscal Inquisition. I doubt whether the Exchequer would come out well in it."

In Neufchâtel, Mirabeau made the acquaintance of Fauche, one of the bookseller-printers of works that could not be submitted to the censorship. He offered him his *Essay on Despotism*. Fauche accepted it and paid Mirabeau fifteen hundred livres. This was the first money Mirabeau gained with his pen. The work was to appear anonymously. In this premature and scarcely articulate work, Fauche discerned the great future talent of a polemical writer. He offered Mirabeau a fixed payment of a thousand crowns a year for his future literary output. A path had opened before Mirabeau. If he were free he could become independent of his father.

On his return, relations with Commandant de Saint-Mauris became strained. Saint-Mauris was one of the first to see through the relations between Gabriel and Sophie. He went about saying malicious things about the young woman. He could report nothing good of Mirabeau to his father.

Gabriel de Mirabeau began to understand the real motives that led his father to keep him in captivity. At the beginning of January 1776 the Marquise de Mirabeau had won her case with a first judgment pronouncing a judicial separation. She wrote to her son: "I sympathize very much with all your troubles." He replied: "Set me free, that is the most important thing for both of us. I could help you, and certainly there would be a change of tone if we were reunited."

Mirabeau was twenty-seven. He felt that he had talent, and he was ambitious. He was consumed with impatience to put his abilities to the test. He was loved. He was ready for anything, as though Sophie's wild admiration had given him fresh confidence in himself. Events were moving fast and were driving him to action. But the two scourges of his existence, debts and affairs with women, were once more fatally at work. A woman who was the commandant's mistress, and whose favours Mirabeau said he had rejected, excited her lover against him.

And one day a Pontarlier shopkeeper, to make sure of his money, brought to M. de Saint-Mauris a bill of exchange signed by Mirabeau to the order of the bookseller Fauche. Although still deprived of legal rights, he had managed to run into debt. The bill of exchange revealed him as the author of a dangerous work. The commandant himself risked being compromised for lax treatment of his prisoner.

There was a violent scene at the Château de Joux. The old commandant was furious, his legitimate indignation reinforced by secret resentment. He forbade his prisoner to leave the fortress. Mirabeau, however, on the ground of avoiding a scandal that would set tongues wagging all over the town, finally secured permission to attend a ball that was being given in his honour. He did not return to the fortress. The incident originating with a little shopkeeper brought about his rash decision to flee. His legitimate desire to recover his freedom, and his justified impatience, took shape in an ill-considered act that put him in the wrong. He wrote to the commandant one of those arrogant and unforgivable letters that proceed from a first impulse of anger. "I am withdrawing, Monsieur, from an authority which, having become tyrannical, has set more traps for me than I should ever have feared from a gentleman. . . ."

He began open war against his father, ranging himself on his mother's side. She herself, in an ill-spelled letter, transmitted a memorial from him to the minister, Malesherbes. The hopes aroused at the outset of the reign of Louis XVI found an echo in this personal plea. "It is well known with what unhappy facility the liberty of the subject was fettered under the late king."

As soon as he took office Malesherbes attacked judicial abuses. He held that *lettres de cachet* should be issued only when the grounds for them had been discussed and approved at a plenary council meeting. He set up special commissions to examine the existing *lettres de cachet*. To one of these commissions the case of Gabriel de Mirabeau was submitted.

The marquis had approved Malesherbes' first reforms, knowing that he was favourable to the Economists. But his good opinion changed as soon as his own personal case was at stake. When he learned of his son's requests, he intervened with the minister. After his visit to him he wrote indignantly to his brother: "This Malesherbes, with his easygoing philanthropy and his fine republican ideas, did he not reply to my reproaches that it was natural to seek one's freedom?"

M. de Marignane hurried to Paris, accompanied by his faithful friend the Comte de Valbelle. Everyone, even the bailli, went to the minister to try to talk him over. "My son is mad," exclaimed the Marquis de Mirabeau. The Marquis de Marignane went one better: "So I think, but I venture to add, in the presence of Monsieur, his father, that if he were not mad he would still be, and is, antisocial in character and wicked on principle."

Emilie was particularly concerned at the news that her husband was at liberty, and her agitation made her ill, as though this was a way out. Her father and her father-in-law settled her fate between them. She was to go back to Provence, with the free disposal of the income from her dowry. The child was to remain with the Gassauds at Manosque.

Open war continued between father and son before the tribunal of a minister whom the marquis taxed with republicanism. The conflict was overshadowed by that of two epochs, by a battle between two worlds. The cause which the marquis was defending was that of a feudal order, of a right based mainly on the power of the father, "a salutary law, which maintains the family and morality." In the long memorial which he addressed to Malesherbes he invoked forty years of life as head and father of a family, years "passed without reproach, witnesses which I prefer to the celebrity and the general marks of esteem with which all Europe has honoured me." His memorial was also a long indictment of "the poor madman." It went back to the "strange passions" and the "vices" of his tender years, and to the evidence of his tutors and masters. He himself felt the fundamental weakness of his argument: "But, it will be said, all this does not merit detention. So I, too, think. He is twenty-seven years old. But since he was eighteen he has always been under detention, and when at liberty he has done more harm and to more people than others could see." At bottom he was asking for preventive imprisonment for his son by painting the deplorable consequences of setting him at liberty. "If he gains his ends, what will become of him? He will live on the level of madmen and incendiaries, he will borrow, despoil, abduct; he is unable to follow any other path." He might have been talking of a monster that must be chained up. "If he is to be left at liberty, I wash my hands of it. I lay on the conscience of the minister all the crimes that will result—the subjects of the king wounded in their honour, in their property, perhaps in their lives."

"My father has pursued me since my childhood with implacable hatred," replied Gabriel de Mirabeau. He drew attention to the same weak point of the marquis' case: "If my father's argument is to be admitted, it will be necessary to place me in confinement for the rest of my life." He asked not for mercy but for the protection of the law against this domestic authority, which he claimed to be blinded by resentment. And he placed himself on impregnable ground: "If I have merited punishment, let that be declared and let me be legally punished." The great struggle for law against despotism, for justice against abuses, which he was one day to carry on, had begun, as with so many memorable combats, for a personal cause.

4

After the ball, the fugitive Mirabeau hid in Sophie's own house, in an unlighted room leading into hers. After a few days he found another refuge with friends in Pontarlier, good souls of the lower class whom he had won over. Sophie sent him food and books. The lovers came together at night.

This game lasted for nearly a month. One evening servants gave the alarm: they had seen a stranger in the house. Mirabeau was surrounded and recognized. But it was not in vain that in his childhood he had played at "pretending." In a haughty voice he asked to see the Marquis de Monnier. The old man, hoaxed but completely unsuspicious, had great sympathy for him. Awakened in the middle of the night, he received his visitor with open arms. Mirabeau embraced him and with perfect unconcern told him that he had come from Berne and was on his way to Paris in order to submit his case in person to the minister, and that he had stopped at Pontarlier in order to greet his friends M. and Mme. de Monnier. With the same unconcern he drew a letter from his pocket which he pretended was from his father, and, in a brilliant improvisation, read out its imaginary contents. The Marquis de Monnier was greatly impressed. At Mirabeau's suggestion he rang for the servants and made them swear to say nothing about this nocturnal visit.

M. de Saint-Mauris, outraged by Mirabeau's insulting letter, sent a priest to tell the marquis about his wife's liaison. Monnier, blundering in his excessive confidence, blundered just as badly in his wrath. He was completely ignorant of the character of the woman he had married. She had duped him in order to enjoy the happiness that was demanded insistently by her twenty years; but dissimulation was repugnant to her nature: she would have liked to shout her love to the whole world. Her principle was "to clear up everything, at once, with everybody." Even the consciousness of her fault did not diminish her fundamental straightforwardness. The marquis wounded her deeply by the line he took. Without any approach to her, he assembled all the servants, made a pathetic appeal to their loyalty, and placed their mistress in their charge. Thereafter Sophie was spied on, watched, and dogged by the servile insolence of the staff. It was an intolerable situation for a proud woman. Mirabeau advised her to take refuge with her own people. Sophie, in her lover's words, was "without any will of her own in face of a being she loved." She followed Mirabeau's advice and signified her resolve to her husband. "I assured him that I should have preferred to be sent to a convent rather than find myself more or less under the tutelage of my servants; that it was not in my nature to put up with humiliation; and that in consequence I requested his permission to return to my family."

But Sophie's situation in her parents' home was worse even than in her husband's. In place of a feeble old man was an authoritarian father, beside himself with rage, a man who had always been Sophie's terror. He would break out into shouts of anger, or avoid her in order to keep himself from violence. Her mother was terrified by the consequences of her daughter's guilty love and sang the praises of the kind Marquis de Monnier. Her sister, a canoness, painted to her the punishments of Hell; her brothers pursued her with their cold and coarse pleasantries.

Elements of comedy persisted in the web of the tragedy that was being woven. There was a grand ball at the house of the provost of Burgundy, M. de Montherot. The Ruffey family were invited. Sophie was accompanied by her faithful friend Mme. de Saint-Belin. The door opened, and a stentorian voice announced a guest with a name that might have come straight from a farce: the Marquis de Lancefoudras [Thunderthrower]. Sophie, half fainting, suddenly saw before her Gabriel de Mirabeau. Her agitation did not escape her mother's watchful eyes. Before the couple were lost to view, she had guessed the truth. "I was in such a predicament," said Mirabeau later, "that I could not do anything right."

Next day Mme. de Ruffey had her daughter's lover arrested. For this Sophie never forgave her. The family's watch over her spared her no humiliation. Her elder sister slept in the same room with her. One night the canoness was replaced by Mme. de Saint-Belin. Sophie slipped away—for a moment, she said—from the bed they shared. She did not return till dawn. According to her friend, the lovers passed that icy night in the garden. "That meeting greatly increased my love," Sophie admitted candidly. "The passions of a gentle woman," said Mirabeau, "may be more slowly aroused, but are infinitely more ardent than those of any others, and are truly invincible when they are thoroughly ablaze."

Pending orders from the minister, Mirabeau was a prisoner on parole in a furnished room in Dijon. M. de Malesherbes ordered him to be taken back to Joux. The Marquis de Mirabeau asked M. de Saint-Mauris to put his son in a healthy, dry prison, "but well locked and bolted and barred," and not to let him write or speak to anyone. It came out that the vindictive commandant was getting ready the Grammont tower, which was dripping with water everywhere, "a dungeon renowned for its hideous aspect and its horrible discomforts."

Mirabeau wrote to Malesherbes: "I beg of your mercy to order that I shall be put in irons to save me from the direst evil. I should be lost and should drag another to destruction if I were left the use of my arms."

In M. de Montherot, Mirabeau found an eloquent advocate. The grand provost of Burgundy had succumbed to his "magic"; beneath the impetuosity of this romantic lover he had discovered great human qualities. "M. de Mirabeau," he wrote to the minister, "is but a flower just opening, and in spite of the few thorns it shows it will become nonetheless precious." As a man of the world he showed indulgence for the indiscreet escapade at Joux, and he asked the minister for a reprieve.

Meanwhile the commission was examining Mirabeau's case. It came to the conclusion that "the first youthful excesses of the Comte de Mirabeau have been punished already." It dismissed the charge made against him by the canteen manager at the Château d'If. It confined its attention to his flight from Joux. Once more Mirabeau's fate was in suspense.

If the minister remained of the same opinion, and if the commission pronounced in favour of his liberation, he would be able to return to normal life and to become of use to his country. Pending the minister's decision he was living at the château of Dijon, under the benevolent supervision of Commandant de Changey, to whom the grand provost had recommended that his prisoner be treated with kindness, and who received him into his own family. The understanding shown to him calmed him; he was now anxious to avoid "a scandal that might end in ruining Mme. de Monnier in the eyes of her husband." He sent letters to Mme. de Ruffey in which he recommended her to show more coolness and prudence in her relations with her daughter. At their first meeting Sophie's mother had found in him a "rustic air." After reading his letters she called him a magician and a demon. "Heavens!" he sighed one day, "when shall I be dull enough for my honesty to be believed in?" He preached the same moderation to Sophie's brothers, who came in secret to see him. He explained to them the violence that slumbered in Sophie beneath her outward gentleness, the energy beneath her amiability. He asked her to return to Pontarlier, to do it as a mark of her attachment to him. But his effort at conciliation brought no more than a moment's halt on the downward path.

Mme. de Ruffey tried to set Sophie against Mirabeau. She told her that her lover was showing her letters to his men friends, and added, hoping to sting her pride, that the friends found the letters "very silly, the letters of an idiot." She was too poor a psychologist to realize that great passions are above petty susceptibilities, and her calumnies merely increased her daughter's devotion. "I told them," she wrote to Gabriel, "that if I saw in your own writing that you loved me no longer . . . I should believe that the writing was forged."

The canoness followed Sophie to Pontarlier, where she busied herself in "taking the whole town into her confidence, going to my friends and making scenes in their homes, using the most shameful expressions." Mme. de Ruffey urged the Marquis de Monnier to apply for a *lettre de cachet* to confine his wife in a convent. Watched and spied on, pursued at the same time by her husband's senile ardour, knowing that her letters were being intercepted and read by third parties, Sophie in her own home was like an animal at bay. "They have not done me all the harm they meant to, but they have certainly done all they could," she exclaimed bitterly. The clumsy meddling of her family had completely isolated her, had poisoned the very springs of her life, and had bound her to her lover by despair. She had come to the point where she saw no other solution than flight with him: "It has got to end, I can't stand it any longer! Again I say, Gabriel or death!"

Everything conspired to drive Mirabeau to a catastrophic decision. The idea of fleeing abroad obsessed him. His father seems to have been the first to suggest it to him. Michaud, the public prosecutor at Pontarlier, whose friendship Mirabeau had won, in addition, apparently, to his sister's regard, had appealed warmly to the marquis. But this irreconcilable father had replied: "From what I can gather about things and men, if the person in whom you are kind enough to interest yourself could go to some country where he did not have to languish, you would do him a great wrong by preventing him from doing so. I know no country today that is more alien to him than France."

"What happened to me when I read that fateful letter," wrote Mirabeau later in reminiscence, "I will not tell you, father; for you used to pretend that when I fainted I was shamming epilepsy. . . . Oh, my father, had I deserved, then, to be chased away from my family and my country?"

The idea wounded him, but it continued to gain headway. "I am indeed tired of prisons," he wrote to his mother. "On the other hand, I am very reluctant to go abroad; it is like renouncing one's country, like giving in, and I neither can nor will do either."

The decision that tormented him was imposed from without. Events entirely unconnected with Mirabeau recoiled on him. There had been a scandal at the French embassy in London. The ambassador, the Comte de Guines, had been accused by his secretary of smuggling under cover of diplomatic privilege, and of profiting by information that came to him through his official position to speculate in government securities. The ambassador was recalled. Powerful friends who had the ear of the queen intervened on his behalf. Royal favour decided the issue in the courts, and his secretary was sentenced for libel.

The incident was exploited by all those who had a grudge against Turgot, all those whose abuses he had combated. Those whom he had offended by his uncompromising methods, those whose susceptibilities he had wounded, used their influence on the queen. In spite of the king's resistance, Marie Antoinette obtained the title of duke for the Comte de Guines and the dismissal of Turgot. Malesherbes, who had worked with Turgot for the recall of an ambassador under too powerful protection, was also sacrificed.

The commission on *lettres de cachet*, which had been occupied with Mirabeau's case, seemed ready to pronounce in favour of his immediate liberation. But on the eve of the minister's fall it seems to have been thinking already, like the other official bodies, of his successor. It did not venture to display too much courage. It decided, "in order to maintain due respect for the king's command and to fall in with the arrangements concerning the Comte de Mirabeau and his family," to take cognizance of only one of his offences, his escape, and to prolong his detention for no more than six months. The Marquis de Mirabeau, aided by a bombardment of petitions to the minister from the Ruffeys, immediately obtained a *lettre de cachet* ordering the transfer of his son to the fortress of Doullens. He was the more determined to incarcerate his son in a well-supervised prison since Louise de Cabris had entered a convent at Lyon. "She has a cooler and a more calculating head than her brother's," he wrote, "but unfortunately for me it works on a wicked heart, which her brother in reality has not. When both are at liberty they have frequent and violent quarrels, but their troubles have united them, and if they got together Hell would emerge from that congress."

He hastened to warn the governor of Doullens against the wiles of his son and his gift of playing "the seigneur and the illustrious victim."

"What was I to expect from this determination to remove me from a place where I was doing well? New persecutions, no doubt, and an austere commandant, prejudiced against me," concluded Mirabeau. The fall of Malesherbes had been "a thunderclap" for him. Before leaving office the minister had transmitted to him a last piece of advice out of his powerlessness—"to go to a foreign country and there to take a degree."

Gabriel de Mirabeau took a desperate course. On the night of May 24, 1776, he fled from the château of Dijon.

<h2 style="text-align:center">5</h2>

"It was entirely my doing," exclaimed Sophie one day. Mirabeau's escape had sown panic among the Ruffey family. Sophie's brother came armed to Pontarlier, as though to maintain a siege. In spite of the family's urgency, the Marquis de Monnier refused to shut up his wife in a convent, for Sophie had declared that "I shall set it on fire." He did not dare to apply for a *lettre de cachet* for her, for, however bad a psychologist he might be, he thought her capable of stabbing herself, as she had threatened to do if she were deprived of her liberty.

Like so many others who are passionately in love with life, Sophie was obsessed by the idea of a voluntary death. Her lover knew that her threats were neither empty nor the morbid play of an excited imagination, but a calm and unshakable resolve: she preferred death to a life without the love that was its *raison d'être*. He said one day, with terrible prescience: "You will see her serene and tranquil a quarter of an hour before the catastrophe, which nevertheless will come if she is reduced to despair."

Mirabeau wandered in flight along the Swiss frontier. He was deeply distressed. "My lot gets worse every minute," he wrote to his sister. Later he admitted to a woman friend: "I knew then just as well as I know today that it was utter madness to carry her off." He was sure of finding abroad, "provided that I went alone, the advantages which my youth, my birth, and my sword could procure for me."

His father would have been satisfied with getting rid of him and would have pursued him no longer. But the abduction of a married woman would rouse two influential families and would close for him every avenue of reconciliation. He was fully aware of the danger he was running. But he was profoundly unhappy. "Here I am, exiled from my country," he wrote to Louise, "without hope of seeing my son again, and lost to all my friends. . . . I have sacrificed everything to love and I have achieved nothing for love. I shall never dare to return to my country when I am able to. Under the insulting pity of those poor creatures who think themselves wise because they are incapable of a passion, what could I do in France? And what should I want to do there, far from Sophie?"

Sophie was not the only one to urge him to take this fateful decision. Louise de Cabris, with her cold heart and her heated imagination, swore to do her utmost to reunite Sophie with her lover, and she herself elaborated plans of flight in order, with the two lovers, to rejoin Brian-con in England.

Her reply to the desperate appeals from her brother was to join him in Switzerland. She was accompanied by her inseparable lover and by a girl whose acquaintance she had made in the convent at Lyon, a sister of the Marquise de Saint-Orens, who had known Mirabeau at Saintes and had yielded to the fascination of his fiery temperament. The romantic young girl felt attracted by this exceptional lover of whose terrible charm she had heard so much. For Louise the escapade was a game whose risks rendered it so much the more exciting.

Mirabeau, absorbed though he was by his passion, was unable to resist the presence of a pretty young girl whom he knew to be so much in quest of adventure. Although she was engaged, the girl allowed herself to be seduced by Gabriel. The two couples lived in a strange promiscuity.

Amid this overexcitement Louise was in her element. She wrote to Sophie: "You had better hurry, you know why." Sophie sent parcels to her containing her dresses and her jewellery. She was accused later of having made use of a skeleton key to steal her husband's money.

The Marquis de Mirabeau sent detectives after Gabriel. He engaged an inspector who was "unique in Europe for this sort of thing," and who undertook, with the aid of two men, to find his son. The marquis was also well served, he said, by his friends, one of whom, the Duc de Nivernois, had become a minister of state. He had prepared a new prison for his son, Mont Saint-Michel, which he believed to be safe, "because there is first the château, then a wall round the mountain, and then a pretty long passage across the sand, which needs guides if one is not to be engulfed in the quicksands."

Mirabeau, dogged by detectives, crossed and recrossed the frontier. "The scoundrel changes his quarters every day," wrote the marquis to Caroline. "He has the secret of baffling lazy or knavish sleuths, and he will ravage the world with his detestable talents."

Mirabeau was helped by adventurers whose acquaintance he had made at Dijon, and who brought danger on him by their indiscreet zeal. He crossed the Rhône with Briançon, who stupidly provoked a quarrel with the boatmen, fired a pistol at one of them, luckily missed, and fled, leaving Mirabeau to struggle alone with a number of furious men.

Louise returned to Lyon; Mirabeau went into hiding at Lorgues, in the house of a friend of Briançon, in a room with closed shutters. After the excitement of constant movement, solitude swooped down on him. Behind the closed shutters, his imagination went roving. He escaped from his troubles, from the burden of isolation, from his longing for activity, and from the privations that tormented him, by writing interminable letters to Sophie. In her absence he wanted her more furiously than ever; he was obsessed by the memory of their intimacy; he imagined her trembling with the same desperate desire as he.

Sophie was curious about all the details of his life, and especially about this sister whose affection filled so large a place in her lover's existence. To appease her unconscious jealousy, Mirabeau compared the two women. He had known little of his sister, who had dazzled him as she dazzled every man who came near her, and the intimacy of their escapade enabled him to see things in proportion. He deflated her deceptive show of intellectual superiority and discovered her moral shortcomings. "Louise has bright ideas, but almost all of them are borrowed," he wrote to Sophie. "She never gets hold of the exact phrase, because she never thinks with precision. Louise is always consistent; she will often astonish, as you rarely do, but you seduce, you go to the heart. . . . As may be seen especially," he added, "in your letters. Everything about Louise is trivial and gigantesque, cold and turbid." The friction between their impetuous temperaments must have produced frequent disharmonies during their journey. "Nobody in the world is more difficult to live with than Louise, and nobody is so sweet and attractive as Sophie."

But Mirabeau did not content himself with contrasting the characters of the two women. He also discussed their physical characteristics, down to the most intimate details. In his indiscreet letter there was even the admission of incestuous relations.

Among the inexplicable impulses to which Mirabeau yielded in his life, this indiscretion was one of the gravest. The letter, with its terrible admission, never reached Sophie. Owing to an imprudent address, it was intercepted and fell into the hands of the Ruffeys. It became a formidable weapon secretly pointed against him. One day it came into the hands of the Marquis de Mirabeau, who held it as a terrible menace over his daughter's head. When Louise learned of it she never forgave her brother. Of all the hatreds that pursued Gabriel, hers was the most implacable. Of all his rabid enemies, she was the most ferocious. Brother and sister were never again reconciled.

Meanwhile detectives were pestering Louise with questions about the fugitive. They alarmed her especially by threats against Briançon. Her lover, in a simple and violent man's fury, swore that if anything happened to Louise the Marquis de Mirabeau should perish at his hand. Louise was distracted. "To betray my brother is more than I can do," she wrote to her mother. "To betray my friend, to leave him in danger —still less can I do that." As yet she knew nothing of the terrible wrong her brother had done her, and yet she was ready to sacrifice him to her lover. She swore that she would have nothing more to do with his affairs. She gave the detectives his address, appeasing her conscience with the reflection that "the best thing that can happen to him now is to be recaptured."

The detectives rushed to Lorgues. But Mirabeau saw them through the interstices of his shutters. He made good his escape in the night. Suspecting nothing of Louise's complicity, he left for Briançon a letter containing his itinerary. But the man hastened to communicate the information to the police.

Once more Mirabeau was in headlong flight. He climbed steep mountain paths, descended toward Turin, crossed the Great Saint-Bernard, and went through the Valais. Drawn irresistibly by his passion, he made for a Swiss village near Pontarlier. A terrible anxiety was added to all the rest: he knew now that the fatal letter had not arrived. He guessed that he had been betrayed by his sister, from whom he asked in vain for his papers and the letters exchanged with Sophie. He felt abandoned, with nothing left in the world but his love.

At this time Sophie informed Mirabeau that she had procured a strong dose of laudanum from a chemist's shop in Pontarlier. Could Gabriel allow her to swallow the fatal dose? He sent her a guide who would conduct her across the frontier by a mountain path. About the middle of August 1776, at nightfall, Sophie escaped from her husband's house. She rejoined her lover in the house of a woman who kept a shop in Verrières. Mirabeau, under his note of this memorable date, put a pencil outline, boyish and touching, of a heart in flames.

6

"When authority becomes arbitrary and oppressive, when it attacks the properties for whose protection it was instituted, when it breaks the contract that assured it its rights and set limits to them, resistance is a duty, and cannot be called revolt."

This justification of the great upheaval of the century preceded it by a dozen years. At that turning-point in history, particularly sensitive beings registered the distant shocks of the future. A man who had suffered from tyranny and injustice could not remain indifferent to any injustice, wherever it might be committed in the world.

Trading in soldiers was a source of important revenue for the German princes. England was buying troops and sending them to repress the insurrection of her colonies in America.

In February 1777 the hereditary prince of Hesse-Cassel had concluded with a representative of England a new contract providing for the supply of a corps of riflemen. Germans torn from their soil revolted when embarking in Holland. Dutch peasants helped them in their escape. But other contingents continued to be embarked at Nijmegen. The incident aroused widespread feeling in Holland. A pamphlet appeared at Amsterdam with the title *Advice to the men of Hesse and to the other peoples of Germany sold by their princes to England.* "You are sold, and for what purpose, ye just gods! In order to attack peoples who are defending the most just of causes, who are giving you the most noble example. Why do you not imitate them instead of trying to destroy them?" A firebrand was smouldering within the pages of this anonymous screed. A German writer replied with a pamphlet entitled *Counsels of reason against the advice to the men of Hesse.* But the anonymous author published in turn a *Reply to the counsels of reason.* The *Reply* proclaimed the right of revolt. "He who exerts himself to recover his liberty, and fights for it, is exercising a very legitimate right." It defined the sovereignty of the people. "The crime of *lèse-nation* is the greatest of crimes, and a people is as superior to its sovereign as the sovereign is to an individual."

It was a new language, the language of the morrow. At the same time there appeared in France a small document, also anonymous, on the same subject, with the title *Letter from Count von Schaumberg to Baron von Hohendorff, commanding the Hessian troops in America.* Its principal weapon was irony. In it a petty German prince recalled to the commandant that England was paying him, the prince, thirty guineas for each soldier killed, and he added that he needed this money for a season of Italian opera. "I am about to send you some new recruits. Don't economize them. Remember glory before all things. Glory is true wealth. Nothing degrades the soldier like the love of money. . . . Do you remember that of the three hundred Lacedaemonians who defended the defile of Thermopylae, not one returned? How happy should I be could I say the same of my brave Hessians!"

The writer of the pamphlet, which was published anonymously in Holland, called himself the Comte de Saint-Mathieu. He addressed himself to the bookseller Marc-Michel Rey, who with Changuyon had founded a French publishing house at Amsterdam in order to evade the censorship: "It matters little to you who I am, or how hotly I have been pursued by my persecutors, but I have no doubt that you would readily seize the opportunity to oblige a man of letters when you find the interest of your business united with the pleasure of doing good. I am the author of the *Essay on Despotism*, of which two editions were issued in six weeks."

But the publishers were suspicious: "Nothing is given away in this country of calculators." Mirabeau wrote to his mother that Rey had told him "that he had been assured that this work was by another person, whom he named to me. The indignation bound to be felt by any honest man at the suspicion that he is telling so cowardly a lie as to claim another's work led me to take a very imprudent step. I wrote at once to Fauche to inform the Dutch publisher whether M. le Comte de Mirabeau was not the author." He also offered to do translations for the publishers: "I know several languages, I have plenty of facility, and I am willing to work and am in need of work."

Holland was "the dearest country in Europe, not excepting London." The Comte and Comtesse de Mathieu rented a modest apartment from a French tailor. They had no friends or relations in this exclusive society. But they were gloriously, shamelessly happy.

Sophie had chosen as the motto on her seal "*L'amour brave le sort*"— "Love braves fate." Mirabeau had had a Latin motto engraved on his— " 'Twas with thee that love began, 'tis with thee that it will end."

A cloud passed over their horizon: Mirabeau's imprudence threatened to cost them dear. Fauche sent him the certificate he wanted, but at the same time hastened to communicate his address to the Marquis de Monnier. Briançon, for his part, denounced him to an inspector of police, Bruguières, who had been vainly pursuing Mirabeau. Louise had learnt, no doubt through the indiscretion of a minister who was very devoted to her mother, that the Marquis de Mirabeau was making use of his son's indiscreet letter, as he had made use long before of his wife's "little papers." Mirabeau replied to his mother's inquiry by denying everything. Louise remained alarmed and indignant in spite of his denials. Briançon, infuriated, took revenge on Mirabeau by setting detectives on his tracks.

To avoid the consequences of his imprudence, Mirabeau acquired the right of domicile in Amsterdam, which he imagined would put him "beyond reach of surprises of any sort." He paid dearly for this right. The little money the two had brought with them had quickly been swallowed up by the purchase of clothes for Sophie and of the books Gabriel could not do without. The publishers kept him waiting for work. The two fell into debt, even for their rent. Their situation became desperate. Sophie suffered especially. "I have an incredible hatred of debts," she exclaimed. But when at that moment a confidential servant of the Marquis de Monnier arrived at Amsterdam with money for her, Sophie refused to see him, knowing that her husband's first condition would be that she should leave her lover.

Little by little, however, their financial situation improved. Mirabeau could translate from several languages. Publishers entrusted him with translations from English. He had an extraordinary faculty for hard work. He started at dawn, difficult though it was for him to get up so early—"We so loved our bed," he sighed later—and worked until nine o'clock at night. The publishers began to "overwhelm him with work." Sophie gave lessons in Italian, made extracts for Mirabeau, read his proofs, did the household work, even found time to do some painting. She was radiantly happy. "Brought up in and accustomed to opulence," wrote Mirabeau later, "she was never so gay, so brave, so attentive, so placid, and so tender as in poverty." Mirabeau wanted to offer her a more luxurious life. It was hard for him to bear the idea that Sophie had to earn money herself, and he showed his bad humour by scolding her for "grammatical stupidities." His jealousy, he admits, "was without limits." He was even jealous of Sophie's pupils. "Your Italian lessons," he admitted to her, "were a torture to me."

He realized himself that he was a difficult man for a woman to live with. "My character is irregular, my susceptibility is prodigious, my vivacity excessive." But Sophie was wholly attached to him, body and soul, and filled with boundless admiration for him.

While Mirabeau was jealous of every man who came near Sophie, she for her part was hostile to everything outside his love for her. She grudged the interests that busied him, and especially those which robbed them of their hours of intimacy, as if she realized that their moments together were limited. Gabriel was for Sophie simply a lover, her lover.

She loved in him only the things that were within her scope. She had no more ambition for him than for herself. Mirabeau said later: "Literally, tending the flocks with me would have fulfilled her highest aspirations."

7

Like all the French aristocrats who were enamoured of the new ideas, Mirabeau was a freemason and a member of the Grand Orient lodge. Sophie greatly disliked seeing him resume contact with these circles in Holland. She detested the "mischievous blackguards of freemasonry," as she detested everything that took him away from her.

Mirabeau was well aware of the part played by fashion in the attraction exercised by freemasonry, a thoroughly ephemeral part: "Those who, lacking a certain illumination of the mind and a certain enthusiasm in the heart, have entered the order of the Free-Masons only through curiosity or for the purposes of some interest, usually find little satisfaction and often leave it." But others were attached to the Order, "men who recognized what utility, what greatness, what worth there is in a universal place from which threads go out to all countries to unite a very great number of enlightened people." To these people he addressed himself with a plan for a reorganization of freemasonry.

The future reformer knew already how to form a group of men for effective action at any desired moment. The future statesman, though he was as yet unaware of his destiny, saw clearly that, in order to carry out necessary reforms, there was need for a plan well prepared in advance and well ripened in men's minds. "The time seems to have come," he wrote in his memorandum, "when the most enlightened and the most magnanimous F. [freemasons] should unite to turn the O. [Order] toward the great aim it is capable of attaining." Mirabeau shared his contemporaries' belief in the omnipotence of universal education in creating the miracle of progress. "It is to defects in education that must be attributed the ignorance of the people of all states." The first aim of the association should thus, in his view, be "care for the extension as far as possible of the sphere of learning, not so much in depth as in area."

The fear of oppression was another obstacle to human happiness. "Despotism and its consequences form one of the great scourges of humanity; and the second main pivot of the association should be the correction of the present system of governments and legislatures."

In this first sketch of a plan for the future there was already all the

boldness that Mirabeau was later to reveal. There was also his spirit
of moderation, allied to his impulses of revolt—his constructive spirit,
concerned to avoid too radical upheavals and destruction. "This correction," he adds, "may be particular or general, insensible or sudden, un-
seen or startling. This latter type should not enter into the spirit of the
association; it is contrary to the statutes of the O. It is dangerous for
humanity itself."

He then gave expression to an idea which he was to make one of
the bases of his future policy: "Ambitious persons take advantage of
disturbed times to impose another yoke, and often a harsher one, on
the human race."

He fixed the rules of the reformed Order. He would have every
prince excluded, "though he were a God in virtue," and he pointed
out the extent to which princes had "spoilt" freemasonry. He wanted
also to exclude bigots: "Every person admitted should be entirely
tolerant and convinced that religion is a matter between God and
each individual man, in which no third party has any right to interfere
against the will of those concerned." He further excluded those who
have "neither property nor talents to assure them against indigence.
Poverty makes men too ready to do anything to escape from it for it
to be possible to entrust such a plan to a man in that state."

It was a complete plan for a future society that he drew up in his
memorandum. The brothers of the superior grade would undertake "to
abolish as far as they can the bond-service of peasants, the tying of
men to the soil, the laws of mortmain, and all the usages and rights that
degrade mankind and are frightful relics of the barbarism of our ancestors."

The man who drew up this bold plan, in which social problems were
approached for the first time and the broad lines of his future policy
sketched, was as yet but a "poor literary hack," exhausted by the labour
for his daily bread. His memorandum, which brought forth no echo
and was without result, seems to have been an isolated excursion into
the field of fundamental reform.

During this struggle with material difficulties his principal relaxation was music. There was very good music to be heard in Holland.
But, wrote Mirabeau ironically, "one goes to a concert in Amsterdam
because it is the means of meeting friends in a country that has no
society; because those who do not like music can admire pretty women
and especially the kind ones; because those who know nothing of the
art of combining sounds are at least looked at."

He preferred instrumental music. In order to defend it as "the princi-

pal object of the composer, the basis of his art, and his prime talent,"
he wrote an essay with an unexpected title: *Le lecteur y mettra le titre*
—*The Reader Will Supply the Title*. But even in this essay on an art he
returns to his main preoccupation: "Despotism destroys the arts after
it has degraded them, for he whose heart is corrupted rarely has an elevated imagination."

A burlesque story in verse, *Parapilla*, which, thanks to its licentious
character, was reprinted again and again, and of which the authorship
was claimed by other contemporary writers, belongs also to the short
period, so laborious and so fruitful, of his Amsterdam idyll.

Gabriel and Sophie were lulled into a sense of false security. "Alas,
yes, we thought our happiness was solid," wrote Mirabeau bitterly at
a later date.

8

The Physiocrats suffered a heavy blow in the fall of Turgot. His failure
meant for them the collapse of their doctrine. Many of their disciples,
such as Dupont de Nemours, were exiled, laughed at, or arraigned.
Everywhere they met with more or less disguised hostility. Not only
did the lukewarm and the hesitant turn away from them, but even their
friends blamed them for the failure of their hopes. "He was simply a
virtuous dreamer, a truly reckless fellow," grumbled the disappointed
Marquis de Mirabeau.

The Marquise de Mirabeau took advantage of her husband's loss of
prestige to push her claim for a legal separation. Her son was abroad,
being unable, she told the minister, "to serve a country as step-motherly
to him as to me." But Louise de Cabris was at her side. Helped and
spurred on by her, the marquise drew up a memorial, "full of horror,"
said the marquis, "in which I am accused of everything conceivable."
And she distributed it "at every door." All her grievances were poured
out in floods of reprobation. Everything was put in, sufferings and
wrongs, real and imaginary; she spared nobody, not even her own children, whom she declared to be in good health while she herself was
infected by maladies of her husband's.

She accused her husband of debauchery and of tyranny, of hypocrisy
and rapacity; extracts taken from his letters showed him in his excessive pride and his harshness. The marquise added in her own writing
a memorandum put together from the letters her son had written, before his flight, to Malesherbes. This was published without Gabriel's
knowledge, and so hurriedly that the letters were inserted without edit-

ing, even the one in which Mirabeau defended himself with indignation against the suspicion of intending to abduct Mme. de Monnier.

The bailli urged his brother to reply to the libels: his silence would surprise his friends and admirers all over Europe. "Reply to whom and to what?" objected the marquis. "Reply so as to attract new lies? It is being said that I am treating the public with contempt—as if the public were my judge!" Actually his hands were tied by the threat that hung over Mme. de Pailly. The marquise had spoken of her in her memorial without naming her. If she were further roused she would attack her directly. Nor could he agree, as was suggested to him, to the legal separation demanded by his wife, for she added "claims for eleven hundred thousand livres for alleged damage and spoliation at my hands, and if I had given way to the first of her demands . . . the others would have followed and would have sought me out at Marseille or anywhere, for, once defeated, Pompey and Antony found nothing but assassins everywhere."

He contented himself with publishing a long memorandum in which he refuted the charge of having squandered the fortune of the marquise, and with circulating "in the seclusion of official quarters," as his son wrote later, the compromising admissions made by the marquise, and representing her as a sensual pervert who would recoil from no infamy.

Mirabeau knew nothing of the shameful certificates supplied by his mother to one or, it seems, more than one, of her lovers. His father had kept them from him, as he himself had not admitted Emilie's betrayal to his father. But he learned that his father was telling "all Paris" that he, Gabriel, had been in bed with his mother. When later he spoke to a friend of his father's—and of his own—he forced this friend to agree that his father "had never believed in this frightful imputation, of which, perhaps, he was not the author, but which he helped to spread and transmitted to all his judges."

Gabriel then, in the first impulse of wrath, drew up a précis in support of his mother's case. In sending it to his mother he added: "I could have done it better if I had had more time, but there is heat in it, and I hope you will not be dissatisfied with it." The document had, indeed, been drawn up, copied, and printed in a week. It was an unconsidered act, accomplished under the influence of violent indignation. Mirabeau tried to justify it as the reply to provocation. "My memorandum will seem moderate to anyone who knows that I wrote with that canker within me."

Like his mother, he spared nothing and nobody. Everything was put in, all the hardships and humiliations of his oppressed childhood and his persecuted adolescence. He, too, did not hesitate to bring in the person dearest to the marquis—without naming her: "One of those intriguing, seductive, dangerous women who, though entirely without the virtues needed for mothers of a family, have sufficient cleverness and impudence to usurp their rights."

He himself felt all the power of his dangerous eloquence. Carried away by the intoxication of this power, he went on to write an anecdote in which he painted the marquis not only as a hypocritical tyrant, but also as an ignoramus who, "though unable to distinguish a grain of rye from a grain of wheat, set himself up as a legislator for kings and agriculturists. . . . The Friend of Mankind was no friend either of his wife or of his children. He preached virtue, beneficence, order, and morality, though he was both the worst of husbands and the harshest and most spendthrift of fathers."

He sent several hundred copies of his memorandum and of the anecdote to his mother, who sent them on to a minister whom she believed to be her protector. But the moment the packets arrived from Holland, the minister hastened to inform the marquis.

The case of the Marquise de Mirabeau was heard in May 1776 before the *Grand'chambre* of the *parlement*. The atmosphere was not favourable to the leader of the Physiocrats. The blow his son had struck was to be mortal for the marquis. His reputation never recovered. Gabriel de Mirabeau had aimed too well. The idol had fallen from its pedestal. The Friend of Mankind remained in the eyes of the general public the enemy of his wife and children, a philosopher-hypocrite.

But the court remained unaffected by the sudden revulsion in public opinion. Mother and son had perhaps gone too far in spreading so gross a scandal. The marquise lost her case for legal separation. "She will always be the dupe of her own violence," her son said of her. Maddened by the judgment, she broke that evening into her husband's house, on the pretence of wishing to resume conjugal domicile. Saying that she was ill, she got into bed.

The marquis fled. But he told the hall porter not to admit the legal adviser of the marquise who had drawn up the insulting memoranda. From her bed the marquise heard the altercation between her lawyer and the *suisse*. Bare-legged and with little more on than a petticoat, she rushed out into the courtyard and threw herself against the door which the *suisse* was just closing against her visitor. Her cries roused the whole street. The Marquise de Mirabeau, clinging to the door, sent her pathetic appeals to the growing crowd that was massed in front of the entrance. It was a pitiable spectacle to see this old woman, with scarcely anything on, caught hold of by a servant and made to go indoors. The excited crowd was ready to intervene. Other servants ran up, and the wretched scene ended amid incoherent, desperate shouting that filled the whole of the rue de la Seine, accompanied by the dull roar of the crowd round the heavy closed door.

"Unhappily she is only half insane," said the marquis. He could not put her into a lunatic asylum as he would have liked to do, but he secured a *lettre de cachet* against her for provoking disorders. The Marquise de Mirabeau was removed by royal warrant and taken to a convent.

9

M. de Monnier now prosecuted his wife for adultery and her lover for the abduction of a married woman. Sophie's family worked for her ruin with ill-considered zeal. They were afraid of seeing the young woman abandoned by her lover in a foreign country, or led by him "from crime to crime." But the family did not know her place of refuge. Mirabeau's letter, transmitted by the publisher Fauche, gave the address to M. de Monnier. The Ruffey family at once applied for Sophie's extradition. They asked the Marquis de Mirabeau to join with them.

The marquis had determined "not to run after the wretch any longer." But when he learned of "his infamous and repeated libels," he lent all his support to the prosecution.

The Minister of Foreign Affairs prepared the act of extradition; the French Minister in Holland, the Duc de La Vauguyon, was instructed to assist the police officer charged with the arrest. This officer was no other than Bruguières, who was out to take his revenge.

The case of the Baron de Villeneuve-Mouans against Mirabeau was heard in his absence toward the end of 1776. Mirabeau was condemned to loss of civil rights and to a fine of six thousand livres. Only his absence saved him from having to listen in the council chamber, bareheaded and on his knees, to the reading of the sentence, which declared him "reprimanded and infamous" and deprived him forever of his civil rights.

While the case of the Marquise de Mirabeau was being heard in Paris, the criminal court at Pontarlier gave judgment in the suit of the Marquis de Monnier against the two lovers. Mirabeau was convicted of the crime of abduction and condemned to death by decapitation. The sentence was carried out in effigy. Judgment was given at the same time against Sophie, declaring her guilty of adultery, and condemning her to detention for life in a house of correction, "there to be shaven and clothed as are the loose women of the community."

The Amsterdam idyll lasted less than a year. Mirabeau was warned of the arrival of Bruguières at the beginning of May 1777, but it was impossible for the two to flee once more. "I owe more than a hundred louis here, and I have not six," he wrote to his mother. "Thus I am chained here. What more can I do? I have done everything I could. I must wait for the bomb and do my best to bury it."

He thought he was protected by his status of burgher of Amsterdam. He did not reckon with the powerful support on which his father could draw.

Sophie was pregnant. The happiness of maternity triumphed over her load of anxiety.

On May 12 the Marquise de Mirabeau lost her case. Two days later Bruguières threw off the mask. The lovers were warned. They prepared to flee separately. Mirabeau had already left the house unobserved. A friend had arranged to take him to a safe place. But Gabriel learned that Sophie had been arrested, and turned back. "My feelings and my principles demanded happiness or unhappiness with her." Sophie recalled later: "Your delicate sensibility did not permit you to flee and to abandon your friend, though you could no longer help her."

Sophie could not endure the thought of separation. She still had the poison she had bought at Pontarlier concealed in her corset. The dose was strong. "It might have served to purge the earth of the tyrants," said one of the detectives later. But Mirabeau warned Bruguières in time. "I was fully convinced that we were entitled to free ourselves from our troubles," he said later, "but I was not persuaded that we had rights over the life of our child." Bruguières, in order to give Sophie something to live for, promised to get a last interview with Mirabeau, and to allow letters to pass between the two lovers, on condition that she handed the poison to him.

There was one last heart-rending meeting between the separated lovers. Mirabeau, as he went away, exclaimed in despair: "I have made you very unhappy." In face of the terrible existence that awaited her, Sophie had the same courage with which she had faced death. She did not turn her head away as Gabriel departed with that lament on his lips. Later she found a reply of magnificent simplicity to that cry of remorse from her lover: "If a man gives us a magnificent palace, and if we are struck by lightning in it, is he to be blamed?"

❧ VI ❦

The Frightful Mutilation
of Existence

"I AM buried alive in a tomb."

Gabriel's father was determined to make the tomb eternal. "Apart from time, which, unfortunately, covers and threatens all; apart also from the idiots who say the king does not want any perpetual prisons for family purposes, that at most he will permit them for reasons of State, my plan is firmly settled; it is that only the authority and I shall know where he is, and that at my death a sealed letter shall inform my substitute of it."

A great menacing tower, high enclosing walls, a very deep moat, smaller towers mounting guard at each corner of the sinister rectangular building, turrets flanking the drawbridge, doors and windows loaded with heavy iron bars—"an enclosure ten feet square is my universe." In the thick wall of his cell there was only a narrow slit that scarcely gave light at any time of the day. Only at sunset did he see a ray pass through it and light up the gloom in which he lived. A tiny fragment of the sky was framed in the slit, which was low and small, so that he sought in vain for a star during his sleepless nights.

At the moment of separation from Sophie, Mirabeau began to bleed profusely from nose and mouth. He had a sudden attack of fever. He continued to spit blood. His robust health had given way when he saw the gates of the sinister fortress of Vincennes close behind him.

For the first weeks he remained bereft of everything, haggard, dishevelled, unshaven, ill, without a change of shirt, without a comb, without paper, without books, going round and round his cell like a wild beast in a cage. The days were interminable, the weeks seemed months, and the months years; time had stopped for him. The same ideas, the same regrets, the same bursts of indignation pursued an infernal dance in his head. He had no illusion as to the duration of his imprisonment; he was too well aware of his father's harshness. Even hope was killed amid this deprivation of all that was dear to him. When one day he became able to communicate with the woman he loved, he put her on her guard against any illusion: "Sophie, Sophie, place no faith in fortune."

2

The royal warrant ordered the transfer of the Marquise de Monnier to Sainte-Pélagie, where prostitutes were imprisoned. The inspector of police was at first full of pride in the success of his mission, and perhaps ready to make the captives feel, after duping him for so long, that now he had got the better of them. But the journey to France lasted long enough for him to feel the "magic" of Mirabeau. "You have made a big change in this man," Sophie wrote later. Before the journey was ended the detective sent to hunt them down had become their friend.

The Duc de La Vauguyon had intervened with the lieutenant of police; Bruguières intervened, in turn, to try to save Sophie from the shameful punishment of Sainte-Pélagie. He did his duties conscientiously, but he could not help thinking that to have fled from an old and impotent husband for a lover like Mirabeau was not an unforgivable crime.

Since Sophie was pregnant, it was decided to send her to the house of correction of Mlle. Douay to await her confinement. Here she was given the special privilege of sharing a room with only four other prisoners, for as a rule there were seven to a room.

In this house in the rue Charonne there were prostitutes who had emerged from Sainte-Pélagie, workwomen, seamstresses, weavers, shopkeepers. Sophie was drawn at first to a woman whose lot seemed to be like hers, for she had been arrested when fleeing with her lover. But she soon found that Alexandrine was only a common adventuress, who had had many liaisons and was consoling herself in captivity with the jailer.

Chance willed it that Alexandrine's husband should be the legal adviser to the Marquis de Mirabeau. When Sophie learned that the woman knew her lover, she made this characteristic comment: "Pardon my question, little man, but I don't think anybody can see you without adoring you. Would it perhaps be a torment for me to find myself here with a woman you have had?"

The house was infested with flies and with bugs. It was a torrid summer. The frequent storms produced panics among the lunatics. In the crowded rooms the atmosphere was suffocating. Sophie, whose pregnancy was proving difficult, complained that the heat was killing her.

But, even more than by her physical sufferings, she was tormented by uncertainty as to the fate of her lover. Bruguières had promised to get letters through. But he was away so she heard nothing. She did not even know where Gabriel was confined. Pending Bruguières' return, she wrote letters for her lover. She cut the paper in advance; at first she used coffee for ink, and later a fluid made by soaking nails in vinegar. She wrote at dawn, behind the drawn curtains of her bed, when her companions were still asleep, on a book supported on her knees, trembling for fear that she would be discovered, and scarcely daring to move the paper.

Her lover, too, was terribly tormented about Sophie; he confided his trouble to the very warders who served him. Sophie learned later with pleasure that all his thoughts were for her and that he "spoke of her to everybody." The warders, touched by his misfortunes, brought him flowers. He wanted to send them to Sophie via Bruguières, but the flowers faded before the police officer returned.

Sophie wrote pathetically: "When I am dozing I look round for you just by me, my lips seek yours. . . . And it is frightful to wake up." But it was about him, always about him, that she was tormented: "Gabriel, I can't help feeling that you will not be able to stand it!" She revolted against their horrible fate: "What crime have we committed? Just to love, to adore each other!" And she added with splendid defiance: "That crime I shall commit all my life, though I were to die for it a thousand times!"

3

"Sire, I am French, young, and unhappy; these are so many claims to interest Your Majesty." From his sombre cell at Vincennes the Comte de Mirabeau wrote to Louis XVI. "Sire, it is not only the kindness of your paternal heart that I seek to interest; I submit to your equity a denial of justice of which Your Majesty is unaware." He did not attempt to deny his errors: "Beyond question there were reprehensible traits in my youth," but "if it were necessary to be irreproachable in order to remain at liberty, it is too true, Sire, that all your subjects would be prisoners. . . . I confine myself to imploring you, Sire, to bring my affair to the knowledge of my natural judges. The magistrates, depositories and organs of the laws, have the time to examine it; this is their responsibility and their duty. I am a man, a citizen, and a father. On all these grounds I claim the protection of my king."

But the voice of the prisoner of Vincennes, eloquent as it was, did not reach the king. Mirabeau had sent his letter under cover to the Minister Amelot. The letter was transmitted to the Comte de Maurepas, brother-in-law of the Duc de Nivernois, who was the best friend of Gabriel's father. "If I were not thoroughly persuaded," wrote Mirabeau, "of your uprightness, I certainly should not venture on the step I am taking today. I am daring to complain to you about you; and I beg you on no account to give vent, on reading this letter, to your first reaction, or, what would be still more fatal for me, to follow the suggestions of friendship." He added, subtly recalling that the minister had himself been a victim of injustice: "Do you not know from your own experience how easy it is to beguile the great? Your long period of disgrace is an irrefutable and a striking proof of it."

But the authorities remained deaf to all the prisoner's desperate appeals. "None of my letters had made any change in my lot," complained Mirabeau. He addressed a new petition to the Comte de Maurepas in November 1778: "The political events that have happened since my detention certainly require that troops shall be sent to America, perhaps to the Indies. I beg you to send me to one or the other of these countries. There are never too many men in these destructive countries, and I am worth using as a soldier."

Meanwhile the Marquis de Mirabeau had obtained no less than four *lettres de cachet* for exiling the Marquise de Mirabeau to a convent, and two more for her landlady and her adviser. He had secured his greatest triumph in obtaining the internment of Louise in the convent of Sisteron. Up to then she had been protected by her wretched husband. But the madness that threatened Cabris broke out violently one night. He roused the village, throwing money and jewels and even his dog out of the window and tearing up precious books and rare prints. Finally he slashed himself with a knife and collapsed. The bailli secured judicial interdiction in lunacy against him in spite of a violent campaign carried on by Louise with the assistance of two of the foremost members of the bar at Aix, Pascalis and Portalis. Thereafter Louise called her uncle "M. le Grand Interdiseur."

The internment of the beautiful Marquise de Cabris particularly revolted public opinion. "I know that if they are to be believed," wrote the marquis to the bailli, "I am the Nero of the century. But what of it? If I had been sensitive I should have been dead long ago. The public is not my judge."

4

Lenoir, lieutenant of police, was no friend of the Economists. At the time of the rioting in 1775 he had been dismissed by Turgot, and he was not restored to his post until after Turgot's fall. Mirabeau played adroitly on Lenoir's prejudice against the secretaries and succeeded in awakening his personal interest.

Lenoir, a man of experience, applied to the prisoners a measure which he considered very wise: "I file letters which I think it better not to transmit," he wrote to the minister. "I have often remarked that these permissions to write are of great help in calming minds overheated by solitude and captivity." But while he buried complaints in the files, he was not insensible to distress. Once his sympathy had been gained for the victim of the Friend of Mankind, he took steps to lighten his lot. Mirabeau was in his debt for a privilege that was inestimable to him, permission to exchange letters with Sophie.

Bruguières had at last returned and set the minds of the lovers at rest; he transmitted their correspondence faithfully. He was not the only one, however, who served them as intermediary. Mirabeau also won over Boucher, the senior confidential clerk who was responsible for the supervision of the prisoners and for the censorship of their correspondence. Boucher was a fervent adept of freemasonry, and this enabled Mirabeau to turn friendly relations into active devotion. Boucher not only saw to the transmission of the lovers' letters, he saved the two from traps, and was prodigal in advice. "How clever you are with your slow wisdom, how much better it is than my turbulent precipitation," declared Mirabeau. Boucher gave support to the two in their trials with a constancy that was never wanting; he never tired of their innumerable agitated requests, and they gave him the well-deserved name of "good angel."

Mirabeau also found at Vincennes a young man whom he had known in the past, one of the cheerful companions of his dissipated youth, Dubut de La Tagnerette. The young man was a typical representative of his age, with its moral indulgence toward the great. Effeminate and curious about other people's affairs, he was greatly interested in Mirabeau's amours. His nominal father was the local postmaster, and he himself was his deputy; he secured accomplices on the staff for Mirabeau, and helped him to arrange the ingenious cipher which the lovers employed to tell each other of their plans and hopes. Sophie transmitted her letters through gardeners, innkeepers, nuns. They had relays of helpers in the country towns, a whole network of complicity.

Thus an uninterrupted two-way flow of open and secret correspondence was established. They wrote in order to tell each other everything, to pour out their affection, to lament their privations, and to escape from despair. Gabriel's letters to Sophie saved his reason.

He wrote first on paper which he procured clandestinely, writing as closely as possible, covering endless pages in the semi-darkness of his cell. Everything came into their letters—recollections of their brief happiness, reminiscences of their youth, the despair of the present, fears for the future, their immense pity for each other, and their impotent revolt. In Gabriel's letters there was the delirium of fleshly hunger, and in Sophie's the "incalculable tenderness" that immolated self entirely. In talking of love, Mirabeau borrowed eloquence from the *Nouvelle Héloïse;* Sophie found in her simplicity cries from the heart that owed nothing to any literary reminiscence: "Anyone who sacrifices everything would sacrifice a thousand times more, and still believe that she had done nothing. . . . I have only one science, my tender friend, that of loving you well."

For Sophie's pregnancy Gabriel was full of advice that revealed great experience and views well in advance of his time. He made her give him minute descriptions of her troubles, and prescribed remedies for her; soon he was giving medical advice to the whole house from afar, and later to the convent to which Sophie was transferred after the birth of her child.

Early in 1778 Sophie gave birth to a daughter, who was given the name of Sophie-Gabrielle. The advice Mirabeau gave for the care of the baby was full of the spirit of an entirely modern hygiene. Whole pages of his correspondence are a manual of child rearing. He wanted the baby to be inoculated in good time, but he was met with objections from Sophie and especially from her companions; these he discussed with great competence. He wrote a whole treatise on inoculation, which was one day to arouse widespread attention, and he sent it to Sophie, telling her that it should suffice, and more, to persuade her.

But she was not allowed to keep the child with her. When she left the house in Paris for the convent of Sainte-Claire at Gien (where she found material conditions that were a great deal better), the child was sent to a foster-mother in the country. "I can no longer stand other people's children," she wrote then. "To see their children and to be deprived of mine drives me crazy."

Mirabeau called for the most minute details of his daughter's health, and sent orders as to the way she should be looked after. He pestered the faithful Boucher to go and see on the spot how the child was being treated. His advice, his exhortations, his anxieties were often more minutely maternal than those of Sophie.

His love for the little daughter who incarnated for him his and Sophie's great happiness and also their terrible sufferings never ,made him forget his son. It needed a great deal of insistence on his part to bring him news in a dry and impersonal letter from Mme. de Mirabeau. But he was not concerned only for the boy's physical health. In his dark cell at Vincennes he began for his son "a very big work which I thought of leaving as a monument of what I should have wanted to do for his education if I had been living with him."

For Sophie he was full of attentions of particular delicacy. He could not heap presents on her, but he took a great deal of trouble to enrich her mind and to fill the gaps in her improvised education. "You have often told me," he wrote to her one day, "that you knew nothing of mythology. So I have compiled for you a work, the substance of which you could have found only in two or three hundred volumes." Sophie avidly assimilated everything that came from him. Infinitely malleable, with no other will than his, she became, so far as her horizon permitted, a faithful mirror of his mind.

5

"I should much rather, I swear to you on my honour, Monsieur," wrote Mirabeau to Lenoir, "have nothing to eat but dry bread, and be in irons, but have books, than have all the liberty that can be accorded here, and be fed from the king's table, but left without anything to read." By dint of vehement petitioning, he succeeded in procuring the books he needed. "Without books I should soon be dead or mad," he said later.

His works were designed primarily for Sophie: "I have also undertaken a very big work for you, perhaps one beyond my powers, a translation of Homer, from Homer, but still more from the magnificent translation Pope has made of him into English verse." He sent her Ovid's *Metamorphoses*, "translated, explained, and with notes," no inconsiderable work. Among the other classics he translated were Tibullus, and the *Agricola* of Tacitus; he compiled an *Essay on Latin Elegiacs*, making much use of borrowed matter but working up everything with his own mental energy and his faculty of assimilation. "I have not ceased busying myself for you," he wrote to her at another time, telling her that he had compiled for her (her ideas of grammar and of spelling were pretty fanciful) "a little treatise on the French language," a "fairly complete" little grammar, which was found later among his papers. He also prepared for Sophie "an essay on ancient and modern literature," giving her his ideas on the art of their time and on the feebleness of modern literature, which to him was a symptom of a general feebleness. From his prison he sketched ambitious plans for the progress of the arts.

He wanted the young king and queen to undertake the patronage of the fine arts. The great gallery of the Louvre should be finished and hung with the king's pictures, "which are solidly piled up in the Versailles storehouse." A parallel gallery, joining the Louvre and the Tuileries, might serve as a home for the royal library. The prisoner whose father intended that he should never again see the lights of the towns dreamed of a modernization and embellishment of Paris. He proposed cutting broad roads from the Place Vendôme to the boulevards, and the opening of a road to be continued past the Panthéon to the Luxembourg. He also called for the building of two wide bridges facing the Invalides and the Jardin du Roi, and also for the removal of the Hôtel-Dieu and the demolition of the buildings attached to it, which hid the river and broke the line of the quays. But he did not think only of embellishment. He called for the making of pavements and of a water supply for Paris. He also considered the social problems which were particularly urgent in a great city. "Thought should be given to those who cannot work. When the royal family gives charity, it leaves its distribution to the lieutenant-general of police, whose knowledge of the city is confined to those who come into contact with the police. The true poor of the capital are those who are not seen. Does anyone suppose that the local officers enter those labyrinths of suffering?"

Mirabeau escaped also into the past. He was particularly attracted by historical studies. The fragments he compiled, intending to make use of them for a more important work, were later put together in some fashion, completed, added to the notes on the development of artistic life and to the advice to the royal couple, and published by an indefatigable compiler, the Abbé Soulavie, under the title *Mémoires du ministère du duc d'Aiguillon*."

Once Mirabeau had begun original work, he thought of tackling a subject that particularly attracted him. But he had doubts of his capacity. "Misfortune," he wrote, "elevates men of courage, but disheartens genius." He felt the demoralizing influence of the terrible monotony of his life and the slow using up of his mental energy, unhelped by any external stimulus. "I know, I know too well, that if sadness softens it also enervates, and that a troubled mind has far less resilience."

But he fought against this invasion of discouragement. "I have always believed," he wrote to the lieutenant of police, "and I shall always believe, that indifference to injustice is treason and cowardice." From his cell he took up the fight against injustice. "Free or not, I shall proclaim until my last breath the rights of the human race. What can be a more natural time for fighting despotism than when one is groaning in its clutches!" he wrote. That was his justification for the work he undertook. Now that books were reaching him, he completed his preparatory work and began to write the book, which bore the title *Des Lettres de cachet et des prisons d'état*.

The point of departure of his work was this cry of revolt: "The height of atrocity, after infringing the liberty of a man and after reducing him to the despair of slavery, is to punish him for anything he does, even with excessive inhumanity, to effect his escape, as if nature and justice demanded that he should respect the life of one who does not respect his property in his own person, as if *everything*, without exception, was not permissible to a man in order to break his chains!"

Mirabeau supported this cry of revolt with a profound study of abuses, with excessively long and frequent quotations, as though he felt the need of the support of authorities in urging his case. Later his authorship was challenged on the ground that it would have been impossible for him to make use in prison of the hundreds of works he quotes. But his memory was prodigious and his capacity for work inexhaustible.

The pleas which Mirabeau advanced in his own defence passed into the claims he made on behalf of the victims of despotism: "The accused person should be judged in the most regular forms; it is necessary that his imprisonment should be legal, and to that end it is necessary that the accused shall be consulted, supported, defended, and informed of everything that may help his defence."

To combat despotism he demanded that judges should be irremovable: "The independence of judges in the administration of justice is as necessary as their freedom in order to guarantee the freedom, honour, and life of the citizen."

His work quickly overflowed the limits of a personal cause. He attacked the whole régime under which the authority of a single individual made law. Like his contemporaries, he exalted the benefits of universal education. But he did not believe in the magic power of the spread of enlightenment through the world. He did not believe that mental forces were in themselves capable of suppressing the acquisitiveness of rival countries or of securing the laying down of arms. Liberty was for him a thing for which one fights and which one defends with one's life.

He wanted the defence of popular liberties and of the national patrimony to be confided to the people as a whole. It was also the people, the whole nation, that must establish its system of jurisdiction: "The law, in order to be just, legitimate, and binding, in a word to be truly law, must have the seal of free and general consent." Ten years in advance of the general call for it, Mirabeau demanded a broad popular representation: "Throughout the state in which the citizens are entirely without any share in the legislative power through the delegation of a body of representatives freely elected by the majority of the nation and subject to the control of their constituents, there is no public liberty at all and can be none."

He sent to Boucher, as a friend "and not in your official capacity," this *livre noir*—this black book. The first part, he wrote to him, had cost a year's work, and, "false modesty apart," he thought it a good work "and entirely new."

Boucher sent it back, saying that this book could not be passed on by him. When one day the marquis gained acquaintance with the book, he described it as "seditious insanity unloosed" in which "he has heaped up everything that can be said against despotism, together with shameless special pleading in favour of ne'er-do-wells." With *Lettres de cachet*, Mirabeau had found himself.

Now that he had learned to use his pen, he acquired literary ambitions. During the brief Amsterdam idyll he had come into touch with various circles, contact with which had confirmed him in his freedom of thought and had swept away the last prejudices he may have entertained. "I despise my birth," he wrote one day to Sophie. "Of all the men of rank in the world, I do not know one who is the equal of the great writers who have gained their living with their pen."

6

"The unfortunate are always wrong; wrong to be so, wrong to say so, wrong to be in need of others and to be unable to serve them," wrote Mirabeau bitterly to Sophie. He had won over the lieutenant of police, but he had found in the commandant of the fortress a harsh jailer on whom he could make no impression. M. de Rougemont, a subordinate officer and a man of illegitimate and unrecorded birth, took his revenge for being a social outcast by making those who were at his mercy feel all his power. Under his rough military demeanour was concealed, according to Mirabeau, "a man of infernal hardness, distrustful, double-dealing, lying." The prisoner of Vincennes continued to endure the worst privations. "I have been reduced," wrote Gabriel to Sophie, "for a whole year to living on bread and mulled brandy, to such a degree was the food and drink given me (and I am anything but fussy) horribly disgusting." He continued also to work like a madman. "I rarely sleep longer than three hours at night," he told Sophie. "You know how active is my brain. . . . So I write or read for fourteen or fifteen hours a day. I succumb, but survive."

Shortage of food, lack of exercise, and mental strain ended by destroying his health. His moral sufferings undermined his constitution; for, he said, "mental sufferings have always affected me a thousand times more than physical ills." The prison surgeon warned him that he was killing himself with work. "I find only one thing wrong with that," he replied, "that I am not doing it quickly enough."

In the summer of 1778 he suffered from grave nephritic colic and from violent haemorrhage. "The regime here is so excessively, I almost said atrociously, severe that it is impossible that I should not perish here if I remain much longer," he wrote to the lieutenant of police. He turned in vain to influential friends, to the Noailles family, who had protected him at court; all his desperate appeals remained unanswered. He decided to write directly to his father. Suffering and debilitated, he mobilized his gift of persuasion and his eloquence in describing the hardships and the injustices he had suffered in order to break down the terrible callousness of the marquis: "It is not worthy of you to be partisan, my father. . . . I have implored you to be judge in your own case . . . to question yourself, with the rigidity of your sense of duty, deep down in your conscience. Have you the right to proscribe me, and alone to condemn me? To place yourself above the laws and the forms of justice in order to destroy me?"

After appealing to reason and to any sense of equity that might still subsist in the Friend of Mankind, Gabriel discussed point by point the charges brought against him, the offences of which his father accused him, and the whole chain of events that had led him to flee abroad. This closely argued plea, this minute justification, united forensic ability with the warm and sincere accents of an intimate confession.

After this bold arraignment of his accuser, Mirabeau tried to touch his father's heart by painting his atrocious situation, his unnatural condition of existence. "Dead to all pleasures, I live only for pain. What a frightful mutilation of existence! . . . I cannot support such a life, my father, I cannot do it. . . . If you give me back liberty, . . . prison will have made me wise; for time, which passes over my head much less lightly than over those of other mortals, has aroused me from my dreams."

But the marquis was in no way shaken by this appeal: he remained insensible to his son's distress. Gabriel's was a clever appeal, and it was that cleverness that set his father against him: "Whether he has to be ape or wolf or fox makes no difference to him—he is either without any effort."

7

Emilie de Mirabeau lived in Provence the life she had always wanted to live. After obtaining the right to administer her share of the joint income at the time of Mirabeau's flight, she sought to complete a legal separation. But the marquis, who had doomed his son to a slow death, defended him against his wife, from family solidarity or pride.

Amid her careless and lively existence Emilie took little thought for the prisoner of Vincennes. She had forgotten her inconvenient husband all the more thoroughly since she had found a large number of admirers and many consolations. The Court of Love at Tourves now had a strong rival in the brilliant society of the château of Tholonet. The vast resources supplied to the Comte de Galliffet by the plantations of Santo Domingo maintained an enormous estate and provided luxurious hospitality for many guests. The young Comte de Galliffet was a widower. He had all the advantages of a seigneur of immense wealth, with the graces of a man of the world and many social gifts. He was passionately fond of dancing and of comedy. He built at Tholonet a theatre at which Emilie could shine. His admiration for the Comtesse de Mirabeau was no secret. One day all Aix resounded with the story of a nocturnal adventure of which Emilie was once more the heroine. A thief, by her account, had fled by the window of her room. Knowing smiles were exchanged as the name of the Comte de Galliffet passed round.

Emilie persisted in her requests to her father-in-law to help her get a legal separation. But the marquis replied: "Ask Victor how he would like to have no father." Small as he was, the child had not forgotten the ardent affection that had been lavished on him, and he would ask for his father, though each time he did so Emilie curtly silenced him. Victor was only in his fifth year. He was a strangely serious child for his age, with the seriousness of children who are unhappy or are doomed to an early death.

Emilie adored this gentle and affectionate child who gave her so little trouble. She knew that his family were jealous of him—the aunts and nieces whose great expectations he had frustrated. She looked after him when she thought of it or when she had time to attend to him. A few days before his fifth birthday the child became ill. Emilie wrote in alarm to the marquis and the bailli. The marquis was terribly disturbed. He seemed to realize for the first time that the whole hope of perpetuating the race of which he was so proud depended on one frail child. In his alarm he consulted Mme. de Pailly. And for the first time he had a faint notion that he ought either to take his elder son out of prison or to get the younger one married. The Chevalier de Mirabeau was difficult to marry. The charming child, "a Mirabeau all over," had become a young man broken by debauchery; the delicate child had become a buck rolling in fat. Women and wine had aged him prematurely. The fire of the Mirabeaus was exhausted in him. The marquis despaired of finding a good match.

News was brought to him that his grandson was better. "I may have taken alarm too soon," he said to Mme. de Pailly, "but it is a lesson for me."

For Victor's birthday there was a great celebration at Tholonet, with a play. Emilie, who was to be the principal lady, was easily persuaded that her son was out of danger. She was on the stage when news was brought to her that the boy was in convulsions. Alarmed, she tried to get away from the fun and excitement around her, but before she could do so a second messenger came with the news that the child was dead. She collapsed on the stage. The audience crowded forward; the Marquis de Marignane fainted.

"I have received news," wrote the Marquis de Mirabeau to his brother, "of the death of our child, the last hope of our name. I thought until now that I had from my mother a soul immune to any major shock. After all I have borne, I believed in my strength. God has willed it that I should be undeceived."

Emilie's indolent mind was filled with terror. She suspected the family of having poisoned her child. She feared for her own life. In her trouble she sought help from the bailli. She went to the château of Mirabeau. "She felt ill when she arrived, and I was very sorry for her," the bailli wrote to his brother. "She can no longer manage for herself anywhere, and wants me to bring her to you."

But in spite of pressing invitations from the marquis, she put off the journey. The bailli, so open with his feelings, may have given her an inkling of the idea that was running in his head. "In spite of the fury and the indignities of the vile libels that have appeared in your wife's name," he wrote to his brother, "people insist on thinking that you are a little hard on your family. Don't you think it might be suggested to this young woman that she cannot go on living with you unless she rejoins her husband?"

When Emilie at last decided to go, there came news of the death of the Comte de Valbelle, which prostrated her father. She therefore went to him.

"I loved my son, Monsieur, so I had to lose him," wrote Gabriel to his father. Sophie trembled for him: "I see your sorrow only too well, although you try to hide it from me. I know too well how you loved him. With what tenderness you used to talk to me about him at the time of our happiness!" She added: "My friend has not changed. What sacrifices has he not made for love! He will also do this, yes, he will live for me and for my daughter; I shall ask him to, and he will not refuse; for he has never refused me anything."

The blow had been terrible. Ill and brought low by grief, Mirabeau felt that his own end was near. He burned private papers, collected his manuscripts into a large sealed packet, and wrote letters which the faithful Boucher was to send to his family. He begged Sophie to live after him for their daughter, reminded his father that he was leaving an unfortunate child in the world, and wrote to his brother, entrusting his daughter to him. "Tired of being unhappy, and that without mitigation, without compensation, and almost without hope, one invokes death. It is cruel to have to say to oneself: *E finito il mio tempo a mezzo gli anni*, but it is my fate. My career is ended at the age at which other men begin theirs." But Mirabeau was not to die in the fortress of Vincennes. His vigorous constitution triumphed once more over sickness.

Above the child's tomb there rose a ray of hope.

8

The bailli claimed for his niece perpetual imprisonment, such as the marquis had claimed for his son. He wanted her place of exile to be unknown, and wanted her to be kept without pen and ink, "recommending that her passionate fits should be restrained, if necessary by means of ox whips." Louise, however, profited by the liberty she enjoyed at Sisteron to prepare a memorial which Briançon took to Paris and submitted to a number of eminent lawyers. In March 1779 this memorial was printed by the presses of the Prince de Conti. It was openly sold at the Palais-Royal. Fifteen thousand copies circulated in Paris alone. This "dog of a memorial," as the marquis called it, made an immense sensation.

The bailli urged his friend the attorney general (*procureur général*) to have the memorial publicly burned by the executioner, but the attorney general objected that "burning is no answer—that is proverbial." The marquis made no attempt to reply. He contented himself, still keeping to official circles, with circulating the terrible letter written by Gabriel. "It was left to this father," wrote Louise bitingly at a later date, "to accuse his daughter of having a lover (a matter not within his jurisdiction), and meanwhile, at the same moment and under her lover's eyes, living criminally with her brother, and, also at the same time, helping to place in that brother's bed a woman for whom he nourished the most violent passion."

The accusation made by the marquis had its effect: sensations had a brief career in Paris, and the effect of the memorial died away. But though Louise's step had produced no practical result, the marquis remained alarmed. And the prolonged detention of his son was also noticed. "The cold-blooded race of frogs who are called friends in Paris were tired or frightened," he wrote to the bailli. Actually, in his brother's phrase, he was possessed by "posteromania." He admitted it later: "It is certain that, so long as my grandson lived, I should have firmly insisted on the undertaking I gave myself, to keep the father locked up and to destroy every trace of him."

His utterances were contradictory, but he took a definite line. Without admitting his brother to his confidence, he got Caroline to put Dupont, to whom Gabriel had written, into touch with the faithful Boucher.

In May 1779 Boucher took Dupont to Vincennes.

His was the first face of an old friend that Mirabeau saw in his gloomy cell, and he was deeply upset by the interview. He spoke hurriedly and confusedly, as though he wanted to make up for his long silence. "The evil spell of solitude has robbed me of the faculty of expressing myself," he complained to Boucher. The presence of an unknown warder added to his trouble. Too many hopes were bound up in this conversation with Dupont. The interview left Mirabeau agitated and in suspense. Indirectly instigated by the marquis, Dupont had touched on a particularly delicate subject. He had informed Gabriel that his father would consent to set him free only "in order to continue the race." The marquis therefore required as a first condition the consent of the Comtesse de Mirabeau to her husband's liberation. But the moment Dupont mentioned Emilie, Mirabeau was up in arms. He revealed to his friend, whom he knew to be loyal and discreet, his wife's odious betrayal, and his generous pardon. Dupont, as a man of the world, was startled. "It is hopeless," he said to Gabriel, "for she will be afraid of you, and fear begets cruelty." Nevertheless he urged an approach to the countess. "We have got to get you free at any cost," he said. "All means to that end are justified." But Mirabeau felt above all one grave scruple. He consulted the Good Angel: "I think and I shall always think that neither honour nor love permits me to return to the home of Mme. de Mirabeau or to induce her to return to mine without the permission and almost the order of Sophie, who has sacrificed everything for me, whose only hope is in me, who wants nothing but me, of whom I am the property only too rightfully acquired, a property with which I have not the right to interfere in the slightest, even in appearance, without her consent."

When Boucher put the facts before Sophie she gave her consent without a moment's hesitation. Dupont urged, put the pen into Mirabeau's hand, brought him paper, begged him, importuned him, until at last the prisoner decided "to put to the test whether it was possible for me to say to that woman something noble that was not colourless." In a painful and humiliating position he succeeded in preserving his full dignity. Admitting his faults and making no attempt to palliate them, he went on: "Are you dead for me? Do you think me dead? I shall on no account ask you to interest yourself in my fate or to give me back my existence. I can count on it, however, only from you, and I have reason to believe that my father would not refuse it to you. To write to you on this subject is to tell you plainly enough that I feel able to appreciate what you do."

"All this will be, or would be, very wise and even for the best," Mirabeau wrote bitterly to Sophie, "if Mme. Mirabeau and I could lose our memories."

But when the reply came from the Comtesse de Mirabeau it proved to be a definite refusal: "I fully realize, Monsieur, the horror of your position; but unfortunately you have made it impossible for me to make common cause with you, by referring to me in your memorial in a manner that is painful to me. I am therefore compelled, Monsieur, to confine myself to hoping that your father will do what you ask; and although I cannot co-operate in making you happy, I shall be charmed to learn that you have become so."

"I feel a secret satisfaction," wrote Mirabeau on receiving her letter, "in seeing how many good reasons I have for despising that vile

and gangrened soul." But he knew that he could do no good by air-
ing his grievances against Emilie, for in doing so he would destroy his
father's hopes and his own chances of liberation. He kept silent, though
it cost him an effort to do so.

9

A heavy atmosphere, presaging a storm, weighed upon the age. Great
ideas were abroad, but they occupied only a few isolated minds. Old
traditions had ceased to cement the social edifice, and fissures ran along
walls that had stood for centuries, yet the walls still stood. A brilliant
society—an infinitesimal part of the nation—still lived within these
walls, as in a closed vessel. But it was troubled by a ferment within it.
Religion no longer offered a moral imperative; worldly priests were indulgent to violations of its commandments, to ridicule of its precepts,
and to a divorce between the principles to which men subscribed and
the life they lived. The sense of responsibility had decayed. The great
restraining influences in the past, the dread of divine punishment, the
fear of social reprobation, and the sense of a dignity to be preserved,
were no longer fully operative. Passions were openly flaunted during
their short and adventurous career. Luxury, the privilege of a tiny
minority, was pursued competitively; minds unoccupied, apprehensive,
lax, sought ever new distractions and sensations. A musty smell of vice
floated in the air. Dulled sensual appetites demanded ever stronger spic-
ing. Perversities were practised as a society game. There was a hunt for
the veiled, the unadmitted, for shameful secrets. It was the epoch of
cynical confessions and smug avowals. Indecencies of language no
longer startled a society that was out to amuse itself at all costs. Books
were published to serve as aphrodisiacs. Sick nerves, strained to the extreme limit, no longer responded to normal reflexes. Pleasure was confused with debauchery as liberty was confused with licence. It was
a descent that dragged along the strong and the weak, the imaginative
and the dull. The atmosphere of the tempest that was to break over
the age was partly made up of this suffocating sensuality, which intoxicated men and women and wore them out prematurely.

Gabriel de Mirabeau was born with a fever in his blood, with violent
and imperious physical needs. Voracious desires that tormented the
whole of the "tempestuous" race were alive in him like wild beasts on
the prowl. But the rich blood of that race was also contaminated by
hereditary maladies; a slow and insidious poison sent some of its members over the border between impetuosity and insanity.

In this same fortress of Vincennes there was imprisoned at this time a man whose "crimes," according to Mirabeau, "astonished even the most consummate scoundrels," the Marquis de Sade. He had twice been condemned to torture and once to be broken on the wheel, but had succeeded in escaping from these punishments; from time to time a prison removed his sexual madness from the world. He was a relative of Mirabeau, a relative who filled him with horror. The two may not have met at Vincennes. But Sade represented the malady of the age in its acutest form, that of criminal insanity, and from his very presence at Vincennes a poison seemed to seep through the walls.

Into the correspondence between Gabriel and Sophie came whispers from fevered nights, sobs of intoxication, avowals murmured into the ear, words suffocated by kisses, the babblings of sensual pleasure. So strong was his force of suggestion that with his morbid imaginings he contaminated so healthy and normal a being as Sophie. Sophie followed him everywhere, even in his sexual divagations.

At first, with the flesh still appeased, Gabriel lived on his memories of love's fulfilment. He set to work to retrace the story. He carved up their passion into dialogues. He dreamed of making of them one of the world's great love stories, over which generations of unhappy lovers would weep. But Mirabeau had not the creative flame that gives universal validity to the details of a personal experience. Simply told, the story of Sophie and Gabriel might have had the warmth of personal confessions. Presented with the rhetoric of the epoch, it had neither the value of a personal narrative nor the quality of a literary work. The *Dialogues* were never finished; Mirabeau must have realized his own limitations. He tried various literary genres, tragedies for example, but only while he was writing them did he deceive himself as to their value. His language of love was the language of sensuality.

Sophie, on whose reserve he harped again and again, replied to him in his own spirit. She praised his body, so handsome, so white, so full-fleshed. "Then," she wrote in ecstasy, "you are superb." She wrote also things that could scarcely be said from the pillow at night. Crude phrases of hers shock one not only because she was a woman, but because one comes to them in cold print, without the inner thrill he doubtless felt. When he asked her for "a new caress" she replied: "I prefer the old one, but today, to satisfy you . . ." She allowed herself to be drawn into the whirlpool of visions in which he delighted. One day he discussed with her his plans for the future of his daughter, and confided "the most secret and most cherished one," in a letter which would never pass the censorship. The plan was simply a defence of incest, to pre-

vent not only in their children, but in the generations to follow, any
mixture of blood, and constantly to re-create the same pair of triumphant lovers, Gabriel and Sophie.

At the instance of the physician, who had prescribed physical exercise for him as the great remedy he needed, he was permitted at the
beginning of 1780 to ride a horse within the precincts of the castle. He
was also permitted to walk in the galleries, "from which," he wrote,
"one can see out a little."

There were several women resident in the castle. At last he saw
feminine figures once more, at the windows, "a passable Provençal
woman, and two very pretty daughters of a lawyer." The captive,
known to be the victim of a great passion, excited lively interest.
Women were brought to see "the curious beast," he wrote. A "very
pretty person" made gentle eyes at him for half an hour. The commandant's sister-in-law, "a very dark brunette," was also interested in
him. The commandant's wife, according to Boucher, was so interested
as to arouse M. de Rougemont's jealousy. She sent him "scent and very
nice things." The physician's wife was also "very pretty." After his
years of confinement any woman must have seemed to him a goddess.

But the beauties of the castle were separated from him by thick walls.
He could use his power of seduction only at a distance, exciting their
curiosity and their tender pity. He began to sing at his narrow window,
with the emotional accents that so easily overcame women. He composed songs. "Since I have been here," he wrote to Boucher, "I have
been making music, weeping bitterly, and this music is good because I
wept." Rougemont's sister-in-law sent him a complimentary message
about his voice and his style of singing, and one day she joined in with
him; duets resounded within the enclosure. His success annoyed M. de
Rougemont, who forbade him to sing "as an act contrary to the regulations of the state prisons." "I told him," wrote Mirabeau to Boucher,
"that I was singing, and should sing until my death, for myself. It is
true that several ladies come to their windows to listen to me, but it
is not my fault if I have a nice voice."

These first contacts with the outer world only disturbed his imagination the more. The "very pretty women" were near-by but inaccessible.
He assuaged his desires in his own way.

He then began to write a novel, which he himself described as "entirely mad," but, he added, "with a singularly new sort of madness;
I cannot read it without laughing." The novel was entitled *Ma conversion*. The subject, which he sketched to Sophie, was indescribable. It
contained the confessions of a philanderer who had decided to make

love his profession. "Up to now I have been a scamp; I have run after the beauties, I have done the difficult thing; now virtue is re-entering my soul. . . . I am going to advertise myself as a stallion to women past middle age." This sort of literature was too strong even for Sophie, and he did not send her the manuscript. "I will read it to you some day, at the risk of having my eyes scratched out." But he assured her that it was a "very funny" book: "all sorts of women and all conditions come into it in turn; the idea is mad, but the details are charming. . . . It is a good skit," he concluded, "on a real book of ethics."

He was quite ready to be unfaithful to Sophie with the first woman he met on the very day he was set free. He put forward to Sophie his theory on "faithfulness of heart," and asked for authorization from her in advance. And Sophie acquiesced at once: "Celibacy kills you. I permit you everything except what may engage your heart; I wish it, I order it!" At the same time he remained fiercely jealous of her. A very young man was brought one day by his aunt to the convent at Gien. He returned to pay a visit to Sophie. This was enough to infuriate Gabriel. "It seems to me so clear that this little gentleman is in love with you that I neither can nor will put up with him, and in this matter I ask of you his formal and definite exclusion." After having deeply disturbed her and set her imagination aflame, he preached to her "decency and the strict duty of your sex." Sophie, who knew his fits of acute jealousy, took fright and reassured him: "The brat does not amuse me any more than you." But Gabriel remained uneasy. He was jealous of every man who came near Sophie, even of the physician who attended her, Dr. Ysabeau, who was "short and ugly." He was jealous of the spiritual director of Sainte-Claire, Father Maillet. He was not reassured about this "monk-sultan" with the gallant manners until Sophie told him of an intrigue that was being carried on under her own eyes and with her help between the priest and a nun.

It was no longer a philanderer recognizing no restraints but to all intents a "quarrelsome husband," in Sophie's phrase, who suddenly made his appearance in his letters—a narrow-minded husband who would have no trifling with morality and who demanded formal assurances of strict faithfulness from her. "These things brook no shilly-shallying," he wrote severely.

In his cell at Vincennes Gabriel was already deceiving Sophie in thought. Since no woman was yet accessible, he set himself to seduce one from a distance. He knew nothing of Julie Dauvers, apart from the story told about her by one of his fellow captives. This was enough to stimulate his curiosity.

Julie Dauvers was the mistress of a former *maître des requêtes*, La Fage. Mirabeau had never seen her. He did not even know whether she was good-looking. But she was "the other one," the woman he had not yet seduced. His "mobile imagination and fleeting tastes," the existence of which he admitted, were used for that purpose from a distance. Soon he was writing to the lady as frequently as to Sophie. But he was refreshing himself with a woman of whose reactions he had no knowledge. In the letters to Julie is to be found the "brightness" which, according to Sophie, enabled him to "have women," and which was lacking in his letters to her. The perfume of adventure excited him, even if it was all his own invocation. Julie was soon his "only friend," she was his "Liriette," his angel whose presence would make him "more truly happy" than could even the delicious delirium in the presence of Sophie. He did not conceal from Sophie his interest in Julie: "I have found another soul worthy of yours," he wrote to her, "and from now on your sex will be composed for me of two individuals."

But even the combination of Sophie's and Julie's affection was not enough for him. The solitude of Vincennes was peopled with other women's faces. Other romances were embroidered around feminine presences that seem to have been purely fictitious.

His eroticism also found an outlet in his writing. He announced to Sophie that he had sent off "a new and very singular manuscript." "Do you think that research could be made in the Bible and in ancient literature on onanism, tribadism, etc., in fact, on the most scabrous subjects that have been treated by casuists, and all this be made readable to the most priggish of people?" This poisonous fruit of the gloom of his prison and of his sexual privations bore the title *Erotica biblion*.

10

"If you had possessed less of the art of persuasion, you would have persuaded me more," wrote the bailli to his nephew. He was, in point of fact, shaken. Mirabeau had implored him: "Would it, then, be impossible, under the same despotism that keeps me here, and subject to my return here if you have the slightest dissatisfaction with my arrangements or my conduct, for me to spend a few months with you at Mirabeau?" The bailli asked his brother to prescribe the reply he was to send: "I will tell you, however, to satisfy my conscience, that if we were sure of catching this bird in the event of his being let out of his cage and deserving to be put back into it, and if the trial he wants to be given in my company were practicable, I should agree and—why should I not say so?—gladly."

Sophie, for her part, did all she could to hasten her lover's liberation. She wrote to the convent of Montargis (where Mirabeau's elder sister lived), to Mme. de Romigny, who had brought up the daughters of the marquis, and begged her to intervene with him on his son's behalf. The letter made a deep impression at the convent, where it was talked about all day long. In the midst of this agitation, the Chevalier de Mirabeau arrived at Montargis on his way to Bignon. He stayed there a long time. He knew that his father did not like to be kept waiting, and to justify his delay he made up a story of having been summoned to Gien by Sophie, who had asked him to intervene on behalf of his brother. He also said she had told him of her correspondence with his brother—of which his father had had no knowledge. He invented various more or less savoury details of his interview at the convent of Gien, amid bursts of laughter.

The marquis prepared to write to Maurepas to put an end to the exchange of letters which was the sole joy of Gabriel and Sophie. The chevalier was amused at the scandal he had created—"I had no idea I could be doing any harm to anybody." He became frightened when he learned that "the king, the counsellors of state, and the devil are mixed up in it."

After long months the negotiations again came to a deadlock. Gabriel's letters to Sophie often expressed regret that he had not been able to safeguard their happiness, and had not put the ocean between himself and his persecutors. "Alas, if we were at Boston, you would now be more or less at ease, I should be useful and esteemed, and my daughter would be an American, that is to say, born in the midst of the most estimable nation on earth."

When he learned that "by a very wise treaty which I had been impatient to see concluded" France had recognized the independence of America, he exclaimed: "So liberty will have an asylum on the earth!" But he added: "Please do not imagine that in congratulating us on the treaty of alliance with the United States of America I meant that I thought it to be in our interest to destroy England. Ah! no, no, interest never lies where justice is not. Come, my Sophie, the interests of nations are indissolubly united in spite of the stupidities of men and of their efforts." He repeated: "Get well into your head that so long as you do not see England and France united by a reciprocal commercial treaty that removes every subject of disagreement, one of the two nations, and perhaps both, will be badly governed." In the fortress of

Vincennes the great idea of his life was taking shape. He formulated it in a letter to La Fage: "If there is a fine plan in the world, it is that of associating the greatness of France with the greatness of England, and setting that enormous power on the basis of equity."

While Mirabeau was dreaming of the asylum of liberty, his brother had embarked with the squadron of M. de Guichen to seek a hero's laurels in America. Emilie, pressed to move on her husband's behalf, advised him to take service "with the insurgents." "The Bostonians are my heroes," wrote Mirabeau to Sophie, "and most of the French who are with them are not."

For himself personally, he felt that he had no ambition left. "At this moment I have not a coat," he wrote to Dupont. "I go bare-bottomed for lack of breeches, and I walk about literally bare-footed in my slippers, because I have no stockings at all. . . . Yet I laugh at all the embroidered garments in the world, and I should need only a thatched cottage and a thousand crowns a year to be the happiest of men."

In those moments of discouragement he was in agreement with Sophie: "You are quite right, it is only in an obscure condition that one can find shelter from evildoers and kings. The nobility that was and always will be the nursery of the satellites of despotism has found its punishment in its very crime. We have been promoters of arbitrary power and are its first victims—and that is just." The lovers sketched plans of future happiness, dreaming of a peaceful asylum abroad, in some little English village. That small corner of the English countryside, which they called "*les M——*," constantly recurs in their letters. They would live there unknown, surrounded with many children, "one every year. A whole school!" They harped on it with the more ardour since they dared not quite believe in it.

In the midst of his dreams of that big family of the future, Mirabeau was constantly anxious about the daughter he had never seen. He was constantly asking for news of her child, and waited anxiously for it, because it was often behindhand. He had a premonition of the unhappy fate of the abandoned child. In the spring of 1780 the little girl died from convulsions due to teething. The faithful Boucher, sent to the child's home, reported that "professional aid had been inadequate." Rougemont took the sad news to Mirabeau. It reduced him to despair and brought on a fever. His first reaction was fear for Sophie. He wrote to Dr. Ysabeau asking him to prepare her and to be with her in that hour of trial. "You loved me in her," he wrote to Sophie; "give me all the love you had for her. . . . Make the sacrifice for me, not of your sorrow, but of its excesses."

Sophie's relatives hoped that the child's death would enable her to come to terms with her husband. Gabriel, too, urged that this misfortune might help her to recover her liberty and might favour their plans of escape abroad. Once more hopes rose above a child's grave. But Sophie replied bitterly to her lover: "Nonetheless, we have suffered a great loss. It may facilitate our entry into '*les M*——,' but what a passport!"

II

Gabriel now played a card which he had already played in the past: he worked upon his influence with his mother. The Marquise de Mirabeau enjoyed the protection of a relative, Sartine, Minister of Marine. A "small private commission" was set up with Sartine as its president and Lenoir as *rapporteur*. The Marquise de Mirabeau published a memorial in which her son was "very warmly and very indiscreetly defended." Mirabeau feared at first that this would injure him with his father, but he thought of a way of turning the new judicial imbroglio to his profit. "If it is still possible," he wrote to Caroline, "to calm my poor mother, I am the one who could probably do it." The marquis pretended to reject this offer, dissembling even to his brother, who was too open: "It is a masterpiece of intrigue, and that is his strong point; I am saying straight out that I will have nothing to do with it; I have no desire for the distinction of having bought over a madwoman by means of a madman."

But he affected to be moved by his son's repentance. In an interview with Dupont he surrounded himself with so admirable an air of generosity that Dupont, in his emotion, kissed his hands. But when Dupont tried to profit by "this fatherly disposition" and asked that Gabriel be set free, the marquis once more brought up the question of "the safeguard he owes to his wife." He "held to his plan." Dupont concluded that "this puts us once more at the mercy of Mme. de Mirabeau."

It was not only with the continuation of his "race" that the marquis was obsessed. "Consider that if we can tame that cross-grained, empty, ferocious spirit, it is by humiliation," he wrote to his brother; "consider that there is no deeper humiliation for it than for him to have to kneel to his wife, to beg from her, and to admit that he owes everything to her—that is what we have to bring him to do; it is still a precarious path, but patience, or it will give way; no matter if it does, it must be that or nothing." He wanted to hit his son at the most sensitive spot. "This man is nothing except through pride; if he is robbed of pride he becomes nothing but a burst soap bubble."

Sophie, too, advised her lover to write once more to Emilie, but "on things that touch her rather than those that humiliate her." Mirabeau made up his mind "to exhaust every path of moderation, conciliation, and patience." He wrote to Emilie, and he wrote once more to the Marquis de Marignane—pitiable letters, the letters of a man fighting for his life and ready to pay no matter what price. He was never to pardon those to whom he wrote for reducing him to this. He tried to move Emilie by a touching picture of his wretched state, and promised her a "heart formed by all these years of misfortunes and sufferings"; he implored her "humanity and nobility." He asked his father-in-law to forgive his faults, and promised him to "bring to my expiatory conduct the same energy of will that ended by plunging me into my present position." But the reply from the Marquis de Marignane amounted to a refusal to negotiate.

Mirabeau asked his father if this refusal meant a "death sentence" for him. The Marquis de Mirabeau used this occasion only to ask Gabriel, through Dupont, to try to effect a reconciliation with the Marquise de Mirabeau. Mirabeau knew how impossible that would be. "The proposal in itself is near to my heart," he wrote to Sophie. He thought he could smooth down his mother and prevent a scandal, but he had not the least hope of bringing the two together. "I find it difficult to believe that a man who is quite familiar with my father's family life could write to me in good faith, 'You ought to succeed.' " He regarded the proposal as a trap, and feared that it was "the veil that conceals from us a new hydra of quibbles and delays."

But another element intervened in his favour.

"It is only too true that the authorities, whom he has been able to influence, would like to force my hand," the marquis wrote to his brother. The imprisonment which the marquis was inflicting on his children was exciting the indignation not only of the public but of influential circles. "Reasonable people regard my frightful detention as very long, of that I have more than one proof," wrote Mirabeau to his sister. The abuse of *lettres de cachet* was regarded as scandalous. The social conscience was deeply disturbed by the prison regime. The king himself was affected by the rising tide of public opinion and ordered ameliorations in the sinister dungeons.

The Marquis de Mirabeau himself perceived the massing of dull discontent. Clear-headed when it was a question of the general interest, he sensed the murmurs of the oppressed. But when it was a question of his private interest he indignantly rejected, as a sign of weakness, every humanitarian consideration.

Mme. de Pailly sensed well before he did the revulsion that was taking place in public opinion. Before long the marquis himself began to realize that his hand would soon be forced. He knew that once his son was free it would not take him long to secure his full rehabilitation. "In three months," he wrote to the bailli, "you will see him secure a royal pardon, break the bones of his creditors, and cut a figure at Versailles; accordingly, I am taking steps." In point of fact it was Mme. de Pailly who took them for him. "But for her," he admitted later to his brother, "he would have perished in irons; she freed him from them."

Emilie herself was moved. "It is only with the liveliest grief that I see the eldest son of this family in the unhappy state to which he has been reduced," she wrote to Caroline; "I would give anything to see him reasonable and happy." But "it is a terrible task for me to speak to papa about the letters from M. de Mirabeau; we are never in agreement as to what I ought to do and to say; he gets annoyed, and when I have written several letters without being able to satisfy him, he always ends by disapproving of the one I have sent off."

At last she wrote to the prisoner a letter that might pass for assent: "From the moment when you think, Monsieur, that my solicitations may have an influence on your liberation, I shall address them to my father-in-law." This was not much, and it committed her to nothing. But it was enough to satisfy the marquis. Mirabeau was delighted. "I am even almost in love with my wife, or you might say enthusiastic," he wrote to Sophie, "and I have written her a charming letter which might have done for the second volume of Anacreon."

His liberation was then decided on. But the marquis was determined "that he shall not come out unless he remains in my hands and well aware of it." He demanded a royal warrant permitting him to dispose of his son "as he shall judge to be fitting." Sophie was indignant: "What, are you to find yourself, at some caprice that may seize him, or through some slander brought to his ears, caught again without hope of recourse to anyone?"

The lieutenant of police himself pointed out to the Marquis du Saillant "how contrary to justice would be this arbitrary proceeding." The negotiations still dragged on; letters went to and fro ostensibly between brother and sister, really between father and son, for it was the marquis who dictated Caroline's replies. Long arguments were carried on between the "goddesses of Bignon," as Mirabeau called them, as to the place to be assigned to him to live in after his liberation. As a *pis aller* they suggested that he should be given quarters in the castle of Vincennes. Mirabeau took alarm: "At the castle I should have to walk on eggs without breaking them. Ten women, more or less amiable, more or less flirts, more or less intriguers, who may be curious about a young man who has been a prisoner for three years because of love." He was afraid of his own famished senses, afraid of adventures, and of quarrels arising from jealousy which would risk plunging him once more "into a dungeon."

But in his longing for liberty he agreed to everything. He even agreed to claim the inconceivable *lettre de cachet* which put him "beyond the realm of the law." He wrote to the all-powerful Minister Maurepas and to the Duc de Nivernois. "He is a man beyond understanding, with his talent for usurpation and domination," his father exclaimed. The marquis considered Gabriel's letters "thoroughly well written" in a spirit of "repentance and submission to his father, but in a tone which Francis I could not have used in prison with more dignity."

On December 13, 1780, the gates of the fortress of Vincennes at last opened. Mirabeau had spent forty-two months in close confinement. His brother-in-law and Dupont were waiting for him at the entrance. So overpowering was his emotion that he was unable to move or to speak a word. His legs gave way under him, and Dupont supported him. His emotion was shared by Saillant, who normally was cool and self-controlled; he, too, gazed in silence at Mirabeau as if rooted to the spot, before he opened his arms to him.

Mirabeau found an asylum in the home of the faithful Boucher. His health was broken. He had not even a name. By his father's order he existed for the world only under his first Christian name, as "M. Honoré."

12

Sophie de Monnier had read the stories of Boccaccio with profit. She had plenty of natural gifts and was able to make faithful friends and to secure both devotion and complicity from the people in her service. In the spring of 1781 she mobilized all the resources of her inventive faculties. She had keys made for the garden gate, but twice they failed in the lock. She then had a key stolen from the abbess's cash-box to serve as a pattern. She made up a gardener's smock. She sent for shoes and for list slippers to go over them to make them noiseless. Victoire (the nun who attended on her), the convent gardener, and Dr. Ysabeau, were in the plot. Her plan of campaign had been drawn up in minute detail. Mirabeau was to spend, undiscovered, five great days at the convent of Sainte-Claire at Gien.

With this chapter of comedy there ended the romance of Gabriel and Sophie. It was the last leap of the flames which were already dying down.

After his emergence from Vincennes Mirabeau eagerly pursued the joys of his freedom. He took great gulps of pleasure and work and money. At the same time he tried to maintain a show of exemplary conduct and to return to his father's good graces. Sophie already belonged to a melancholy past. "Your letters are becoming dreadfully rare," she wrote reproachfully. Gabriel pretended that they got lost, but Sophie felt that these incidents of negligent servants, of pockets with holes in them, of irregularities of the post, recurred too often. "I confess that I am terribly tired of beginning all my letters with complaints of your silence," she repeated six months later. Dupont had been obliged to write to her to excuse her lover: "If his business, his urgent duties, sometimes compel him to write more briefly or involuntarily to miss a post, let not your noble and sensitive heart be in any way alarmed. Tell yourself that your friend is doing what he can and what he must do, and do not ever fear that your empire over his soul has diminished. You would be doing wrong to both of you." He added pompously: "I shall go bail for him with you as I do with his parents."

It was not the impatience of a lover that took Gabriel to Gien at the risk of his liberty, but the tenderness of a friend who was gently preparing a sensitive woman for his abandonment of her. Shut up in a tiny room, listening intently for the slightest sound from outside, both of them risking their freedom, the two lovers were once more joined together in their last passionate embrace. "I love you as I loved you in the past," he wrote to her immediately after leaving her.

Gabriel's mad escapade did not pass unobserved. A friend, son of his former tutor, seems to have denounced him. Indiscreet confidences had been followed by an indiscreet quarrel: "Try, my beloved, to have no more squabbles with anyone," was one of the last pieces of advice that Sophie was to give him. Dupont, alarmed, himself went to tear Gabriel from the arms of his mistress.

In the whirl of existence after his release, Gabriel made fresh debts, while still burdened by old ones contracted in prison. He had even accepted a loan of five hundred livres from Julie Dauvers, whose father demanded payment and brought him into court. Once more Mirabeau was struggling amid great financial embarrassment, and

Sophie, herself entirely without resources, was obliged to ask him several times to send her one or two louis. "Alas!" she sighed, "I have always thought that debts would destroy you!"

She realized that all these difficulties were barring their way to "*les M*——." Her courage was revealed magnificently at the moment when she saw fading away the vision that had supported her through so many dark years. She saw the future as a low, dull horizon over which the last rays of light were dying.

She thought now of the one thing that was most repugnant of all to her, a return to her husband. She wrote him a letter which her mother had drawn up. Her fund of humour did not abandon her even at this moment of trial. When she had copied the last phrase in the letter, in which she assured the Marquis de Monnier that she had loved him and would love him always very tenderly, she commented on it in a letter to her lover: "I thought at first that it was going to finish like the song —'Always, always, always the same!' "

Her declarations of contrition arrived too late. The Valdahons had regained all their hold over the old man, now weak and blind and more dependent than ever on his daughter. But Sophie had been more afraid of his consent than of his refusal. She had thought he would consent "if only to make me his housekeeper or to have the pleasure of tormenting me." The thing that troubled her most was the idea that Gabriel seemed to want her to take the step. "I could not conceive your wanting me to do that," she wrote to him, while actually complying with what she believed to be his wish.

She was ready to efface herself from his life with but a tender plaint on her lips.

She knew in the end that she had been sacrificed to the thing she was afraid of—"that ambition may wrong love in your heart. It is so easy for you to go to all lengths when you wish to, and I know so well that these two passions cannot live together." The lover of Vincennes was no more.

The ashes of a great love marked the introduction to a great destiny.

☙ VII ❧

The Dealers in Lies

" AT LAST, on May 18, they killed me," exclaimed the Marquis de
Mirabeau. The Marquise de Mirabeau had succeeded in leaving
the convent. But she refused to listen to Gabriel's plea for reconciliation with the marquis. "Never have I seen such obstinacy and refusal
to listen to reason," he wrote to Caroline. In the struggle carried on
by the marquise against her husband, Gabriel was thenceforward resolutely on his father's side. He seems to have learnt for the first time of
the contents of the "little papers" that distracted his mother. In place
of her accomplice he became her accuser. He had written violent memorials against his father; he now wrote them against his mother. He
never did things by halves, and now he devoted the same energy to
opposing her as he had devoted in the past to her defence.

Gabriel had, in fact, a feeling near to pity for this proud old man so
cruelly tried by fate. His work on behalf of his father on the eve of
his great lawsuit had nothing about it of the perfunctory. As always,
he was entirely absorbed in the task of the moment. He had the gift
of letting unpleasant or inopportune considerations lie dormant, at least
for the time. "A quarter of an hour afterwards he has forgotten and
forgiven everything," noted the marquis, not without disapproval as
a man who was vindictive and proud of it.

But all Mirabeau's efforts on his father's behalf came up against a
barrage of hostility. "The star of the *ami des hommes* is paling," Sophie
had written a year earlier. The eloquent appeals of the prisoner of Vincennes, vain though they had been, had set the public against his father.
The reputation of the marquis had been shaken. His protectors had
grown tired. The grievances put forward by the Marquise de Mirabeau
found credence so much the more easily. The hardest blow of all had
been struck by the memorial of Louise de Cabris.

The fall of Sartine had disorganized the small tribunal set up to examine the case of Mme. de Cabris, but powerful influences were still

working on her behalf. And she neglected no means of agitating for her liberation. The marquis was afraid of her early release: "I blush internally and feel a ferocious element of character up in arms within me at the idea of seeing that creature here flaunting intrigue and prostitution," he wrote to the bailli.

But he knew that now he was losing on all sides. The atmosphere of the *parlement* was unfavourable to him. The public, which crowded the court, noisily demonstrated its hostility. The passages in the counsel's argument that denounced the tyranny of the marquis were greeted with applause. On May 18, 1781, the Marquise de Mirabeau obtained a judgment in her favour. Her son, on hearing the judgment pronounced, said aloud to his father's counsel: "I call that putting a crown on vice."

Ten days later Louise de Cabris was set free, and her emergence from the convent of Sisteron was greeted with acclamations and celebrated with music and fireworks.

The Marquis de Mirabeau was ruined. All the costs in the case were levied against him. The marquise pitilessly drew up a list of her claims and lists of the alleged damage done to her property. She ended by seizing even her husband's furniture. But the ruin of the marquis did little to enrich her. When his turn came to seize her assets, she was found "in a hovel, gaming on the straw, and surrounded by knaves." The Marquis de Mirabeau had lost everything, a great name, a great reputation, a great fortune. He now benefited only from the one reasonable investment he had made in his whole career, when he had provided for the bailli: the only means of living that he had left was the annual income of fifteen thousand livres which the bailli assured to him for life.

2

Caroline du Saillant now tried to reinstate her brother, who, since his liberation, had been living with Boucher, for the marquis' house was closed to him. After the loss of the case, she urged her father to receive his son. She and her husband argued that "since the intriguers have publicly declared that success alone would secure his reinstatement, now is the moment to prove them wrong." Boucher also intervened in favour of his friend. "Boucher is an experienced man, cool and sensible," wrote the marquis. "After dinner he appealed to me; suddenly, with his chest swelling and his eyes filling with tears, he said to me amid sobs: 'Monsieur, I will go bail to you for Monsieur your son; you would be pleased with him, and if I have merited anything at your hands . . .' At these words he got up to go, overcome; I followed him to the door and, embracing him, assured him that although my plans had been quite different, he himself should present him to me."

On the next day there took place the first interview between father and son.

A friend of the marquis who was present at the meeting exclaimed when Gabriel came in: "It is the prodigal son!" The marquis held out his hand and delivered a little speech he had prepared for the occasion. At the same time he watched his son keenly. He found him "grown much bigger, especially in the shoulders, neck, and head." He found also, a great compliment coming from him, "that he is of our form, build, and manner."

Mirabeau took up his abode at Bignon. The marquis made "a great effort at fatherliness." He had found a mission. The bailli urged him to leave Paris, "that most infectious sewer, whose black vapours and unclean reptiles the sun lights up with its rays." But the marquis declared that he could not turn his son into the street. "I am trying to pour out my mind, my soul, and my heart over that man." Since Gabriel's emergence from Vincennes, the marquis had begun "to fill him, by correspondence, with principles and with everything I know." Before he had seen him, he had written that "in his long solitary studies he has only augmented the medley in his head, which is a library turned topsy-turvy."

The bailli laughed at these belated efforts at education: "So there you are, thanks to your hindsight, busy teaching a chicken thirty-two years old! Do you really deceive yourself with the idea that you can make him anything but what he is?" "He is no more thirty-three than I am sixty-six," replied the marquis, adding: "One cannot cut off a son like an arm. If that had been possible I should have been one-armed long ago." He had undertaken "to turn the swimmer that he was into a diver."

Gabriel submitted with docility to the spiritual guidance of his father, who was trying to make of him a substitute for his lost followers. In his delight, indeed, at returning to a full life, nothing troubled Gabriel, nothing discouraged him. He showed all his natural gentleness and kindness. The servants adored him at Bignon as they had done at the château of Mirabeau.

He entered energetically into the regime of a fresh air life. With magnificent optimism he was ready to make a fresh start. He plunged into family life as his natural element. "Honoré," wrote his father, "seems to be solely occupied in playing the tame duck and in saving me trouble." For the second and last time, father and son passed several months in the intimacy of a stay at Bignon. Mme. de Pailly was away. A strange entente was established between the retributive father and the son who was so capable of forgetting everything. There was even a new family celebration, for which Mirabeau composed an "Intermezzo"— verses set to music. He rendered homage to his father—

> . . . *à sa force et à sa fermeté*
> *que tout le monde admire* . . .

The verses were bad, but the marquis was flattered by his son's good intention. He was very pleased with his son: "Far from being difficult to live with and from having the complaining, restless, inimical temperament for which he used to be blamed, he is cheerful, easygoing, and thoroughly good-natured," he wrote to the bailli.

Gabriel busied himself with the Bignon estate, to which his father was so attached, and with the tenants for whom the marquis was concerned. He thought of installing an observatory, taking advantage of the visit of a learned astronomer to Bignon. At the same time he worked on the revision of the translations he had made in prison. He worked hard, even, he admitted, too hard, in order to satisfy an incessant urge to activity.

3

The marquis was obstinately set on reconciling Gabriel with his wife, but he had imprudently committed himself with the Marquis de Marignane: "I give you my word of honour that I will never agree to my son ever approaching Madame your daughter, unless you order it or give your permission. In this matter our interests are the same. I could not be suspected of desiring to acquire by any means a child of a madman."

The marquis now hastened to rectify that judgment. "I know that from now on I shall not by any means have a madman to present to you," he wrote to Emilie. He sent the bailli to ascertain the attitude of the Marignanes. His brother wrote indignantly to him: "We have to deal with people who are not without intelligence, but who have no more feeling than the Chinese pagodas with which their good taste surrounds them. They think only of their pleasure. They have a society, or comedy, music, and indeed everything they can imagine to take their revenge on time by killing it, since it kills them." This feverish social activity had been redoubled since the liberation of Mirabeau, as if to exorcise a ghost.

When Emilie reproached the bailli for no longer coming so often, he replied with his sailor's bluntness that soon her residence and her name would be known no longer, and that she would "in future be called Mme. du Tholonet and not Mme. de Mirabeau." Not only did the bailli no longer believe in the possibility of the reunion of the couple, but he considered that it would be disastrous.

Gabriel himself no longer expected any great happiness from a resumption of conjugal life with Emilie. But for the second time in his life she represented for him the only means of entry into an assured existence. He could not remain too long dependent on his father, who was now a ruined man. He was troubled by a vague anxiety in spite of his rooted optimism.

The idyll of Bignon did not last long. The marquis tired of his effort at fatherliness. He tried to get rid of his son by sending him to stay with the bailli. "If this dislocated creature can ever be sewn up, it can only be by you, and since he wants shaping I could never give him a better employer than you. I give him to you as a young fellow with a rare future."

The bailli replied caustically: "Today you are trying to romance about good order at home, as you used to romance about the social order. I am no good at romancing. Honoré is the worst of all the misfits of your moulding."

The explanation of this sudden desire on the part of the marquis to be rid of his son was simple: Mme. de Pailly, who had been in Switzerland, was returning to Bignon. Gabriel was *de trop* in his father's home.

Once more a controversy over the intruder clouded the relations between the two brothers. The marquis eagerly defended his mistress, who had heaped kindnesses on him and had devoted herself to his family: "Her property, her attentions, her time, have all been at my service; my houses, my furniture, everything has been her care, at the time and in the way I have wanted, even against her judgment and even against her interest. During the storms when everybody was abandoning me because I was supposed to be submerged, she openly showed her constancy, even putting up with personal outrages and forgiving them, she who is so sensitive."

She was in truth, then and thereafter, the only friend who remained to him from the brilliant society that had lauded him in the days of his greatness. "Without her, I should long ago have been isolated."

"Even if it was true, as you think," the bailli replied, "that you owe her a great deal of gratitude, it is nonetheless true that in my eyes and in the eyes of those who are interested in the matter, although she may have done so very innocently, herself blinded to the facts, she has certainly done a great deal of harm to you and your family, for she has never been mentioned to me except in derision."

The greatest proof of the friendship between the two brothers is that it survived that outburst. The marquis no longer pressed the bailli to take charge of his son. But he seemed to blame Gabriel for having been the cause of so painful a controversy. He suddenly looked at him without friendliness, as though through the critical eyes of Mme. de Pailly. Suddenly everything about his son jarred on him, even his submissiveness. It irritated him to hear his own opinions voiced by his son. He cut him short, pulling his watch out of his pocket and remarking dryly: "It was this morning, or yesterday, at such and such a time, that I said that to you." He had only just been rejoicing to see him willing and confident. Now he objected to his adaptability—"He is magpie and jay by instinct."

Gabriel needed all his adaptability to live in his father's house under that hostile regard, which weighed on him as it had done in his childhood. He had to secure a revocation of the Pontarlier sentence that had condemned him to "death in law." He needed this revocation also for material reasons, for the sentence also condemned him to pay forty thousand livres in damages to M. de Monnier within five years from the date of the sentence, a period that expired in 1782.

In order to win this decisive struggle, he needed all his father's support. But his sincere and arduous efforts to win him over had been in vain. He was painfully conscious of his father's hostility when he left his house. He knew as well as the bailli did that he owed that hostility to "the Fury whom fate has unleashed against our house."

For the second time an effort at reconciliation between Gabriel and his father had failed—and for the same reason. It was the last attempt. Gabriel left to try to regain his civil existence, his wife, his position. He never returned to Bignon.

4

On his arrival at Pontarlier Mirabeau had himself arrested. He ran a great risk, in the hands of the judges, as a man who had been executed in effigy. His case was precarious. The Marquis de Monnier was an important magistrate. The deputy, Sombarde, was a relative of his. The magistrates of the court of the little town were all interrelated, connexions of the notable families of the region, agents for important personages; they formed a clan that defended the interests of a narrow social stratum. "I do not think there has ever been anywhere in the world such an example of universal corruption," wrote Mirabeau to his friend Vitry. "There is nobody, down to the lowest usher, who is not sold to the Valdahons."

Mirabeau could have appealed for a royal pardon; the marquis was sure he would succeed, "for all the secretariats are made of butter, and the authorities of brass." But since that would liberate only his person, he refused. His father offered guidance from a distance. He sent him "with all imaginable emphasis" the advice given by an illustrious Economist, "who told us what we have long known. We were a little astonished," added Gabriel caustically, "that the result of this eagle's-eye view, which took in at once the crucial point in the affair, was the recommendation to wait for the death of the husband, who is as hale and hearty as I am."

Mirabeau had been condemned for *rapt de séduction*—abduction with consent—an offence punishable by death; adultery had not been alleged. He concentrated his defence on the fact that in the wording of the law *rapt de séduction* has no reference to the carrying off of a married woman. He took the audacious line of denying adultery. "The fabricated compilation of public rumours wounded the *amour-propre* of an easygoing, affectionate, and perhaps amorous old man," he wrote in his memorial, and he added cuttingly: "He had the rights of a husband, the desires of a lover, and perhaps the pathetic humiliations of old age." He quoted the advice he had received: "The Pontarlier sentence is frightful, the procedure, I am told, terrible, the crime of which you are accused entails loss of civil rights; appeal to the king's clemency and ask for a royal pardon." He refused, for "my heart, my conscience, and my memory tell me that I have nothing to fear; I will go in search of my judges." He added menacingly: "If I found none but assassins, well! there are still men of my name to avenge my memory on my slanderers and their satellites."

He summarized the charges brought against him: "The charge of *rapt de séduction* cannot stand. Adultery is not proved and could not be; and if it had been, there is neither charge nor accuser. What remains against me? Nothing.

"Well, then, such is the case that for five years has brought desolation to two families! Such is the case that has robbed me for five full years of my civil existence! Such is the case that has armed three families against one another and filled society with hatreds and scandals."

His adversaries tried to wear him out. A single confrontation with two witnesses for the prosecution lasted ten hours; but Mirabeau "paid them out well in their own coin." M. de Monnier's counsel declared openly at a hearing: "We shall tire out the Comte de Mirabeau." But Gabriel's power of resistance had been underestimated. The most dangerous rock for him would have been the depositions of witnesses of Sophie's arrival in Switzerland. He fought tenaciously to prevent their admittance. He got into touch with the Council of State at Neufchâtel, which would have to give the witnesses an authorization to appear before the French courts. He obtained a result important to him: their depositions would be authorized only on condition that they were not interrogated concerning any offence committed on the territory of their country. Part of the case for the prosecution had crumbled; the court decided not to call these witnesses. But it made up for this with the witnesses from the little town, who were intimidated by the imposing machinery of the law. Mirabeau again appealed to the tribunal of public opinion: "Crimes and calumnies ought to be exposed to full daylight; it is to the public that favouritism, obscure connivances, secret subordinations, and vexatious treatment of details, should be denounced," so that "the voice of decent people may make good the imperfection of the laws."

The Marquis de Mirabeau was distracted at the noisy publicity the case was receiving, although he had learnt, to his great surprise, that the first memorial of the "infallible" had had great success and had been praised in Paris. "You have no idea of what he calls his defences," he wrote to his brother. "I have never seen him so extravagant! He has humiliated witnesses, annoyed the judges, insulted everybody; and he believes himself, in good faith, to be innocent, oppressed, moderate, magnanimous."

Although he was "bitterly thwarted," he pleaded his cause with an animation that often brought a laugh in his favour. "Gentlemen, I am charged with seduction," he said to the magistrates. "My only reply and my only defence is to ask that my portrait may be placed with the papers in the case." The clerk to the court did not see his point: "Ass," said a magistrate bending over to him, "look at the gentleman's face."

Fiery, haughty, contemptuous in turn, Mirabeau was spurring himself to a great effort. His adversaries had secured from the *parlement* of Besançon (whose counsellors were also mainly friends or relatives of M. de Monnier) the suppression of his first two memorials. But the Keeper of the Seals refused to approve their destruction. In defiance of his enemies' chicanery and his father's prohibition, Mirabeau published a third memorial, the most violent of all.

"In the immense volume of the documents in the case there is not," he claimed, "a single item of evidence that is not equivocal, there is not a presumption that is not uncertain, not a conjecture that is not doubtful." But he did not content himself with a daring and haughty defence: he attacked the inspirer of the proceedings, "her father's jailer," and exposed "the insulting vanity, the satirical humbug, and the sordid, insatiable cupidity of Mme. de Valdahon."

One of his most active enemies was a king's counsel, Pion, whose slanderous talk was overheard on a journey by an English friend of Mirabeau, who visited him in prison. Mirabeau described him in his memorial as "unworthy, because of the daily scandal of his life, to be a member of a legal body." Above all he attacked the deputy Sombarde. Michaud, the attorney general, a very conscientious man, had been closely associated with Mirabeau during the latter's detention at the fortress of Joux; of him Mirabeau had said that "he never speaks without first reflecting for an hour." He had suddenly withdrawn from the case as a relative of M. de Monnier. His substitute had not had the same scruples. "Sombarde, perfidious Sombarde, come here," wrote Mirabeau in his memorial. "I am going to expose your crime and let it be known whether I slandered you when I called you a liar. You are a relative of M. de Monnier; you have extorted writs of summons in foreign countries; you have menaced, seduced, suborned witnesses; you have helped to draw up their depositions; you have paid them from your relative's money."

This violence, from a man whose resistance they had expected to break with ease, disconcerted his adversaries. In the atmosphere of a little town with its unavowed jealousies, its secret grudges, and its appetite for scandal, Mirabeau's memorial turned the accusers into the accused. He was very pleased with the effect he produced. "If that is not eloquence unknown in our slavish age," he wrote to Vitry, "I do not know what is that gift from Heaven, so seductive and so rare."

Grotesque incidents brightened the dark surface of this fight of a man for his future. Mirabeau had brought with him a valet who seemed to have come out of a comedy of Molière. He had nearly killed his master by accident when hunting at Bignon, and was all the more passionately devoted to him. His attachment was equalled only by his insolent familiarity. He shared good and evil fortune with his master, and even, it seems, his amorous conquests. Confidant and accomplice in his adventures, always zealous and often blundering, he put up with Mirabeau's fits of anger and played often the part of Providence for him and always that of buffoon. This was the faithful, cunning Legrain, whom Mirabeau had sent to Neufchâtel to secure the council's pronouncement.

He had acquitted himself well on that occasion. Legrain shared all his master's hatreds. Riding one day along a road from Pontarlier, he met Pion returning from the chase, surrounded by his hounds. Pretending to defend himself from the pack, Legrain flourished his whip so violently that he lashed the lawyer full in the face. In court he defended himself with a cheapjack's fluency, pretending that he had been dazzled by the sun. "Did I really have the misfortune to catch Monsieur the King's Counsel instead of the hound? It is incredible."

The violence of Mirabeau's memorials produced a reaction in his favour. But the marquis lost patience. He sent Saillant with instructions "to do in my name and his the exact opposite of what has been done so far." Mirabeau swore that not even the sight of the scaffold facing his window would make him accept any proposal in prison. He wrote indignantly to his brother-in-law: "I have told my father, and I repeat it to you, that nobody has the right before God and men to interfere in my affair against my will." But Saillant succeeded in appeasing his susceptibility. He started negotiations with the Valdahons.

The proposals made in the name of M. de Monnier seemed to Mirabeau "reasonable and decent." The sentence of the Pontarlier tribunal was to be considered null and void. A judicial separation would be granted, and a life pension assured to Sophie, on condition that she remained at the convent until her husband's death. Mirabeau was satisfied. "I do not think it is possible to emerge with more honour from so melancholy an affair."

"You have no idea how the fellow can impress the court," the marquis wrote to the bailli, "for I am well informed, and I know that it is generally thought that he would have secured an arrangement without Saillant, with all his extravagance; and perhaps—indeed, people are saying beyond doubt—a more advantageous one." He went even further: "In fact, it is possible that his mad memorials won the day for him, and that they will serve him further." But this avowal did not bring any change of heart. He refused to pay the debts his son had contracted in prison.

When Caroline congratulated her brother on the issue of the proceedings, he replied bitterly: "I am very far from being able to credit the favourable auguries which your good heart sent me. My own heart is torn, and the wound will never close. My father's contempt and hatred have at last been unmasked; he is showing them without disguise; the contempt may be forced, but in that case the hatred is only the more violent." Gabriel was profoundly discouraged. "What can I do?

What should I do? Unless I forestall his judgment and his prophecies by exiling myself forever from my country and my family."

5

The Marquise de Malleroy was the salvation of the poor at Gien. The little town saw her riding about in a donkey-chaise, distributing aid to suffering families and caring for children with the tenderness of a mother who had not had the happiness to keep her own child. Under that borrowed name and amid that activity which brought her the esteem of the whole neighbourhood, the sinner Sophie de Monnier sought oblivion. She had had no wish to leave Gien, which had sheltered her in her sorrows and in her last days of happiness with Gabriel. Her tormented past seemed to survive in her only in solicitude for those who were in need. But not with impunity had she loved Mirabeau. She was one of love's uprooted, retaining beneath a deceptive appearance of serenity her eternal nostalgia for a passion. She sought in vain for Gabriel de Mirabeau in the men who approached her. But she could not live without being loved, and least of all without immolating herself in a love.

An officer much older than herself became one of her intimates. He was regarded as a lover, but a neighbour bore witness that he was only a friend, and the society of the neighbouring châteaux received him with Sophie. One of these châteaux belonged to an ex-cavalry captain, M. de Poterat. He was still young, a widower and a consumptive. He was a man of the world, and a man of wide culture, a thing of which Sophie must have felt the need after the disappearance of her encyclopaedic mentor. But he was in need of a woman's solicitude, of devoted care, of vigilant affection. He attached himself to Sophie with the passion of a man who knows himself to be doomed, and he settled at Gien, in a house facing hers. He wanted to marry her in order to leave her his fortune. The day of the marriage was fixed. Sophie believed herself to have found happiness again in an ardent sacrifice for an invalid. But his emotion seems to have been too strong for his diseased heart: M. de Poterat died suddenly at the beginning of September 1789. On the morrow of his death, Dr. Ysabeau returned to Gien from a morning round in the countryside. A messenger ran to meet him, shouting that the Marquise de Malleroy had been assassinated.

Sophie's faithful friend hurried to her house. He found her in her dressing-room, with the windows closed, and in front of her two braziers of burnt-out charcoal. Her face was livid; her body, already stiff, was bound hand and foot to her easy chair. Dr. Ysabeau recalled a recent conversation with Sophie in which she had talked of reflexes of desperate people that drive them at the last moment to open their windows. Sophie had been afraid of that last impulse of the will to live and had bound herself. She had always played with the idea of a voluntary death. She could not live a loveless life. She had been consumed in the flames of a passion that was too much for her. She had tried in vain to survive it. Mirabeau understood that she had died for him and not for M. de Poterat.

Dr. Ysabeau sent the news to his brother-in-law, the Abbé Vallet, member of the National Assembly. The abbé went with it to the Comte de Mirabeau, his political opponent; he watched the effect of the news on the face of the great man of the Assembly. He thought it excessive, and believed it to be feigned. For the last time Gabriel, the passionate lover, rose from the past. Abruptly he left an important debate to weep for Sophie.

6

"Savages of bellicose tribes may prefer to bury themselves wholesale in a common death; but a commercial people simply calculates its assets," said Clavière, one of the exiles from Geneva, bitterly. Neufchâtel, the refuge of thinkers, had become a place of asylum for the leaders of the democrats of Geneva. The city had prepared to defend itself against the armed coalition of France, Sardinia, and the Canton of Berne, whose aim was to re-establish by force of arms the rule of the aristocrats, who had been overthrown by their adversaries. Geneva had fortified itself and had mounted guns on its ramparts against the enemy. Ardent young people were ready to die in the defence of freedom.

But Geneva could not have much hope of long resisting the army of the French general, the Marquis de Jaucourt. The city was in danger of being sacked, and also of reducing itself to ruins by blowing up houses in its fierce defence. The leaders of the popular party were democrats and not revolutionaries. They had a horror of bloodshed. "We may have a right to dispose of our own lives," Clavière said, "but who gives us any right to dispose of the lives of ten thousand women and children?" The democrats considered it more honourable to "sacrifice" themselves. Only their adversaries tacitly agreed with them. Their partisans accused them of cowardice and pursued them with gunfire.

These men had taken refuge temporarily at Neufchâtel; embittered, eloquent, and disunited as leaders in exile often are, they loaded each other with mutual reproaches and argued about their plans. They wanted to found, somewhere in the world, a new Geneva. The Prussian Emperor offered them permission to establish themselves at Constance, but they distrusted an absolute government.

From Switzerland, whither Mirabeau had gone after his case at Pontarlier, he wrote the French Foreign Minister responsible for intervention, asking his protection. He was filled once more with his old terror of his father. A letter from the marquis had given him reason to fear that his return to France would be "the first step to a new prison." He prayed the minister to make an end of that arbitrary regime. "Thirty-eight *lettres de cachet* have already descended upon my family. I have been the victim of some of these orders; I cannot reconcile myself to being the thirty-ninth." But he did not approach the minister as a humble petitioner alarmed by the prospect of imprisonment. He promised him as "the first evidence of my gratitude an important memorandum on the affairs of Geneva."

The memorandum which he drew up for Vergennes was his first effort in the field of foreign policy. He gave evidence from the outset of courage and political wisdom in addressing himself directly to the men responsible, in order to win over the most redoubtable adversaries. It was to the man who was most hated by the Genevese exiles that Mirabeau addressed himself to ask him to reconcile them with France.

"The troubles of Geneva are not the work of the party sacrificed," he wrote, "they are the masterpiece of Machiavellism of the other party. Permit me to say that if you had said *sotto voce* to the aristocrats that the faults of the ruled are generally those of the rulers, perhaps the mere sound of your beneficent voice would have calmed the Genevese and put an end to their discord. . . .

"Do not deceive yourself. The Genevese who are humiliated at present are the part of their little nation which is the most esteemed all over Europe." He advised the recall of French troops and preparations to make peace. It was a lesson in foreign policy offered to a powerful minister for whose favour he was begging. The lesson was not listened to. The Genevese exiles scattered over the world, to return to France in her critical hours. They were but a handful of men, but their influence was to be one of the forces that would one day bring down the existing political system, the old order, the society which Vergennes represented.

Mirabeau had already been corresponding with the Genevese democrats from his prison in Pontarlier. When he met them at Neufchâtel he gained friends for life, collaborators who were to help him to lay the foundations of his great reputation. In France nothing was known of him but his notorious amorous adventures and his quarrels with his father. Nowhere had he sufficient backing to justify the assurance with which he spoke to the exiled democratic leaders. But he dazzled them with the picture he painted of conditions in France. They never forgot his vision of future political changes and of his own role. "In 1782," one of the Genevese recalled later, "he spoke to us of the States General of France as an event that could not fail to come: 'I shall be a deputy . . . and I shall re-establish your country!'"

His father, who accused him of being blind to his own interests, admitted that "never was man so clear-sighted about other people's business." Jacques-Pierre Brissot, then a young journalist and much among the Genevese, was struck by "that accurate and piercing vision, which saw through men and foresaw events, that ability to assimilate all the talents."

Brissot had arrived at Neufchâtel at the moment when the democrats went into exile, and he established relations with one of the most important of them, Clavière, who was to play a decisive part in the life of Mirabeau.

When Mirabeau made his acquaintance at Neufchâtel, Clavière was nearly fifty years old. Clavière's dream was to become, like Necker, the French Finance Minister. One day in 1780, when in Paris on business for the Republic of Geneva, he had stopped in front of the residence of the Controller General of Finance and said to his travelling companion: "My heart tells me that one day I shall live there."

He was to realize his ambition a dozen years later, with the aid of that modest journalist Brissot, to whom he had given hospitality. As though he suspected that a great upheaval was necessary for him to be able to fulfil his destiny (which ended beneath the guillotine), he sought out men capable of unhinging an epoch.

"Clavière liked Mirabeau," wrote Brissot. "I think he liked him best of all his friends. The cause of this attachment lay, if I am not mistaken, in the unconquerable urge that carried the Genevese toward revolutions and toward those who could engineer them."

Clavière was not only won over by Mirabeau's personality, the dangerous quality that even his father recognized in him; he was also drawn to him by his ardent humanity, his vehement indignation against social injustice. "He is a great man in intellect and in his moral resources," he said of him. At the time when Mirabeau met him, Clavière was of the type well described by Brissot as "an inexhaustible mine of crude diamonds; what he needed was a setter." This was the role Mirabeau later assumed; for, to quote a phrase of Goethe, "he had the gift of perceiving talent, and talent felt attracted by the demon of his powerful nature and willingly submitted to his direction."

But that was in a future that then seemed distant and almost inconceivable. Mirabeau's existing position was obscure and desperate. He tried to earn a little money with his writings. He sold to Fauche, the publisher of his *Lettres de cachet*, *L'Espion dévalisé*, on which he had collaborated with Badouin, a fellow-prisoner, while at Vincennes; he tried also to pass off a manuscript of his father's, *L'Instruction d'un prince;* Fauche refused it, but Mirabeau had no scruple about publishing it later without mentioning the marquis. The *Lettres de cachet* began to sell widely in France. Mirabeau's old protector, Lenoir, the lieutenant of police, became alarmed, remembering his former prisoner's earlier intention of dedicating the work to him. Fearing that he might be suspected of complicity, Lenoir, like a true police official, denounced the work to Vergennes, though without mentioning the author's name. He also denounced *L'Espion dévalisé* and the libertine novel *Ma conversion*.

Vergennes transmitted the denunciation to Goltz, Prussian ambassador at Paris, for Neufchâtel was under Prussian sovereignty. The first edition of *Lettres de cachet*, nine thousand copies, had been sold out, and four thousand copies of the second edition had already been distributed when the police raided the publishers. The presses were then stopped, the publishing premises placed under seal, and the printers imprisoned. The censor took alarm on examining the work, which had not been submitted to him. He found that "the author has sought to destroy religion by treating it as a human invention, and seems further to be inviting the French to set limits to the authority, described as absolute, of their sovereign."

The affair produced great activity among subordinate officials. The French ambassador at Berlin remarked that it was "impossible to speak of a trifle in more portentous language." Vergennes himself intervened and asked for the seals to be broken. Frederick II, for his part, declared that the penalty of three days' imprisonment inflicted on the printers was sufficient. The publishers, questioned by the police, finally admitted that they had returned the manuscripts to the Comte de Mirabeau. Mirabeau was not disturbed: he knew that it was impossible to prove that he was the author of the book concerned.

He had worse troubles. "Here I am, free! What can I do with my freedom?" he wrote to his sister. "Reprobated by my father, forgotten and perhaps hated by my mother, dreaded by my uncle, waited for by my creditors, not one of whom has been paid although every penny was taken from me on the pretext of satisfying them; threatened by my wife, or by those who rule her; destitute of everything, of income, of status, of credit." The money he earned in Switzerland melted rapidly in his hands. He was distracted about his debts at Pontarlier. "My lawyers must certainly regard me as an ingrate. I must appear in a most unenviable light, since I am offering no return to those who helped me in so capital an affair," he complained to Vitry. He had no wish to return to Provence with "a double bankrupt's reputation."

At that time of discouragement he had no knowledge of the victorious progress his ideas were already making. His *Lettres de cachet* was stirring men's consciences. One of the most brilliant men at court, the Comte de Vaudreuil, friend of Mme. de Polignac (who was an intimate friend of Marie Antoinette), had the courage a little later to lend the book to the king. Public opinion was so moved that in the end the government was obliged to evacuate the fortress of Vincennes. In the autumn of 1784 a chronicler noted that "all Paris" was trooping through Vincennes to see the hateful traces of an "ancient barbarism."

7

"We must at all costs have a house and prosperity," declared the marquis. It was with this feeling that he permitted his son to re-enter France in freedom.

The bailli fought hard against the burden his brother was imposing on him. "I have taken a surprising aversion to that man," he said, adding that Gabriel's only proper home was with his father. Since the reunion with his wife could only be effected in the course of a stay in Provence, however, the bailli submitted, though he thought it "quite impossible to get used to him."

The return of Mirabeau to the château, "the home of my fathers for four centuries," as he declared with more pomposity than truth, was a triumphal entry. "My uncle did his best," he wrote to his sister, "to give me a tepid reception, but he did not succeed." The peasants assembled in crowds along his route with fifes and Provençal drums. They received him with harangues, with fireworks, with salvos and wild music. "I think you ought to have prevented these village celebrations," wrote the marquis, annoyed, "for it is a flouting of the decree and the creditors."

The bailli was himself astonished at "the joy of these people at seeing him arrive, although he owes money to some of them; but they are very fond of him, and I have been touched by the lively expressions of some of them on this subject."

A few days of his nephew's presence at Mirabeau sufficed to make the bailli write that "M. Honoré seems to have sobered greatly in his ideas" and that he was "very agreeable and very docile." A fortnight later he was resolutely taking his nephew's side against his brother. "I am seeing to it that your son shall not catch sight of your letters, for I begin to think that you are being made to set him down as rather worse than he is, and I am very pleased with him, except for his rather lively air, though not too much so, and perhaps some stories that are very much embroidered but which I cannot be sure are false; finally, I will hide nothing from you, but also I will not try to set you against your children. Somebody else looks after that and will go on doing so."

Thenceforward the bailli was leagued with the children of the marquis against Mme. de Pailly. He assured the Saillants that he had never been able to bear her presence in his brother's house, "because, far from realizing the way she ought to behave, she persisted in playing the part of mistress of the house," arousing furious jealousy in the Marquise de Mirabeau. In spite of his realistic resignation, he flattered himself that he could influence his brother: "Perhaps we shall manage to undermine the confidence he has in that woman."

But the marquis was seriously offended. When Gabriel, too, permitted himself a remark on the subject of Mme. de Pailly, he roughly snubbed him: "I have told you, my son, that there is a subject on which I have no intention at all of listening to anybody, a subject that gets my back up and deeply wounds me; I have told you that; only from my brother can I listen to anything connected with that subject, because I owe him respect, and because without knowing it he is jealous."

Gabriel's arrival spread dismay in the clan of the Marignanes. He learned that Emilie's first impulse was to rejoin him at Mirabeau, but that her father made a violent scene and, so Mirabeau learned, "told her in front of the servants that he would renounce her if she went away." Emilie was not the woman to struggle for a man, especially a man of whom she was afraid. She gave way at once and adopted the views and the suggestions of those round her.

Mirabeau sent a servant to Marignane with letters for Emilie and her father, "very polite" letters, "very measured, but very firm and quite unanswerable." The replies the man brought back were dry and negative. "You must feel yourself," his wife wrote, "that the events that have happened will always form an insurmountable barrier between you and me," and that she would defend her liberty "with the aid of the law." She told the bailli at the same time that her father "is very determined that I shall never live with M. de Mirabeau." She added: "I may perhaps flatter myself that I contributed to his liberty. He is enjoying it. It would be very extraordinary if he made use of it to attack mine."

Emilie also sent a letter, dictated by her father, to Caroline complaining of Gabriel. She told her that they had decided to institute proceedings for a separation: "Papa will spare neither his fortune nor any means to get me away from a man so little master of himself." She added: "I am quite sure that my father-in-law will not support him in the steps he says he is taking against me. My father and I have, indeed, his word guaranteeing it." She concluded with the threat of a "scandalous case."

The marquis was very vexed at this reminder of his undertaking. "I said nothing of the sort to the girl. I still remember it, and I was glad that they did not do me the honour of replying, for an undertaking not accepted is an undertaking not given." In his embarrassment he burst into reproaches against his son: "If he had wanted his wife he would have had her, but it would have taken years of prudence to reconquer her, and of gentleness and respect." The bailli answered impatiently: "Years of prudence, yes; but heirs? Would you have demanded them from this woman when she was sixty? Gentleness? but how to give evidence of it to people who will not see you and do not read your letters?"

The Marignanes sent their legal adviser, Gassier, who was at the same time a friend of the bailli, to Mirabeau to "convince us that we are wrong." Mirabeau listened calmly to all the complaints his wife brought against him. This calm of a man well known for his bursts of temper was so impressive that the bailli said several times: "You can see that I am less self-controlled than my nephew."

In reply, Mirabeau showed Marignane's envoy the letters from Emilie. He also revealed his wife's lapse. The lawyer was dumbfounded. He saw that in the eyes of the public the Comtesse de Mirabeau might have more to answer for than her husband.

Mirabeau learned that the lawyers engaged by the Marignanes—there were twenty-three of them—had told their clients plainly that they had "not the shadow of a case for a legal separation." "All the difficulties with which we are meeting," he wrote to his sister, "proceed from a dozen letters of my father's in which he paints me as the most villainous of men, and from two others in which he gives his word of honour that he will never permit me to claim her return." But when, to palliate the effect of his father's terrible screeds, Gabriel de Mirabeau asked him to send him letters from his daughter-in-law that spoke in his son's favour, the marquis took offence and invoked his old principles. "I have always considered that letters are a deposit of confidence and that in consequence a letter addressed to me should never be shown in court with my consent," he wrote to the bailli.

He also wrote to his daughter-in-law in this tone of laboured facetiousness, which he assumed when he did not want to admit that his conscience was uneasy. He reminded her, too, that letters are a deposit of confidence which must never emerge from the desk of an honest person, and he added: "I wrote of things as they were at the time, and so I shall always do."

The marquis wrote a very pointed letter to M. de Marignane: "What personal advantages have I sought in your alliance? What have I asked from you? None of the rights that were given me by our laws and by the usages of Provence. I left you to dispose of the funds and the revenues of Madame your daughter as you thought fit. When she came to me, my house was unreservedly thrown open to her, without any payment for board. . . . When she wanted to keep her son with her, in spite of the steps I had taken for his education, did I not leave him with her, this boy who was the only hope of my race? He perished in her hands, in a strange house, in the midst of celebrations, and far from my allowing the slightest complaint to escape me in my deep affliction, all I thought about was to console the mother in her just grief."

Before the struggle became envenomed, Mirabeau also made a last appeal to Emilie. He brought into play all his persuasiveness. He was himself moved in his effort to move her: "Emilie, listen to me: it is a matter of your happiness and mine. You loved me, you loved me very much, and the first man a woman has loved is never indifferent to her love. . . . Poor Emilie, listen to a man who loves you, a man whose interests are yours, Emilie, and consider. This moment may decide your whole life."

Painful as it was for Mirabeau to appeal to her, in his eloquent supplication he preserved his full dignity. "Certainly I do not want a woman against her will, but certainly also I owe it to myself not to allow my house to fall in order to allow my wife the pleasure of being a star in a comedy troupe." Emilie had tried to intimidate her father-in-law with the fear of scandal; her husband showed her that scandal threatened her too: "Oh, you, whom I have seen so honourable, so decent, so sensitive to public opinion! Does not that scandal and all that may result from it make you tremble? You know what dealers in lies and insults there are among lawyers. They will choose you a madman. He will attack me scurrilously; he will do all he can to make it impossible for me to live with you. And what will happen to you? Are you going to live always from day to day? All the hope of your happiness will rest upon one single man, whom may Heaven long preserve, but who is neither very young nor of very robust health. . . . No, you will not come into court, or I little know you." Like all his appeals to Emilie's heart, this one, too, was in vain. It was sent by a messenger, and seems to have been sent back to him, for it was found among his papers.

All means of conciliation failed. The bailli asked his brother whether he had decided to go to law. "A wife isn't to be got through a writ-server," the marquis replied.

The bailli lost patience. "I want a yes or a no," he wrote. "I am too old to be trifled with. Make up your mind; but in God's name, decide for yourself, and without any female opinion."

The Marignanes were sure that the marquis would recoil from a law-suit. "There has always been correspondence between a certain person, whom you do not know well enough and I know only too well, and this woman here," wrote the bailli to the marquis later. "You will not be-lieve me, but it is certain that your distaste for going to law has always been known here. It has been confidently assumed that you would prevent us from taking proceedings."

The marquis, driven to a decision, yielded to his brother's represen-tations. "I have no right to prevent that gentleman from starting pro-ceedings," he replied, embarrassed. "And as he knows as well as I do that this is the way to get separated from his wife, I do not for a mo-ment want him to be able to charge me with having stood in his way." Resigned to the worst, he gave his consent. "I can see that it is my fate to be dragged by my hair into the abyss."

8

"When I came to Aix, everybody fled from me; I was Antichrist."

The brilliant society was horrified to see Mirabeau reappear, like a ghost, and "crowded tenderly round the kind woman who was their delight, and that, too, at her own expense." The Marignanes had threat-ened to boycott anybody who received him, and only Mme. de Vence dared to brave the threat.

The whole town seemed to be holding its breath as if at the approach of a catastrophe. "A costumier said the other day," wrote the bailli, "that a gentleman had come who was upsetting the balls and the the-atricals at Tholonet, and that business had come to a stop." It was as though an elemental force had been unloosed and had made a void around itself. But so much had been said about the violence of the Comte de Mirabeau that those who approached him were almost disappointed. "He has greatly changed," said a wit; "he has become very reasonable. If he became more so he would be a bore."

Mirabeau displayed, in fact, remarkable patience and moderation. He sent New Year greetings for 1783 to the Marquis de Marignane and to Emilie, to which no reply was sent. He wrote to them again at the end of January; the bearer brought back a message from the Marquis de Marignane: "I have no reply to give; M. de Mirabeau will do what he chooses." Mirabeau further proposed, as a last resort, a conference with his wife, alone, with the bailli and her father in an adjoining room. Emilie asked for twenty-four hours to consider this, and replied on the following day that the conference seemed to her to be impossible and useless.

Mirabeau allowed another month to pass. Then, at the end of February, he informed Emilie that, to his deep regret but as a matter of honour, he would take legal proceedings. The letter was returned to him unopened. In a province in which "I had few relatives left, few secret friends, and scarcely a single open one," wrote Mirabeau later, "I proceeded to fight against the family of the highest repute, and against the individual in the town of Aix who was considered to have the most pleasant company, the most powerful friends, and the best cook." M. de Marignane had, indeed, spared no effort to seize every possible advantage; Mirabeau could find no lawyer of reputation to take charge of his case; he had to be content with a young barrister who was beginning his career.

Once the struggle had been decided on, Emilie seemed to take pleasure in the general excited anticipation of the great event. She felt herself to be the centre of attention, the principal heroine of a play, which she regarded as comedy rather than drama. She herself had discussions with her lawyers, always in the company of the master of Tholonet, the young Comte de Galliffet.

Her leading counsel was Pascalis, a man of fifty, with the fire of a Provençal and the roughness of a self-made man of humble origin. He was sufficiently conscious of his strength not to be moved easily by anything or anybody. His vigour of speech, sometimes brutal, was helped by his physical appearance, his height, his marked features, and the blazing glance that came from beneath his bushy eyebrows. His pleadings were battles in which he thrust at his adversary as though in mortal combat. He was pleased when he learned that Mirabeau, helped only

by the young Jaubert, had decided to conduct his own case: "We shall
have to goad him: he will rear up like a stallion, and we shall have him."

Another of Emilie's counsel was Portalis, a younger man than Pascalis.
He was no less violent than his colleague, and still more personal, pitiless, and sarcastic, searching with the skill of a fencer for the weak spot
in his adversary's armour. The eloquence of Pascalis was a matter of
sledge-hammer blows; Portalis distilled his words like drops of poison.

On the day that the Comtesse de Mirabeau returned her husband's
letter unopened, Mirabeau sent his petition to the lieutenant general of
the seneschalsy of Provence "that an injunction may be issued for Mme.
de Mirabeau to return to her husband within three days." M. de Mirabeau appealed and sued for a separation.

The sensational case had opened in that month of February 1783.
The private life of two noble families was to be exposed to full daylight in its most intimate weaknesses. The case of Aix became one more
exhibition of the evil that was eating away the social edifice; it revealed
hidden cracks and threw discredit upon those who claimed to be pillars of society. With so many other celebrated cases of the time, it was
one of the sources that nourished popular contempt and promoted
revolution. It brought nearer to the small man the bearers of great
names, who until then had been entrenched in their inaccessible existence. In this eagerness of great families to expose their vices there was
a sort of unconscious urge to suicide.

On March 20 Mirabeau addressed the lieutenant general of the
seneschalsy. It had to be determined where the Comtesse de Mirabeau
should reside during the hearing of her appeal. His pleading was prefaced
by a memorial entitled "Observations on behalf of the Comte de `Mira-
beau," which opened with a quotation from one of Emilie's letters—
"May God bring us together again soon, for we are not made to be
separated." The memorial was made up of letters received from his
wife in 1774 and 1775. "Without you the world is a desert for your
Emilie," she had written in one of these. After each quotation Mirabeau
commented: "And Mme. de Mirabeau, since writing that, has never
seen the husband from whom it is claimed that she wants to be separated."

The lawsuit at Aix, which was to end in so resounding a manner,
opened quietly enough. The public so crowded into the court that the
atmosphere was suffocating. Mirabeau was accompanied only by Lord
Peterborough and by another English friend. "Not a Frenchman dared
to show himself" at Mirabeau's side. Mirabeau complained of this os-

tracism in his pleading. "An effort has been made to turn the simplest of claims into a party suit, to rouse the public, to close every door to me, to prohibit me from seeing even my oldest and dearest friends; an effort has been made to rob me of all aid and all advice."

He pleaded with a warm, engaging voice, modulated to a tender melancholy, for the return to him of a loving but straying wife. Emilie's lawyers reproached him with having defamed her. But Mirabeau declared with chivalrous ardour: "Emilie de Mirabeau is capable of all honourable feelings and actions, she is capable only of those . . . and I have so much esteem for my wife that I confide my defence to her. In fact, gentlemen, for my whole argument, as its whole art and eloquence, I have had printed the only letters she has written me since the storms of my life separated us from each other." He added: "Just God! On what may a man's reputation depend! Eight months ago I did not possess one of these letters. Buried among the papers abandoned a thousand times in my unfortunate wanderings, they have been preserved for me by the faithful vigilance of a friend . . . and if they had not been brought back to me, I should have had to bend my head beneath the weight of an unanswerable slander. A town, a whole province, would have repeated it and credited it."

As he spoke his vibrant accents won over his audience. The Marquis de Marignane had taken stock of him at first with a sneer. But soon he was seized with concern, his expression changed entirely, and he listened with bent head. Mirabeau was pleading for Emilie's withdrawal from her father's influence, because "she cannot be called free in a house to which her obsessors are admitted, while the voice of her husband cannot be heard there." And he exclaimed ardently: "Thou who hast always loved me and hast never departed from my heart! Thou whom one glance would have brought back to me! Oh! blame only our common enemies for the melancholy past which thou art forcing me to play here. I groan under their compulsion, and never wert thou dearer to me. Have no fear of my victory, it is necessary to thy happiness or I should not want it. . . ." He was trying to move the woman who had trembled in his arms; to move the mother who had mourned his son. "Victor, the unhappy Victor who, if he were living, would ask for me, is he not crying to the depth of your soul, 'He is my father, and you are thrusting him away!'"

He had found words that went straight to men's hearts. Even the Marquis de Marignane, the bailli declared, wept in spite of himself.

The verdict of the court ordered Mme. de Mirabeau "to rejoin her husband provisionally or to retire to a convent where she should receive his visits." The public, which had been prejudiced against him, received the verdict with loud applause.

The Marignanes appealed to the *parlement*. But, said Mirabeau, "the counsellors of the *parlement* are accustomed to finding at the house of the Marquis de Marignane a family devoted to them, among whom they are regarded as the best of company." The young men of the *Chambre des Enquêtes* proved their own importance to themselves by openly pronouncing in salons and cafés against the Comte de Mirabeau. The *parlement* ordered a stay of execution.

Mirabeau presented a petition in reply to that of his wife, in which he contended that all the arguments she employed were irrelevant to the case. Emilie, for her part, introduced a demand for a separation. Her lawyers had now to speak. They prepared a terrible blow. Portalis, who was drawing up a memorial for the Comtesse de Mirabeau, had no scruple about making use of the letters from the Marquis de Mirabeau. Emilie communicated this memorial to the bailli as a last attempt at intimidation. She demanded that he should decide at once. If he did not agree to the separation the memorial would be issued to the public. The bailli, although he had known of these letters and was well aware of the excesses of his brother's pen, was dismayed at the violence of the resentment revealed by every phrase: "Where did you find all that you say here, declaring that I have the proof of it all, which is not the case? The devil of scribomania must have strangely possessed you when you wrote in that style." He saw once more the influence of his brother's "fatal entourage." But he returned the memorial without replying.

Distribution began at once. Through the good offices of the Comte de Galliffet a copy was placed in the nobles' café and another in that of the bourgeois. The public pounced upon it. Its success extended beyond the limits of the town. It was read with avidity in Paris. It was circulated beyond the frontiers. Copies were called for in London and Berlin. A few days after its publication it had to be reprinted.

"This scandalous attack," the Marquis de Mirabeau wrote to a friend, "made me go pale for the first time in my life." To a publication made up of quotations of love, Mirabeau's adversaries had replied with a collection of extracts of hatred. They denounced Mirabeau as "a bad father, a bad son, a bad husband, a bad citizen, and a dangerous person." In addition to this printed abuse, they neglected no means of attacking him. They succeeded in bringing his creditors into the field. "To prevent them from putting my nephew into prison for debt," the bailli wrote, "I have just pledged my cross"—the diamond cross of the Order of Malta.

But they did not succeed in ruffling Mirabeau. In his reply, entitled *Observations on a Defamatory Libel*, a document of two hundred pages, there growls the terrible wrath of a man who has kept perfectly cool. The *Observations* opened with a quotation from Cicero's Philippics: "What man, not deprived of all honesty, of all humanity, of all respect for the proprieties, what man will consider himself relieved by an unexpected disagreement from the duty of keeping secret the letters he has received?

"In our burning climate," wrote Mirabeau, "in which all the affections of the soul tend to excess and passions are roused to the point of atrocity, father-in-law and son-in-law have been seen duelling, and nature has trembled. But I do not know whether a father-in-law has ever been seen to constitute himself an informer against his son-in-law through the medium of his daughter, and on the strength of pretended proofs acquired through letters sent by his son-in-law's father. . . . Let the coward who would not prefer to be attacked with a dagger rather than with slander from his own family, let him who would not feel it easier to forgive the assassin who attacked his life than the libeller who attacked his honour, find this parallel exaggerated!"

As for the letters from the marquis, "obviously dictated by the wrath of a father justly irritated by the bad conduct of his son, but who, like all fathers, exaggerated both that misconduct and his own indignation," he declared that even if those letters were not contradicted by his disavowal, by his efforts, and by subsequent facts, "it would still be the most cowardly of outrages to have them published by the woman who bears my name. . . . What subtleties, what distinctions, what sophisms will disguise that infamy?" Yet, although wounded to the quick, he still showed consideration for Emilie. "The laws cannot refuse me my wife. I should be glad to get her away from those who are so greatly interested in separating us; I wanted to get her away and not to tear her to pieces."

9

The hearing opened with great solemnity in the Grand Chamber of the *parlement*. Since Mirabeau's arrival at Aix there had been a turn in his favour in public opinion. He had been supposed to be guilty of every sort of crime, and overweening in his claims, but the violence of his adversaries had put him in the position of a victim. However, the tribunal before which the struggle was taking place was more concerned for the interests of a clan than for justice.

It was in an atmosphere in which, as the daughter of Mme. de Vence put it, all the judges were "parties in this affair," that Portalis attacked Mirabeau. "Better be defamed than praised by you," was his opening thrust. He announced at the outset that he had "horrors" to reveal. He filled two entire hearings with them. It was a supreme bid in violence. He continually addressed Mirabeau instead of the court. He went beyond all limits.

The marriage with Mlle. de Marignane, he said, had been for Gabriel de Mirabeau one that exceeded his hopes. He had been led into it by the greediest and most sordid interest, the vilest cupidity. In support of what he said, Portalis produced with the triumphant address of a conjuror a letter from the Marquis de Mirabeau to his son, written at the time of his marriage, which had fallen, nobody knew how, into his hands. In this letter the marquis urged his son to conclude the marriage "by every possible means." Mirabeau interrupted with a request to be shown the letter. It was promised, but was never communicated to him.

His whole existence, Portalis continued, was due to Mme. de Mirabeau. But on the very day of the marriage he got drunk and ill treated his wife. Portalis enumerated a whole series of outrages, of infamies, of daily scenes, and of assaults on his victim. He spoke of debts, of extravagant living; but at the same time he alleged that Mirabeau had condemned his wife to hunger, even refusing her a soup for which she asked. When the young woman remonstrated, the brutal husband cuffed her.

After abusing her fortune and her person, he deceived her. After deceiving her, he defamed her.

But Portalis did not content himself with presenting Mirabeau as an unworthy husband. He painted him after their separation as a highwayman, lurking in the forests, disguised sometimes as an ecclesiastic, sometimes as a foreigner "wearing decorations," living in Holland at the head of a band of brigands. He painted him even as a murderer, and went on to attack the father as well as the son.

From then on it was for himself and for the honour of his family that Mirabeau fought. He prepared his reply to Portalis, no longer held back by any scruple. The bailli, too, was disgusted by the speech of Portalis and wrote to his brother: "The only reply now must be a refutation of these infamies and not a demand for that woman, who, believe me, must not enter our mother's house."

On May 23 Mirabeau made his speech in court. He went to the heart of the judicial issue, the suspension of the sentence that had ordered Mme. de Mirabeau to rejoin her husband. But at the same time he denounced the life Emilie was leading, the indulgent moral code of her father, and the habits of her associates.

Portalis had said that it would be unjust, indecent, and insulting to order Mme. de Mirabeau into a convent. Mirabeau took this up: "Yes, no doubt it is supremely just that a young and amiable woman should be the darling of a society to which all the young people of the town are admitted and from which her husband alone is excluded. . . . It is decent that a young woman who is suing for a separation should be the heroine of clubs and suppers and concerts, and even the heroine of a theatre."

He refused to enter into the war of insults that had been launched against him: "I have to be judged upon facts defined with precision, and not upon epithets." One by one he took up the grounds for complaint alleged by Mme. de Mirabeau in support of her suit. He quoted them, dissected them, ridiculed them, always with skill, admitting what he could not deny and minimizing it by his admission. Still with the same impressive calm, he refuted one by one the chapters of Mme. de Mirabeau's "defamatory work of fiction." Thoroughly master of himself, after quoting each item he said: "Let us take a breath and reply."

The voice was strong but always harmonious and well modulated, one of those sensuous voices that evoke multiple overtones in the human soul, stirring it and capturing it before the reason has been convinced. Everything served him in his art of oratory, even the defects with which he had been continually reproached—the vivacity of his reactions, an imagination that carried him away before it carried away the public, the skill with which he disposed of troublesome arguments from his adversaries, and the daring of a born gambler, who had the knack of transforming a bad card into a winning one.

He showed this daring in taking up the accusations contained in his father's letters. His father, he claimed, was not sufficiently detached to be able to discern the truth, "because he was accumulating at a distance all the gossip that was afflicting his fatherly heart, the gossip of which so many reckless voices have been the echoes in this province, the gossip which perhaps was born in its entirety here . . . so that my defamers, in relying on my father's letters, are relying as a rule on their own assertions."

But he did not confine himself to defence: he had decided to attack. "Mme. de Mirabeau accuses me of having slandered her. For whole years I have drunk to the lees from the inexhaustible cup of misfortune for not speaking ill of her, and I have slandered her! I had pardoned her, I wanted still to pardon her, but pardon would be cowardice today when my father has been outraged." He prepared to read a letter from Emilie. "Without any question, this letter would never have seen the light of day if Mme. de Mirabeau had not to expiate new faults, faults much graver in my eyes, before she can claim to resume the rank and the rights of a wife."

He read the letter breaking off relations with young Gassaud; it contained the admission of her adultery. Had Emilie informed her lawyers of her own lapses? Did she think her husband would never dare to accuse her? It almost seemed as if, with her capacity for dismissing anything from her mind, she had forgotten the very existence of this compromising document. The letter had the effect of an explosion. Emilie's lawyers were in consternation. The public was excited at the unexpected turn the case had taken. Evil tongues now got to work at Emilie's expense. All the concealed jealousies and secret envy pounced on this unexpected meal. Soon rumours were spreading throughout the province, swelled by invention.

Mirabeau recalled the circumstances of Emilie's lapse and of his pardon. "Mme. de Mirabeau paid homage to my moderation and praised my generosity, she who has just traced the most monstrous picture of my atrocious brutality."

He returned to his point of departure. "Well, gentlemen, shall we still be told that Mme. de Mirabeau should be sequestrated at her father's home, shall we still be told that that house is the sanctuary of morals, the chief asylum of innocence? . . . The man to whom the letter I have just made known was addressed lived for a whole winter at M. de Marignane's house, in the room that was intended for me—a room separated from that of Mme. de Mirabeau only by a dressing-room. . . . Such is the majesty, such is the sanctity of her father's house. The saintly and majestic father is too hospitable."

He came to the crucial issue, but in a manner dangerous to his own success. "Can a man who in examining his life includes the proceedings I have indicated . . . can he deign to call by the name of wife a woman capable of such ingratitude, capable of unheard-of perfidies that are an outrage upon me and my family?" He caught himself at once: "But it is not at the request of such a woman that a separation should be pronounced—or from now on wickedness will be a guarantee of success and the title of wife a patent of impunity for the most horrible calumnies and defamations." With this speech Mirabeau in very truth separated from Emilie.

Mirabeau now turned wrathfully upon the lawyer. "And you who interrogated me at such length through two whole hearings, answer now in your turn: Are not you the real author of this lawsuit?"

Mirabeau gave free reign to his long-suppressed indignation. All the humiliations he had suffered, all the outrages he had endured in silence, were now thunderously voiced. His wrath had the vehemence of the blind forces of nature. Everything in him seemed to serve these tempests of indignation—his Herculean stature, his swelling bull's-neck, his great head with its immense shock of hair, the swoop of his square shoulders, his broad and sonorous chest, and the powerful breathing that resounded as in a brazen bell.

Immobile on his bench sat Portalis, growing more and more livid under the claps of thunder that were breaking over him. Mirabeau spoke of the sublime mission of the lawyers who devote themselves to the defence of the oppressed. "But if one of them, sheltered by the impunity accorded and due to their profession, of which independence is the soul, is known only for the culpable ability, imbued always with alien passions, that is roused and calmed at their bidding, if his only eloquence is in vomiting abusive declamation, lies, passion, calumny, if he truncates or falsifies every document he quotes . . . such a man degrades himself from the freest of occupations to enslavement by the most servile of passions, and Martial has defined him for me: he is a dealer in lies, in rhetoric, and in abuse."

Portalis listened with tears of weakness or of rage in his eyes, and at the end of the hearing he collapsed. He was carried, insensible, out of the court. "Your brother," the marquis wrote to Caroline, "has won over the whole country, people and good judges; it is astonishing how that scallawag captures everybody."

His speech at Aix was the first step Mirabeau took in his climb to celebrity. He had carried on his own case, had taken revenge on Emilie, and had made her lawyer pay dearly for his infamies. But it was not his judges alone that he had addressed. He was aware that his words would have a wider influence, and one of more importance in his eyes.

10

Marie Antoinette's brother, the Archduke Ferdinand, governor of Milan, and his wife were travelling through France under the names of

Comte and Comtesse de Nollenbourg. The great attraction at Aix was the Mirabeau case. They expressed the desire to be present. The presence of the august visitors had its influence on the course of the proceedings, and especially on the attitude of the opposing party. Emilie was ready for the compromise which her husband proposed—a separation for two years, during which she would retire to a convent, on condition that at the next hearing he would exonerate her from the faults revealed in the letter he had read.

The arrival of the royal personages abruptly tilted the balance toward conciliation. Portalis, who had been in bed for some days, had spoken at the hearing on the day before. The tempest that had shaken him had brought wisdom. His tone had changed. From Mirabeau's violent accusations he drew the inference that "the husband has declared that he no longer wants Mme. de Mirabeau." He could not deny the existence of the compromising document, and contented himself with insinuating that the letter "was not written voluntarily and freely."

Mirabeau had prepared a rejoinder which he himself described as "vehement." The presence of the illustrious visitors, and the condition put forward by Emilie, made it necessary for him to redraft his speech. The threads that had seemed broken still held. Mirabeau seemed to hesitate to make a final break with his past aspirations and with all the facilities represented by his wife's fortune and social position. When he pronounced his great speech, he had felt, just as the bailli had done, that any further life together was impossible for the couple. But the chance that had brought the archduke to Aix seemed to give value to a destiny which would not be the same when he had lost Emilie. He seemed suddenly to recoil from a future in which he would find himself once more without money or support.

On June 17 the public crowded into the court. As he opened his speech, Mirabeau fixed his gaze on the archduke. Ferdinand greatly resembled his sister. The Comte de Mirabeau had no suspicion as yet that his path and the queen's would cross one day. But for him, as for so many other young aristocrats of the time, she was the very embodiment of grace and caprice and seduction. She was a sovereign and at the same time enveloped with a perfume of femininity. She herself had thrown down the barriers that surrounded her, and haunted unbridled imaginations, elusive and provoking, a delicious mirage for the frivolous and the ambitious.

Her image had now been brought into the proceedings at Aix. Mirabeau, as an accomplished courtier, saluted it. "Which of us, if he wished to consecrate here the living image of justice and to embellish it with all the charms of beauty, would not place here the august effigy of our queen? A happy chance offers us here her adored features, re-traced by nature herself. . . . We have all caught with delight that striking resemblance, and how it reassures my heart!" In the course of his speech he also slipped in a eulogy of the Empress Maria Theresa, as a model of love and of conjugal devotion. At the bar of a provincial tribunal, Mirabeau was showing his aptitude for the salons of Versailles.

But the influence of the visitors was yet more subtle. It suggested to him not only well-turned compliments, but emotions, perhaps forced, which ended by gaining control of him. In the presence of these illus-trious spectators, the temptation was great for him to play a handsome part. He displayed himself to the public as a magnanimous husband, sad-dened at having been obliged to overwhelm his wife. "Why did Mme. de Mirabeau, in her demented infatuation, choose to compel me to reveal all our domestic secrets? Oh God, God! What would I not give to be able to bury them in eternal oblivion? Why did she want to extract from me all these frightful truths? Why does she force me to speak to her only by addressing you, gentlemen, and the public?"

It was the voice of what his age called sensibility that was raised be-fore that audience by Mirabeau, tender, persuasive, emotional, and almost sincere, in his desire to win his case and to win over his public. He already possessed that art of the great orators, and also a certain ab-sence of shame that is a condition of it, the art of creating in the pres-ence of a numerous audience the factitious intimacy of a tête-à-tête.

For the last time he spoke directly to Emilie, for the last time he used the intimate "thou": "My passion for thee was too real not to penetrate thy soul. Thou art burning for me and thou hatest me, thou art tearing me. Nature has shown thee so sweet, so touching. Thy voice, thy gaze, soften a man and penetrate his soul. Can nature have lied so cruelly? There remains for thee one resource, there remains one alone, that of tearing thyself away from the vortex that has corrupted thee."

The plea of that ardent voice won men's hearts, and impressionable ladies wept over a great love misjudged. But Emilie was not deceived as to the quality of an emotion paraded before the public. She did not consider that she had been cleared of suspicion as Mirabeau had prom-ised; and she felt crushed by his tenderness no less than she had been by his wrath. She considered herself to be no longer bound by the compromise. The negotiations that had been proceeding out of court were broken off.

Mirabeau made one last effort to gain his wife. He printed a memorial which he addressed to his fellow-citizens and his judges.

But it was too late to bring his wife back to him. She seems to have nourished the ambition to bring her social talents into play in a vaster theatre than that at Aix, and to have dreamed of a place at court. She was angry with Mirabeau for having humiliated her in the presence of the brother of Marie Antoinette. The gulf between them was deepened yet more by the weight of a frustrated ambition.

Mirabeau worked obstinately to win his case out of *amour-propre* no less than because of the uncertainty of the morrow. In a last plea he addressed himself to his judges. He tried to move them by reminding them of the consequences their judgment would have for the *ami des hommes*. "Can anyone desire to inflict on that illustrious and unfortunate man in his old age the horrible grief of having immolated his son through an excess of confidence in his daughter-in-law?" He tried to fill them with pity for his own fate: "Are the sweet names of husband and father to be no longer applicable to me? And yet I was both! And it would be impossible for them to be pronounced any more in front of me without tearing my heart!" He foresaw the argument that his own accusation was liable to separate him forever from Emilie: "I offer her honour and peace, I forget her faults, I forgive even her calumnies. I have in no way inflicted such wounds on her soul as cohabitation must make worse. On the contrary, reunion alone can repair all the ills of the past; reunion alone can remove the slurs cast on her honour; reunion alone can bring forgetfulness for her imprudence."

At the moment when the hope of a home was eluding him forever, he felt all its value. "I shall be a good husband," he swore before his judges, "because, battered for so long by the billows of fate, I know better than anyone else that there is no other happiness than domestic happiness; all else is transitory." He also swore to them, "in the presence of the public that is giving me its good wishes, to regard the justice you are about to do me as a benefaction, and never to give reason to any man of feeling to regret what he has done as an inflexible magistrate."

The hearings ended. Nine magistrates deliberated on the judgment. The *avocat general* of the *parlement* of Aix had special reasons for gaining the favour of the Marignanes. He had belonged in the past to the brilliant company that assembled at Tholonet; he had played in theatricals with Mme. de Mirabeau; he had been excluded from that circle of the elect, and his one concern was to get back into it. "I need to be right forty times over," Mirabeau had said to his judges, "to win my case."

On July 5, 1783, they pronounced in favour of a separation. The magistrates of those days gave no reasons for their judgments, but from the notes left by one of them the tribunal had taken no account of the allegations of maltreatment or of notorious adultery on the part of the husband, and had based its judgment solely on a juridical pronouncement under which a husband who accuses his wife has no right to demand a reunion.

The judges also considered the question of the future residence of the Comtesse de Mirabeau. Opinions were divided among the prejudiced though they were in her favour: half of them demanded that she should be relegated to a convent. But a fresh vote was taken, and she was granted full liberty of movement.

In bitterness the bailli wrote to his brother: "It is Paris that ruined us here. It was your fine, useful traffic in letters that spoilt everything."

Mirabeau was staggered. He was tossed between violent resentment and utter discouragement. But if he had lost his case, he had won renown. "The ancients were right," he wrote to Brissot later, "in deifying the talent of oratory. The public, always extreme, ranged itself on my side to the point of idolatry. Applause pursued me at the palace, on the promenades, at the theatre. In fact, I have become a sort of demagogue of the province, and the winner of the case is in flight, while the loser is proclaimed aloud the illustrious unfortunate." But he ended in discouragement: "You may well imagine that these melancholy successes do not turn my head, especially as an insurrection never amounts to anything in France."

The Comtesse de Vence consoled him with the shrewd vision that comes from a great attachment: "Enthusiasm can carry far the man who has the good fortune to be its object."

II

The lawsuit at Aix ended with what the Marquis de Mirabeau maliciously called "a breaking of wind." On the evening of the day when judgment was given, Mirabeau provoked a duel with the Comte de Galliffet. He charged him with having defended Emilie's interests with too much warmth. He was also concerned to clear himself of a suspicion that weighed on him, arising from a letter from his father, inserted in the memorial of the Comtesse de Mirabeau, in which the marquis insinuated that his son would not go in search of fights because he had no love for them.

The duel caused a sensation at Aix. The Comte de Galliffet was slightly wounded in the arm by a sword thrust. Mirabeau wanted a second meeting, but the authorities intervened. Mirabeau then went to the fountain of Vaucluse, in the papal territory. But he waited for his adversary in vain. Next day the Comte de Galliffet received a present of crabs, "because nobody can teach them better than you how to walk backwards."

This time, too, public opinion was on Mirabeau's side; the populace was "ready to stone" his adversary.

But the glorious loser at Aix was faced once more with agonizing uncertainty about the future. He was more alone than ever. The bailli, deeply discouraged, abandoned him. "I have never succeeded in anything," he wrote, "whatever zeal and care, constancy and devotion, I have expended on it. Always I have thought only of my family, never of myself. I put up with the first extravagances of my nephew's marriage, and here is the result." He felt that his brother blamed him for the loss of the case. "Well, the thing is lost and our name is extinguished. There remains an appeal. You must send for your son to try that. Besides, there is nothing more for him to do here, or for me: the affair has cost me six months of my time, and my repose, and my health, and about twenty thousand francs thrown away; so, let him go to you; it is your turn; I have done more than my share."

But the Marquis de Mirabeau never forgave a defeat. He would not forgive his son for the fading away of his dreams of posterity. He refused to admit his share of responsibility. Curtly he informed his son, once for all, that he would have nothing to do with an appeal. "If he comes to my door, he will find there a letter for him signifying my intentions. . . . He will stay where he likes, not with me. For the rest, I will receive him when he wants to speak to me, so that he shall not knock at every door to be admitted. Apart from that, nothing more, for I have not the slightest desire to hear further about his affairs, either in white or in black."

This was the end of the stormy relations between father and son, definitive rupture. "His ways are no longer mine," the marquis wrote to the Minister Amelot. "I must return into your hands a warrant by which my son was put under my orders in regard to his place of residence. He is thirty-four years old. I can no longer serve him or guide him or answer for him."

Mirabeau decided to continue the struggle alone, and to appeal to the Council of State at Versailles. He gained the support of some distinguished jurists in Paris, including a future minister, and with their aid he printed a memorial which he sent to the members of the Council of State.

"An upright man," he wrote, "can only want to remain on the scene when there is a possibility of serving his fellow-men. Nevertheless, when the injustices which one brings before the tribunal of the public (the tribunal that judges all the judges, all the great of the earth) concern individual liberty, the dearest property of every citizen, in a word, the supreme rights of human nature, then the repugnance which a man possessed of a measure of shame feels at occupying others with his private affairs must give way before the duty of speaking, of sustaining, of publishing every useful truth to the defence of which his situation calls him."

This was a new language, these were the ideas of the morrow, and they easily obtained support from a public more and more conscious of its role of supreme tribunal.

The Marquis de Marignane took alarm. He hastened with his daughter to Paris to fight his son-in-law on the spot. He secured from the Keeper of the Seals the suppression of the memorial. Mirabeau asked for an audience with the Keeper of the Seals, M. de Miromesnil. He tackled him on this "arbitrary" suppression.

"Begin, Monsieur, by striking out of your dictionary the word 'arbitrary,' " said the Keeper of the Seals.

"Monsieur, I knew that you were the head of the administration, but not that you were the censor of my dictionary," retorted Mirabeau.

"But, Monsieur, this word 'arbitrary' is very strange."

"Yet, permit me to tell you, it is one of the most used in the country," was Mirabeau's biting rejoinder. He added: "I know nothing more alarming than to see united in the same person the character of magistrate and that of satellite of despotism. I know nothing more horrible than to be assassinated by the authorities."

M. de Miromesnil explained with much patience to his vehement visitor that a regulation of the Council prohibited the printing of petitions of appeal until both sides had been heard, and he took refuge behind this usage.

"There cannot be at the very foot of the throne a usage contrary to the laws," exclaimed Mirabeau. "Everybody prints memorials in appeal cases, as you know; you approve it, you even recommend it to those whom you protect. For me alone, you recall today that there is a regulation that can deprive me of the only means of rebutting calumny and of being heard in my defence. Certainly the method is not new; but the custom is cruelly ingenious."

"Monsieur, you are not a judge of customs," said the Keeper of the Seals, losing patience.

"No, Monsieur, but the king is."

"Very well, Monsieur, go and complain to him of his regulations."

Mirabeau thus entered into open conflict with the authorities. He was carrying on at the same time a struggle with his father. He wanted to regularize his financial position. But the father claimed that Gabriel was liable for the very heavy expense incurred for the services of the police in tracking him down. In the end Mirabeau obtained an annual allocation of three thousand livres. The final settlement was the subject of a lawsuit that dragged on for years.

While M. de Marignane was carrying on his campaign in Paris, Emilie suddenly felt a desire to revisit the room she had occupied in her father-in-law's house. The Marquis de Mirabeau, although he was away from Paris, refused to give permission for this. But at the same time he profited by her move to suggest to Caroline that she should induce her brother to make one last approach to his wife. But Mirabeau was much more anxious to win his case than to regain the stake involved. When Caroline spoke to him, "he replied by laughingly changing the subject and talking of his memorial."

"I am persuaded and even certain that he has more or less duped the whole lot of us, and that he did not want his wife at all," the marquis wrote later.

Mirabeau addressed a letter to the king, in a tone as far removed as possible from that of a supplication; it never reached the monarch. With a haughtiness that nothing seemed yet to justify, he declared: "I announce, and my prediction will not be belied: a day will come when the whole nation will know the story of my case, and my voice, long used to bold truths, will disclose all the details of the most odious hatreds that have ever dishonoured the judicial order and the temple of justice."

Mirabeau was to keep his word. Through him the lawsuit at Aix, one of the numberless cases of his time, passed into history.

But at that time his voice was stifled yet once more. His petition in appeal did not even reach the Council of State, being rejected at the outset by the officials. The Marignanes had powerful friends not only in Provence but at Versailles.

In spite of this set-back Mirabeau went on with his struggle against arbitrary jurisdiction. He had his memorial reprinted in Holland, "out of respect for the king and for justice," adding to it his lively exchange with the Keeper of the Seals. The denial of justice he had suffered drove him along the path of revolt. Thenceforward he identified himself with the mass of the oppressed. He felt that he had with him all the victims of despotism. Each one of those who had suffered from injustice "can

and should consider himself thereafter as a defender of society," he said
in the introduction to his memorial; "each one should see in his own
cause that of all his fellow-citizens."

⊰ VIII ⊱

Here the People Count

WHEN Franklin reached Paris, one of his first visits was to the
Marquis de Mirabeau. He fascinated the marquis, as he did all the
Economists. They extolled him particularly because he was a living confirmation of their theories on the virtues of an agricultural country,
which he represented, and on the philosophic dignity of a rural life as
opposed to that of the trading English, crowded together in big towns.
"Even in the palace of Versailles," wrote Mme. de Campan, the queen's
lady-in-waiting, "at the exhibition of Sèvres porcelain, where the king
himself could see it, Franklin's medallion was being sold, with its legend:
'*Eripuit caelo fulmen sceptrumque tyrannis*'—'He tore down the lightning from heaven, and their sceptres from the tyrants.' "
This motto was the work of the king's minister, the Economist Turgot. But it was especially the women, the women of society, who made
of the American sage the idol of the salons, and who made a nation of
pioneers the height of fashion. This craze was illustrated by an incident recorded in the police registers: a libertine, who had been courting
a belle without success, painted wrinkles on his face and, dressed as a
Quaker, won the favour of the lady. The Duchesse Diane de Polignac
was one of the most ardent of Franklin's women admirers. Louis XVI,
with his homely good sense, felt instinctively the danger for the French
monarchy of this exaltation of the apostle of the American Republic.
He ridiculed it in his coarse way. According to Mme. de Campan, he
"had a chamber-pot made at Sèvres with the medallion and the famous
motto reproduced inside it, and he sent it as a New Year's present to
the Duchesse Diane."
In his house in the suburb of Passy the sage of the New World received all Paris like a sovereign. His judgments, always balanced, his
dicta, full of sturdy common sense, were like a breath of fresh air

brought into the perfumed atmosphere of the salons. His unshakable optimism was contagious; the two little words which he had used so often in talking to his French friends in America in the darkest hours of his country's struggles, "*ça ira*"—"so it goes"—caught on in Paris. Very soon those two words were to become the refrain of a song of the Revolution.

Young aristocrats were among his most faithful disciples. The young Duc de La Rochefoucauld saw in him a prophet of a new faith; he offered his services as Franklin's secretary, and translated into French those evangels of freedom, the constitutions of the new American states. There were other adepts of this new faith in the powerful Noailles family. The grand old man's violent hostility to any sort of aristocracy did not worry these disciples. They were ready to forget his curious calculation, destroying the very basis of pride in lineage, that the ancestral blood disappears after a few generations.

Franklin's attention was drawn to the Comte de Mirabeau. In the villa in Passy after the establishment of the Order of the Cincinnatus in America, Franklin talked with Mirabeau about his hostility to this anti-Republican trend in the newly formed republic, and Franklin passed over to him what he had written on the subject and gave him all necessary data. When Mirabeau set to work on the material he felt that he was simply expressing his own ideas.

2

There was nothing in the circumstances in which Nicolas-Sébastien Roch Chamfort came into the world that could suggest either his career or his end. Everything about him, including his name, was borrowed, as though modelled on a greater destiny. He was an interloper in a social class, out of his element in its prosperity, out of his element in that century, of which he was an outstanding intellectual representative, out of his element even in the mode of his death. He came into the world without rank or fortune, "without birth," as the phrase then went. He won prosperity and celebrity, and tired of them so quickly that he applauded the cause that robbed him of them, as though he had been impatient to lose all that he had gained.

He was the son of an unmarried mother, a lady's companion of Auvergne, who managed to get him a bursary at a college in Paris, where he was known simply as Nicolas. He distinguished himself there by his precocious intelligence and by a dangerous independence of mind. He and another youth ran away from the college to seek their fortune in Normandy. He returned from his escapade sobered by his first contact with life's problems. He had no choice but to become an abbé: in his phrase, it was a costume, not a calling.

"I shall never be a priest," he said to the principal of the college. "I am too fond of ease, of philosophy, of women, of honour and true glory; and not fond enough of quarrels, of hypocrisy, of honours and money." Here was the whole programme of his life in the mouth of this adolescent.

In order to carry it out he fought his way through poverty, hackwork, sermons written for preachers, obscure journalism. He often went short of necessaries to lighten his mother's hard lot.

Nature had compensated him for having come into a hostile world so naked and destitute of everything. She had given him regular features, a rare physical and moral grace, a charm and wit that were to be the undoing of women and the admiration of a society that exchanged epigrams like precious gifts. With his precocious sureness of judgment he saw his way clearly before him. At a time when he was almost penniless he said to a friend: "Here am I, just a poor devil; well, do you know what will become of me? I shall gain a prize from the Academy; my comedy will succeed, I shall find myself launched into the world and welcomed by the great whom I despise. They will make my fortune without my doing anything, and then I shall live as a philosopher."

His programme was carried through to the letter. He received the prize of the Academy, and had success with a pleasant comedy of no great moment. A conventional tragedy brought him the protection of the Prince de Condé and material security. Women made it their business to transform his literary repute into celebrity.

The wits raved over him. He was irreplaceable, unique in a world that knew but one social vice, that of being dull. His literary production was of no particular value, but he himself was a living masterpiece of cultured wit. "He is the flint I needed for my musket," said Mirabeau when the two became friends.

Chamfort owed perhaps his greatest success to the open contempt he showed for those who made his success. A society that took nothing seriously, least of all itself, loved laughing at its own expense. His free and easy manner stopped short at nothing and at nobody. Marie Antoinette said to him one day: "Do you know, Monsieur de Chamfort, you have pleased everybody at Versailles, I will not say *by* your wit, but in spite of it." "Quite simple," replied Chamfort. "At Versailles I resign myself to learning lots of the things I know from people who don't know them."

This fundamental contempt of the environment to which he owed everything, of the epoch of which he was himself the incarnation, and of the prosperity he enjoyed, became Chamfort's dominant trait. His best friends were amiable representatives of the abuses and vices of the time. After escaping with a great deal of trouble from his dependence on the Prince de Condé, he accepted the hospitality of the Comte de Vaudreuil, who owed his position and his fortune to being the lover of the Duchesse de Polignac.

He was over forty when he allied himself with Mirabeau. Their friendship seems to have grown with lightning rapidity. Chamfort declared to Mirabeau one day that he was "one of those who have best understood me." Amid the flagrant contradictions of Chamfort's life, Mirabeau had realized the inflexibility of his character, with a feeling almost of envy. In the presence of this man, not much older than himself, he felt his own youthful uncertainty, his ill-regulated passions, his unformed ideas; he felt backward for his age. His contribution to this friendship was his enthusiasm, his expansive affection, his almost tender solicitude for his friend's health and for the sentimental perplexities amid which Chamfort was always struggling.

But he received more from Chamfort than he gave him: Chamfort enabled him to find himself and showed him his path. Mirabeau, who could be almost passionately ardent in friendship, received proofs of affection that showed how he had suffered from indifference. To him Chamfort was more than an oracle of taste, of literary mastery, and of social *savoir-faire*. But Chamfort, in spite, or perhaps because, of the ease with which he had made his way in a world he despised, still felt the resentment of the de-classed. In his epigrams, his anecdotes, his maxims, he distilled social criticism like a poison. He precipitated his friend's reactions. He was revolution incarnate, in spite of his enjoyment of what revolution would destroy. He awaited its coming, warned by the acute sensitiveness which his friends later called a prophetic vein. He was to acclaim it as men welcome personal deliverance.

From putting ideas into the heads of his friends in the aristocracy, he proceeeded to coin slogans for the revolutionary forces. He endowed the troops who were fighting for the greatness of a new France with one of those phrases that win battles—"War on the castles, peace to the cottages." He sacrificed nothing of his independence to an absolute regime, and later he refused equally to bend to revolutionary despotism. He satirized the vagaries of a popular government with the same wit with which he had castigated the vices of an aristocratic society. Coming to an inscription traced on the walls everywhere, "Fraternity or death," he remarked with a smile: "Be my brother, or I'll kill you."

He had been a revolutionary in the palace of the Comte de Vaudreuil, he took the risk of figuring as an enemy of the people under the Terror. The zeal of an informer brought him to prison. After a few days he left prison with the horror of a man who preferred death to any infringement of his liberty. When he believed himself to be threatened with re-imprisonment, he escaped from his watchers and tried to blow out his brains. All he did was to destroy one eye. Finding himself mutilated but still alive, he seized a razor and tried to cut his throat. His trembling hand did no more than inflict deep wounds. He tried then to open a vein. But it was not given to him to die a classic death. He had the strength to jest on his failure as a suicide: "In honour of Seneca I tried to open my veins; but Seneca was a rich man; he had everything he could want, a good warm bath, and, in short, every convenience; as for me, I am hard up; I have none of those things; I have hurt myself badly, and here I am still."

A little later he succumbed to the effects of his attempt. But he died, as he had been determined to live, with this declaration: "I am a free man."

The Revolution was speaking already through the mouths of Mirabeau and Chamfort in the year 1784, from which their friendship dated. The revolutionary writers found no more violent terms for castigating the aristocracy than are to be found in the pamphlet on the Order of Cincinnatus, written by Mirabeau with the assistance of Chamfort. Mirabeau read the pamphlet to Franklin in July 1784, in the presence of his friend, in the villa at Passy. Franklin expressed his approval.

3

"To lend six francs one must have them, and on my honour I haven't as much," wrote Mirabeau to a friend. He was obliged to pawn at the Mont-de-Piété his "coat embroidered with silver with vest and breeches and his half-mourning vest of cloth of silver, and all his winter lace." He tried desperately to get money. He had urged Chamfort to expedite the work on the Order of Cincinnatus, for he was "dying of hunger and speculating on the pamphlet."

The disorder of his finances was equalled only by that of his amours. At the beginning of the year he had received a letter from a lady whom he had not seen for fifteen years; in it she artfully revived pleasant memories of the past. Mirabeau had perhaps forgotten her, but on receiving this tender letter he imagined that he had always loved her. He replied with his customary effusiveness; the correspondence went on, and flames leaped from the ashes. The Marquise de Saint-Orens asked him to visit her on her estate in Dauphiné. Mirabeau was in the throes of painfully carving out a new existence in Paris. But never in his life could he resist an amorous adventure. Abruptly he abandoned his work and left Paris to shut himself up with her in the country for a whole month.

The adventure threatened to turn into tragedy. His mistress had a jealous husband, whose suspicions had been aroused. He followed Mirabeau to Paris and demanded an explanation.

The old Marquise de Mirabeau, who had quarrelled with her son over money matters, revenged herself by taking an unhealthy interest in his amours. "Hell," wrote Mirabeau to a friend, "is vomiting perfidies and horrors of every sort on my path. After trying in vain for a fortnight to force me into a duel with M. de Saint-Orens, whom I threatened yesterday to throw out of the window if he came near me again, my mother has been trying to embroil me with the Baron de Martzan. She has told his wife that I had said to her, and to you and your wife, who were ready to certify it, that I had been in bed with the baronne, and that I had talked outrageously about it."

Mirabeau was still busy with his appeal in his wife's lawsuit. He was faced with responsibilities which he could see no means of meeting. One of his many liaisons of the time following his release from Vincennes, when he had lived like a famished animal, had left him with a child on his hands, a little boy of three, repudiated by the man whose name he bore. Mirabeau had taken the child into his care.

At this moment when "everything was against me, parents, friends, and fortune," at the very moment when "everyone had abandoned" him, destiny placed salvation in his path in the guise of a pretty woman.

4

In the Maison des Petites-Orphelines, a secular convent, the refuge of so many well-to-do solitaries, a young foreigner had taken shelter. Almost a child, she was alone in the world, without family, without social position, almost without a name. She was the illegitimate child of a Frenchwoman of obscure origin and an illustrious Dutchman. Her father, Willem van Haren—statesman, philosopher, humanist, and well-known poet—after an eventful life, a life of distinction and luxury and many amorous adventures, in the course of which his fortune had melted away, succumbed to the persecutions of his enemies and killed himself. His three-year-old daughter was cared for after his death by his brother, Onno Zwier van Haren, himself a celebrated poet, patriot, and statesman, one of the shining lights of the Dutch democratic party. But he, too, died prematurely. The young girl settled in Paris, with a small income sufficient for her needs.

From the sorrows that had saddened her childhood and the trials she had suffered there had emerged a softly radiant being, as though woven of light on a background of gloom. She had a slender figure, with a deceptive appearance of fragility; a long face with finely chiselled regular features; a mass of ash-blond hair with golden glints; and sparkling blue eyes, lent a darker shade by their contrast with a clear, almost transparent complexion. She was touching in her pale loveliness, making an unconscious appeal to the protective instinct of the men who made her acquaintance.

The Marquis de Mirabeau wrote: "All who have seen her say she is charming and has a pitiful candour." She had all the qualities her appearance promised—a good-heartedness easily called into play, a smiling sweetness, a ready adaptability, an unfailing courtesy. But she was not merely an example of charming and fragile femininity. Under the influence of the distinguished man who had watched over her childhood, her own character had developed and strengthened. Obliged at an early age to count only on herself, she had acquired a sense of responsibility, and responsibilities seemed, indeed, to attract her rather than frighten her. The sufferings of her youth had so steeled her that misfortunes and weaknesses in others moved her more than force impressed her. Her physique and her position seemed to call for protection, but in truth the longing to give protection was her dominant trait, a maternal instinct as strongly developed in this young girl as in a mature woman, a tenderness, not entirely free from a sense of superiority, that rejoiced in its own exercise. She seemed a skein of silk thread, lustrous and flexible; but she was fundamentally steel.

Into the tranquil convent in which Henriette Amélie van Haren was living there came like a whirlwind one fine morning the Marquise de Saint-Orens. She had formed a friendship with the young girl some years earlier; she knew her kindness and good nature, and thought she could make use of her as an excuse to her husband for her sudden departure for Paris. The girl was away when the marquise arrived, and on her return she found the marquise installed in her quarters, with her maid and lackey, expecting her lover. Henriette had the greatest difficulty in the world in making her visitor understand that she could not stay at the convent because men were not admitted there after dark. The marquise sent a letter to her lover telling him of her young friend's refusal.

Mirabeau arrived fuming against an insignificant being who was thwarting their plans. He did not make a good impression at that first meeting. Henriette, expecting to see a man whose seductive qualities could bring an upheaval in a woman's life, saw before her a monster of ugliness, whose atrocious frown made him all the more repulsive. "I found his face inconceivably unpleasing; I recoiled in fright," she confessed later. But the monster himself, calming down, or trying to efface an unfavourable impression, smiled with "a smile full of grace" and suddenly revealed in his ravaged face "a charming mouth." Lit up by that smile, his strong features showed their mobility, in accord with his vivacity and his vibrant accents. His voice was the more eloquent since he was trying not only to win over his mistress's friend but to bring her to do a thing that was repugnant to her. Their first conversation was a pitched battle. Henriette van Haren showed him from the very first her own strength of will. The Marquise de Saint-Orens did not stay at the convent. But Mirabeau succeeded in persuading the young girl to join the marquise in furnished rooms, and to write to the husband to explain his wife's departure and to persuade him to join her in Paris.

This arrangement brought the two together frequently. Mirabeau had warmed the girl's heart by speaking with ardent and sincere admiration of her uncle, whom he had known in Holland. With the emotionalism of that epoch, which wept easily and was proud of it, he was himself moved to tears at the sight of her weeping for the protector of her childhood.

It may be that Mme. de Saint-Orens had not noticed that her young friend was dangerously pretty. But she soon discovered that Henriette had an intelligence that impressed her lover, and the intellectual seductiveness which, in a pretty woman, makes a man think that he has never been so well understood, so deliciously appreciated.

Henriette was not in the least on her guard against her friend's lover, who was for her "sacred, a brother, a friend." He himself may not have known yet that he loved her, that her presence had become indispensable to him. But Mme. de Saint-Orens had the intuition of jealousy. Henriette found her suddenly changed and astonishingly frigid. She felt herself in the way and left her friend, without explanation and without reproaches. Her departure marked the end of an old friendship and the beginning of a new passion.

Thereafter Mirabeau went every day to her convent. Often he spent four or five hours with her. He had been too delicate or too clever to speak of his love so long as she was living with his mistress. "I should have been furious," she said with her liking for straightforwardness, which made her so concerned for moral principles and even for the conventions. In the austere surroundings of a convent parlour with its grille, she seemed to him so pure and so inaccessible that his desire was transformed into sincere affection.

Henriette was impressed by this assault of strong and true feeling, but she resisted. Mirabeau's eroticism awakened no echo in her placid soul. In her girlish dreams love had never appeared to her in this form of ardent passion. The hero of her dreams was not to be supplanted by the tormented features of Mirabeau. "I felt sure that he was not quite the man my heart needed," she said in her precise, measured, almost banal style.

In face of this resistance a passion took root in a heart tired by easy conquests. The contempt for women which Mirabeau owed to his unhappy childhood still existed alongside his furious thirst for love. But this girl, with her mixture of reserve and trusting openness, inspired respect in him. She was an infinitely precious thing in his eyes, a thing he never tired of adoring.

The tempest in his spirit did not catch up Henriette; his adoration touched her, "but I was not in love with him," she said later. "What determined my course above all else was his misfortune."

In telling the story of their love many years later, Henriette certainly idealized herself, but she was not far from the truth. She did not yield to Mirabeau out of readiness for sacrifice, as Sophie had done. Amid the tenderness inspired in her by his material and moral distress, her consciousness of her own value, her pride in strength of soul, was confirmed. She yielded because she knew that he needed her, and because that conviction exalted her. "I was all that remained to him," she said, "and I intended to take the place of all else for him."

In her hatred of Henriette, Mme. de Saint-Orens allied herself with the Marquise de Mirabeau. The two did their utmost to destroy this girl. One day Mirabeau disappeared again from Paris, and a friend, who was also an intimate friend of Chamfort, the Comte d'Antraigues, received a letter dated from Brussels, explaining this precipitate departure. "In her mad jealousy my mother so distorted everything with everybody that I suddenly found myself leaving for Brussels simply in order to carry off a pretty woman menaced with a *lettre de cachet*." Henriette relates that she had gone away with him as a friend. She returned from the journey as his mistress. She was free to do as she chose;

there was nothing to deter her and nobody to dissuade her. "I sacrificed a tranquil life to join in his stormy career with the peril that surrounded it."

In Belgium Mirabeau printed the memoir against his wife that had been suppressed in France by the Keeper of the Seals. Henriette van Haren was caught up in the difficulties and disorder of his existence. From the first she courageously faced their material difficulties. In Brussels they were without resources, and she found herself obliged to await the arrival of a regiment in which she had relatives from whom she hoped to get financial assistance.

When they returned to Paris—the danger of a *lettre de cachet* seems to have been conjured up or exaggerated by her lover's imagination—they took with them the edition of the memoir which had been printed at Maastricht and stored it near the city. Mirabeau had forbidden Henriette to take charge of that compromising work. But when they had sufficiently got past the barriers he was sorry he had done so. "We might at least," he said, "have got a dozen copies through with us. God knows when I shall be able to get the package, and distribution is becoming urgent."

"Don't worry," she replied. "There are two hundred in Paris at this moment." Without a word to her lover, lest she should alarm him, she had squeezed copies into their trunks, beneath the cushions of their carriage, and under her own clothes. Mirabeau overflowed with gratitude. He never departed afterwards from this attitude of exuberant admiration for her. Henriette wrote that she had "sworn to exist only for him, to follow him everywhere, to expose herself to anything in order to do him service in good or evil fortune." She kept her word. "I swear to you, my friend," Mirabeau wrote to Chamfort, "I swear to you in all the sincerity of my soul that I am not good enough for her, and that her soul is of a superior order in tenderness, delicacy, and goodness."

5

Mme. de Nehra—so she called herself from then on, in an anagram of her father's name, and so she passed into history—took her lover's affairs into the firm and capable control of her own fair hands. She made him leave an expensive flat and install himself in a modest one. He let her have her way, though he did not hide his discontent, complaining of the distance from his business and his colleagues: "I would just as soon be in Siberia." She looked after the housekeeping herself. Her solid bourgeois virtues proved a precious asset in their state "of the cruellest penury." She took pride in the humblest household tasks, including looking after his washing. All the bills passed through her hands, and he gave her all the money he got.

A spirit of order came into Mirabeau's existence, for the first time. Her unshakable good sense reduced to proper proportions the excesses of his imagination. He was never to have a peaceful existence except during the time he lived with Henriette-Amélie, whom he called by the melodious pet name of Yet-Lie. Months passed in a calm happiness that triumphed over financial difficulties.

Nothing could diminish the devotion or the courage of Yet-Lie. Soon she was looking after her lover's child, whom its mother had abandoned. Jean-Marie-Nicolas, said Gabriel, was nominally the son of the sculptor Lucas de Montigny, who had made a bust of Mirabeau. The child had been so neglected that at three years of age he could scarcely walk or talk. He was a little savage who had to be tamed. "That child," said Mirabeau to a Genevese friend, "has a fierce soul." And his friend remarked maliciously: "He thought that whoever had Mirabeau blood in him was bound to be extraordinary. I caressed the child and I was quite surprised that the little animal took my hands not to bite them but to kiss them. . . . He seemed to me gentle and easy to manage with a little care and affection." Yet-Lie lavished affection on this child of another woman. In spite of her youth—she was barely nineteen—she managed the child with the skill of a mature woman and the unfailing tenderness of a mother. She saved him from the over-severity from which Gabriel de Mirabeau had suffered. Thanks to her, the child had the happiness of a kind home.

Amid this comfort and felicity Mirabeau lost the combativeness with which he had started his fight against Emilie. He now took little interest in the matter, scarcely went near the judges, and perhaps had become afraid of winning the case. At all events he was not disturbed in the slightest when he learned that he had lost it. But his memoir had infuriated the Keeper of the Seals. Mirabeau learned that the minister was seeking vengeance and threatening him with a *lettre de cachet.* "This news," wrote Mme. de Nehra, "true or false, we never knew the truth of the matter, was sufficiently important to send us in search of a refuge."

In this hour of distress Mirabeau remembered his childhood friends from England. Hugh Elliot, the younger of two brothers who had been with him at the Abbé Choquard's school, was now Minister Plenipotentiary at Copenhagen. The sensation produced by Mirabeau's *Lettres de cachet* had interested Elliot in his former schoolfellow. He asked a friend whom he met at Copenhagen to ask Brissot, who was then in London, to give him news of Mirabeau. Youthful memories awakened in the English diplomat his old affection for his turbulent friend. He sent a message to him that he would be glad to offer him asylum in England and the protection, if needed, of a diplomatic career.

Brissot hastened to communicate this generous offer to Mirabeau. The letter reached Mirabeau at the moment of the failure of his appeal in the Aix lawsuit. It touched him deeply. "Only that nation," he wrote to Brissot, "shows such traits of humanity and generosity; and even in that nation it must be rare for a young man—Elliot is no older than I am—to be moved by the sufferings of a friend whom he has not seen for seventeen or eighteen years, and to want to wrest from despotism a victim foreign to his country."

But he could not accept Elliot's offer, and he gave Brissot a long and frank explanation of the reasons. "If it had been in my power to realize the smallest part of the fortune that must come to me one day, the sight and touch of a slave country would not have polluted me much longer. . . . But I cannot be a burden on anybody, on Elliot no more than on anybody else." He saw, however, a possibility: "If Elliot has sufficient credit at the court of Copenhagen or with any other prince in the north to get me some sort of appointment. . . . The career is less brilliant, no doubt, than in England, but it is less exclusive, if I may say so. In England one has to be English; in the north it is often enough to be French."

Brissot communicated Mirabeau's reply to Elliot. But Elliot's readiness to be of service seemed to have evaporated. Mirabeau was deeply disappointed. But at the moment when he believed that he was threatened with a *lettre de cachet*, he had no other choice left. He decided to try his luck in England, though without much hope.

6

"When I feel myself getting annoyed, I recall the Arab fable: 'I had always complained of the blows of fate and of the unkindness of men. I had no shoes and no money to buy any. I went to the Mosque at Damascus. There I saw a man who had no legs. I praised God, and no longer complained of having no shoes.' " So wrote Mirabeau to Chamfort from London.

Shortly after reaching London, Yet-Lie fell ill. She had attacks of intermittent fever, followed by a nervous breakdown; she became extremely weak, and they were obliged to call a doctor, at heavy expense.

Still, Mirabeau was enthusiastic about England. "We have been going through the most beautiful country in Europe, in its varied landscapes and verdure, in the beauty and richness of the fields and the tidiness and elegance of each property," he wrote to Chamfort. "The approaches to London are of a rural beauty of which even Holland shows nothing comparable (I should be more inclined to compare with it some of the Swiss valleys). I was strongly and profoundly moved at the sight of these rich and prosperous scenes, and I asked myself, why this novel emotion? These country houses, compared with ours, are country cottages; many French cantons, even the most ordinary ones, and the whole of Normandy, through which I have just been, have certainly more natural beauty than these fields . . . and yet I am much more enchanted by them than astonished by the others! . . . The universal care and neatness is an eloquent symptom of well-being. . . . Everything tells me that here the people count, that here every man is able to develop his faculties and to make free use of them, so that here I am in a different order of things."

London, "apart from the superb Thames (which must not be compared with anything because nothing is comparable with it)," seemed to him, in spite of its size, "ordinary and almost mean." He was impressed only by the pavements: "Praise God! here is a country in which the pedestrian is looked after."

The couple installed themselves in furnished rooms looking over Saint James's Park. They had brought Yet-Lie's maid and Mirabeau's valet-secretary, Hardy.

Hugh Elliot was still at Copenhagen. Sir Gilbert, his brother, had sent his family to Bath to escape the heat of London, but he himself returned to the capital from time to time. Sir Gilbert wrote to his brother after the first meeting that he had found "our persecuted old schoolfellow as ardent as when I left him, and as little changed as could be by twenty years of which six were passed in prison and the rest in domestic and personal upsets. His talents, which are really very great, have ripened a good deal, and he has acquired a great fund of knowledge." But he found him "as direct in his conversation, as awkward in manners, as ugly-faced and badly turned out in his person, as dirty in his clothing, and with all that as self-satisfied, as we remember him at school twenty years ago; yet I liked him then," he added, "and so did you, although he recognizes that sometimes you argued with him because you had not always as much patience as I to accept his excessive pretensions. His courage, his energy, his talents, his application, and above all his misfortunes and his sufferings, should rather increase than diminish our

affection for him, and I have been really happy to give him a good welcome, and perhaps to serve him here."

But in spite of his kind intentions he found it difficult to secure for
Mirabeau the reception he would have liked. He had the experience
so often suffered with foreigners met abroad, who seem completely
changed when met again in one's own country. Mirabeau, conspicuous
even in an environment accustomed to exuberance and vivacity, was
a sensational figure in an English home. He produced a disastrous impression.

Sir Gilbert told his brother about it with comic despair, mitigated
by his sense of humour. "I took Mirabeau with me the other day to
Bath. He paid court so precipitously to Henrietta [his sister], whom
he counted on subjugating in a week, so absolutely dumbfounded my
John Bull of a wife who understands no more about the French than
does Molly the chambermaid, so horrified my little boy by caressing
him, so completely disposed of me between luncheon and supper, so
astonished all my friends, that I had great trouble in keeping the peace
in the vicinity, and if he had not been recalled unexpectedly to the city
I am sure that my wife's patience, I don't wish to say her politeness,
would not have held out."

Mirabeau had gone alone: he had not dared to present Mme. de Nehra
to the ladies of Bath. Sir Gilbert had found her, as he wrote to Lady
Elliot, "a modest woman, ladylike, virtuous," with "at least the merit
of remaining faithful to one of the ugliest and poorest men of Europe."
But Mirabeau considered that "the state of mind of these ladies needs
to be known beforehand." Lady Elliot seemed to him "kindness itself;
she is indulgent as are all virtuous women who have no need of indulgence."

While Sir Gilbert's insular family misjudged Mirabeau, he for his
part was blind to the subcutaneous reactions, so to speak, of English reserve. He hardly noticed that he had sown horror in a British home.

As if to make up for this, Sir Gilbert introduced Mirabeau to all his
political friends. He himself belonged to the Opposition; Mirabeau made
interesting acquaintances—interesting rather than useful—among the
Whigs.

7

The year of Mirabeau's arrival in London was that in which William
Pitt came into power. Pitt, heir of an illustrious name, had had as
sheltered an existence as Mirabeau's had been stormy. He had been all

that Mirabeau had been unable to be. Destined from the cradle to a high career, he had been brought up by his father with a view to his future mission. He had all that Mirabeau was never to have—means, standing, a moral reputation beyond attack, a precocious wisdom sheltered from passions.

Mirabeau was to know Pitt only through the eyes of the Opposition, made up of the most capable men in the country, who were resentful of the position of this young man, scarcely twenty-five years old, whom they derisively called the "infant prodigy." Pitt took the place of a disastrous coalition, that of the Tory Lord North, protégé of the king, with his fiercest adversary, the Whig Charles Fox. Mirabeau had no idea that he was witnessing a turning-point in English history.

The Opposition, discredited by the coalition, raged in vain against Pitt. In vain was he defeated in Parliament eighteen times during the first months of 1784; he refused to resign, convinced that the situation of his country made it his duty "to defend it like a fortress." Five years later, at a critical time, Pitt was still in power. He tried to prevent a disastrous war by sending to the most influential member of the French National Assembly, the Comte de Mirabeau, a special envoy, who was none other than his old friend Hugh Elliot. But when he was in London Mirabeau was associated with Pitt's great adversary, Burke, whom his friends the Elliots venerated. It was in Burke's company that Mirabeau was present at the opening of Parliament in January 1785. He noticed Lady Warren Hastings, in her finery, and quoted to Burke a passage from Pliny the Younger condemning the luxury of the wives of men in public office. Burke, who was only awaiting his chance to denounce the exploitation of the Indies, remembered Mirabeau's quotation and made use of it in his savage attack on Warren Hastings. His relations with Mirabeau were so cordial that he invited him to Beaconsfield, where he entertained with generous hospitality.

Some years later, when Burke had become the bitter enemy of the French Revolution, and the Abbé Maury, fleeing from the Terror, sought asylum in England, he invited the abbé to his country house, adding that it had undergone "purifications" since the "revolutionary demon" had stayed there.

Mirabeau met again in England some of the Genevese exiles, including Francis d'Ivernois, who in spite of his youth—he was scarcely twenty-seven—was one of the leaders of the Democrats, and who was himself to become one day one of the bitterest adversaries of revolutionary France. D'Ivernois introduced him to Samuel Romilly, the liberal jurist, with whom Mirabeau became closely associated; Romilly was one of those whom Mirabeau saw every day. According to a Genevese friend, Romilly, though of Huguenot origin, never spoke of the revocation of the Edict of Nantes "without blessing the memory of Louis XIV, thanks to whom he was an Englishman."

After his arrival in London, Mirabeau askèd Benjamin Franklin, through Chamfort, for an introduction to Franklin's intimate friend Doctor Price, hoping to interest him in the work on the Order of Cincinnatus. Dr. Price was so interested that he wanted to collaborate in the book. Feeling sure that it would make a sensation, he asked Mirabeau to insert in it a letter sent to him by Turgot, and also his pamphlet *Observations on the Importance of the American Revolution and the Means of Making It a Benefit to the World*. Mirabeau set to work at once on the translation of the pamphlet. "It is not excellent," he wrote to Chamfort, "but I have been much importuned." The additions delayed publication, but Mirabeau could not venture to offend an influential protector. A further contribution was added to this miscellany. In London Mirabeau met Target, a lawyer who had been in the *parlement* of Paris; his energetic pleading in a lawsuit against the Jesuits had made him famous, but his independence of mind led him to renounce a forensic career. He made a great reputation as a consultant. He was given charge of famous lawsuits, such as the affair of Cardinal de Rohan. He became responsible for procuring the edict that restored civil rights to the Protestants. He lived on his manifestation of independence as a man lives on his capital. His attitude of *frondeur*, due, perhaps, more to circumstances than to natural inclination, filled him with unmeasured pride.

Mirabeau found him "a perfectly decent man, good, warm, sensitive, pure, incorruptible." He explained his enthusiasm: "He did me an important service which I had not even asked of him." He asked Chamfort to work for Target's election to the Academy: "I know all that there is to be said against him. . . . He has few literary claims or none at all. . . . But who is being proposed, a few titled blackguards or a few literary nonentities?" And he concluded with this strange remark: "Target has done much better than write bad or feeble works: he has written none at all."

Mirabeau's *Considérations sur l'ordre de Cincinnatus* written in 1785, was at once translated into English by Samuel Romilly. It had a great success. It was the first book by Mirabeau that appeared under his name. The boldness of its ideas was well matched by his trenchant style. "Yes, it is that nobility of barbarians, the prize of blood, product of the sword, fruit of conquest, that the Cincinnati want to establish in their country, though they did not conquer it, and though it had been entrusted to their defence," he wrote in indignation. "Honours created by savage chiefs—these are the ambition of the heroes of a free people and an enlightened age." The orders of chivalry "always created ranks extending into the nobility, founded a new patriarchate in the patriarchate, a new pride amid pride, new means of oppression amid oppression, new instruments of despotism round thrones always ready to alienate the rights of nations and to sell a people for a ribbon. . . . In monarchy all tends to elevation; in the republic all should tend to equality. In the former, ranks are necessary; in the latter, virtues."

The American experience, he wrote, of a republican government was being won in such favourable circumstances as had never been met with in any part of the globe. "New land, inexhaustible, endowed with all the wealth of nature, encircled by immense seas, easy to defend; favourable principles and even prejudices, the draft of a considered and not a fortuitous constitution: men of genius, valiant leaders. . . ." As for the issue of the great experiment, "America can and will determine with certitude whether the human species is destined by nature to liberty or to slavery."

8

Brissot had his troubles in London. His plan to set up a Lycée Français and a literary journal had brought him to prison for debt. He was the victim of the manoeuvres of a journalist, Théveneau de Morande, editor of the *Courrier de l'Europe*.

The *Courrier de l'Europe*, a journal published in French in England, had been founded by a certain Latour, who had made a fortune in London out of a patent medicine. His knowledge of mass psychology and his instinct for publicity had led him into journalism. He had seen that during the war between England and America the French public had been particularly eager for news from abroad. His scheme was to send into France a journal printed in London, so evading the severe censorship. The French government was inclined to be indulgent. Vergennes himself needed to know what was going on in England. The journal gave him more information than a hundred secret agents. The *Courrier de l'Europe* spread with extraordinary rapidity and brought in a fortune for Latour and for his sleeping partner.

When the American war was over, the journal passed into the hands of Morande, who had made a profession of blackmail. He speculated on men's lower instincts and on their fear of scandal, and gained as much

money from the pamphlets with which he threatened the French government as from those he wrote. But his silence did not bring in enough
to please him, and he began to get money for speaking. "I can assure
you," wrote Mirabeau to Chamfort, "that in London the French are
just as much under the inspection of the Paris police as in France itself. The rascally adventurers who soil the press here are the most corrupt spies in existence. . . . There are also Englishmen sold to the
Paris police; witness the vile owner of the *Courrier de l'Europe*, who is
just as despicable as the editor. The latter, after living on scurrilous libels, has become a hired spy."

Among French journalists of this sort there was no room for such
a man as Mirabeau. He negotiated with the booksellers for an important
work that should appear in English and French, and for which he
would receive a monthly payment. "The idea is nothing less than to
inform these gentlemen and keep them informed of all the sound notions
of political economy which up to now they have called empty meta-
physics. I maintained that the greatest service, in my view, that could
be rendered to literature today was to summarize and to guide the
choice amid the immensity of printed lies, errors, and truths." He
proposed to give analyses, not extracts, of good books of all kinds. He
knew that it would be "a severe and disagreeable task," but he added
with the resignation he had acquired in England: "Better men than I
have been condemned to just as evil slavery."

The plan came to nothing. Mirabeau wrote bitterly that "French literature is so unfamiliar here, labour so dear, and the booksellers so timid,
that the best way to die of hunger here is to be even a good French
writer."

He was ready to try anything. A Genevese exile was working on a
history of the revolutions of Geneva. He urged Mirabeau to edit his
book. In less than a week Mirabeau presented to him an abstract of the
first volume. "This masterly abstract was energetic, rapid, interesting,"
said a Genevese. But the author had a sudden fit of *amour-propre,* and
the collaboration came to an end. Mirabeau jumped at every opportunity. He made the acquaintance of a French geographer and embarked
at once on the immense project of a universal geography. "If anyone
had cared to give him the elements of Chinese grammar, he would
have written a treatise on that language," a friend said of him. But all
these plans were so many autumn leaves swept away by the wind of
indifference.

In spite of Elliot's friendly efforts, Mirabeau had not succeeded in
making his way into English circles, in overcoming the initial distrust

felt for all who come from abroad, a distrust that is often suddenly transformed into lively curiosity. He had found too few Englishmen of influence ready to help him. The Frenchmen he met did him more harm than good.

In the end the failure of his efforts embittered him. The great success of his book had done little to improve his situation. He confessed to Chamfort that he was getting into difficulties. He wrote bitterly to him: "You are disturbed about the state of my affairs, and I, too, am not very reassured, especially as regards my good-tempered companion. . . . The talk about the generosity of the English is not true. Accustomed to calculate everything, they calculate even talents and friendship; most of their writers have almost literally died of hunger. As for anyone who does not belong to their nation—!"

9

Joseph II cast his quixotic eye over the map of Europe, trying to heap benefits on the provinces of his kingdom. The Austrian Netherlands were keenly interested in securing freedom of navigation on the Scheldt. The Emperor decided to secure this for them at the expense of the Dutch Republic. Mirabeau realized at once the dangers of the situation. "The Austrian shepherd," he wrote to Chamfort "ought to have at his side a Sancho to repeat incessantly to him: 'Grasp all, lose all!' " The Dutch surprised the Emperor by their energetic resistance; they fired on an Austrian vessel that tried to force a passage out of the Scheldt, and Joseph II found himself obliged to resort to arms. He tried to open negotiations with France. His head was filled with a bizarre mixture of principles of absolutism with democratic aspirations, and he regarded peoples as a merchandise that could be moved at will. In his secret negotiations he proposed that Holland should be exchanged for Bavaria. Marie Antoinette was alone in France in supporting her brother's projects. Mirabeau probably knew nothing of the negotiations between the cabinets, but he knew enough of the Emperor's projects to raise an alarm. In the course of a month he drew up and had printed a work of over two hundred pages, *Les doutes sur la liberté de l'Escaut, réclamée par l'empereur, sur les causes et les conséquences probables de cette réclamation—Doubts concerning the freedom of the Scheldt, demanded by the Emperor, and concerning the causes and probable consequences of that demand.*

The presence of Henriette at his side had no doubt had something to do with the warmth with which he defended the Dutch cause. It was an exile treading the hard pavement of London in search of employment, and already dreaming of a return to France, who dared to attack with extreme vehemence the brother of his queen: "Joseph II has the reputation of an ardent, incoherent man, full of wild ideas, without system or order, a man whose activity often looks like delirium. Like the child who saw the moon at the bottom of a well and said 'I want the moon,' the Emperor says: 'I want commerce,' without knowing how or whence, or what shall be its artery, or what shall be its foreign source, or for whom or what or precisely about what he is working. He wants commerce and he is an enemy of freedom. There is not to be found in the annals of the Roman emperors, there is not to be found in the code of the Inquisition, a more terrible law than his edict against the freedom of the press in the Netherlands, to which country he wants to sell the navigation of the Scheldt."

Mirabeau addressed himself to Vergennes, the liberator of America, who "will not cravenly desert the cause of Holland." He urged him not to emulate the alleged greatness of Louis XIV. "No doubt Louis XIV was great, but Caesar was greater, and what honest man does not detest Caesar? Louis XIV was great, but all the illustrious scourges of the earth were great, and they merit only the execration of mankind. Louis XIV was great, but with the greatness that desolates and dishonours humanity." He added: "Woe to the minister, ill-advised or perverse, who should set such a model before the young king, for whom his conscience is still a judge, a witness, a friend! Woe to him who should give the king false ideas of glory!"

Mirabeau realized the instability of the existing situation. He envisaged for the future the constitution of an independent Belgian state, but he saw it in the form of a federated republic. He thought that a Dutch republic would then be ready to grant to an independent state what it was refusing to an imperial province.

The part he assigned to his country in the event of a conflict breaking out was to establish, by the simple deployment of its armed forces, "a durable peace, based on the interest of all." But he asked himself whether France was capable of playing that noble part. Nobody at that time doubted the power of France, which the clever policy of Vergennes in the war between England and America had consolidated. But Mirabeau asked, and the questions seem the more striking in the light of later events: "Can France count on ten years of prosperous government? Who can promise her regeneration? What is there to give her in place of the routine that is prolonging and protecting her decay?"

He did not content himself with expressing doubts of the solidity of a structure whose weaknesses were not suspected. He had not only an exceptional critical lucidity, but already the constructive mind of a statesman who indicates future solutions. He regarded an alliance with a great power as a necessity. In conflict with the tradition prevailing in France in the conduct of foreign affairs, he sought that alliance at the side of England. He proposed the conclusion of a commercial treaty that should "make national jealousies disappear forever." The general course of the future policy of the Comte de Mirabeau was traced already in this first work of his on international affairs. A commercial treaty such as he envisaged would serve as basis for an alliance. This alliance he wanted to see "solid, sincere, eternal."

The *Doutes sur la liberté de l'Escaut* made Mirabeau widely discussed. The queen was long resentful of his attack on her brother. The work also had a certain financial success. "Now I am saved for a couple of months," wrote Mirabeau, relieved. Breathing more freely, he was able to judge more fairly the country that had proved inhospitable: "Nothing perfect can come from the hand of man, but there is less evil, much less evil, in England than anywhere else."

10

Hardy, the secretary-valet whom Mirabeau had brought from France, suffered from his master's terrible fits of anger. "It must be admitted," wrote Henriette, "that M. de Mirabeau was subject to fits of rage; the young man's stupidity and laziness continually provoked him." Hardy consoled himself for his troubles with the scum of the French refugees in London, men who were always in search of profitable secrets. He also consoled himself with the chambermaid, who, according to her mistress, was a thief. The two went to work together; the chambermaid took things belonging to Henriette, Hardy took papers of Mirabeau's, "important papers in which a large number of people were interested." It became necessary to prevent a scandal. On the advice of Elliot, Mirabeau brought Hardy into court.

An amusing hearing gave the incident an unfortunate publicity. Elliot himself intervened to explain the motives that had led Mirabeau to prosecute his secretary. Mirabeau announced that he would be content with the recovery of his property and would drop the prosecution, and in the absence of legal proof of the thefts Hardy was acquitted.

He avenged himself by a vicious libel. The future adversaries of Mirabeau drew liberally from this source of calumny. Henriette de Nehra, who had to appear several times as witness, was so upset that she fell ill.

"The horrible worries" told greatly on Mirabeau. It had become impossible to stay any longer in England. "I don't want to die of hunger here, where Rousseau would have perished of that sad malady if he had only had his talents to mortgage to his butcher and his baker, and yet it is very difficult in France, because I am refused means of living there." He did not dare, indeed, to return.

Henriette was his principal support during this time of torment. A young French physician who was friendly with them gave an enthusiastic description of that "celestial creature," who with her sweetness and placidity was able to calm the "storms of irritation" of her lover. She had the courage of great devotion. She left alone for France to seek assurances that Mirabeau could return freely. He asked Chamfort to help her in her efforts: "If the Comte d'Antraigues is in Paris, let him know of my friend's arrival, and as he is an ardent and discreet petitioner, both of you discuss matters with him."

Henriette had scarcely left when the terrifying rumour spread in London that plague had broken out. Fortunately it proved a false alarm. But the news Henriette gave Mirabeau threw him into the utmost anxiety. "I found a flood of hostility beyond description," she wrote later. "Friends and enemies were all united against the unfortunate man. Everyone regaled me with a story as slanderous as absurd, as absurd as slanderous." Dupont warned her "that there was talk of imprisoning the count on his return, and that I myself was running the greatest risk because it was taken for granted that I had a share in M. de Mirabeau's works and that he was writing against the government. Everybody advised me to take care of myself and let all else go."

Fearing official action against Henriette, Mirabeau wanted to return at once to Paris, but Elliot, although ill, did his utmost to persuade his friend to remain with him. Mirabeau wrote urgently to Henriette: "Don't stop a moment in Paris. What do I care for public opinion in comparison with your safety? Go away to a free country and under friendly protection where you can brave slanderers and tyrants."

But Henriette was less impulsive than he; and beneath her fragile exterior she had unexpected resources of daring. "It always seemed to me," she wrote later, "that the others would not bring to bear the same ardour or the same eagerness as I when it was a question of my friend. So I decided to do my own petitioning."

Mirabeau took alarm when she told him of her decision. "You have decided to go to Versailles. Good God, what will you do there? What reception will you have? What a strain on you! What a place for your simplicity! How little nature has fitted you for such a spot! You, so sweet and so proud, I so hail-fellow-well-met but so intractable in face of haughtiness and duplicity, both of us so fond of domestic happiness and peaceful enjoyments."

Henriette applied direct to the minister, the Baron de Breteuil, though she did not know him, and she was received by him. The minister was touched by her innocence and charm. "He expressed his astonishment that at my age I had been ready to associate my peaceful existence with the continual storms that surrounded Mirabeau."

The Baron de Breteuil, who had a daughter whom he loved greatly, was filled with an almost paternal pity for this charming young being, whom he thought led astray by her passion. "He urged me many times to return to the convent, and told me that my needs would be provided for."

Mirabeau's friends had not exaggerated the risks he ran. "The Baron de Breteuil did not conceal from me that the king was irritated and the queen was displeased by the work on the Scheldt." But these warnings and counsels were in vain. Henriette de Nehra would not abandon her friend; she pleaded for him with all her warmth and by her very presence. Breteuil may have said to himself that a man who had been able to win such love from so innocent a creature could not deserve his bad reputation. In the end he gave way to her, promised to see the king, and asked her to come again in the evening. At dinner he talked about her visit, and his daughter was very interested in this romantic young woman. Breteuil assured Henriette that Mirabeau might return without anxiety, provided that he lay low. The young woman's presence at his side seemed to the minister a sufficient guarantee.

In London Mirabeau lived in suspense, waiting for news from her. "The slightest commotion in the house makes me tremble." The slowness of the postal communications was a terrible trial for him. "My God, must I still be deprived for a long time of you and of news from you? What a change in my life, what a burden for my heart, for my head! It is too much for me, I am wretched to the point of hating life."

At last he received Henriette's account of her interview with Breteuil. "Bless you, bless you a thousand times for the courage with which you exposed yourself at Versailles in my interest. But what authority would have dared to lift a sacrilegious hand against such an angel as you? My whole life shall be consecrated to blessing you for it, and all the feeling in my heart, all the devotion in my soul, all the resources in my mind shall be a tribute of my gratitude."

He was in a hurry now to return to Paris. The disappointments he had suffered had given him a strange humility. "Why should not the same government that encourages, that maintains, that subsidizes here vermin of the vilest and most venomous species, let *me* live?" he wrote to Chamfort.

He was filled with bitterness by his experiences in England, and was inclined to visit his disappointment on a whole people, reversing the favourable judgments he had earlier expressed. But he drew a lesson for the future, which he summarized in a letter to Chamfort. "No, my friend, I am not at all enthusiastic about England, and I know enough about her now to tell you that while her constitution is the best that is known, her administration is the worst possible. I think that, speaking individually, we are of more worth than they, and that the land of wine is better than the land of coal, even in its influence on morality. Without agreeing with M. de Lauraguais that the English have no other ripe fruit than baked apples and nothing polished except steel, I do think that they have no justification for their fierce pride. But what is liberty, when the little that there is in one or two good laws places in the front rank a people so little favoured by nature?

"What cannot a constitution do when, though incomplete and defective, it saves, and will save for a time yet, the most corrupt of peoples from its own corruption? How great is the influence of a few favourable gifts on the human species when this ignorant, superstitious, obstinate people (for it is all that), acquisitive and of doubtful good faith, is worth more than most known peoples because it has civic liberty? That is admirable."

≥ IX ≤

Instructor of the Nation

"IF YOU know the four rules of arithmetic, and can conjugate 'to have,' and work hard, you are an eagle in finance," wrote Mirabeau to Chamfort. He had quickly assimilated Clavière's teaching. He also owed to Clavière his entry into the financial world and his acquaintance with Clavière's compatriot Panchaud.

Panchaud, with a Scottish partner, Clonard, had founded the Caisse d'Escompte in Paris. As a prudent man he had been careful not to follow the example of John Law and his short-lived Banque Générale (1716–1720), and his bank was not empowered at first to issue notes payable at sight. But it did so later, when its credit was established; and the government, by demanding advances on too big a scale, swelled the note issue until the moment came when the bank was unable to continue redeeming the notes.

It was a time of feverish financial speculation. Bearer bonds, which had been put into circulation in 1783, facilitated speculation on the Bourse, into which the Caisse d'Escompte had thrown itself. Trading in futures was not authorized under any conditions; it was carried on nevertheless. Fortunes were made and unmade. At moments of crisis, when great establishments were tottering, the government intervened and, by a decree of the Council of State, declared deals in futures null and void. Fortunes and hopes were sunk.

When the Caisse d'Escompte was threatened with ruin, Ormesson was dismissed and M. de Calonne became Controller General in his place. Calonne set out to save the Caisse d'Escompte by repaying its advance to the government, so enabling it to meet its obligations in cash. The reorganization of the bank was carried out jointly by Panchaud and Talleyrand, the Agent General for the clergy. Panchaud, who was highly appreciated by Calonne, left the Caisse d'Escompte to become banker to the court, and so one of the intermediaries through whom the Treasury negotiated its bills.

Mirabeau, too, was profoundly impressed by the great banker. "He spent all his time at Panchaud's," wrote Henriette de Nehra. He spoke of the banker's eagle eye, and soon counted him among his three dearest friends. Later, when Panchaud was dismissed from his post of banker to the court, Mirabeau was in consternation. His affectionate admiration for Panchaud does not seem to have been fully reciprocated. He thought he had mastered the mysteries of finance, but the banker remarked maliciously that nobody could "talk so well as Mirabeau about things about which he knew nothing." Yet it was of that very eloquence that Panchaud and Clavière decided to make use.

Clavière was alarmed at the speculation in government stocks, and he needed help in combating it. He knew his own lack of lucidity. "His ideas were excellent," wrote Brissot, "but he needed someone to express them for him." Mirabeau was chosen by Clavière and Panchaud (the latter had joined in the bear speculation in the shares of the Caisse d'Escompte) for an attack on speculation.

Henriette had conceived a very wise plan for her friend: "I thought that in the state of his affairs a year or two of retirement would do

him a lot of good. I advised him to shut himself up either at Mirabeau
or elsewhere, but in the country, to remain there with me, to occupy
himself on a big work, to give it every care, and when it was perfected
to reappear suddenly with it." It was this project, accepted with enthusiasm, that had hastened Mirabeau's departure from London. "We
had agreed to leave Paris at once, and our trunks were packed," writes
Henriette. At that moment their little boy "Coco" fell ill. The negligence from which he had suffered in his early infancy had rendered him
particularly susceptible to infection. For so frail a child, smallpox might
easily be fatal. Mirabeau had always been a fervent believer in inoculation. Henriette shared his ideas. "It was decided that the operation
should be carried out at once, and that we should wait for his recovery
before leaving. During this interval M. Etienne Clavière did his utmost
to induce Mirabeau to remain in Paris."

Mirabeau gave way to his friend.

2

Brissot watched, not without jealousy, Mirabeau's advance in the affection and esteem of Clavière. He had himself found shelter with his
Genevese friend after his many misfortunes. He had been arrested in
London for debt, and, seeing all his projects founder, had returned to
France. There he was at once arrested and imprisoned in the Bastille.
He had been preceded by the calumnies of Morande and of other secret
agents. "These scoundrels," Mirabeau had written from London in regard to Morande, "are afraid of getting no money if they make no accusations, so that they make them right and left." But Brissot had imprudently given a handle to calumny. He was too careless in confiding
in crooks, and too impulsive, alike in his ready good nature and in his
resentments. Only the powerful intervention of the entourage of the
Duc d'Orléans procured his liberation from the Bastille.

When Clavière decided to enlist Mirabeau's help he only asked him,
according to Brissot, for the use of his name; but that name, Brissot
added, "in view of his bizarre adventures and daring character, always
attracted and riveted attention; that name was worth a great deal, and
it was a wise and sound speculation to buy it." He claimed to have written two chapters in the book on the Caisse d'Escompte which Mirabeau
edited at Clavière's request; another chapter was supposed to have been
written by Dupont.

Mirabeau himself described the work as "very elementary." But he added that, hasty and imperfect as it was, "it has saved many decent people whom rogues had set out to dupe." He fought against speculation by showing its fatal consequences, but demanded that the government should abstain from intervention, and denounced a recent decree declaring all past dealings in options and futures null and void. "God himself," he wrote, "cannot make a retrospective law a just law."

3

At this time *"grand seigneur"* was a synonym for a man in debt. Mirabeau, whom Brissot reproached for "that constant disorder in his private affairs, out of which gentlemen almost make themselves a title of nobility," was only a typical representative of this epoch. The balancing of income and expenditure was a monopoly of the middle class. The seigneurs lived in the style of adventurers, from hand to mouth, waiting for an inheritance, for a miracle, or, more likely, for intervention by the court to save them from ruin. The great estates were mortgaged to the hilt, and "expectations" were consumed in advance, delivered over to usurers. The most ostentatious luxury was a sort of social obligation, to which were sacrificed age-old family estates and the whole fortune of the humble. The sense of honour formerly so strong seemed to be eclipsed in money matters. Dressmakers, hairdressers, menials went unpaid, while fortunes disappeared in a night's festivities or at the gaming-table. From time to time a disaster showed society its precarious situation. One of the most illustrious families of France was that of the Guéménées, a branch of the Rohans. They held the highest appointments in the kingdom. The Prince de Guéménée, Grand Chamberlain, was believed to be one of the richest personages in Europe. His bankruptcy in 1782 had brought distress all over France. Guéménée had dragged down with him in his fall his friends, his tradesmen, his relatives, his servants, and small men who, dazzled by his splendour, had trusted him with all their savings. Cardinal de Rohan exclaimed with a mixture of despair and a sort of pride: "Only a king or a Rohan could have such a bankruptcy."

When the king dismissed the Guéménées from their high appointments at court, all the great families were indignant. The Duchesse de Guéménée had been *gouvernante* of the king's children; her loss of the post was attributed by the leaders of society to the queen's desire to appoint her favourite, Mme. de Polignac, in her place. For this the queen was never forgiven.

The queen was blamed also for the fall of the Controller General, Ormesson, for he had refused to pay the debts of Mme. de Polignac. The Comte de Vaudreuil made a violent scene and said threateningly as he left: "Very well, Monsieur, if you will not do it, someone else will." "M. de Vaudreuil followed up this affair," wrote a courtier, making light of the gravest matters in the current fashion. "The king was annoyed and dismissed Ormesson." "M. de Vaudreuil was determined on M. de Calonne; the entourage of Mme. de Polignac worked hard for him; the queen wanted him, the king resisted; the queen had a miscarriage, and M. de Calonne was nominated."

Calonne granted the court all that his predecessor had refused it. He paid the debts of Mme. de Polignac and of M. de Vaudreuil. He expended, wrote a courtier, "fourteen millions for Rambouillet, fifteen millions for the Comte d'Artois, six for the Comte de Provence, and another five or six for other people." He was himself deeply in debt when he came into power.

At the time when Mirabeau was editing *La Caisse d'Escompte*, he sent to Calonne a letter on the subject of the re-establishment of the Compagnie des Indes, which the minister had just decreed. His purpose, Mirabeau wrote later, was "to prevent the Compagnie des Indes from extending further than its privileges permitted and becoming a monopoly destructive to all national industry and commerce." Calonne's chief weapon was his amiability. He replied to Mirabeau with an invitation to come to see him. He succeeded in impressing him. With regard to the principal object of this visit he maintained a prudent silence, but he was all the more flattering in what he did say. He told Mirabeau of his keen desire to see him spreading enlightenment on various economic matters. But when Mirabeau wanted to print *La Caisse d'Escompte*, he was able to do it in only the petty state of Bouillon, whence it was smuggled into France.

The success of the book recalled Mirabeau to Calonne's memory. "I was sent for, praised, caressed." The minister covered him with compliments, but asked him to soften some rather too forcible criticisms of decrees of the Council. To his astonishment he received the proud reply: "I shall pursue to the death every retrospective law." But Calonne was not a man to take offence at a refusal. "The victory was mine," wrote Mirabeau, "the distribution of my book was publicly authorized." The Controller General knew well where his interest lay, and felt that a Mirabeau with a grievance would be a dangerous enemy.

4

The day came when Mirabeau could say with pride: "I have frustrated speculation in every form, speculation that was swallowing all the currency of the kingdom, was discouraging all honest industry, and finally, when it had infected the court, was threatening to inundate France with new corruption." Calonne was interested at the moment in bringing down the price of shares in the Banque de Saint-Charles, which the Caisse d'Escompte had taken under its protection. The bank had been founded in Spain by a naturalized Frenchman, Cabarrus, father of the future Mme. Tallien; it was invested with all the prerogatives that could be conferred on it by an absolute regime; it exchanged its own notes for notes of the state that had been issued at a fixed premium; it possessed several monopolies; and it controlled a subsidiary, the Compagnie des Philippines, which had every privilege in colonial trading.

Clavière, too, was preoccupied with the dangerously powerful position of this Spanish bank, though for different reasons from those of the Controller General; he was preparing with Brissot an attack on the Banque de Saint-Charles. Part of this work was already in proof.

Calonne, judging from *La Caisse d'Escompte*, considered that Mirabeau's attack would be more effective than that of Clavière and Brissot. He wrote to Clavière urging him to turn over his work to Mirabeau, offering at the same time to indemnify him in full. Clavière, who "saw that this was in the public interest," agreed at once and sacrificed his work, to the great disappointment of Brissot, who remarked bitterly that "Mirabeau had the honour of it and kept the money, while Clavière paid the expense." The attack on the Banque de Saint-Charles—a book of three hundred twenty pages—was finished in four days and published in a week. "It was, perhaps, no small achievement, but the peril was immediate," wrote Mirabeau to a friend.

In this book, *De la Banque d'Espagne*, Mirabeau dwelt on suspicious analogies between Law and Cabarrus, between Law's system and the Banque de Saint-Charles, which had made play with imaginary profits in Philippine trade as Law had done with a fictitious development in Mississippi and Louisiana. Mirabeau had a good knowledge of his subject, or was well informed by Clavière. He published the original charter of the Banque de Saint-Charles, of which neither Calonne nor his agents had the text. He also published the memorandum transmitted by Cabarrus to the Spanish court. Mirabeau considered his hasty work "infinitely better, more profound, more orthodox," than *La Caisse d'Escompte*. He fiercely attacked monopolies and privileges, and, faithful to the teaching of the Economists, fought for freedom of trade. He flattered himself that in this voluminous pamphlet he had given "the theory of public banks."

The Bank of Spain got wind of the attack that was in preparation. It was ready to pay Mirabeau "all the gold I might be ready to accept" for silence. The fact was attested later by one of Mirabeau's friends, a man of absolute integrity. The moment was particularly difficult for Mirabeau. He declared that he received from Calonne nothing but the cost of printing his pamphlet, and was obliged to borrow money from Clavière and Jeanneret, which he was unable to repay for a long time. He prided himself later on never having entered into any sort of speculation, on having lived by his work, with help from his friends, without having ever "staked a crown or received a sou as a present."

His attack on the Banque de Saint-Charles had a crushing effect. "Not only did I cure a fatal mania and arrest the excessive purchases of shares in Saint-Charles, but I entirely prevented the introduction of shares in the [Compagnie des] Philippines, which today are more discredited in Spain than those of Saint-Charles itself." The shares in the Bank of Spain, which had risen to nine hundred francs, were thrown on the market a week later at four hundred.

The powerful protectors of the bank were up in arms. Calonne took fright at the tempest he had unloosed. Le Couteulx de La Noraye, head of an important Paris bank and all-powerful in the Caisse d'Escompte, brought all his influence to bear to secure the suppression of Mirabeau's book. Calonne gave way, lest he should be suspected of having engineered the fall in the shares. He defended himself later by pretending to Mirabeau that that decision had been "wrangled" out of him by the Keeper of the Seals. A decree of the Council of July 17, 1787, prohibited the book "as the work of one of those individuals who venture to write on important matters of which they are not sufficiently well informed to provide the public with useful information."

Mirabeau was exasperated by these contemptuous words. Yet Calonne claimed to have "immensely reduced the harshness" of the wording of the decree. What was of more importance, he held out the hope of a fresh task. "The book by the ill-informed man," Mirabeau commented bitterly, "had no sooner been suppressed by decree of the Council than the Minister of Finance asked him to do another one on loans." The Austrian ambassador, Mercy-Argenteau, a man particularly well informed, a confidant of the queen, confirmed that Calonne had asked Mirabeau for a book on the state loans, promising him a fee of six thousand livres. But the minister did not find in Mirabeau the docile instrument he wanted. All he did was to soften his wrath, or rather to hold him in leash, ready to jump at any moment—to secure his silence for the time.

Mirabeau contented himself with publishing a violent diatribe against Le Couteulx de La Noraye. The pamphlet was published with Calonne's knowledge; he had read the proofs and asked Mirabeau to make a few changes in it. Two editions were quickly exhausted. But the financier got to work and secured a decree of the Council suppressing the pamphlet. Calonne again claimed that he had been powerless. Mirabeau was indignant. If, he said, Calonne had not had the courage to stand up for the work after he had given it his approval, he should at least have prevented the mortification of the author. But Calonne, still smiling, soothed him with his characteristic unconcern: "After all, what does a decree of the Council amount to?"

5

Pauvres gens! je les plains, car on a pour les fous
Plus de pitié que de courroux.

"Poor people! I pity them, for we are more sorry for the insane than angry with them." Mirabeau gave this motto, borrowed from one of La Fontaine's fables, to his next work, *Sur les actions de la Compagnie des Eaux de Paris*—On the shares of the Paris waterworks company. He contrasted foreign securities, with their riskiness, with solid French shares. But he was up in arms against the monopolies granted to certain French companies, and against the boosting of their shares. Those of the Compagnie des Eaux, issued at twelve hundred livres, had risen to thirty-eight hundred. His pamphlet resulted in their fall to two thousand, which they did not again exceed. Calonne, who had a considerable holding of these shares, was furious. He sent for Lauzun, a friend of Mirabeau, and told him to tell Mirabeau that the queen was very upset by his book on the freedom of the Scheldt, the king was upset by his attack on the Compagnie des Eaux, and everybody at court was thoroughly annoyed with him. He added that he had defended Mirabeau for two whole days, but on the third he had been obliged to abandon him.

Calonne added threats to his warning. If Mirabeau gave the slightest further cause for dissatisfaction to the administration, not only would Calonne no longer defend him, but he would have him punished as severely as he could. Calonne did not venture, however, to attack Mirabeau directly, but tried to intimidate his friends. The book on the Compagnie des Eaux was signed by Mirabeau, but it was found convenient to attribute it to Clavière. One fine day Clavière found himself summoned before the lieutenant of police, who "informed him of the king's strong disapproval, and conveyed to him a prohibition of any further writing on matters of administration."

The Compagnie des Eaux also acted, by means of an anonymous reply from a man who was the hero of the day, Caron de Beaumarchais.

Son of a humble watchmaker, and himself a watchmaker by trade, Caron de Beaumarchais belonged entirely to his age; but at the same time he was a precursor of the living forces of a power of the morrow —the middle class. He had acquired noble rank, of which he said: "Nobody would dare to dispute my title to it, for I have the receipt." He had acquired a fortune through the support of a good cause, the independence of the New World; he was a born organizer, ready to exploit every opportunity. He became a secret agent of the government, employed on difficult missions, and later its influential adviser, consulted by the Minister of Foreign Affairs and the Minister of Finance, consolidating his position everywhere and succeeding in everything by his characteristic mixture of audacity and amiability.

In some famous lawsuits in which his ability, his wit, and his bold eloquence triumphed over an all-powerful magistracy, he earned the reputation of a redoubtable opponent whom no one could provoke with impunity. He owed his celebrity as an author to a play which he himself called "my night-cap's wildest dream." He triumphed over the king, who declared that the *Mariage de Figaro* was detestable, and over the Keeper of the Seals, who prohibited it, thanks to curiosity cleverly aroused in the very environment whose abuses his play stigmatized. "There is one thing wilder than my play," said Beaumarchais, "and that is its success."

Such a great organizer and brewer of big schemes as Beaumarchais could realize better than Mirabeau the possibilities opened up by a water supply for Paris. When the brothers Périer erected their fine pump on the heights of Chaillot, he came to their support, financed them, and helped them to organize the Compagnie des Eaux de Paris, of which he became one of the chief shareholders and administrators. Mirabeau was not unaware that in attacking the Compagnie des Eaux he was offering provocation to the redoubtable creator of Figaro. Beaumarchais was, in fact, up in arms at once, though anonymously, against Mirabeau's pamphlet. But his reply to it seemed to the public curiously mild. He contented himself with contradicting Mirabeau's figures and insinuating, though with perfect courtesy, that the motives that led the friend of Panchaud and Clavière to take up his pen might not be disinterested. There was only one spark of wit in his reply: "Formerly, when criticisms were really harsh, they were called philippics. It may be that one day some cynic will adorn them with the name 'Mirabelles,' after the Comte de Mirabeau who *mirabilia fecit*."

The first passage at arms had not been fierce. In this duel with the most feared literary antagonist of his time, it might have been expected that Mirabeau would be mercilessly slaughtered. He came out of it scarcely scratched. He returned to the fight at once with redoubled violence in the *Réponse à l'écrivain des administrateurs de la Compagnie des Eaux de Paris*. He called the idol of the public an adventurer and "Reynard the Fox." He exposed his relations with the master black-mailer Morande, whose friendship was a disgrace.

This second attack was a thrust into the void. In this sensational duel Mirabeau had the last word. To the great surprise of the public, Beau-marchais remained silent. Had he, with his quick perception, recog-nized the superior strength of Mirabeau, or did he, dazzled by his suc-cess, lull himself in a contemptuous and fallacious security?

In a vehement personal passage in his *Réponse*, Mirabeau had con-cluded: "My only aspiration is to win honour to the day of my death from my friends and my enemies." His work on the Compagnie des Eaux brought him unexpected friends. Mirabeau, little versed in tech-nical questions, had treated as a chimera the idea of bringing water into every house in Paris. But if it was possible, what, he asked himself, would become of the water-carriers? His book had no sooner appeared than the water-carriers, of whom, no doubt, not one had read it, learned that a great champion had arisen to defend their interests.

The news spread, with that occult faculty of intercommunication which the masses possess, that the oppressed had found an eloquent voice to speak for them. When the Savoyard porters found themselves threat-ened by a scheme for starting a transport company, they met together to deliberate. One of them stood up on a tub and shouted: "My friends, they are trying to do us an injustice. But don't worry: there is a man in Paris who will support us. A little while ago he saved the water-carriers from being starved to death. He will do as much for us. Let us go and see him."

They all went to the furnished rooms Mirabeau was occupying. In vain were they told that he had left the night before; in their disappoint-ment they searched the whole building. Their simple faith in Mirabeau was expressed in this sentence: "He always takes the part of the weak against the strong."

6

"That gentleman is now in the pay of the speculators," wrote the Marquis de Mirabeau to his brother. "They make use of him like a vicious dog who is set at the legs of every passer-by, and always ready the moment it is a question of biting." Mirabeau had emerged from his controversy with Beaumarchais with a considerably enhanced reputation, but even his fame offended his father. When the marquis was told of the great success of his son's writings, he replied: "When Persepolis was burning, the roisterers were more eager to obtain a brand than the most precious jewels." His undying prejudice fed on every calumny circulated against Gabriel: "That personage and his venality, in a man of quality, make of him a phenomenon as curious as debased." There were no longer any direct relations between father and son, whose lawsuit was still in progress, but the marquis watched the man as he had watched the child, with an almost physical repulsion.

At this time all Mirabeau's wrath was directed against Calonne. The Controller General's threats and the censure inflicted on Clavière had deeply irritated him. In his anger he wrote a pamphlet against Calonne, in the form of an open letter, with this motto, borrowed from the *Letters of Junius:* "I would pursue him through life and try the last exertion of my abilities to preserve the perishable infamy of his name and make it immortal."

Calonne learned of the fierce attack in preparation. He sent a message to Mirabeau that he had better keep quiet, or Calonne would find himself obliged "to have him punished as severely as possible." Friends urged Mirabeau to go discreetly with this powerful man: in his uncertain position he could not permit himself to run grave risks. Mirabeau gave way, for the moment. But the dream of a great mission continued to haunt him. His friendship with Clavière had led him to occupy himself with financial questions, and he felt bound to fight against the corruption that was being favoured by the government. He had realized that the deplorable condition of the state finances was a reef on which the kingdom would founder. He made it his duty to advocate a healthy morality in finance, to be "the instructor of the nation."

7

"Mirabeau always loved me, and even more tenderly every day," wrote Mme. de Nehra, "but he was frequently unfaithful to me; if he saw a pretty little face, or if a woman led him on, he took fire at once. His intrigues were not lasting; sometimes he was so bored by them that he asked my advice about getting out of them with decency. He took no pains," she added, "to hide these affairs from me, and they did not trouble me. This man, who has been painted as so false, was on the contrary so straightforward, and I was able to read his soul so well, that any attempt at constraint would have been useless. I was at peace with regard to his liaisons because I was sure of his heart."

But in that summer of the year 1785 a more serious intrigue threatened to disturb the peace of this household. Henriette described the intruder as "a stuck-up, vain woman, who despised everybody who had not a hundred thousand livres a year." She led Mirabeau into extravagances; he engaged a valet, started using a coach, and provided himself with a lackey for carrying letters.

Mirabeau's arrogant mistress did all she could to belittle Henriette in his eyes. She looked for things to ridicule and sneered at her economical ways. In spite of her solid good sense, the woman in Henriette suffered from this disdain and from the jokes about her simple way of dressing. The lovers quarrelled, but never for long. The intruder soon came under a cloud, and peace was restored. After this, Mirabeau sought only passing distractions. He found them in the company of the Duc de Lauzun.

"Handsome, brave, generous, and witty," the Duc de Lauzun had, according to Talleyrand, "every sort of brilliance." If his century had wanted to mirror itself in its most amiable, most artificial, and most frivolous aspect, it would certainly have chosen Lauzun to be its incarnation in the eyes of posterity.

Armand de Gontaut, Comte de Biron, and later Duc de Lauzun, had come into the world to shine in it. "At twelve years of age I knew," he himself wrote, "that I was destined to an immense fortune and to the finest position in the kingdom, without needing to take the trouble to behave myself." Endowed at birth with an illustrious name, with relations with the most powerful families of the kingdom, and with a great fortune, he was also endowed by nature with the bearing of a hero, with a lively wit, and with a romantic soul. He had but to let himself live in order to succeed. But his great potentialities, which might have responded to stern trials, were whittled down, in that period of affectation and effeminacy, to amorous prowess; his fine ardour, capable of brilliant deeds, was expended on the small coin of love-making. Thus he wasted youth, fortune, and a generous nature to add to his list of sentimental conquests, squandering ambitions that might have been far-reaching on satisfactions of vanity.

When the day came for him to sketch the course of his life, all he could do was to call up a procession of women of all countries and of every social class, monotonous and boring in its frivolity. Knowing himself to be irresistible, he dreamed of seducing the queen. But Marie Antoinette took offence at the pressing and perhaps deliberately indiscreet court paid to her by Lauzun. The handsome duke exchanged his rank of favourite to play the part at Versailles of victim of a royal caprice, until he passed over to the ranks of the enemies of the court.

Mirabeau had met Lauzun in the Corsican campaign. They met again as guests of Panchaud. Mirabeau, so sensitive to distinction of mind, was conquered by Lauzun's brilliance, heightened as it was by the laurels he had won in the American War of Independence.

Lauzun owned a "folly" at Montrouge, where he gave wanton parties. Mirabeau was often there. Apart from the frivolous element in their relations, the two men were united in their ideas on serious matters. Lauzun's dissipated life had not stifled his broad political views or his serious ambitions. He was one of the most ardent proselytes of the Anglomania then current. Although he had fought for American independence, Lauzun had not lost his English sympathies. He had made prolonged visits to London and had many friends there. As with many of the young aristocrats, his opposition to the court increased his enthusiasm for constitutional liberties and his realization of the need to improve relations between France and England, strained as they had been by French help to the American insurgents.

He found Mirabeau—who had already written from his cell at Vincennes of the necessity of a treaty with England—in full agreement with his ideas. In the end he persuaded the government to entrust him with the negotiation, as a first step, of the commercial treaty which Mirabeau had suggested as the preliminary to a treaty of wider range. Mirabeau gave him constant encouragement in his truly important plan to devote all his energies to "a change of system, without which," wrote Mirabeau, "Europe will always wander at random between the agonies of periods of a bad peace, which will be no more than an indefinite truce imposed by reciprocal exhaustion, and the horrors of indecisive and ruinous wars." The two discussed at length the idea, "alleged," said Mirabeau, "to be chimerical," of an alliance between France and England. This was Mirabeau's great idea, the keystone of his system of European pacification. He continually found new persuasive arguments to send to the negotiator in London.

In 1786, thanks to Lauzun's efforts, a commercial treaty was signed, for ten years, between France and England. The treaty represented great sacrifices on the part of French industry. But opinion was so roused on both sides of the Channel by this breach with tradition that the treaty, favourable though it was to England, raised a storm of disapproval in London. The political atmosphere there was so hostile to France that there were public demonstrations, and a great crowd marched, with Lord George Gordon at its head, to burn a copy of the treaty in front of the French embassy.

8

"Those who did not live in the years approaching 1789," wrote Talleyrand, "do not know what the pleasure of living is." But across that bright light shadows were passing as though cast by coming events. The sensitiveness that had been cultivated as a social pastime awoke to human misery. Men's minds were "intoxicated with philanthropy," said a contemporary. Among those who saw most clearly the necessity of radical change were the most unbridled beneficiaries of the existing system, the young aristocrats, spoilt children of their day. The day was to come when the Duc de Lauzun would command the armed forces of the Revolution, as General Biron, with the task of repressing counter-revolutionary disturbances in the Vendée. But in spite of the services he rendered he was one day to die, as a former aristocrat, on the scaffold.

There came a day when some of those who had been in revolt before the Revolution took fear of the forces they had unloosed and fanatically threw themselves against them. Among the habitués of the Montrouge "folly" was Comte Louis de Narbonne. This man was deeply attached to the court. He was generally supposed to be a natural son of Louis XV, and had received the education of a prince. A very rich marriage wiped out his debts and gave him a life of affluence. He had every reason to be attached to a social order of which he had known only the advantages. But the journeys he had made for his education as a cosmopolitan *grand seigneur*, and especially his prolonged visits to England, where he was on friendly terms with the English liberals, including Fox, had enlarged his horizon, and the very serious studies in which he had engaged had filled him with aspirations for a better social order. He was handsome, in the rather ponderous and spectacular style of the Bourbons; he was brilliant, even more dazzling than his friend the Abbé de Périgord; he tried to please and charm all who came near him. But, as Talleyrand said, there was nothing light about him except his conversation. He put his heart into his liaisons, and his confiding soul into his care for the public weal. Loyally attached to the royal house by ties of blood and by gratitude for benefits received, Narbonne was to work obstinately to save it in spite of itself, in spite of its recalcitrance and its bad faith. As Minister of War at the most critical moment in the destiny of his country, he succeeded in escaping from the wave of terror thanks to his mistress, Mme. de Staël, and to the devotion of a young German. Faithful always to his urge to serve something or someone greater than himself, he was to end his adventurous career as a confidant of Napoleon, sacrificed by the emperor in an exposed position.

Among those who gravitated round Lauzun, Mirabeau found one of his friends of the past, the Comte d'Antraigues, who was closely associated also with Chamfort.

Louis de Launay d'Antraigues, whom Mirabeau chaffed about the ancient noble lineage on which he prided himself, was an embodiment of the restlessness of his age and its search for novelties in every field of thought. He had been associated with Jean-Jacques Rousseau at the time of the latter's obscure beginnings. In Paris he associated with men of learning and with inventors such as the brothers Montgolfier, keeping always on the track of the sensation of the day. At court he aroused the enthusiasm of the women by the boldness of his philosophical ideas and the eloquence with which he preached liberal principles. He seems to have aspired, like Lauzun, to the favours of Marie Antoinette, who is said to have told him not to appear again in her presence. His disgrace at court sent him, like Lauzun, to join the queen's enemies, and brought him into close relations with the king's brother, the Comte de Provence, whose secretary and secret agent he became.

The Montrouge "folly" was not the only meeting-place of these courtiers with secret resentments and open hostility to the regime. Lauzun, Narbonne, Antraigues, Mirabeau, met also at Panchaud's. The great banker was ambitious to found and lead a school. He took his role so seriously that he neglected the affairs of his bank in order to "propagate his ideas." It was under Panchaud's guidance that these bright and frivolous young men were initiated into the signs of the financial decline of the regime.

9

Mirabeau, who claimed that he could "tip the balance of the Bourse at will," was living from hand to mouth; there were those who would have been glad to pay him large sums to keep silent, while he went in search of employment, any employment, even in a subordinate capacity.

He sought it in journalism, though he admitted that his idleness took fright at any regular work and that journalism was distasteful to him. The journal to his taste would have been based "on the idea, novel perhaps and, I think, not without utility, of occupying itself with old books, as ordinary journals occupy themselves with new ones." He wanted to edit the memoirs of the Académie des Belles-Lettres, to extract "from that muddle all that may be of interest to philosophers, men of letters, and men of the world, without crushing them beneath the weight of an ostentatious erudition."

He drew up a prospectus of a journal on these lines, but the subscriptions seem to have been inadequate. In vain did he deal gently with Calonne in order not to lose government support; in vain did his friends seek to obtain a post for him. Bitterness overcame his fundamental optimism. He thought once more of emigrating, and of founding a paper abroad. He wanted to try the possibilities in Germany. He may have thought of the sort of career his uncle had been able to achieve there. He also conceived the idea of a work on Prussia. Frederick II was ill, perhaps dying. The position of Prussia, the possibilities of the succession to Frederick, occupied men's minds. Mirabeau prepared for a new journey. Once more he realized bitterly that there was no place for him in his native country.

10

"People always speak either too ill or too well of me; I enjoy the honours of exaggeration," once wrote Charles-Maurice de Talleyrand. He had come into the world as the bearer of an illustrious name, and was related to the greatest families of France. As first-born, he was predestined to a brilliant career. But the clumsiness of a nurse who let him fall in early childhood altered the course of his life. A crippled leg closed the military career to him. For the neglect that had left him in infancy to a stranger's care, instead of bringing him up at home, he never forgave his parents. As a child he was terribly jealous of all who were free from defect, including his younger brothers. He was destined by his parents for the priesthood, the only career open to a semi-invalid. His companions remembered him striking his club-foot and shouting: "There's my vocation!"

Of his years at the seminary he wrote later: "Everything I did went against the grain. I felt a grievance against my superiors, against my parents, against institutions." Already, he added, he acted as "a little Bonaparte." He was frank with himself and with others about his absolute lack of any religious feeling. He was born with strong appetites, with avidity for enjoyment and a sensuality that bred a taste for conquests. Regarding himself as disinherited, he forged a weapon out of his humiliation. He prepared a fierce revenge upon destiny. Endowed with a rare lucidity, he cultivated a biting and pitiless humour that shocked and fascinated. He did his best to unite his genius with a monstrous insensibility. At an early age he found pleasure in "caressing scandal," said one of his friends, "and despising the opinion of respectable people."

He had liaisons even at the seminary, and later, according to the Duchesse d'Abrantès, he belonged "to the cohort of the clergy who exploited boudoirs and the streets." He deprived himself of nothing that was forbidden to his cloth. He even knew the joys of paternity. In 1785 his mistress, the Comtesse de Flahaut, gave birth to a child who was his and who was to become the lover of Queen Hortense and father of the celebrated Duc de Morny.

But while he lived the careless life of the young men around him, there was a point at which he differed fundamentally from them. While his friends squandered fortunes or ran ruinously into debt without thought for the morrow, he was haunted by the idea of poverty. And he was one of the first of his class to realize the power of money. At a time when the privileges of birth seemed to be the only ones that mattered, he devoted himself to the worship of that new divinity. Money became a passion with him, for its own sake. Initiated by Panchaud into the problems of finance, he took at once to the subject, finding it "full of charm." He showed his capacity when he was appointed director of the General Agency for the Clergy, at that time virtually the Catholic Ecclesiastical Commission. He performed his duties all the better since they enabled him to make a fortune for himself, by devoting himself, as he admitted, to "financial speculations that were not too remote from the position I occupied."

Round-faced and full-cheeked, with prominent cheekbones, and a snub nose that would have been ridiculous but for the smile of disdainful superiority that played about the down-turned corners of his mouth, he had, in the words of a contemporary, "the face of an angel with the expression of a devil."

He was six years younger than Mirabeau, but when the two met Mirabeau fell at once under his ascendancy; it was Mirabeau who introduced him to Calonne in a letter that reflected his blind admiration and affection: "M. l'Abbé de Périgord unites with a very real and practised talent a profound circumspection and a secrecy that is proof against anything. You could never choose a safer man or one more conscientiously loyal in gratitude, more assiduous in well-doing, less concerned to share the glory of others, or more convinced that this belongs and should belong to the man who can conceive and can dare to carry out his conceptions. He has," Mirabeau added, "another advantage for you, his ascendancy over Panchaud, which represses the latter's defects, concerning which the attempt has been made to alarm you."

This able and emphatic letter produced its full effect. Their turn of mind and their lack of scruple were bound to bring the two men together. The Abbé de Périgord was only at the outset of his career and had much to learn; Calonne made that his care. Talleyrand, wrote Lord Holland, served his political apprenticeship under Calonne and soon outstripped his master.

Talleyrand had quickly recognized Mirabeau's capacity. He said one day that Mirabeau, "with his vigorous intelligence, would have been able to carry the world like Atlas." Mirabeau responded to this appreciation with his natural exuberance. Once, when publishing an important book, he had four special copies made, as he wrote to Henriette, "for those who are dearest to me in the world—for you, the Abbé de Périgord, the Duc de Lauzun, and Panchaud."

II

"You know M. de Mirabeau's intelligence," wrote the Duc de Lauzun to Calonne, "you know his persuasiveness in speech and writing, and how much interest he will arouse in Prussia when he talks of you." Talleyrand, too, had quickly recognized Mirabeau's faculty of rapid adjustment to a new environment and his special aptitude for questions of foreign policy. He actively encouraged him in his project. Lauzun did the same; and he did more—he undertook to find the funds for his journey. He went to work with Calonne in a very shrewd way, bordering on extortion. "His poverty," he wrote in a letter to the minister, "will drive him to start a periodical that will rather hurt his pride. The freedom with which he will permit himself to write will have its drawbacks for you and for your ministry, in a distant country in which you are highly regarded; he needs to be made to keep silent by sending him money, not from you, so that he shall not think that he has been bought, but from one of his friends who will insist on his keeping quiet. It will be easy for me to arrange this for you."

It was under these none too honourable auspices that Mirabeau left to explore a country of which he knew nothing—an exploration of the highest importance to his future conduct in foreign policy. Before leaving he examined the existing conditions in his own country. He felt that "a crisis threatens the peace of Europe." He asked himself what would then be the situation of France, and what potential of power she had at her disposal. As soon as he reached Germany he summed up his conclusions in a letter to Talleyrand. They were melancholy, almost desperate conclusions: "More than two hundred and forty millions of advances, sixty millions excess of expenditure over revenue, our royal funds in the dirt; speculation ruining Paris, which is draining the kingdom dry; the people exhausted and discontented, commerce embittered and discouraged, disunion in the country and discredit abroad; a fleet without crews and impossible to renew in case of disaster; the troops incomplete and incontestably the worst among the good ones; the alliance with Spain which has never done anything but hinder us in our operations; the unnatural alliance with Holland, which will be the first firebrand of war. . . ; not a friend in Germany; universal distrust in its place; the most profound ignorance of the plans of our enemies; the most inactive diplomacy in Europe, although the best paid; in a word, the truly decrepit and fatal situation of unfitness to maintain peace and unreadiness to sustain war."

❧ X ❧

The Country
of the Human Machine

"SIRE, it is perhaps presuming too much to ask Your Majesty for an audience when one cannot talk of any matter that might particularly interest Your Majesty. But if you will pardon a Frenchman, who, from his birth, has found the world filled with your name, the desire to see the greatest man of his age, and of so many others, more closely than one ordinarily sees kings, you will graciously grant me permission to come and pay my court to you at Potsdam." So wrote Mirabeau, almost on the morrow of his arrival at Berlin, to Frederick II.

He had left Paris on Christmas Day 1785 with all his "horde," as he put it—Mme. de Nehra, Coco, their adopted son, and even a little dog Gabriel had given her, a great pet of hers. It was a very cold winter. The journey was trying. They went by way of Nancy, Frankfort, and Leipzig. In spite of the very short stay at Frankfort, Mirabeau succeeded in having an "intrigue of gallantry" there.

The French minister at Berlin, the Comte d'Esterno, was ill-pleased at Mirabeau's arrival. He was the traditional type of diplomat, "too cold, too stiff, too ministerial," who took fright at any departure from the paths of routine. Mirabeau had obtained a letter of recommendation from Vergennes, the Minister of Foreign Affairs. Esterno took offence at this and complained to the minister: "Without that letter I should not have taken it upon myself to present here a man with regard to whom I have had reason to make complaints in this court, on the occasion of the libels he printed at Neufchâtel."

Vergennes, alarmed at this unusual vehemence, hastened to disavow Mirabeau: "The letter from me which M. de Mirabeau transmitted to you commits you to nothing in regard to that gentleman, and nothing should prevent you from conducting yourself in regard to him with the reserve you may consider necessary. It would be wise not to show him any personal friendship." Mirabeau, however, had no need of the representative of France to procure him introductions in Berlin. Frederick II, with his careful attention to foreign opinion, had a list sent to him every day of the new arrivals who entered their names in the Guards' office at the entrance to the city. The name of Mirabeau struck him, and, no doubt, recalled to him that of the uncle of Mirabeau whom he had charged with an important mission at a particularly difficult moment for him. He at once sent the secretary of the Academy to ascertain the motives of his journey. When Mirabeau, unsupported by any recommendation, asked for an audience, Frederick answered without delay, in the most courteous terms: "I shall be very pleased to make your acquaintance, and I appreciate the offer you have just made to come here for that purpose."

From the information he had received, the king had already formed an opinion on his visitor. "So far as I can judge, he is one of those satyr-like effeminates who write for everybody and against everybody," he wrote to his uncle, Prince Henry. "It is said that this man intends to seek asylum in Russia, where he will be able to publish with impunity his sarcasms against his country."

On January 25, 1786, Mirabeau arrived at Potsdam. The "satyr-like effeminate" made his first appearance before the king as a humble petitioner. In this first audience in the presence of witnesses, he did not venture to speak directly to the king. But he was encouraged by the reception given to him. Frederick II found him very different from the doubtful adventurer he had expected. He seems to have received a favourable impression. Mirabeau sent some of his writings to the king. Frederick II instructed his aide-de-camp, Graf von Goertz, to thank him, and added in his letter to the count: "I admit that I shall be very curious to know by what happy chance this traveller has come here, and I shall be pleased if you will let me know." Mirabeau, sensing the king's interest, sent him a second letter in which he put the best face he could on his situation at the time.

"Very poorly rewarded for the truly great service I have rendered in France, compromised in my safety and almost in my reputation by the present minister, because I was unwilling to co-operate either in his last loan or in his manipulation of the louis . . . tormented by the desire, not, perhaps, very reasonable, to make myself regretted in France, I have left the country . . . with the firm resolve of not returning so long as I am young and capable of anything, unless to take over the considerable heritage of my father. Accordingly I shall push on to Russia. . . . I should certainly not have sought that immature nation and that wild country, did it not seem to me that your government is too completely organized for me to be able to flatter myself that I could be useful to Your Majesty. To serve you, and not to take my ease in academies, would undoubtedly have been, Sire, the first of my ambitions. But the storms of my first youth and the disappointments of my country have turned my ideas for too long away from that fine purpose, and I fear that it is too late."

This mixture of braggadocio and eagerness to profit by the king's welcome must have made a bad impression on Frederick II. Ignoring the undisguised offer of service, he contented himself with replying by a courteous letter in which he invited Mirabeau to remain in Berlin until the arrival of Mirabeau's brother, who had asked permission to be present at the spring manoeuvres, and meanwhile to come again to see him "a couple of times."

Mirabeau had nothing in him of the courtier. He did not allow himself to be dazzled by the glory that was already weaving a legend around the dying king, but he had a fresh and youthful enthusiasm for true greatness. Beneath the deceptive prestige of success he saw the arduous path by which Frederick II had climbed to the summit, and he realized the mental labours that had fashioned him.

2

It was entirely through personal ascendancy that Mirabeau succeeded in entering Berlin society. Esterno did him bad disservice, but he gained the friendship of a Frenchman who facilitated his access to the court. The Marquis de Luchet, "well known for the amiability of his character," according to Henriette, was the editor of a French compilation that had had a large sale in Germany, the *Conteur*, and he was also the author of novels widely read by women. He was, according to Mirabeau, "an avowed and fanatical protector of the French system." He eagerly welcomed every Frenchman who travelled in Germany. "Thus," complained Esterno, "beings almost imperceptible among us make a sensation in other courts and especially in this one, in which the liking of the royal house for foreigners gives them greater importance of a sort than anywhere else."

This was written with reference to Mirabeau. The minister noted bitterly, in a report to Vergennes, that "Prince Henry began by becoming infatuated with this man, and when he spoke to me about him I felt that it was due to my attachment to his Royal Highness that I should say nothing to confirm him in his decided taste for M. de Mirabeau."

Mirabeau became one of the friends of Prince Henry; he was received as a guest at Rheinsberg, the prince's summer residence; he felt that he was listened to when he explained things to the prince or lavished advice on him. Esterno was annoyed by the tone which the prince allowed his protégé to adopt. But he was unable to do as much harm to Mirabeau as he would have liked, for Prince Henry considered that France, which he so admired, was not worthily represented in Berlin. He would have liked to have a less narrow-minded personality sent there, or at all events a more sagacious observer attached to Esterno.

It was a grave moment; the king might die at any time; the start of a new reign called for special attention; Prince Henry wrote to this effect to some of his friends in Paris. In point of fact, he was trembling for his own influence and preoccupied with his own position. The French government counted on the influence of Prince Henry over the successor to Frederick II in maintaining a policy favourable ·to France.

Mirabeau seems at first to have shared that hope. But he soon discovered that "he can neither lead nor be led," and he warned his French friends to place no trust in the prince.

3

"He possessed the art of questioning to such a degree that it is difficult to give any idea of it to those who have not become familiar with his conversation," said Christian Wilhelm von Dohm of Mirabeau.

Mirabeau gave himself up entirely to discovering the preponderant influence in Prussia and the true features of the German leaders and people. He was determined to see everything for himself; he was interested in everything, and concerned to penetrate everywhere and to familiarize himself with every class of society. His friends found that he made very rapid progress in German; soon he was able to read newspapers and periodicals, and to devour the most important literary works with his customary avidity. He became able to follow conversations, to obtain information at first hand, and to check it by drawing from all sorts of sources.

He made friends with Dohm, who as a historian and diplomat was in particularly good position to enlighten Mirabeau on Prussian home policy and on the preliminaries of the League of Princes, the last great success of Frederick II. Dohm's friend Nicolai, publisher of the *Allgemeine Deutsche Bibliothek*, introduced Mirabeau to German literature, and Mirabeau adopted all his views. His new friends represented the intellectual clarity and rationalism of the Germany of that day and the solid good sense of the German middle class, which dominated the world of literature and the arts. They represented an enlightened liberalism, a reformist tendency that placed all its faith in the march of rational progress and was opposed to revolutionary upheavals.

4

"Milord Dalrymple," said Mirabeau of the English ambassador to Berlin, "is a man of honour and of sense, boring sometimes because he is always bored, but endowed with more intelligence than might be imagined by those who have not carefully watched him, and, indeed, by nature dependable, generous, liberal."

Mirabeau was much with the "very Britannic" secretary of the British embassy, Ewart. He mixed with foreign diplomats and with all classes. His picturesque silhouette became familiar to many Berliners. The young romantic poet Ludwig Tieck remembered his penetrating as far as a remote tavern frequented by artists, at the foot of the Kreutzberg. He was particularly well received in Jewish society in Berlin. The Jews, only recently tolerated, and only recently arrived at a certain prosperity, were eager for intellectual enfranchisement, as though trying to make up for centuries of backwardness. Only just escaped from the shadow of the ghettos, they pursued enlightenment in every direction. In this new city of Berlin, destitute of tradition, they were a sort of leaven that threw up about them the society of the morrow. The Jewish colony of Berlin formed circles in which poets and artists gathered in their search for a new art. The salon of the beautiful Henriette Hertz, and later that of Rahel Levin, transplanted to Berlin the traditions of Parisian cultural centres. Mirabeau was present at the lecture on physics of Marcus Hertz, and was received by his wife, in whose salon he met Prussian junkers alongside bearers of purely French names, descendants of Huguenots but themselves ultra-Germanic; leaders of the rationalist school alongside young representatives of the *Sturm und Drang* movement. In these alert and forward-looking circles the visitor from abroad excited lively curiosity. Years later, Henriette Hertz remembered that she "had never heard anyone speak in so ravishing a manner."

The only Jews Mirabeau had met until then were money-lenders. He was now meeting an intellectual élite. He had never thought about the Jewish problem. He now read Lessing's *Nathan the Wise*, and learned from Nicolai, who had inspired him with lively admiration for that author, that Lessing's Nathan was drawn from the Jewish philosopher Moses Mendelssohn, who had died in the early part of that year, 1786. Nicolai, who had been closely associated with Mendelssohn, interested Mirabeau in his work.

Dohm's pamphlet on Jewish emancipation also produced a deep impression on Mirabeau, who was alive thereafter to the burning problem of anti-Semitism. The first fruit of his stay in Germany was the work *Moses Mendelssohn et la réforme politique des Juifs*, based largely on Dohm's pamphlet and on articles by Nicolai and Engel. In the conclusion of the pamphlet he wrote:

"I exhort the adversaries of the Jews (I wish the word 'enemy' could be banished from every tongue) to ask themselves in good faith whether, in this important discussion, they have not always justified oppression by its consequences, sought the causes in the effect, published calumnies by way of explanation, suppositions by way of proof, predictions by way of rejoinder. I exhort them to ask themselves whether it is not very reprehensible levity to reinforce by frivolous objections . . . a prejudice so barbarous as this, which mutilates a numerous group of the human species, and degrades it below the rank which Nature assigns to her children. Human nature is much the same everywhere. The Jews will be what the other citizens are in each state in which the same rights are accorded to them and the same obligations imposed on them."

The book on Moses Mendelssohn was one of the first of his son's writings that found grace in the eyes of that redoubtable critic the Marquis de Mirabeau. "That scamp," he commented, "has not only thoroughly acquired the use of the tool of speech, but also of that of thought, a thing of which I did not think him capable, and, save for a totally irreligious basis that shows itself in details, the work would be good."

5

Mirabeau realized the importance of the information he had gathered and the contacts he had established, especially when he compared them with the narrow horizon of the official representative of France. His awareness of his own capacity and of the impossibility of employing it embittered him. He was without news from his friends. He felt "treated as an exile who has earned proscription." He nursed his resentment against Calonne and gathered material for an attack on him. He acquired evidence "that all our coinage of 1784 and 1785 was debased," and he informed a journalist of this "brigandage," which was one day to become the basis of a charge against Calonne. While in Berlin he received the reply of the Banque de Saint-Charles to his pamphlet; it attacked him in an insulting manner. In his rejoinder he thundered against "the speculators and their leader." Deeply injured, he was determined to make the minister who had duped him feel his power; he felt strong enough to force the minister into an ignominious abandonment of his post by exposing his baseness before the nation. He completed his open letter to Calonne. Indignation still guided his pen: "A speculator who holds a principal place in the King's Council, a Minister of Finance who speculates, is the cruellest scourge that Providence can let loose upon an unconstituted kingdom like France."

Mirabeau sent the manuscript of his open letter to his friends in Paris. They informed the minister. Calonne, alarmed, sent a message inviting Mirabeau to come to see him. Mirabeau, still plagued with financial worries, decided to accept the invitation. Before his departure he wrote to Frederick II. The king replied at once: "You would give me pleasure, should you be passing through here, by letting me know of your arrival in this town."

On April 17 Mirabeau was received for the second time by Frederick. He found the king exhausted by the morning's drive: "He went at such speed that he killed two of the horses." Frederick, huddled in his easy chair, was breathing with great difficulty, struggling against suffocation. But this worn-out body was inhabited by an indomitable spirit, the sick organism was whipped up by a will of steel. "It is impossible to imagine a brain more alert or a conversation more amiable," wrote Mirabeau to Henriette.

Mirabeau, with his habit of going to the root of difficulties, broached the problems that were occupying him at the moment. He had noted the king's indifference to German literature. "Why," he asked him point-blank, "has not the Caesar of the Germans been their Augustus? Why has not Frederick the Great deigned to associate himself with the glory of the literary Revolution of his day, to speed it on, to warm it at the fire of his genius and his power?"

Frederick II parried with his sceptic's subtlety: "But what could I have done for the German men of letters that would have served them as well as I did by leaving them alone?" he replied. Mirabeau remembered that argument, and later, in an account of this conversation, he added the comment: "In comparison with that benefit, I regard as very small the loss that German literature may have suffered by being deprived of the support of the great and of sovereigns. Literature is like commerce, it hates constraint, and constraint is the inseparable companion of the great."

"Tell Dohm," he wrote to Henriette from Potsdam, "that we had a good talk about the Jews and about tolerance. I do not recommend the superstitious to get up against him."

Mirabeau was the last foreigner admitted into the presence of Frederick II. He left Potsdam just as fascinated as he had been at the first audience. It was only later that he said to himself: "Let us seek in him the limitations of a great man."

On his way home he stopped at Magdeburg, where he was warmly received, thanks to letters of recommendation from Minister von Hertzberg and from Dohm. He stayed a few days at Brunswick, in the hope of meeting the Duke of Brunswick. "I was received with much kindness at this court, and even fêted," he wrote to Henriette; but he could not afford to stay long enough to meet the duke. He had not wasted his time, however. He met a friend of Dohm, Jakob Mauvillon, a man

of French origin who had become an enthusiastic German while retaining his affection for his former country. Mauvillon was a major in
the Engineers and professor of tactics at the Carolinum, an indefatigable
worker, equally versed in political economy and in military science. His
respect for authority, inculcated by his German education, had not
stifled his liking for freedom of thought. The two men became warmly
attached to each other; their chance meeting gave birth to a lifelong
friendship—in the phrase used later by Mirabeau, a "marriage of souls."

6

Mirabeau reached Paris when the courts were occupied with the Affair
of the Necklace.[1] He realized that the case involved not only a duke, a
crook, and an adventuress, but a whole regime. Marie Antoinette had
refused to follow the advice of the Minister of Foreign Affairs and
the Keeper of the Seals to hush up the affair. She had been determined
to punish her slanderers and to satisfy her hatred of the cardinal, which
dated from the time when Rohan, as ambassador at Vienna, had transmitted reports charging her (she was then wife of the Dauphin) with
frivolity.

Marie Antoinette failed to realize that she could not use her influence
as queen to satisfy a private resentment. "Thirty years ago," wrote
Mirabeau, "the cardinal would have been lost without hope of redress;
fortunately we have learnt to overthrow authority in its elements of
absurdity." He mixed with the crowd that had been awaiting the verdict
since dawn. The courts, the approaches to the Palais de Justice, and the
neighbouring streets were thronged. When the cardinal's acquittal was
pronounced the crowd mobbed the members of the *parlement:* "The
people stopped them, kissed them, caressed them; five hundred persons
prostrated themselves; it was a scene of delirium."

Mirabeau had the same feeling as the people when he saw in this
case a whole society unmasked in its cynicism and its credulity, its
boundless love of luxury, and its intrigues around an arbitrary power.

[1] Cardinal de Rohan, anxious to overcome the queen's aloofness, allowed himself
to be duped by the intriguing Comtesse de La Motte. The countess told him that
the queen was anxious to possess a necklace worth 1,600,000 francs, which the king
had refused her. The Cardinal bought the necklace and sent it to the countess for
the queen, but it disappeared. Rohan was unable to pay and the affair came into
court. He was sent to the Bastille but acquitted, though he was exiled from Paris.
The Comtesse de La Motte was whipped, branded, and imprisoned in the Salpêtrière.
The queen had had no part in the intrigue, but the scandal of the affair did not leave
her unscathed.—Translator's note.

A regime had been judged, a society, then all-powerful, had been condemned without appeal. "What a country," exclaimed Mirabeau, "what men, what flabbiness, what corruption!"

Calonne was the typical representative of a period that was living on expedients and saving the present at the cost of collapse on the morrow. But Mirabeau could not come forward to accuse him. His financial difficulties were too great; he had assumed too heavy responsibilities for the woman he loved and the child. He allowed his silence to be bought. "M. Calonne finds it is safer to give me employment," he said bitterly. He allowed himself to be "muzzled," while trying to safeguard a few shreds of his dignity.

Calonne obtained from Vergennes a secret mission for him, at Calonne's expense. Talleyrand had been the chief agent on his behalf, becoming a sort of personal guarantor for him with Calonne. But at the very moment when his secret mission was bringing the two still closer together, an incident occurred that risked embroiling them. Mirabeau, in his uncomfortable role of a man whose mouth has been stopped, was concerned to appear before Calonne as an irreplaceable adviser, knowing everything, and possessing a solution for every problem. Calonne was preoccupied with the question of the provincial assemblies, on the organization of which a report had been presented by Necker. With the rapidity of a conjurer, Mirabeau submitted a detailed plan to Calonne, but without telling him that the plan was not his own but was the work of Dupont, who had passed to him his report on provincial assemblies and elective municipalities, drawn up for Turgot at the time when Mirabeau was a prisoner at Vincennes.

He also showed this manuscript to Clavière, who thought it had been written by Turgot himself, and Clavière passed it on to Brissot. Mirabeau suddenly learned that Brissot, without asking anybody's authorization, and without informing Clavière, was getting it printed. Mirabeau, angered at this "infinitely grave imprudence," let Brissot know that the divulgation of the manuscript would do him irreparable harm, and that he would find himself obliged to proceed against Brissot. Brissot defended himself with this specious argument: "I believed, I believe, and I always shall believe, that this work, which may be useful to the public, the work of a man no longer living, of a man who throughout his life sacrificed himself to the welfare of mankind, belongs to the public."

The work appeared later, this time, apparently, with Mirabeau's assent, at a moment when he was dogged by money troubles, as a posthumous work of Turgot. Dupont then publicly protested against this abuse of confidence: "He gave it to M. de Calonne as a work of his own, and I was driven to present to the minister the original in my handwriting to show him how Mirabeau writes some of his works."

During this stay in Paris, Mirabeau was obsessed by cares. Humiliating negotiations, anxiety for the future, and overwork so fatigued him as to bring on violent haemorrhage, followed by serious exhaustion.

The mother of his son called on him one day and declared that her husband "would not leave him in peace or quiet until he had this child." Mirabeau sent for the husband and tried to reason with him. Mirabeau was very fond of the child, who had become for Henriette, as Mirabeau wrote to her, "a need of your heart, an occupation of your life." He secured a momentary respite by promising the nominal father to resume the discussion on his return from Germany.

He was also haunted by anxiety for Henriette's health; she feared that she was consumptive. "I wake up in the middle of the night asking in a sort of nightmare how you are."

At this time Talleyrand, always haunted by his dream of an immense fortune, confided to Mirabeau, apart from his political mission in Berlin, negotiations for the founding of a state bank, for which he was to mobilize capital in Prussia, and also for the investment of public funds. On his return to Berlin Mirabeau became associated with the Dane Struensee, a former professor of philosophy and mathematics who had become financial adviser to Frederick II and later became Minister of Finance under the new king.

Struensee regarded the projected bank as "a great and superb organization that cannot but succeed," and promised his support for it.

7

"His features show depth and subtlety, and the desire to please, tempered by firmness and even severity." Such was Mirabeau's description of the Duke of Brunswick. "He is polished to the point of affectation; he speaks with precision and even elegance, but he does so with a little effort and often misses the exact phrase. He can listen and follow up one's replies with further questions."

On his return to Germany Mirabeau had stopped again at Brunswick, where the duke made him stay for dinner. After the meal the duke took him into an alcove and talked with him for two hours. The duke was very reserved at first, but the vehemence with which his interlocutor questioned him overcame his reticence. He was apprehensive with regard to rumours that Vergennes was to go and that his place was to be taken by Breteuil, whom the duke knew to be pro-Austrian. Mirabeau reassured him: "Europe and ourselves in particular are so concerned for peace that our relations with Austria can only contribute to it."

Mirabeau expressed apprehensions in turn about the change which the king's death might bring in Prussia, which was "today on the Continent the pivot of peace and war." His interlocutor would, he said, be "almost the only one to decide the issue." He added shrewdly: "I was convinced that, having been the god of war sufficiently, he would in future be the angel of peace." The duke emphatically denied ever having been a lover of war. Mirabeau did not yet know what he was to discover later, that "war is the national industry of Prussia."

The duke seemed very interested in his visitor, or very concerned for his publicity in France, for he kept Mirabeau again for a long conversation on the day of his departure. He broached the subject dearest of all to Mirabeau: "Asking my opinion with the air of fearing that I should regard as an absurdity what he was going to say to me, he inquired whether I should really treat as an impracticable chimera the project of an alliance between France, England, and Prussia, of which the solemnly avowed purpose would be to guarantee its possessions in Europe to each power." Mirabeau enthusiastically agreed: "This idea, which I have been turning over in my head for seven years, is too great not to be seductive; it will infallibly immortalize the sovereign who carries it through and the minister who is able to second it. It will change the face of Europe, and entirely to our advantage."

Mirabeau saw his great idea making its way and assuming concrete shape. He was aware that if it was to triumph, French policy must be less inert. On his arrival in Berlin he drew up a report in which he reviewed the European situation. "The King of Prussia is dying; he may be dead at the moment I am writing. It is impossible that he should live another two months. With him will fall the keystone that held in position the political arch of Europe." He assessed at its true value the military power of Prussia: "Two hundred thousand men who form the best army in Europe, beyond all comparison, and a great general of known character, as influential in peace as in war, who may be eager to gather laurels for himself."

In Berlin he discussed his project with the diplomatic representatives of England. Unfortunately he was unable to make proposals in the name of the French government. "I spoke of it philosophically," he wrote to Lauzun, "with the English legation, and I found Milord

Dalrymple and even his very Britannic secretary of legation far nearer to these ideas than I should have dared to hope."

Placed by chance, as a result of shady scheming, at so important a spot for observation as Berlin, Mirabeau strove in vain to inspire the French government with confidence. He sent urgent letters to Talleyrand and lavished encouragement in his vehement way on Lauzun, who he knew shared these ideas.

After his interview with the Duke of Brunswick, he wrote to Lauzun: "I discussed with him that 'chimerical' idea of an alliance between France and England; he regards it as the salvation of the world, and as presenting no other difficulty than the prejudices of pseudo-science and the indifference of pusillanimity." The tragedy of centuries to come lay in that one phrase.

8

With the journalist's instinct for looking ahead, Mirabeau arranged for the French government to be informed immediately when the death of the king should take place. To this end he set a whole organization on foot. He bought two pairs of carrier pigeons and placed them in a farm four miles from Berlin. He informed the Comte d'Esterno that he had safe means for despatching news. The reply was: "The Comte d'Esterno has the honour to send his thanks to M. le Comte de Mirabeau; he will not profit by his obliging offers."

"I am keeping this letter as a curious memento," commented Mirabeau. He imagined that Esterno must have sent a courier or received orders not to send one. "Thus I discovered that we were not rich enough to throw away a hundred louis, and . . . I set free my pigeons." The French Foreign Minister learned of the death of the King of Prussia from the Leyden paper.

Moved as he was, Mirabeau was greatly surprised at the impression made on the public by the king's death. He walked up and down the streets of Berlin with Henriette to watch the reactions of the crowd: "Everybody was gloomy, nobody sad, everybody concerned, nobody afflicted. Not a face that did not reveal relief and hope, not a regret, not a sigh, not a word of praise. . . . Is this the end of so many battles won, so much glory, of a reign of almost half a century filled with so many high achievements? Everybody wanted it to end, everybody is glad that it is over. . . . The people have been so oppressed, so harassed, so weighed down, that they cannot but feel relieved."

9

"Sire, you are King. The day has come when God has willed to confide to you the destiny of several million men. . . . Sire, your figure, your features, recall the heroes of antiquity; this is much for the soldiers, it is much for the people, who associate high qualities of soul with physical beauty." Mirabeau wrote this to the new King of Prussia on his accession to the throne. It was no courtier's letter. He omitted none of the critical reflections suggested to him by the death of Frederick II. "Your predecessor certainly gained battles enough, perhaps too many; he over-tired the hundred voices of fame. Frederick conquered the admiration of mankind; never did he win their love; it can belong in its entirety to you." Rarely has a man ventured to speak in this style to a sovereign.

"This age is gaining enlightenment day by day. . . . It is extending its influence over your nation, which so many circumstances have kept backward. Everything today is judged with severe logic. The men who see only a fellow-man beneath the ermine, and who demand from him the virtues of a fellow-man, are more numerous than ever; it is no longer possible to dispense with their suffrage." But what he was asking of the new King of Prussia was a state of mind well in advance of his time. "For you, Sire, while it is good always to govern well, it is worthy of you not to govern too much. . . . A furious succession of regulations marks the character of small minds, fed by timid ideas and ridiculous apprehensions."

The reforms he demanded from Frederick William II, in the categorical and imperious tone of a man confident of the victory of his ideas, went beyond what the most progressive government of his age could have granted. He invited the King of Prussia to proceed in the first place to "the abolition of military slavery." He was no pacifist dreamer demanding the abolition of the army, but a citizen of the morrow, conscious of the strength of a people defending its liberties.

With great daring, Mirabeau demanded of a country so proud of its militarism as Prussia that it should "make war on the prejudice that sets so great a distance between military and civil functions. . . . In such a state as yours, it is possible that the military should have first consideration; but it must not have exclusive consideration; or you will have an army but never a kingdom."

He demanded for the middle class the right to acquire land belonging to the nobility. "Wherever the bourgeoisie can acquire property, wherever commerce is in honour, the country offers a picture of abundance and prosperity." He also demanded access for the middle class to all official posts. "Abolish, Sire, those prerogatives that fill great posts with men of little merit, to say no worse, and destroy the interest of the great bulk of your subjects in a country in which they meet with nothing but restrictions and humiliations."

Faithful to his convictions, he launched into a violent diatribe against the nobility. "Distrust that universal aristocracy, scourge of monarchical states, which, from one extremity of the globe to the other, oppresses mankind. Ah! whence comes the strength of the prince if not from the people?"

It was the language of an age approaching revolution. But Mirabeau did not content himself with a struggle against abuses. "Prompt and gratuitous justice is clearly the first duty of sovereigns." He demanded independent judges, "paid from the public revenue." In an entirely modern spirit he put forward the principle of the right to work. "Be also the first sovereign in whose state every man who wants to work finds work. All who breathe should be nourished through work. It is the first law of nature, a law anterior to any human convention; it is the bond of every society."

Mirabeau saw clearly the consequences of the reign of Frederick II. Europe was exalting the hero king and celebrating in every tongue the independence of mind of the philosopher king; the age took pride in him. But Mirabeau judged him from the reactions of his people; and he judged him severely, on the very morrow of his death. "Frederick II was much more an almost unique example of the development of a great character set in its place than of a genius elevated by nature high above other men. . . . Having turned all the forces of his talent to forming a great military power out of disunited, fragmented, and mostly infertile states . . . he thought mainly of money."

The future legislator was already speaking in Mirabeau. It was the tragedy of every absolute sovereign that he was exposing, the dangers from which no man can escape when he holds unlimited power in his hands. He pointed out Frederick's "habit of suffering no contradiction and of allowing no discussion of his extreme contempt of men, which perhaps explains all his successes, all his faults, his whole conduct, the sense of superiority that confirmed him in the fatal resolution to see everything, to settle everything, to order everything." After exposing the king's weaknesses as a man, which nobody had yet dared to discuss, Mirabeau—the only critic to do so for a long time—threw doubt on the excellence of his work. "What did this great man achieve as king, at the cost of such efforts? Did he leave you wealthy, powerful, happy states? Take away their military reputation and the resources of their treasury, which may be dissipated, . . . and there is very little left."

Following Talleyrand, Mirabeau attacked the Prussian lotteries, that so-called "free and voluntary tax." "What a tax!" he exclaimed, "basing its chief production on delirium or despair. . . . This horrible invention, which poisons everything, even hope, man's last asset."

He fought for the ideas that were dear to him, ideas for which he never ceased fighting in the days when he had in his hands the power of the legislator. "The most complete liberation of the press should be one of your first operations," he wrote. His great voice grew particularly eloquent when he raised it in favour of tolerance: "But, Sire, a great, a first and immediate operation which I ask of Your Majesty, in the name of your closest interest and of your glory, is a prompt and formal declaration, invested with the most imposing character of sovereignty, that unlimited tolerance shall be accorded forever to all religions. . . . Grant it in the edict that shall accord every civil liberty to the Jews. This boon, which from the first moments of your reign will make you surpass in religious tolerance your illustrious predecessor, himself the most tolerant prince who ever was, this boon will not be without reward. Amid the large increase of population and capital that it will infallibly bring you, at the expense of other countries, from the second generation the Jews will become good and useful citizens."

"The king," Mirabeau wrote to Talleyrand, "simply acknowledged it, adding that I might be sure that everything that came to him from me would always give him pleasure, and that the kind things that reached him would never seem more flattering than from me."

This polite answer revealed nothing of the impression produced by Mirabeau's letter. But since the sovereign to whom it was addressed had failed to express indignation, Esterno charged himself with that duty: "The Comte de Mirabeau has further injured the nation by his presumption in tracing a plan of government for the King of Prussia," he wrote to Vergennes. "In this plan, in the guise of a philosopher who makes it his duty to speak the truth to the king, who did not ask him to do so, he wrote things that were very out of place and very disagreeable."

Esterno was excited to the point of asking, in the name, he said, of Prince Henry, "that no Frenchman should be allowed to come to this court. . . . Mirabeau might well be made to leave the Prussian states." This statement was contradicted by Mirabeau, who reported that the king had had him sounded about entering his service. It seems especially discredited by the fact that Prince Henry continued to receive him in the intimacy of his palace at Rheinsberg, and that he charged him with the negotiation of a reconciliation with "his implacable enemy" the Minister von Hertzberg.

On September 2, 1786, Esterno had demanded in Prince Henry's name the expulsion of Mirabeau; on August 18 Mirabeau had written to Talleyrand: "Prince Henry has asked me to say that the Comte d'Esterno is far too cold, too stiff, too much the minister, for the new king." It is possible that both statements were true, and that Prince Henry played a double game. Mirabeau said later of him: "His whole life is just petty, base, dirty intriguing."

Mirabeau prided himself on two immediate results from his letter to Frederick William: the suppression of the lotteries and consideratior of the case of the Jews. He wrote later to his sister: "The King of Prus sia is occupied with giving full civil liberty to the Jews, and my re- quests were not greater than are his concessions."

One evening at supper the king spoke to Mirabeau on the question of the lotteries. "In this matter I owe you an apology, for it is one of the good bits of advice in a certain manuscript." Mirabeau bowed low. "But you must excuse me a little longer," the king went on. He explained that the suppression had been delayed by the funds involved and by existing agreements. "Sire, none of those are violated," replied Mirabeau; "and besides, so much use has been made of despotism to do harm, if for once it could be used to do good—"

"Ah, you are getting a little reconciled to despotism?"

"One must, Sire, in a country in which a single head has four hundred thousand arms."

10

"They are quite satisfied with your reports; I am told so every day," wrote Talleyrand to Mirabeau. "The king reads them with much in- terest. M. de Calonne thanks you for your exactitude, and for the care with which your messages are drawn up. I have made good use of your statistics; the merit of this work has been fully appreciated." Between his return to Berlin on July 21, 1786, and January 19, 1787, Mirabeau sent to Paris sixty-five reports, in addition to memoranda and extracts from German papers. Talleyrand received his letters. Before passing them on he toned down Mirabeau's energetic manner. He gave his direct and often verbose style diplomatic conciseness and discretion. He sup- pressed too heated criticisms of the incoherence of the French government's foreign policy, as well as over-free anecdotes of the court of Berlin.

Mirabeau drew up his letters with especial care, but he submitted with a good grace to Talleyrand's censorship. He thanked him, indeed, for "the sensation my reports have produced after being expurgated. arranged, and embellished by you."

He was a "superstitiously conscientious" observer. His life in Berlin was made up in part of what he called "an idle activity." He plunged into every throng, into "the most fastidious societies, into the loss of time usually involved by the whirl of German circles, which are called intimate when there are only thirty persons present." He often went to bed at one o'clock, but rose at five and started work at once.

Mirabeau had a rare talent for discovering intelligent collaborators. whose help enabled him to get through an immense amount of work His collaborator in Berlin was a young baron from Courland, M. de Noldé, a lieutenant in the French service in the Royal Swedish Regiment, esteemed and liked by his chiefs. He had distinguished himself on active service, but he preferred study to the "melancholy service of a junior officer." Mirabeau had also a secretary, Sambat. "Never have I seen young men more sober, more steady, harder working, or more good-natured," wrote Henriette de Nehra.

It was inevitably an expensive life. In sending Mirabeau to Berlin. Calonne had asked what salary he wanted. "I shall only spend for you so you will pay what I spend," replied Mirabeau. "In eight and a half months," he wrote later to his father, "I have spent forty-two thousand livres, including various secret expenditures, the luxurious clothing needed in northern courts, and the horses of every sort indispensable in Berlin. Of this amount the king owes me twelve thousand which I shall probably never get."

As always, his life was made up of external luxury and domestic straits, with even heating inadequate, for Mirabeau complained of having no fire in his own room. It was a life of hard work for sixteen to seventeen hours a day. Amorous adventures seem to have been lacking. In this foreign city Mirabeau had found a home. A mistress, an illegitimate child, and two young foreigners living under his roof formed a circle of domestic happiness, of middle-class peacefulness, in which he relaxed from the tension of his former hectic existence. It was the brightest period of his life, a brief interlude. Mirabeau's best qualities showed themselves in serenity. The future statesman ripened in Berlin. He said later with justified pride: "I predicted no Prussian event that did not happen, and none happened that I did not predict."

11

"I believe . . . that the king has conceived the idea and the hope of becoming a great man by making himself German, purely German, and so flouting French superiority." Mirabeau saw in this attitude the influence of the Minister von Hertzberg. He assumed that he had said to the king: "What will you ever be as a Frenchman? A poor imitation of Frederick II. As a German you will be original, you will yourself be revered in Germania, adored by your people, extolled by men of letters, and highly respected in Europe."

The positive policy pursued by Frederick II had demanded great concentration. Frederick William's attitude was negative, that of following the path of least resistance. The big body of the young king was filled with an incurable lethargy, interrupted by sudden tempers which he himself took for manifestations of strength. Mirabeau had gained knowledge of the intimate life of the king: "Not a paper is in order, not a memorandum commented on, not a letter personally opened; no human power can make him read forty consecutive lines." This lethargy was shaken off only "by a brutal sensual appetite, an unrestrained thirst for pleasure, without discrimination or delicacy."

The king's amours occupied a large place in Mirabeau's reports. Prince Henry speculated on his nephew's sensuality. He wanted ("for," said Mirabeau maliciously, "great men do not disdain little expedients") to have "a blonde, rather plump, sent here, especially one with musical talents," to win the king over to the French cause. She should be "readier to grant favours than to reveal needs," for the king was miserly, or rather, "a worshipper of gold, not so much from avarice as from the passion for possessing." But a French adventuress who came to Berlin with aims on the king proved too much in a hurry.

The general disillusionment paved the way after Frederick's death for the mystics whom his scepticism had kept at a distance. The Rosicrucians, with their cult of the elixir of life and of the philosopher's stone, gained enthusiastic adherents. Their challenge to rationalism and enlightenment brought them support from all reactionary sources, and they proclaimed themselves the stern defenders of the throne and of the established order. Their power was due especially to the ability of two men who made use of the sect to serve their own ambitions.

Wöllner, son of a country pastor, originally a rationalist and freemason, was brought into the Rosicrucian sect by his ambition and by a sense of persecution. While tutor in the family of a Prussian general of noble rank, he had seduced the general's daughter in order to force her into marriage. Frederick II, who objected to misalliances, had him thrown into prison. He became the determined enemy of everything Frederick II represented, of the doctrines he favoured, of his cosmopolitanism and of his spirit of tolerance.

Chance brought him into touch with a Saxon officer, a brilliant man of the world, who was a convinced mystic and a fervent adept of the Rose-Cross. This officer, Bischoffswerder, was a friend of Frederick William, then Crown Prince of Prussia, and cured him of a grave malady by "the supernatural virtues of a medicament of which he claimed to have received the secret from his order." In his boundless gratitude, Frederick William at once joined the order. So illustrious an adept at once brought success to the Rosicrucians. Under the able direction of Wöllner the order spread quickly and gained power, especially in Prussia, through "the attraction of the mysterious . . . and of good jobs to be had."

Wöllner neglected no means of maintaining his hold over Frederick William II. He called up spirits amid thunder and lightning. A clever ventriloquist appeared in turn as Marcus Aurelius, Leibnitz, and Frederick II. Esterno reported to Vergennes that at a séance of "masonic illuminati" at which the king and the Duke of Brunswick were present, the shade of Julius Caesar was evoked. Wöllner, "always surrounded," wrote Mirabeau, "by obscurity, mystery, intrigues, accomplices," soon wrested from the king two edicts against freedom of conscience and freedom of the press. It was no longer possible to discuss politics; scientific research was stifled. The universities became citadels of reaction, which, to capture men's minds, united an aggressive nationalism with a hatred of everything French.

"Who now is master?" Mirabeau asked himself, after tracing this sombre picture of intrigue around the throne. "One might well be tempted to say King Log. . . . Rottenness before maturity; I am much afraid that that is the motto of the Prussian power."

12

"The French cause is lost in Berlin," was Mirabeau's conclusion. It was at Berlin that he dreamed most ardently of the alliance with England, it was from Berlin that he sent his most pressing letters to Lauzun. He feared that France's position would become untenable the day Prussia formed an agreement with the Austrian Emperor.

He wrote to Paris: "Hasten to oppose to that coalition . . . the system of union with England, which will save the world. . . . Think of

Poland. What they did there (if they got no more it was because they got all they wanted), they will do again, even without the intervention of Russia, that sleeping giant whose awakening may change the face of the globe."

But he found only "redoubled symptoms of extreme inattention." He received no news from Paris. His most important questions were left without reply. "I should learn a thousand times more if I were better instructed," he complained.

At this decisive moment he left for Brunswick and had long talks with the duke, one of the few persons in Germany whom he esteemed and thought capable of piloting the future. But a time came when he asked himself: "Has the duke disgracefully deceived me?" The admission hurt his self-esteem and was a blow to his affection, and he did not hesitate to communicate his suspicions to Paris.

This bitter experience was only one of a long series of disappointments. In his daily growing dislike of the leaders of Prussia, he made only one exception: "The Crown Prince will soon deserve watching; this young man may have great destinies," was his conclusion. "And if he should be the pivot of some memorable revolution, far-seeing men would not be surprised." Once more Mirabeau showed his extraordinary psychological penetration. He was no longer alive when the future King of Prussia revealed, in an hour of tragedy for his country, the qualities which this foreign observer had noted in him.

After a few months in Berlin Mirabeau wrote that he was thoroughly tired and disgusted. The longer he stayed, moreover, the more difficult became his "nebulous position." At the end of January 1787 he suddenly decided to leave; Henriette and the child remained there.

13

Having failed to make any useful contribution to current policy in Germany, Mirabeau contented himself with collecting "exact results in a country which is of the same importance for the understanding of despotism as Egypt was to the ancients. We may, perhaps, glean from it a singular theory of the human machine, and of his usefulness to those who make use of him, in preference to the man who is free."

He brought away another lesson, which he was to publish in a big work, *La Monarchie Prussienne.* He advised his countrymen "to reflect on the constitution of the Prussian army."

≽ XI ≼

The Century Has Joined Him

"**M**Y HEART has not aged, and if my enthusiasm has been damped, it has not been destroyed," wrote Mirabeau from Berlin to Talleyrand. "I had good evidence of this today; I regard as one of the best days of my life the day on which you informed me of the convocation of the Notables, which no doubt will soon be followed by that of the National Assembly. I see in it a new order of things that may regenerate the monarchy."

Talleyrand replied: "You cannot praise M. de Calonne too highly. He must be supported by general praise in order to make a success of this great matter and to show him especially the glory he will gain."

The king shared the same illusions. When, toward the end of 1786, Calonne proposed to him that an Assembly of Notables should be convoked, Louis XVI was at once attracted by the project. "I did not sleep last night," he wrote to him, "but my wakefulness arose from pleasure."

The truth was that Calonne had brought himself into a hopeless situation; and in order to mask his failure he had seized on this idea, which several persons, Mirabeau among them, claimed credit for suggesting to him. He had found himself obliged to admit to the king a deficit of a hundred millions. To induce the nation to accept new sacrifices, he submitted to the king a plan that included the suppression of certain flagrant abuses, a more equitable distribution of burdens, massive economies in the king's household, and the alienation of part of the crown domains. "But you have come straight from Necker with all this," exclaimed the king. "Sire," replied Calonne with his habitual coolness, "as things are there is nothing better we can give you."

In suggesting the convocation of the Assembly of Notables, Calonne was yielding to a powerful current of public opinion, which demanded the collaboration of a larger number of responsible persons in the determination of the burdens imposed by the state. For Calonne, everything was a matter of deals: he proposed to barter reforms for new revenue. He hoped by this great gesture for the general good, this concession to the new spirit, to secure immunity for his imprudent administration, his culpable complaisance, and his depredations.

Mirabeau, fascinated by the result, did not discern so clearly Calonne's intentions. He was far away. But the French public was not deceived. It was taken for granted that the government was convoking the Assembly only in order to make it shoulder the responsibility for new and crushing taxation. Parisian scepticism found expression in bills posted everywhere, even on the door of the Ministry of Finance: "The new troupe of comedians raised by the Sieur de Calonne, which will make its first appearance on the 29th instant, will present as its main piece 'The Confidence Trick' and for the smaller one 'Forced Consent'; these pieces will be followed by an allegorical pantomime ballet entitled 'The Sieve of the Danaïdes.' "

In Paris Mirabeau found a very different situation from that which he had expected. He had hoped to gain a seat in the Assembly, and had written to Talleyrand that he would feel "honoured a thousand times" if he could be "its junior secretary." He thought he was entitled to this as the father of the idea. But two secretaries had already been nominated, including Dupont, who also claimed paternity.

The general scepticism further increased his personal disappointment. The composition of the Assembly of Notables seemed to justify the worst expectations. Of the hundred and forty-six notables, seventeen were princes of the blood, seven archbishops, eight marshals of France, twelve dukes, thirty-four presidents of courts of justice or provincial attorneys general, and twenty titled gentlemen. The Assembly was criticized and derided even in court circles. One day the queen was present at a comedy in which the principal part was that of a king who ran out of money on a journey. A squire asked: "What can we do?" "Assemble the Notables," shouted a voice in the pit. A print widely circulated represented a farmer who collected his poultry and said to them: "My dear creatures, I have assembled you to deliberate on the sauce with which you shall be served up." Vergennes at this moment deprived Calonne of "his sole prop," wrote Mirabeau to Mauvillon: the Controller General was going "to be occupied solely with battling for his personal safety and not with organizing the nation; in consequence he needed concocters of manifestos and not collaborators, intriguers and satellites and not citizen aides-de-camp. All this was not by any means to my taste: I am entirely unable to say, still less to prove, what I do not think, or to defend what my conviction accuses. So when the Minister of Finance sent mutual friends to sound me I asked straight out to be allowed to stand aside, and as in the circumstances that was almost impossible for me while here, I repeated my request to be sent abroad." He hoped to obtain a new mission, especially to Holland, where, thanks to his personal relations, he could do useful work. But Calonne was too absorbed in his own difficulties, too contemptuous of those whom he paid, and aware that Mirabeau was struggling in "embarrassments of every sort." Mirabeau's friends returned to the charge and pointed out that Mirabeau was "not a man to make discontented." Calonne replied with calm disdain: "I will arrange all that with money." This was more than Mirabeau could endure. He had been hurt at the most sensitive, because the most vulnerable, spot. He was determined to be revenged for this "inexpiable outrage." He would prove to Calonne, who had "thrown away the lemon while it still had juice in it," how redoubtable he, Mirabeau, still was. He still felt a mission to enlighten the nation, and to his care for the public good there was added, as he wrote to Henriette, the desire "to show a certain personage that if it was a good thing to take me, it was not good to drop me."

2

The Vicar General of Sens, the Abbé d'Espagnac, was typical of the misplaced careers of his time, one which maintained traditions at the cost of moral degeneracy. If Espagnac, a man of good family, son of the governor of the Invalides, had been able to choose his own career, his gifts and his speculative daring would have made him one of the great financiers of his time. As a professional financier he might have retained some decent scruples. But, having been educated for spiritual functions, in the financial operations that attracted him he went to work without either rule or restraint. "He speculated on everything," wrote a contemporary, "and would have done so with souls if he had had the chance."

Calonne, driven to extremes by the growing deficit, decided to make use of the Caisse d'Escompte, whose share capital he increased by eighty million francs, of which seventy million were paid over to him. Bargains for future settlement were entered into under his orders by two companies, one operating in the shares of the Compagnie des Eaux and the other in those of the Compagnie des Indes. These shares had to be deposited in pledge with the bankers, who lent to the two companies the funds they needed. Espagnac had sold shares in the Indes to agents of Calonne, but he knew that the minister could not pay for the shares he had acquired. He entered into forward purchases of them at an enormous profit. More were sold to him than were on the market, at a loss on the purchase price; shares were sold to him that had not been paid for and were not actually held. The clerical speculator soon had Calonne's agents at his mercy. In order to carry through the immense operation, the abbé tried to bring in other speculators. He drew up a secret plan. The rumour of this operation spread on the Bourse at the moment when he wanted to carry it out.

Mirabeau succeeded in getting hold of the confidential document. This "villainous enterprise" supplied the battleground he needed. He denounced it in a pamphlet addressed to the Assembly of Notables, which was shortly to meet. But he hit out not only at the dishonest speculators, but at the invisible hand that was protecting this swindling scheme: "How can operations so immense and at the same time so scandalous be carried out? Whence can help come for them?" he asked. Calonne's name was not mentioned, but he wrote of a minister "to whom every principle of good faith, of fidelity to engagements, of respect for property is unknown, whose morality is entirely odious, whatever idea may be formed of his supposed talents."

His *Denunciation of Speculation to the King and the Assembly of Notables* was written and printed in three weeks. The work was not merely a denunciation, but urged constructive reforms—a free press, the sound organization of the finances of the state, and above all popular representation and provincial assemblies. It had, wrote Mirabeau to Mauvillon, "an unexampled success which it was far from meriting as a work, but may have merited as a service rendered with courage and dignity."

The sensational work was being attributed to the Marquis de Mirabeau, who wrote to his brother: "I am being constantly obliged to disown it and to reply to a crowd of letters that I have no knowledge either of the book or of its author." But—for the first time—the marquis saw his own influence in his son's work: "It is impossible not to recognize his father in his present style—assuming his father to have become a rhetorician."

Calonne, shaken by the general indignation, was obliged to move against the speculators. He exiled his compromised agents and the Abbé d'Espagnac. One of his intermediaries committed suicide. But Calonne could not do without his exiled agents or the abbé in liquidating the crash that followed. The shares of the Compagnie des Indes slumped. The Caisse d'Escompte was tottering. To prevent final ruin, Calonne had to make a deal with the abbé and to draw twelve millions from the Treasury to compensate him.

3

"Perhaps in all epochs of history," wrote Mme. de Staël one day, "there are personages who may be considered as the representatives of the good and the evil principle. Such were Cicero and Catiline in Rome; such were M. Necker [her father] and Mirabeau in France." Yet she admitted that her father's adversary was endowed "with the utmost mental energy and breadth. Mirabeau knew everything and foresaw everything."

In contrast with Gabriel de Mirabeau, whose father had done his best to destroy his self-confidence, Necker, always praised by his family, had the proud self-assurance of a self-made man. While Mirabeau had inherited from the "tempestuous race" a southern exuberance and Latin clarity, Jacques Necker, son of a German lawyer, had the rather pedantic Teuton ponderousness and the rather narrow and unconciliatory Teuton rectitude.

Differences more fundamental even than those of their origin and upbringing produced an inevitable antagonism between the two men. Necker was ruled by rigid moral principles; Mirabeau was the plaything of his passions. The world of the Genevese banker was solid and simple, resting on the basis of an unshakable social order, and illumined by a firm and absolute faith. In contrast with Necker's semi-feudal, thoroughly conservative world, that of Mirabeau was mobile and fluctuating, a world whose old beliefs and old abuses were dying. The strength of Necker lay in his sureness of everything; the extraordinary prescience of Mirabeau was born of the general uncertainty which was reflected in his own life.

The Assembly of Notables opened at Versailles at the end of February 1787. Calonne announced a deficit of eighty millions; later he was obliged to admit that the true figure was a hundred and twelve millions. Many notables were fervent Neckerites, and recalled his excess of revenue of ten millions. Calonne threw doubt on Necker's calculations. Necker asked the king to let him reply to Calonne's allegations, adding that if his statements were disproved he would abandon his fortune to the royal treasury. The king refused permission, but Necker nevertheless entered into public controversy on the question. Mirabeau had had no intention of intervening in the dispute between the two ministers, but he foresaw that Necker's financial policy would be the policy of the morrow, and he considered it important to pronounce upon it. He published a pamphlet entitled *Lettres sur l'administration de M. Necker.*

Necker's celebrity was well established; Mirabeau had only a quite recent notoriety. As he himself said, his attack might seem impious. For the universal cry was: "M. Necker made war without taxes! He is a god!" But the impious critic said: "What you impute to him as his glory is a crime. What you regard as his benefaction has been an aggravation of your evils. To borrow without taxing is to deliver a nation to the usurers; for they alone lend without security; it is deceiving a whole people about its true situation, and intoxicating governments by presenting to them as simple the plans of destruction and of expenditure that render mankind desolate." Panchaud furnished him with the data that demonstrated that Necker's loans had been the worst organized and the most ruinous that France had ever contracted. Necker himself was obliged to admit in his work on administration: "I had to borrow on unfavourable conditions, being unable to do otherwise."

The Marquis de Mirabeau shared his son's opinion of Necker. This attack was a belated vengeance for his friend Turgot. But, inconsistent as ever, he felt a secret irritation that made him write to the bailli: "There has just appeared another pretty strong pamphlet from the coryphée of the turbulent. . . . The remarkable thing about it is the indefatigable talent of a sponge that that man has for collecting whatever there is in his path of the nature of dirty water and expectoration and garbage . . . He goes on throwing stones at every passer-by. . . . That wretch cannot let his name rest in peace for a whole week."

4

"The Notables are behaving wonderfully well," wrote Mirabeau to Henriette. "Men are always straightforward the first time they are brought together. They are showing energy and wisdom, breadth and foresight. This epoch will remain a glory to the king and a boon to the nation."

From the very first this Assembly, so criticized in advance, gave evidence of a considerable change, of the approach of new times. Calonne himself, in his opening speech, adopted a modern phraseology that sounded strange in his mouth. He spoke of the abuses that had to be abolished for the public good, of the "most considered and most protected," whose existence weighed on the productive and labouring class; he spoke also of the "inequality of the subjects of the same sovereign"; he even spoke of the rigour and the arbitrariness of the collection of taxes. A new age, he announced, was beginning for France, and the old formula "Thus wills the King, thus wills the law" would thenceforth be replaced by "Thus wills the people's weal, thus wills the King."

All this only served to mask the imperative need for replenishing the Treasury, which he had exhausted. It served only to veil the decisions of absolutism, for Calonne, sure in advance of the acceptance of his plans—he declared that they had become those of His Majesty in person—had already had the edicts printed.

The Notables belonged to the privileged class, but they did not dare to protest against Calonne's plans on the score of their personal interests. To combat him they made use of the same method which he had used against them. They masked their repugnance to the loss of their privileges by a display of indignation at the minister's arbitrary proceedings. Public opinion, which had believed them to be in Calonne's pocket, ranged itself on their side when one of them exclaimed: "Do you take us for sheep and cattle, to be brought together simply to give our assent to a plan already matured?" There was competition in the advancing of new ideas, which disguised the true nature of the debate. The Notables pronounced in favour of provincial assemblies and of the suppression of the *corvée*. But they refused to vote the subvention proposed, and demanded that Calonne should first indicate the causes and the exact amount of the deficit, with supporting documents. Calonne attacked them in turn by circulating a pamphlet in which the Notables were represented as enemies of "the well-being of peoples." They retorted by sending a memorial to the king, in which Calonne was accused not only of wasting public money, but of converting considerable sums to his own use.

With the energy of despair, Calonne turned to intimidation. He got rid of the Keeper of the Seals, whom he believed to have served him ill, demanded the dismissal of Breteuil, who was a protégé of the queen, and prepared thirty-nine *lettres de cachet* for the most vehement members of the opposition in the Assembly.

The struggle against Calonne continued. The Currency Court soon furnished the proof of what Mirabeau had stated while in Germany, that Calonne had ordered the debasement of the coinage. The criminal carelessness of his administration came increasingly to light. Louis XVI realized the extent to which he had been deceived, and, weeping with disappointment, ordered proceedings to be started against the Controller General.

But Calonne still hoped to triumph over his adversaries and busied himself with removing every troublesome obstacle in his path. The presence of so eloquent a denouncer as Mirabeau seemed to him to be undesirable. "My success was greater than could be forgiven," he wrote to Henriette. Mirabeau, warned that he was to be arrested, was firmly resolved to face the storm; but he learned that he was to be imprisoned in an old fortress in a remote province where he would be lost and forgotten. Talleyrand was involved in this sinister and enigmatic affair. He seems to have been pursuing some personal design with which Mirabeau's presence interfered, no doubt some shady financial operation. One fine day he called on Calonne, accompanied by Dupont, and suggested to him that Mirabeau should be informed, as from Calonne, that a *lettre de cachet* had been issued against him.

A *lettre de cachet* had in fact been signed and sent to the lieutenant of police. Talleyrand made use of it to frighten his friend. "I gave way to the urgency of the excellent Abbé de Périgord, who had returned from Versailles and who exorcized me for five hours on end to make me go," wrote Mirabeau to Henriette, unaware of the actual part played by his perfidious adviser. He left at once for Belgium. On learning that a *lettre de cachet* had been issued against the author of the *Denunciation of Speculation*, Chamfort made the caustic comment: "In France those who are guilty of arson are left alone and those who cry 'Fire!' are persecuted."

5

Henriette and Coco were unable to leave Berlin for lack of money. But Mirabeau's friend Jeanneret came to his aid, sending Henriette the money needed for her journey. Antraigues and Luchet informed her of Mirabeau's precipitate departure. She joined him at Liége, patriots of that city having invited him to spend his exile there.

Mirabeau was deeply discouraged by his financial difficulties and his forced inactivity and resigned himself to taking no further part in public affairs. In a letter to Talleyrand he asked only to be able to remain in Paris in complete obscurity and to escape from his "wretched celebrity, collecting in silence my material and my ideas. That is all I want, and never to occupy the stage." He begged Talleyrand to negotiate with the minister for his return to Paris, and to give him whatever assurances he wanted.

Reassured as to his state of mind, Calonne promised to intervene in his favour with the king, who "is too just to want you to be the only victim when your adversaries have made themselves a rampart out of the enormity of their crime." He insisted that Mirabeau's silence be the condition of his return. "It would be beneath you to hinder the good

of the state for the sake of personal vengeance." He promised, moreover, to concern himself not only with Mirabeau, but also with Mme. de
Nehra.

On her arrival at Liége, Henriette questioned her friend about his
personal situation. One of the reasons for his departure from Berlin had
been the lawsuit which was dragging on between himself and his father. But Mirabeau seemed no longer to realize that he ought to pay
attention to his case. "Yes, of course," he said, as though suddenly
emerging from absent-mindedness, "I wanted to ask you how I stand."
In reply to further questions he admitted to Henriette that he had not
even seen his trustee.

Henriette prepared to go to Paris to look after his affairs and to try
to get the *lettre de cachet* cancelled. At the last moment Mirabeau decided to go with her. He had not seen her for three months and did
not want to be separated from her any longer. He promised her that
he would stop at Saint-Denis. But Henriette had scarcely reached Paris
when Mirabeau unexpectedly arrived. He thought he might remain unnoticed. His powerful voice resounded in the passages. One of Panchaud's valets recognized him. "I was dying of fear," relates Henriette.
She secured an appointment with the Baron de Breteuil. She learned
from him that the king himself was very annoyed with Mirabeau. Trembling for her imprudent friend, she took the risk of admitting to the
minister that Mirabeau was in hiding in her rooms. Once more her love
triumphed over ministerial routine. The *lettre de cachet* was not cancelled, but she obtained at least a promise that no use would be made of
it. "Dear friend," wrote Mirabeau, "I have had only one happy day in
my life, the day when I came to know you and you gave me your
friendship."

6

Mirabeau was still in Paris when the Assembly of Notables came to its
end, in May 1787. He wrote with pride: "I have had the honour to see
the Notables and the king turn my theory into decrees and laws."
But this was but a poor consolation for a man who felt that no use could
be made of him. The Assembly had brought down Calonne. Mirabeau
was so far from being vindictive that he was distressed. When, later,
the *parlement* ordered the prosecution of Calonne, who had fled to
England, Mirabeau had so completely forgotten his resentment that he
was concerned only with the public issue: "I do not understand how
ministers can resolve to make an example of one of their colleagues.

. . . The prosecution of a Minister of Finance might perhaps have been really useful to the public cause, but in that case it would have to be done frankly, directly, with energy, but above all impartially."

One of Calonne's bitterest adversaries among the Notables had been the Archbishop of Toulouse, Loménie de Brienne, and the king had reluctantly made Brienne Minister of Finance.

Mirabeau's hopes of the new Minister of Finance were soon disappointed, for the archbishop had his *Lettres sur l'administration de M. Necker* prohibited by a decree of the Council. Mirabeau concentrated all the more on his big work on the Prussian monarchs, for the preparation of which he had gone to Brunswick early in June. Mirabeau was so tired of struggling with material difficulties and of seeing all his aspirations frustrated that he thought he could content himself with a life in obscurity. The months he passed at Brunswick were devoted to a sedentary labour that did not even allow him sufficient exercise. Plunged in his work, with no other society than that of a petty German court, he felt "as aloof from all that is happening elsewhere as if I were an inhabitant of Kamchatka, and this is embarrassing and shameful."

In the introduction Mirabeau explained the reasons that had led him to undertake it. "A similar work on England would have been a thousand times easier, more brilliant, in greater demand. But it was for that very reason that, without renouncing that fine plan, I felt it my duty to begin with what is within the reach of fewer Frenchmen, in view of our limited familiarity with the German language and the very little knowledge we have of Germany."

As he made progress in his work, Mirabeau began to hope for great, success: "My friend, when this work appears I shall be little more than thirty-eight," he wrote to Henriette. "I venture to predict that it will make my name. It may be that it will make my country feel some regret at leaving in idleness such an observer and at having paid badly for his labours." Mirabeau was one of those whom success renders generous. He thought his work would show their mistake to all those who had had doubts of him, of his talents and of his capacity for work. He thought especially of that pitiless critic his father. He may also have thought of what he owed him as his initiator into economic science.

The old Marquis de Mirabeau was a forgotten man, a figure of the past. Sensational lawsuits had destroyed his reputation forever, and his son's violent attacks had made him half odious, half ridiculous. He was poor and alone, with his ageing, soured mistress. He was mortally at feud with his younger daughter, and he had sent away his elder son. His oldest friends had abandoned him. "We ought to do justice to my father, as a political philosopher, for it has really been forgotten to the point of ingratitude what services he rendered," wrote Mirabeau. With his easy forgetfulness of wrongs done him, and also with a fancy for fine gestures, he dedicated *La Monarchie Prussienne* to the Marquis de Mirabeau.

With this dedication the long and painful struggle between father and son came to its end. But it was only Gabriel who had laid down the arms of his rancour. The marquis still clung to his old prejudices. He was secretly flattered by the dedication, "but when I am told that I ought to be very satisfied, I reply that one must first know what there is in this big book." The marquis took the trouble to read attentively its four quarto volumes, each six hundred and fifty pages. Still on the defensive, he began by expressing his objections to his brother: "I am greatly shocked, to begin with, at one thing that wins for him the noisy innovators and alienates from him forever the men of wisdom; it is the affectation of philosophism that I detest." He long resisted the attraction of the book. "It should be noted that when he has something stupid to say, he summons up energy and what they call eloquence," he commented maliciously. But as he read on through "this vast work" ("in which the devil must surely have taken a hand, in view of the little time this man was in Germany, though we know his talent for drawing from everywhere, lifting up and appropriating everything"), the marquis was filled with involuntary admiration. He declared that his son was "a centaur of work, be it only as collector, compiler, editor," and his admiration ended by wringing from him this avowal: "I regard him as the rarest man of his century, and perhaps one of the rarest whom nature has produced—if at the same time rightness of outlook had been granted him."

With this final reservation, the Marquis de Mirabeau brought himself at last to do justice to this son whom he had slandered throughout his life.

With *La Monarchie Prussienne* largely completed, Mirabeau left for Hamburg, where the son of Fauche, the Neufchâtel publisher, had set up for himself. He signed an agreement with Fauche, who offered him twenty thousand francs on delivery of the manuscript. He wanted Mirabeau to remain in Hamburg to see the work through the press. They agreed later to print in concert with French publishers, including Le Jay. Mirabeau was in a hurry to return to Paris. "I no longer have the courage to stay away," he wrote to Henriette; "my soul is too cast down, my spirit too mortified, my heart too tormented."

7

"Poor Netherlands! Of how many bloody executions are they to be
the theatre." Immersed in his work, knowing nothing of all that was
happening in France, Mirabeau watched from afar the affairs of Holland. Above all, he watched from close at hand the principal actor in
the future drama, the Duke of Brunswick. When the duke was appointed a field marshal, Mirabeau sent him a letter of congratulation.
He continued to be on very friendly terms with him, but distrusted
him, seeing in him the future adversary of his country. "It is important
that we should not be supposed to be paralysed, as our army reform has
made him think, perhaps as much as and more than the statement of
our deficit," he wrote to Henriette.

Public opinion in Holland grew more and more agitated. The Prince
of Orange, strong in the protection of his brother-in-law, was capturing more and more power every day. Patriots were maddened by his
usurpations. They believed themselves to be protected by France, but
the King of Prussia, knowing the weakness of the French government,
felt sure that it would not attempt to intervene in Dutch affairs. The
cabinet in London was fanning the flame, as though it wanted to be
revenged on France for the humiliation suffered in the American war;
it felt equally sure that France had neither the money nor the troops
nor the generals to risk armed intervention in favour of the Dutch patriots.

The Dutch democrats were asking themselves anxiously whether
the help they hoped for from France would be efficacious, for they
knew that they were powerless by themselves against a Prussian army.
In their fear of a general apathy they wrote to Mirabeau, whose "courageous eloquence," they said, "is consecrated to the defence of the rights
of man." Mirabeau was unwilling to believe that France had abandoned
the Dutch patriots to their fate: "A moment of torpor and of error
has made us unable to help you; everything proclaims that in France
the nation is going to count for something, and the nation is entirely
for you." He added: "A people has never been long enslaved unwillingly.
Persevere, then, my friends! Persevere! . . . The logic of events always
wins mastery over men in the end, and the ultimately invincible pressure
of rightly conceived interest here seconds your efforts."

But when the Duke of Brunswick entered Holland at the head of
his troops, no help came for the Dutch patriots. Their lack of military
preparation revealed itself at the first contact with regular troops, and
the good Dutch bourgeois were as economical with their blood as they

were preoccupied with their property. The democrats filled them with fear through their revolutionary aims, and there were bourgeois who secretly preferred the maintenance of order to the maintenance of liberty. No resistance was offered to the foreign invasion. "We have struck our blow magnificently in Holland," triumphantly declared Baron von der Goltz, Prussian minister at Paris. "The French ministry knows well that, bitter as the draught may be, it is better to put up with it than to make war on Prussia."

After this, Holland allied herself with Prussia and England. In addition to the loss of her ally, France lost her prestige in Europe. The abandonment of a friendly country and of a cause cost her dearly in foreign policy. "France has fallen," commented Joseph II, "and I doubt whether she will rise again."

The Dutch patriots, now the prey of pitiless vengeance, fled into exile. They pressed again for Mirabeau's intervention. One of their leaders, van Kussel, wrote to him: "You have already spoken for my country when it was threatened by a foreign despot. Could you abandon her when she is being enslaved by a crowd of subordinate tyrants? You could not have a more important subject or one more capable of doing honour to your talents." The Dutch democrat was alarmed at the rumour that Mirabeau had in preparation a great work in praise of Prussia, that he was devoted to the king and especially to the Duke of Brunswick, and that he was unwilling to intervene for fear of displeasing them. "What an opportunity," van Kussel insisted, "for confounding your enemies!"

"No, I cannot compound with violence and iniquity," replied Mirabeau. He frankly admitted his keen interest in the Prussian monarchy and even his attachment to it, his esteem and even his affection for the Duke of Brunswick. But when a king "deserves to become the subject of a crusade," nothing could induce him to keep a cowardly silence. "No, no motive can impose silence on me concerning an infringement of the rights of man, other than the uselessness of my speaking." He knew that a work of the sort proposed would have no effect at the moment. He suggested that it should be reserved for a day when it would have more practical value.

Van Kussel considered Mirabeau's reply so eloquent that, being unable to get the work he wanted from him, he published the letter with his own. Some months later, Mirabeau saw that Vergennes' successor was favourable to the cause of the Dutch patriots, and that the fatal effect of France's default had disturbed many people. He considered that the moment had come for encouraging resistance among the half-hearted and the hesitant in Holland. In April 1788 he published an *Addresse aux Bataves sur le Stathoudérat.*

Generous as was this intervention in favour of a lost cause, and courageous as was the attack on a sovereign whose striking success had just confirmed his power, the value of the *Address to the Batavians* lay especially in the boldness of its constructive part. Mirabeau offered to the "unfortunate Batavians" in their subjugation "the picture of the rights that belong to you as men." He was writing not only for the Dutch but for all peoples in the world who had not yet become aware of "the rights anterior and superior to all agreements; the inalienable, imprescriptible rights of every people that desires liberty."

The *Address to the Batavians* was really an address to the French. To the fiery denouncer, the keen critic, had been added the statesman, disguised as yet in the part of adviser of a handful of foreign democrats; for the moment had not yet come when he could sketch a constitution for his own country.

"All men are free and equal by the intention of Nature; they are so also in the primitive aspiration of all societies," declared the first article of the early Declaration of the Rights of Man appended to the *Addresse aux Bataves.* "Since all power emanates from the people, the different magistrates or officers of the government, invested with any sort of authority, legislative, executive, or judicial, owe an account to it at all times," said the second article. "The people, for whose well-being the government is instituted, has the inalienable right to reform it, to correct it, or to change it entirely when the people's well-being so requires," daringly affirmed the third article. The right of free elections was also solemnly laid down, together with that of assembly "to consult on the common good"; the people "has the right to give instructions to its representatives." Mirabeau demanded that justice should be dispensed "promptly, gratuitously, completely," that no citizen should "be exiled or deprived of life, liberty, or his property save by an authentic judgment," and that the citizen should be "secure from all search or seizure of his person, his papers, and his possessions." His knowledge of human weaknesses suggested to him to demand a suitable salary for the members of the magistracy, for "their independence and their integrity are the best guarantees of the rights and the liberty of citizens."

Tolerance, the admission of every form of worship, and freedom of the press, were to him sacred principles. In this spring of the year 1788 he claimed that "the military power should always be severely subordinated to the civil authority," and that every citizen should have the right to possess and to carry arms for the common defence; and he added: "When the citizen loses this habit, some ambitious person soon appears and sets everything in motion to profit by it." As early as this the future creator of the first revolutionary militia declared that "a well-regulated militia is the appropriate, natural, and sure defence of a free government."

Seen in the light of later events, the *Addresse aux Bataves* has the air of a sort of dress rehearsal for the great part which Mirabeau was before long to assume.

8

Mirabeau returned from Hamburg toward the end of August 1787.

Since the close of the Assembly of Notables a more and more violent struggle had been in progress between the king and the *parlement*, which, called upon to register the new edicts, registered without opposition the one that instituted the provincial assemblies and another suppressing the *corvée*, but refused to sanction the new taxation. One of the magistrates declared that only the nation, united in the States General (the parliament of the three estates), should pronounce on the country's taxation. Two concepts were at issue at this critical moment. The younger brother of Louis XVI, the Comte d'Artois, careless and cynical and ignorant of all the changes that had taken place in the country and of the force of public opinion, declared, as if he were proclaiming an axiom: "Gentlemen, you know that the king's expenditure cannot be regulated by his revenue; his revenue must be regulated by his expenditure."

The dispute was envenomed by questions of competence. The *parlement* wanted to know the state of the finances before giving its judgment; the king, stiffened in his attitude by his advisers, refused to communicate it, declaring that it was no part of the functions of the *parlement* to enter into this question. Angered by this refusal, the *parlement* declared in its sitting of July 30, 1787, by seventy-two votes to four, that "the nation is alone entitled to grant subsidies, the need for which should be clearly demonstrated."

The *parlement's* opposition brought a sudden return of its old popularity. Paris followed with passionate interest the phases of the drama, the implications of which were not realized even by the participants.

The queen urged the king to resist. She was influenced by the Baron de Besenval, commandant of the Swiss guards, who insisted that it was "high time for the king to show that he is master; failing that, he will have to lay down his crown and perhaps never again put it back on his head."

On August 6, 1787, the *parlement* was ordered to proceed to Versailles for a "bed of justice" (a formal session), at which the king had the fiscal edicts registered. On the following day the *parlement* reassembled in the Palais de Justice, which was surrounded by an immense crowd of excited people, and issued a formal pronouncement that the registration had been extorted and was null and void. The crowd acclaimed the magistrates as saviours of freedom. Marie Antoinette, alarmed by the noisy demonstrations, exclaimed: "Ah! what harm M. de Calonne did to this country with the Notables."

The king's Council met but failed to agree. Malesherbes, who had entered the Council after Calonne's fall, was one of the few who understood the spirit of the time; he opposed rigorous measures and called for the convocation of the States General. But the Council decided to publish the challenged edicts. The *parlement* declared the publication null and void. The government replied by exiling all the members of the *parlement* to Troyes.

The Archbishop of Toulouse profited by the confusion to secure appointment as Prime Minister. He came into power at the moment when the Dutch affair was inflicting a painful defeat on French policy. He did not feel strong enough to face the double peril at home and abroad, and preferred to come to terms with the *parlement*, even at the cost of a humiliation for the government. The edicts which the *parlement* had refused to register were revoked. The *parlement* was brought back from exile. The people of Paris celebrated with fireworks and illuminations this capitulation of absolutism. In the Place Dauphine an excited crowd burned in effigy the queen's confidante, Mme. de Polignac. Popular hatred was concentrated on Marie Antoinette, who was believed to be the inspirer of the arbitrary measures now defeated. At the Comédie Française there was wild applause of the verses of Racine's *Athalie* about the queen animated by

> . . . *cet esprit d'imprudence et d'erreur,*
> *De la chute des rois funeste avant-coureur*

—that spirit of imprudence and error which is the fatal forerunner of the fall of kings.

The revolutionary drama had begun well before the raising of the curtain.

This double capitulation, of which Mirabeau learned on his return, made him realize that "some great revolution, whether for good or for evil," was inevitable. "This revolution cannot long be delayed," he wrote, soon after reaching Paris, to a young man, Soufflot le Mercy, whom he had met in Germany. Mercy, who had become chief clerk to Loménie de Brienne, had gently reproached him through Caroline for not coming to see him on his return. "Public affairs," replied Mirabeau, "seemed to me to be at so active a crisis, and the sanctuary in which you now are seemed so obsessed by men and things, that, being unable to believe that anyone would want me to be of use there, I should have felt importunate and out of place." But in his letter he made an undisguised offer of his services: "I feel that it would be too easy and even too natural to give myself to the man who gives us hope that France will secure a constitution and consequently regeneration."

In an interview with M. de Montmorin, Minister of Foreign Affairs, he frankly stated his desire for rehabilitation, and asked for appropriate employment. "Warsaw, St. Petersburg, Constantinople, Alexandria, anything will suit me." If Montmorin had realized the worth of this petitioner, the Revolution would have found Gabriel de Mirabeau peacefully at work in some distant diplomatic post. But a prudent minister is deterred by a too insistent suitor; Montmorin was kind enough to hold out some hope, for Mirabeau wrote to him later: "You were the first man in a high position who was ready to be my benefactor, and above all the first to reveal to me the only desire that could really flatter me, that of assigning me to my natural existence, and revealing me as I am."

The only result of this appeal was the permission Mirabeau secured to publish a periodical, of which he had elaborated the plan much earlier. He felt that it was more and more necessary to maintain continuous contact between the English élite and enlightened circles in France. In November 1787 he founded, with Clavière and Brissot, *Analyse des papiers anglais*—a publication intended to rival the *Mercure de France*. The publication created a sensation. But Mirabeau's material situation scarcely improved. He renewed his appeals to Montmorin.

The conflict between the government and the *parlement* entered an acute phase. Brienne, abandoning hope of securing the registration of the fiscal edicts, was driven to asking for a loan. It was a considerable one—four hundred and twenty million livres, spread over five years. In order to induce the *parlement* to sanction the loan, Brienne promised to convoke the States General at the end of the five years.

"It is impossible for that date to inspire the citizens with confidence," wrote Mirabeau to a young magistrate of the *parlement* (the fragment of the letter preserved does not show his name). "The generality of citizens will regard it as truly derisive. Deeper observers will see in it collusion between the authorities and the *parlements* in order to continue governing in the absence of the nation. Where will you be then, Ministers and Magistrates?"

9

Louis-Philippe-Joseph, Duc d'Orléans, was one of the richest men in France. Both fortune and nature had loaded him with gifts. But he had been born a prince of the blood. And the kings of France were more suspicious of the princes of the blood than of any other of their subjects. He was kept out of everything. "Am I condemned, then," he complained, "to eternal idleness?" He satisfied his big sanguine body's need of movement by frequent journeys, distractions for the moment, and vast projects for the future. Prodigal with his wealth, he plunged into business matters, scientific research and spiritualist séances in which he called up the devil with the aid of Cagliostro. He indulged his vigorous temperament by a life of debauchery. But when a great passion entered into his life with Mme. de Buffon, daughter-in-law of the illustrious savant, the orgies of Monceau and the suppers with prostitutes and companions in debauchery such as Lauzun and Talleyrand came to a sudden end; the duke remained subjugated by the disinterested love of a woman of gentle and self-effacing charm.

The Duc d'Orléans had tried to find useful employment in the army. But he was pursued by the queen's resentment for what she regarded as cavalier treatment on her arrival in France as wife of the Dauphin. When he asked to be allowed to follow Lafayette to America, the queen sent him a curt refusal. Marie Antoinette was to pay dearly for her hostility; she had no more implacable enemy than the Duc d'Orléans. His hatred of the court became the duke's one consistent idea, his one true feeling, apart from his attachment to Mme. de Buffon.

On November 19, 1787, as Mirabeau had foreseen, the *parlement* refused to register the loan. In this grave hour it was to Montmorin, "the honest man in the ministry," that Mirabeau turned, as "a good citizen and the personal friend of the king." "It is said that the government intends to resort to extreme measures, and to decree the suspension of payments, since funds are refused it. . . . What is to become of the many unfortunates robbed of the fruit of their thrift, . . . free from every curb, from all moral restraint? Could they be anything but incendiary enemies of the state and above all of the king? Is the fanaticism of property or that of destitution less burning, less inextinguishable, than that of religion? . . . I ask whether there has been thought given to the measure of the convulsions of hunger, the genius of despair? I ask who will dare to answer for the consequences for the personal safety of all who surround the throne and of the king himself?" It was on November 20 of the year 1787 that this warning was written, summing up in a few words the sanguinary tragedy of the years to come. The king had but to choose between two courses: "Either a ministerial *coup d'état* with its infinite perils or an indispensable act of beneficence. . . . Can there be any hesitation over this alternative? . . . There must be an announcement in precise and formal terms of States General in 1789; they can wait no longer. . . . Yes, with this one phrase, States General in 1789, we shall see credit resuscitated and a fulfillment of the loans necessitated by the present state of affairs.

"Speak, then," Mirabeau continued; "tell everything; and if you are not understood, resign, so as not to survive in office the honour of the government and not to be under the reproach of having been present at the sitting that decreed the shame of France. . . .

"The time is no more when the favour of a king sufficed to create the renown of a minister and his disfavour to destroy him. Today the sources of true glory are elsewhere and higher; it is now the nation, the nation alone, that will make political fortunes."

Mirabeau's warning was issued in vain. The king had decided to break the resistance of the *parlement*. He summoned it once more to a "bed of justice" at Versailles. Esprémènil appealed to the king in a speech that moved him. Louis XVI admitted next day that he had been on the point of forgetting the resolutions of the Council and of granting the States General. But the Keeper of the Seals spoke to him in a low voice. Undecided, distrusting his own impulses, Louis XVI ordered the registration of the loan.

The sitting was over. But a voice was raised. The Duc d'Orléans protested against the illegality of a forced registration. It was his entry into political life. It was his début in the history of the Revolution. Louis XVI replied in an authoritarian tone that masked his secret uneasiness: "It is legal, because it is my will." Next day the Duc d'Orléans was exiled to his estate of Villars-Cotterets. Two other members of the *parlement*, who were associated with him, were arrested and taken to a fortress.

The exiled duke became the idol of the crowd. Mirabeau did not then know him, but he realized the part he was destined to play. He wrote to the duke the day after his intervention: "If the nobility had syndics to express its aspirations, if the nation, with its rights restored,

had legal representatives, these and those would be calling on Your
Most Serene Highness to express their inacquittable gratitude for the
high and magnanimous act of patriotism by which you yesterday supported their rights, their magistrates, and holy liberty."

10

"I have always thought that between the king and the *parlement* there
was a poor obscure little party, called the nation, to which people of
good sense and of good faith ought to belong," wrote Mirabeau a few
months later. His first enthusiasm had vanished; he realized the motives
that had brought "those aristocrats in black gowns" into action, and
he was soon to set them down as "insatiable privileged persons who
want to despoil the king, but only in order to keep the spoil for themselves." But his critical attitude made him very unpopular. "I am the
prey of every sort of slander in the world, because in conversation I
do not echo the fanaticism for the *parlement*, and because I have not
written a single line for the opposition party," he wrote to his German
friend.

He still believed, as he had written to the Duc d'Orléans, that bad
advisers had reduced the king to actual fraud. But among these advisers
was the Keeper of the Seals, Lamoignon, who tried to win over Mirabeau and succeeded. "I like him personally, I esteem his character, I revere his courage," he said of him later, but added: "He showed me
that he really wanted to make a revolution for the good of the nation,
but he had neither the talent nor the grit."

This remained his attitude toward Lamoignon, and also toward Montmorin, during the struggle between the throne and the *parlement*. The
two Orléanist counsellors of the *parlement* were released, and the duke
returned to his country house near Paris, but the three were still forbidden to stay in the capital. The blow struck at its members seems to
have revealed to the *parlement* for the first time that there existed abuses
of authority; it insistently demanded the abolition of *lettres de cachet*:
"Sire, liberty is in no sense a privilege, it is a right; and it is the duty
of all governments to respect that right." The *parlement* spoke with
more and more daring. It declared that "in finance it sees for the nation
only one resource, the nation itself. . . . Kings are men and fallible;
and it is in order not to abandon the nation to the fatal effects of random
caprice that the constitution requires the verification of laws by the
courts, and in the matter of subsidies the prior approval of the States
General."

To combat the growing prestige of the *parlement* among the public, Lamoignon and Montmorin approached Mirabeau. The offer from the ministers reached him at a moment of particularly acute material distress. But, harassed as he was, he had "no intention to sell himself." "Is this the time to denounce to France an aristocracy of magistrates, when the king has not disdained to denounce it himself?" he asked Montmorin. "I shall never make war on *parlement* except in the presence of the nation." He concluded: "Do not compromise a zealous servant who will account his dangers as nothing on the day when he must devote himself to the country, but who would not for the price of all the crowns prostitute himself in an equivocal course of which the end is uncertain, the principle doubtful, the direction alarming and sinister."

But, whether the ministers had put strong pressure on him, or whether he thought he could ignore the objections he had stated so clearly, shortly after sending his eloquent letter he decided to write a pamphlet attacking the *parlements—Réponse aux alarmes des bons citoyens.* The opinions he expressed were not imposed on him, for he had long expressed them.

His friends, especially Lauzun, criticized the pamphlet hotly. He tried to justify himself in a long letter to Lauzun. On May 8, 1788, the king proclaimed the suppression of the *parlements* for an indefinite period, forbidding them to meet for any public or private matter. He also instituted a plenary court to which he would dictate his orders; it would be empowered to register loans.

Liberal circles in Paris were in consternation; they seemed paralysed by the very excess of rigour in these measures. But movements of resistance broke out all over the kingdom. There were refusals to carry out some of the orders of the government; there were attacks on officials, and collisions between crowds and the military. The royal palace was transformed into a barracks; on its walls were posted placards: "Palace to be sold, Ministers to be hanged, crown to be given away." Revolution was brewing beneath an apparent general despondency.

Mirabeau wrote to Lauzun: "On the day when it becomes necessary to strike at despotism because of its perfidy or tyranny, I shall strike with all my strength, reinforced by my past caution and my vain advice."

❧ XII ❦

Between a Dunghill and a Palace

"THERE is always coming into my head," Mirabeau had written to Henriette, "a profoundly true thing you said to me one day. Our ideas had clashed, and you had reason to think that I did not sufficiently realize the motives and the value of your friendship. 'My poor Mirabeau,' you said, 'you have only one friend in the world—me.' I have felt this thousands of times, and my heart, equally prompt to surrender and to grow irritated, has sworn to forget it no longer."

At the beginning of 1788 Mirabeau fell gravely ill. Mme. de Nehra cared for him with tranquil and self-effacing devotion. Herself of frail health, she was just recovering from an illness when Mirabeau's state demanded her constant attention. He called the illness cholera morbus. The physicians of his day knew no other treatment to save his life than excessive bleeding. They took twenty-two basins of blood from him in the space of two days. He had never taken care of himself, never husbanded his strength. His organism was exhausted by this violent cure.

Day after day Henriette de Nehra sat at her patient's bedside. But the sick man's need for a woman's constant presence, and the sweetness of sacrifice for a loved being, were the last chapter of their great love and their greater friendship. A hostile presence came between them.

La Monarchie Prussienne had been printed in Paris by the publisher Le Jay. Mirabeau was frequently in touch with him. Le Jay himself was an invalid, devoured by care, weak, and incapable of efficiently carrying on either his business, which was in a precarious state, or his private life. His wife, remarkably beautiful, had a passionate temperament and a cold and calculating brain.

Every beautiful woman awakened desire in Mirabeau, and the beauty of Mme. Le Jay was particularly exciting. Both of them lived under the same sensual urge and had the same habit of yielding to it. Their meeting was bound to awaken strong passion. It might have been just one more of the many brief and stormy adventures that had broken the calm of Mirabeau's love for Henriette. But Mme. Le Jay was determined to be more than a passing fancy for this man. She called up all her feminine experience, all the resources of her active intelligence and her psychological subtlety, to capture Mirabeau entirely. In order to do so she had to destroy the influence of Henriette de Nehra. She began cunningly to throw doubt on Yet-Lie's feeling for him, and exploited the placid Dutchwoman's lack of sensual passion, to which Mirabeau had learnt to adjust himself. Mme. Le Jay also excited his natural suspicion, and especially the feeling that was never absent from his love, his furious jealousy.

Instead of humouring him, Henriette de Nehra did the worst possible thing with a man of such violent character: she overwhelmed him with reproaches. "Protestants love preaching; I am passionately one of my sect, and I shall always protest against what may injure you and compromise you," she wrote to him one day. She saw Mirabeau curse his "physical madness" in his lucid moments; always mistress of herself, she did not take into account the subjection of his senses by a woman whom he knew to be unworthy of a great passion, but whom he could not prevent himself from passionately desiring and from admiring in order to justify his desires. Henriette treated her rival with all the haughtiness of her moral superiority. She tried to open Mirabeau's eyes, while he, to preserve a vestige of self-esteem, clung to his blindness. She knew Mme. Le Jay to be greedy for money, and she knew that Gabriel was being exploited. "I am constantly afraid of your being involved in some big swindling affair of which the profit will belong to others and the odium fall on you," she wrote to him one day, no doubt repeating what she had said to him many times.

Her worst fears were to be justified, but Mirabeau, for the very reason that he shared her apprehensions, would not listen to her. Stormy scenes incessantly followed their passionate reconciliations. Henriette's health suffered. The lovers separated—temporarily, they thought. Mirabeau had furnished for Henriette, to whom he still remained deeply attached, an elegant little suite at Passy. Henriette continued to preach to him by letter as she had done face to face: "Your liaison dishonours you, you are in execrable hands. You do not understand as I do all that may be thought of it. I shall not sacrifice my friend's honour and reputation to considerations of interest; I shall do my duty, I shall tell him what is thought of his extreme weakness."

All she did was to make him quarrel with his friends, isolate him still more, and deliver him over to the fatal influence of his mistress. She realized that he was escaping entirely from her. She had asked him in vain to sacrifice her rival to her, to choose between Mme. Le Jay and herself. But if she was to lose him, she wanted at least to rescue him from the claws of a woman of whom she said: "Why is it impossible to mention the name of the Comte de Mirabeau's mistress without getting the reply, 'Pah! She's trash!'?"

All that was good and trusting in Mirabeau, his desire for rehabilitation and his need for reflection for the tasks of the morrow, bound him to Henriette. She was still at all times that which was "dearest in the world" to him. But his sexual wildness and the taste for risks and even for the dramatic that formed part of his natural vehemence drove him into the arms of Mme. Le Jay.

Torn by a terrible internal conflict, he lost mastery of himself. There were painful scenes. "I was exposed at that time to the most violent storms," wrote Henriette later; "even death faced me . . . when, suffocated with tears, I saw him, beyond himself, pistol in hand, in an access of rage; any involuntary movements might have sent off the shot, leaving him to die of remorse and regrets."

Henriette de Nehra had not the strength to fight her way through the storm. Unhappy and disheartened, she chose the easier course, that of flight. One August evening she made up her mind. Her face bathed in tears, she kissed her sleeping child good-bye and left the house. For fear of further violent scenes, she placed a frontier between herself and her lover. She took refuge in London. And Henriette de Nehra passed out of Mirabeau's life.

2

"Ministers and even sovereigns will pass, but France will remain," wrote Mirabeau to Montmorin at the time of the conflict with the *parlement*. "It is out of the question to try to substitute the power of the bayonet for that of laws, the resources of oppression for those of confidence, the credit of leeches for that of the nation." He saw but one path open to the nation. "Give, give this country a constitution! Oh, what great, fertile, imperishable wealth will there be lavished on you by this soil which you imagine to be exhausted, this people that seems to you discouraged. Substitute the credit of the state for that of its ministers. Has Great Britain, so astonishing in the incalculable abuse of its credit, ever had any other lever for the support of its enormous expenditure and the deployment of its power than the right to vote or refuse taxes and the inviolable respect for public faith? A constitution—that is the basis of all economy, of all resources, of all confidence, of all power."

This eloquent appeal was made by Mirabeau in a pamphlet entitled *Suite à la dénonciation de l'agiotage.* He was once more accusing the more and more active speculators who were sending up to fictitious prices the shares of establishments whose privileges were imaginary or illegal. But primarily he was defending Panchaud's interest in the *Chambre d'Accumulation,* which had been attacked by one of the privileged companies, the *Compagnie de l'Assurance sur la Vie.* Mirabeau's fidelity in friendship never failed. He had remained deeply attached to Panchaud, whose recent loss of his post of royal banker made Mirabeau "roar with anger," and who was not only financially shaken but the prey of slanderers.

In this summer of 1788 Mirabeau made the acquaintance of a young man belonging to the category of the declassed, which particularly attracted him, through compassion and perhaps through a secret sense of affinity. The young man's family, a very old one highly esteemed in Provence, had been ruined by military service, lawsuits, and bankruptcies. Young Comps, transplanted to Paris, dreamed of a career that would rehabilitate himself and his family. He was one of those impressionable and enthusiastic young men whom a strong personality will capture and exalt.

Mirabeau spontaneously suggested that Comps should become his secretary. "I have only obeyed the impulse arising from your youth, your misfortunes, and what I fancy I have seen of your character and intelligence." In his honesty he was concerned to dissipate any illusions the plan might inspire in Comps. "Your association with me has no present advantages save for your instruction, and the future is obscure. But the time is coming when the power of talent will become greater and less precarious. Believe me, with a growing public spirit the convulsions of despotism are no longer to be feared by those who can speak at the tribunal of public opinion."

For the moment these assurances had no solid basis. "The reputation of the Comte de Mirabeau stood at the lowest possible level,"—so stated the Genevese companion of an Englishman with whom Mirabeau had been associated in London, Sir Samuel Romilly. Romilly had come to Paris with his friend Etienne Dumont in this summer of 1788; and in the "respectable houses" which he visited Mirabeau's name was mentioned, according to Dumont, "with disdain." Romilly asked himself whether he had not been mistaken in regard to the man to whom he had given such a good reception in England. "Almost ashamed of his past friendship," wrote Dumont, Romilly decided to avoid so compromising a personage. But he relented, and they met frequently. "We became again," Romilly wrote, "very intimate, and passed many hours in his most captivating society."

Etienne Dumont, a former pastor of Geneva, was a man of rigid character, downright, clear-headed, methodical, but with a tendency to pedantry and moralizing; very sure of himself, very critical of others. He seemed too free from weaknesses to be generous; he was also without ambition and unwilling to assume great responsibilities.

Dumont frequently met Mirabeau at the house of Clavière. The relations between Clavière and Mirabeau were stormy. Clavière, like Brissot, and like Dumont himself at a later date, claimed the chief credit for Mirabeau's literary successes. Each of them claimed the paternity of one or more of his works. Mirabeau was well aware of this. One day there was a violent scene between Mirabeau and Clavière. But what struck Dumont was that "in the midst of their anger the two men maintained a regard for each other's feelings that surprised me."

Dumont impartially summed up the two men: "Clavière tried to treat Mirabeau as a jay who was being stripped of his fine feathers, but this plucked jay was still armed with a very powerful spur, and he could take flight above the whole of the literary farmyard." He found that Mirabeau "had so well established himself in public opinion that his colleagues could not have diminished the reputation they had won for him. I compared him," he added, "to a general who makes conquests through his lieutenants, and who thereafter subjects them to the authority of which they were the founders. He had the right to regard himself as the father of all these writings, because he had presided over their execution, and because without his indefatigable activity they would never have seen daylight."

Mirabeau amassed everything of which he might have need, like a financier who neglects no opportunity of a good investment; it was this habit, adopted at an early stage, that enabled him to be one day master of an immense stock of knowledge on the most varied subjects.

Dumont concluded: "He studied a subject by writing a book; he needed a collaborator only to provide its basis; he knew how to employ twenty others for additions and notes, and would have taken charge of an encyclopaedia if he had been well paid for the enterprise." In the end Dumont was captured: "I have never known a man who when he wished could make himself more agreeable and more attractive than Mirabeau. His conversation, very interesting and very animated, was like a grindstone of which he made skillful use to sharpen his tools."

Himself austere and, indeed, prudish, Dumont admitted that Mirabeau "preserved even in his lapses a certain elevation and dignity."

Dumont brought away from his visit the memory of a personality distinguished by his "strength of character from all those spineless men, all those shadows, whom we found in Paris."

3

"Among the most serious evils of society I count indifference to the most deplorable excesses when they are repeated day by day in our sight. We live in the midst of a mass of oppression and misery that leaves us little moved; if we turn away our heads it is out of good taste and not out of commiseration. It does not occur to us that this levity renders us answerable, in proportion to our social influence, for all the evil which the rousing of public opinion might prevent, and for all the good it might do."

This magnificent declaration, revealing all the acuteness of Mirabeau's civic conscience, this eloquent accusation of social complicity, appears in a small book *Imité de l'Anglais par le Comte de Mirabeau*, and is preceded by a letter from Benjamin Franklin: "Observations of an English traveller on the prisons of Bicêtre, followed by reflections on the effects of severity of punishment and on the criminal legislation of Great Britain." A letter from Romilly to a friend, in which he described La Salpêtrière and Bicêtre provided the basis of the work. Romilly found at Bicêtre a mixture of hospital and prison such as might well "engender maladies and give birth to crimes." His moving description of the hideous misery of the prisons was read by Mirabeau, whose indignation was of the sort that finds expression in action.

"As soon as he had seen it, its translation and publication was the concern of a day," wrote Dumont. Mirabeau added to the little volume a description of penal administration in England and a recent memorandum by Romilly on the organization of prisons. He explained in his introduction why he spoke of the laws and the judges of Great Britain: "In England, at least in this respect, there are in my view only things that want putting right, whereas what we need is a completely fresh start." The future legislator warned the legislators of the day not to let the laws be "armed with such severity that nature cries out to us that it is a virtue to frustrate the law." While the description came from another pen than his, it was to him that credit was due for having denounced this revolting spectacle and roused public opinion; for the little work produced a great impression. Dumont mentioned its "rapid success."

But it is not only the indifferent and the self-centred who are responsible for social evils. There are also very many decent people who in their timidity dread any change. It was to these that Mirabeau addressed a few months later another "imitation of the English," in defence of one of his closest concerns, the liberty of the press. This small pamphlet, *La Liberté de la presse*, was written on the occasion of an appeal from the government to all the corporations in the kingdom and all the savants of France to give it advice on the method of convoking and assembling the States General, whose last assembly had taken place at so distant a date as 1614.

4

"The king was deceived. The laws were without ministers and twenty-five millions of men were without judges. The public treasury was without funds, without credit, without means of preventing a general bankruptcy. The authorities had no respect for the liberty of the individual and no force for the maintenance of public order. The people had no other resource than the States General, but were without hope of getting them. To these political scourges, nature, in her wrath, had come to add her own. Fields were ravaged and desolate and famine was appearing already on the horizon, menacing part of the kingdom." It was a moderate, a conservative, Lally-Tollendal, who drew up a year later this picture of the summer and autumn of 1788.

Public opinion was awake everywhere to the dangers of the situation. "The ferment of minds is general," wrote Count von Fersen to his father; "the only talk is about a constitution, the women especially join in, and you know as I do what influence they have in this country. It is a craze; everybody is an administrator and talking of nothing but progress. In the antechambers the lackeys are busy reading the pamphlets that come out; every day there are ten or a dozen of them."

But the agitation went deeper than the queen's lover imagined; it was no mere matter of sensation-seeking *grandes dames* and curious lackeys. Anonymous writings which the court despised warned it in vain of what would come on the morrow. In one of these we read: "Frenchmen, awake! The epoch has arrived of that Revolution which will determine the regrets or the admiration of posterity, according as we leave to our sons slavery or freedom."

The police were reinforced; there were new arrests every day. The people were arming themselves. The nobles, it was being said, had stored considerable quantities of arms.

"I have provided for everything," said Brienne, "even civil war." The country was no less disturbed than Paris. To the war of the *parlements* against the throne there was added the agitation of the nobles of certain provinces for the restoration of their suppressed autonomy. Provence recalled that she had been united by his own friend to the crown of France on the death of the last Comte de Provence, and claimed the status of "co-state united with and not subordinate to the crown."

The nobles of the province of Dauphiné declared that if the court did not renounce its illegal enterprises, the province would recover its independence and the son of the sovereign would cease to bear the title of Dauphin.

The *lettres de cachet* issued against members of the provincial *parlements* had simply spread exasperation outside legal circles. At Grenoble the people forcibly opposed the removal of the magistrates. The troops of the garrison were attacked by an excited crowd that stoned them with cobbles and with tiles torn from the roofs. The violence of the Day of Tiles was the prelude to rioting that broke out all over the kingdom.

It was also from Grenoble that another movement started, a movement that was later regarded as the first signal of the Revolution. Deprived of its *parlement*, Grenoble convoked an Assembly of Notables. There was a judge at Grenoble, Mounier by name, whose poor health had kept him from the exercise of his profession. Mounier, a conscientious student, had acquired a profound knowledge in the domains of legislation and foreign policy; a chance friendship and his natural bent had aroused in him a predilection for British liberalism. Moderate by temperament, conservative in feeling, he had the obstinacy of men of poor health who have triumphed over their circumstances through a rigorous self-imposed discipline. He had also the courage given by his sense of indisputable competence. In the Assembly of Notables this man of inflexible integrity played the part of counsellor and guide. The Assembly petitioned the king for the convocation of the provincial Estates. Without waiting for the royal permission, it convoked the Estates for June 21, 1788. This Assembly of Vizille, which demanded the convocation of the States General, the reopening of the courts of justice, and the re-establishment of the provincial Estates, was the first act of insubordination toward the royal power.

Mounier, his secretary, and his principal orator, escaped arrest only because of the governmental crisis. He immediately became the apostle of the new evangel of liberty. All France fixed its gaze on the province of Dauphiné. Mounier was soon to be a moderating element in the political life of the kingdom; disturbed by every excess, alarmed by every blow against the established power, he was to try in vain to restrain the movement he had started. But after the meeting at Vizille "it might have been said," wrote a contemporary, "that the province of Dauphiné ruled all France, and that Mounier ruled Dauphiné."

At about the same time there appeared a *Memorandum on the States General, their rights, and the manner of convoking them*. The memorandum started with an incendiary phrase: "No doubt it was in order to give the most heroic virtues a country worthy of them that Heaven willed that republics should exist; and perhaps it was in order to punish human ambition that it permitted the rise of great empires, of kings and masters." The memorandum vehemently attacked the nobility with its mistaken ideas of feudalism. Its author, hardly disguised by a transparent pseudonym, was the Comte de Launay d'Antraigues. The Third Estate had found in Antraigues the first great spokesman of its claims: "What is the imprescriptible right of the Third Estate? That of the great number over the small number; for this order is to the two others as a hundred thousand to one. That of fertile labours on sterile properties, since without industrious arms the earth would be but a planet and never an empire. That of antiquity itself, since the plough existed before the coat of arms, the crook before the crozier, workshops before tribunals, the trader before the treasurer, the simple farmer before the farmer general, the unprivileged before all those who have become privileged through the favour of kings." Antraigues became celebrated overnight. His pamphlets were circulated and quoted and graven in men's minds and hearts.

Brienne struggled in vain amid inextricable financial embarrassments. In vain did he ask for subsidies from the Assembly General of the Clergy. He was compelled, as Mirabeau had feared, to suspend payments. In this desperate situation it was decided at last to convoke the States General for the beginning of 1789. Mirabeau, in a letter to Mauvillon, made no secret of his exultation. "The nation has stepped forward a century in twenty-four hours. Ah! my friend, you will see what a nation this one will be on the day when it is constituted; the day when talent itself will be a power." And he concluded with the proud knowledge of his true value: "I hope that in this epoch you will hear your friend favourably spoken of."

5

"It is my fate to bring misfortune," wrote Marie Antoinette to the Austrian ambassador. She had wanted to get rid of Necker and had favoured Brienne. The confusion in public affairs at last forced the archbishop to resign. He was so discredited that a few months later he killed himself. The queen now worked for the recall of Necker, who toward the end of August came back as Controller General, with the place in the Council which in the past had been refused to him. "Here at last is M. Necker as King of France," commented Mirabeau.

Necker was, as Mirabeau said, "the god of the day." The king had charged him with the preparations for the convocation of the States General. The *parlement* entered Paris in triumph and registered the royal edict setting up the States General; it deliberated on the method of convoking them. "Let us beware especially of erudition," Mirabeau had written on the morrow of the royal edict; "let us ignore what was done in the past and seek what is to be done now." The *parlement*, as though to belie its reputation for liberalism, declared, against the opposition of a minority led by the young counsellor Adrien Du Port, that the convocation and assembly should take place in the forms observed at the last meeting in 1614.

"If," wrote Mirabeau, "the precedents of 1614 are followed, as the *parlements*, which only want to render the States General useless, are so strongly insisting, we shall become once more, as far as is possible, a feudal people. . . . One part of the nation will be able still to attempt to oppress the other; but in the end this other part will feel its hurts and will measure its rights by its real power."

Necker was now the arbiter of the country's destiny. He could get anything from the court, thanks to the fear inspired by his popularity. If he had had the courage, he could easily have carried through the boldest reforms. But this citizen of Geneva was by temperament opposed to any sudden breach with an established order, and he still felt the deference of a parvenu toward the privileges of the nobility. He tried to gain time and elude his responsibilities; instead of himself determining the method of convocation of the States General, he left the task to an Assembly of Notables: he confided to the privileged the task of determining their own sacrifice. Like the *parlement*, the notables turned to the precedents. "Our trouble comes from having preserved those old archives," commented Mirabeau in a letter to Mauvillon. He offered Montmorin a "fixed and solid plan, which the representatives of the nation need but to sanction." But even if Montmorin had realized better the dangers of the situation and the value of Mirabeau's advice, he would have been alienated by the insistence with which Mirabeau pleaded his personal cause. "Without at least the secret help of the government, I cannot be in the States General," he wrote. The arrival of Necker threatened his most ardent ambition. Montmorin made no reply, and no longer permitted Mirabeau to approach him. Mirabeau was consumed with anxiety: "There will be every possible opposition to my presence in the States General," he wrote to Mauvillon.

In this desperate situation Lauzun, now become Duc de Biron through the death of the marshal, once more devoted his capacity for intrigue to his friend's cause. He intervened with Montmorin in his favour. "Please commit me with M. de Montmorin to anything to which you would commit yourself in my place, and to nothing else," Mirabeau wrote to Biron. "I can promise to spare individuals. I cannot undertake to respect or take account of other principles than my own, but it is very true that in the National Assembly I shall be a very zealous monarchist, because I feel deeply how we need to kill ministerial despotism and to augment the royal authority."

Mirabeau alternated between hope and discouragement. There were rare moments when he thought of abandoning everything, leaving with Mauvillon for England, and there writing a big book like the one on Prussia. His financial situation grew so much worse that he confessed to Mauvillon that he did not know what he would live on in the following year. His resolve not to commit himself on questions of the moment prevented him from earning money. He tried to get a publisher for a small work on legislative questions, for which Mauvillon sent him an analysis of the proposed Prussian code. A Strasbourg publisher, Levrault, sought means of getting him elected in Alsace; in a letter which Mirabeau wrote to him on this occasion, he revealed that it was his ambition not only to sit in this foremost tribunal of the nation, but to dominate it by the force of his personality and by his talents. This assembly would necessarily be numerous, but so much the easier to lead. "Five or six persons will always settle the way the herd goes," he wrote to Levrault. But his efforts to get elected failed.

6

The old Marquis de Mirabeau was seventy-three years of age. He had been obliged to sell his property at Bignon and to hand over his Paris house to Saillant: he no longer wanted to live with his eldest daughter.

Thenceforward he lived alone with Mme. de Pailly in a house he rented at Argenteuil, or rather in two wings separated by a court, saving appearances, even at his age, in regard to a woman who was approaching her sixtieth year. Mme. de Pailly was financially independent of him. She had inherited from her husband and from her sisters-in-law, and she had been granted a pension by the king.

At the beginning of 1788 the marquis had been seriously ill. His son, although then very ill himself, had sent three times a day to ask after him. He had wanted to improve their relations by settling the litigation between them and renouncing all his claims.

Mirabeau, who was on good terms with Mme. du Saillant, had become reconciled with his younger brother. The marquis had retained his predilection for the vicomte, whom he considered to be "of our race and sort."

The vicomte had fulfilled the desire of the marquis for posterity by marrying, in the summer of 1788, Mlle. de Robien. But the marquis was furious when his elder son called on the young vicomtesse without asking his permission. He still nourished vestiges of rancour against him, ready to blaze up on any occasion.

Mirabeau was not unaware of his father's state of mind. After vainly doing all he could to get into the States General, he thought of trying to secure election in Provence. For this he needed the help of the marquis. For lack of other support, he secured through Montmorin the intervention with his father of M. de Thémines, Bishop of Blois, a connexion by marriage. The marquis, who no longer found many people ready to listen to him, profited by the occasion to tell the bishop all about his son. He chewed over his old grievances, repeated the old abuse, went back to the benefits he claimed to have heaped on Gabriel in his youth and his son's bad behaviour to him, even "the assault on my own person." He repeated the accusation of venality, of being "in the pay of the bankers," and then of Calonne, "whom he betrayed and attacked when he saw him fall." "And this is the man who is to be brought to see me, a man whom I know to be physically and incorrigibly bad and mad." The bishop did his tactful best to appease the old man, and asked nothing more for Gabriel than "simply to be able to say that he had been received by his father." The marquis obstinately refused. "Since the ministers are interested in him, let them give him a chance of rehabilitation by doing some services, let them make a man of him, and then I could see him as a public man." The bishop pointed out that it was in order to make himself a public man that his son needed to be able "to boast that he had not been rejected by his father." The old marquis at last allowed himself to be persuaded and, with certain reservations, gave his consent.

"All I felt, my father, at this news, all that I feel at the first ray of hope that there are no longer eternal barriers between you and me, is beyond expression," Mirabeau wrote, with the exuberance his father detested in him.

Father and son had not seen each other for ten years. In face of this redoubtable parent, Mirabeau felt once more all his childish terror. In this decisive hour, with his destiny at stake, with everything dependent on the help the marquis might agree to give him, he made use of the same means to win him over which he had employed to gain forgiveness for his naughtinesses as a child or his imprudences as a young man, by making show of extreme submission. He came through the room with three profound bows. The marquis was very much at his ease in his part of the magnanimous father. "Three times is too much," he said humorously. He also cut short the little speech which Gabriel had prepared, saying: "My jurisdiction is over, and as father I can only give advice." Gabriel de Mirabeau had come to discuss with the marquis his election in Provence. Instead he heard a harangue on his book. Manifestly very pleased with himself, the marquis wrote to his brother: "You will not believe how effectively and how abundantly I showed him the childishness and the triviality of his objections, the feebleness, in the matter of religion, of taking the nut for the plant." After these amiabilities, the marquis declared: "For the rest, I treated him well."

The question of election to the States General had not been touched on.

7

"This sheet was in the press," wrote Mirabeau in a postscript to his pamphlet on the liberty of the press, in December 1788, "when the resolution of the Paris *parlement* of the 5th of this month was published. Its profession of faith is beyond all ambiguity:

"Equitable representation clearly indicated.

"Responsibility of ministers, as the sole basis of the inviolable respect for the royal authority, clearly established.

"Individual liberty of the citizens imperiously demanded.

"Legislative power recognized to the nation, under the presidency of its king.

"Liberty of the press, sole guarantee, sacred guarantee, of these fine rights, liberty of the press as the only prompt and certain resource of the good against the bad."

After Necker's return the political clubs, prohibited during the disturbances of the past year, had been permitted to reopen. The Constitutional Club had been formed by Adrien Du Port and met at his house. Son of a counsellor of the *parlement* of Paris, Du Port de Prelaville, he became a counsellor himself at the age of nineteen. This little man of delicate health, who was to die young from consumption, had the firmness of tempered steel. Lucid and penetrating in his judgments as a magistrate, he had come under the influence of mysticism and had become an ardent disciple of Mesmer. He had a taste also for intrigue and manoeuvring.

Adrien Du Port—he was one of the first to renounce the titles of nobility that were his due—had pursued Calonne with all the severity of a man who knows his own incorruptibility and has a keen sense of responsibility. His influence had weighed heavily in the condemnation of the minister, for, though young, he was a power in the Paris *parlement*, according to Brienne the most indomitable of the magistrates. "He had opened a sort of school of republicanism, to which his friends were active in bringing high-minded persons." The left wing of the *parlement*, known as the American faction, was grouped round him. Panchaud had brought into the club, which was often called the "Du Port Committee," his faithful disciples Talleyrand and Mirabeau; the latter brought in Biron, who was followed by all the nobles of the left wing, the Duc d'Orléans, Aiguillon, Rochefoucauld, Luynes, Clermont-Tonnerre.

With the Duc d'Orléans came his recently appointed secretary, Captain Choderlos de Laclos, author of a celebrated novel, *Les Liaisons dangereuses*. Tall and thin, with narrow shoulders, a yellow complexion, dark eyes, a bony face with a pointed chin, and a small, silent mouth that rarely showed a smile, he had the style of a conspirator and seemed to reserve himself for secret activity. A model husband, he bore ill the reputation for cynicism and depravity with which his great literary success had burdened him. His ambition took cover beneath the shadow of a carefree and debonair prince. His enigmatic gaze, so skilled in discerning human motives, scrutinized the men of whom he might one day make use. The Duc d'Orléans may not have known the part to which his secretary destined him. Nor, probably, did the duke suspect the importance of the events in progress. He followed them with worldly scepticism, and even made a bet of a hundred louis with Biron that the States General would one day disperse with nothing done, and without even abolishing *lettres de cachet.*

"We shall have a constitution," said Mirabeau, clearer-sighted and jubilant, "since public opinion has made such conquests; we shall have a constitution, perhaps even without great civil disturbances, which, after all, matter less than a bad legal order." Always suspicious of the privileged, Mirabeau feared the influence of the *parlement* on constitutional change; he feared even the influence of members so advanced as Du Port on the deliberations of the Constitutional Club.

Lafayette, covered with glory as hero of the American War of Independence, proposed in the club that nobles with advanced ideas should seek election as representatives of the *Tiers Etat*, the Third Estate. Mirabeau contended that they should seek election by their own order, the better to defend the cause of the Third Estate, and the political reasons he gave were loudly applauded; his motion was adopted. The hazard of the elections was to send him to the States General as a member of the *Tiers.*

At the moment, however, with the elections very close, he still did not know where he could find the money needed for the electoral campaign. Biron vainly urged Montmorin to help his friend, mingling declarations of loyalty with vague threats of "other resources" which Mirabeau had refused: "It seems to me that you owe it to his resolutions to be faithful to you not to expose him to the dangers of a cruelly imperious necessity."

This last expression was no exaggeration. Henriette de Nehra had been right in fearing that one day Mirabeau would be involved in some swindling affair under the fatal influence of Mme. Le Jay. The publishing firm of Le Jay was threatened with bankruptcy. Mme. Le Jay pestered her lover to find the sums needed to save her husband. He had in his hands a sensational manuscript, the sale of which might save the firm and meet his election expenses. But its publication would be a grave lapse and abuse of confidence. It was Mirabeau's copy of the reports he had sent from Berlin to Talleyrand and Lauzun. He resisted his mistress's suggestions and fought against the temptation of so dangerous an expedient. He distrusted her, and distrusted his own weakness. The manuscript was too ready to hand in emergency. He confided it to his young secretary, Comps. He enjoined him to place it under lock and key in his own home. He told him to refuse to give it up to anyone, even Mirabeau himself. But one day, it appears, its receptacle was broken open in Comps' absence, and the manuscript was stolen.

According to one version, Le Jay or his wife had broken into the room and committed the theft. According to Luchet, Mirabeau "weakly delivered his correspondence to a commercial firm which was in deadly fear of the disgrace of bankruptcy." The Marquis de Luchet, one of the persons hardest hit by the indiscreet publication, for it was he who had introduced Mirabeau to Prince Henry, seemed likely to know the true story. Le Jay, it appears, went to Alençon to hand the manuscript to the printer. The proof corrections were not in Mirabeau's handwriting. But Mirabeau must himself have gone to Alençon at a certain moment to superintend the publication. The document was put into the form of letters from an anonymous traveller who had died. The actual names of his correspondents were suppressed. The work bore the title *Histoire secrète de la cour de Berlin*.

The publication of this secret history was an abuse of his political mission, and also an abuse of the names of his friends, Lauzun and the Abbé de Périgord, who were given only the transparent disguise of their initials.

When the scandal aroused by the publication broke over him, he did his utmost to escape from admitting responsibility for the publication. He complained in a letter to Mauvillon as if he had been victimized: "A strange destiny, mine—to be always the engineer of a revolution, and always between a dunghill and a palace!"

8

Necker, who had tried in vain to gain time, or to evade his responsibility, now found himself obliged personally to settle the formalities of the future States General. He did so in a verbose, diffuse report to the king's Council. He was careful not to touch on the thorniest problems. The Third Estate represented ninety-eight per cent of the population of the kingdom; consequently it was entitled to the same number of deputies as the two other orders (nobility and clergy) together. He left unsolved the question whether the Third Estate might choose its deputies among members of the other orders. He left unsolved, above all, the thorny question whether the States General should vote as a single body or as separate orders. The king's Council proclaimed by decree of December 27, 1788, the result of its deliberations. It was generally assumed that it was in favour of the Estates voting as a single body.

The elections that began to take place under this decree started from a misunderstanding of which the consequences were to be disastrous. Mirabeau, always made clear-sighted by his hatred, issued a small pamphlet, *Correspondence between M. C—— and the Comte de Mirabeau on M. Necker's Report and on the Council: Resolution of December 27th.* Once more it was a correspondence published without the knowledge of those concerned—an exchange of letters between him and a fervent apologist for Necker, Cerutti, an unfrocked priest. Mirabeau had realized that the Necker plan brought the Third Estate "defeat under the appearance of victory." He also attacked Necker's financial policy. Necker had secured a secret advance of fifteen millions from the Caisse d'Escompte, fixing in return the price of its notes. The arrangement was prolonged for six months under the decree of December 27. Mirabeau accused the all-powerful minister of "pretending to perform miracles" while only "doing tricks and not good ones." He rightly foresaw a new flood of paper money based on a loan. Cerutti, in a letter published in the Paris *Journal,* accused Mirabeau of a breach of confidence. On his friends' advice, Mirabeau published no reply. He had intended to attack Necker in a big work, to "disembowel" him. But he refrained because "Necker's popularity is needed for the formation of the States General."

He may also have felt that the time for personal combats had passed. At this turning-point in his life he had self-control and tolerance. A long letter to Mauvillon reveals him endowed with the sense of the possible that was to make of him a man of action: "Three roads should lead us to the most unqualified indulgence: the realization of our own failings, the prudent fear of being unjust, and the desire to do good, making do with men and things as they are. I think I am obliged now to exercise this extreme tolerance of all philosophical and religious opinions. In a certain sense, in fact, everything is good so far as I am concerned—men and things and opinions: everything has a handle, a lever. I am becoming too old to use. up my remaining strength in warfare: I want to use it to help those who are helpful. Let us not excommunicate anyone, and let us associate ourselves with anyone who has one companionable hair."

≥ XIII ≤

Tribune of the People
Despite Himself

"IT IS as if the Destroying Angel had visited the whole kingdom," wrote Mirabeau to his father, in the course of his tour of Provence, at the beginning of January 1789. "Every scourge has been unloosed. Everywhere I have found men dead of cold and hunger; and that in the midst of the wheat, for lack of flour. All the mills are frozen."

When he reached Aix, he found the town in ferment. Particularism in revolt against government interference had led in the preceding year to the re-establishment of the Estates of Provence. But amid this apparent union social differences had shown themselves with all the more force. Pascalis, Mme. de Mirabeau's vehement counsel, had drawn up a memorial for the first session of the Estates, in which he showed that the land belonging to the nobility and clergy formed one-sixth of the whole of the province. "If you do not contribute to the taxes in proportion to your property," he said to the nobility, "what return will you make to the state in payment for its benefits, in compensation for the security it gives you and the laws that protect you?"

On his arrival Mirabeau wrote: "I have never seen a nobility more ignorant, more greedy, more insolent." Imbued with the feudal spirit, the majority of the nobles were in revolt against the royal decree of December 27, and drew up a protest against the equal representation granted to the *Tiers*, the Third Estate. The Assembly of Vizille had had a great repercussion in the country. The *Tiers* of Provence also demanded a general assembly of the three orders. The municipal council of Aix, following the example of Grenoble, convoked a meeting of all the citizens of the town. More than twelve hundred persons assembled, but the clergy and the nobles possessing fiefs kept away. The Third Estate was paralysed in face of these intractable adversaries. Mirabeau watched it with contempt: the assembly of the three orders was essential to it, but it was "far from having the boldness needed to get it."

Mirabeau was well remembered in this town. His conjugal troubles had seemed to be a closed chapter, but the people now realized that he had been fighting against injustice, in the name of all who suffered from it. Now, in their hour of difficulty, the people knew that he was entirely with them. "My arrival brought an explosion," he wrote to his father. "The *Tiers* shouted that I had come to be its advocate; people flocked together with proposals of acclamations, of petitions, of twaddle, and I am being given the melancholy, ephemeral, perilous honour of the tribuneship."

Faithful to the doctrine he had advanced in the Constitutional Club, Mirabeau tried to get elected by the nobility. But the nobles were set yet more against him by the acclamations of the *Tiers*, whose expressions of confidence and enthusiasm Mirabeau found "very imprudent for their own cause." He tried to escape from them and vainly multiplied his assurances that he had not come to destroy. "The nobility, between you and me, are truly frightened," he wrote. "But I neither disarm nor reassure them."

He was refused a seat in the Estates of Provence on the pretext that he had failed to send in his proofs of noble rank a month in advance. He saw at once that he had no chance of getting into the National Assembly by this path. "My line will be this: we have got to have States General. A month ago I should certainly have secured election; today my only chance lies clearly with the *Tiers*," he explained to his father, and concluded, in exasperation with the nobles: "These people would make me become tribune of the people despite myself if I did not hold myself in." For the moment he won his case. "I am in the Estates," he wrote to Comps, "and it has required more intriguing and scheming to secure that than for the most important affair. The nobles showed deep cowardice and infernal perfidy in their efforts to exclude me. They did not dare to when they saw that I was determined to fight."

A child watched with curiosity the procession that preceded the opening of the provincial Estates. He was the young brother of another of Emilie's lawyers, Portalis. The child was only eleven years old, but Mirabeau made a lasting impression on him. "He walked more or less between the nobility and the Third Estate, the last of the nobles. His piercing eye roved over the crowd of spectators, and he seemed to be interrogating the multitude with his provocative gaze. He carried his head high and thrown back. He rested his right hand on the pommel of his sword, and held under his left arm a hat with a white feather. His thick hair, brushed up above his broad forehead, ended in thick curls at the level of the ears. The rest of it, collected behind his head, was brought into a big black taffeta bag, which hung above his shoulders. There was something imposing about his ugliness."

2

"The time has come to be less easygoing and much more thoughtful," said Mirabeau on January 21 in the assembly of nobles. He was supporting the motion that every subject of deliberation should be proposed twenty-four hours in advance. The motion was rejected. Mirabeau did not take an active part in the debates. His position was precarious. The nobles had exhumed a regulation of 1620 that the possession of a fief was a necessary condition of eligibility. On January 23 Mirabeau supported the protest of the nobles without fiefs against this regulation. "The nobles without fiefs form a large part of the Provençal nobility, and they enjoy neither the rights of the Third Estate nor the principal prerogatives of the nobility. Yet they are citizens, notable citizens, and there are even among them men whose names, celebrated in history, shine still with the purest radiance. It is not at a time when it is proposed to resist so many millions of men of the Third Estate that we should isolate ourselves from our peers."

He was alone in defending that position. He realized that his election to the States General would depend on the elections being made by an assembly composed of the three orders. In the session of January 30 he threw doubt on the legality of the assembly of nobles. He demanded a representation of the first two orders (nobility and clergy) and the *Tiers* in equal number and power.

He asked "whether the king had convoked the nobility or only the possessors of fiefs," and whether "the clergy or only the prelates." He asked who were the representatives of the commoners, "that order of such importance that without it the two first orders certainly do not form the nation." But his appeal to reason and generosity among the Provençal nobility was in vain. His intervention, however, produced a sensation among the public. Next day peasants came to offer their services to the defender of the commoners. A crowd collected outside the assembly. It knew nothing of what was going on in the session, but it knew that the attempt was being made to stifle a voice that had been raised in its favour.

The fury of the nobles was redoubled by the applause of the *Tiers*. Mirabeau was accused of "preventing an agreement that was ready to be concluded, by his incendiary motion, of inciting the people to war, and of professing principles that challenged the authority of the king."

The session became more and more stormy. In their alarm the *commissaires du roi* suspended the debate and adjourned the Estates. Outside the crowd growled threateningly; it booed the members of the nobility and the clergy as they left, and insulted even the Archbishop of Aix.

"Such was their terror," wrote Mirabeau to Comps, "that they did not dare to hear me again in the Estates on their protest and receive my counter-protest." Mirabeau then published the speech he had been unable to deliver "on the illegal representation of the Provençal nation in the present Estates and on the necessity of convoking a general assembly of the three orders." He also published a *Reply to the protests made in the name of the prelates and the possessors of fiefs of the Assembly of the present Estates of Provence against the earlier speech.*

"What have I done that was so culpable?" he asked. "I wanted my order to be so wise as to give today what will infallibly be taken from it tomorrow." His whole position lay in that phrase. Again and again he was to issue that warning, and never was he listened to. "I am much more culpable than is supposed, for I believe that when the people complain, they are always right, that their untiring patience constantly waits for the last degrees of oppression before resolving on resistance . . . that they are too unaware that to render themselves redoubtable they have only to remain immobile." His magnificent self-assurance gave him prophetic eloquence: "Nobles of Provence, Europe is attentive: weigh your answer." He concluded: "Woe to the privileged orders, for privileges will cease, but the people are eternal."

3

After the sensation produced by Mirabeau's widely circulated *Reply,* the nobles were continually seeking means of eliminating so troublesome a critic. On the eve of a great upheaval they elaborated a feeble intrigue.

The plot was hatched at a big dinner at the house of one of the syndics, to which the whole of the nobility were invited. On the next day Mirabeau, who had no longer been called to the sittings, received a curt summons. "I am going against the advice of all my friends," he wrote to Comps, "such an opinion have they of those fellows. My own feeling is that if they are such cowards that they will get the hundred and eighty of them together to insult a single man, they will not have sufficient courage to assassinate him; and, to tell truth, my funeral might have been a bloody one."

The session was opened by the Marquis de La Fare, first consul of

Aix, who asked Mirabeau to state his fiefs. Mirabeau replied that he had not been prepared for this and "had not his archives in his pocket." He claimed fiefs through marriage, and also referred to a regulation issued on January 29 and made applicable to Provence admitting gentlemen without fiefs to vote among the nobles. The genealogist was sent to find Mirabeau's marriage contract. Mirabeau himself knew that the contract conferred no actual property in fiefs.

The nobles had counted on rousing him to some indiscretion. But he left the humiliating meeting perfectly cool and with undiminished dignity. He knew that he could appeal in future to a wider tribunal. After the sitting he set to work on a manifesto, *To the Provençal Nation*. "It seems to be my fatal destiny to be always obliged to do everything in twenty-four hours," he complained. "I cannot write a line without thirty interruptions." But this "centaur for work" succeeded in getting his manifesto of fifty-six pages printed on the following day. "It is not the quality of possessor of a fief that gives me the right to be of use to my country. Provençal, man, citizen—I make no other claims."

4

A woman was following the stormy debates over his election with lively interest. The passion for politics was *à la mode* among society women, and Emilie always followed the fashion. Mirabeau no longer felt either affection for or hostility to her. His indifference was so profound that he would even have been ready, as he had said to his father, to resume living with her. But he had too much else to do, too many anxieties and far too much going on round him, to be able to think about Emilie. And, indeed, if she remembered the past, he had completely forgotten it. If he had remained a deputy for the nobility, Emilie de Mirabeau and the Marignane clan might have been of some use to him. But he had broken with his own class.

The good people of the region had a vague feeling, however, that an injustice ought to be set right. At the beginning of March peasants arrived at the Marignane mansion and urged Emilie to rejoin her husband. *Aco es trop bello race serei pecca que manquei*—it is too fine a race, it would be a shame for it to die out—they said to her as their supreme argument. The countess's family remained adamant, but Emilie was no longer so easy to influence.

"No doubt you are aware," one of his fervent admirers wrote to Mirabeau, "that Mme. la Comtesse wants very much to return to the arms of her dear and glorious husband, in spite of her family's opposition." She now saw her husband glorified by popular enthusiasm, defying dangers, a man of magnificent courage and overflowing with energy. She thought tenderly of him. "The little woman," the same young friend wrote to Mirabeau, "has continual visions of you bleeding at a turn in the road, or in bed with your throat cut."

But Mirabeau was uninterested. Emilie was a forgotten shadow of the past. She never saw him again.

5

The *parlement* of Paris had to consider the anonymous *Histoire secrète de la cour de Berlin*. Maître Antoine-Louis Seguier, king's counsel, denounced the work. He remarked bitterly that "simple prohibition only adds to the celebrity of the author, quickens the sale of the work, doubles its price, and gives greater publicity to imposture and calumny."

The book had created a great sensation in the capital. Although the police had been informed at once about it, twenty thousand copies had been sold clandestinely. The *parlement*, sitting as a court of justice, ordered the two volumes of the work to be "torn up and burnt in the court of the palace, at the foot of the grand staircase thereof, by the Executor of High Justice."

The scandal was most awkwardly increased by the presence in Paris of Prince Henry of Prussia, whom Mirabeau had treated worst of all. Montmorin, extremely embarrassed, transmitted his regrets at once to the court of Berlin through the Prussian ambassador, von der Goltz. The Prussian ministers demanded exemplary punishment of the man "who is attacking all the most distinguished persons in Europe like a mad dog." Montmorin also soothed Esterno, of whom Mirabeau had drawn a malicious portrait, by assuring him that Prince Henry did him "the most flattering justice. His opinion may compensate you for that of M. de Mirabeau." Esterno was in fact jubilant at seeing his dangerous critic and possible rival discredited. He reported to Montmorin that the president of the Berlin police "sent for all the booksellers in this city and signified to them that any of their body who received copies of the work attributed to M. le Comte de Mirabeau and who did not instantly place them in the hands of the police would be taken to the fortress of Spandau."

In spite of the threat of detention, the booksellers continued to sell the prohibited work. "The secret letters of M. de Mirabeau," Esterno reported to Montmorin a few months later, "having been reprinted at

Frankfort, are circulating in Berlin and all over Germany on an immense scale. I have heard from several quarters that the King of Prussia was furious about this work, and stamped several times, saying: 'That's what they're like, Frenchmen travelling in my states.' "

The most magnanimous man was the one who had been hardest hit, Prince Henry himself. The Marquis de Luchet, who also was terribly confused, ran to see the prince, who was in Paris under the name of Comte d'Oels. He told him despairingly of the publication of the work. Prince Henry was concerned to show himself as a really great man. He may have been more intelligent than Mirabeau thought, or his vanity may have made him rise to the occasion. "Why worry?" he said to Luchet. "Fortunately, or unfortunately, I was born with a rank that devotes me entirely to historic truth. If what M. de Mirabeau says of me is true, he is only getting a day ahead of history, and there is nothing to complain about in that. If what he says is untrue, I need not trouble about it, history will avenge me."

He made another grand gesture. He asked Luchet to buy him sixteen copies of the work. He took fifteen away with him to distribute to his friends. "Here is a work," he said to them, "in which I am very badly treated. Will you oblige me by reading it and considering carefully whether I resemble the portrait given of me in it."

The French government, and especially Montmorin, was furious with Mirabeau and wanted to prosecute him. The printer and publisher of the work got away with a reprimand—the "unknown author" was not touched. Montmorin assured Esterno that the government was letting nothing be forgotten "in supplying the *parlement* with the necessary material for pushing on with this affair. But it seems that M. de Mirabeau has protectors in that company who will profit by the slowness of procedure in order to save him from punishment and the penalties that would ensue from it." Montmorin conceived the idea of having Mirabeau arrested in Provence and embarking him at once for the East Indies. This project, Mirabeau declared later, was rejected energetically by the king himself in Council.

Mirabeau had not foreseen this storm. His faithful secretary informed him of the general agitation and of his own friends' reprobation. Mirabeau quickly took the measure of the trouble he had brought on himself. He took the audacious step of denying everything in a letter to Comps, which he asked him to correct, modify, even scrap for another if necessary, and distribute among his friends. He also sent a formal disavowal to the Paris *Journal;* but it deceived nobody.

The publication of the letters to Cerutti, under Mirabeau's name,

further added to the public disapproval. The agitation in Paris spread
to Aix. "You have no idea of the horrors that are being circulated about
these two works," he wrote to Comps. "I am nothing less than a mad dog
in whom the people of Provence cannot place the slightest trust." He
boldly faced the violent agitation: "To those who have said this to
me I have replied: 'A very good reason for electing me: if I am a mad
dog, despotism and privilege will die of my bite.'"

Seeing the agitation increase, he decided to go to Paris to face the
storm.

On his arrival he found such an atmosphere that he did not venture
to show himself in public. He spent a few days in his country house at
Polangis. There he saw only a few friends of proved fidelity, Panchaud,
Lauzun, Dupont de Nemours, and even the Marquis de Luchet, who
seems to have forgiven his indiscretions. He wrote to Montmorin
in an attempt at self-exculpation and asked for an interview. Montmorin
replied cuttingly: "It seems to me at least useless to receive you
here."

Mirabeau did not reply to this insulting letter until later, when his
personal situation had changed.

Apart from the circumstances of the publication of the secret history,
its indiscretions, and the wrong done to his friends, the work itself
speaks for him. Twenty years later Chateaubriand, then ambassador to
Berlin from the court of Louis XVIII, wrote of the work: "The future
of Europe is in every line of it."

6

Bells were pealing wildly and fireworks were being let off. A crowd
was massed at every stopping place of the post. Men and women, priests,
peasants, soldiers—the crowds were vibrant with joy. They shouted
with all the force of their lungs and all the resonance of their throats:
"Long live the Comte de Mirabeau, long live the Father of the Country!"

He was a sovereign entering his kingdom, and that kingdom was the
heart of the people. The crowd mobbed his carriage. Men gesticulated,
shouted themselves hoarse, laughing and crying, and bustled about the
horses to unharness them. Mirabeau stopped them. His great voice dominated the uproar: "My friends, men were not made to carry a man,
and you carry too many already."

It was Mirabeau's first experience of the dizzy heights of popularity.
He was so moved that tears ran down his ravaged cheeks. With a chok-

ing voice he exclaimed: "I see how men became slaves: tyranny was grafted on gratitude."

As soon as he reached Provence, in every town, every village, the same scenes were repeated. Couriers who had gone to meet him gallopped to Aix to tell the town he was coming. A cavalcade of young townsmen was to have set out to meet him, but it was formed too late. A dense crowd poured out of the town. From a hilltop the human tide was seen afar. It was a crowd rejoicing, with Provençal flutes playing festive airs, Provençal drums beating time for the crowd's joyful shouting. When Mirabeau got down in the Place des Prêcheurs he was seized by strong arms and carried to his lodging. The crowd remained outside and called for him until he appeared on the balcony. He spoke to this mass of anonymous friends of the gratitude "which a people never owes, because the debt to it is never paid." He also said: "Hate oppression as much as you love your friends, and you will not be oppressed."

A great hope had come into the humble life of each of these men. They clung to a man who for them was the pledge of a better future with all the faith of simple hearts. They followed him as if they feared to lose him if they let him out of their sight. When he went out to dine with his former counsel Joubert, in a moment his sedan-chair was covered with wreaths. Musicians accompanied him everywhere. The trills of the flutes and the beating of the drums mixed with the acclamations of passers-by. Throughout the dinner the musicians remained outside Joubert's window. When night came, a thousand lights scintillated in the town, which had been illuminated in his honour. The theatre was besieged by two thousand people who hoped to see Mirabeau at the play. The managing director, driven crazy, sought him out, ran to Joubert's house, and begged Mirabeau to come: "Promise, then, for tomorrow, or I don't know what will happen."

That day, according to an eye-witness, "not one of the nobles dared to show himself."

On that same evening a grand dinner was given by the nobles' syndic. His windows overlooked the Place des Prêcheurs. Attracted by the noise of the overjoyed crowd, the syndic looked out of the window. The crowd recognized him. The acclamations changed to booing. Threatening shouts penetrated into the dining-room like a coming storm.

Mirabeau's election at Aix seemed assured. But at this great moment in his life he would run no more risks. A few days after his return from Paris he left for Marseille, where he also sought election. For Marseille as for Aix, his arrival made a fête-day. The guards rendered him military honours. The flags of all the vessels in the port floated over his lodging.

Amid this effervescence Mirabeau did not lose sight of his own interest. He published an anonymous *Letter from a citizen of Marseille to one of his friends on M. de Mirabeau and the Abbé Raynal,* another candidate. He knew that he had to strike the popular imagination. Already he was a public man. He no longer had the reticences or the timid scruples of the private individual. Under the cover of anonymity he glorified himself and painted himself as he wished to be seen by the masses. After a few words on Raynal, he painted his own portrait and career in crude and striking colours. "North America, after winning liberty by hatred of oppression, started to lose it through gratitude, by creating a body of nobles. At once he thundered against hereditary nobility, exposed to free men the abuses of aristocracy, and the establishment of the Order of Cincinnatus was abandoned. . . . For fifteen years, in works that will live as long as bronze and brass, he has been engraving the most sacred rights of man, liberty and equality.

"It should be added," he remarked in his panegyric, "that this good citizen is the most eloquent man of his time; that his voice dominates public meetings as the thunder overbears the booming of the sea; that his courage arouses yet more astonishment than his talents, and that there is no human power that could make him abandon a principle."

7

"The general destitution exceeds the idea we had formed of it," Pascalis had written in August 1788. The hard winter increased it. The orange trees were frost-bitten. One-third of the olive trees were frozen. There was a shortage of wheat. Owners and sellers had sent up prices, speculating on the scarcity. The high cost of living was sent up further by such taxes as the *piquet,* a duty on flour, crushing for the townsman and ruinous for the peasant. The excitement of the crowd that acclaimed Mirabeau was born of distress.

March 14, 1789, was market day at Manosque. There was no wheat. The crowd was indignant. The Bishop of Sisteron, M. de Suffren Saint-Tropez, came into the market. He was himself a large landowner. It was he who had drawn up the protest of the clergy against Mirabeau's speech in the provincial Estates. He was not popular in his diocese. He was suspected of holding up wheat in complicity with the sellers. His appearance brought down upon him the exasperation of the crowd.

Fists were raised in threat. "We are poor, you are rich, we want your property." Clods of earth flew in the air. The booing redoubled in violence. The bishop took to flight beneath a hail of stones.

The incident at Manosque was the signal for rioting that spread from place to place like a forest fire, from the big towns to isolated hamlets. Châteaux were attacked, houses pillaged. A noble who fired on his assailants was hacked "into little pieces," reported M. de Caraman, commandant of Provence. The bishop's palace at Riez was besieged, and the crowd threatened to burn it down. The bishop escaped from that disaster at the cost of a ransom of fifty thousand livres. The bishop's palace at Toulon was sacked while four thousand soldiers and sailors passively looked on.

"The population is attacking the ecclesiastic, the noble, the bourgeois, without distinction," wrote the intendant of Provence. "There is open war here on landowners and on property," reported the advocate general of the *parlement*, M. de Montmeyan. It was a war of principles, not a spontaneous outbreak of popular wrath. The people felt entitled to carry out these acts of summary justice. "The peasant is continually announcing that the destruction and pillage he is committing are in conformity with the will of the king," said the intendant. In its revolt against the most hateful of burdens, the taxes on consumption, the people still remained respectful to the throne. The office of the collector of duties on leather at Brignolles was pillaged amid shouts of "*Vive le Roi!*"

"Never were the people so inflammatory and so ready to work together," wrote Caraman. It was no longer a question of "isolated riots as at ordinary times. The process is directed by uniform principles. The same errors are shared universally."

Some fifty insurrections took place during the third week of March. One commune remained aloof from the agitation, that of Mirabeau. When it drew up its list of grievances, it simply remarked that it was "fortunate in still having as its seigneurs the Riqueti, such as the *ami des hommes*, and such as M. le Comte de Mirabeau, the *ami du peuple*, whose name will always be dear to the Provençal nation and in particular to this community, which will never forget that he was the only one in his order to plead the cause of the Third Estate."

8

"Marseille has been and continues to be the focus of all the insurrections that have broken out in the various communities," noted the intendant of Provence, De La Tour. He himself was the most detested man in the town. He was accused of having sent up the cost of living. According to Blanc Gilly, a Marseillais writer who later became administrator of the Bouches-du-Rhône, a pound of meat cost five sous at a distance of eight leagues from Marseille, while the cost in the town was nine to ten sous. The people were more and more incensed. Placards, in handwriting, were posted all over the town demanding reductions in meat and bread prices. The demands were followed by threats. At the end of February notices were put up on three consecutive days that the port would be set on fire if no relief was given to the people.

"This warning was ignored," wrote Mirabeau; "yet the people were complaining loudly of the administration of the farmed taxes of the town." The time had come when threats quickly gave place to action. On March 23, 1789, on the eve of the day when the electors, chosen in the primary assemblies, were to meet, gatherings took place all over the town. Very soon there were armed men among them. Others brandished sticks. It was the signal for action. A dangerous crowd made for the house of the farmer general. But with one of the unexpected turns resulting from some chance phrase uttered by an unknown person, the mass of people changed their mind. The growing flood of rioters made for the town hall, where the mayor was deliberating with the city magistrates. The windows were smashed. The doors were broken in. The crowd shouted that it wanted bread and meat at its own prices. The municipal council promised all that was asked and was compelled to send the town criers into every quarter to trumpet the victory of the people. A group of rioters pursued the mayor and the assessor, who escaped across a roof. They fled from Marseille in the night, in disguise. The population was wild with joy. The people had secured justice; their conscience was clear. When the military commandant reached the town from Aix at nightfall, he was met with welcoming shouts of "*Vive le Roi, vive le Comte de Caraman!*"

The military commandant harangued the masses. He knew nothing of the changing humour of the people. He was misled by the reception given him; he imagined that calm had been re-established. He did not realize how dangerous is a crowd that has once tasted success won by violence. He took no precaution, and in the middle of the night he quietly left for Aix, satisfied with his personal success.

But a young friend of Mirabeau, Brémond-Julien, sent an urgent message to Aix in the evening. "All is lost if we have to give way to the people; all is destroyed if force is used," he commented, more clear-sighted than the commandant. "Perhaps your presence would calm things down," he wrote to Mirabeau, imploring him to come.

Scarcely had the commandant's carriage left Marseille when disturbances broke out again with increasing violence. The intendant's house was broken into and sacked. The crowd tried to force the wheat stores. The house of the farmer general, spared earlier, was attacked with fury. It was pillaged, even the furniture was taken away, and everything that could not be taken was destroyed. Day broke on a town in worse disorder than the day before, with a seething mass of people ready for any excess. Agitators were inciting it to break open the prisons. At any moment released criminals might be able to join a people thirsting for vengeance.

Mirabeau had received his young friend's letter in the course of the night. He communicated it to Caraman, asking his advice and, indeed, his orders. The mission which Brémond-Julien wanted to entrust to him was a dangerous one. He felt all the weight of his responsibility. Caraman replied: "What is said to you, Monsieur le Comte, is true, and I have done what was required of me to prevent a worse evil." He realized that the disorder must at any price be calmed without resort to force. "What shall I advise you, Monsieur le Comte? To do what your heart and your abilities dictate to you for the public good. It is indeed a critical moment, and your success will carry the price of its importance."

Mirabeau left at once for Marseille. The town had a threatening appearance. "Yesterday," he wrote to Caraman, "the movements seemed to you to be considered and arranged. The people wanted only to get justice; in the night, however, and this morning, Genoese and foreigners, that is to say many bad characters, caused the tumult and seemed to be trying to profit by it." But he found also the first signs of reaction against the disorders. A number of young men of good family had joined together to form companies. One of these had been spontaneously named Compagnie Mirabeau.

From the moment of his arrival Mirabeau assumed the responsibilities and the functions of the public authorities, which had been delegated to him, and at the same time he dismissed the military commandant and the intendant and appointed others in their place. "The fall in prices," he reported to Caraman, "instead of calming the people, continues on the contrary to excite them, for they would like to keep it and yet do not themselves believe it to be possible to do so. What proves this is that several individuals have visited the bakers with sacks and asked for bread to last them a fortnight. Moreover, if bread and meat were kept

below their real value at Marseille, all the inhabitants of the surroundings would come to buy. I have been preaching the necessity of an
increase wherever I had influence."

He knew that he must see first of all that nothing was lacking to this
agitated population. Caraman had authorized him to take any steps to
bring in grain and meat. Mirabeau learned in the course of the day that
a ship loaded with grain was ready to leave the port. He ordered its
departure to be suspended, and negotiated for the purchase of the cargo.
He had scarcely been initiated into the administration of the town, and
was giving evidence of more foresight than its official administrators.
"Really," he wrote to Caraman, "I am astonished at the sense of security
of this town. Very often it has only a few days' supply of wheat. What
does it rely on then? On the east wind that brings it grain ships? How
can it forget that the west wind continues for whole months, and that
the port cannot then be entered?"

He called on the excited crowd to be calm; he explained its own interests to it: he was looking after its needs, and he promised it that justice would be done and that the farmer general's activities would be
submitted to an inquiry. He promised to examine whether the farmer
general's conduct was as blameworthy as was supposed: "I believe that
the people are never mistaken in their complaints, but they may be mistaken in their imputations." He did not content himself with simple
measures of administration. Nothing had been done to prevent worse
disorder in case suspicious characters should take over the direction of
the infuriated masses. In the neighbourhood of Aix and Marseille there
were only two regiments of infantry and a small detachment of cavalry.
Marseille had not seen troops inside its walls within human memory.
The military commandant had not dared to appeal to armed force, for
fear of a general rising. Mirabeau took advantage at once of the goodwill of the young men who had begun to organize before his arrival.
But he knew also, although this was the first time he had been face to
face with disturbances, that what was needed was a force drawn from
the people themselves to keep them in order. He needed strong fists,
redoubtable muscles, honest men speaking a language which the crowd
could understand, and not only sons of good families. He appealed to
the "truly respectable" corporation, as he called it, of the stevedores,
and within a few hours he had organized an imposing force. It was the
first time a citizen militia had been created on French soil. Later, in
the National Assembly, Mirabeau was able to claim with justice "the
honour of having anticipated the establishment of national militias" in
this improvisation at a critical moment in Marseille.

While the new militia men, wearing red rosettes or feathers, were patrolling the town, Mirabeau wrote to Caraman: "The evening has been quieter, but the people are still excited, and we are by no means entirely free from anxiety; it is thought, or at least hoped, that my presence may calm men's minds."

On that same day he prepared an address which was posted up next day all over the town. It was headed simply *Notice from Mirabeau to the People of Marseille*. He dropped his title and his particle. But this was not in order to renounce them or to let them be forgotten. The simple name "Mirabeau" was already a power. In that form he was closer to them. He spoke to them as an equal, as an elder brother, without a shadow of condescension or superiority, to his younger brothers:

"My good friends, I have come to tell you what I think about what has been happening these three days in your proud city! Listen to me, I only want to be of use to you, and I do not want to deceive you. Each one of you desires only what is good because you are all honest men; but each one of you does not know what needs doing. One often makes mistakes even about one's own interest. Let us first consider bread. Two things are needed for bread, first that there shall be some, and then that it shall not cost too much."

He recalled the hailstorms that had destroyed crops everywhere. He recalled also that wheat had to be imported. "At the present moment, my friends, tell me, since wheat is dear everywhere, how could it be cheap at Marseille? You are just and reasonable. Let us reason together about this." He tried even to make the people understand the necessity for a tax so hateful as that on flour, the *piquet*. "The town of Marseille, like every other town, pays something toward the expenses of the kingdom and toward the support of our good king. Money is taken a little from this source and a little from that." He tried also to explain to the masses, in a few very simple words, the interdependence of the national economy, and the functioning of the complicated mechanism of the administration of the state. He chose words that would make the man in the street who spelled out his manifest or had it read to him say: "There, that is quite true!"

It was Franklin's style that he adopted from the first, with the same suggestive force of common sense. He asked the masses only for "a little patience. It is impossible to change at once everything that wants changing; if it were otherwise, we should not be men, we should be angels."

It was absolutely necessary to increase the price of bread above that which the rioters had imposed. It had to be increased at a moment when the agitation was barely calmed and still simmered dangerously. The municipal council fixed the price at about three sous. The decision was arrived at while an immense crowd was massed round the council hall. The atmosphere was tense. When the people were deprived of part of their conquests, they might react violently. "In any other conditions," Mirabeau explained on the next day, "it would have been dangerous to run the risk of a crisis at half-past eight at night. But I felt that it would be more dangerous still to allow men's minds to run in another direction."

He had the decision announced that night. But he neglected nothing to prevent any untoward effect. While he spoke to the people in the language of reason, he knew that it was also necessary to strike their imagination. Instinctively, although entirely without experience, he realized the importance of a tactful presentation. He had the proclamation read by the leaders of the citizen patrols who "took responsibility for everything." He had it read by torchlight. He took the precaution of disseminating everywhere men who were loyal to him as "applauders" to give voice to "the public joy." His measures were entirely successful. The people "showed themselves more grateful for having secured a moderate price, that is to say the real price of the thing, than they had been for a drop on which they had foreseen that they could not count."

Liberty, or Marseille Saved, was the name given to a play staged a couple of months later by a Provençal author, Le Blanc, in a Paris theatre. The action took place in the sixteenth century, but the hero was a Riqueti, who, at the time of the League, saved his native town from a popular revolution.

9

The first consul of Aix, M. de La Fare, stood at the door of the town hall. It was March 25, 1789, the day of the three primary assemblies, those of the country people, of the inhabitants of the suburbs, and of the townsmen. The voters on their way found the roads packed with people. A crowd was massed round the town hall—agitated women, peasants, workers, the poor in their rags who had no right to vote. The surging crowd, noisy and excited, incendiary material which the slightest incident might set aflame, was demanding the lowering of bread and meat prices and the suppression of the *piquet* duty. The crowd became threatening and hurled insults. The presence of the first consul at the door of the town hall exasperated it. There were jeers and shouts of hatred. But La Fare refused to go back into the building. He did not propose to give way to a mob of the lower orders. Women were pressing close on him. One of them was insistently demanding bread from him. In irritation he replied: "Horse dung is good enough for you."

The remark was heard, perhaps distorted, and repeated. A wave of indignation ran through the crowd. Threatening fists were raised. La Fare took a gun from a soldier and raised it to his shoulder. A hail of stones fell on him. He fled inside shouting, "*Sauve qui peut.*"

The big square was now a whirling mass of revolt in which everyone was caught up, peaceful voters, women, children. The commandant ordered a detachment of infantry to clear the square. He himself led the troops. He was popular at Aix. The crowd greeted him with acclamations. But from the depth of this human whirlpool stones were thrown at the soldiers. There were pistol shots. As in every violent scuffle, nobody knew who fired first. No order to open fire had been given. The troops, provoked, spontaneously charged the crowd. Over the corpses strewn in the square a mass of furious men threw themselves upon the soldiers. Two soldiers collapsed, dead; eleven were wounded. The commandant himself became involved in the mêlée. Shouts of fury were mixed with the groans of the wounded. There were cries of "Ah! if M. de Mirabeau were here! We should get justice! We should not be killed!"

But Mirabeau was not there. The commandant changed his mind and gave the signal for retreat to avoid a massacre. Slowly the big square emptied.

But the rioting, which seemed to be ending in the centre of the town, broke out violently in the neighbourhood of the wheat stores. The crowd broke in the doors and carried off sacks of grain. At the sight of the pillagers loaded with booty, peasants and women rushed in turn to carry off wheat. A woman and two children were suffocated by the pressure of the crowd. In less than three hours the stores were emptied; pillagers had carried away even the doors. The rioting continued through the night; a gang stoned the house of a grain merchant; other grain merchants were pillaged. Alarming rumours spread of violence in preparation.

The next day was a market day. Nobody doubted any longer that there would be a great upheaval. The night was one of terror in the town.

Caraman wrote Mirabeau of the rioting that had broken out at Aix. Marseille was scarcely reduced to calm. Mirabeau rode during the evening to inspect all the guard posts. He took note of their means of defence and strengthened their arrangements. "When I felt perfectly sure of everything I sent for the post horses and went full speed to Aix."

He reached Aix a little after three in the morning. He hurried to the commandant. But Caraman was asleep. He had not expected Mirabeau until six. "I let him sleep," Mirabeau told his young friend Brémond-Julien next day. "And after getting some information at his house that showed me that his staff could not distinguish men from flies, I went away to arrive at an understanding with the principal citizens."

Everything indicated the probability of new and very serious disturbances. About half-past five Mirabeau returned to Caraman's house. "Prepared by our enemies, all his military dispositions had been made, and all of them were changed. I persuaded him to withdraw all the troops from Aix and to leave its protection to the police and to a citizen militia, and to rely on me for the safety of the town and the market. The danger was so extreme that he took my advice."

In this grave hour Caraman transferred all his responsibilities to Mirabeau. He was left to do as he thought best. He formed citizen pickets as he had done at Marseille. He asked them to choose their own leaders; he made the troops give up to him all the posts that had been placed in their charge, and replaced them with his improvised militia, whom he placed within the town at judiciously chosen spots. "At eight o'clock in the morning," he triumphantly reported to his young friend, "I was already master of Aix, with no fear of plot or brigandage."

He was told that a crowd was gathering. He ran there at once. He addressed a mob in revolt, excited by its own violence, as though he were speaking to thinking persons. "I put the people on their honour to be sensible, and to ask or compel others to be sensible." After awaking in the crowd a sense of responsibility, he knew that he could trust it. "I was obeyed like an adored father." He was told how the crowd had shouted for him on the previous evening, after the salvo from the troops. He saw this same faith looking to him from all these simple hearts. "Women and children bathed my hands, my clothes, my steps, with their tears." Wild cries of gratitude streamed toward him.

About one in the afternoon, order had been restored in Aix. Mirabeau rode through the town. "Not the slightest vestige of unrest," he reported. He had fully justified the trust placed in him by the people and by Caraman. But though the people had yielded to his arguments, difficulties arose from another quarter. Scarcely had calm been re-established when the nobles, "who had not been seen for thirty-six hours, reappeared, armed, insolent, claiming appointments as officers of the citizenry." The nobles were not in the least grateful to Mirabeau for having saved their properties and their lives and having prevented terrible bloodshed. They claimed that Mirabeau had roused the masses. They went about shouting: "It is M. de Mirabeau who has done all the harm." "Strange logic, that of hatred," commented Mirabeau.

He had spent himself without stint. He had stopped two riots. He had called up all the resources of his talent and had staked his whole vehement personality. He was proud of the task he had accomplished. But he was tired and disgusted. "There you see the human heart," he concluded. "Human nature horrifies me."

10

"One good thing has resulted from our misfortunes," wrote M. de Caraman a few weeks later, "the suppression of the municipal taxes that were most burdensome for the people. The well-to-do class has been made to shoulder what was beyond the strength of the poor journeyman; it is a pity that this reform was the fruit of fear."

The fear had been salutary. Even the most uncompromising had realized that it was dangerous to drive the people to excesses by insolence.

But the influence of the night of terror at Aix, and Mirabeau's influence, spread further. The nobility split into two groups. The possessors of fiefs having refused to attend the assemblies, the minority had the upper hand in the deliberations of the nobles. This minority had ranged itself from the outset behind Mirabeau and had protested against his exclusion from the assembly. Its very presence had shaken the feudal edifice. The list of demands of the gentlemen of the seneschalsy of Aix was one of the boldest drawn up. Mirabeau, although a candidate of the Third Estate, seems to have inspired the demands of the nobility, which included: majority voting; "the suppression of the humiliating distinctions that degraded the Third Estate in the last States General"; liberty of the press; the entire suppression of *lettres de cachet*; "the responsibility of Ministers"; and even the re-establishment of elections for the choice of bishops.

The nobility of Provence, haughty, insolent, behind the times, was to be represented in the States General by a man without a fief, M. d'André, a counsellor in the *parlement* of Aix. Mirabeau's election by the *Tiers* was scarcely contested. He headed the list, with two hundred and ninety votes out of three hundred and forty-four.

The elections at Marseille were livelier than at Aix. No deputy obtained a clear majority. Mirabeau had a serious rival, a merchant of Marseille who was at the same time a writer and a member of the Academy. He was the candidate of the upper middle class which distrusted Mirabeau. But Mirabeau's young supporters were determined to get him elected at any cost. They surrounded the Carmelite convent in which the Third Estate was deliberating. The voting was prolonged. Not until midnight did the electors, intimidated by the presence of the crowd outside, agree on the list of deputies. Mirabeau was elected, but only in the fourth and last place. Next day he wrote to Marseille that he was compelled to make his choice at once, and he chose Aix. The municipal council voted him by acclamation the freedom of the city.

Marseille gave an ovation to the man who had almost been its representative. He was especially the hero of the young men to whom he had first spoken of their responsibility, and whom he had given the chance to distinguish themselves by preserving public order at a critical moment. When he left in the evening, several hundred young men on horseback escorted him, each holding a torch. The long procession was greeted with shouts of enthusiasm.

Aix, which had been able to keep him, was not to be outdone by Marseille in its demonstrations of attachment to its deputy. Mirabeau, in order to avoid too spectacular a departure, had proposed to leave secretly for Paris. Late in the evening he had sent his valet to order post horses for the middle of the night. But a crowd had collected round the house in which he was lodging. The adjacent streets were full of people. He scarcely lay down that night, but the people, faithful to their idol, kept vigil also. A dense crowd followed him until he left the town.

Mirabeau at the time of the French Revolution

L'*Ami des Hommes*,
Mirabeau's father

Le Bailli, Mirabeau's uncle

Sophie de Monnier

Costumes of the Three Orders of the States General, 1789 Left, *Clergé;* center, *Noblesse;* right, *Tiers Etat* (CONTEMPORARY PRINT)

Mirabeau presiding at the Jacobin Club (CONTEMPORARY CARTOON)

Louis XVI and Marie Antoinette on a Paris street during the
Revolution

The National Assembly taking the "Oath of the Tennis Court,"
June 20, 1789

FROM A CONTEMPORARY PRINT, IN THE LOUVRE

The Storming of the Bastille

FROM A CONTEMPORARY PRINT, IN THE LOUVRE

Mirabeau's funeral

FROM A CONTEMPORARY PRINT, IN THE LOUVRE

Book Two

In the Revolution

❧ XIV ❧

We Are Beginning the History of Men

ALL Paris crowded into Versailles to see the procession of the States General on May 4, 1789. All along the route of the procession, from the church of Saint-Louis to Notre Dame, the houses were decorated with brilliant tapestries. Gobelins were hung across the side roads. Against this brilliant background stood out the bright uniforms of the royal guards. The tall forms of the "Hundred Swiss," made yet taller by their plumed hats, dominated the crowd; they wore their picturesque wide breeches and harlequin tunics. Falconers followed them, with decorated falcons perched on their fists. But in the sumptuous cavalcade it was above all the nobles who attracted the eyes of the crowd, their coats sparkling with embroidery and a foam of precious lace on their breasts. They wore black breeches, white stockings, and cloaks of black silk with broad golden borders. Their diamonds flashed, and on their hats, turned up in the style of Henry IV, tall white plumes waved to and fro as they strode along. It was the last public display of an age of luxury on the point of extinction. All the illustrious names of France defiled before the crowd, immortal echoes of past glories. But no name any longer aroused its admiration or even its respect. Then suddenly applause broke out. A majestic Bourbon figure had come into view. The people proclaimed a friend in this prince of the blood, the Duc d'Orléans.

In the procession of the clergy, with its fifty archbishops and bishops, bright splashes of sacerdotal vestments broke the monotony of the black cassocks. But the Third Estate with its many deputies moved on in a dark mass, wearing the coat and breeches of black cloth, the black stockings, and the short cloak prescribed by royal regulation—the costume of subordinate officials, with each detail fixed by a tradition dating back more than a century and a half and resuscitated to humiliate.

"The distinction in the costumes assigned to the deputies of the different orders was generally disapproved," said Mirabeau, by the pen of a journalist whom he had engaged, in his first letter to his constituents. "But not everybody is able to appreciate its political consequences: most people see in it only a humiliation for the deputies of the commonalty because they are allowed neither plumes nor lace. . . . But is not the prescribing of costumes, of whatever sort, for the members of the legislative body the extreme of despotism and of debasement? What matters the elegance or richness of the clothing? Is not the servitude the same? And can men born to be free lend themselves to this shameful degradation? . . . When we see such symptoms in a nation, we may be assured that it no longer has anything to lose, and that it is completely enslaved."

After the dais that bore the sacrament came the king; the finest diamond of his crown was blazing on his black hat with its great white feathers. The crowd, which up to then had been silent, broke into shouts of enthusiasm. Silence, this time hostile, returned at the approach of the queen, impassive and haughty. There was an isolated shout of "Orléans forever!" It was a shrewd thrust against Marie Antoinette, but only a slight twitch of her features betrayed her feelings.

2

On May 5 more than two thousand spectators were crowded in the bays and galleries of the Salle des Menus Plaisirs, the hall in which the master of ceremonies had been busy all the morning placing the deputies. The members of the nobility and the clergy were the first to enter. They came in by the main entrance. The Duc d'Orléans was loudly applauded. He was the only prince of the blood present as a deputy. The Comte d'Artois, who had been elected at Tarbes, had resigned by the king's command.

The deputies of the Third Estate were kept waiting for several hours in a shed. They entered the hall one by one, by a little door, when the others were already in their seats. The ceremonial of 1614 was rigorously observed, with the exception of one detail which was not ventured upon: the spokesman of the *Tiers Etat* was supposed to address the king on his knees. It was arranged that he should not speak at all.

Mirabeau was greeted on his appearance with some applause, but it was cut short by murmurs.

The king appeared, and a few moments later the queen, with some ladies of the court. The princesses and princes of the blood took their places right and left of the king. The officials in their brilliant uniforms were ranged in a semicircle.

All the deputies, including the humiliated members of the *Tiers*, were sincerely and deeply attached to their king. When Louis XVI took off his hat to read his speech, all eyes were fixed affectionately on his placid face. But it was a haughty and even a censorious speech: "A general unrest and an exaggerated desire for innovations have taken possession of men's minds, and would end by leading opinion entirely astray if we did not hasten to stop them by a meeting for wise and moderate counsel." The king appealed to "the sentiments of a generous nation whose love for its kings has always been its distinctive characteristic." "He is interrupted in the reading," wrote the ambassador of the United States, "by acclamations so warm and of such lively affection that the tears start from my eyes in spite of myself."

Mirabeau, according to one of his friends, had come to this royal session with the intention of speaking, in spite of the etiquette that forbade speaking in the king's presence without permission. This friend, Frochot, later prefect of the Seine, preserved among his papers the speech which Mirabeau had prepared but had been unable to deliver, according to him, because the king, seeing him stand up, stood up at the same time and put an end to the session. But it is not very likely that at that moment, at the very opening of the States General, Mirabeau intended or would have ventured to commit such a sensational and provocative act. In the course of this undelivered speech Mirabeau urged the king to settle the question that was agitating all minds in the Assembly: "Shall the orders separate or remain united?" The answer given to that question "will decide the fate of the Assembly and," added Mirabeau, with striking prevision, "perhaps of the monarchy."

From the superb entourage, in uniform or court dress, that formed a semicircle round the king, a man in plain civilian clothes emerged. He was himself a member of the humiliated Third Estate. But he spoke as a minister of the king, of an absolute monarch. It was Necker.

His speech was in fact the true reason for the convocation of the States General. It placed in front of the nation the deficit which the government was unable to cover. The situation was, however, by no means desperate. In his long account, which lasted nearly three hours, exhausting Necker and compelling him to turn it over to a reader to finish, he admitted a deficit of fifty-six millions. But he demonstrated at once that, thanks to his financial skill, he would easily cover it.

"The general inference from the speech," wrote Mirabeau, "is that Necker thought he could be not only the moderator but the legislator of France, and that the only thing for which he wanted States General was to provide the necessary sanction for his conceptions. His domineering tone was resented."

Disappointment had not yet been voiced, and this opening session ended in a thunder of acclamation. The crowd outside the building took up the Assembly's warm applause with shouts of "Long live Necker!" and he was escorted to his house by a procession. But the enthusiasm died down as soon as his adversary's sharp criticism appeared. "Thanks to the blows Mirabeau rains upon him in the second of his periodical sheets, the man and the speech have been torn to pieces in Paris for the last week," noted a friend of Necker.

Mirabeau had ended with a warning of which Necker, to his misfortune, took no account: "Let us hope that the Minister of Finance will understand that the time has passed for manoeuvres; that it is impossible to resist the current of public opinion; that it is necessary to have its aid or go under; that the reign of intrigue and charlatanism is over; that the cabals will perish at his feet if he is faithful to principles, and will quickly beat him if he departs from them; that, strong in an unprecedented popularity, he has nothing to fear but his desertion of his own cause."

3

"His Majesty having made known to the deputies of the three orders his intention that they should assemble today, May 6, the deputies are informed that the place assigned for their reception will be ready at 9 A.M." The nobility and the clergy met separately in the places assigned to them. The *Tiers*, the most numerous, was assigned the great hall. It went there on the morning of May 6, and, profiting by the ambiguity of the royal convocation, which seemed to imply a joint meeting of the three orders, awaited the arrival of the other deputies. The government realized its tactical error, but could no longer remedy it.

The *Tiers* stopped where it was and waited—to the obvious confusion of the enemies of the popular cause, as Mirabeau wrote in his account of the sittings of May 8, 9, and 11. In his journal he gave this picture of these first meetings of the *Tiers*: "Picture more than five hundred individuals thrown into a hall, without knowing each other, brought together from all parts, without a leader, without a hierarchy, all free, all equal; none of them with any right to command, none of them feeling any call to obey, and all, in the French way, wanting to be heard before listening." This mass of men, undecided yet as to their course, wanted above all to prevent any appearance of being formed into a chamber. Mirabeau inserted in his journal a reply to criticisms of the deputies: "So much the better that you find it difficult to set yourselves in order; so much the better that you have men of strong feelings among you, and fiery speakers. Time and experience will correct all these short-comings. But if the must in a tun does not ferment violently, if it does not fight against its container almost to the point of breaking it, the resulting liquor will never be anything but a flat and insipid beverage."

He wanted to give these inexperienced men precedents in parliamentary procedure to consider. Etienne Dumont, who had returned to Paris to obtain, with support from "the divinity of the moment," Necker, the rehabilitation of the Genevese exiles, was asked by Mirabeau to translate a work by Romilly on the rules observed by the House of Commons. Romilly had compiled it with a great deal of labour, for no written record existed. Mirabeau had the translation printed at once and placed copies in the office of the Assembly. But if the deputies were embarrassed by their inexperience, they were ambitious to create something new and unprecedented in history. "We are not in England," they said. "We are not English and have no need of Englishmen."

There was ardent discussion in the Salle des Menus Plaisirs. But the discussion was no less heated outside the Assembly. Everywhere committees were being formed. Everywhere amateur legislators were delivering speeches. Dumont was present at one of these committees, in Clavière's house, and he brought away from it a deep disgust for "all the babbling of these windbags." Yet this severe and rather pedantic critic was infected in spite of himself by the passion for big general ideas and for the public weal: "I was electrified amid this nation emerging from the circle of its frivolities."

These men of the Third Estate, summoned for the first time in the history of their country to express their opinion, were helped by the experience of the bar. More than half the deputies were lawyers or magistrates. But their eloquence, which they had so much pleasure in displaying, was frustrated at first by the impossible arrangements in the hall. Mirabeau wrote in his journal that "only a stentorian voice can make itself heard. And to limit ourselves to the strong lungs is to deprive ourselves of many good heads." He called for semicircular rows of seats as in an amphitheatre; but the indispensable reforms in seating were not effected until later, with the energetic intervention of Dr. Guillotin, after his election to the Assembly as a deputy for Paris.

Mirabeau also recommended that the deputies restrain their "French itch to speak without listening and to interrupt those who are speaking."

Especially he recommended patience: "At the moment your method of action is to keep still: your army is excellently encamped; be careful to make no movements: beware of eagerness to act; to temporize is not to lose time but to gain it. France and Europe are watching you attentively, but not impatiently; do not yourselves grow impatient. Begin by settling your rules; determine your methods of taking action and of speaking; take a fortnight, if necessary, over these preliminaries; a fortnight is nothing in the age-long history in which you figure."

4

"*Novus rerum nascitur ordo*"—"A new order of things is coming to birth"—was the motto of the journal *Etats généraux*, published by Mirabeau from the opening of the Assembly. It aroused attention at once among the public, and among the foreign diplomats; the Genevese minister wrote to his secretary of state: "I will send you a journal which Mirabeau is making of the operations of the States; it will be curious on account of the author's freedom and critical spirit."

On May 7 the journal was suppressed by a decree of the Council. Mirabeau was indignant: "It is true, then, that, far from enfranchising the nation, all that is being attempted is to rivet its shackles!" From the first he made the clearest distinction between the government and the king. "It is fortunate, gentlemen, that these prescriptions, which the circumstances render yet more criminal, cannot be imputed to the monarch. No one today is unaware that the decrees of the Council are eternal falsifications, to which the ministers do not hesitate to put the king's name."

"Twenty-five millions of votes demand the liberty of the press," he wrote. "The nation and the king unanimously demand the collaboration of all the enlightened. And at this moment, after lulling us with an illusory and perfidious tolerance, a ministry, claiming to be popular, has the effrontery to place our thoughts under seal, to favour the traffic in lies, and to treat as contraband the indispensable exportation of the truth."

Braving prohibitions, Mirabeau brought out on May 10 the first of the *Lettres du Comte de Mirabeau à ses commettants—Letters of Count Mirabeau to His Constituents*—beginning with a vehement protest against the prohibition of his journal. The protest awoke passionate echoes. Target denounced the decree of the Council at the meeting of the electors of the Third Estate for the city of Paris, which joined in his protest and claimed the liberty of the press. The government found itself obliged to give way. On May 19 the Keeper of the Seals notified the press that "the government approves the reporting by journalists of what goes on in the States General, but they must abstain from all comment."

Thereafter Mirabeau's *Lettres* were published undisturbed, in spite of their often violent commentaries. Mirabeau felt a legitimate pride in his victory.

He had been disappointed, however, with his reception in the Assembly. The reputation that had preceded him aroused as much distrust as curiosity. After his triumphs in Provence he met in Paris the frigidity of moralists and the slanders of the envious. There were allegations of unworthy manoeuvres that had secured his election, and even suggestions to annul it during the verification of mandates.

In these first days of May 1789 Mirabeau was, in fact, ill. He had exhausted himself in Provence. He was suffering from attacks of fever, and from jaundice, to which he paid no attention and from which he never entirely recovered. A state of morbid overexcitement rendered him particularly sensitive to the attitude adopted toward him. Even insignificant details wounded him. With a feminine susceptibility he felt every pinprick as a wound. He was faced by a conspiracy of mediocrities that was difficult to evade. But from the first he stood up before his colleagues as a mentor. He sharply criticized their naïve enthusiasm and their confirmed respect for the authorities. "Let us hope that in future the representatives of the nation will have a better sense of the dignity of their functions, their mission, their character—that, in fact, instead of giving Europe the spectacle of young schoolboys escaped from the rod and mad with joy because they are promised an extra day's holiday in the week, they will show themselves men and the elite of a nation which needs nothing but a constitution to make it the foremost in the world." He spoke of his colleagues, says Dumont, with the utmost disdain, "and foresaw that all would be lost through their vanity and their jealousy of any signs of distinction."

But Mirabeau was one of those whom disappointments stimulate. Exhausted, he multiplied his efforts. Rebuffed, he exhibited indomitable courage. He promised himself that he would "make them see that they will have to reckon with me."

5

"Let there be no repeating of pompous commonplaces about the necessity for conciliation," said Mirabeau on May 18 from the tribune of the Assembly. "Nothing is easier than for the thoughtless, or even for good citizens more conscientious than well informed and more zealous than far-seeing, to be caught by that quack remedy; for all who are good-hearted want concord and peace; but the clear-sighted know also that a durable peace can have no other basis than justice."

It was his first intervention in the Assembly. The question of the verification of mandates was being hotly debated. The *Tiers* demanded joint verification. The two first orders, meeting separately, informed the *Tiers* that the nobility had pronounced by one hundred and eighty-eight votes to forty-seven in favour of verification by the orders, and the clergy, more divided in opinion, by one hundred and thirty-three to one hundred and fourteen. The deadlock had now lasted ten days. "The commons have persisted so far in a system of immobility which, by means of the omnipotence of inertia, will bring them victory over everything and everybody if they can keep to it," wrote Mirabeau to Mauvillon.

But the *Tiers* were impatient. Rabaut de Saint-Etienne proposed the appointment of commissioners to confer with those of the nobility and clergy. Mirabeau opposed the motion, which, he said, "takes no account at all of the arrogant conduct of the nobles. If," he proceeded, "we want to pursue farther the paths of conciliation, it is to the clergy . . . that we should address ourselves." Saint-Etienne's motion was, however, adopted. The first meetings between the commissioners of the three orders produced no result.

"The nobles' arguments," said Mirabeau on May 27, "may be reduced to these few words: We do not want to meet to judge common mandates. Our reply is very simple: We want to verify mandates *in common*." He called for a formal and numerous deputation to the clergy, to ask them to join in a fresh effort with the nobles. His motion was adopted, and a deputation was sent. The parish priests were for agreeing at once, but the bishops preferred to temporize.

The king himself then intervened, though, wrote Mirabeau in his journal, "we have not given the slightest pretext for the intervention of authority. . . . Such a mediator as the king can never leave real freedom to the parties whom he *desires* to conciliate. . . . Who does not feel how difficult it is to say no to him who for so long has said, without discussion and without participation, '*It is my will*?'"

No member of the *Tiers* yet dreamed of disturbing the immense prestige of the king; at a much later date even Robespierre vehemently disclaimed republicanism. But Mirabeau saw in the king's intervention a trap laid by those who "have given him an incorrect account of the situation. A trap if the king's desire is deferred to; a trap if it is met with refusal." He proposed to the Assembly that an address to the king should be drawn up; but the Assembly decided instead on a deputation. The elections for Paris had ended on May 25 and had brought an important accession to the commons of personalities such as Bailly, author of a history of astronomy, who was soon elected its *doyen*. It was he who was to ask for an audience with the king. Mirabeau energetically objected to going through the master of ceremonies and induced the Assembly to resolve that deputies of the commons could not recognize any intermediary between the king and the representatives of his people.

This new rule (Mirabeau was always to be particularly jealous of the dignity of the Assembly) came as a surprise to the court. But the dauphin's illness caused a postponement of the audience. The dauphin died. The audience was fixed for the beginning of June. In court circles it was seriously discussed whether the representatives of the *Tiers* ought to kneel before the king; but no one dared to impose this on them. When the deputation from the commons was received by the king, Bailly delivered a loyal message, but the king confined himself to generalities; all the orders of the States had "an equal right to my bounty, and you may count on my protection and my benevolence."

Conferences continued without producing any result. Necker put forward a plan that the orders should proceed separately to verification of mandates and should communicate the results to each other; cases in dispute should be submitted to a mixed commission and in the last resort to the king's arbitrament. Mirabeau hotly opposed the plan as "an attack on the rights of the nation."

More than a month had passed since the opening of the States General. "The time lost in appearance," wrote Dumont, "had been made good use of by the deputies of the *Tiers*. They had secured public favour; the people, seeing only the surface, regarded the nobility and the clergy as obstinately refusing everything. . . . The people of Versailles had acquired the habit of insulting in the streets and at the doors of the Assembly those whom they called the aristocrats. The people of Paris, so easy to govern, so docile when they are calm, were gradually being filled with inflammable gas like a balloon."

But Mirabeau knew that the decisive battle had not yet started. He wrote to Mauvillon: "The horizon is so clouded that it would be more than rash to predict what will happen. But the few true citizens and enlightened men in the rabble of the National Assembly will do well to win the great course of the Revolution or to flee to America; for if the judicial aristocracy at least is not killed, the vengeance of feudalism and of judgery will be endless and boundless."

6

"Mirabeau is not yet listened to, though he speaks a lot," wrote the Vicomte de Mirabeau in the satirical review he had founded about the beginning of June, *La Lanterne magique*. He had been elected to the States General by the nobility of Limoges. He took the line diametrically opposed to his brother's. He had no other means of making his mark. He was a wretched speaker, stammering pitifully if he had to read a speech, but he had a gift of ready repartee. This mass of flesh—he weighed over sixteen stone—exuded humour seasoned with malice. In the shadow of that colossus his brother, the only part remaining for him was that of Falstaff, but he had higher ambitions. His pitiless father, however, in spite of his marked preference for him, quickly disillusioned him. According to one of the friends of the viscount, he submitted to his father one day the manuscript of an important speech; the old marquis sent it back to him with the remark: "If I had a brother like yours in the States General and if I were you, I should let my brother do the talking and keep my mouth shut."

The viscount revenged himself by loading his brother with sarcasms. He drew upon his intimate knowledge of him for sharp thrusts that went home, envenomed slanders and cruel mockery of his weaknesses. But Gabriel de Mirabeau never replied to these attacks from so inferior an adversary. He treated him with an indulgence that covered, perhaps, not only contempt but some affection.

The viscount had observed with the accuracy of family hatred: though Mirabeau had spent himself during that first month of the Assembly, he was not yet listened to. To the nobles a renegade, to the *Tiers* he was suspect from the very fact of his origin. His bourgeois colleagues, Mounier for instance, called him Monsieur le Comte with malicious intent. One day a deputy referred to this. Mirabeau exclaimed: "I attach so little importance to my title of count that anyone who wants it may have it; the finest title, the only one of which I am proud, is that of representative of a great province and of a large number of my fellow-citizens." The remark was repeated by the gazettes, and added to the number of his enemies among the nobility; the old marquis thought it improper.

Duroverai, who had drawn up the Genevese code, was thoroughly familiar with the routine of popular assemblies. He was not always easy to work with; he imposed his advice with peremptory authority and sometimes with asperity. But, according to Mirabeau, Duroverai and Dumont were men "of the first order," "men of gold." He induced them to work for him by stimulating their ambition through the very vehemence of the confidence he showed in them. He took Duroverai "in a way as mentor, and consulted him on every step of any importance," said Dumont.

In these first days of the Assembly, when visitors entered without difficulty, the two Genevese followed Mirabeau into the hall during sittings. Duroverai, full of his duties as mentor, whispered advice, and even passed chits to him when he was speaking. One day a deputy asked his neighbour who the stranger was. The answer he received led him to suppose that the time had come for making a sensation. He asked that individuals other than deputies should be made to leave, and added: "There is one especially, a foreigner, proscribed by his own country . . . with a pension from the King of England, whom we have seen for several days writing notes and sending them about the hall, and it is particularly this man that I denounce."

In the tense state of the Assembly this denunciation unloosed a storm. There was a confusion of shouts from all sides: "Who is he? Where is he? We must have his name." Fifty deputies rose to speak. So serious an accusation, at that time of taut nerves, might have cost Duroverai dearly. Dumont was "frozen with fear."

Mirabeau's voice, calm and powerful, was heard from his seat: "Gentlemen, I recognize with the last speaker that no individual who is not himself a deputy, whether he be a native or a foreigner, should be seated among us. But the sacred rights of friendship, the most holy rights of humanity, the respect I show to this Assembly of children of our mother-country and of friends of peace, alike require me to separate the reminder in regard to public order from the denunciation, the really hateful work of the informer, which the last speaker did not hesitate to add."

Mirabeau, redoubtable in his calmness, dominated the unrest. With his vibrant voice he described the man who had been denounced as "one of the worthiest of respect among the citizens of the world. Never did freedom have a more enlightened, a more hard-working, a more disinterested defender." He spoke of the law of which this man was the author, "a law that consecrates this great truth, that all states have perished, or let us rather say that they deserved to perish, for having oppressed their subjects and failed to realize that one preserves one's liberty only by respecting that of one's brethren."

The courage with which Mirabeau faced the storm of indignation to defend a friend, the courage that impresses any popular assembly, gained him a hearing from all present. He did not deny that Duroverai had been given a pension by the English government. "It was a sort of civic crown awarded by the modern nation which the tutelary genius of the human race seems to have placed more specially in charge of the worship of freedom."

Mirabeau concluded: "In other days a man in peril embraced the altars, and found in them an inviolable sanctuary: this hall is to become the temple which in the name of the French people you are erecting to liberty! Will you suffer a martyr of this liberty to suffer an outrage within its walls?"

Duroverai was saved. Frenzied applause broke out on all sides. Mirabeau was the centre of universal enthusiasm. "Nothing of such force and dignity had yet been heard" in the Assembly, wrote Dumont. Mirabeau's first great success as an orator was due to a spontaneous reaction of friendship.

7

"We must put an end to inaction. Cut the painter, the time has come!" declared the Abbé Sieyès on June 10 amid general enthusiasm. He had been elected a deputy for Paris, the twentieth and last in the list at the third ballot: the man who was to give the Third Estate its doctrine nearly missed membership in its representative body.

He had become the oracle of the *Tiers* since the publication of his pamphlet on the eve of the States General, under the title which Chamfort claimed to have suggested: *Qu'est-ce que le Tiers état?*. "What Is the Third Estate? Everything. What has it been until now in the political order? Nothing. What does it demand to become? Something." He had given it the theory of the *tabula rasa*, so seductive for new men: "It seems to me that to judge what is happening by what has happened is to judge the known by the unknown. It is more correct to judge the past by the present, and to agree that the pretended historic verities have no more reality than the pretended religious verities."

Sieyès brought into the chaos his cold logician's clarity. The fifth child of a land agent at Frejus, near Cannes, he had shown from childhood a special aptitude for mathematics. Poverty drove him into the Church. But, as in the case of Talleyrand, his superiors soon saw that he was quite unsuited to clerical life. This unwilling abbé devoted his brilliant intellect to the study of social problems. Politics was for him an abstract speculation concerned not with an unpredictable human being, but with some invariable mathematical unit.

His language, too, was that of a scientist, lacking the emphasis of his time. He despised the eloquence of his contemporaries. Disappointing as an orator, and later embittered by his lack of immediate success, he sat through these early Assembly debates with his thin lips disdainfully compressed, an enigmatic and solitary figure. But he imposed his theory. In his pamphlet he had already maintained that the nobility and the clergy had mandates from only two hundred thousand individuals, while the deputies of the third order represented twenty million. The conclusion he drew was: "The *Tiers* alone cannot form the States General. All the better! It will form a National Assembly."

The nobles had saved the *Tiers* the trouble of rejecting the conciliation proposals put forward by the royal commissioners by making reservations that showed the uselessness of continuing the negotiations. In his intervention of June 10 the Abbé Sieyès called for the dispatch of a last summons to the privileged chambers to unite with the Third Estate in the Hall of the States, and to inform them that during the day there would be a roll-call of all the orders.

An address to the king was drawn up to explain the commons' decision. But next day it was learnt that the king had not yet received it "because he was hunting."

The alphabetical roll-call of nobles and clergy proceeded in silence. But when Poitou was reached three curés presented themselves with their mandates and passed them in to the office. "This action was loudly applauded. The three venerable pastors were embraced by their co-deputies," Mirabeau reported in his journal. And on June 14 more curés presented their mandates to the commons.

The Assembly was virtually constituted. Bailly changed his title of *doyen* to that of president. Officers were appointed; minutes of the proceedings were drawn up, and the journal of the Chamber was printed.

"The absentees who have been summoned cannot prevent those present from exercising full powers," declared the Abbé Sieyès on June 15, "especially when the exercise of those powers is an imperative and pressing duty." The Assembly declared that the common task of national restoration "can and should be begun without delay by the deputies present, and they should pursue it without interruption." This sitting of June 15 had been, said Mirabeau's journal, "one of the most remarkable yet held, in the gravity of its business and in the number of persons who took part." It lasted from nine o'clock in the morning until ten at night, and was witnessed by Arthur Young, who was then travelling in France. Accustomed to the traditional discipline of the English Parliament, he was indignant at the applause and noisy demonstrations of approval or disapproval permitted to spectators in the galleries. He was also shocked by the disorder in the hall. "At one time today there were a hundred members on their feet, and M. Bailly was unable to restore order."

Mirabeau was ill that day and not in possession of his normal energy. "I have never been less capable than today of discussing an important question and speaking before you. . . . I ask therefore for great indulgence for what I am going to say," he said as he came to the tribune. But Arthur Young declared: "M. de Mirabeau spoke without the help of a single note, for nearly an hour, with a warmth, an animation, an eloquence that should give him the right to be called an orator."

Mirabeau asked the Assembly to pass at the same time a series of resolutions in which principles should be established, among others "that no tax can legally exist without the express consent of the people through its representatives and that in consequence all the present taxes are illegal and are declared by the Assembly to be null and suppressed by law."

In spite of his eloquence, and perhaps because of an instinctive reaction against it, Mirabeau did not carry the day. Arthur Young, although a foreigner, quickly perceived this anomaly: "Among all sorts of people you will hear praise of the talents of the Comte de Mirabeau; he is the foremost writer, the foremost orator of France. Yet he could not count on six votes of confidence in the States General."

8

The foreign visitor noticed particularly in this sitting of June 15 "quite a young man" who "improvised with a great deal of warmth and animation; some of his phrases were so happily turned, and he spoke so eloquently, that he received a great deal of applause." This young man was Barnave, son of a lawyer of Grenoble, and himself a lawyer when he was only nineteen. He was now no more than twenty-eight, and looked younger. Through his mother he was of noble extraction. Launched early into public life, he devoted himself to it to the exclusion of every other interest. The family fortune sheltered him from material cares.

He gained the sympathy of the Assembly from the first. "No one," he explained, "saw in me a rival, and everyone could see in me a useful pupil or adherent." But as soon as he discovered that someone was trying to win his allegiance, he became refractory. One of the persons whose influence he most distrusted was Mirabeau, toward whom he showed hostility from the first. In this sitting of June 15 Barnave attacked Mirabeau for the first time, warning the Assembly against an eloquence that might arouse terror and indignation. Mirabeau did not depart from his courtesy in rejecting "the opinion ventured by a previous speaker whose youth may well add to my esteem for his talents; but that is no title to impose them on me." Barnave had questioned the need for the royal sanction. "For my part, gentlemen," exclaimed Mirabeau, "I think the king's veto so necessary that I would rather live at Constantinople than in France if he had not one. I can imagine nothing more terrible than the sovereign aristocracy of six hundred persons, who tomorrow might make themselves irremovable, next day hereditary, and would end, like the aristocracies of all countries, by invading everything."

At bottom, Mirabeau had a sort of indulgent sympathy for a young man so well endowed; he knew himself to be sufficiently superior to him to be able to forgive his aggressiveness. But later he noted in a single phrase the limitations that made of Barnave's great promise a transitory glory and a second-rate man: "There is no divinity in him."

Debates on the name to be chosen for the Assembly continued in a tense atmosphere. The various motions were put to a vote; and, as often happens at times of tension, the solution came unexpectedly from an undistinguished source. An obscure deputy, Legrand, had proposed on the first day the adoption of the title already in common use, "National Assembly." On June 16 Sieyès accepted Legrand's motion, and the title was adopted by an overwhelming majority.

Alarming rumours began to spread. A contemporary wrote: "It was rumoured that a certain number of deputies were to be arrested; beds had been prepared in the Bastille and at Vincennes, and the orders had been signed. Some took up arms to resist, others slept away from their homes; terror reigned in the Assembly. In the evening the deputies said as they separated: 'Till tomorrow, if we are still here.'"

The Assembly parried the danger of repression by adopting Mirabeau's proposal and declaring all existing taxes illegal; it granted legality temporarily "until the day of the first separation of the Assembly, from whatever cause."

The lower clergy, carried away by the daring of the *Tiers*, decided on June 19 to join it. The nobles sent an address to the king, lamenting that the *Tiers* had assumed the rights of the king and of the other orders.

The bishops also hurried to the king to try to prevent the clergy from going over to the *Tiers*.

9

"Mirabeau was, perhaps, the only man in the Assembly who saw the Revolution from the first in its true spirit, that of a total subversion," wrote Malouet in his *Mémoires*. Malouet was the only intendant elected by the *Tiers*; an enlightened conservative, he was to be overwhelmed by events. He was one of those upright officials who make the greatness of a country. He had been an administrator at San Domingo and in Guiana, and everywhere he had made the regime he represented popular. The brilliant career that he owed to his own capacity, without the protection of royal mistresses or of courtiers, had enabled him to preserve the fundamental idealism of a man who believed in the virtue of reforms and the might of reason: "I had so firm a belief in all the improvement possible in the government of France that I would have sacrificed everything, except honour, to secure election as a deputy." But after being elected at Riom in his absence he was disheartened by his first contact with his constituents. "I was on the point of resigning after I had seen *petits bourgeois*, entirely uninstructed practitioners and lawyers, discussing public affairs, quoting Rousseau, declaiming vehemently against tyranny and abuses, and each of them bringing forward a proposed constitution. I thought of all the disaster that such extravagances could produce in a wider theatre, and I came to Paris very discontented with myself, with my fellow-citizens, and with the ministers who were precipitating us into this abyss." He was a thoroughly honest man, second-rate but with excellent intentions, with a fine intellect but limited by an ingrained conventionality; his fate had thrown him into surroundings that were too much for him.

He was horrified by Mirabeau's vehemence and what he called his lack of moral sense. Mirabeau for his part ridiculed in his journal Malouet's timorous appeals to the Assembly. But Duroverai was in touch with Malouet, whom he had known at Geneva, and induced him to give assistance to the Genevese exiles. He arranged a meeting between Mirabeau and Malouet. To Malouet's great surprise, he found in the man whom he regarded as a dangerous tribune ideas very close to his own. Mirabeau met him in his usual style with direct flattery: "I know you are one of the wise friends of freedom, as I am myself; you are afraid of the storms that are gathering, and I am no less so." He described the dangers of the situation with an eloquence beyond Malouet's reach. "There are hotheads and dangerous men among us as well as in the two first orders; not every man of intelligence is possessed of common sense, and among the duffers I know more than one who are capable of putting a match to the powder barrels. Thus the question is whether the monarchy and the monarch will survive the coming storm, or the mistakes made, and the others that will infallibly be made, will engulf us all." He knew that Malouet was very devoted to Necker; he knew, too, that he was a friend of Montmorin—the two ministers who "virtually form the whole of the king's council." "I do not like either of them," Mirabeau proceeded, "and I do not suppose that they care for me; it matters little whether we like each other if we can come to an understanding. They must have a plan of supporting or opposing certain principles. If this plan is reasonable within the monarchical system, I undertake to support it, and to use every means at my disposal and all my influence to prevent the invasion of democracy."

Mirabeau's sincerity and urgency impressed Malouet. He went in search of Necker. He found him with Montmorin, who remembered Mirabeau's recent indiscretion in the publication of his secret history. Necker, with his big head thrown back and his eyes on the ceiling, declared with a superior and indifferent air that Mirabeau had no standing and could not have any. In the end he yielded to Malouet's pressure and granted Mirabeau an interview for the next day. Montmorin pretended that he could not be present. He suggested that Malouet, too, should not trouble Necker with his presence. Malouet, who gave way to this precaution for the moment, grew angry about it later, "as if M. de Mirabeau had been a man who would grossly and cravenly sell himself." Later he bitterly regretted his absence. He saw Mirabeau arrive next day at the Assembly in flaming wrath. Stepping over the deputies' benches, Mirabeau rapped out: "Your man is a fool, he will hear from me." Necker had received Mirabeau with an air of condescension and had let fall, with a lordly sneer, these words: "Monsieur, M. Malouet tells me that you have proposals to make to me. What are they?"

"My proposal is to bid you good day," replied Mirabeau hotly as he went to the door.

Duroverai continued to lavish advice on Malouet and to make use of his influence with Necker. "Duroverai," wrote Dumont, "formed the plan of a royal session. Its object was to do by royal authority what the commons had done by destroying the royal authority, and to order the nobility and the clergy to join the Assembly, so that this union should be the work of the king and not of a decree of the *Tiers*. Malouet entered entirely into the views of Duroverai and secured Necker's agreement. The plan was adopted by the king."

The king was then at Marly, where he gave the order for the Council to meet. Necker was so self-centred that he took no account of the state of mind of those whose interests he was serving. The Marquis de Ferrières wrote to his wife: "You could not imagine the frightful fury of the leaders, the financiers, the *parlements* against Necker: slanders, pamphlets in which he is denounced to the king as the most dangerous of men; others in which he is covered with ridicule." In the end their arguments penetrated the obtuse mind of Louis XVI. Just when Necker was submitting the plan for the royal session and the declarations he had drawn up, the king, according to Barentin, Keeper of the Seals, was becoming alive "for the first time to the depth of the abyss to the edge of which M. Necker had brought him."

Necker had understood the *Tiers* no better than he had understood the aristocracy. He had thought up to the last moment that Sieyès' motion would be rejected. At Marly he met with an opposition the violence of which he had had no suspicion. Barentin fought his proposed declarations as "infringing the fundamental laws of the kingdom and bound to lead to the destruction of the monarchy." Necker wanted to accept in silence as an accomplished fact the constitution of the National Assembly. The court party was revolted by the idea. "The presence of the king," wrote Barentin, "kept our indignation within bounds." When the Council resumed its sittings at Versailles, with the king's brothers present to support the diehards, Necker, discomposed by their presence, gave way, according to Barentin, to every suggestion.

Mirabeau knew nothing of the scheme his friends had elaborated. Clavière, "who could never keep a secret," told Mirabeau at the moment when the Council had made its decisions. He was furious. "Duroverai," he exclaimed to Dumont, "did not think me worth consulting. I know he thinks me a madman with lucid intervals. But I should have told him at once what advantage would be taken of his measure. These brutal forms cannot be employed with an elastic character like that of the French. To suggest such devices to M. Necker, of all men!" And, to Dumont's consternation, he positively added: "That is the way kings are led to the scaffold."

10

On June 20, in heavy rain, the deputies of the *Tiers* found the doors of the assembly hall at Versailles closed and guarded by soldiers. The heralds-at-arms announced that the sittings were suspended until the 22nd, when there would be a royal session.

The closing of the Salle des Menus Plaisirs had been decreed in order that the necessary preparations might be made for the decoration of the throne. Nothing better than a brick had been devised for damming an irresistible current. The deputies, informed of the king's intentions, according to Bailly, "as the inhabitants of a town are informed of the closing of a show," gathered in the rain. Bailly induced the guards to let him enter to take away some papers. Indignation spread from group to group. These hundreds of men, representing more than twenty millions of the king's subjects, found themselves shut out like naughty schoolboys; they were filled with the sort of anger that does not die down. The day before they had still been disunited; now they were unanimous in their indignation. The prudent and the timorous were carried away with the most violent. Complete agreement, such as weeks of discussion could not have achieved, was cemented by this humiliation.

The deputies went in search of shelter. Dr. Guillotin, always practical, proposed the Tennis Court. "They encouraged each other as they went, and promised never to separate, and to resist to the death," wrote Rabaut de Saint-Etienne.

The Tennis Court with its high bare walls added, in its incongruous nudity, a strange majesty to this grave hour. Bailly ·refused a chair in front of his standing colleagues. "The people who besieged the door," continued Rabaut de Saint-Etienne, "showered benedictions on their representatives. Soldiers disobeyed in order to come and guard the entrance of this new sanctuary of liberty." The great sonorous shell echoed the hum of voices. There were indignant shouts demanding, says Bailly, "that the Assembly should transfer its session to Paris and leave at once on foot in a body."

Sieyès was already drawing up a motion to this effect. But Mounier proposed an oath which at that moment should bind all the deputies. Mounting a table hastily brought up, he read the oath, couched in terms of juristic precision: "All the members of this Assembly shall at once take a solemn oath never to separate, and to assemble wherever circumstances demand, until the constitution of the kingdom has been established and consolidated on firm foundations."

All raised their arms, and the hundreds of voices pronouncing the oath rose to the high roof, with its golden fleurs-de-lis on a blue field. The voices were heard in the street and were welcomed with frenzied applause. But the crowd's cry was "*Vive le Roi!*"

Courtiers prowled about the Tennis Court, alarmed, "to try to discover what diabolical machinations were under way." "It is Milton's
pandemonium," one of them said; "it is the opening of a Long Parliament, and the only thing now is to find out who is its Cromwell."

The Duc des Cars hurried to the Comte d'Artois. He suggested to
him that the Tennis Court should be surrounded by troops, and "the
mutineers arrested and sent to the *parlement*, which will administer
prompt and proper justice to them." The count at once found his way
to the king's Council. But he was opposed by Necker. "The cursed
Genevese objected to everything," he reported, pale and disfigured
with excitement. Necker still had sufficient standing to be able to prevent the king from taking violent action, which in any case was repugnant to the king's natural indecision.

The alarm raised by the courtiers engendered grave rumours. The
news spread that all the deputies were to be arrested. The intoxication
of the moment was followed by alarm among the weaker-kneed. But
when the deputies confirmed their oath by their signatures, only one
of them evaded doing so. He ran the risk of being torn to pieces, and
Bailly whisked him away through a back door.

But the very apprehensions of the deputies stimulated their courage;
"the most timid shouted loudest," commented Dumont, that conservative who had strayed into a great upheaval. "Men were scared out of
their minds; the oath was a pledge of honour, and the deputies of the
Tiers were thenceforward confederates against the royal power."

II

The sumptuous preparations for the opening of the States General were
started again. But there was deployed in addition, said Mirabeau in his
journal, "the full display of arbitrary power. A numerous guard surrounded the hall of the States General; barriers were set up, and at a
moment when everything should have inspired confidence, the only
thought was for instilling terror. The door of the hall was opened
again to the representatives of the nation, but admittance of the public
was severely prohibited." The good King Louis was fortifying himself
against contact with his people.

While the atmosphere of confidence was no longer present, the spirit
of trickery remained. The errors of May 5 were repeated. The two
privileged orders were admitted by the main door. The deputies of
the *Tiers* waited under a wooden gallery, outside a door that was

closed. The gallery was too small; many waited in the rain. They waited a long time. Bailly knocked again and again on the closed door, without result. The deputies threatened to go away. Only when they began to carry out this threat was it decided to let them in. The master of ceremonies explained the delay by the sudden death of one of the king's secretaries. When the deputies entered they found the other two orders already in their places.

Dumont saw the royal procession form: "I remember the hostile and triumphant looks of several persons on their way to the château: they imagined that the victory was already won." He saw the king leave the château with the princes of the blood, attended by his bodyguard, his pages, and his falconers. "The bearing of the Comte d'Artois was full of pride; the king seemed sad and gloomy; there was a large silent crowd when the king entered his carriage; we heard the beating of drums and fanfare, but no cheering from the people, not a single 'Vive le Roi'; fear alone prevented expressions of hostility. These brilliant costumes of the nobles, this magnificence of the throne, seemed the accompaniment of a funeral ceremony."

The royal session was deferred from the 22nd to the 23rd. This day's postponement enabled the *Tiers* to make great progress. On June 22, in the nave of the church of Saint-Louis, which had granted hospitality to the Assembly, the majority of the clergy joined the Third Estate. At their head were the Archbishops of Vienne and Bordeaux and the Bishops of Chartres and Rodez. Two nobles also had the courage to break with their order.

Next day the *Tiers* silently entered the Salle des Menus Plaisirs. At the foot of the platform on which the throne had been set were the ministers; one chair was empty—Necker's. After inspiring this royal session and discussing the king's declaration in Council, he had changed his mind.

The proceedings were more like those of a "bed of justice" than the debates of a free parliament. Louis XVI, after complaining that the "disastrous division is creating universal alarm," read two declarations: "The king wills that the old distinction of the three orders of the state shall be preserved in its entirety, as essentially bound up with the constitution of his kingdom; that the deputies freely elected by each of the three orders shall form three chambers, deliberating order by order, and able, with the sovereign's approval, to agree to deliberate in common; they alone can be considered as forming the body of the nation. In consequence, the king has declared null and void the delibera-

tions of the deputies of the order of the Third Estate on the 17th of
this month, as well as those which may have followed, as illegal and
unconstitutional."

After the condemnation of its proceedings came the condemnation
of the very purpose of the Assembly: "All properties without exception
shall be constantly respected, and His Majesty expressly includes under
the name of property the tithes, quit-rents, feudal and seignorial rights
and duties, and generally all useful or honorific rights and prerogatives
attached to lands and fiefs or belonging to persons."

"The king," Mirabeau commented in his journal, "declares himself
the arbiter of that which is property and that which is not, independently of the nature of things. Here we may observe that at the reading
of this article some of the nobles had the indecency to applaud, so
demonstrating that they had too much pride for their avarice or too
much avarice for their pride. Only by dint of cries of *paix-la* [order]
were they induced to restrain themselves."

The debates of the Assembly would no longer be open to the public,
declared the king. "Good order, decency, and the very freedom of
voting, demand that His Majesty should prohibit, as he does expressly,
the presence of any person, other than the members of the three orders
making up the States General, at their deliberations, whether these proceed in common or separately."

"What is the meaning," asked Mirabeau, "of these words 'decency,'
'good order'? Here indecency would lie in mystery, disorder in the
secrecy of our operations. This irregular prohibition can have been
conceived only by those who are afraid that their guilty manoeuvres
may be unmasked and who could not show themselves without blush-
ing."

"You have come, gentlemen, to hear the result of my arrangements
and my views," the king continued; "they are conformable to the lively
desire I have to effect the public good; and if by a misfortune far from
my thought you abandon me in this fine enterprise, I shall work alone
for the good of my people; I shall consider myself as alone their true representative and, knowing your briefs, knowing also the perfect agreement that exists between the most general desire of the nation and my
beneficent intentions, I shall have all the confidence that should be inspired by so happy a harmony and shall proceed to the end I desire to
attain with all the courage and firmness with which it should inspire me."

"But," commented Mirabeau, "to attain such an end was it not useless to assemble the representatives of the people? If the monarch is

free to make laws on the basis of the various provincial representations, the ministers need only arrange to have these sent by post."

Louis XVI proceeded, in the spirit of absolutism: "Reflect, gentlemen, that none of your projects, none of your arrangements, can have the force of law without my special approval. Any mistrust on your part would be a great injustice. It is I who up to the present have caused all the happiness of my people; and it is perhaps rare that the single ambition of a sovereign should be to secure from his subjects that they shall at last agree to accept his benefits."

"As if the rights of peoples were benefits from kings," commented Mirabeau.

Louis XVI concluded: "I order you, gentlemen, to separate at once and to go, each of you, tomorrow morning, to the chambers assigned to your orders, to resume your sittings; in consequence, I order the grand master of ceremonies to prepare the halls."

The king rose. The session was ended. Behind the king went slowly the concourse of guards, courtiers, nobles, ministers, and some of the clergy. The deputies of the *Tiers* remained in their seats as if petrified.

Workmen arrived to take down the decorations. They removed the throne and the dais, the stools and the bunting. The noise of their heavy steps, of hammering and the shifting of planks, echoed in the silence. Suddenly, in the presence of the motionless deputies, the men stopped their work. Vaguely they realized that great things were in preparation in this strange calm.

The master of ceremonies, the Marquis de Dreux-Brézé, came in to see that the king's orders were being executed. He came in with his hat on his head. He was received with howls.

He went up to Bailly. "Monsieur, you heard the king's command?"

"Monsieur, the Assembly adjourned after the royal session; I cannot dismiss it until that has been discussed," replied Bailly.

"Is that your reply, and may I inform the king?"

A voice interrupted this dialogue. It was a powerful voice, but a witness was impressed by its silvery tone.

"Go and tell those who sent you that we are here by the will of the people, and that we shall not leave except by force of bayonets."

Mirabeau, who had jumped up from his seat, had no authority at all to speak in the name of the Assembly. Bailly resented his doing so. But at that moment Mirabeau incarnated the will of a whole people. Next day, in reporting his intervention in his own journal, he amplified his words and at the same time softened them. But witnesses heard only that short sentence. It remained indelibly graven in their memory, and it is in that form that it has passed into history. Vehement shouts came from all the benches: "That is the wish of the Assembly!"

Even a master of ceremonies, familiar only with tradition and the virtue of precedents, understood that something was happening that was beyond him. Those words had sounded the knell of the regime he represented. They had sounded the accession of a power of which as yet he knew nothing. Embarrassed, the Marquis de Dreux-Brézé withdrew, walking backwards, as the ceremonial required of him in the royal presence.

Sieyès, cold and logical, recalled the deputies to the next business: "Today you are what you were yesterday; let us continue." Mirabeau proposed that the inviolability of deputies should be decreed at once. Bailly opposed, thinking that the precaution would be taken as a sign of weakness. But Mirabeau replied with vivacity: "You do not know to whom you are exposing yourself! If you do not carry the decree, sixty deputies will be arrested this night, and you first of all."

The Assembly followed him by declaring by four hundred and ninety-three votes to thirty-four that all those who dared to prosecute or arrest a deputy for a crime of opinion were "infamous, traitors to the nation, and guilty of a capital crime." Mirabeau, who expressed so entirely the feelings of the nation, knew equally well those of the court.

As soon as the master of ceremonies had reported the reply given him, "the order was given," wrote André, deputy for the nobility of Aix, "for two or three squadrons of bodyguards to march on the Assembly and, in case of need, to use their sabres to eject it."

At the moment when these troops were on the march, several members of the nobility were gathered together on a terrace on their route. Among these nobles were the two Ducs de Crillon, the Marquis de Lafayette, the Duc de La Rochefoucauld-Liancourt, and André himself. All of them belonged to the enlightened elite of their order. André exclaimed: "What, could we be such cowards as to permit the throats to be cut before our eyes, without vigorous action on our part to prevent it, of men who are giving us such an example of staunchness and devotion! Let us go ahead of the squadrons and save the deputies of the commons or perish with them."

They went at once to the road and barred the way of the troops, sword in hand. They declared to the commandant that he would have to pass over their bodies before he could reach the deputies of the commons. The commandant replied that he knew only the orders he had received. He made a gesture for the cavalry to advance. The group of nobles did not budge. The commandant saw that they would allow themselves to be massacred rather than give way. He returned to the palace to ask for instructions. The court, alarmed at this unexpected resistance, ordered him to recall the guards.

12

The *coup d'état* suggested to Louis XVI had failed. On June 25 forty-seven deputies of the nobility, with the Duc de Clermont-Tonnerre at their head, entered the assembly hall, in which the deputies of the *Tiers* had carefully kept vacant the seats occupied by the other orders at the opening of the States General. The Duc d'Orléans was among the new arrivals. It was a sign of the times that struck the popular imagination that a prince of the blood should take part in an assembly presided over by a commoner. A few days later, on the expiration of Bailly's term of presidency, the office was offered to the duke, but he refused it, saying: "I should be unworthy of your kindness if I accepted, knowing my unfitness for the office."

Mirabeau had drafted an address to the Assembly in which, faithful to his theory of extreme tolerance, he had written: "The number of our enemies is greatly exaggerated. Many of those who do not think as we do are far from deserving that odious title. Fellow-citizens who, like ourselves, are simply in search of the public weal, but who seek it by another path . . . men who, enchained by the prejudices of education and upbringing, have not the strength to stem the current; men who, seeing us in an entirely new position, have been afraid of exaggerated claims on our part and are alarmed about their properties and afraid that liberty may be but a pretext for licence; all these men deserve consideration from us; some need compassion, others time to come round; all need enlightening and avoidance of any degeneration of the differences of opinion inseparable from the weakness of the human mind into disputes involving self-esteem and a war of factions. . . . Our fate lies in our wisdom. Violence might jeopardize or even destroy the liberty which reason assures us."

Did the court realize the fermentation of the country? Or did it feel too weak at the moment, with insufficient troops, to impose its will? Did the king, always irresolute, yield to a sense of impotence after allowing himself to be led into a vain exercise of his authority? There came a sudden revulsion. Barely four days after the royal session, on June 27, Louis XVI addressed a letter to the deputies of the clergy who were still resisting and urged them to join the commons. He told the

Duc de Luxembourg that he wanted the nobles to join the *Tiers:* "I desire it, and if need be I will it." The majority of the nobles, who, according to Gouverneur Morris, the ambassador of the United States, "possess neither the strength, nor the wealth, nor the talents of the nation," were incensed. But, with good grace or bad, the representatives of the two first orders complied with the command.

The Revolution had triumphed. It had triumphed over the king and the privileged classes. It had won by its strength and its firm unity. The people knew they had won a great victory. There were illuminations at Versailles and at Paris. Great bonfires were lit all over the capital. There were frenzied shouts of "*Vive le Roi!*" This first act of the Revolution was without a shadow. "It will be to the glory of France and of ourselves that this great Revolution is costing humanity neither penalties nor tears," wrote Mirabeau. "History has related only too often actions like those of wild beasts, among whom heroes have been few and far between; let us hope that we are beginning the history of men."

≥ XV ≤

The Ancient Edifice Has Fallen

"TWELVE hundred and fifty legislators," wrote the Marquis de Mirabeau, "all new to any sort of administration, are going to make a marvellous state constitution, with Green Hat [his son] at their head and the romancer [Necker] for guide. All the little dodges of sedition are being used in an agitation of unexampled fury and impunity. The government, as absolute a nullity as was the municipality of Marseille at the time of the plague, shows itself only in suave and fervid invocation of Saint Anarchy, and meanwhile, save for scandals in details, Saint Routine keeps at it, so that what the nation seems to want is a very Masaniello."

It was the last letter the marquis wrote. It was dated July 8, 1789, a few days before his death. The Friend of Mankind died in deep disagreement with his time, and still jeering at his elder son, for whom he felt a strange mixture of involuntary admiration and obstinately nourished contempt.

But his judgment of the government was sound. "The nobles deeply feel their situation," wrote Gouverneur Morris, the United States ambassador, on July 1. "The king, after siding with them, was frightened into an abandonment of them. He acts from terror only." What was most likely to terrify Louis XVI was the defection of his troops. "In effect," added Morris, "the sword has slipped from the monarch's hands without his perceiving a tittle of the matter." The Gardes Françaises were leaving their barracks in Paris and going into the taverns to fraternize with the people. "The king can no longer count on his own bodyguards," noted Salmour, the minister plenipotentiary for Saxony, at the end of June.

Some soldiers of the Gardes Françaises, charged with insubordination, had been arrested and taken to the Abbaye prison. The rumour spread that they were to be transferred to Bicêtre. The soldiers were no longer the organ of the oppressor but the defenders of the people. Those who had been fraternizing with the soldiers decided to rescue their new friends. They broke in the gates of L'Abbaye, freed the soldiers, and took them to the Palais-Royal. An immense crowd watched over them. The military authorities could not tolerate this defiance. If necessary they would recapture the soldiers by force. A deputation of citizens of Paris asked the Assembly to intervene with the king on the soldiers' behalf.

The Assembly could not sanction an act of violence; but it was equally unable to disappoint the people who were turning to it as to a new sovereign. Mirabeau considered that there was no justification for deliberating on an affair "so clearly remote from our mission," and proposed to calm the masses with an address which he had prepared. But on this first of July he was ill; his voice scarcely carried; the address was largely unheard and was not discussed. The Assembly decided to send a deputation to the king to "enlist his clemency." Louis XVI pardoned the soldiers, who had been taken back to prison, but at the same time he warned the Assembly: "Licence and insubordination are destructive of every bond, and if they should grow not only would the well-being of all the citizens be affected, but in the end they might produce a false estimate of the value of the generous labours to which the representatives of the nation are devoting themselves."

Since the day on which he had given way to the Assembly, the king had steadily surrounded himself with a powerful force. He no longer trusted any but foreign troops, and brought these to Versailles and to Paris. The commander of these troops, the Baron de Besenval, declared that the château was "being turned into a headquarters and the garden into a camp." Swiss and German troops defiled at night into the Place d'Armes, beneath the king's windows. "There was deep silence everywhere," wrote Alexandre de Lameth; "no drums, not a command from the officers, not a word from the spectators; only the monotonous sound of the parade march, which, in view of the ideas that were filling all men's minds, had an element of the sinister and seemed to presage tragic events."

The most alarming rumours spread in Paris as to the use to be made of these forces. It was declared at the Palais-Royal that the members of the *Tiers*, in danger of assassination by the nobles, were asking for help. Several thousand men were ready to go to Versailles to protect them. Rumours grew more precise: the court intended to seize the Assembly by force; the hall was to be occupied by the military; the most turbulent of the deputies were to be executed, and the rest dispersed. At a dinner given by the Duc de Liancourt, Vicomte Mathieu de Montmorency announced to some deputies of the nobility, known for their liberal ideas: "Gentlemen, I shall not have the honour of being in the first batch, but I can answer for it that I shall be in the second." Mirabeau was particularly marked down. The king's entourage did not realize that in the Assembly he was what he had planned to be, a "zealous monarchist," provided that the royal power showed itself to be enlightened and constitutional. His reply to Barnave on the question of the royal veto had struck the Keeper of the Seals, who had drawn the king's attention to it, but the court had in no way revised its prejudices against him. One day, toward the end of June, Mirabeau was dining with the Comte de La Marck. He strongly criticized Necker and the other ministers, but he added: "The day the king's ministers consent to reason with me, they will find me devoted to the royal cause and to the welfare of the monarchy." After the dinner he said privately to his host, whom he knew to be in the queen's confidence: "Do see to it that at the château they shall know that I am more with them than against them." But the court persisted in believing him to be its bitterest enemy.

"Already a large number of troops surrounded us. More have come and are coming every day; they are arriving from all quarters. Thirty-five thousand men are already distributed between Paris and Versailles. A further twenty thousand are expected. Trains of artillery are following them. Points have been designated for batteries." Mirabeau ascended the platform on July 8 to denounce these signs of a coming *coup d'état*. He expressed the alarm of the Assembly and the people. "Public events, hidden facts, secret orders, hasty counter-orders, preparations, in a word, for war, are in striking evidence and fill all men's hearts with indignation."

He was the one most threatened and the strongest in attack. He pointed unhesitatingly to the persons really responsible. "When had the fermentation begun? With the movement of soldiers and the military display of the royal session. Before, all had been peaceful; the agitation had begun on that sad and memorable day. Are we, then, to be held responsible if the people have taken alarm at the sight of the instruments of violence directed not only against themselves, but against an Assembly that needs to be free if it is to occupy itself freely with all the causes of their sufferings? How could the people fail to grow agitated when they are given reason to fear for the one hope they have left?"

He pointed out the danger of bringing soldiers near the Assembly, "of electrifying them by contact with the capital, of interesting them in our political discussions. . . . French soldiers are not just automata. . . . They will see in us their relatives, their friends, their families. . . . Such men, such Frenchmen, will never entirely abandon their intellectual faculties; they will never believe that their duty is to strike without inquiring what the victims are. . . . Have the advisers of these measures foreseen the consequences they entail for the very security of the throne? Have they studied in the history of all peoples how revolutions have begun? . . . Have they observed the fatal sequence of events that has thrown the wisest minds beyond all the limits of moderation, and the terrible impulsion under which a fevered nation is being precipitated into excesses of which the first suggestion would have made it tremble?"

In the frenzied applause that greeted his speech, prejudices were effaced and suspicions softened. Mirabeau had made himself the spokesman of the Assembly in its hours of difficulty.

He proposed an address to the king demanding the dismissal of the troops. His motion was adopted with enthusiasm. The only thing that was suppressed was its appeal for the organization of a citizen militia. No one knew better than he how serviceable it could be—he had proved it at Marseille—but his proposal seemed premature. A few days later citizen guards were formed spontaneously in Paris.

The address to the king was printed by order of the National Assembly. "I drafted it and Duroverai drew up the resolutions containing the proposed measures," boasted Dumont later. But Alexandre de Lameth, though hostile to Mirabeau, declared that "as a member of the drafting committee I saw this famous address drawn up almost entirely under my eyes." A fragment was preserved by Mirabeau; it bears corrections and additions in another hand. The Bishop of Chartres, in his account of the labours of the committee, declared: "The author accepted the changes we thought necessary with the readiness proper to men of genius." Not only was the inspiration Mirabeau's, but the style is his, with the rich and headlong rhythm of his eloquence and a quality of emotion peculiar to him. He expressed what was then felt by the whole of the Assembly: "The danger, Sire, is pressing, is universal, is beyond all the calculations of human prudence. The danger is for the people of the provinces. Once they are alarmed about our liberty, we know of nothing that can hold them back. The danger is for the capital. How will the people, sunk in poverty and a prey to the cruellest anxieties, take the snatching of the last of their food by a threatening crowd of soldiers? The presence of the troops will produce excitement and rioting and a universal fermentation, and the first act of violence on a pretext of maintaining public order may begin a horrible succession of evils. . . .

"The danger, Sire, threatens the labours which are our first duty, and which can have full success and real permanence only in so far as the people regard them as entirely free. There is, moreover, a contagion in passionate movements; we are but men, and our distrust of ourselves, our fear of seeming weak, may carry us beyond the mark; we shall be obsessed by violent and extreme counsels, and calm reason and tranquil wisdom do not deliver their oracles amid tumult, disorder, and scenes of faction. . . . Great revolutions have had less striking causes; more than once an enterprise fatal to nations and kings has been ushered in with less sinister and less formidable symptoms."

2

"The nobles in their anxiety are cursing Necker, who in point of fact is less the cause than the instrument of their sufferings," noted Morris in his diary at the beginning of July 1789. "His popularity depends now more on the opposition he meets with from one party than any serious regard of the other."

Louis XVI had never liked Necker. He now blamed him for the failure of the royal session. Marie Antoinette detested him. After June 23 the king had made Necker promise that he would quietly retire the day he was asked to do so. On July 11 he sent by messenger a letter to Necker reminding him of his promise and calling for his prompt retirement "without giving rise to any commotion." Necker faithfully complied. He preserved the deepest secrecy even with his entourage. Accompanied only by his wife, he left for Brussels.

On the previous day the king had received a deputation composed of six members of the clergy, six of the nobility, and twelve of the Third Estate, to present the Assembly's address. "In this salon soiled with the base adulations of Louis XIV from his courtiers, and harbouring at this very moment the conspirators who proposed to arm Louis XVI against his people, Frenchmen have at last spoken to their monarch the language of free men," wrote Mirabeau in his paper. While the Comte de Clermont-Tonnerre, deputy of the nobles, read the address, Louis XVI kept his eyes fixed on Mirabeau. Louis replied evasively, talking of evil-intentioned persons who were trying to deceive the people as to the true motives of the precautions taken. He suggested that the States General should be transferred to Noyons or Soissons "if the necessary presence of troops in the environs of Paris continues to cause them umbrage." So great was the king's prestige that this reply "produced a noticeable effect of tolerance and almost of security in the National Assembly; so ready are the French to place unlimited confidence in their monarch," wrote Mirabeau in his paper.

He attacked that blindness from the tribune of the Assembly. The king's word, he said, was "a poor guarantee of the ministry's conduct." He firmly rejected the king's proposal to move the Assembly. "We did not ask for flight from the troops, but only for the troops to be kept away from the capital. And we asked this not for ourselves, and certainly not out of fear, but, of course, from consideration of the general interest." When he spoke he was unaware of Necker's dismissal and of that of the chief ministers. When he described the imminent evils and the perils of the existing situation, he was unaware of the extent to which they were to be aggravated by the choice of the new ministers. Among these was Marshal de Broglie, the organizer of the military display, and Baron de Breteuil, the artisan of the Austrian alliance and the queen's confidant. Their nomination was a defiance of the popular effervescence.

On Sunday, July 12, the deputies, who had learnt the news, met very early in the morning. "They were plunged into consternation," wrote Mirabeau's paper; "they measured with terror the abyss of evil into which the previous day's resolution might lead the country." But Mirabeau himself was absent from this sitting. On the previous evening the Marquis de Mirabeau had died.

At the funeral the two brothers met. The viscount had been made sole heir and legatee. A crowd witnessed the funeral procession, but not in honour of the old marquis. From the line of anonymous friends rose shouts of "Long live Mirabeau the Pockmarked."

3

Paris learned the news of Necker's exile on the afternoon of July 12. "It is impossible to describe the immense excitement that at once filled the city," wrote Rabaut de Saint-Etienne. "All that must be expected was foreseen—the National Assembly dissolved by force and the capital invaded by the army." A dense crowd assembled at the Palais-Royal, the nerve centre of Paris. Men told each other in consternation that a formal attack was in preparation. Troops were encamped on the Champ-de-Mars, and those at Courbevoie and at Saint-Denis would move up. But the groups that formed there "were not quite ready for a rising," wrote Camille Desmoulins. He was a young briefless barrister, poor and ambitious. There was little about him to suggest the popular hero or the leader of crowds. He was small, with thin legs supporting a short body. Thin wisps of hair swept his agitated brow; his black eyes were uncannily filled with the dream of great deeds far from his true bent. But he had the superficial sensitiveness that could anticipate developments and was to make of him an excellent journalist, with a redoubtable pen for polemics. He was to be one of the first republicans of the Revolution.

In the dismayed throng at the Palais-Royal Camille Desmoulins complained aloud of "the cowardice of the whole lot of us." "Three young fellows came along hand in hand," he told his father, "shouting 'To arms!' I joined them. My zeal was noticed; I was surrounded and pressed to get up on a table." Small and frail as he was, from that table he dominated the crowd. He overcame his usual stammer, and his agitated features cleared. He found words that electrified his hearers: "Citizens, you know that the nation demanded that Necker should remain, and he has been dismissed! Can you be more insolently defied? After this stroke they will dare anything; this very night they may be arranging a Saint Bartholomew for patriots." Inflamed by the general excitement, he shouted: "To arms! To arms! Let us all take green cockades, the colour of hope!"

Nature had not by any means endowed him with exceptional physical courage, but with his nerves tense he was ready at that moment to brave the world: "The scoundrelly police are here! Very well, let them watch me! Let them observe me well! Yes! here I am, calling my brethren to freedom!"

This firebrand set the common fury ablaze. "The citizens," wrote Rabaut de Saint-Etienne, "took a bust of M. Necker; they added to it that of M. d'Orléans, of whom it was being said that he, too, was to be exiled; and they carried them round Paris, followed by an immense multitude."

It was not only such incendiaries as Camille Desmoulins who unleashed an irresistible movement of revolt; nor were the crowds made up of the ragged and destitute: they included a mass of well-to-do citizens, disturbed and anxious about the rumours that were circulating. Since July 10 repeated stories about the movement of troops round Paris had driven down the price of the notes of the Caisse d'Escompte. When the news came of Necker's dismissal, the stockbrokers met and decided that to prevent panic selling the Bourse should be closed next day. Speculators spread a rumour that at the same Council meeting at which Necker's dismissal had been decided on, it had been resolved to declare national bankruptcy. "The capitalists, through whom the Revolution began," wrote Rivarol, "were not so difficult in the matter of a constitution, and they would have given their support to anyone so long as they were paid. Sixty thousand capitalists and the swarm of speculators produced the Revolution."

But if obscure motives inspired the work of spreading alarm, when the crowd poured into the Champs Elysées it represented simply the protest of a whole people against despotism. In a moment this demonstration turned into revolt. In the Place Louis Quinze the crowd came into collision with soldiers of the Royal German Regiment who had received orders to charge. Soldiers struck the two busts with their sabres. Several persons were wounded. The people replied with a hail of stones. Prince de Lambesc, commanding the regiment, rushed into the Tuileries and wounded an old man who was walking there. Guns were fired, and then all Paris was afoot, shouting "To arms!" At nightfall the barriers outside the farmer general's office were seen to be burning. The crowd forced its way into the theatres and demanded that they should be closed in sign of mourning. Repressive measures were expected during the night. To guard against any surprise, lights were placed in every window. The Revolution began with festal illuminations.

The Assembly sent a deputation to the king to express its regret at Necker's dismissal. Louis XVI sent the answer that it was for him alone to judge the need for the measures adopted and that he could make no change in them. "The Assembly was in consternation, frozen with fear at this reply," wrote Bailly. Mirabeau told his Genevese friends that a proscription list had been drawn up and that "Sieyès, Chapelier,

Lafayette, Lameth, he himself, and several others, were to be arrested."

The Parisian crowd armed itself by sacking the armourers' shops. Terror gave birth to desperate courage. Several thousand people rushed to the assault of the Hôtel des Invalides. They hurled themselves into a moat twelve feet broad and eight deep, helping one another across. They seized muskets and powder and cannon. "The Generals," wrote Salmour, Saxon minister plenipotentiary, "concluded that it was impossible to subjugate Paris, and that retreat was the only prudent course." In spite of this warning, the court continued its intrigues, without the king's knowledge. The Duc d'Aiguillon told the American ambassador that on July 14 "the Queen, Count d'Artois and Duchess de Polignac had been all day tampering with two regiments, who were made almost drunk. . . . The Maréchal de Broglie was tampering in person with the artillery. The plan was to reduce Paris to famine and to take two hundred members of the National Assembly prisoners."

Next day Mirabeau addressed from the tribune of the Assembly a deputation which was to seek an audience with Louis XVI. He said: "Tell the king that the foreign hordes by whom we are invested had a visit yesterday from the princes, the princesses, and the favourites, and received their caresses and their exhortations and their presents; tell him that throughout the night these foreign satellites, gorged with gold and wine, predicted in their impious songs the enslavement of France, and that they gave brutal expression to their intention to destroy the National Assembly. Tell him that in his very palace the courtiers danced to the sound of that barbarous music, and that such was the prelude to Saint Bartholomew."

4

"The masons have rebuilt one-third of the capital in the past twenty-five years," wrote Mercier in a *Tableau de Paris* in 1785. "The centre of the town has undergone metamorphosis from the indefatigable mallet of the stone-cutter. The Bastille alone has the appearance of standing fast and of intending incessantly to shock our gaze with its hideous visage."

The Bastille was the point of crystallization of the resentment of every social class. Nobles or commoners, everyone had one day had a relative or friend behind its sombre walls; everyone felt that one day he himself might perish there. It was the incarnation of despotism. The members of the nobility of Paris inserted in their *cahiers*—their lists of grievances: "His Majesty will be begged to order the demolition of the Bastille."

On the morning of July 14, 1789, numerous deputations of the citizen militia spontaneously constituted or organized by the assembly of the electors of Paris called on Launay, the governor of the Bastille, to give up his arms to them. The last of the deputations was received with musket fire.

This it was that brought into action the great multitude massed outside the Bastille. Those who rushed to the assault on it were mainly inhabitants of the suburb of Saint-Antoine, workers, tradesmen, and students, with a few young writers. Most of them had never handled a firearm, and yet, wrote later the author of a counter-revolutionary publication, the *invalides* (army pensioners), "who had been in many sieges and many battles, have assured us that they never saw a musketry fire served like that of the assailants." Among them were some old soldiers like Elie, a non-commissioned officer with twenty-two years' service, who had never had a chance of further promotion because of his humble origin. His resentment of those years of persecution by noble officers found vent now; at the sight of the assault on the fortress he ran home to put on his uniform and returned to take his place in the front rank. He and another man pulled away burning hay-carts to free the entrance. Among them was also Jean Rossignol, a man knowing nothing of politics, one day to be a revolutionary general. Lives that would have passed in dull obscurity yielded on this day the full measure of human courage. In front of this formidable block of black stones, blacker and more formidable still behind its curtain of flames and smoke, men whose only care until then had been to secure a humble existence by their labour revealed a greatness of which they themselves knew nothing, in a supreme urge for sacrifice for a cause whose nature they only vaguely sensed.

The fortress, reputed to be impregnable, was taken within four hours by these inexperienced men, of whom, it was said at the time, "each one was leader and followed only his own passion." Of these obscure fighters a hundred were killed and sixty wounded. The spilling of blood aroused blood lust. Launay, the governor of the Bastille, was struck down on the steps of the Hôtel de Ville. Provost de Flesselles was shot. But in spite of these acts of violence the taking of the Bastille became at once to contemporaries the symbol of the triumph of bare fists over armed force, of the spirit of liberty over the citadels of oppression. The taking of the Bastille was not an event subsequently magnified by the memory of the humble men who accomplished it or by the revolutionary leaders: it was regarded at the very moment as a miraculous achievement. "The taking of the Bastille," wrote Gouverneur Morris on that day, "is among the most extraordinary things that I have met with." "Thus," wrote the Duke of Dorset, the British ambassador, two days later, "was accomplished the greatest Revolution of which history has preserved the memory. . . . From this moment we may regard France as a free country, the king as a monarch whose powers are limited, and the nobles as reduced to the level of the rest of the nation."

That afternoon the Assembly was in session. Mirabeau was urging insistence on the recall of the troops when the Vicomte de Noailles arrived from Paris with the news of the fall of the Hôtel des Invalides and the siege of the Bastille.

The Assembly decided to send a numerous deputation to the king to demand the immediate removal of the troops. "The audience was long and the wait cruel," wrote Mirabeau. The king's reply was again evasive. A second deputation was sent "to obtain the definite dismissal of the troops." But the king merely declared that it was incredible that his orders to the troops could be the cause of the misfortunes of the capital. "This nebulous reply was far from satisfying us," wrote Mirabeau. "We resolved to prolong our sitting throughout the night."

That night Versailles echoed with the rattle of arms and the shouts of the soldiers, of whom the watching Assembly seemed to be prisoners. In the middle of the night the Duc de Liancourt took it upon himself to wake the king, who was still in ignorance of all that had happened on this fourteenth of July: "Sire, it is not a revolt but a revolution." If the troops were not moved, all would be lost. Louis XVI gave way, too late as always. He decided to go himself to the Assembly to announce the removal of the troops.

Mirabeau had called for a third deputation, and this was about to start when the Duc de Liancourt announced the king's arrival. The Assembly realized that the king had capitulated and received the announcement with enthusiasm.

The king appeared at the Assembly without ceremonial. He spoke standing and uncovered. He had come, he said, "with confidence into the midst of his representatives, to testify to his concern and to invite them to find means of restoring order and calm. I know," he continued, "that mistaken suspicions have been aroused; I know that it has actually been asserted that your persons are not in safety: can it be necessary to reassure you concerning such reprehensible rumours, negatived in advance by my known character?" The king ended with the announcement that he had given the order to the troops to move away from Paris and Versailles. His speech was received with loud applause.

Louis XVI returned on foot—a sign of the times—to the château. A large part of the Assembly and a wildly excited crowd filled the air with shouts of benediction. "This scene, sentimentally interesting," noted Mirabeau (who had disapproved the Assembly's enthusiasm), "has nothing to offer to politics."

He gave this summary of the events: "The whole of the ancient edifice, worn-out and worm-eaten buttresses, has fallen at the first shock, never to rise again; and when the site has been cleared it will be possible to plan a new building and to erect it on the unshakable foundations of the eternal rights of peoples."

A few days later Mirabeau went to see the ruins of the Bastille. "We visited every accessible quarter," wrote Dumont. "We descended into a dungeon into which Mirabeau's servant was not allowed to go. The poor fellow burst into tears and implored me to keep an eye on his master, who might be killed in those dungeons." The crowd had recognized their great defender and made way for him. "Verses and flowers were thrown to him; his carriage was filled with books and manuscripts that had been carried off during the first days. This visit to the Bastille was for Mirabeau a triumphal procession."

"Were it not that France is dishonoured by too many palaces," wrote Mirabeau in his paper, "and that the Assembly needs no other monument than the imperishable constitution which it has to propose to the country, I should ask that on the place where the Bastille stood until recently, insulting the rights of mankind, a building should be erected to receive in future the representatives of the nation and that its only inscription should read:

> In the reign of Louis XVI
> On the ruins of a state prison
> Consecrated to ministerial vengeance
> And destroyed by the people of Paris
> The National Assembly of seventeen hundred and eighty-nine
> Has raised this Temple to Liberty"

5

On July 16 Mirabeau proposed that the Assembly should send an address to the king demanding the dismissal of the ministers, but Louis XVI had forestalled this move: before the end of the sitting the dismissal of three ministers was announced. The king also officially communicated the prompt withdrawal of the troops and the recall of Necker. He announced that he would himself go on the next day to Paris. "Whoever advised that step," Mirabeau remarked to Dumont, "is a man of sense; without it Paris would have been lost to him. Two or three days later he might not have been able to enter the city." The king, said Bailly, went to the capital to reconquer the community that had conquered him. The triple row of spectators along the whole route received the king with shouts of "Long live the nation! Long live liberty!" On his return, Dumont remarked: "As if the lesson had been finished, shouts of 'Long live the king!' resounded all along his route."

Paris received her sovereign as a great power newly established. She was organizing herself and giving herself a municipal constitution. Bailly was appointed mayor of Paris, and Lafayette commander of the citizen guards.

There were savage summary executions in the capital. The Assembly was alarmed by the barbarity with which popular justice was being carried out. Comte Lally-Tollendal proposed an address to the people calling for the maintenance of order. But terror had bred terror; benevolent warnings were no longer enough.

Mirabeau showed that the "formidable dictatorship" exercised by the people was a threat to public liberty no less than were the plots of the enemies of the people. "Society would soon be dissolved if the multitude, growing accustomed to blood and disorder, was to place itself above the magistrates and defy the authority of the laws. Instead of advancing to liberty, the people would plunge themselves into the abyss of servitude; for too often danger brings support to absolute domination, and amidst anarchy even a despot seems a saviour."

"The whole entourage of the queen is in flight and dispersed; several of her ladies have abandoned her in a very disgraceful way," wrote Count Salmour in his dispatch of July 29. "In general, all who had to reproach themselves with abuses of the favour of Their Majesties and of the princes, or who were afraid of being charged with them, have fled." All their adherents were abroad. All the princes of the blood with their courts, except the Duc d'Orléans; all the Lorraines, all the Rohans, the whole of the Broglie family, all the general officers of the Broglie army, all the Polignacs, all the Ossuns, the Gramonts, the Guiches, and a number of other prominent Parisians, had left the country, together with a multitude of financiers, lawyers, and country gentlemen, and many bishops. Fear had scattered a brilliant society in all directions. All who had helped to light the conflagration that was reddening the horizon had been seized with terror at the first approach of the flames.

Often they fled in ridiculous disguises and with borrowed passports. But their insistence on comfort and consideration aroused suspicions, and they gave themselves away at the first challenge; local police made arrests all over the kingdom. Then the fugitives sent pitiful messages to some relative or friend in the Assembly, who publicly supported their claims. Mirabeau opposed exceptional measures, and while he had little sympathy with the great and the responsible now in flight, he energetically opposed every violation of individual liberty. He was up in arms against the employment of "the maxims and the procedure of tyranny." Among those arrested was the Baron de Castelnau, French ambassador at Geneva. Letters found on him, including one to the Comte d'Artois, were sent by Bailly to the Assembly. A heated debate arose on the inviolability of letters.

Two stages of the Revolution came into collision at this sitting of July 25. "Of course letters are inviolable, I know they are, I am convinced of it, but when a whole nation is in danger, when there is scheming against liberty, when respectable citizens are being proscribed, what is a crime at another time becomes a praiseworthy action." The speaker, a man slightly pockmarked, with common features, a livid complexion, and deeply sunken eyes, had nothing about him to command attention. His clothes were threadbare, and his bearing had the embarrassed stiffness of a man unused to a big audience. No one dreamed that in the person of Maximilien Robespierre the early future of France was speaking.

Mirabeau vehemently opposed him. It was not fitting that "a people who wish to become free should infringe morality after being so long the victims of those who had violated it. Let those vulgar politicians," he continued, "who set above justice what in their narrow scheming they call political security, let those politicians at least tell us what we shall learn from the shameful inquisition into letters. . . . Is it imagined that plots are transmitted through the ordinary couriers? Is it supposed that even political news of any importance passes through that channel? Thus no useful purpose would be served by violating the privacy of families, communications between those separated, the confidences between friends and men's confidence in one another. This last asylum of liberty has been violated by those very persons whom the nation delegated to assure all its rights." Mirabeau's appeal was so eloquent that even at that moment when mass emigration was arousing such resentment the Assembly was won over to his view.

Among the émigrés was the Duchesse de Polignac. She had abused her royal friend's affection without scruple for the benefit of her whole family and all her friends, and she was the first to abandon her. When she reached Basle, the first stage in her exile, she met in her hotel the man to whom she had done the worst disservice with the queen— Necker. He, too, was in exile. The duchess was never to turn back, never to see France again. But Necker received at the moment of their meeting a letter in the king's hand recalling him to his post. It was a triumph for the man who had been ignominiously dismissed. He had no illusions, however, as to the difficulties of his task. "I am returning to France," he wrote to his brother, "but as a victim of the esteem with which I am honoured. It seems to me that I am re-entering the abyss." On his way back he learnt that Besenval, commandant of the troops which had been intended for the *coup d'état*, had tried to flee from the popular wrath but had been stopped by peasants.

Paris prepared a triumphal reception for Necker. All along the route from Versailles to the Hôtel de Ville he was received with wild enthusiasm. He profited by the popular emotion to save a single person. "In God's name, gentlemen, let us have no more judgments, no more proscriptions, no more sanguinary scenes," he urged. "On my knees I ask you that neither toward M. de Besenval nor toward any other person shall there be shown such rigour as I have been told of."

In those days the mob was entirely unaccountable, and equally ready to use violence or to respond to generous promptings. Necker's appeal, doubly pathetic from so pompous a man, brought from all sides shouts of assent. In the midst of the general emotion a member of the assembly of Parisian electors proposed that a statue of Necker should be erected outside the Hôtel de Ville. It was Necker's apotheosis. He never knew a day of greater glory.

Next day the Oratoire district, where Mirabeau had lately been living and where he exercised great influence, declared that Besenval's amnesty constituted an abuse of power. The district of Blancs-Manteaux passed a similar resolution, which Mirabeau supported in the Assembly. The Assembly agreed with his argument and ordered that Besenval be sent before the tribunal of the Châtelet. The judges realized that the Assembly trusted to their impartiality. Besenval was acquitted in spite of the crowd's demand for his execution.

"Mirabeau," wrote Mme. de Staël bitterly, "in wresting from M. Necker the palm of internal peace, struck the first blow at his popularity." Necker found that the man whose influence he had denied earlier might become a serious enemy. "Mirabeau, who knew everything and foresaw everything," continued his daughter in her resentment, "made use of his thunderous eloquence only in order to secure a place in the front rank, from which his immorality had debarred him."

Mirabeau had now acquired an influence that disturbed his enemies. Especially his immense popularity in Paris was feared. Sometimes he went twice in the day to the capital, and this caused alarm. Bailly was assured that Mirabeau wanted his place. Mirabeau had proposed that deputies should be sent to calm the districts, and this was interpreted as an attempt to gain control of the districts through their deputies.

The capital did in fact need the help of the deputies living in it in order to elaborate its municipal constitution. But this mattered little to those who had decided to hit out at Mirabeau. On August 1 Regnault, deputy for Saint-Jean-d'Angély, brought forward a motion forbidding any member of the Assembly to enter any district of Paris unless on a special mission. Mirabeau replied to this proposal with scathing irony. It had been received with some applause "in defiance," he said, "of rule or reason. We are the most natural supervisors of public affairs. I ask how those of us who are domiciled in Paris can be forbidden to communicate their knowledge and their aspirations to the districts, or to fulfil the duties of simple citizens, if possible, at the same time as the functions of public men."

This time Mirabeau defeated the intrigue by the vigour of his argument. Regnault himself no longer upheld his motion. But he was only the precursor of those who were ready to use any means to undermine Mirabeau's growing influence, even at the cost of the public weal. From this session dated Mirabeau's revolt against the despotism even of a representative body. The incident may seem of no importance. But from that moment the positions were taken up. Mirabeau showed his independent spirit by hurling this defiance at the Assembly: "The true friend of freedom never obeys decrees that injure it, from whatever authority they may emanate."

6

The *Letters of Count Mirabeau to His Constituents* had been transformed into a regular newspaper, which appeared three times a week under the title *Courrier de Provence*. Mirabeau had often elaborated publishing plans that were to bring him in a fortune but never got beyond the state of projects. But this time his success even surpassed his hopes. "The subscriptions so crowded in, though the subscription price was high," wrote Dumont, "that we were already seeing in imagination mountains of gold. Within a few days our list ran beyond three thousand. The demand from the provinces was in proportion."

From its first issue the *Courrier de Provence* was assured of great success. It gave faithful and impartial reporting of "all the effective speeches." Mirabeau, who knew his colleagues' habit of writing out their speeches, asked them for the text, which he corrected and cut down before insertion. "Anyone would think we speak like oracles," said Le Chapelier to him one day, "when we appear stripped of all our verbiage and all our stupidities." The high level of the paper was partly due to the care taken to avoid personalities. Mirabeau was especially tender with his colleagues. One day Sieyès complained of some critical remarks. "Don't on any account," Mirabeau told his colleagues, "get me embroiled with that man—he has an implacable vanity."

"Mirabeau himself," wrote Dumont, "though his extravagances were toned down, got no flattery." On the other hand, the Assembly was censured with striking boldness.

Mirabeau formed a publishing company. The profits were to be shared between Dumont, Duroverai, Le Jay, who was the publisher, and Mirabeau himself. The Genevese drew a reasonable monthly sum for their expenses. Le Jay also received a considerable share for printing and commission. Mirabeau gave up his own share to the Le Jay couple, though he was in a difficult financial position. "As yet we are rich only in hope," he wrote to Mauvillon. He was so short of money that he did not know how he would be able to pay his servants.

"If Le Jay had had a head," wrote Dumont later, "and if his wife, who managed everything, had had a little orderliness and honesty, their fortune would have been made." But Le Jay was an imbecile who would promise anything, and he trembled like a child before his wife. Mme. Le Jay looked upon the enterprise, as she looked upon Mirabeau himself, as her own to exploit. "She had fitted up her house out of her profits, she had stocked her shop; from a poor little pamphlet shop it had become a substantial bookshop; everything spoke of a new opulence in her condition." She concealed the account-books from her partners; she refused to make payments to them, hoping to tire them out by endless chicanery. Mirabeau, worn out by his mistress's proceedings, said to her one day in Dumont's presence: "Madame Le Jay, if honesty did not exist it would have to be invented as a means of growing rich." But with all her cleverness in exploiting men and her unscrupulous greed, she had not the sense to manage her affairs properly. To her greed—her rapacity, said Dumont—she added negligence.

Subscribers soon began to complain. Deliveries became more and more irregular. Subscribers in the provinces sometimes went unsupplied for a fortnight or even a month because Le Jay had not the money to pay the postage. The booksellers loaded him with reproaches. The printer himself was soon paid irregularly and threatened from time to time to suspend publication; in the end Mirabeau found himself compelled to advance money. His colleagues could not get paid. Mirabeau could do nothing with Mme. Le Jay. "Violence was useless against her coolness; her only reply to his reproaches was to scoff at him." The Genevese thought of taking proceedings, but Mirabeau advised them not to. "She would be more than a match for the whole bar; I defy the wiliest prosecutor to cope with her wriggling."

"She was in fact too dangerous and too vicious," said Dumont, "for him to venture to fall out with her." There was no bond any longer between Mirabeau and this woman who had excited violent sexual passion in him. His senses were sated. His widened sphere of interest detached him more and more completely from her. He seemed to be uneasy about her presence in his new life. But she would not so easily give up a man whom in her fashion she may have loved, and who could be useful to her. She had too strong a hold over him. She was mixed up with a whole side of his life which he would have been glad to forget. One day, exhausted, Mirabeau declared that the whole National Assembly was easier to deal with than a woman who had made up her mind. Mme. Le Jay was part of the penalty Mirabeau paid for his free and easy morals. His reputation stuck to him like a Nessus' shirt. He "was so sure that if he had enjoyed personal consideration all France would have been at his feet," wrote Dumont, "that there were times when he would have been ready to pass through fire to purify the name of Mirabeau. I have seen him lament, half choking with grief: 'I am cruelly expiating the errors of my youth.'"

His sphere of activity was growing every day to the point of eclipsing his personal existence. With Mirabeau's entry into public life, his private life seemed no longer to count.

"If I had not lived with him," wrote Dumont, "I should not have known all that can be done with a day, all that can be got into twelve hours. A day was worth more to him than a week or a month to others: his total output was prodigious; from project to execution not a moment was lost." He relaxed only in friendship. "Conversation alone could entice him, and even then he made it a means of working; it was almost always as a result of some conversation that a task was begun and writings prepared." From the opening of the States General he received so great a quantity of letters that the porter, unable to advance the cost, told the postman to bring a bill. At the end of a week this account totalled over a thousand francs. When the bill was taken to him, Mirabeau contented himself with writing at the foot: "I the undersigned acknowledge the receipt of the letters for which the amount is stated above, and I promise never to pay anything." The Baron d'Ogny, intendant general of posts, submitted this singular receipt to the king himself. "After that," wrote Dumont, "there was no longer any question for Mirabeau of paying for the carriage of letters."

This enormous mail Mirabeau read, or at least glanced through, himself. He made it his duty to reply to all his correspondents. The courtesy of a reply to every letter received, he told his secretary, is even more strictly required from a public man than from a private individual. He induced Comps to draw up replies so concisely that they kept to a single page, so that he could read as he signed. And he read them conscientiously. Sometimes he stopped in the middle of a signature and put his pen through the letter. "Very sorry, my friend," he would say to Comps, "but I do not repeat myself. Here is a phrase that is exactly the same as one I used about three months ago in writing on this same constitutional question. The idea it expresses is good and right; keep to it, but give it another colour." His prodigious memory retained even insignificant details. He had been a ravenous reader in the past, but no longer had time to read much. But he read very rapidly, and in each work he ran through he saw at once what was new and interesting. He always had at call all that he knew. And he purified and dignified every idea he expressed. Dumont conceded, with seeming reluctance, that "his imagination loved the great; his intelligence seized the true." Mirabeau had, he added, especially "a sense of his powers which had sustained him in positions that might well have been the destruction of another character." It was this awareness of his capacity, this faith in himself, never dimmed by any doubt, that gave him constantly increasing power in these first months of the Revolution. He also had a passionate faith in his country's destinies. He ended by identifying them with himself. That faith removed every obstacle.

7

The Great Fear was making its way throughout France. The number of beggars and tramps was increasing because of unemployment in the Paris workshops. When these famished men were refused work or relief, they were ready to cut down the growing corn or to burn farmsteads.

The peasant, suspicious by instinct, was also in terror of reprisals after the victory of the Third Estate, and this fear was increased by the news of plans attributed to the nobility for breaking the deputies' resistance. Men's minds were full of the fear of an aristocratic conspiracy. The *émigrés* were reputed to be seeking the aid of foreign troops, and France was filled with the fear of invasion.

In this atmosphere of auto-suggestion, everything was amplified, everything was believed and shouted abroad. Labourers quarrelling on a farm, the arrival of some marauders, even the appearance of an unknown figure at the crossroads, presaged the approach of brigands. The tocsin was sounded furiously; women and children fled from the villages and wandered in the woods, even in torrential rain; men seized what weapons they could, scythes, forks, sticks, if they had no firearms —and the brigands made no appearance.

In and around the capital the current tale was that these invisible brigands were in the pay of England. Mirabeau fought this rumour in his paper as incredible. "Pitt is too jealous of his glory to heap on his head the execrations of centuries to come, too enlightened not to feel that free peoples have even more interest in uniting for the maintenance of their independence than have despots in fighting to extend their domination. And even if the minister did not think thus, the English nation has a wisdom independent of its government: the morality of states and universal benevolence are for that nation no chimera."

But nothing could stop the panic terror. Each village had its own Bastille a few leagues away, the château with the aspect of a fortress, and its detested seigneur. The peasants proceeded to follow the example of the Parisians and to execute justice themselves. They marched on the nearest châteaus. They knew that the king had been reconciled with the Assembly and with the capital; it was in accord with the king that they went out to destroy the feudal regime. They knew that the victory of the *Tiers* meant the end of aristocratic privileges; to hasten the end they burned the old parchments that fixed their dues. They would pay neither tithes nor quit-rents nor taxes.

Inevitably there were incidents. Peasants and soldiers invaded a château near Vesoul to celebrate the fall of the Bastille, pretending to have been invited by the owner. During the night a powder-barrel exploded, probably through the carelessness of some drunken man. But the owner of the château was one of the die-hard nobles who had not joined the Assembly. The news of a "terrible crime" spread through France. Mirabeau referred to it in the *Courrier de Provence*. "The very atrocity of the crime," he wrote, "had in our eyes every element of improbability." But next morning the whole estate was sacked. The agitation extended from village to village. Soon the whole country was in flames. Archives were burnt, châteaux sacked, their inhabitants molested if they offered any resistance. In the wake of the Great Fear came devastation.

"Who does not know," wrote Mirabeau in the *Courrier de Provence*, "that the passage from evil to good is often more terrible than the evil itself? The insubordination of the people results in frightful excesses. In trying to mitigate evils they make them worse; in refusing to pay dues they impoverish themselves; in suspending work they prepare a new famine. All this is true, even commonplace; but when it is added that despotism was better than anarchy and bad laws than no law, a false, extravagant, detestable principle is advanced. History shows us no nation that has persisted in anarchy; the need, the disturbance, the very suffering leads men back to law. . . . Such will be France's lot: she will certainly not perish, not be subjugated; the present disorder will hasten the moment of her freedom, because it will lead the privileged classes to make the necessary sacrifices."

The peasant revolts prepared the way for the night of August 4. The Duc d'Aiguillon, descendant of Cardinal Richelieu's sister, was, according to Lameth, "after the king the richest seigneur of France in feudal properties; he enjoyed full crown rights in the provinces of the Agennais and the Condonnais, which the weakness of Louis XIII had conceded to Cardinal Richelieu's nephew." He was also the son of the minister of Louis XV whose memory was bound up with hateful measures of repression. He seems to have set out to redeem that reputation. He was one of the first to demand the reunion of the nobles with the *Tiers*. In these terrible times of the Great Fear and the attacks on the châteaux, Aiguillon decided to give an example of the necessary sacrifices on the part of the privileged classes which Mirabeau expected. His motion was elaborated at the Braton Club. The Vicomte de Noailles learned of it. The vicomte, Lafayette's ambitious brother-in-law, had nothing to sacrifice. The youngest of his house, he was known to his friends as Jean Sans Terre—John Lackland. La Marck maliciously called him "the busybody of the Revolution." At the sitting of August 4 he was the first speaker, trying to take the wind out of Aiguillon's sails. He proposed the abolition of the *corvée* and other unpaid services to the feudal lord, and the purchase of feudal rights by the communities. The people, said Aiguillon in his turn, "are trying to shake off a yoke that has burdened them for so many centuries, and it must be admitted, gentlemen, that this insurrection, though blameworthy (for all aggression is that), may find its excuse in the vexations of which they are victims." These vexations were mentioned by several deputies— the obligation, for instance, of vassals "to beat the water of the marshes when the lady of the place is in labour, to save her from annoyance by the croaking of the frogs," or the horrible barbarity of the right mentioned by the *Courrier de Provence* "under which the seigneur was authorized, in certain cantons, to have two of his vassals disembowelled on his return from the chase, so that he might refresh himself by putting his feet into the bleeding bodies of these unfortunates."

In the atmosphere of indignation created by recalling these horrors of the past, Aiguillon's proposal was accepted with wild enthusiasm. The sacrifice he proposed represented for him personally a renunciation of a hundred thousand livres a year, and of this the whole Assembly was aware. One after another the nobles mounted the tribune to divest themselves of their feudal rights. The meeting lasted until late at night.

Mirabeau was not present; he had been kept away by a family meeting to discuss questions of inheritance. He was disturbed by this haste— this "electrical storm"—and the excessive hopes it would raise. The *Courrier de Provence* echoed a day later the criticisms that had been made of this orgy of generosity. But, critical as he was of the method, Mirabeau knew that what had been done could not be reversed: "All these resolutions of the Assembly are irrevocable; they are under the sacred guarantee of honour."

8

"The National Assembly is entirely abolishing the feudal system." So Dumont summarized the results of the night of August 4, 1789. At the news of the decrees adopted, strangers embraced in the streets and the countryside resounded with shouts of joy.

Aiguillon had declared that the feudal rights were a property and that all property was sacred; their value should therefore, in his view, be redeemed at thirty years' purchase. In the course of the sitting the question was raised of the purchase of ecclesiastical tithes. A deputy at once rose to object that "ecclesiastical properties belong to the nation." At the sitting of August 10 Mirabeau defended the same principle: "No, the tithe is not a property. Tithes have never been for the clergy anything but annual revenues, simple possessions revocable at the will of the sovereign. Not only that, the tithe is not even a possession as it has been called: it is a contribution intended for that part of the public service which concerns the ministers of the altars: it is the subsidy with which the nation pays the salaries of the officers of morality and instruction."

His words brought indignant exclamations. "I hear many murmurs at the word 'salaries,'" Mirabeau continued, always at his best when improvising or replying to an interruption; "it may be thought to wound the dignity of the priest. But, gentlemen, the time has come, in this Revolution that is giving rise to so many just and generous sentiments, to abjure the prejudices of proud ignorance that make the words 'salary' and 'salaried' despised." It was the breath of a new world passing suddenly through the Assembly, a social conception of the future evoked for the first time. Mirabeau concluded: "I know only three ways of existing in society, begging, stealing, or drawing pay."

Sieyès, this time more an ecclesiastic than a defender of the Third Estate, tried vainly to prevent the simple abolition of tithes. He contended that the people would not profit, only the rich landowners who had bought their properties after deducting the value of tithes and would thus now gain ten per cents. Feeling that his arguments were having no success, he exclaimed mournfully: "They want to be free, and do not know how to be just." Mirabeau retorted, as the abbé descended from the tribune: "After letting the bull loose you are complaining that he is using his horns."

9

The committee of the Assembly for the drafting of the constitution was formed on July 14. Almost all the *cahiers* or memorials of the Third Estate and several of those of the clergy and the nobility had called for a declaration of rights to be proclaimed as a preamble to the constitution. The Paris *cahier* had demanded that "it should be laid down in a formal fundamental law," that "all men are equal in rights." On August 1 the committee decided to draw up the Great Charter of mankind.

Lafayette presented the first draft of the declaration of the rights of man to the Assembly with these words: "For a nation to love liberty, it is enough that it should know it; for it to be free, it is enough that it should wish to be." This optimistic faith in the power of ideas was reinforced by the influence of foreign examples, the English Magna Charta and the American Declaration of Independence. The enthusiasm aroused by the Virginian Declaration of Rights was still fresh in men's memory. The American ambassador laughed at this faculty of enthusiasm in the deputies: "They all have that romantic outlook and all those romantic ideas of which, happily for America, we were cured before it was too late."

Mirabeau had already drafted a declaration of rights in his *Addresse aux Bataves*, but in France's existing situation he considered it premature. The force of example, however, was too powerful. "It was an American idea," wrote Dumont, "and there was scarcely anyone who did not regard such a declaration as an indispensable preliminary. I remember that long discussion, lasting weeks, as a period of deadly boredom. . . . The Assembly was turned into a Sorbonne in which all the apprentices to legislation brought along their essays on these puerilities."

The Assembly failed to agree, and a special committee was charged with the elaboration of a new draft. Mirabeau was one of the five members. He was fully aware of the difficulties of the task. "The project of reciting the broad principles of liberty is one of the most tempting for a friend of mankind; but as soon as he tries to get to work on it he finds himself among the reefs," wrote the *Courrier de Provence*.

But in spite of his objections, Mirabeau could not withdraw from his task. "Mirabeau had the generosity to take this work upon himself and to give it to his friends," wrote Dumont slyly. "So, there we were, Duroverai, Clavière, and himself, drafting, discussing, adding a word, taking out four, exhausting ourselves in this ridiculous task and at last producing our bit of marquetry, our mosaic of pretended rights that had never existed."

The result corresponded to the ill-humour of the collaborators and the multiplicity of efforts. Mirabeau felt some embarrassment in offering it to the Assembly. His draft was coldly received. "Of all human affairs," he said in excuse, "I know only one in which despotism is not only good but necessary—drafting; and the words 'drafting' and 'committee' howl with fright at finding themselves linked together." He proposed—as an individual and not as the *rapporteur* of the committee —that the declaration of rights should be deferred until the constitution had been completed; the proposal was received with a storm of indignation. The Assembly proceeded at once to consider the draft offered by Lafayette. Of Mirabeau's draft nothing was left but the preamble.

In the course of the discussion Mirabeau insisted on the necessity of inserting in the declaration of rights the principle of the responsibility of all public officials: "If the law of responsibility were not extended to subordinate agents of the authorities, no nation would be better fitted than ours for slavery. There is no country that has been more insulted, more oppressed by despotism. The law that lays down that no citizen may be arrested except in virtue of the law is recognized everywhere, and yet it has not prevented *lettres de cachet*."

His most vehement intervention was in favour of a principle for which he had fought all his life: "I have not come to preach tolerance. The most unlimited liberty of religion is in my eyes a right so sacred that the word 'tolerance,' which is intended to express it, is itself in a way tyrannical; for the existence of the authority that has the power to tolerate is an attack on freedom of thought, through the very fact that it tolerates and thus might not tolerate. . . . I urge those who fear disorders from the introduction of freedom of worship to consider that tolerance (to make use of the consecrated word) has produced no poisoned fruits among our neighbours, and," he added humorously, "that the Protestants, inevitably damned in the other world, as everybody knows, are very comfortably installed in this one, no doubt by a compensation due to the kindness of the Supreme Being. Thus we who have only the right to concern ourselves with the affairs of this world may permit freedom of worship and sleep peacefully."

He also dealt trenchantly with an expression frequently used during the debate, "dominant form of worship." "Dominant! I do not understand that word, and I need a definition of it. Does it mean a form imposed by oppression? But you have outlawed that word, and men who have assured the right of freedom will not claim that of oppression. Does it mean the form followed by the prince? But the prince has not the right to dominate over consciences or to regulate opinions. Is it the form followed by the majority? But worship is an opinion; this or the other worship is the result of this or the other opinion. And opinions are not formed as the result of voting; your thought is your own, it is independent, you cannot enter into any engagement concerning it.

"Finally, an opinion held to by the majority has no right to dominate; the word is a tyrannical one that should be banished from our legislation, for if you admit it in one case you must admit it in all cases; you will thus have a dominant form of worship, a dominant philosophy, and dominant systems. Nothing must dominate but justice. Nothing is dominant but the right of each man; all else must give way to it; and it is an evident right, already laid down by you, to do that which cannot injure others."

But the Assembly was not content with that sole restriction. After declaring that "no one may be disturbed on account of his opinions, even his religious opinions," it added: " . . . provided that their manifestation in no way disturbs the public order established by law."

10

"Observers of the sittings are shocked at the noise, the tumult, the use-less harangues, the rapidity and sometimes the excessive slowness of the decisions, the defects of procedure by which small minds are al-ways the most upset," wrote Mirabeau, himself so critical of the As-sembly, yet always ready to defend it against outside critics. "Do they not see that these very defects are implicit in liberty? Would they have an assembly of free men in which such great interests are at stake, such great questions at issue, as submissive and disciplined as a regiment of Prussian soldiers? Of course regulation is good, but freedom is a thousand times better; tumult is a great evil, but the greatest of all is to shackle deliberations and to enslave the political body."

The Assembly was discussing the articles that were to serve as the basis of the constitution. There was no dispute as to the form of gov-ernment, but passions were aroused over the delimitation of the execu-tive power. "In the best organized monarchy," said Mirabeau in his speech of September 1, "the royal authority is always the object of the fears of the best citizens; he whom the law sets above all others easily becomes the rival of the law."

He remained faithful to the principle with which he had entered the Assembly. He wrote to his uncle: "I have always thought as you do, and now more than ever, that the monarchy is the one sheet anchor that can save us from shipwreck. And what efforts I have made, and am still making every day, to support the executive power and to com-bat the mistrust that makes the National Assembly go too far!"

He made a very clear distinction between the essential rights of the crown and its traditional attributes. In the discussion of August 7 on the king's right of hunting outside his domains, he had declared: "The royal prerogative has nothing in common with what are called the king's pleasures. I think much too highly of the royal prerogative to agree to make it consist in a futile and oppressive pastime." In his speech of September 1 he exerted himself to dissipate the fears aroused by the royal veto: "Certainly on a merely superficial view there are great objections to the idea of a veto exercised by any individual against the wish of the representatives of the people." But the danger was suffi-ciently guarded against by certain guarantees, which he summarized as "annual meeting of the Assembly, annual provision for the army, annual taxes, and ministerial responsibility." The nation's watchful-ness was the guarantee of these.

The question of the royal veto particularly excited popular passion.

Agitators gave this definition of it: "You want your soup, and the king tells you to turn your bowl upside down. That is the veto." Anonymous letters threatened the deputies who dared to vote for the veto with the worst of reprisals. "I shall never forget," wrote Dumont, "going to Paris with Mirabeau on the day or the morrow of his speech on the veto. People were waiting for his carriage in front of the Le Jay shop, and they threw themselves in front of him, imploring him, with tears in their eyes, not to suffer the king's possession of the absolute veto."

Mirabeau tried in vain to stem the strong popular current. He evoked in vain, in the *Courrier de Provence*, the English example. In the Assembly Mirabeau braved the wrath of his excited colleagues; he jeopardized his popularity with the masses. "He could have moderate principles, this man who maintained them with passion," wrote Mme. de Staël later. "A true friend of liberty, he believed that the existence of a king, armed by the constitution with sufficient force to provide for the execution of the laws, was necessary to France."

But Necker gave way to the agitation in Paris. He hoped to calm men's minds by asking, instead of an absolute veto, for a suspensive veto. Necker's memorandum to the Assembly won over the hesitant and the lukewarm, and the suspensive veto gained a big majority.

II

"I shall never consent," wrote Louis XVI to the Archbishop of Arles, "to the despoiling of my clergy and my nobility; I shall never give my sanction to decrees despoiling them; if I did, the French people would be able one day to accuse me of injustice or weakness." Louis XVI was hostile from the first to the enthusiasm that was creating a new world, and he submitted to its laws with a bad grace.

The Assembly was impatient at the king's delay in sanctioning the decrees of August 4. Mirabeau thought it had been impolitic to submit these decrees to the king, and asked whether the royal sanction was necessary to the validity of the acts of the legislative body. The resistance which the Assembly guessed that the king was offering exasperated the left wing. The debates became tumultuous. The president went to the king to ask for his agreement. Louis XVI realized that he could no longer evade a decision. He sent a letter to the Assembly making certain criticisms, and to gain time he asked that the decrees should be submitted to him in the form of laws.

"We need not have asked the king," declared Mirabeau energetically, "to sanction the decrees. But since that was done, and since if they were contested today the public distrust, the almost universal discontent, would be greatly aggravated; since the clergy, which would lose by law any compensation for the tithes, would not have lost it any the less in fact; since the nobles, who might refuse to negotiate as to the feudal rights, would see themselves deprived of them none the less by the insurrection of opinion, we are all interested in the pure and simple sanction of these decrees re-establishing harmony and concord." He asked his colleagues, however, for a generous comprehension of the difficulties; and he appealed also to the spirit of concord. "No doubt none of us wants to start the conflagration for which the materials are so notoriously in readiness from one end of the kingdom to the other. If we substitute . . . distrust for discussion, petty and passionate hatreds and bitter reminiscences for regular debates aiming at mutual enlightenment . . . we are leading the monarchy whose interests are confided to us to dissolution and not to constitution." After this debate the king realized that his resistance was vain. He reserved his sanction to the decrees, but authorized their publication.

Mirabeau's repeated interventions assured him a growing ascendancy over the Assembly. But his ascendancy disturbed his irreconcilable adversaries. The Comte de Volney proposed that there should be an immediate election of a new Assembly, to substitute "a truly national representation for a vicious and contradictory one." The Vicomte de Mirabeau supported this motion with enthusiasm: it proposed that "no member of the existing Assembly may be re-elected." He made merry with the idea that the influence of the most eminent of the deputies would thus be eliminated, and thought of his brother's broken career. His noisy satisfaction was distasteful to the Assembly. "I have always regarded it as a very good characteristic," replied Mirabeau, "to take one's profession gaily; thus I am far from reproaching the last speaker for his joyousness in circumstances that call forth only too many melancholy reflections and sombre thoughts." Against Volney's motion he set the oath taken in the Tennis Court, which committed the deputies to go on with the preparation of the constitution till it had been completed. To call on the provinces "to send us successors because we are at issue and cannot agree—is that, gentlemen, the language we ought to speak? We shall be admitting that our *amour-propre* is more sacred than our mission, our pride dearer than our country, and our obstinacy stronger than reason, impenetrable by our good faith, and totally exclusive of peace, concord, and liberty. Ah! if that were the truth, we should not even be worthy to speak it."

He did not hesitate to oppose energetically the exclusion of the existing deputies: "Thus we are to be giving orders to the nation! From now on there will be law in elections other than trust." He expressed what others less sure of their powers did not venture to declare for fear of seeming interested and ambitious. "We are approaching peace; and if we put other deputies in our place, this first moment would still be for them one of war. Let us remain, then, at our post; let us profit even by our faults and gather the fruits of our experience."

Writing to Mauvillon on his activities, Mirabeau gave this summing-up: "I have been more consistent than perhaps any other mortal in trying to carry out, to improve, and to extend a Revolution which will do more than any other for the advancement of the human race."

≥ XVI ≤

The Mob Will Trample Their Bodies Underfoot

"ON THE platform he stood motionless. Those who saw him often know that the waves swept round him without disturbing him, and that he retained self-mastery even under every sort of insult," wrote Dumont. Mirabeau's voice was full, masculine, sonorous; "he made himself heard just as well when he lowered his voice as when he raised it; and he pronounced his final words with such care that one never lost his conclusion. Generally he dragged a little. He began with some embarrassment, and often hesitated, but in such a way as to arouse interest. One could see him, so to speak, searching for the most suitable expression, rejecting, choosing, weighing his words, until he became animated and the bellows of the forge were working. At the most impetuous moments, the earnestness that made him stress his words to bring out their force prevented him from speaking rapidly; he had a great contempt for French volubility and the pseudo-warmth which he called operatic thunderstorms. He never lost a senatorial gravity, and his defect was perhaps a little affectation and pretentiousness at the outset; he raised his head with too much pride and sometimes showed his disdain to the point of insolence."

Mirabeau had attained complete mastery of his oratorical powers. Barnave, who distrusted his influence because he was afraid of succumbing to it, called him "the Shakespeare of eloquence."

"Picture a man of prodigious strength with an enormous load in front of him, which he wants to shift," wrote a contemporary. "He brings all his energy to bear; you can see him placing his limbs, can see his muscles swelling, all his features growing tense, the fire in his eyes. The resistance only excites his courage; the pride of his movements proves his confidence in success; and in the end the load gives way to his efforts. In this picture I think I have drawn a fairly faithful likeness of what Mirabeau was on the platform."

He was always isolated, as he had been at the outset. But it was his own disdain of mediocrities, of incoherence in some and weakness in others, that isolated him. "He had no phalanx of followers," said Dumont. Yet he was a power. In great hours, or dark hours, his eloquence was deployed in all its vigour; he was then the whole Assembly.

One particularly grave hour had struck. Mirabeau had foreseen it. On August 19 he warned the Assembly that little money was being subscribed for the loan. "Do not let us wait to be told that it will not be subscribed at all." He recalled that it was the king's fidelity to the creditors of the state that had led him to convoke the States General, and that "if he had been willing to constitute himself a defaulting debtor he would have had no need to deliver us from our shackles." He spoke of the involuntary injury done by the Assembly itself to the loan. "Let us forego vain declamations against financiers, businessmen, bankers, and capitalists"—the Assembly had fixed too low a rate of interest. The Minister of Finance "counted on a patriotic movement, and his opinion weighed with us." But, he concluded, "we cannot count on the credit either of the king or of the Minister of Finance," only on that of the nation.

On August 27 Necker sent a report to the Assembly on the disastrous result of the loan: out of thirty millions, only two and a half had been subscribed. He proposed in place of this failure a new loan of eighty millions, repayable in ten years. On September 19 a deputy announced "a terrible and pressing danger, an incalculable disaster threatening the state." The second loan had failed. France had lost foreign confidence. Mirabeau supported the proposal of the president of the finance committee to devote two days a week to financial questions.

Five days later Necker gave a report which, he said, "it tears my soul to have to present." He proposed a patriotic contribution of a quarter of income, the authorization of the receipt by the mint authorities of silver vessels from those who were ready to invest their yield in the national loan, and for the future the conversion of the Caisse d'Escompte into a national bank. Mirabeau had been informed in advance of this last proposal and had prepared a long technical speech, due, no doubt, to Clavière's pen, to attack his old enemy. But he did not deliver the speech. The moment was too grave for polemics. He limited himself to publishing it in his paper. Necker had revealed that the Treasury would have only three or four millions in hand at the beginning of October, against requirements of thirty millions for the month and sixty millions up to the end of the year.

Necker's appeal to the patriotism of the French was warmly echoed by the Assembly. "There is enthusiasm enough for a vote," remarked Dupont de Nemours, "but only the wealthy can pay; and wealth sufficient to pay a quarter of its income does not seem to me to exist at present among most of our wealthy people. Obviously it does not exist among our poor."

"The revenues of the state are destroyed," said Mirabeau from the tribune of the Assembly on September 26; "but it seems to me impossible either to offer a plan to the Minister of Finance or to examine the plan he offers. . . . The mere verification of his figures would take whole months." To the great surprise of the Assembly he went on to say: "The unbounded confidence which the country has shown at all times in the Minister of Finance is sufficient authority, it seems to me, for you to show him unlimited confidence in these circumstances."

The Assembly burst into frenzied applause. It was entirely ready to adopt a decree unanimously. But Mirabeau urged it to weigh the terms carefully. He was asked to withdraw to draft it. But during his absence the Assembly changed its mind. Those who had yielded to the force of his eloquence went over to an unreasoning hostility.

Between September 1789 and April 1790 the patriotic contribution yielded only nine million instead of a hundred and fifty million livres. "It should have been a forced contribution to bring success," he proceeded. "And let no one say that such a contribution was impossible. Either we can still count on sufficient public feeling for the public welfare, or we cannot. If we can, a wisely ordered contribution would succeed; if we cannot, its failure would matter little, for it would have proved that the evil was approaching its last stage." To dissipate suspicion, he concluded: "Woe to those who do not wish the Minister of Finance all the success of which France has such exceeding need! Woe to those who could let their opinions or their prejudices weigh against the country! Woe to those who would not abjure all rancour, all mistrust, all hatred on the altar of the common weal!"

But his appeal was lost in the tumult of the Assembly, which continued the discussion for hours. Mirabeau was disgusted by this atmosphere of petty suspicions, this debate squandered on trivial objections and timid reservations and conflicts of *amour-propre*.

The debate went on till late in the evening. Then Mirabeau came to the tribune a third time. He wanted to put an end to this tournament of futilities. He spoke under the spur of indignation, his strongest stimulant. No one could boast later of having prepared his speech for him or suggested its argument to him.

"I, too, do not think M. Necker's methods the best possible; but may Heaven preserve me, in our critical situation, from setting forth my own in opposition to his methods," he said in a direct attack on the opponents of the Necker plan. "It would be vain for me to claim my methods as preferable; there can be no competing at short notice with a prodigious popularity, won by striking services and long experience, and the reputation of the highest talent of any known financier." The only alternative remaining, if the Necker plan were rejected, would be "the infamous word bankruptcy. To those who may be entertaining the idea of failing to meet our public engagements, from fear of excessive sacrifices, from terror of taxation, I would say . . . what else is bankruptcy but the cruellest, the most iniquitous, the most unequal, the most disastrous of taxes?"

He spoke with warmth and urgency, as though from man to man, adopting the intimate tone which the eloquence of genius could foster between himself and a numerous audience: "My friends, listen to one word, just one word. Two centuries of depredation and brigandage have created the abyss in which the kingdom is in imminent danger of being swallowed up; and that frightful abyss must be closed. Here is the list of French landowners: choose from the richest among them, so as to sacrifice fewer citizens, but choose; for is it not necessary that a few should perish to save the mass of the people? Come! These two thousand notables have the means to meet the deficit; strike, immolate these unhappy victims, cast them into the abyss, it will close. . . . You recoil with horror? Inconsistent men! Pusillanimous men! Why, do you not see that in decreeing bankruptcy, or, what is still more hateful, making it inevitable without decreeing it, you will soil yourselves with an act a thousand times more criminal? For, after all, that horrible sacrifice would at least make an end of the deficit. But do you think, because you have not paid, that you will not owe anything? Do you think the thousands, the millions of men who will lose in a moment, through the terrible explosion or through its repercussions, all that was the consolation of their lives, and perhaps their sole means of sustenance, will leave you in peace to profit by your crime? Stoical onlookers at the incalculable evils which that disaster will bring upon France; impassive egoists imagining that the convulsions of despair and destitution will pass like so many others, and the more rapidly for their violence, are you really sure that all these men without bread will leave you in peaceful enjoyment to those dishes of which you have not been willing to diminish either the number or the delicacy? No, you will perish, and in the universal conflagration which you do not shrink from starting, the loss of your honour will not save a single one of your detestable delights.

"That is the way we are going," thundered Mirabeau. "I hear talk of patriotism, bursts of patriotism, invocations to patriotism. Very magnanimous, indeed, is the effort to give part of one's income to save all one possesses. Yes, gentlemen, it is to the most ordinary prudence, to the most elementary wisdom, it is to your crudest interest that I appeal. I tell you, you will all be caught in the universal ruin, and those who are most closely interested in the sacrifice the government is asking of you are yourselves.

"So, vote this extraordinary subsidy, and may it suffice! Vote it because if you have doubts as to the methods proposed, vague and imprecise doubts, you have none about its necessity and our inability to propose anything in its place. Vote it because the public circumstances brook no delay and because for any delay we should be responsible. Don't ask for time, misfortune never grants it."

When he had finished, one single feeling possessed the Assembly. Ferrières noted this unanimous, imperious feeling: "As though each deputy was in a hurry to escape from the heavy responsibility with which Mirabeau threatened him, and had suddenly seen in front of him the abyss of the deficit calling for its victim, the whole Assembly rose, called for a vote, and unanimously passed the decree."

A single deputy had asked to speak in reply to Mirabeau, but he remained standing, his arm raised, as if petrified by the emotion that had overpowered all. One man made his way toward Mirabeau. Out of professional habit, he had recovered the faculty of speech sooner than the rest. He was Molé, an actor at the Théâtre-Français. "Heavens, Monsieur le Comte," he exclaimed, "what a speech! And spoken with what expression! Heavens! haven't you missed your vocation!" Mirabeau smiled, flattered.

The *Journal de Paris*, in giving extracts from the speech, recalled the words of Aeschines about Demosthenes: "What would you have felt, what would you have said, if you had seen and heard that monster?"

2

Mirabeau met the Duc d'Orléans for the first time at the end of 1788, at a dinner given by the Comte de La Marck. Mirabeau, wrote La Marck, afterwards told him "several times" that he did not care for the duke or trust him. Toward the end of September 1789 the two met again at La Marck's house. Their host noted the same reserve between them.

Mirabeau then saw more often the man whom the British ambassador described as dominating the duke, "as far as it is possible to govern so flighty a man"—Choderlos de Laclos, the author of *Liaisons dangereuses*. As an officer belonging to a family but recently ennobled, Laclos could not aspire to high rank in the army; he found opportunities of action and of a career by exploiting the weaknesses and stimulating the ambitions of the duke, whom he made one of the secret springs of the Revolution.

Laclos and Mirabeau collaborated in an amusing series of portraits, *Galerie des Etats généraux, 1789*, which had a great success. Mirabeau was undoubtedly sought as a great acquisition for the Orléans party; but he does not seem to have been in the confidence of Laclos, who saw that Mirabeau was "for the king."

If Laclos, as was believed, aimed at overturning the monarchy, he had but to draw on the material within the bounds of the Palais-Royal, which was a rendezvous for all the discontented, the declassed in search of rehabilitation, and the fishers in troubled waters. While Paris was settling down, organizing her administration and consolidating her militia, the Palais-Royal remained a centre of agitation, "the States General of the Revolution." A giant dominated its excitable crowds. The Marquis de Saint-Huruge, a ruined·debauchee who had nothing more to lose and everything to gain, lent his voice of thunder to every incendiary movement. It was believed at the Palais-Royal that Mirabeau was to be silenced. On August 30 Camille Desmoulins shouted at the Café Foy that the aristocrats were planning to assassinate Mirabeau. He added that the queen wanted to arrange for the royal family to flee, and that the king must be brought to Paris to make sure of his remaining in the country.

The Palais-Royal received with a shock the news that the veto had been adopted, and that the heads of the best patriots were in danger. Fifteen thousand men, thundered Saint-Huruge, were ready to march to Versailles to disperse the enemies of the people in the Assembly. Paris was getting ready to dictate to Versailles.

The gulf between the king and the nation grew deeper and deeper. "Since the decrees of August 4, almost the whole of the governing part of the nation has become our enemy and that of liberty," wrote Barnave on October 4.

The *Chronique de Paris* of September 25 proposed that "the king and queen should be invited to come and spend the winter in Paris."

The *Révolutions de Paris* of October 1 wrote: "A second access of the Revolution is needed; everything is preparing for it."

Mirabeau was acutely aware of this tension between the court and the nation. He may have thought at this time that the Duc d'Orléans, if he succeeded in imposing himself on the court, might play the part of an intermediary between the throne and the people. But he knew above all that it was necessary to close that yawning gulf. One of his adversaries reported hearing him say: "We shall not take one step toward liberty so long as we do not succeed in effecting a revolution at court."

3

Mirabeau felt that he had the strength to control events if he could gain power. He had the impatience of the man of action who is not merely ambitious but wants to grapple with outstanding problems. He was not one of those who are content to direct affairs from the background, to be the power behind the throne: he was too big a man, too far-seeing, and also too indiscreet, to play a secondary part. Nor was he one of those whose strength is in opposition or criticism. He had the creative flame that has to find an outlet. The desire for power grew in him with events, fed by the incapacity of the holders of power and exasperated by the country's distress. It was one day to become an obsession and a torment.

His ambition was well known, even too well known. He readily spoke of it. He used it to soothe his creditors. He had owed money to the Hôtel de Varsovie ever since his marriage; he confided to its proprietor that he would soon be a minister. One day he recounted to Talleyrand, who had become Bishop of Autun, the essential qualities, in his view, of the statesman of whom France had need at the moment. Talleyrand listened and then remarked coldly:

"You have forgotten one thing."

"What?" asked Mirabeau, surprised.

"That he must be pockmarked."

4

From the first days of the Revolution, from the day of his harangue at the Palais-Royal, Camille Desmoulins had acquired an enormous reputation. "One part of the capital names me among the principal authors of the Revolution," he boasted boyishly to his father; "others go so far as to say I am its author." He was one of those who can formulate what is in process of formation, say what has not yet been said, crystallize the chaos of feelings and thoughts. He was a born journalist. He was to speak out all his thought and more, for he was not held back by any scruple or any sense of responsibility.

He had unbounded admiration for Mirabeau. One day he called on him to offer to work for his paper. Mirabeau asked him to dinner. Desmoulins, his days of poverty and obscurity fresh in his memory, wrote: "I think myself lucky to have become a guest of Mirabeau." He attached himself to him. Toward the end of September he spent a fortnight with Mirabeau at Versailles. "We have become great friends," he wrote to his father; "at all events, he calls me his dear friend. He is always seizing my hands or thumping me on the back; then he goes to the Assembly, resumes his dignity as we enter the vestibule, and works wonders; after which he returns to dine with excellent company and sometimes his mistress, and we drink excellent wines." Mirabeau liked in Desmoulins his youthful, undisciplined ardour: he supposed that the young man would be sobered in time by contact with realities. "I draft motions," wrote Desmoulins, "and Mirabeau calls that initiating me into high policy."

It was not without qualms of conscience that Desmoulins tasted the delights of his stay at Versailles. "I feel that his table is too loaded with delicacies; I am being corrupted. The Bordeaux and his Maraschino are of high price, and I try in vain to forget it; afterwards I have all the trouble in the world to resume my republican austerity and to detest the aristocrats, whose crime is to go on having these excellent dinners." He soothed his conscience by sowing dismay with his ideas, which were in advance of his time.

Toward the end of September Mounier, visiting the studio of the painter Boze at Versailles, found Mirabeau there, posing for a portrait. Mirabeau was surrounded like a sovereign with a numerous suite—Mme. Le Jay, Target, Dumont, Desmoulins.

It was at about this same time that Mirabeau became more intimate with a man who was not only one of the pillars of a doomed regime, but represented the opposite pole of humanity to that of Desmoulins— Auguste, Comte de La Marck, Prince d'Arenberg. La Marck belonged to one of the most illustrious princely families of Europe, a family whose origin dated back to the twelfth century. Descendant of an Austrian on the father's side and a German on the mother's, born and educated at Brussels, he had inherited from his maternal grandfather a regiment which had been in the French service since the days of Louis XIV. He took possession of the regiment and installed himself in France at the time of the marriage of Marie Antoinette. As German princes of reigning houses did not rank in the French court, he inherited by special favour the title of Grandee of Spain which had belonged to his grandfather, placing him on an equality with the dukes and peers of France. Married to a rich French heiress, La Marck became a great landowner in France. He acclimatized himself with the adaptability of a foreigner who conscientiously savoured all that that country could offer in the pleasantness of life.

Covered with honours from his childhood, cradled in affluence, with his ambitions sated and his health wrecked, La Marck had the wisdom of a man with no aspirations and no ambitions who could permit himself the intellectual luxury of shedding every prejudice.

La Marck had made Mirabeau's acquaintance in 1788. Everything about the man seemed to La Marck, at their first meeting, to be extravagant and forced. His own distinction and taste for half-shades was offended by Mirabeau's ostentatious luxury. The buttons on his coat, of coloured stones, were too big, the buckles of his shoes too voluminous. It was Mirabeau's own world, but he gave the impression of a parvenu trying to force an entry. His manners also had an element of affectation. "In trying to show politeness he exaggerated his bows; his first words were pretentious and rather vulgar compliments. In a word," La Marck concluded, "he had neither the forms nor the language of the society in which he was moving; and although by birth he was the peer of his hosts, one could see at once from his manners that he lacked the ease given by familiarity with high society."

La Marck, although a foreigner, held a French fief, and, thus gratified, had been elected a representative of the nobility in the States General. He was not the only foreigner elected. The clergy, who could elect foreigners exercising ecclesiastical authority in France, counted among their deputies the Prince de Salm, Bishop of Tournay, and the Comte d'Arlberg, Bishop of Ypres.

Mirabeau sought a government which he described as "more or less like that of England." If that meant a constitutional monarchy, La Marck was ready to agree with him. Louis XVI seemed to him to be particularly fitted to play the part of a constitutional king. His vacillating character would lend itself well to the functions of a limited authority. La Marck even thought the king would be glad to be relieved of a crushing responsibility.

But La Marck reckoned without the influences at work on the king. He also failed to discern a good part of Mirabeau's motives. He saw only the satisfaction of a man who had reached by his own powers the place he occupied. He heard him exclaim: "The time has come when men must be valued by what they have in this little space—on the forehead, between the eyebrows." He accounted for Mirabeau's revolutionary ardour as the result of injured self-esteem. His revolutionary language seemed to La Marck to be inconsistent with his monarchical conviction. "My popularity is my strength," Mirabeau replied to him. He hoped to make use of La Marck as an intermediary between king and nation.

But soon a stronger bond was to unite the two men. Mirabeau, who was already a power in the new order of things, was still battling with financial difficulties. One day, in September 1789, he called on La Marck very early, with a worried and preoccupied air.

"My friend," he said, "it depends on you to do me a very great service."

"Tell me."

"I don't know which way to turn. I haven't a crown piece. Lend me something."

La Marck held out a roll of fifty louis, apologizing for having no more at the moment.

"I don't know when I can pay it back," Mirabeau honestly warned him.

La Marck begged him not to trouble about that and added that he would be happy to be able to oblige him and so to contribute to assuring the independence of his talents and his character. More even than the immediate help, the free way in which it was given deeply touched Mirabeau. He assured La Marck with emotion that he had never in his life met anyone who had shown himself so truly his friend.

"From that day," wrote La Marck later, "he did not cease to show me a gratitude which was not belied to the day of his death. He was a true friend, confiding and devoted."

The liveliness of his gratitude revealed to La Marck both Mirabeau's eternal financial embarrassment and the delicacy of his feelings. La Marck went surety for his friend. "I gained the certainty that this man, whom everybody described as venal, had never sacrificed any principle for money."

He understood that a certain amount of luxury was a necessity for Mirabeau and offered on his own initiative to place him beyond reach of the troubles caused by his incapacity to live economically. "I told him that if he would promise me never in such cases to have recourse to anyone but me, it would be a real pleasure to me to lend him fifty louis a month, which, with his emolument as deputy, might suffice for his current expenses."

No friendship of Mirabeau's was so deep as that for La Marck. He had had more admiration for Chamfort, had profited more from the friendship of Mauvillon, had submitted more, often unwillingly, to the influence of Talleyrand; but no man, and perhaps no woman, held in his life the place thenceforth occupied by La Marck. In the rapid development of his own power, this friendship was for him a sort of brake. By his very limitations, by his prudence and discrimination, La Marck was a sort of stand-by for Mirabeau. The more his existence gained in richness and in responsibilities, the more Mirabeau needed the relaxation he found in his friend's company.

Their friendship, made closer by the disturbed times, was one of strange serenity, shining against the stormy background. Auguste, Comte de La Marck, one of the many *grands seigneurs* of his time, was saved from oblivion by his gift of friendship. He has won lasting remembrance in the company of a great man as a beneficent influence. He gave Mirabeau the little comfort he knew during his last years.

As the disagreement between the king and the representatives of the nation became more acute, Mirabeau saw the fate of the monarchy grow more sombre. His judgment of the passing day was so exact that he drew from it a prescience of the future. "In seeking the characteristic trait of his genius," wrote Dumont later, "I find it, after long reflection, in his political sagacity, his prevision of events, his knowledge of men, which he seemed to me to possess in a rarer and more eminent degree than all other intellectual qualities. There were times when he would say that he felt himself to be a prophet, and it did indeed seem that he had inspired glimpses of the future."

Toward the end of September Mirabeau said again and again to La

Marck in talking of the court: "What are these people imagining? Do they not see the abysses that are opening on their path?" One day he exclaimed: "All is lost, the king and queen will perish, and you will witness it: the mob will trample their bodies underfoot!" And when La Marck started up in horror he repeated obstinately: "Yes, yes, they will trample their bodies underfoot."

La Marck was shaken in spite of himself. The prophecy seemed inconceivable. But Mirabeau insisted that he should let the court know the dangers of its position. Although such a courtier as La Marck would not willingly be the bearer of an alarming message, he decided toward the end of September to go in search of one of his friends, a woman who had the queen's confidence, her lady of the bedchamber, the Comtesse d'Ossun. He seemed to be more anxious to justify himself than to warn the court. He had associated, he said, with Mirabeau only in order to moderate his revolutionary promptings. This friendship must not inspire any doubt of his devotion to the royal cause. He was trying to prepare Mirabeau to be useful to the king on the day when the ministers found themselves forced to come to an arrangement with Mirabeau, which he believed to be inevitable. Mirabeau's passionate appeal was reduced, as it passed through a *grand seigneur* and a lady of the bedchamber, to a discreet murmur. But even thus attenuated, it offende royal ears. Marie Antoinette made a point of giving her reply personally to her devoted servant. "I have never doubted your sentiments," she said graciously to La Marck, "and when I saw that you were associating with Mirabeau I felt sure that your intentions were good; but you will never be able to do anything with him, and as for what you think necessary on the part of the king's ministers, I do not agree." And she concluded haughtily: "We shall never be so fortunate, I think, as to be reduced to the painful extremity of going for help to Mirabeau."

5

On October 1 the Bodyguards gave a banquet to the Flanders Regiment, which had entered Versailles. "When heads are heated," wrote the *Courrier de Provence*, "by a sumptuous feast, by the excitement of a large gathering, and by prodigality with wines and liqueurs, conversation becomes unbridled. A chivalrous idea brought the folly to its height. The queen, to show her appreciation of the homage rendered to her, had appeared for a moment before this excited multitude with the little dauphin in her arms. The band struck up the familiar air 'O Richard! O my king, all are forsaking you.' Amid the general emotion some voices, perhaps paid, shouted imprecations against the National Assembly. A grenadier dashed into the midst of his comrades and, accusing himself of faithlessness to his prince, tried several times to stab himself with his sword. His blood flowed, carrying the excitement to its height and producing almost convulsive movements. The national cockade, that emblem of the defenders of liberty, was torn to pieces and stamped on, and another sign put in its place."

At the sitting of October 5 Pétion denounced the banquet. Mirabeau proposed that the Assembly should prohibit these so-called patriotic feasts, "which are an insult to the poverty of the people and of which the consequences may be disastrous." An over-zealous monarchist threw himself into the breach. Thinking to embarrass Pétion, he asked him to put his denunciation into writing and sign it. It was Mirabeau who thundered the reply: "I begin by declaring that I regard the denunciation just proposed as highly impolitic; nevertheless, if the demand for it is insisted on, I am ready to supply full details and to sign them; but before this I ask that the Assembly shall declare that the person of the king alone is inviolable, and that all other individuals of the state, whoever they may be, are equally subject to and responsible to the law."

In the horror-stricken silence someone shouted: "What, the queen!" As he came down from the tribune, Mirabeau said quickly, but in a voice that travelled like a stage aside: "I should denounce the queen and the Duc de Guiche" (one of the captains of the Guards). The inopportune intervention was at once withdrawn.

This sitting of October 5 began in the morning with the reading of the king's reply to the requests for his pronouncement on the constitution. "In accordance with your wish, I give my consent to these articles, but from one positive condition I shall never depart—that the executive power shall remain entirely in the hands of the monarch. I will not discuss," the king proceeded, "your declaration of the rights of man; it contains very good guidance for your labours, but principles susceptible of differences in application and even in interpretation cannot be rightly appreciated, and need not be, until their true meaning is fixed by the laws to which they are to serve as a first basis."

The royal declarations were received in gloomy silence. A few isolated cheers from nobles and clergy were answered by murmurs. "The king's reply," declared Robespierre, "is destructive not only of any constitution, but of the national right to have a constitution."

"The consent which the king has just given raises doubts as to his sentiments," said Mirabeau. "It is of the utmost importance to the monarch, for success in securing public tranquillity, that our decisions shall be accepted, and especially that they shall seem to have been accepted willingly. . . . If the king persists in his refusals," Mirabeau added, "the germ of patriotism would soon be stifled, and anarchy will begin the moment the people realize their power sufficiently to notice that it is desired to restrain it." He proposed that an address to the king should be drawn up, to make clear to him that his opposition was dangerous and useless—an address "in which we shall speak to him with the candour and the veracity of one of Philip's fools when he said: 'What would you do, Philip, if everybody said no when you say yes?' "

A few hours later the king's hand was forced. At the moment when Mirabeau was speaking public tranquillity was already being disturbed.

6

"Mounier, Paris is marching on us." Mirabeau was bending over the president's chair. It was between eleven o'clock and noon on October 5. For some days Paris had been simmering with revolt. The harvest had been good, but the wheat was reaching Paris only slowly. Queues were forming outside the bakers' shops. The scarcity was "partly artificial, partly real," according to Lafayette. What excited the people was more the fear of wheat shortage than any actual privation, and especially the persistent rumour that the court intended to starve Paris. The banquet to the Flanders Regiment had spread alarm. The insult to the national cockade was an insult to the nation. It was said that the agitation was partly engineered. Women in rags and seedy-looking persons had been seen pulling big silver coins out of their pockets. "It is said that the Duc d'Orléans has been bribing the populace," wrote Mme. de Staël. "But whether he has or not, only those who have no idea of the Revolution could imagine that the money, if it was given, had the slightest influence. A whole people is not set in motion by such means. The great mistake made by the people of the court has always been to seek in a few details the cause of sentiments expressed by the whole nation."

For some time Paris had been in tne habit of threatening on the slightest pretext to march on Versailles. In disturbed times violent ideas quickly make their way. "To Versailles! To Versailles!" the crowd shouted all the morning in front of the Hôtel de Ville. Market women took charge. Forcing their way into the town hall, they seized muskets and even cannon. They went round the city making all the women, even aristocrats in their carriages, join them. The National Guards came on the scene to prevent pillage. The women urged the Guards, imploring and even threatening them, to go with them to Versailles to bring the king to Paris, and with him bread and peace. The tocsin sounded. All the shops were closed. The frightened population barred its doors. Workmen and soldiers wandering in the streets of Paris joined this army of militant women.

"Paris is marching on us," said Mirabeau to Mounier. "I know nothing about it," replied Mounier, not trusting him.

Mirabeau had been informed that the fermentation in Paris was increasing. "I had no need to know the details to believe it," he said later. "I inferred it from an augury that never misleads, the nature of things." "Believe me or not," he said to Mounier, "I tell you that Paris is marching on us. Say you are ill; go to the château and give them this information; say if you like that you have it from me, but put an end to this scandalous controversy. Time is pressing, there is not a moment to lose."

"Paris is marching on us," replied Mounier. "Very well, so much the better. We shall be all the sooner in a republic."

"It is a pretty word," replied Mirabeau, "but if the royal family is injured or reduced to flight I can no longer answer for the consequences."

Mounier regarded Mirabeau as the firebrand of Paris. He attached no importance to his warning, or thought he was raising the spectre of insurrection for demagogic purposes.

The Assembly decided to send a deputation, headed by Mounier, to ask the king to give his "acceptance pure and simple" to the articles of the declaration and of the constitution which had already been presented.

The effervescence continued to grow in Paris. The surging masses pressed Lafayette to take the lead in their movement. But he did not dare either to lead it or to stop it. He let himself be carried along by events.

In Paris there broke out "the most violent and most general riot that I have seen in my life," said Lafayette, and he could no longer resist the appeal of the wild crowd. To cover himself he had the order to march on Versailles confirmed by the municipality. He placed himself, "more dead than alive," at the head of the National Guard, which advanced to the beating of drums, with flags flying.

The women, soaked in rain and mud, reached Versailles about four o'clock in the afternoon. They had brought a spokesman, one of the conquerors of the Bastille, and demanded to be heard by the Assembly. "We have come to Versailles to ask for bread and also to get the Body-guards punished for insulting the patriotic cockade."

Another deputation from the Assembly was preparing to leave for the château. It was instructed to ask for measures to assure the provisioning of Paris. But the women wanted to speak to the king themselves. Fifteen of them went with the deputation to the château. The king was hunting. A messenger was sent after him in haste. The queen was walking alone, as though lost in her dreams of the Petit Trianon.

Mirabeau was with his friend La Marck that afternoon. He knew that the king was being advised to go to Metz, and he insisted on the dangers of such a step. "The dynasty is lost," he said to La Marck, "if Monsieur [the Comte de Provence, the king's brother] does not remain to take over the reins of government." La Marck had failed with the queen through a courtier-like inability to insist; he hoped to find more understanding in the Comte de Provence.

In the quiet of La Marck's house no sound of the uproar outside penetrated. The two friends did not know that the Paris crowd had already invaded Versailles. About six o'clock La Marck took Mirabeau back to the Assembly.

In the absence of Mounier the assembly hall had been invaded by the women, who had been admitted out of pity. They filled the galleries and the surroundings of the hall; one of them had even taken possession of the president's chair. On entering the hall they had sought in vain for a familiar figure and had shouted: "We want our little mother Mirabeau."

But Mirabeau, after a glance at the hall, went home at once.

The king returned from the hunt. He received the deputation of women. He loved his good city of Paris too well, he said in reply to their complaints, to let it lack anything. So long as he had been responsible for its provisioning, he thought he had been very successful. But since these gentlemen—he pointed to the deputies who were present at the interview—had tied his hands, "it is no longer my fault." He gave a fatherly promise to take the necessary steps and embraced one of the women delegates. The women went away moved and flattered to such an extent as to arouse the suspicions of their comrades, who sent them back to get assurances in writing.

Mounier was still waiting for the king's reply. Louis XVI was not prepared to give Mounier his adhesion to the constitutional decrees. The ministers advised him to leave for Rambouillet. "Sire," urged Saint-Priest, "if tomorrow you are taken to Paris, your crown is lost." But Necker opposed this. "At the worst," he said, "if His Majesty thought it necessary to establish himself in Paris, he would be revered and respected there by his people, who adore him."

Hours passed. The king's one thought was for the safety of the queen and the children. About nine o'clock the queen's carriages were in readiness. But Marie Antoinette refused to leave the king.

Mounier intimated several times that he was about to go. The king asked him to wait.

Outside, the crowd saw the arrival of the carriages and grew agitated. There were shouts of "the king is going away." The Bodyguards had been ordered to re-enter the château. The crowd thought they were preparing to charge and pursued them across the park.

Mounier was still waiting to be admitted to the presence of the king.

There was a first clash at Versailles, between some women and a detachment of Guards. The "Bastille volunteers" fired and killed several Bodyguards. At that moment—after five hours' wait—the king sent for the president of the Assembly. "He had heard the firing," wrote Mounier. "Judge his emotion, judge mine."

The news spread that the National Guards were approaching. Was Lafayette coming as friend or enemy? The château was horror-stricken. The king called for the convocation of the Assembly. It suddenly appeared to him a safeguard between the unleashed people and an army whose intentions he did not know. The drum beat to recall the deputies. Drums were also beating as the army of the National Guards advanced by torchlight. "Sire," said Lafayette, as he bowed to the king, "if I had thought I could serve Your Majesty better today by laying down my head on the scaffold, you would never have seen me here." The king, with all his ponderous dignity restored, assured Lafayette that he was always glad to see him as well as his good Parisians. Lafayette occupied the château with the National Guards.

The assembly hall was filled with a crowd soaked by its long wait in the rain; muddy, famished, tired out, it was still excited and vociferous. In vain were efforts made to send the crowd away. From the gallery Dumont saw a woman giving the lead to a hundred others. The women shouted in unison: "Who is that talking down there? Stop the babbler. That doesn't matter, what matters is to have some bread. Get our little Mirabeau to speak, we want to hear him."

In that hour of confusion the prestige of the Assembly and the ascendancy of the elected of the nation had sunk to nothing. Suddenly the scene was dominated by a voice of thunder: "I should just like to know why it has been thought fit to come and disturb our sittings."

Mirabeau stood up commandingly, disdainful of the popular wrath. At the sound of his great voice the crowd was silent. He asked the president to preserve the dignity of the debate by ordering "the strangers scattered about the hall," to retire to the galleries. The crowd recognized its great man. It listened with respect. "The representatives of the nation cannot carry on any intelligent discussion in the midst of a scandalous tumult, and I hope the friends of liberty have not come here to interfere with the liberty of the Assembly."

This was language the crowd could understand. It was won over and broke into applause. Calm was restored.

At midnight the king's declaration was read: "I accept purely and simply the articles of the Constitution and the Declaration of the Rights of Man and the Citizen which the National Assembly has placed before me." The king had concluded peace with the representatives of the nation.

The king, reassured by Lafayette that the National Guards had taken every precaution for the preservation of undisturbed tranquillity, sent for Mounier. He had no more need of the Assembly now that Lafayette had promised to guard him against the "pretended brigands supposed to have reached Versailles."

The Assembly adjourned till next day. La Marck, who had stayed late at the château, offered to take Lafayette back in his carriage. He heard him say that he was tired out: he must have some hours' sleep now that order was definitely re-established.

The king and queen, relying on Lafayette, returned to their apartments. The sentinels were at their stations.

Round the railings indistinct figures prowled. The night was disturbed by unfamiliar sounds. Lafayette slept. Rivarol later called him General Morpheus.

7

"Were the events of that night misfortunes or crimes?" asked Mirabeau later. "Were the crimes the result of a plot, or of imprudence, or of chance?" The enigma of the night of October 5-6 was never solved.

At the dawn of a grey day, the crowd had come into collision with some Bodyguards. Shots had been fired and there had been an explosion. In its pursuit of the Guards the crowd had forced its way past the railings, broken into the château, and penetrated as far as the queen's apartments; she had fled to the king. The château had been besieged by a surging mass of people shouting "*Vive le Roi!*" and "To Paris! To Paris!" The court had been seized with terror. Those shouts of "Long live the king!" were shouts for the death of the queen. The Bodyguards in the hands of the furious mob were to be massacred like those whose heads had already been brandished on pikes. Lafayette, belatedly rushing up, pleaded pathetically for the men to be pardoned. It was at that point that the royal power capitulated to the Paris mob. Versailles with its splendours, a setting of harmonious luxury built to exalt the royal house, became no more than an empty shell, an abandoned stage.

Louis XVI appeared on the gilded balcony, above a sea of heads, an armed and threatening multitude. At that decisive moment, when he was undoubtedly thinking of how to avoid extensive bloodshed, and certainly of how to save his wife and children, his ponderous, thick-set figure had a dignity that was felt even in the midst of the mass hysteria.

"My friends," he said, "I am going to live among you with my wife and children."

Lafayette, profiting by the effect of the king's words, brought the queen with her children to the balcony. "My friends," he shouted, "peace has been made."

Two deputies of the nobility came to the Assembly asking its members, in the king's name, to present themselves to him. Mirabeau loudly declared that "the president cannot make the deputies go to the king without deliberation." The sitting was opened. Mounier was still shaken by the tragic hours through which he had just passed; he asked that the Assembly should fall in with the king's desire without delay. "I oppose that," said Mirabeau; "it is not consistent with our dignity, it is not even sensible, to desert our post when dangers, real or imaginary, seem to threaten the common weal."

Mounier was irritated. His was a timid spirit of reform, and he was distracted at the outbreak of a violence he had not suspected. On the morrow of these tragic days he was to flee from his responsibilities to a safe refuge in a foreign country, confining himself to censuring events instead of influencing them.

He was so revolted by Mirabeau's attitude that he spoke from the chair, breaking the rule of presidential non-intervention in debate. He urged the Assembly to go to the king, who had need of its advice: "Our dignity consists in fulfilling our duties; I consider it a sacred duty, at this moment of danger, to be with the king." Nobody rose to refute this, but when the motion was put he had the majority against him. Mirabeau spoke again: "I ask that it be decreed that the king and the National Assembly shall be inseparable during the present session, and I observe to the Assembly that a healthy policy should determine it to perform freely an act of such importance." His proposal was unanimously adopted.

Versailles was to be no longer the seat of the first popular representation of the country. The Parisian crowd took back with it Louis XVI and the royal family. It was a strange procession, with the carved and gilded carriages of the court in the middle of it. Soldiers of the National Guard marched alongside women armed with muskets or sitting astride cannon, waving flags and wearing grenadiers' caps. Horses from the royal stables were harnessed to bread carts. Saveloys were hung on the tips of bayonets. The crowd was excited by the wine that had flowed freely in the taverns, and still more excited by its triumph. It bawled: "We shall not go short of bread any more, we have got the baker, the baker's wife, and the baker's boy."

The women proudly wore tricolour cockades. A Versailles shopkeeper's accounts included: "Supplied on the 6.x. to the ladies of Paris coming on behalf of the queen, 150 cockades"; and another: "Supplied to the ladies of Paris coming from Paris, 150 cockades at 1 fr. = 150."

On the next day Mirabeau prepared a memorandum reminding the court of the dangers that surrounded it. More disastrous even than the impotence of the ministers was the loss of prestige of the Assembly, the king's last remaining protection. "The National Assembly," he wrote, "is finding that the confidence in its labours diminishes daily. Each day a portion of public opinion is turning away from it. Today we are only tired and discouraged; it is the moment of despair that must be dreaded. If Paris has great strength, it also harbours great causes of effervescence. Its populace in agitation is irresistible: winter is approaching, food may be lacking, bankruptcy may arrive; what will Paris be in three months' time? Certainly a hospital, perhaps a scene of horrors."

8

The Duc d'Orléans and Mirabeau were named as the persons chiefly responsible for the events of the fifth and sixth of October. Testimony against Mirabeau came from all sides—chance confidences, imprudent language, remarks torn from their context. Dumont, whose attachment to Mirabeau so often resembled hatred, said that if he had been an accomplice in the revolt he could not have acted differently. At the moment, in an atmosphere laden with suspicions, every evil rumour spread by Mirabeau's friends or his enemies was credited. He referred to them in a letter to the bailli:

"If it were not you to whom I am writing, my very dear uncle, I should make no reply to the calumnies that leave here for Provence or return here from there. Anyone of sense ought to see that it might be possible for many obscure or unknown intriguers to be long guilty and to escape from prosecution, but it would be impossible for the Comte de Mirabeau, surrounded at all times with implacable enemies, to make a single false step with impunity." Later, when these accusations became the subject of a prosecution, Mirabeau reduced them to their true proportions. La Marck, who was so devoted to the queen, bore witness to his friend's innocence. He confirmed that Mirabeau had passed the day with him, and revealed also that at the time when Mirabeau was accused of having received money from the Duc d'Orléans, he was asking him for a loan of a few louis.

Mirabeau triumphed over the campaign of calumny. The attitude of the duke remained equivocal. Mirabeau does not seem to have believed in his guilt. His principal accuser was Lafayette, who, in an interview in the presence of Montmorin, intimidated the duke into agreeing to leave at once for London on a mission to the English government. The duke may himself have been frightened by the headlong course of events, and was certainly tired of conspiracies, for which he was temperamentally unsuited. He may also have felt that the Revolution had already cost him too much.

Mirabeau was alarmed by this decision. It would immensely increase the prestige of Lafayette. The duke's flight "left without rival the man whom chance had just given a new dictatorship, the man who at that time, under the banner of liberty, possessed a police more active than that of the *ancien régime* . . . and who, by imposing departure on M. d'Orléans instead of having him judged and condemned, if he was guilty, by this alone eluded the inviolability of the members of the Assembly." Under the influence of his friends the duke retracted his promise to Lafayette. But Lafayette insisted on a second interview and extracted from the duke a promise to leave in twenty-four hours. The vacillating duke changed his mind a second time and asked Biron to consult Mirabeau.

"M. d'Orléans," said Mirabeau, "is to leave, without judgment, the post his constituents have confided to him. If he obeys, I denounce his departure, and I oppose it; if he remains, I denounce the authority that is taking the place of the laws; let him choose between these alternatives."

The duke wrote once more to Lafayette to take back his word. But Lafayette took him to the king and bound him irrevocably by making him announce in the king's presence that he accepted the mission.

Lafayette wanted to get rid of Biron as well. But Biron replied: "If I am guilty, let me be judged." Lafayette hustled the Duc d'Orléans off that very night.

≥ XVII ≤

In France You Never Can Tell

THE FIRST sittings of the Assembly in Paris were held in the archbishop's palace. They moved later to the inconvenient and illventilated Salle de Manège, the Riding School, near the Tuileries. Dr. Guillotin, who watched over the health of the Assembly with philanthropic zeal, found the Riding School appalling from the point of view of hygiene and went to a great deal of trouble to introduce a few improvements.

At the first sitting in the palace, Bailly, in the name of the municipality, and Lafayette, in the name of the National Guard, welcomed the Assembly and promised to watch over its peace and safety. In proposing a vote of thanks to them Mirabeau was not entirely disinterested. He well knew Lafayette's hesitations, his facile optimism, and especially his easily wounded vanity. The political ideas of the two men had become more similar since the events of the night of October 5–6. Lafayette, who before the Revolution had been openly republican in his views, said again and again that the events of that night had turned him royalist. And Mirabeau agreed with deputies of the left like Barnave, Du Port, and the Lameth brothers, that a change of ministry was necessary and that it could not be effected without Lafayette's help. Nevertheless there was a certain amount of antagonism between them.

Barnave and Du Port arranged a meeting with Lafayette at the house of the Marquise d'Aragon, Mirabeau's niece, Caroline's eldest daughter. But the meeting did little to improve the relations between the two men. Lafayette made his disapproval of Mirabeau's immorality quite evident; Mirabeau sought in vain to disarm him. Mirabeau, with his feminine susceptibility, reacted by trying, as Lafayette recorded, to "make himself out blacker than he really was." His sense of humour, in the face of Lafayette's complete lack of it, found play when Lafayette burst out with a declaration that Mirabeau must give up agitating against the queen if he wanted to have any relations with him. Mirabeau replied: "Very well, General, since you wish it. A humiliated queen can be of some use, but a butchered queen is good only as the subject for a bad tragedy."

But in spite of all this the interview seems to have served its main purpose. Lafayette agreed as to the need for forming a new ministry that could ride out the storm. He proposed, however, not to proceed to the formation of a new ministry until after the departure of Necker, who, he said, would be going in a couple of months. "If," Mirabeau objected, "he must go after irremediable harm has been done, it would be preferable, since the state matters more than a single individual, that he should go at a time when it is still possible to save everything. In two months the state will be lost or saved for good."

Lafayette, shaken by Mirabeau's arguments, went with him to see Montmorin; but Montmorin had been annoyed by Mirabeau's attacks on the court and the ministry and was non-committal. Necker asked Mirabeau to see him. In the list of proposed ministers which Mirabeau had sent to Lafayette he had put at the head: "M. Necker, Prime Minister, because he must be made as powerless as he is incapable, and yet his popularity must be kept for the king's benefit." In this list the Archbishop of Bordeaux was proposed as Keeper of the Seals; La Marck for the Ministry of Marine; Montmorin to have a governorship and a dukedom and his debts paid; Lafayette to be marshal of France; and Mirabeau to be in the Council without department. But Necker would have nothing to do with the plan. At the end of the interview, which lasted five hours, Necker said to Mirabeau: "My strength lies in morality; you have too much intelligence not to feel some day the necessity of that bulwark; before then it may suit the king in present circumstances to have you as a minister, but it is impossible for us to be ministers together." Necker made one of his worst mistakes in keeping Mirabeau out of office at the time when he might have been able to change the country's course.

After Necker's refusal the conversations with Lafayette were resumed on another basis. In a further interview, "we agreed," wrote Lafayette, "to leave the ministry as it is, except for his attack on M. de Saint-Priest, from which I could not dissuade him."

2

A baker had been killed in Paris on suspicion of withholding bread. A deputation from the municipality came to the bar of the Assembly to ask for martial law to be decreed. Only a few days earlier Mirabeau had called for this, together with a tribunal for the punishment of crimes of *lèse-nation*. He objected, however, to the proposal now made. "I know of nothing more alarming," he said, "than motions arising out of dearth. All are silent and should be, all give way and should, before a hungry people. What can martial law do if the crowds shout: 'There is no more bread in the bakers' shops?' What monster would reply with gunfire?" Other action was necessary. "Let us call on the executive to say definitely what resources it requires from us in order to assure the food supply of the capital; let us give it these resources, and from that moment let it be responsible for administering them."

The president informed the Assembly that Necker had stated that the municipality had stopped all communication with the ministry in connexion with the provisioning of the capital. But Mirabeau's harsh criticism corresponded so entirely with the general feeling that the ministry was asked to report to the Assembly.

The ministry was indignant at this attack. One of the ministers, Saint-Priest, had been denounced by Mirabeau to a committee of the Assembly for saying, it was alleged, to the women at Versailles: "When you had only one king you were not short of bread; now that you have twelve hundred kings, address yourselves to them." Saint-Priest energetically denied having said this and contradicted the evidence of witnesses. But within the cabinet he was the representative of the counter-revolution; he had "despotism in his soul," and in attacking him Mirabeau was attacking all those who stood in the way of a rapprochement between king and nation.

After the sanguinary days of the beginning of October and the murder of the baker in Paris there came a calm. There was a reaction especially among the Parisian middle class, a desire to maintain order and respect for property. Relations between court and people grew less strained. But there was a lack of comfort in Paris: the king pointed out later that "more than a hundred years had passed since the kings of France had made the Tuileries their normal residence. Nothing had been done to prepare it for the king, and the royal apartments were far from providing the convenience to which His Majesty was accustomed in the other royal houses, and which every individual of means can enjoy."

Marie Antoinette, however, rejoiced in the improved relations. She wrote to the Austrian ambassador, Mercy d'Argenteau: "If we forget where we are and how we came here, we are bound to be pleased with the change in opinion. I talk to the people, to militiamen and fish-wives; all are friendly." One woman slyly spoke a few words in German, but the queen replied that she no longer understood German; she had become "so good a Frenchwoman that I have actually forgotten my mother tongue." There were shouts of "Bravo!" from all sides. The queen was assured that there would be no more shedding of blood. A crowd stayed long outside the Tuileries shouting "Long live our good queen!"

In those conditions a capable and enlightened ministry would easily have reconciled the king and the Revolution. But the ministers, in a printed memorandum addressed to the Assembly in reply to Mirabeau's attack, disclaimed responsibility, pointing to the confusion through-out the kingdom—a confession, wrote the *Courrier de Provence,* of impotence.

3

Once more material needs threw shadows over Mirabeau's path. Incapa-ble of personal economy, he had also embarked on expenditure which he thought indispensable in his position. "I am retaining three first-class men," he explained, "two of whom, if I did not keep them, would already have returned to England." In addition to the two Genevese to whom he was referring, he had engaged a young lawyer from Pro-vence, Pellenc, who had asked for him in the Aix proceedings. In October Pellenc, no doubt in view of Mirabeau's growing reputation, had hur-ried to Paris "with a very young and very pretty wife," said Dumont. His hope had not been vain: he became one of Mirabeau's most hard-worked helpers. Dumont, who seemed to regard Mirabeau as a Genevese monopoly, made allegations against Pellenc's past; La Marck, who had no feeling against Pellenc, found him clear-headed and concise. Although a southerner, he was reserved and discreet, and so self-effacing that he "almost disappeared in Mirabeau's presence." But his stolidity, his rather unimaginative prudence, and his sometimes rather laboured logic, made of him an invaluable assistant. Mirabeau treated him very much as a subordinate, often adopting a tone that surprised Dumont, who knew how useful the lawyer was. Mirabeau, usually so trustful, harboured a secret suspicion of Pellenc, as if he expected to find him at any moment turning against him. He shouted angrily one day that no doubt he would rather make speeches against him than for him, and he confided to La Marck that Pellenc had played two or three nasty tricks; but his anger passed and he continued to employ him, and even to overload him with work.

"So long as I have ambitious plans, I cannot dismiss my staff," Mirabeau declared. "If I am to attain office, these fellows are men of gold; and we must always remember that a government will never get anywhere without subordinates." He was ready to assume the responsibilities of office and believed he could attain it with or without Lafayette's help. But on the very day when he wrote to tell him proudly that he resumed freedom of action, he received a threatening letter that brought him back to sordid reality. The banker Jeanneret reminded him in brutal terms that his debt to him amounted to nearly twelve thousand livres, and he added: "I have always detested the airs of a *grand seigneur*, and I should feel degraded in putting up with them from anybody, still more from you."

Mirabeau was so preoccupied by his material difficulties that he could not help mentioning them at his first interview with Lafayette, to La Marck's regret. With great devotion and no less skill La Marck had himself undertaken to negotiate material aid for his friend, which Lafayette offered to procure for him. "I cannot accept important help without an appointment that justifies it, and a small aid would gratuitously compromise me—there's the rub; there I have so much the more need of your wisdom, which is more of this world than mine is."

La Marck did indeed do useful service, by securing from Lafayette a promise that next time he saw Mirabeau he would begin by offering him fifty thousand francs. La Marck explained that his friend needed a fixed income, and he negotiated with Lafayette as to the form it should take. Lafayette proposed "a written engagement for an important embassy, to Holland or England. Constantinople would have been possible eight months earlier." "I rejected everything," declared La Marck. Under the influence of this good friend, Mirabeau recovered his spirit. "I rejected with all due pride everything connected with money," he reported to La Marck, like a good child that had learnt his lesson carefully. But he was in real distress. "I know your embarrassing position," wrote La Marck, "but between the objections to receiving and the objections to declining there should be a way out. Meanwhile, for the moment," added this never-failing friend, "I still have three hundred louis at your service."

Finally Montmorin transmitted to Mirabeau through Lafayette a pompous proposition: he was to be appointed ambassador to Holland or England, "not to go there but to decorate me, and to make me worthy of the supreme honour of putting in my pocket a note from the king assuring me that I should be a minister in May."

"Accept it all," advised La Marck. "Your enemies will find you all the harder to deal with. Your affairs will involve you no longer in petty embarrassments, and then you will be entirely at your full worth, that is to say, superior to all."

4

The Archbishop of Bordeaux, Champion de Cicé, Keeper of the Seals, heard of the negotiations between Mirabeau and Lafayette. He would have been ready himself to enter into relations with Mirabeau, but Mirabeau had good reasons for distrusting the archbishop. Champion de Cicé quickly noticed his coolness and turned against the man of whom he had proposed to make an ally. Mirabeau soon had proofs that the author of the vehement pamphlet directed against him, *Domine salvum fac ragem*, had been "inspired, indoctrinated, paid for, etc., by the Keeper of the Seals." The pamphlet denounced part of the court, which, it alleged, had been intriguing to induce the king to leave for Metz, to proclaim the Duc d'Orléans lieutenant general of the kingdom, and to make Mirabeau mayor of Paris or a minister, and Talleyrand Keeper of the Seals or Minister of Finance.

One of the most active intriguers was Gouverneur Morris. This ambassador of the Promised Land of liberty had come to France with one fixed idea: "A democracy. Can it last? I think not. I am sure not, unless the whole people are changed." Such influence as he had he employed in insisting on the dangers of a democratic constitution. This son of the country of new men noted with pride that he was frequently quoted by the aristocrats as being one of their party. He urged Lafayette, with whom he had a certain influence, to preserve some constitutional authority in the body of the nobility. For pride in nobility he had the respect of a parvenu. His snobbishness had in it an element of religious fanaticism. He was implacable against renegades from their class. Mirabeau was for him the John Wilkes of France. He pursued him from the first with violent hatred. He never spoke of him except as "scoundrel" or "rascal," and incessantly denounced his immorality. But Mirabeau's worst offence was for Morris his abandonment of the society into which he was born, to make common cause with the riffraff.

Morris's indulgence in the matter of morals was extreme in the case of those whom he considered as men of the world. He was a frequent visitor to Talleyrand's mistress, Mme. de Flahaut, and tried to be Talleyrand's rival. His morality was also lax in money matters; his integrity was little disturbed by the proposals he noted in his diary after a dinner with the Bishop of Autun and Mme. de Flahaut. "We converse about the public affairs and she tells us that if he is minister we must make a million for her."

He had, moreover, a sort of strange affection and even devotion for the lover of the woman he loved. He served Talleyrand's ambitions with ardour, although he knew that Talleyrand wanted to be in the government, and especially Minister of Finance, only in order to make a fortune. As soon as he heard of the negotiations for a new ministry he rushed to see Lafayette to recommend the Bishop of Autun as Minister of Finance. Lafayette considered his protégé "a bad man, false," but Morris urged that through Talleyrand he could win over Mirabeau. Lafayette thought it would be simpler just to take Mirabeau. If he did, said Morris indignantly, every decent Frenchman would ask the cause of that strange coalition. He followed up his visit with a vehement letter and returned to the charge in several further visits. He took Talleyrand to Lafayette. They discussed different persons, wrote Morris, and "*par hazard*, Lafayette asks whether Mirabeau's influence in the Assembly is great, to which the Bishop replies that it is not enormous."

On the morning on which Lafayette was to talk with the queen, Mirabeau found him less decided than ever. The indefatigable Morris had had full success, Lafayette had abandoned his plan of collaboration with Mirabeau. But Lafayette was too deeply committed, had promised too much. He felt that he was at least bound to keep his promises of material aid and sent Mirabeau twenty-three thousand francs, "a ridiculous and unexplained remittance which does not even enable me to pay my debt to you," he wrote to La Marck. La Marck, no less indignant, replied: "I hope you sent back the twenty-three thousand francs."

5

The Abbé Maury had the worship of eloquence in his blood. It was for him the lever of public affairs and the key to personal success. The son of a bootmaker, he was confident from the first, in spite of his humble origin, of an exceptional destiny. "A single passion dominated him —ambition," said a contemporary, "and there was no post, however elevated, to which he did not claim to rise." In the diligence that took him for the first time to Paris, he discussed with other ambitious young-sters their future careers. "I shall become chaplain to the king, and one of the forty of the Academy," he said. A favourite saying of his was: "You can do anything, if you want to." He had neither mystical en-thusiasm nor faith in men. "For thirty years," he said, "I have found men so evil, as individuals and taken one by one, that I expect nothing good from them in public and taken collectively."

The motion introduced by the Bishop of Autun for the nationaliza-tion of ecclesiastical properties set the Abbé Maury fiercely on the alert. The clergy were ready at once for any sacrifice to avert the dan-ger. They knew that the emigration of so many nobles and moderates had robbed them of a majority in the Assembly. The prelates did not, like Maury, count on eloquence to win over the undecided among the deputies. They tried other methods of gaining support. They ap-proached Mirabeau, who had given Talleyrand the support of his powerful oratory.

The Prince-Cardinal Louis de Rohan had ranked, since the fatal af-fair of the necklace, as a victim of absolute power. At this moment, when the prelates were desperately facing the Revolution, he thought of his past relations with Mirabeau. "He came to see him several times," wrote Legrain, Mirabeau's valet; "he was always alone with him, and I locked them in and told all his people to go away." Legrain, like all Mirabeau's valets, was on a strange footing of familiarity with his mas-ter. Devoted and insolent, curious about everything, he was quite ready to listen at keyholes. "I heard them discussing together the properties of the clergy," he candidly confessed. The style of his memoirs, and the bizarre spelling, difficult to decipher, reveal an illiterate who would not be capable of inventing these discussions: they were beyond him. "I listened to the cardinal who told M. de Mirabeau to drop his mo-tion, that the clergy would give four hundred millions to pay the debt of the state and ten millions for him, that he would be paid in cash without anybody being able to find out."

It was a time when Mirabeau was in the gravest financial difficulties. "Monseigneur, I am supposed to love money, I should like to have it to pay my debts," was what Legrain heard. "I accepted the place in the *Tiers Etat* for the people, I will not be false to my oath." And Legrain ended his picturesque story with the words: "He came back again several times, same result."

Mirabeau was not muzzled. He was concerned to prevent the pos-sessing classes from taking alarm. "The consideration of the public in-terest," he said in the Assembly, "however important it may be, would not suffice for decreeing that the properties of the clergy belong to the nation, if that meant violating the properties of an important part of its members." He stated the principle that nothing is expedient that is not just, and put the Assembly on its guard against the danger of seeming to sanction a usurpation. But the nation had the right "to examine whether it is fitting that the ministers of its religion should form a political aggregation . . . capable of acquiring and possessing. I should say further," he added, "that if the properties of the Church are consecrated to public worship, the temples and the altars belong to society and not at all to their ministers. . . . I should remark that all the members of the clergy are officers of the state, that the service of the altars is a public function, and that, since religion belongs to all, for that very reason its ministers should be in the pay of the nation, like the magistrate who judges in the name of the law, and like the soldier who, in the name of all, defends the common properties."

The prelates tried to meet the blow with ingenious arguments that left the Assembly unmoved. Then it was that the Abbé Maury pounced on his adversaries. He had never been so eloquent as on that day, and he never surpassed this effort. He was convinced that a revolting injustice was being committed. He was defending twenty thousand livres a year of his own. He defended them by going over to the attack, or, rather, by creating a diversion. He exploited the latent conflict between the provinces and Paris. "Let it not, then, be so lightly proposed to us, gentlemen, to sacrifice the property of the countryside to that devouring abyss the capital, which already swallows the richest portion of our territorial income." He exploited the working class's distrust of capital. He exploited especially the general indignation against the schemings of speculators, as his opponent Mirabeau had done in the past. "The motion of the Bishop of Autun has suddenly revealed their design. The ruin of the clergy is their great speculation; they are waiting for that rich prey, which is silently being prepared for them." He went on to mobilize anti-Semitism: the Jews "are asking you, gentlemen, at this very moment for a civil state, so as to confiscate together the title of citizen and the possessions of the Church." He exploited also the inveterate anxiety of the middle class: "Property is one and sacred, for you as for us. Our properties guarantee yours. We are being attacked today, but be not deceived: if we are despoiled, you will be in your turn."

Mirabeau had prepared a long speech, whose slow and laborious development seems to be the work of a collaborator, but it was not delivered, the debate closing before Mirabeau had an opportunity to intervene. The speech was edited by Dumont and published in the *Courrier de Provence*. Mirabeau did not allow Maury to go off at a tangent and constitute himself the advocate of the working class. "Do you think that if the clergy were not landowners religion would be less holy, public morality less pure, and the morals of the clergy less severe? Do you think the people's respect for the ministers of the altars would be less religious, or that their confidence in them would be less shaken, if they were not forced to compare the opulence of the clergy with their own indigence?"

6

A riot had broken out at Marseille. The national militia had been re-organized and recruited among the elements which the people suspected of hostility to them. There were clashes and bloodshed, and several Marseillais were charged with inciting to disorder. The provost had them arrested and brought them before a tribunal of officers of the new militia. In virtue of a decree of the Assembly on the reform of criminal procedure, the prisoners, who had been transferred to the Fort d'If, claimed to see the documents in the case. The provost rejected this application although the new law was in force.

Mirabeau was particularly attentive to events in Provence. "Through what strange event did the Assembly's decree fail to reach the provost or the municipality of Marseille?" he asked. "Do the ministers wish to render your decrees null and void? Or can the administrative bodies and the tribunals dare to hinder the publication of your laws?"

His denunciation produced further complaints from all quarters; deputies of different provinces hastened to report other abuses to the Assembly. One deputy, seeing how the agitation was growing, proposed that the motion should be adjourned. "If you were about to be hanged, Monsieur," retorted Mirabeau, "would you propose the adjournment of an examination that might save you? Very well! Fifty citizens of Marseille may be hanged any day." His motion was at once adopted.

On November 6 Mirabeau spoke on the precarious financial situation, "the aggravation of which may render all our labours useless." The most serious symptom was the disappearance of the currency. "It is now an advantageous traffic to send our louis and crowns abroad." He denounced the Caisse d'Escompte, which "is inundating us with paper money in the most alarming way, since its manufacture remains in the hands of a company that is in no way accountable to the state." He asked whether the food troubles of Paris were not "as much the effect of the scarcity of currency and the alarm it spreads as of those shadowy plots, so difficult to understand, so impossible to prove, to which they are obstinately attributed. We can collect wheat in the countryside only with money in our hands." He proposed also that the finance committee should be called upon to draw up a plan for a national bank.

The country, he said, was full of confidence in the Assembly, but "there is a troublesome lack of agreement between the government and the Assembly," which "look on each other as enemies and are afraid to discuss public affairs together."

Mirabeau had reached the main point of his intervention. "Let us seek means of putting an end to all these disagreements, which will not cease to arise so long as the king's ministers are absent from the Assembly." He invoked the example of England, where the presence of ministers in Parliament was considered "not only as absolutely necessary, but as one of its great privileges." The speech was loudly applauded, but the motion concerning ministers was adjourned to the following day.

7

The ministers knew that they were threatened. With the voting of their admission to the Assembly the barrier between the executive and the legislative power would be levelled, and very soon members of the Assembly would be sitting on the ministerial benches. Mirabeau, as he had announced to Lafayette, would be able to form a new cabinet. He would be in power. That night of November 6–7 was dominated by the redoubtable shadow of Mirabeau. The right wing was not alone in its fear of him. There were ambitious persons to whom he was an incubus, young deputies who objected to the dominance of any individual, idealists distrustful of all who were suspected of making terms with practical realities, and intriguers who exploited all these apprehensions for the benefit of powerful patrons. There was the Keeper of the Seals, Champion de Cicé, with his secret relations with members of the Assembly and with the police. And Champion de Cicé was working, according to Lafayette, against Mirabeau, although he had assured him of his support. There were also the lukewarm and the hesitant who held aloof—like Lafayette—from the battle that was about to begin. And there was the mass of deputies who had not realized all that underlay the debate.

The Comte de Montlosier, as he himself admitted, was meeting the suggestion of a friend of the Keeper of the Seals when he rose to ask the Assembly to take care, for Mirabeau's proposal had an unrevealed purpose. A young deputy from Rennes followed him. His name would have been forgotten but for his intervention on that day. Lanjuinais was a man of the left, sincere, apparently, but limited. If, as Mirabeau alleged, he was under influence, whether from the Keeper of the Seals or from Necker, he was not consciously so: they may have presented the issue to him in terms of the public weal. He exclaimed: "An eloquent genius is leading you on and subjugating you; what would he not do if he were a minister!" Applause released the secret feelings of mediocrities who were ill at ease under the sway of a strong personality. Lanjuinais proposed a decree that "the representatives of the nation shall not during the life of the legislature of which they are members, or during the following three years, obtain from the executive power any place, pension, advancement, or favour." An amendment was proposed that "no member of the Assembly shall henceforth pass into the ministry during the whole period of the session."

Mirabeau came to the tribune to defend his motion, spoke with eloquence and scathing irony, ending his speech with a proposal for an amendment which would exclude him from the ministry. But he knew in advance that the issue was decided. "Nothing," wrote the *Courrier de Provence*, "inflames men's minds like the personal element when it invades any question, and here the motion itself was personal."

But his scathing irony and his eloquence alike failed with a prejudiced Assembly. The first amendment was voted. On that day, November 7, Mirabeau's political career was broken. He remained faithful to his general policy, which aimed at bringing king and people together, but he could no longer effectively promote that reconciliation; he could no longer pursue its realization in full daylight. The decision of November 7 threw him into intrigue, and his great destiny suffered its fatal deviation. He no longer incarnated the pure flame of the Revolution. He was disheartened by the outcome of that day: "Do not speak to me of these hatreds, too stupid if they are not atrocious," he wrote to his sister, "and do not be troubled about us but about the good of the state and of the Revolution, which they do not understand."

Not only his friends and his family were indignant and distressed at this decision which barred his way. A woman was following his career from afar. Her interest seemed to increase in proportion as he drew away from her. Emilie de Mirabeau still corresponded with Caroline du Saillant. She understood what that fatal vote meant for Mirabeau, and she greatly deplored it. Caroline showed her letter to her

brother, who found it "very good-hearted, with a broad-mindedness
and a thorough reasonableness that I like, that is to say, seasoned with
grace and character."

Caroline had never ceased to hope for a reconciliation between her
brother and Emilie. She profited by the interest Emilie showed on this
occasion to suggest it to her. She spoke of Mirabeau's state of mind
after his set-back. "He is certainly tired," she wrote, "and has said
so to me, but I think I gathered that he would no longer be so heedless
if he retained hope of a direct family. Oh, my friend! how what might
have been for you the subject of such glory and pleasure has become
for you simply a source of disquiet!" She added by way of opening:
"And could nothing alter this decree of fate?"

At times of discouragement and of financial difficulty, Mirabeau became more responsive to the idea of resuming married life, that solution
of lassitude. He gave way to Caroline's urgent advice and at her request dictated her reply to Emilie. "In the torrent that is carrying him
along," his sister wrote, "he is never able, with the best will in the world,
to count with any certainty on an hour to himself. At last I managed
to carry him off to dinner with my daughter and I talked to him."
Mirabeau dictated this statement for Emilie: "She thinks me ambitious;
she is mistaken, at least in the ordinary sense of the word. I have never
been ambitious for administrative posts or gold lace or dignities. I
wanted to prepare, to hasten, perhaps to determine, a great revolution
in human affairs for the benefit of the race; and, helped by the spirit
of the age and by inconceivable circumstances, I have succeeded up to
a certain point, and more than an ordinary mortal, for whom his own
faults and those of other persons had raised so many obstacles, could
have hoped." With the recollection of that distant past, with its passions
and sufferings, a little emotion seemed to awake in him; he revealed to
Emilie more than he need have done of his fundamental ideas and his
motives. "I was so cruelly provoked by the nobles of Provence that it
is very natural to suppose that my conduct was influenced by a certain
spirit of vengeance. That is a mistake. The incapacity and the bad faith
of the government on the one hand, and on the other the imbecility
and the wrong-headedness of the enemies of the Revolution, carried
me more than once farther than I intended, but I never deserted my
principles, even when I was forced to carry them to excess, and I have
always desired to remain at or to return to the golden mean."

He confirmed Emilie's supposition that his failure was a fruit of
Necker's intriguing. With a sincerity touched by emotion, mixed with
a little diplomacy, he continued: "I am approaching the evening of my

life; I am not discouraged, but I am tired. Circumstances have isolated me; I am more eager for peace and quiet than is supposed, and I shall accept it gladly the day I can do so with honour and security. I shall try then, if my fortune is sufficiently restored, to be happy even if just playing skittles. If I have not enough, I think it is difficult to suppose that I could not still secure an embassy, and that will be an honourable and pleasant retirement for me. But one must begin by doing one's job and completing it, and I am convinced that it would be to desert it and not to finish it to enter the Council with men with whom it has become impossible to do any good." The pleasant and honourable retirement was no more than a passing aspiration, born of great fatigue. In any case, he retracted it at once. He still had his fighting spirit. And in the fight his personal fate was associated with the triumph of a cause: "The decree about ministers must be revoked. It will be revoked or the Revolution will never be consolidated."

8

On November 14 Necker presented once more to the Assembly what Mirabeau called a crude conjuring trick. After admitting the melancholy fact that he must at all costs secure at once an extraordinary subsidy of one hundred and seventy millions, he returned to his old expedient, the transformation of the Caisse d'Escompte into a national bank. He called for "the full and entire guarantee of the nation" for the restoration of the Caisse d'Escompte, which was in a critical situation. In justification of this demand he recalled the services it had rendered and the advances it had made, totalling one hundred and fifty-six millions. This, wrote the *Courrier de Provence*, was "a palliative that will prolong the malady."

"No, gentlemen, we are no longer in the times of political miracles," exclaimed Mirabeau contemptuously from the tribune. He pitilessly dissected Necker's memorandum, article by article. "What painful efforts, what uncertain and contradictory measures for giving the Caisse d'Escompte a new existence, for rejuvenating a sullied and discredited virgin!" he exclaimed. "Say no more about its services—it is by them that our public faith has been violated, it is by them that our exchange, since I predicted its continual fall, has worsened every day to a degree which nobody would have dared to envisage!"

The close argument furnished by Clavière, the mordant irony, and the vehemence of Mirabeau's speech produced such an effect on the Assembly that the speech was ordered to be printed. But the Caisse d'Escompte had eloquent defenders in the Assembly, like Lavoisier, a co-opted deputy on its council, and Dupont de Nemours, who still saw in it the creation of his master Turgot. The Assembly appointed a commission to study the position of the Caisse d'Escompte.

When the question came again before the Assembly on December 19, Necker's idea of utilizing the Caisse d'Escompte was adopted, but its transformation into a national bank was refused. At the same time the Assembly decreed the sale of crown and church properties. Mirabeau wrote that day to La Marck of "the unspeakable stupidity of the Minister of Finance, who makes you decree the sale of four hundred millions of church estates, in the present circumstances, to buttress the Caisse d'Escompte and postpone bankruptcy for a few weeks. A strange destiny," he concluded, "that of a mortal who advances to glory on the crutches of famine and paper money!"

9

"Monsieur," the king's brother, the Comte de Provence, although troubled by his stoutness and his heavy gait, had a more royal manner than Louis XVI. He had intellectual interests that did not appeal to the king. A prodigious memory that enabled him to retain long passages he had read and to make happy quotations had given him the reputation of a well-read man. He wrote verses which he published anonymously in the *Mercure*. He sought especially the society of men of intelligence and of erudition. His pedantic airs repelled the queen. His scepticism, his indolence, and his habitual glumness made him few friends. But he was the only Bourbon "indicated not only by nature but by necessity," said Mirabeau in a memorandum, "as able to form a link between the king and the nation. Let the king announce in good faith his adhesion to the Revolution, on the one condition that he is its leader and its moderator, and let him oppose to the egoism of his ministers a representative of his dispersed family: at once we shall see confidence or at least hope reborn, the popularity of the monarchy restored, and the parties who in good faith do not want to see the French empire in dissolution or the scene for half-a-century of the sanguinary struggles of ambitious nobodies or insensate demagogues rally round a Bourbon who has become the king's counsellor and the chief of the friends of the royal authority." But this advice gained no hearing.

"Nothing very striking here except the aggravation of the symptoms of dissolution," he wrote to La Marck, who was in the Netherlands. Belgium had risen against the domination of the emperor. Joseph II, full of the ideas of the age, wanted to introduce reforms into Brabant, and these ran counter to the people's attachment to their old customs and traditions. This revolution imposed from above was replied to by a rising of aristocratic patriots led by a lawyer, van der Noot, whom the people of Brabant called the Belgian Franklin. The machinery of the Austrian administration, under the impulsion of that authoritarian democrat the emperor, continued to grind down the popular resistance by terrorist methods. Mirabeau had long expected to see an independent Belgium, and he saw with joy the constitution of a Belgian Republic. Public opinion in France, more and more hostile to the court of Vienna, was following events with impassioned interest. Camille Desmoulins started a periodical, *Révolution de France et de Brabant*, in which he brought his incendiary wit and eloquence to the support of the Belgian rebels.

La Marck was in a painful dilemma. He was Belgian at heart and deeply attached to the customs of the country. He was an aristocrat and traditionalist by instinct. But he was also devoted to the Habsburgs, and it was hard for him to belie his loyalty to them. A personal motive contributed to his decision. His "beloved sister," the Duchesse d'Ussel, was the victim of unjust persecution by the Austrian government. La Marck placed himself at the disposal of the revolutionary government.

Mirabeau "quite naturally" approved of the Belgian revolution. He corresponded regularly with La Marck and kept him informed of his relations with the Comte de Provence. "At the Luxembourg" [the residence of Monsieur], he wrote, "they are afraid of being afraid. At the Tuileries the king has settled in; the queen maintains her aloofness. The General [Lafayette] is the most cheerful stickler and sidler in the world. M. Necker knows neither what he can do nor what he wants to do nor what he ought to do. What a collection of dupes! What a noble game of goose!" The Assembly alone maintained its prestige. "Toulon, which had refused to obey Saint-Priest's letter, at once obeyed our decree. So the great colossus amounts to something, and so long as that illusion is fostered it will produce welcome realities."

An inquiry had been opened into the events of October 5. In the calm that had followed the king's entry into Paris, a reaction had set in. To safeguard future order, the punishment of the ringleaders was demanded. A grave complication arose. Brissot announced triumphantly one evening, in the course of a dinner, to Dumont: "Now! You are always laughing at our committee of inquiry and our discoveries of plots, but this time you will laugh no longer. We hold all the threads of a conspiracy."

Next day, December 26, Mirabeau wrote to La Marck: "M. de Favras was arrested, with his wife, on the night of December 24–25, and at once Paris was full of the news that he had proposed to raise thirty thousand men to assassinate M. de Lafayette and the mayor and to cut off the food supply of the capital; and that Monsieur was at the head of the conspiracy."

Thomas de Mahy, Marquis de Favras, married to a German princess of Anhalt-Schomburg, was one of those eccentric beings who are brought to the fore in disturbed times. He was an ardent royalist, disgusted with the state of affairs, credulous, talkative, and burning to take action; he was convinced that the daring of a single individual could divert the course of events, and he dreamed of his own providential intervention in the country's destinies. To satisfy his taste for adventure he thought of organizing an expedition to Brabant. The Duc de Biron put him into touch with Mirabeau, to whom, according to him, he communicated his project of "going to Brabant to assist the revolution." Mirabeau later deposed in the proceedings that Biron had presented Favras to him as a man "with great knowledge of financial matters," and that he had seen him "on different occasions with regard to certain financial plans" in the presence of other persons. He does not seem, in any case, to have taken Favras seriously.

Favras had talked indiscreetly to *agents provocateurs,* and they had denounced the plot. A sheet printed and sold in Paris accused Monsieur of having been at its head. A letter from Mirabeau, the authenticity of which is not definitely established, seems to have reference to this obscure affair. "Do, do calm down an impatience that will wreck everything. It is precisely because your birth placed you so near the throne that it is difficult for you to make the one step that separates you from it. We are neither in the Orient nor in Russia to be able to take things so lightly. Nobody in France would submit to a palace revolution."

Everything about this melancholy affair was deliberately buried in mystery. Victim of his illusions, Favras may also have been the victim of promises that were not kept and of responsibilities eluded. From the admissions of Favras, Talon collected details of the personal cooperation of Monsieur. Favras, said Talon, had not been ready to content himself with direct instructions from Monsieur; he had demanded the participation of the queen herself, and he was promised that the queen would walk on the terrace on a given day and speak certain words agreed on in advance. Talon, who visited Favras in prison, claimed to have deterred him from making his admissions public: "Doesn't it occur to you that a thousand avenging arms will be raised all over Europe to punish you for having directed to the heads of Monsieur and the queen the sword that menaces you?" Overcome by that appeal to his chivalry, and intimidated by threats, Favras gave way after what Talon called three hours of struggle and promised silence. As a good policeman, Talon had taken away the compromising document. A document was, in fact, in his possession, and he showed it one day to La Marck and to Mercy-Argenteau. La Marck wrote to the queen: "The part of this document which might compromise Your Majesty is only the result of a perfidious machination, but it is nonetheless certain that this document, which has a sort of authenticity, deserves serious attention in the existing circumstances."

Favras was executed in February 1790; he had hoped to the last to be reprieved. He took his secret with him into the tomb. Dumont, always ready to speak ill of his friend—and writing at a time when Mirabeau was no longer there to contradict him—remarked that Mirabeau's praises "of Favras' intrepidity in his last interrogation made me suspect that his death had been no less a relief to his friends than to his enemies."

But at the moment when the Favras plot had been exposed and Monsieur accused of having fomented it, Mirabeau preserved the calmness of an innocent man, or at least of one who was sure of not being compromised. The situation was grave. Mirabeau stepped immediately into the breach to save the Comte de Provence and induced his distracted highness to defend himself by going over to the attack. "Monsieur," Mirabeau wrote to La Marck, "sent for M. de Lafayette and said to him in front of several people: 'M. de Lafayette, this sheet is being distributed in Paris. You have great credit in Paris, M. de Lafayette, and I have no doubt that you are doing something to destroy a slander by which the evil-minded will say that you are profiting. I am going this evening to give an explanation to the municipality of Paris; I hope you will be there.' "

Mirabeau did not content himself with advising that bold step; he drew up the letter in which the Comte de Provence informed the president of the National Assembly of his intentions; he also drew up the letter inviting the municipality to an extraordinary meeting and prepared a speech for the count. All these documents, in his handwriting, are extant among the papers which La Marck preserved.

Mirabeau made the king's brother speak as a simple citizen addressing his "fellow-citizens." Monsieur denied having had political relations with Favras, who had been indicated to him as a man who could help him to secure a loan to pay his debts. But Mirabeau did not confine himself to a simple denial. He made Monsieur recall his liberal past, which rendered incredible his participation in so base a crime. "Since the day when, in the second assembly of notables, I declared my position on the fundamental question which then divided men's minds," said the Comte de Provence in the speech prepared for him by Mirabeau, "I have not ceased to believe that a revolution was ready; that the king, because of his intentions, his virtues, and his supreme rank, should be its head, since it could not be of advantage to the nation without being equally so to the monarch; and finally that the royal authority is the rampart of the national liberty and the national liberty the basis of the royal authority." It was no longer a justification but a whole programme, having in view the part which Mirabeau wanted Monsieur to play. Lafayette, whose popularity had been enormously increased by the revelation of the plot, had no great liking for this intervention, which he knew to have been advised by Mirabeau and which he called "one long platitude."

But Mirabeau's hold over the Comte de Provence did not last long. "He has the purity of a child, but he has the weakness of one, and it is extremely difficult to make him understand that if he would let himself be guided just for twenty-four hours he would be a second Duc d' Orléans," wrote Mirabeau to La Marck. Mirabeau soon realized that he could not count on the credit of the king's brother at court. "The queen treats Monsieur as a little chicken to be caressed through the bars of a coop but carefully kept in it, and he puts up with that treatment."

But Mirabeau knew of no one else to remedy a situation which he saw deteriorating almost every day. "Never has our government been more incapable," he wrote to his absent friend. "The moment for the reconstruction of the political system of Europe has at last arrived. My plan is ready in every detail and has at least the merit of a universal and durable pacification and of extreme simplicity. But they have neither the capacity to conceive it nor, above all, the good faith to listen to it."

He finally induced Monsieur to present to the king at the beginning of January 1790 a memorial in which he asked that he might be "the nominal pilot of a new crew without which the vessel can no longer sail." A copy of this memorial was found among Lafayette's papers. A draft of an agreement to be negotiated through the intermediary of the Comte de Provence between the king and Mirabeau accompanied this document. The whole probably came into Lafayette's hands through one of the police officers in his pay, perhaps Talon, who was indefatigable in double-dealing.

Mirabeau began to regain hope of being able to set his personal affairs in order at the same time as the affairs of the state. The agreement with the king was conceived on the same lines as the agreement proposed some months earlier by Lafayette. The king was to promise Mirabeau an embassy and to give him meanwhile a salary of fifty thousand livres a month, for four months at least, while Mirabeau undertook to aid the king with his intelligence, his ability, and his eloquence in whatever Monsieur considered of service to the state and to the king's interest; and "in the event of M. de Mirabeau not being convinced of the soundness of the reasons which may be given him, he would abstain from speaking about that subject." The agreement remained a mere proposal. "What they want," wrote Mirabeau to La Marck, "is amphibious beings with the talent of a man and the soul of a lackey."

Mirabeau was being gradually worn out. His first experience of relations with the court thoroughly disheartened him. He described his disgust to La Marck with a vehemence that was painful for a courtier to hear. "At court, oh! what balls of cotton! what groping! what pusillanimity! what indifference! what a grotesque assemblage of old ideas and new projects, of petty repugnances and childish desires, of wills and nills, of abortive loves and hates! . . . And when they have not followed any of my advice, or profited by any of my conquests, or taken advantage of any of my operations, they weep for themselves and say that I have done nothing to alter their position and that they cannot count much on me."

His first attempt at collaboration with the court to save the monarchy came to an end about January in this deep discouragement. He had realized the uselessness of his efforts. "Always reduced," he wrote, "to giving advice, never able to take action, I shall probably have Cassandra's fate—I shall always give true predictions and shall never be believed."

10

"In enslaved countries all the peoples are treated by their masters as by enemies, all have compared their rights and their situation, all have been weighing their shackles," wrote the *Courrier de Provence*. "Watch that restless movement in all Europe. A subterranean murmur announces an earthquake, and it will perhaps be by the horrible light of a universal conflagration that the peoples will march to freedom." Mirabeau was persuaded of the influence of the French Revolution on every country in Europe. "I see that heads are fermenting in your Germany," he wrote to Mauvillon, "and I know well that if a spark falls on the combustible matter it will be a coal fire and not one of straw as elsewhere." He was less sure, however, than so many idealists of his time that under the revolutionary impact all the old political systems of Europe would crumble, and he knew Germany better than they did, for he added: "But although you may be more advanced educationally, you are not so ripe as we, who, indeed, were ourselves scarcely ripe. You are not, I say, because emotions have their roots among you in the head, and the heads have been used from time immemorial to slavery; the explosion will take place among you much later than in a nation in which everything is dramatic and momentary and in which the same quarter of an hour may offer the heroism of liberty and the idolatry of servitude."

His personal disappointment, the bitterness of his experience, and the discouragement he suffered from the very character of the nation with its rapid oscillation between extremes, did not destroy his confidence in the vital forces of his country.

Toward the end of that first year of the Revolution, a "memorable year" marked by "great and immortal events," he summed up in a letter to Mauvillon his great anxieties and his still greater hopes: "The monarchy is in danger more because of the failure to govern than because of conspiracies. If no pilot presents himself, the vessel will probably run aground. If, on the contrary, the force of events compels the summoning of a man with a head and gives the courage to overcome all the false human valuations and the petty jealousy that continually oppose it, you have no idea how easy it will be to set the ship of state afloat. The resources of this country, the very mobility of this nation, which is its capital vice, offer so many expedients and facilities that in France you never can tell."

⊭ XVIII ⊯

The Art of Daring

"IF I were to write a book on the military art, the chapter on Enthusiasm would not be the least extensive," we read in a fragment found among Mirabeau's papers. "If I were to write a treatise on politics, I should deal thoroughly with the Art of Daring, which is no less necessary for the success of civil enterprises than for that of military operations—and also for giving the measure of the author of the enterprise; for it is the wider or narrower limits of the possible that determine the differences between men. In reading history I note that almost all the mistakes made by leaders of parties come from half-hearted adherence to principles and failure to go straight ahead. Revolt is half-hearted, loyalty is half-hearted; men do not dare either to leave their duties entirely unfulfilled, or to sacrifice their passions entirely to them. The first steps are hesitating and diffident, whereas they should be the firmest; men leave open a way of retreat, they try different ways of arriving at their end. The very dodges that are the favourite resource of commonplace politicians are a result of that timidity of mind or heart; they negotiate to disguise their aims, to attract partisans, to make a show of moderation, whereas they should act and follow the shortest route to their goal. What happens always? That the one who sets out to deceive is deceived; the critical moment is missed, and no one has been persuaded. Just as extremes are unreasonable in the ordinary conduct of life, so half-measures are insufficient in critical events; and the most dangerous as well as the most inconsistent course is to divest oneself of only half of one's prejudices. But there are almost as few resolute evil-doers as resolutely upright men; most men lack character."

This art of daring which Mirabeau praised was eminently his own. He always acted, never lost sight of his goal. But in those months of calm filled with a secret malaise which followed the violent agitation of October 5 and 6, 1789, everyone around him seemed to grow petty. "Lafayette plots little revolutions for us, Montmorin little intrigues, the Tuileries and the Luxembourg outdo each other in turn in poltroonery, indifference, and fickleness," he reported to La Marck. "Never did more invisible animalcules try to play a greater drama on a vaster stage. They are mites imitating the combats of giants."

It is in his letters to La Marck that he reveals his whole self, with his impatience and his enthusiasm, his aspirations and his repugnances; he knew that if he was not always approved he would always be understood. He needed someone in whom to confide entirely and was conscious of the value of this friendship to him. In summing up his personal experience of "this memorable year," he wrote to La Marck that among the great and immortal events "a very fugitive detail for everybody else and for you yourself will never be forgotten by me, the circumstance that brought us closer together and began an association, based on relations of courage and character, which has been cemented by esteem, and which, I at all events am sure, will become the most imperishable and the most devoted friendship."

To this impetuous outburst of affection La Marck replied in his measured way, covering a feeling no less deep and sincere than Mirabeau's: "I am honoured in my own eyes by having been able to come closer to you and to render homage to your rare and often unappreciated qualities. The friendship that attaches me to you finds a further attraction in the justice I do you, and my own self-esteem is gratified by the superiority, so to speak, which I acquire over those who have not been able to appreciate you or who have refused to; for there is envy wherever there are men, and it is never more exercised than in regard to men of a higher type."

The year 1790 opened for Mirabeau in lassitude and disillusion. "What are we really doing?" he wrote. "We are playing blind man's bluff, and the result of the game seems to me entirely undesirable. As for me, I am keeping still as far as I can, because I have often said to myself that a man walking at night whose torch goes out must stop until light returns." He did not stay long, however, in that frame of mind, so contrary to his temperament and his convictions. Indeed, he added at once: "But you know that immobility can only be relative, and that in our state of things it is impossible not to be compromised by the very faculty of existence."

2

"What are all these efforts of pygmies straining to make abortive the finest and greatest of revolutions, the one that will infallibly change the face of the globe and the destiny of the human race!" Mirabeau's great voice thundered from the tribune of the Assembly. The question under debate was the refusal of the Chambres des Vacations of Rennes to register the decree suspending the *parlements*. Mirabeau nursed an old grudge against the *parlements;* he had never been misled by their attitude of opposition to absolutism. "You of the privileged class," he thundered, "stop pretending to be representatives of the provinces of which you are the oppressors. Stop talking of their liberties while you enchain them and enslave them."

But it was late, and the deputies were tired and anxious to get home for dinner. The opposition secured an adjournment till the next day. Mirabeau had been speaking for an hour and a half and was bathed in perspiration. He went out into a cold January evening. "I was caught by a gust of wind," he wrote to La Marck, "which that very evening gave me a terribly inflamed left eye. Next day I did not want to do anything, but I had a sick friend; I went out although I could not open my eyes and had been unable to get a moment's respite from the most intolerable pain." Finally he sent for the doctor, who decided to bleed him at once. But he was "quite determined not to lose the battle of the Bretons." In spite of his doctor, who "moved heaven and earth" to dissuade him, he went to the Assembly, with his eyes bandaged. He kept up the battle until eight o'clock in the evening, speaking several times, and with spasms of pain shaking him. He succeeded in getting a majority. The magistrates of the Rennes *parlement* were excluded from all official civil activities. The victory cost Mirabeau dearly. "I went home on Monday," he wrote to La Marck, "absolutely done up; leeches, blisters, the devil. Yesterday was frightful." And he commented in resignation: "Will power can do anything against pain, but it cannot cure a local trouble—indeed, it aggravates it."

At the same sitting of the Assembly a foreigner submitted the first application for naturalization. "The applause that followed this request," wrote the *Courrier de Provence*, "seemed to announce that France would give asylum to all the friends of freedom." Mirabeau saw his country becoming, by its adoption of foreigners, the benefactress of Europe; and he made his paper say: "A good naturalization law will be worth more than the conquest of several provinces."

"The Revolution is too far advanced for any serious setback," La Marck had written to Mirabeau. "That is true," Mirabeau replied, "in the sense that systematic despotism will not return in peace. It is not true in the sense that the French monarchy will remain as it is and that its rule will be free and active under a reasonable and compact constitution. It is possible (though doubtful) that counter-revolution by force has been renounced. It is certain that it is being prepared by negotiation." He remained suspicious and ready to pursue the counter-revolution along all its tortuous paths.

He devoted all his energies to the troubles at Marseille, though he had not fully recovered and the terrible attack had left him very much afraid of a relapse. But he had not learned, and never did learn, to spare himself. He explained to La Marck the reasons for his persistence: "(1) Because the counter-revolution is at work there; (2) because what is at issue is the enslavement or liberation of Provence for all time; (3) because this affair has become my affair." He had prepared, with Pellenc's assistance, so complete a statement that his speech when printed made a pamphlet of ninety-one pages. This immense labour was finished scarcely half an hour before he went to the tribune. He spoke for three hours. He described Marseille as "the first city in the kingdom to manifest the desire for a successful revolution; the first to arm in resistance both to its oppressors and to the brigands that might threaten its peace. But only a few months later a single judge in a single case has made of a generous and a free city a city trembling and desolate." After a long list of the various counts against the provost, Mirabeau concluded: "Whether innocent or guilty, whether the direct agent of his oppressive administration or the passive instrument of those who instruct him, what do I care? I separate his case here from a greater one. It is no longer one more individual that we have to prosecute; what we have to do is to save the friends of freedom at Marseille. What we have to assure is the success of the revolution."

He triumphed in spite of his exhausted condition. He wrote to La Marck in the course of the fierce battle he had been fighting: "We have to show to all these myrmidons that in spite of their united efforts, in spite of the aristocratic party of Marseille with an army behind it, in spite of Lafayette's cabal and the rage of the right wing in the Assembly, and of the activity of the ministers, who have brought to bear all their means of corruption, the National Assembly does its duty on important occasions, so that my intervention is never pointless."

3

The chief guilt for the financial crisis, in Mirabeau's view, was Necker's. In his letters to La Marck he gave expression to all his bitterness against him: "If M. Necker is there for another month, nobody in Paris will know what a crown piece looks like . . . and you will see the awful results of the sublime invention of paper money."

Necker himself felt his popularity waning; he was alarmed at the influence Mirabeau had gained over Monsieur, and he tried to gain the friendship of Lafayette, who also felt that his popularity was vanishing. In the fear of isolation and the fear of Mirabeau, Necker and Lafayette joined forces. The Swedish ambassador, Necker's son-in-law, reported to his government: "Monsieur, who had engaged in a little intrigue with M. de Mirabeau in order to enter the Council and to make himself the head of the popular party, has been cleverly thrust aside. M. Necker and M. de Lafayette, now fairly closely associated, may thus be regarded as the two sole departments of the government."

The two worked upon the king in concert, trying to rouse him from his lethargy. Necker succeeded in persuading the king that he could dissipate suspicion by a solemn act of adherence to the Revolution. Mirabeau had always advocated that adherence and felt rather nettled at its accomplishment independently of him.

On February 4 the king came to the Assembly. At that solemn moment Louis XVI seemed to commit himself entirely to the Revolution. His declarations, ably drafted by Necker, left no room for doubt. "Time will reform such defects as may remain in the collection of laws that has been the work of this Assembly, but every scheme tending to undermine the principles of the constitution itself, every plot that may aim at overthrowing them or weakening their beneficent influence, would serve only to introduce in our midst the frightful evils of discord." The king entered into this solemn engagement before the Assembly: "I shall therefore defend and shall maintain the constitutional liberty whose principles the general wish, in accord with my own, has consecrated. I shall do more and, in concert with the queen, who shares all my feelings, I shall in good time prepare my son's heart for the new order of things which circumstances have brought about."

The left wing broke into applause. The moderates were taken by surprise and almost embarrassed. There was consternation in the ranks of the intransigent partisans of absolute monarchy. The sensation created by the king's strong and precise declarations was weakened by the excessively long speech that followed, and by his insistence on the necessity of maintaining the honorific distinctions of the nobility. But the fervent monarchists realized only that the king was coming to terms with the Revolution.

The Vicomte de Mirabeau, always prompt in manifesting in public his violent opposition to his brother's ideas, came to the tribune and there, in a theatrical gesture, broke his sword, exclaiming: "Since the king renounces his kingdom, a gentleman no longer needs a sword to defend it."

There was wild enthusiasm in Paris. A new oath of fidelity to the nation, the law, and the king, "and of obedience to the constitution decreed by the Assembly," was taken in all the district assemblies, following the National Assembly itself. The oath was taken in the public squares; university students went through the district of Saint-Etienne-du-Mont, stopping from place to place to repeat its solemn words. Next day a *Te Deum* was chanted at Notre Dame in the presence of the National Assembly. That evening all Paris was brilliantly illuminated.

Mirabeau did not share this general enthusiasm. "You have seen the king's action, his strange speech, the oath, the pantomime, and what all these things really amount to," he wrote to La Marck. He wanted this adherence of the king to the Revolution to be without reservation. He was afraid of some trickery that would lull the nation into a false sense of security. He communicated his doubts to La Marck: "We have come to the most critical moment of the Revolution, the time when we must defend ourselves against the nation's and our own impatience and lassitude, and when our tendency to emotionalism is being taken advantage of to make of each event, great or small, the occasion for reinforcing the executive power and giving it all the instruments necessary for preventing the completion of the constitution."

Once more his vision was accurate.

The *jacqueries*, or peasant risings, that occurred in Brittany and in the southwest alarmed the Assembly. The committee on the constitution presented a proposed decree aiming at "restoring order and peace in the different parts of the empire and assuring the receipt of taxes." A deputy of the right, Cazalès, profited by it to paint a black picture of the state of the country and to propose that the king should be invested for three months with unlimited executive power.

Mirabeau vehemently protested: "Dictatorship! In a country of twenty-four million souls, the dictatorship of a single person! In a country working at its constitution, a country whose representatives are met together, the dictatorship of a single person! Dictatorship is beyond the strength of any one person, whatever his character, his virtues, his talent, his genius. . . . Read, read these lines of blood in the letters from Joseph II to General Alton: 'We must take no account of a few drops of blood more or less when it is a question of pacification.' That is the code of dictators; that is what has been unblushingly proposed."

4

"Interfere with the ideas and the habits of an individual who has devoted himself to a certain profession, compel him to do what he has never done, what the blind fear of injuring his fortune prevents him from attempting, and he will exclaim that the whole of society is being overturned. . . . He wants to be rich and then, if possible, free, but let him imagine that his interests are being compromised and he will prefer despotism. That is why men who generalize their own ideas seem to be at war with the human race."

Mirabeau, speaking at the Jacobin Club, was attacking the slave trade. He was one of the founders of the Société des Amis des Noirs, founded in February 1788 and associated with the British Society for the Abolition of the Slave Trade.

Mirabeau had given hospitality in his paper to this Société, of which Brissot had been the inspirer. After his election to the States General he remained actively devoted to the cause of the Negroes, although the traders of Marseille, as of every important seaport trading with the colonies, vehemently protested against the abolition of the slave trade as ruinous to the colonies and to French commerce.

The bitterest opponents of abolition were the colonial capitalists, united for the defence of their interests in a society known as the Massaic Club. Before the opening of the States General one of the representatives of the Massaic Club had asked the king to prohibit the meetings of the Société des Amis des Noirs. "Have these poor Blacks, then, friends in France?" asked Louis XVI, astonished. "So much the better. I will not interrupt their labours."

At San Domingo a few thousand whites reigned over four hundred thousand slaves. There was a large mulatto population, mostly free and owning about one-third of the properties. At the sitting of July 3, 1789, twenty elected colonial deputies demanded admission. Mirabeau challenged the number, which had been arbitrarily fixed. The colonists claimed representation according to the population of the island, but he asked why, in that case, there were no coloured deputies among them. "If the colonists want to regard the Negroes as men, let them enfranchise them. Otherwise we shall point out to them that in France, in proportioning the number of deputies to the population, we have not taken into consideration the number of our horses and mules."

The proclamation of the rights of man aroused magnificent hopes in the colonies. In October 1789 a deputation of coloured men owning land in the French colonies claimed from the Assembly "these imprescriptible rights based on nature and on the social contract." The colonists tried to prevent the Assembly from considering the question. They redoubled their vigilance in the colonies. They repressed uprisings in Martinique and San Domingo and brought about the arrest of a magistrate who had dared to say that Negro slavery was irreconcilable with natural law.

Successive deputations of shipbuilders declared to the Assembly that to interfere with slavery would mean losing the colonies, and that that would be the loss of the whole fortune of France at a moment when she was on the verge of bankruptcy.

The colonists saw in Mirabeau the gravest threat to their interests. One day one of the deputies from San Domingo had a lively altercation with him and proposed to him to settle the matter outside the Assembly. Some prelates intervened. The fiery deputy exclaimed: "Nay, gentlemen, spare yourselves all this trouble; I will answer for it that he has no intention of coming out." Mirabeau did in fact refuse every provocation to a duel. He noted them and promised to take them up after the end of the Assembly. "It is not right," he said one day, "that I should expose a man of intelligence like myself to a fool like him." "And, strange to say," remarked Mme. de Staël, "even in France this conduct did not injure him; it did not even make his courage suspect. There was something so martial about his spirit, so bold about his ways, that it was impossible to accuse such a man of fear."

Indifferent alike to threats and pressure from the colonists, Mirabeau imperturbably pursued his campaign. In the autumn of 1789 Thomas Clarkson visited the Société des Amis des Noirs. He gave Mirabeau an engraving representing a section of a slave ship, which Mirabeau kept constantly before him. He was haunted by the terrible lot of these victims of human cupidity. In the one year 1788, 29,506 Negroes were sent from the shores of Africa to San Domingo. The Negroes died rapidly in the hot and unhealthy climate, and each year new cargoes of human beings were delivered to destruction.

Mirabeau saw that it was necessary to act in accord with England. At the beginning of 1790 he wrote to Wilberforce, to enlist Pitt's cooperation. But circumstances compelled him to act before Wilberforce could reply. The Assembly, which had long hesitated to approach so thorny a problem, decided to refer it to a colonial committee. Barnave, who was *rapporteur* of the committee, was not the sort of man who might have been expected to defend the slave trade. But he was an intimate friend of the Lameths, and a brother-in-law of Charles de Lameth was owner of one of the biggest plantations in San Domingo. On this question Barnave took up a position that threw a shadow over his reputation.

Mirabeau wanted to intervene before Barnave reported, but the Assembly adjourned the discussion. He decided, therefore, to speak to the Jacobin Club. Among his papers is a speech prepared for the Assembly. The affirmation that the traffic was not carried on in an inhumane way was belied, he said, by precise figures. Great Britain, for example, exported annually more than a hundred thousand Negroes, of whom at least one-fifth perished on the way. "Whence comes this terrible mortality?" He showed Clarkson's engraving, with the inhuman conditions between decks, the crowding, the lack of air. "And this traffic is not inhuman! Each slave ship carries a stock of poison; it is useful in revolts. With the poison the crew rids itself of the slave who is difficult to control. You shudder, but the fact is certain; it is one of the necessities of the traffic. And this traffic is not inhuman!"

He ended with the proposal that "His Majesty shall be petitioned to communicate to the King of Great Britain the desire of the National Assembly to come to an agreement with the British legislature to carry out in a peaceful and durable manner the entire abolition of the Negro slave trade." The speech, delivered to the Jacobin Club virtually as prepared for the Assembly, had immense success. Dumont, who this time did not boast of writing the speech, was impressed by the poignant description, but he added maliciously: "Impatient to receive applause, Mirabeau read this speech to the Jacobins, where it produced so great an effect that all those interested in the slave trade made every effort to prevent the subject from being discussed in the Assembly. They were afraid that Mirabeau's speech would cause the abolition of the slave trade by a decree passed in enthusiasm."

Some days later Mirabeau tried in vain to oppose Barnave's report. Barnave secured the passing of a decree declaring that the colonies were not subject to the French constitution, leaving to the colonies the initiative to establish their own constitution, and passing in silence over the thorny question of the enfranchisement of the mulattoes.

Mirabeau tried several times to open a debate in the Assembly on the Negro problem, but prejudices and interests always united to bar his path. Not until May 1791 did the Assembly, against Barnave's advice, confer civic rights on Negroes born of free parents. But Mirabeau was no longer there to see the partial triumph of a cause which he had passionately pleaded.

5

One day Mirabeau was at a bookseller's with a friend who had just had a quarrel with a third person whom he had called "as stupid as this morning's Assembly."

"This morning's?" asked Mirabeau. "Why put a date?"

He now adopted this tone of contemptuous irony toward the Assembly. He used it also against the man whom he regarded as both the chief obstacle to his ambitions and the author of the financial troubles of the kingdom. He urged the Assembly to call for a report from Necker: "All we know is that we have confidence in the minister and that all is going badly: we are sleeping only because one can sleep at the foot of Vesuvius. There is a saying which I have never forgotten and the application of which I leave to you: Caligula's horse was consul, and that astonishes us only because we were not there to see."

He took little further interest in the legislative work of the Assembly; his interventions became briefer and fewer. During March 1790 he spoke only three times apart from the Marseille affair, and very briefly. Only a great occasion would break his silence.

On April 13 Dom Gerle proposed that Roman Catholicism should be decreed the national religion. The moment was well chosen. The Assembly was discussing the conditions of the sale of church properties and preparing the civil constitution of the clergy. The motion might well pass by inadvertence or through fear of giving offence to great masses of the faithful.

There was a stormy debate. The Vicomte de Mirabeau swore that he would end his life rather than abandon Dom Gerle's motion. A deputy of the nobles recalled Louis XIV's promise to tolerate Catholic worship alone. "There is no doubt," replied Mirabeau, "that under a reign marked by the revocation of the Edict of Nantes, a reign as to whose quality I will say nothing, all sorts of intolerance found approval; I will observe further that what despots did cannot serve as a model for what should be done by the representatives of a people that wishes to be free. But since in the motion under consideration references to past history have been indulged in, I will make just one. Bear in mind, gentlemen, that from here, from this same tribune from which I am speaking, I can see the window of the palace in which bigots, uniting temporal interests with the most sacred interests of religion, induced a weak king of the French to fire the fatal arquebus that gave the signal for the massacre of Saint Bartholomew."

For a moment, spellbound by his words, his gestures, and his flaming eyes, the Assembly remained silent as though overwhelmed by the vision he had evoked. The applause that then broke out seemed, said a witness, to mark the end of a nightmare.

At the end of the sitting a colleague pointed out to Mirabeau that from the tribune of the Salle du Manège, at the end of the terrace of the Tuileries, he could not see the windows of the Louvre. "Maybe," Mirabeau agreed, "but at that moment I saw them."

Mirabeau remained on the alert against any counter-revolutionary attempts. Some of the deputies had been elected by their constituencies for only a year. The committee on the constitution proposed a decree (1) that the Assembly could not be renewed until the Constitution had been completed, and (2) that qualifications of mandates were annulled so far as regarded the duration of the session in progress. This proposal met with furious opposition from the right wing. The Abbé Maury vehemently urged that the deputies represented their constituencies before they represented the nation, and that in consequence they owed obedience to their constituents.

"I cannot but feel deep indignation," said Mirabeau, replying with equal vehemence, "when I hear malevolent rhetoricians constantly opposing the nation to the National Assembly, as if it were not through the National Assembly that the nation has recognized, recovered, reconquered its rights; as if, surrounded by monuments of our labours, our dangers, our services, we could become suspected by the people or a danger to the liberties of the people; as if the gaze of the two worlds that is fixed upon us, the fanatical rejoicing over a great revolution, the gratitude of so many millions of men, were not a sufficient guarantee of your fidelity, your patriotism, and your virtues!

"One speaker asked how out of simple representations of the constituencies we were suddenly transformed into a national convention. I reply: on the day when, finding the hall that was to receive us closed, bristling with bayonets, we hastened to the first place in which we could gather, to swear to perish rather than allow such an order of things to continue; the deputies of the people formed a national convention when, by an act of truly sacrilegious insanity, despotism tried to prevent them from fulfilling their sacred mission; they formed a national convention to destroy arbitrary power and to defend from all violence the rights of the nation.

"The crimes of despotism, the perils we have countered, the violence we have repressed, these are our titles: our successes have consecrated those titles, the oft-repeated adherence of all parts of the empire has legitimized them, sanctified them. Brought into being by the invincible tocsin of necessity, our national convention is superior to any imitation and to any authority; it owes no account to any but itself, and can be judged only by posterity."

He concluded with these words, which no contemporary could forget: "Gentlemen, you all know the retort of that Roman who, to save the Republic from a great conspiracy, had been compelled to exceed the powers conferred on him by the laws. A captious tribune called on him to swear that he had respected them—hoping by that insidious challenge to face the consul with the alternative of perjury or an embarrassing admission. 'I swear,' the great man said, 'I swear that I saved the Republic.' Gentlemen, I swear that you have saved the commonwealth."

6

"It has been suggested to me that I should come to an understanding with M. de Mirabeau," wrote Lafayette on the day of Favras' execution.

"I said: 'I do not like him, I do not esteem him, I am not afraid of him. I see no reason to seek an understanding with him.' " At that time Mirabeau hoped to be able to make use of Monsieur, and he, in turn, thought that he could do without any help from Lafayette. But a bitter disappointment threw Mirabeau back once more on his more fortunate rival. His private affairs were still in the same disorder. He was living on a small scale and, as usual, was in need of money. At a time when public affairs called for bold action, he saw opportunities irremediably lost.

He learned that relations between Lafayette and Barnave, Du Port, and Lameth had cooled. From the depth of discouragement in which he had lost even the will to fight, he decided toward the end of April to write to Lafayette. "I parted from you," he wrote, "because your associations at the time were not worthy either of you or of me. . . . These motives no longer exist; Barnave, Du Port, Lameth, and the like, are no longer tiring you with their active inaction."

He eloquently painted the perils that threatened the state, and added: "I am forgetting the worst one, the inaction of the one man who could prevent them." To this deliberate inaction he opposed his own desire for action, so lamentably paralysed, and also the repugnance he had had to overcome before speaking to Lafayette in this way. He revealed to Lafayette all his distress: he spoke to him of the "obstacles my enemies incessantly place in my path, either by setting rather long-continued errors in my life against my public conduct, or by tormenting my domestic existence in order to take me away from my work and to rob me of the confidence of those men who know no other virtues than order and economy."

Mirabeau seems to have lost even his magnificent confidence in his future in resigning himself to accept an offer which he had disdainfully refused a few months earlier: "What in other times I disdained would find me less indifferent today, because the political horizon of Europe has entirely changed. I see at this moment at Constantinople the lever of an entirely unrecognized influence. There, perhaps, exist the only means of hastening for France the restoration of her political prestige, almost without the employment of any of her resources."

The observation was in itself entirely accurate; but the fact that he was ready to leave the great theatre in which his country's destinies were at stake, to abandon a position of great power in the Assembly in order to work in a secondary field, shows the deep wound made by his disappointments, the decay of his unutilized powers.

Nothing at all came of Mirabeau's letter to Lafayette. Immured in his suspicion and his vanity, Lafayette was neither responsive to Mirabeau's broad views nor touched by the extent of his confidence. "This move was a stroke of genius," we read in Lafayette's memoirs, "for it gave its author the right to attack the general while keeping him fettered by his delicacy."

7

The ambassador of the court of Vienna was an Austrian subject only in consequence of the treaties of 1714. He bore a French name, Florimond-Claude, Comte de Mercy-Argenteau. He had become naturalized in France, and he retained that status although he remained in the Austrian service. He had risen rapidly in his career. At thirty-five he was already Austrian ambassador at Turin. He had the full confidence of the empress. "To Mercy alone, whom I esteem as my friend and minister, have I opened my too oppressed heart," wrote Maria Theresa. He remained for twenty-four years ambassador at Paris, the most important post for the Viennese court. He was there also in the secret capacity of adviser to Marie Antoinette both as dauphine and queen. In fact, his principal function was to play the difficult part of guardian angel to Maria Theresa's daughter.

He was well equipped for positions demanding extreme prudence and unfailing reserve. In default of imagination, he had the experience of a long career. In default of agility of mind, he had in his favour his professional knowledge, his assiduity, and his familiarity with society. Kaunitz, the Austrian chancellor, admitted that Mercy lacked brilliance, but he appreciated his qualities as a diplomat with wide social experience and "a thorough knowledge of the court and of Paris society."

In spite of his cold and reserved manner and his rather pompous style, Mercy was supple enough to bend to changed circumstances. His devotion to the empress's daughter sometimes served him in place of clear-sightedness. Toward the middle of March, La Marck received at Brussels a letter from Mercy asking him to come immediately to Paris for a talk on matters of the highest importance. La Marck lost no time in returning.

"You are in intimate touch with the Comte de Mirabeau?" asked Mercy.

"Yes," said La Marck.

"The king and queen have felt that in keeping in touch with him you had the intention of being useful to them."

"They have not been mistaken."

"Their Majesties," pursued the ambassador, "have instructed me to ask your opinion as to the present attitude, as it seems to you, of M. de Mirabeau."

La Marck explained to Mercy Mirabeau's devotion to the cause of the monarchy.

Many things had changed since the queen had haughtily declared that she had no expectation of ever being reduced to asking help from Mirabeau. "The king and queen," the ambassador continued, "have decided to call for the services of the Comte de Mirabeau. They leave you to settle the conditions and do not wish to have any relations with the count except through you. You will be their sole intermediary."

He mentioned particularly that the secret must be kept from Necker. "The queen counts particularly on you," he concluded.

"M. le Comte," La Marck replied, "the harm already done is very serious, and I doubt whether Mirabeau himself can repair what he has been allowed to do." He was sceptical as to the result of this belated and secret step; and, having a good acquaintance with the fickleness of court circles, he was afraid of the responsibilities that were being placed on him in the guise of a mark of favour. He consented to be an intermediary in the negotiation only on condition that Mercy himself took part in it and had an interview with Mirabeau. But the prudent ambassador was afraid of compromising himself and asked for time to reflect.

On the day after his arrival in Paris La Marck went to see Mirabeau. He found him even more dissatisfied with the state of things and more discouraged than when he last saw him. "Mirabeau," he wrote later, "felt that every day the work of restoration would become more difficult, even for him, and that the delays would end in making the evil absolutely incurable." But Mirabeau eagerly accepted La Marck's first very discreet overtures.

Mercy succeeded in overcoming his hesitation to meet Mirabeau; or rather, the worsening of the political situation conquered his diplomatic scruples. At the beginning of April 1790 he agreed to the interview suggested by La Marck. It was surrounded by measures that gave it a conspiratorial air. The meeting took place in La Marck's house in the rue du Faubourg Saint-Honoré, the Hôtel Charost. The old house had a second entrance through the garden into the Champs Elysées. Mirabeau came to his friend through this garden door. The ambassador arrived by the main entrance. La Marck's servants were foreigners, mostly Germans, and had no knowledge of the identity of the visitors and but a poor acquaintance with the language in which the conversation was carried on.

At the table of a foreign aristocrat the ambassador of the court of Vienna met the man who in the eyes of so many courts incarnated the French Revolution. As a conservative, Mercy considered that revolution a disastrous event and the prelude to yet more terrible disasters. He seemed to see in Mirabeau a failure who had taken the revolutionary path out of rancour. He could not believe, he told him, "that he would persist in compromising his talents and his genius by favouring such disorders." But, according to La Marck, "his mind was free from the narrow prejudices that would have prevented him from recognizing certain useful consequences of the Revolution." In spite of all their divergences of view, the two men felt a strange reciprocal esteem. Mirabeau realized, as Mercy did, the dangers of the situation and the necessity of removing the royal couple from the excited Parisian mob. The king must be got away from Paris, he declared to the ambassador, though not from France.

But Mirabeau did not know of another fear that haunted the ambassador. Mercy had a better knowledge than he of the influences at work on the royal couple, and he was alarmed at the readiness with which they lent themselves to the most absurd projects, which the *émigrés* were continually putting before them. In vain did he warn the queen against the danger of these chimerical plans. On May 15 he wrote to her: "The Turin projects make one shudder at the levity with which the risk is run of compromising the future of the state, and, I must say frankly, the personal existence of the sovereigns. The proposed move would be stopped at the first step by the cruel disaster of finding the whole royal family seized and at the mercy of a furious populace, whose ferocity is beyond calculation."

He was the more entirely in agreement with the suggestions Mirabeau made because he knew of those with which Turin was pestering the court. Worst of all, he wrote to Marie Antoinette, was the scheme of carrying off the king by force: "Those who dared to attempt it would deserve capital punishment." He took trouble to describe the exact position, knowing the dangerous illusions harboured by the royal couple. "There is absolute lack of stores, arms, munitions—in fine, all that is indispensable to the arming of any body of troops, to rendering it mobile, and to supporting it in the field"—in face of three or four hundred thousand of the national militia "more or less disciplined, but well armed and enthusiastic," cutting off every avenue of escape. "How, in this state of things, could it be possible to carry off the king and the royal family? How can anyone face the thought of the danger the monarch and his august spouse would run if they were stopped en route, and this they certainly would be, before attaining a place of safety? The pen falls from one's hands when one envisages the incalculable results of such a disaster."

About a year later the terrible previsions of Mercy were to be realized with frightful exactitude. Now there might still be time to save the royal couple, though it was late for the step they had embarked on. At the end of the interview with Mirabeau, Mercy deplored "the long delay in having recourse to so eminent a man, who had been allowed to become dangerous when he might have been so useful."

Next day the queen secretly received La Marck in the rooms of her chief lady-in-waiting at the Tuileries. She told him that, jointly with the king, she had decided about two months earlier to approach Mirabeau. Marie Antoinette scarcely realized how precious was the time that was passing, with opportunities missed that would never recur. She admitted to La Marck one of the reasons that had made her hesitate. She asked him "with a certain accent of curiosity and embarrassment whether he thought Mirabeau had had no part at all in the horrors of the 5th and 6th of October." La Marck answered for his friend's innocence, stating that he had passed the greater part of those two days with him. Marie Antoinette expressed pleasure at that reply: "I badly needed to be undeceived on that point; for after the rumours that were current at the time I had felt, I admit, a horror of the Comte de Mirabeau which contributed not a little to retard our decision to approach him."

At that moment the king came in. With his usual brusqueness, which masked the flabbiness and indecision of his character, he asked La Marck whether he thought Mirabeau had the intention and the power to be of service to the court. "It is very late to begin," replied La Marck. "At the opening of the States General the ministers ought to have enlisted in the interest of the king the deputies who were known for their talents."

"Ah," replied the king, "there is nothing to hope for on that point with M. Necker. Everything that is done through Mirabeau must be kept a profound secret from my ministers, and I count on you for that."

"I was horrified by that reply," wrote La Marck. "I could not understand how the king could think of employing such a man as Mirabeau without his ministers' knowledge. But his courtier-like restraint imposed silence on me." It was agreed between him and the royal couple

that Mirabeau should place in writing his ideas on the means of serving
the court, and that La Marck should transmit them to the queen. Marie
Antoinette was so pleased with this arrangement that she was particularly gracious toward her faithful servant.

La Marck had difficulty in dismissing the impression of childishness
and inconsequence left on him by this interview. "I was frightened by
what I had heard," he wrote. What a poor dyke to hold up a revolution
was this secret procedure. But he was careful not to communicate his
fears to Mirabeau. He confined himself to telling him "what the king
and queen thought of his talents." He was surprised and, indeed, disappointed to see how strongly Mirabeau was impressed: "The effect
this overture produced on his self-esteem did not escape me. I saw
this man, who thought himself, and rightly, so high above others, nevertheless influenced by the sort of magic which royal persons can exercise when they show favour."

Though he felt flattered, Mirabeau placed no confidence in the royal
promises. Like La Marck, he kept his doubts to himself. He wrote his
pessimistic letter to Lafayette after the negotiations with the court had
already begun. His scepticism was justified. Weeks passed without anything further happening in regard to the great project. There was no
change in his difficult position. At the beginning of May 1790 La Marck
wrote to him: "The more I think of the troubles that threaten you, the
more I am revolted! Ah, my dear count, it is characteristic of great
men to have contemptible enemies."

8

"It would be repugnant to me to play any part at the present time of
strife and confusion if I were not convinced that the re-establishment
of the legitimate authority of the king is France's first need and the sole
means of saving her," wrote Mirabeau in a memorandum intended for
the court. "But I see so clearly that we are in the midst of anarchy, that
we are sinking further into it every day, I am so indignant at the idea
that I should have contributed to nothing but a vast demolition, and the
fear of seeing another head of the state than the king is so insupportable
to me, that I feel imperiously recalled to affairs at a time when I was
more or less vowed to silence and though I could aspire only to retirement."

Mirabeau's period of discouragement passed as soon as he was consulted. But he was concerned to define his position and to leave no

doubt as to his convictions. "Here, then, is the profession of faith for which the king asked, and this statement will remain forever my declaration or my witness: I undertake to serve with all my influence the true interests of the king; and, in order that this assertion may not appear too vague, I declare that I believe a counter-revolution to be dangerous and criminal, and I consider equally chimerical in France the hope or the project of any sort of government without a leader invested with the power necessary for the application of all the public force to the execution of the law."

After this unequivocal declaration Mirabeau sketched his programme of action in favour of the monarchy: "I need two months to collect, or even, if I may say so, to make my own resources, to prepare men's minds, and to win over to reason the good citizens necessary to the service of the king. My progress will be by invisible stages, but I shall take a step every day. A quack will promise a quick cure and will kill; a true physician observes, acts especially through the regimen, doses, measures, and sometimes cures."

He concluded: "I promise the king loyalty, zeal, activity, energy, and a courage of which people may be far from having any idea. I promise him, finally, everything except success, which never depends on a single person and which it would be a very rash and very blameworthy presumption to guarantee in the terrible malady that is undermining the state and threatening its head."

From the first he reserved to himself great latitude in his activity: "There must never be a partial judgment of my conduct either on an act or on a speech. It is not that I refuse to explain anything, but it is possible to judge only by the total result. It is impossible to save the state each day."

This memorandum was transmitted by La Marck, under seal, to the Comte de Mercy-Argenteau. La Marck, more clear-sighted than the others concerned, did not conceal his scepticism from the ambassador: "I told the Comte de Mercy that, whatever might be my confidence in Mirabeau's great talents, I could not but regard the French monarchy as lost, at all events for a very long time. Nor did I hide from him that I even doubted whether Mirabeau could be of any service at all, in view of the manner in which the king proposed to employ him."

But the king and queen were delighted with Mirabeau's memorandum. When La Marck was next received by the queen at the Tuileries, she repeated to him that the king had no desire to recover his authority to the full extent of the past. To have won over Mirabeau seemed to her so great a diplomatic success, and she was so pleased with herself, that she quickly recovered her old sprightliness, her unthinking high spirits. She kept La Marck more than two hours. She was sparkling with the graciousness that charmed men and with the natural gaiety of which La Marck, as an amiable courtier, said that it "took its source equally in the goodness of her heart and in the sweet roguishness of her mind." She refused to talk of serious matters. The conversation was like a dance among the reefs of the dreadful problems of the moment. "The purpose of my audience had almost been lost sight of," La Marck recorded; "she tried to brush it aside. When I spoke of the Revolution, she became serious and sad, but the moment the conversation turned to other subjects I found again her amiable and gracious humour." No enemy of Marie Antoinette has expressed a severer judgment on her than did this faithful servant in tracing this striking portrait of her levity amid the dangers that surrounded her on all sides.

When the queen sent for La Marck again a few days later, the king was present during the conversation. He repeated to La Marck that Mirabeau's memorandum had given him "entire satisfaction." "He seemed," noted La Marck, "to have even greater confidence in the future than the queen had; he thought it would be easy to set things back on a bearable footing." La Marck described him as asking little for himself personally and as ready to get rid of some of the heavy burdens of absolute power. "He thought that if ministers were in future to have more difficulties and problems, he himself would have less responsibility, and in consequence more tranquillity. The king," he added, "saw in his personal relations with Mirabeau a means of assuring that tranquillity in advance." But when La Marck observed that in his opinion it would be necessary for the relations with Mirabeau to be extended to the ministers, the king changed the subject. All those concerned, even Mercy, the reserved and prudent diplomat, were full of hope, as if the appearance of Mirabeau had suddenly cleared the horizon.

La Marck was the only one to mingle the discordant voice of pessimism with the joyful chorus. He pointed out to Mercy that in reality nothing had changed, that Mirabeau had always defended monarchical principles. "But we shall succeed," Mercy replied, "in forming another and a better ministry; it will come to an understanding with Mirabeau, and things may improve." Big clouds seemed to have been dispersed and the storm to have become distant.

In her lively gratitude to the man who had brought her peace of mind for the moment, the queen inquired of La Marck "as to what would be the best thing to do so that Mirabeau should be satisfied with her and with the king." La Marck admitted to her that his friend was often without the barest necessaries. The most urgent thing, he thought, would be to pay his debts. Mirabeau made a list of them. They totalled two hundred and eight thousand francs. Not even his wedding clothes had yet been paid for. Mirabeau did not dare to hope that he could be freed from so crushing a liability. But the sum seemed a trifle to the ambassador. "When I informed Mercy of the amount of Mirabeau's debts," wrote La Marck, "he said: 'If that is all, the king will do well to settle the whole bill. I will suggest it to the queen.'"

When the king next saw La Marck, he gave him the original list written out by Mirabeau. "You will keep it," he said, "together with these four notes of mine, each of two hundred and fifty thousand. If, as he promises, M. de Mirabeau serves me well, you will give him, at the end of the session of the National Assembly, these notes, for which he will receive a million. Between now and then I will have his debts paid, and you will yourself decide what is the sum I should give him every month to meet his present difficulties." La Marck proposed six thousand francs, with a further three hundred francs for the copyist.

The Archbishop of Toulouse, M. de Fontages, formerly almoner to the queen, was the only person let into the secret apart from Mercy and La Marck. He was authorized to make the payments. Mirabeau "burst into wild exultation," wrote La Marck, "the extravagance of which, I admit, surprised me a little, but which was explained naturally enough, first by the satisfaction of emerging from the penurious and haphazard existence he had led till then, and second by the justified pride at the thought that at last he was being consulted."

In Mirabeau's view there was no inconsistency between his public and his secret activities. As La Marck pointed out to Mercy, Mirabeau had professed the same principles before being retained by the court. He regarded the pecuniary aid given by the king as a homage to his talents and a means of making his ideas triumph. His friends were not alone in exonerating him from any charge of venality. Mme. de Staël, in spite of her resentment against her father's implacable adversary, wrote: "Mirabeau, whether or not he accepted money from the court, was quite determined to make himself master and not the instrument of the court." Even Lafayette gave this homage to his sincerity: "Not for any sum would Mirabeau have sustained an opinion that would have destroyed liberty and dishonoured his spirit."

9

"Above all, let us not mistake the fervid advocacy of principles for their sublimation," remarked Mirabeau in the Assembly on May 3, addressing a warning from the tribune to a man who was later to carry this confusion to an extreme—Robespierre. The young lawyer from Arras at that time played no important part in the Assembly. "Many of his enemies regarded him in 1790 as a virtuous madman," said Gorani in his *Mémoires*. His speeches were laboured, in an old-fashioned literary style, which he elaborated with conscientious zeal as if he were competing at some provincial academy. He provoked ironic smiles more often than indignation among his opponents. The newspapers were fond of mangling his name, hurting him a good deal. Until the time when his name began to strike terror, it appeared in the reports of sittings as Robert-Pierre or Roberspierre or simply as "a member."

By his own admission he was "prostrated by a childish timidity" when approaching the tribune, and "almost paralysed with agitation when he began to speak." Dumont described him as never looking people in the face and blinking distressingly all the time. With his stiff and awkward manners, his affected language, his sing-song voice, and his one and only olive-green coat, he was redolent of the provinces.

Mirabeau, with his ease, the fascination of his eloquence, and his power over the Assembly, was for Robespierre a model as yet far out of reach. One of his first biographers related that he liked to sit near Mirabeau, followed him in streets, and even tried to copy his coiffure, so that the time came when the papers called him "Mirabeau's Ape." "It was Mirabeau," said Gorani, "who first set me watching Robespierre." With his rare psychological gift he discerned in him from the first a dangerous force. "Mirabeau told me in 1790," Gorani added, "that Robespierre was dominated by an incalculable ambition and that he wanted to elbow his way to the throne. Mirabeau was a little afraid of him. 'I defy Robespierre,' he said to me, 'to rob me of my popularity.'" From the first, Robespierre was a man of abstract and absolute principles. He defended the poorest and the humblest, and was the spokesman of the masses, but he spoke of them as a mathematical quantity.

Mirabeau was as hostile to a popular dictatorship as to the abuses of monarchical authority. During a debate on the election of judges Maury had waved in front of the Assembly the spectre of republicanism. "Republics," replied Mirabeau, "are in a sense monarchical; monarchies are in a certain sense republics. There are only two sorts of bad government—despotism and anarchy: I beg your pardon, they are not governments but the negation of governments."

The Marquis de Crillon, chosen by the king to repress the disturbances at Marseille, asked Mirabeau's opinion on the latest events. As soon as the troops had left the town, the people and the National Guard had taken possession of the forts, and a superior officer had been killed. "The people," Mirabeau explained to Crillon, "believed that the leaders of the troops were ill intentioned, the forts provisioned, and the batteries in the forts directed on the town. If that was the reason for their action, they must be charged with panic terror and not with rebellion." It was sufficient, he proceeded, to know the causes that had determined the people's action: "I say to know them, not to judge them; to know them, in order to determine not whether the people were right or wrong, but whether they were loyal, or thought they were. I insist on this point, because history is full of examples of impolitic steps, of violence with no other cause than the mistake of the leaders, a first wrong idea about an event which would have gone no further but which, through their determination to inflict exemplary punishment they turned into a general upheaval." But "account must be taken of the opinion of the enemies of the commonwealth concerning this same event. If they treat it as a revolt, that does not make it a revolt; if they call for troops, if, in the hope of getting troops, of inflicting punishment, they are glad of the excuse of the insurrection at Marseille, the troops must not be sent, there must be no punishment; for the people would see in the punishment inflicted by the law simply the vengeance of their enemies."

Crillon was unable to profit from Mirabeau's advice because the Assembly opposed his appointment as incompatible with his position of deputy. Mirabeau repeated his defence of the municipality of Marseille in answer to a proposal to summon the municipality. "It is too clear," he said, "that there has been great fermentation at Marseille; but you will only increase it by bringing away from the town its only pacific moderators." But he did not content himself with exonerating the municipality. He passed on to a remarkably bold attack: "But what is this balance in which actions of the same nature, inspired by the same circumstances, are weighed so differently? Why should October 5 be innocent and April 30 at Marseille guilty?"

These words created an uproar. "Every word was interrupted by abuse from the right," noted Dumont. Mirabeau stopped for a moment and turned to the most furious of the interruptors. "I am waiting, gentlemen," he said in a honeyed voice, "for the end of these compliments." In the sudden silence he went on quietly to say he knew that he himself was being accused of being the instigator of the disturbances at Marseille by "these people who have never fought me except with the stiletto of calumny; these people who have not been able to turn me for a moment from the true principles; these people who would have condemned me to a silence inspired by contempt if there existed none but men of their own sort. . . . I gave peace at Marseille; I am giving peace to Marseille; I shall continue to give peace to Marseille."

10

Montmorin, Minister of Foreign Affairs, wrote to the president of the Assembly demanding credits for the arming of fourteen ships of the line. "We have to show Europe," he said, "that the establishment of our constitution is far from placing any obstacle in the way of the development of our forces." A very distant event had produced this concern for French rearmament. In the other hemisphere, off the coast of California, the English and the Spaniards were bitterly disputing over fishery rights. An English vessel had been arbitrarily seized by a Spanish officer, and relations between the two countries had been suddenly embittered. War seemed likely. France, bound by a family pact to Spain, might at any moment be asked to come to her aid. An incident entirely remote from the interests of the country threatened to drag it into war, destroying the great work on which, amid terrible internal difficulties, it was engaged.

Montmorin's request, his reminder of old obligations, and the continuation of the traditional foreign policy which he proposed, were heavy with consequences for the future. The Assembly realized this at once. Deputies jumped up from their seats and demanded to speak. The president told them, to their great surprise, that a list of speakers had already been drawn up.

The ministry, in order to make sure of support in the Assembly, had divulged Montmorin's letter the evening before to the deputies favourable to the government, who had then sent in their names as intending to speak in the debate. The Assembly was wildly excited. The deputies who were supposed to have been in the secret were violently taken to task by their colleagues. A quarrel between Barnave and Noailles was settled the same evening by a duel with pistols in the Bois de Boulogne, without serious results.

Barnave and his friends formed the most active opposition to the government's move. This group was known as the Triumvirate—Mirabeau called it the *Triumgueusat*, the Triumvagabondate—and was the subject of a familiar saying: "Du Port thinks, Lameth acts, Barnave speaks." There were in fact two brothers Lameth, both elected by the nobles, who intervened jointly in the Assembly. The four Lameth brothers, born of an ancient Picardy family which proudly traced its origins back to the Crusades, were orphaned at an early age through their father's death on the field of battle and were brought up by their mother, a sister of Marshal de Broglie, who received a pension from the court. It was to the court's protection that they also owed the high rank they gained in the army. But like so many other young nobles of their time, they had taken part in the American War of Independence, from which they had brought back honourable wounds and democratic convictions. Charles de Lameth, who had had the influential position of gentleman-in-waiting to the Comte d'Artois, threw it up when he was elected deputy. He and his younger brother Alexandre, in full agreement in their ideas and both close friends of Barnave and Du Port, formed with them the most advanced section of the Assembly, which grew more and more distrustful of the royal authority. The publication of the Red Book that revealed the grants made by the court to their mother interfered with their popularity for a time, though they hastened to repay the whole of the sums received. The Triumvirate were united also by a common hatred of Mirabeau.

The threat of war brought their group into action. When Dupont de Nemours proposed that the debate should be adjourned for three weeks, Barnave exclaimed that in three weeks France might find herself at war. Charles de Lameth summed up the secret fears of the left wing: "If an army is built up, the malcontents will take refuge in it. The rich people, for it is the rich who make up the number of the malcontents, will employ all their resources for spreading disorder." After this demagogic argumentation he ended with this threat: "But they will not win, for if they have gold we have steel, and we can use it."

Right-wing speakers, including Cazalès, tried to revive the secular hatred of England. Alexandre de Lameth raised a question which Montmorin had not anticipated—whether a sovereign nation ought to leave to the king a decision of peace and war. This gave the signal for one of the most violent discussions ever held in the Assembly. "Make of the rule of the monarch," said Mirabeau toward the end of a long speech, "that which it should be, and fear no longer that a rebel king, himself abdicating his crown, may expose himself to a progress from victory to the scaffold."

There were murmurs from the right. Espréménil jumped up. "I ask that M. de Mirabeau be called to order; he forgets that the person of the king has been declared inviolable."

Mirabeau replied calmly: "You have all been listening to a supposition, that of a despotic and rebellious king, coming with an army of Frenchmen to conquer the place of tyrants; now, a king in that case is no longer a king."

The hall rang with cheers; but after rousing the right, Mirabeau brought the left upon him when he put this question: "I ask you, shall we be better assured of having none but just and equitable wars if we delegate exclusively to an assembly of seven hundred persons the exercise of the right of making war? Have you considered the lengths to which passionate impulses or a false sense of dignity may carry imprudence and claim to justify it? We have heard one of our speakers propose to you, that if England waged an unjust war on Spain, we should at once cross the seas, throw one nation against another, and stake our last crown piece and our last man in London against proud Englishmen; and we all cheered: a gust of oratory sufficed for a moment to lead us astray. You will not be led astray by ministers; will you never be led astray by yourselves? People talk of the brake of public opinion on the representatives of the nation; but public opinion, often misled, even by praiseworthy sentiments, will then serve only to mislead. The Roman who, carrying war in the folds of his toga, threatened by unfolding it to shake out all the plagues of war must have felt the full importance of his mission. He was alone; he held in his hands a great destiny; he was the bearer of terror; but had the numerous Senate, who despatched him in the course of a stormy and passionate discussion, felt the terror which the formidable and precarious future of a war should inspire? Look at the political assemblies: it is always under the driving force of passion that they have decreed war."

II

"Treason of the Comte de Mirabeau discovered," was being shouted in the streets of Paris. The throng at the Palais-Royal eagerly bought the pamphlet. It was discussed in the streets and in the garden of the Tuileries. It was passed from hand to hand at the very doors of the Assembly, and men read: "So your crimes, you clever impostor, have at last been found out. We had had only suspicions of your conduct in the National Assembly. Today these suspicions are confirmed. When you put forward your motion for the National Assembly to be constituted an Assembly of the Representatives of the People, you wanted it adopted only because you wanted to gain supporters for your entry into the ministry; you declared yourself a supporter of the absolute veto only because you wanted gold and honours. You wanted the abolition of the Negro slave trade, an abolition that might involve the ruin of the National Assembly; you wanted it only because you had been promised gold. Finally you have just carried your crimes and your perfidy to the last extreme by bringing forward the insidious motion to grant to the executive power the right to slaughter us and to invade our properties, on the specious pretext of the apparent good of the people, and on the pretext of preserving for the legislative power a derisory share in that terrible right." The pamphlet ended with incitements to the murder of Mirabeau.

"You are right, it is an infamous libel," Mirabeau wrote to his sister, "but it is the evil side of a good thing [the liberty of the press] which compensates for all possible evils; and do not tell me that we must renounce the good because of the evil."

The anonymous author of the libellous pamphlet was soon discovered to be an obscure journalist named Lacroix. An artisan reported that he had been in a café and had heard a man "reproaching M. Lacroix for publishing the libel entitled *Trahison découverte du Comte de Mirabeau*; M. Lacroix contended that he had nothing to fear and that if the said M. de Mirabeau attacked it before any tribunal he would uphold it, that he had people to uphold it, and he named four persons; the witness only recalled the names of three, who are Du Port, Lameth, and Barnave; that all those who were in the café molested and abused M. Lacroix, who was obliged to leave the café."

On July 3, 1790, Mirabeau brought an action at the Châtelet in Paris against "an atrocious libel . . . of which the intention can have been no other than to discredit the plaintiff's principles . . . by inflaming the people and inducing them to commit criminal violence against the person of the plaintiff." The case, however, was dropped; Mirabeau was not greatly concerned to punish so petty an adversary when he could not touch the instigators whose protection Lacroix claimed.

Adrien Du Port attacked him directly at a sitting of the Société Patriotique de 1789. This society included among its members the municipality of Paris, the general staff of the National Guard, deputies such as Talleyrand, Sieyès, Barnave, Du Port, the Lameth brothers, and a number of financiers and writers. Almost all Mirabeau's friends were members, including La Marck, Chamfort, Clavière, and Duroverai.

The journal of the society was edited by Condorcet. In it André Chénier published his "warning to the French of their true enemies." The principal aim of the society was to spread the ideas of the Revolution in France and abroad. Mirabeau had opposed this tendency since the foundation of the society. "If impetuous daring is necessary for the victory of a revolution, moderation alone can consolidate it," he had said in a speech. The same members who had cheered that speech showed impatience when at a meeting on May 21, 1790, he had repeated that "the French should have no other aim than to establish the constitution on unshakable foundations." Calumnies against him found credit which would have been dismissed in the past with a shrug of the shoulders. Some considered him to be in the pay of Austria, bribed by the Comte de Mercy to work against the Belgian cause; others regarded him, together with his friends Dumont and Duroverai, as in the pav of Pitt.

12

"If the commencement of hostilities constituted the nation at war, it would no longer be either the legislative or the executive power that declared it," said Barnave on May 21, 1790, from the tribune of the Assembly; "it would be the first civilian or the first officer who, by attacking an individual or resisting his attack, acquired the right to make war." He accused Mirabeau of having tried to confuse the commencement of hostilities with war, acts of war with the state of war. On this 21st of May the battle seemed lost for Mirabeau. Barnave's speech produced an immense effect on the Assembly. Realizing this, he became more and more ironical and biting against Mirabeau.

Mirabeau was unmoved by Barnave's insolence and abuse. He listened silently to Barnave's arguments, which were so strongly impressing the whole left wing of the Assembly. At one moment he said quietly to his colleague Frochot: "I've got him." He borrowed a pencil from him and wrote: "I have heard enough, let us go out." He walked up and down the Terrasse des Feuillants with Frochot, and they met Mme. de Staël. He had a long talk with her. They spoke only of subjects remote from the day's events, although he had in his hand the pamphlet denouncing him, and although in the Salle du Manège Barnave was still speaking.

From the hall of the Assembly the excitement spread to the crowd. The people had little understanding of the subtle difference between according rights to the executive and to the legislative power. They thought the king would in future have full power to launch a war of vengeance which would deprive them of their liberties. As in the case of the veto, they had made their own the struggle against the monarchy.

Cazalès, fearing a vote under the immediate influence of Barnave's speech, proposed that the debate should be adjourned and that at the same time it should be decided to close it on the following day. "I ask for an explanation," said Mirabeau, "of those words—'The debate shall be closed.'" He had re-entered the hall, determined to make a direct attack on Barnave. He demanded that the discussion should be continued next day: "My principal argument at the moment is the heat with which my demand is being opposed."

Alexandre de Lameth wrote: "An immense crowd collected during the sitting" of the next day, May 22; "more than fifty thousand citizens filled the Tuileries, the gardens of the Feuillants and the Capucines, the Place Vendôme, the rue Saint-Honoré, and the adjacent streets. During the sitting some people had climbed up to the windows and let down on a string from time to time a sort of bulletin with particulars showing the fluctuation of opinions. These bulletins were copied and distributed and maintained among the crowd a ferment beyond imagining."

The crowd acclaimed Barnave as a saviour. When Mirabeau appeared, he was pursued with howls of "*A la lanterne!*"—"String him up!" Lacroix' pamphlet was still being hawked in the streets. The surging crowd was ready for any excess. The mounting hostility increased Mirabeau's fighting spirit. As he entered the hall he shouted to a friend: "I shall be carried out of the Assembly in triumph or in bits." As he went to the tribune a deputy shouted: "Well, Mirabeau, yesterday in the Capitol, today on the Tarpeian Rock."

Mirabeau hit out at his adversaries. "It has been noised abroad for a week that the section of the National Assembly that wants the royal will associated with the exercise of the right of peace and war is the parricide of the public freedom. Allegations of perfidy and corruption have been broadcast, and popular vengeance has been invoked to maintain tyranny over opinions. It might be inferred that there can be no two opinions, save by a crime, on one of the most delicate and most difficult questions of social organization." He stigmatized the deplorable blindness "of the men who in this way substitute exasperated self-esteem for the love of our country." Turning to Barnave, he thundered: "I, too, but a few days ago was to be carried in triumph, and at this moment 'The High Treason of the Comte de Mirabeau' is being cried in the streets." He repeated the words shouted to him on his way to the tribune and commented: "I had no need of that reminder that it is but a short distance from the Capitol to the Tarpeian Rock; but the man who is fighting for reason and for his country does not so easily give in." One of those present recorded Mirabeau's proud glance at the Lameth brothers as he continued: "He who knows that he has deserved well of his country, and, above all, that he can still be useful to her; he who does not feast on an empty celebrity and who disdains ephemeral success but pursues true glory; he who is determined to tell the truth and to serve the common weal independently of the fickle changes in public opinion—that man finds his services their own reward, his labours their own delight, and his dangers their own prize; for his harvest, for the only destiny that interests him, the destiny of his name, he looks only to time, that incorruptible judge. Let those who a week ago were spreading my opinion abroad without comprehending it, and who now are slandering my speech without having understood it, accuse me of burning incense before powerless idols at the moment when they have been thrown down, or of being the base beneficiary of men against whom I have not ceased to battle; let them denounce as an enemy of the Revolution a man who, it may be, has been of some service to it, and who, if the Revolution was not an element of his glory, might find safety in that one fact. Let them deliver to the fury of the fooled populace the man who for twenty years has fought against every sort of oppression, who was speaking to the French of freedom, of a constitution, of resistance, when his base slanderers were lapping up the milk of courts and living upon every dominant prejudice —what matters it? These underhand blows will not stop me in my career. My reply is: Answer if you can, and then slander as much as you like."

He replied point by point to Barnave's argument and then continued: "He declaimed against the evil that kings may do and have done, and he was careful not to remark that under our constitution the monarch can no longer be a despot or do anything arbitrarily; and he was especially careful to say nothing of popular movements, although he had himself given an example of the ease with which the friends of a foreign power might influence the opinion of a National Assembly by rousing the people around it."

He dealt vigorously with the critical issue in the debate: "I cannot prevent the depositary of all the national forces from being in possession of great resources and of opportunities of abusing them. Do you propose, because royalty has its dangers, that we should renounce the advantages of royalty? It is possible to maintain anything except inconsistency; tell us that we must not have a king, do not tell us that we may have only an impotent and useless king. I do not believe," he concluded, "that men who are to serve the public cause as true brothers-in-arms do well to fight as base gladiators; to do battle with imputations and intrigues instead of talents and enlightenment; to seek in mutual ruin and disparagement guilty successes, ephemeral trophies injurious to all and even to glory. But I say to you: among those who maintain my doctrine you will find all the moderate men who do not believe that wisdom lies in extremes or that the courage to destroy must never give place to the courage to rebuild; you will find among us those tribunes of the people whom the nation will count for a long time yet, in spite of the yappings of envious mediocrity, among the liberators of the country."

The whole Assembly broke into a long ovation. In this reply, improvised by utilizing the attacks on him, turning his adversaries' arms against themselves, Mirabeau revealed the full measure of his eloquence. He had spoken in his own defence and had identified it with the preservation of the regime. He emerged with increased reputation from a trial that might have been fatal. The Marquis de Ferrières wrote: "Mirabeau descended from the tribune amid redoubled applause, to the manifest chagrin and confusion of Barnave and the Lameths, leaving hatred and vengefulness in their hearts; no one attempted to reply to him."

Mirabeau himself, however, asked that Barnave should be heard, but his reply was feeble. Lafayette, as if he wanted to make up for the past, supported Mirabeau in his hour of triumph. He shouted: "I feel that I cannot better pay the immense debt I owe to the people than by not sacrificing to ephemeral popularity the advice which I think most useful to it." Mirabeau's motion was adopted with an amendment that was a compromise. But if Mirabeau had to give ground to his adversaries, he had secured the maintenance of the royal initiative. He realized the measure of this victory. He made a point of establishing the facts in a pamphlet made up of his speeches, preceded by a covering letter to the departmental administrators.

Mirabeau's adversaries were in confusion. They went feverishly to work to mitigate their defeat. Alexandre de Lameth published a reply in which he accused Mirabeau of having introduced important changes in printing his speech. Pétion, too, published an open letter to Mirabeau; Charles de Lameth entered into a newspaper controversy with Lafayette; and Barnave drafted a letter which, however, he refrained from publishing. One of the most unbridled of the attacks on Mirabeau came from his former admirer Camille Desmoulins, who, a few days later, found himself face to face with Mirabeau on the Terrasse des Feuillants. "I was with one of his great enemies," Desmoulins told Clavière and Brissot, "all of us giving vent to our patriotic disgust; I threw Mirabeau a glance as full of contempt and indignation as I could manage; he greeted me out of the corner of his eye, smiling, and in a manner that invited me in such a friendly way to come and have it out with him that I was carried after him and followed him at a distance, uncertain whether to beard him and cover him with reproaches. He saw me coming and stopped. 'Do you really dare,' I said, 'to go about the streets so calmly in the middle of the day, and aren't you at all afraid of being strung up? You must agree that if the executive power has not given you a hundred million crowns for your last harangues, it is robbing you.'" But Mirabeau contented himself with smiling "in an undefinable way," and at once, Desmoulins continued, "putting his arm through mine, he took me as far as the rue de l'Echelle, making me promise to go and see him the next day but one, and assuring me that I should be satisfied with his explanation; the explanation was a charming dinner."

Mirabeau's real explanation was given in his letter to the administrators of the departments—an explanation that was also a warning: "Those alone will be the true friends of the people who teach them that the action we have had to take in order to escape from chaos must be followed by conceptions suitable to our permanent organization; that after having sufficiently distrusted one another, and especially after clearing away plenty of wretched rubbish, what is needed is the bringing of all our minds to reconstruction; and, finally, that the time has come to pass from a state of legitimate insurrection to the lasting peace of a true social order, and that freedom is not preserved solely by the means that won it."

His appeal was lost in the discordant clamour of the day. It was a time of agitated unrest. "All Paris is still in ferment," wrote William Taylor on May 14. "The last sound which dies away upon the sleeping ear is the rattle of the patriot drums, and the first murmur which disturbs our rest is the martial music of the national militia. It is like living in a citadel besieged. In every street you are surrounded by hawkers of pamphlets with terrific titles, and every hour is startled with some new tale of terror."

Mirabeau summed up these weeks of upheaval in a letter to Mauvillon: "We are in a real crisis, and it will not be the last; but, whatever may happen, your friend will live and die as a good and perhaps a great citizen."

≈ XIX ≈

My Existence Is My Strength

MIRABEAU had passed his fortieth year before he was able for the first time to satisfy his terrible hunger for living, his frenzy for work, and his passion for luxury. He was able for the first time to spend money at will without a bad conscience and without getting into inextricable difficulties. "There was in him," wrote La Marck, "an abundance of intellectual and physical faculties which continually worked upon his impetuous nature and constantly sought to find expression."

With his debts paid, the money he received from the court permitted him to set up a comfortable household. He allowed no consideration and no friendly warning to keep him within bounds. "Instead of taking a more decent flat than that which he had occupied until then," wrote La Marck, "he was determined to have a whole house to himself." Tired of furnished rooms, he rented from one of his friends, the actress Julie Carreau, later the wife of Talma, a little house in the rue de la Chaussée-d'Antin. "In place of the one servant he had had," continued La Marck, "he engaged a *valet de chambre*, a cook, and a coachman, and bought horses; and yet everybody knew that until recently he had been desperately hard up." In vain did La Marck try to make him understand that his enemies would not fail to inquire into the sources of his new opulence. "He put up with all my remarks and even my reproaches with the utmost good humour, and promised to be more cautious in his expenditure." But even when he was making that promise, Mirabeau knew that he would not be able to keep it. "Mirabeau was like a child," said Dumont, "he coveted everything and could not deny himself a fancy; money seemed to be an embarrassment of which he was in a hurry to rid himself." His friends were amused at his discussions with his secretary, Comps, who was responsible for looking after the day-to-day expenses and who tried to resist his employer's extravagant ideas. Mirabeau cut short all the young man's remonstrances with, "Don't trouble me with tiresome details."

2

"With you I would undertake anything," wrote La Marck to Mirabeau; "without you I shall run no risk except with a calculable expectation." He wrote this, emerging from his reserve, on May 20, 1790.

Mirabeau had the greater need of La Marck's friendship because
his Genevese collaborators abandoned him. They had begun by no
longer getting on with each other. Dumont complained that Duroverai
left him too big a share of the work. The difficulties created by Mme.
Le Jay exhausted their patience. She thought she had a monopoly of
the newspaper and could change its collaborators without any risk to
the quality of the publication. More and more frequent friction led
Mirabeau himself to break off his connexion with the newspaper.

In March 1790 Dumont left Paris for England, carrying with him a
dull resentment against Mirabeau and disappointed hopes. "When I
came to know him too well, Mirabeau no longer inspired me with the
same feelings." He complained of finding his name associated with
Mirabeau's by the public and in libellous publications. "I found very
estimable persons cool toward me as a consequence of the contempt
they felt for Mirabeau." He was also influenced by the attitude of his
English friends, among whom a reaction against the French Revolution was beginning to set in. But the true reason for the rupture was one
that he seemed to reveal involuntarily: "There was nothing flattering
to one's self-esteem in the reputation of a subordinate agent." The day
came when he took his revenge by claiming the principal part in Mirabeau's work. He conceded that Mirabeau "abounded in striking expressions, and even made a particular study of them." He conceded also
that he had "quick apprehension, sure tact, and a gift of at once de-
tecting the true mind of the Assembly and of applying his whole
strength to the point of resistance, instead of wasting it on side issues."
He added: "Nobody achieved more with a single word, nobody hit
the target with more precision, or more frequently carried the general
opinion with him, either by a happy insinuation or by a stroke that
intimidated his adversaries." But after that Dumont, in his *Souvenirs*,
presented Mirabeau as the spokesman of his, Dumont's, ideas, a sonorous
trumpet marvellously performing airs composed by Dumont.

Mirabeau himself reduced to its just proportions the part played in
his work by his collaborators. He refuted their claims in the portrait,
signed Iramba and apparently from his pen, in the *Galerie des Etats
généraux:* "The common herd of writers, echoing the thoughtless multitude, dispute his credit for part of his works. A mistake if ever there

was one. He conceived them all, created them all. The architect will not have carved the columns or painted the ceilings or carried out the ornamentation; but he will have designed the plan, distributed the rooms, chosen the type of decoration; and it is he who will have made the palace and who receives the praise or suffers the criticism." Mme. de Staël pointed out that after Mirabeau's death none of those who boasted of having done his work "could have written what he was able to inspire in them."

La Marck described him at this happiest period of his private existence as a great river flowing toward its estuary "in a state of splendour. He did not allow himself a moment's rest. Now in the tribune, now in his study, on the lookout for everything that was happening and everything that was being said, dictating to his secretary, writing himself, revising the manuscripts compiled at his request; starting discussions for the sake of the new ideas that would emerge; taking possession of those ideas, instructing others to base their work on them, and on top of all this not forgetting his pleasures."

3

"I professed monarchical principles at a time when I could see nothing at court but its weakness, and when, having no knowledge of the thought of the daughter of Maria Theresa, I could not count on that august auxiliary," wrote Mirabeau in a memorandum intended for the court and dated June 1, 1790. "I fought for the rights of the throne at a time when I inspired nothing but distrust and when a poisoned malignity saw in all my actions so many traps. I served the monarch when I was well aware that I could expect from a just but deceived king neither benefits nor recompense. What shall I do now, when confidence has restored my courage and gratitude has made of my principles my duties? I shall be what I have always been—the defender of the monarchical power as regulated by the laws, and the apostle of liberty as guaranteed by the monarchical power."

Did he really think he was trusted? Fersen expressed the attitude of the royal couple in his over-simplified way: "Mirabeau has been completely won by the court, and this without Lafayette's knowledge or consent. I think he will be able to be very useful to them, and he has pretty despotic ideas, but he is a great rascal and will have to be watched with suspicion. He needs a lot of money to distribute." As if unaware of this atmosphere of suspicion, Mirabeau continued to dream the great dream of his life. "He directed all his ambition to the ministry of France," wrote Dumont, "and hoped to put all past ministries into the shade; he felt strong enough to attract every man of distinguished capacity; he wanted, he said, to give himself an aureole of talents whose brilliance would impress all Europe."

The obstacle to his great dream was still the man whom he called Grandisson-Cromwell, "an ambitious incompetent who wants to enjoy supreme power without daring to seize it or having the means to do so." His animosity did not blind him in the least to certain qualities of Lafayette, especially his coolness: "All the talent he has is always at his command," he said of him. But he was conscious of his own superiority: "M. de Lafayette has an army, but my head is also a power."

The principal purpose of his memorandum of June 1 was to discredit, and to mobilize the resistance of the royal couple against, "the idol of the day, the pretended general of the Revolution, the monarch's rival." He described Lafayette, whom the sovereigns feared and detested, as likely to become still more formidable than he was already. "He is master of the Parisian army, and if ministers devoted to his ambition refuse him no means of influence, will he not become through this army of Paris the most absolute and the most formidable of dictators? Lafayette's strength rests upon the confidence he inspires in his army. He inspires that confidence only because he seems to share the opinions of the multitude. Since the city of Paris is the one in all the kingdom in which public opinion, directed by a mass of writers and by a still greater mass of intelligent laymen, is the least amenable to the control of a single individual, it follows that Lafayette, having acquired his influence simply by adopting the tone of Paris, will always be forced, in order to retain it, to swim with the torrent of the multitude."

It seemed to Mirabeau that it would be easy to undermine Lafayette's prestige and to destroy him by depriving him of his resources. "What would become of him if he were reduced to his own capacities, if he were unable to win support by his wealth or to corrupt by his credit, if he had nothing but the inertia of his thoughts and the nullity of his talent? There is an opportunity now to oppose to him a dangerous rival. M. de Bouillé, if he wanted to be popular, would soon be more so than Lafayette."

Mirabeau congratulated himself on the skill with which he thought he had entered the struggle against his rival; in a covering note sent to La Marck with his memorandum, he wrote: "I have been delivered of some pretty fine children." The queen, too, was very pleased. "The negotiation is still proceeding," she wrote to Mercy-Argenteau, "and if he is sincere I have every reason to be satisfied with him."

4

Meanwhile Mirabeau made a last effort to win over Lafayette, or perhaps to lull his suspicion. If he was playing a double game, it was because he was by no means sure that his advice would be followed by the court. His letter to Lafayette was a mixture of subtlety and sincerity, an ingenious manoeuvre which, according as he succeeded or failed, might turn into close collaboration or open war. But the letter produced no result. The court must be induced to act. "When the king is tired of being a prisoner, we shall see," wrote Mirabeau to La Marck when telling him what he had done. He added at once, to make sure of not being misunderstood: "But remember, my dear count, that in any case we must have nothing to do on any pretext with an escape, and that if a king goes away he must do so in broad daylight if he is still to be king."

He seems to have realized that the court would not enter into an open struggle with Lafayette. He proposed to the queen that she should intervene personally and talk to Lafayette in this sense:

"Your functions entirely absorb your individual faculties. For political affairs you are obliged to refer to those around you, and those around you are weak, and you are waiting for a new ministry to strengthen you, and clearly the delay is injurious to us. You have, and we have, the conviction that apart from his talent M. de Mirabeau is the only statesman in the country; nobody has his combination of qualities, his courage, his character. Plainly he does not want to have a part in making an end of us; we must not run the risk of his being constrained by circumstances to want to do so; he must be on our side. For him to be on our side, we must be on his." In this speech, drawn up for the queen with a particular purpose, Mirabeau incidentally supplied the key to his own character. It was given in full in a further phrase, which Marie Antoinette is very unlikely to have adopted: "He needs a great purpose, a great danger, great resources, great glory. We are resigned now, or resolved, to give him the confidence of despair." This was followed by an ultimatum for the queen to present to Lafayette: "I ask you, I demand, that you should collaborate with M. de Mirabeau, and should do so entirely, daily, openly, in every question."

The queen cannot have been either able or willing to use such language. The Archbishop of Toulouse edited the text—"to change the style and not the matter." La Marck promised that "if this helpless captain shuffles, we will say straight out: 'I demand.'"

A few days later La Marck let Mirabeau know that he had received from the queen "a letter several pages long about an interview with Gilles César [Lafayette]; you will like it." But, either because the queen was less firm than she had promised to be, having been intimidated by Lafayette or unwilling to commit herself so deeply in Mirabeau's favour, or because Lafayette was less impressed by her intervention or too obstinate to give way, the interview was without result. Lafayette, under the influence of his friends, continued to vacillate; for a moment he would draw nearer to Mirabeau, and then at once he would hold himself aloof.

About this time there was a motion in preparation in the Assembly calling for the abolition of titles and rank, which, according to Charles de Lameth, were incompatible with true freedom. Mirabeau found his friends "very scandalized by the motion against insignia and hereditary nobility and anxious to settle a plan of battle, at which I laughed." When the motion came up, Lafayette supported it "with all his heart." The Assembly hastened to throw every distinction into what one deputy called the tomb of vanities.

5

On June 11, 1790, Mirabeau, at Lafayette's request, pronounced from the tribune of the Assembly a funeral oration for Benjamin Franklin, who had died in April. The speech deeply impressed the Assembly and it was ordered that it should be printed. For three days all the deputies, except one who was called to order, appeared in mourning clothes. Robespierre, who had only one suit of clothes, had to borrow a mourning suit from a friend who was much bigger than he. Mirabeau had spoken in spite of great physical suffering. He had for some time been afflicted with ophthalmia. "I thought I was going to lose my sight," he wrote to Mauvillon, "and my eyes were all the more in danger because, except for ten or a dozen days when I was entirely prostrated, I followed the business of the Assembly."

In another letter written to Mauvillon about the same time, he described the disquieting general situation and his own part: "We have here a lot of men who are simply out to create disturbance. Their audacious turbulence imposes on the timid, alarms the sensible, carries away the inflammable, and rallies the factious. We have had to form, guide, and bring to triumph a truly monarchical party, and it was not easy in a nation so fickle, which acts only under emotion or following a fashion. And the things that are at present the fashion are licence and anarchy."

In his satirical review, the *Lanterne magique*, the Vicomte de Mirabeau made a practice of bringing his elder brother under the "lantern's" deforming lens: "See how the people cheer him, it is the great Comte de Mirabeau; admire his head of hair, the most elaborate of all, and see how pleased with himself he looks; he smiles at his backers, he will repay them in motions for the benefits they are good enough to heap on him." The viscount's friends thought him witty and collected his jests in pamphlets. He was a great friend of the Comte de Montlosier and dined with him every day at the Palais-Royal. He was full of sallies and witticisms and malicious remarks, especially after a very copious dinner washed down with plenty of wine and a whole bottle of liqueur. It was in the course of one of these dinners that the royalist sheet *Les Actes des apôtres* came to birth.

The viscount was an easy prey for pamphleteers and caricaturists; in the prints of the day he appeared as a great tun, with arms that ended in wine bottles. One of these prints had the legend, "Tun Mirabeau, brother of Thunder Mirabeau," and the nickname stuck.

At a loss on the tribune, entirely ignorant of public affairs, he was essentially a soldier out of employment, a feudal warrior rusting in time of peace, a grotesque survival of a dying period. But he was a born soldier, responsive to any appeal from his valorous past. He had particularly at heart his old Touraine Regiment. He had been adored by his men though he had maintained rigorous discipline. In June 1790 he learned that his regiment, in garrison at Perpignan, had on its own initiative dismissed two of its officers and had filled their places. Revolted by this lack of discipline, he set off in haste, on the impulse of the moment, for Perpignan. He described his mad escapade in a humorous account, *Le Voyage national de Mirabeau cadet, 1790*. On his journey he fell in with a fête of the National Guard. "The commandant, coming up to me to clink glasses, recognized me and exclaimed: 'It is M. de Mirabeau!' At once there were shouts of 'Vive le Comte de Mirabeau!' In these cases I am the only one of the family that is known. I thought it my duty to point out that I was not the count but the viscount, and to remark that it was as well to know with whom one is drinking. A few persons said: 'It is the aristocrat.' That rather damped the enthusiasm."

On his arrival at Perpignan he reprimanded the mutinous soldiers in his old tone of authority. But he no longer inspired the old respect in them. Their attitude sent him into a violent temper. He unsheathed his sword and wounded three soldiers. Officers came up to support him, and they put the regiment to flight. But his prestige was entirely lost.

That evening he was a guest of the mayor of Perpignan, the Marquis d'Aguylas. Next morning he disappeared. In the room next to that in which he had slept, the regiment had stored its flags. It was discovered that the viscount had carried off the regiment's bows and tassels. His intention, according to his account, had been to take them to the king, who could have sent them to a town a long way from Perpignan, telling the soldiers to go and join them. The good soldiers would have gone and the bad ones remained behind.

When the regiment discovered the disappearance of the bows and tassels, it mutinied. It seized the mayor and held him in the citadel as a hostage. The municipal officers of Perpignan sent a complaint to the Assembly. The Vicomte de Mirabeau was arrested at Castelnaudary, with the bows and tassels in his trunks.

He had a narrow escape from being torn to pieces by the crowd. As soon as he learned of the danger his friend the mayor was in, he returned the bows and tassels to the regiment. The Assembly, following the denunciation from the municipality of Perpignan, called for the viscount's transfer to Paris under escort.

His brother intervened. "The Assembly cannot have forgotten," he said, "that one of its most celebrated decrees, in the circumstances that led to the opening of the National Assembly, established the inviolability of its members. The Assembly has no authority to charge the executive power with the arrest of one of its members; it has none to place M. de Mirabeau the younger in the double danger of an escort and of the loss of his rights. I said Mirabeau the younger, for I am not saying a word on behalf of my brother; I claim for him only what I should claim for any member of the National Assembly."

The Assembly complied with his request and reminded the municipalities concerned of the decree on inviolability. The viscount was called upon to defend his conduct before it. Deputations from the Touraine Regiment and from the municipality and the National Guard of Perpignan were heard first. A delegate of the National Guard gave an eloquent description of the soldiers' dismay at the disappearance of the regimental bows and tassels, which "the oldest soldier in France" had followed "for eighty years under three victorious kings."

Before the case was debated there was an interview between the two brothers. It was to be their last meeting. With the viscount was Cazalès, the most intelligent of the members of the right. Cazalès seems to have realized that the great revolutionary tribune had joined the defenders of the throne. To trap him he said that he knew of his relations with the Archbishop of Toulouse. "Who told you that yarn?" replied Mirabeau, laughing. But the viscount had no suspicion of his brother's position. At the moment when their aims were much the same, he deserted his post and, without knowing it, left to his brother the effort to save the monarchy. When the case came before the Assembly, the Vicomte de Mirabeau had already left France. Once more his brother undertook his defence, asking that he should be tried by court-martial, "which will be able to decide with justice who is the aggressor, a mutinous regiment or a colonel who wants to keep it loyal." But the Assembly decreed that Mirabeau the younger was a "thief of bows and tassels," and also, as an *émigré*, an enemy of the people.

The Vicomte de Mirabeau carried on his activities outside the country. He raised a troop of mercenaries on the Alsatian frontier; he called them the Death Hussars and equipped them at his own expense. Soon he had three thousand men under his orders. He felt himself to be a power, and made his companions in exile feel it. His hectoring manners produced quarrels, and Prince Hohenlohe expelled him from his domains. In his exile he lost the last remains of mental balance. For a time he wandered in Germany in quest of asylum, turned back by the Austrians and threatened by the Bishop of Spires. He continued to drink and to settle at arms his drunkard's quarrels. In September 1792 he died suddenly at Freiburg im Breisgau. The death certificate specified a fit of apoplexy. Actually he fell victim to a brawl with an *émigré* officer. The officer had come from the Prince de Condé and was the bearer of a conciliatory letter. The viscount would not listen to him, refused to admit him, and, throwing himself upon him, transfixed himself on the other's sword.

The *émigrés*, who had rejected him in his lifetime, buried him with the honours due to field marshals, near Salzbach, at the very spot where Turenne was killed.

Near the Swiss frontier, in a little village in the Jura, the inhabitants set up at a crossroad an obelisk to mark the entrance into the new country of liberty. On one face of the obelisk were engraved the names of those who had earned the love and gratitude of France—Mirabeau, Sieyès, Chapelier, Barnave, Grégoire, Robespierre, Talleyrand, Bailly. On the opposite face figured, among those who had disgraced humanity, Maury, Mirabeau the younger, Esprémenil, Malouet, and the tribunal of the Châtelet.

6

"The king has only one man, his wife." Mirabeau was directly addressing Marie Antoinette, abandoning the reserve of court etiquette. "There is no safety for her except in the re-establishment of the royal authority. I should like to think that she would have no desire for life without a crown; but," he added, as though reading the future, "of one thing I am very sure, that she will not keep her life if she does not keep the throne.

"The moment will come when, building all her hopes on the queen, at the risk of wounding the king's self-esteem, the moment will come, and soon, when she will have to see what can be done by a woman and a child on horseback. For her it is a family method, but meanwhile it will be necessary to go cautiously, and not to suppose that it will be possible, either by chance or by contrivance, to emerge from an external crisis through ordinary men and means."

In this second note, addressed to the court on June 20, 1790, he gave an eloquent picture of the dangers of the moment. "There must be no disguising the fact that the political crisis is at its height and is becoming complicated in a very alarming manner. The army, to begin with, is providing the instruments for brigandage for anyone contemplating robbery on a grand scale. I do not think that the throne, and especially the dynasty, has ever run a greater risk." There were resources still left, and he knew them. He had a plan, but "it would be gratuitous rashness to attempt it or even to confide it without seeing some means of success."

Mirabeau proposed that a negotiator should be sent to Spain to secure a revision of the treaty which would permit of its ratification by the Assembly. For this mission he suggested the young Comte de Ségur. He knew that for his advice to carry weight he must strike the queen's imagination and excite her to employ her hold over the king, so far as anybody could have influence with so elusive a being. He built great hopes on a personal interview with the queen. "It is essential that I should soon see her," he said repeatedly to La Marck, who fully agreed and did all he could to secure an audience.

Mirabeau proposed to the court that it should secure a man like Desmoulins, who was "very responsive to offers of money." He worked at the same time to dissipate the apprehension felt in regard to the return of the Duc d'Orléans. "To prevent him from returning would be a false step," he wrote on July 1, "and it is always a great mistake to give orders when one is not sure of being obeyed." Moreover, "the former party of the Duc d'Orléans no longer exists, and circumstances have changed. That party was in search of a leader, and that prince is no longer anything but a wraith." And he added, with the extraordinary psychological subtlety that gave such value to his advice: "To serve him is to weaken him; to humour him is to kill him, him and his party."

The king bowed to his arguments. As a proof of his goodwill, he decided to give the Duc d'Orléans the rank of admiral, which was one of the duke's ambitions. Louis granted him a long interview, with which he declared himself very pleased. But he forgot to give instructions to his courtiers. When the duke appeared at the king's levee, insults were heaped upon him; courtiers mobbed him and trod on his feet. He found the same reception in the queen's apartments. Dinner was ready, and as soon as the duke entered, the courtiers treated him like a poisoner, shouting: "Gentlemen, watch the dishes." He was hooted on leaving and even spat upon. The duke left the château convinced that the king and queen were the instigators of these outrages.

7

"Nothing shall stop me, I will die rather than fail to keep my promises," Mirabeau exclaimed to La Marck on July 4, 1790. He had passed the night of Friday, July 2, at the house of his niece, the Marquise d'Aragon, in Passy. On Saturday morning, July 3, he went into the country. His nephew, the Comte du Saillant, served as postillion on this mysterious drive. The carriage stopped at the gates of the palace of Saint-Cloud. It was early—particularly early for visits to a royal palace—scarcely half-past eight in the morning; but the visitor was quickly admitted.

"I have found a place that is not very comfortable but will suffice for seeing him and palliating all the inconveniences of the garden and the château," the queen had written to Mercy. The queen, said Mme. Campan, "went alone into her garden, to a crossing of the paths that still exists on the heights of the private garden of Saint-Cloud." Mme. Campan, a none-too-reliable witness, seems this time to have given a correct account. The interview actually took place in the park. Mirabeau spoke later of "two grenadiers who saw the two persons strolling in Saint-Cloud."

On that July morning, beneath the foliage of Saint-Cloud, the queen and the tribune of the people met for the first time. "The queen admitted to me," wrote La Marck, "that when she first saw Mirabeau she was overcome for a moment with horror and fright." His presence was such a shock that she was near fainting.

But she quickly recovered, with the self-mastery that often gave her a distant and haughty appearance. She addressed Mirabeau with a phrase prepared in advance. According to Mme. Campan, whose memory is not always to be trusted, she said: "In the presence of an ordinary enemy, of a man who had sworn the destruction of the monarchy, without appreciating its usefulness to a great people, I should at this moment be taking the most ill-advised of steps; but when one is speaking to a Mirabeau . . ."

Her woman's instinct seems to have dictated to her a shade of expression to which Mirabeau was particularly sensitive. "This poor queen," said Mme. Campan, "was delighted at having found this way of setting him above all others, and in confiding to me the details of that interview she said: 'Do you know, those words, "a Mirabeau," seemed to flatter him immensely.'"

Mirabeau had come to Saint-Cloud with the intention of rousing the queen from her somnambulist's walk along the edge of the abyss, of gaining her trust while danger threatened. But much of what he meant to say he did not say, or softened down. Mirabeau seemed to forget the queen's defiance of public opinion, her lack of comprehension of great events, her pitiful efforts to arrest the march of time with her ineffective feminine hands. He regretted later that he had only said to her, "with some energy but perhaps with too much brevity, that all was lost if she concentrated on a veto which could only add to the king's indecision, instead of making up her mind always to prompt him." "Each individual," he explained to her, "has but a limited measure of attentiveness and of will-power."

The atmosphere of Saint-Cloud inspired him with the reticence of a courtier; he stopped suddenly and contented himself with saying that "the king and queen, harassed by deliberations that lead to nothing, apply less activity and energy to those which should lead to something."

"He came away from Saint-Cloud full of enthusiasm," wrote La Marck. "The queen's dignity, her infinite grace, her affability when, with an emotion mingled with remorse, he accused himself of having been one of the principal causes of her sufferings, everything about her had charmed him altogether beyond words. The meeting inspired him with fresh zeal and further increased his eagerness to repair his errors."

The interview deeply affected both Mirabeau and the queen. They never met again; but the hour they spent together seemed to them a turning-point in history, in their own destinies and in that of their country. Both drew exaggerated hopes from it. When Mirabeau bent over the queen's hand, he exclaimed, as if carried away: "Madame, the monarchy is saved!"

According to La Marck, Louis joined them for a time. The placid king drew a certain grandeur from his unshakable apathy. When he spoke of the country's affairs, his disdainful expression changed to animation, his pale eyes lost their habitual cold and distant look. He was no absolute monarch fiercely attached to his privileges, no despot resolved to reconquer power against the wish of his own people. Mirabeau, perhaps over-impressed by the royal presence, saw a dignity where there was only an incapacity to feel anything deeply. "He was no less touched," wrote La Marck, "by the king's calm resignation and the moderation of his views on the re-establishment of the royal authority." The meeting at Saint-Cloud ended in cordial agreement.

"The first time I saw the queen again after that interview," wrote La Marck, "she assured me at once that she and the king had gained from it a conviction of Mirabeau's sincere devotion to the cause of the monarchy and to their persons." She was so pleased with the reception she had given Mirabeau, so full of the sense of her own magnanimity, that she expected to see him overflowing with gratitude, subjugated for all time. The Archbishop of Toulouse urged some such acknowledgment on him, and La Marck wrote to him: "I know that the queen is expecting a nice letter of thanks; I feel I ought to let you know, so that it may be carefully written and sent off without any delay." Louis XVI was no less pleased with that third of July. He had gained from it, said La Marck, "a still more exaggerated confidence in the assistance Mirabeau was giving, and abandoned himself too much to the sense of security inspired in him by that support."

The interview at Saint-Cloud did not remain unknown. "Some rumours are spreading about Saturday's drive," noted the archbishop on July 5; "so far they seem to me to be nothing more than gossip." Two days later Mirabeau informed the court that a letter had been sent to the investigating committees. "The letter," he said, "is badly written and so filled with misspellings that they seem to me to be deliberate. It is pretended that it was found in the park of Saint-Cloud on Monday or Tuesday, the day before, or two days before, the day to which my pretended interview is assigned."

The *Orateur du peuple* published the sensational news that Mirabeau had had an interview with the queen. In the *Ami du peuple* Marat wrote: "News has just come of secret intrigues of Riqueti the elder at Saint-Cloud." An anonymous sheet was distributed in Paris, headed: "Nocturnal interview of Gabriel-Honoré Riqueti, former Comte de Mirabeau, with the king at Saint-Cloud on July 2, 1790."

"I know beyond any possibility of doubt," said Mirabeau in his note to the court, "that the Lameths, Du Port, Menou, Aiguillon, and even

Pétion de Villeneuve, are very busy collecting evidence that I had a meeting at Saint-Cloud. I do not think that all their machinations can do me any serious damage in the Assembly, but they may compromise me and disinfluence me." But though he escaped being "disinfluenced" by the interview at Saint-Cloud, he failed to achieve his principal purpose. He had wanted to make the queen realize the gravity of her situation. But, said La Marck, "her kindly character led her to think that we exaggerated the perversity of her enemies, and she took for granted that all the king could lose in the struggle would be some of the prerogatives of his royal power."

Another point of capital importance which Mirabeau had intended to raise in his interview with the queen also failed to be secured—a change of ministers. "Thus," wrote La Marck, "all our resources were concentrated in the Comte de Mercy. He shared our view of the importance of this measure; he tried to get it adopted by the court." In the end the queen, who had entire confidence in her faithful servant, was convinced; but she met with insurmountable resistance from the king. The king, concluded La Marck, "was surrounded by people who gave him other advice; always undecided, unable to resolve on anything of his own accord and to persevere in the resolve, he listened to everyone's advice and followed no one's completely, or adopted the worst."

8

> *Ah, ça ira, ça ira, ça ira!*
> *Les aristocrates à la lanterne!*
> *Ah, ça ira, ça ira, ça ira!*
> *Les aristocrates on les pendra.*
> *La liberté s'établira,*
> *Malgré les tyrans, tout réussira.*[1]

The song raced victoriously through the Champ-de-Mars. It burst from the lips of two hundred thousand citizens. It was born of a strange alliance between a favourite air of Marie Antoinette's, the *Carillon national*, and a constant expression of Franklin's during the American War of Independence, "*Laissez faire, ça ira.*"

[1] It'll get done, 'll get done, 'll get done!
The aristocrats, string 'em up!
It'll get done, 'll get done, 'll get done!
The aristocrats 'll be hanged.
Freedom, we'll get it for good,
In spite of the tyrants, we'll get it all done.

On the Champ-de-Mars people of all classes, all ages, all walks of life, were crowded together, the song on their lips and shovels or picks in their hands. Deputations' flags floated in the wind. One banner showed a big knife with the inscription: "Tremble, aristocrats, here are the butcher boys." While the men's vigorous arms levelled heaps of stones, a chain of women formed to drag along piled-up carts; among these the Duchesse de Luynes pushed her mahogany wheelbarrow. Between the folds of the charcoal burners' standard was to be read the inscription: "The last sigh of the aristocrats." Alongside them was the deputation of the Carthusians, at work with Dom Gerle at their head. Mayors, wearing their tricolour scarves, had brought deputations from distant villages. A delegation of actors and actresses was headed by their manageress. Rough hands and white hands, wrinkled hands, arthritic hands, hands with broken nails and with manicured nails, plump hands that had never touched a tool, bare arms with muscles standing out, wrists surrounded by foaming lace, all were at the same work with the same ardour, as though in some strange fever. It was the intoxication of union with the mass of the people, of fraternization in joy and of united labour. A whole past of age-long divisions seemed to be buried in this preparation for the celebration of the first anniversary of the taking of the Bastille. Above this vast and humming workplace of the Champ-de-Mars floated invisibly the magic word incarnated for the first time in this swarm of voluntary workers, the word "equality."

The Revolution was marking a stage in its victorious march. It was allowing itself the respite of a festival in order to contemplate its work. The organizers of this festival of the Federation, or covenanting, in which the whole country took part, were out to triumph over all the enemies of the Revolution by this gigantic demonstration of national unity. "Already the division of the provinces no longer exists, the division that made of France almost as many different states and peoples," said Bailly, in the name of the municipality of Paris, in an address to the Assembly. "All the names are giving place to a single one; a great people knows now only the name of 'Frenchman.'" But their aim was also "to win respect for the laws of the empire and for the authority of the monarch." The tumults, the indiscipline that was eating away the army, and the underground agitation of the masses who were known as "passive citizens" and were excluded from the franchise, alarmed the revolutionary bourgeoisie, whose only desire now was to enjoy its conquests in peace. The moment was favourable for the reawakening, by means of that satisfied bourgeoisie, of the sentiment of loyalty to the throne in the masses of the French people, for rallying the king to the Revolution and the Revolution to the king.

Mirabeau fully realized the importance of the occasion. He had advised the king to speak at the festival of the Federation, to reserve to himself the initiative in that great demonstration, and, amid what would be a movement of indescribable enthusiasm, to put the seal on the solemn union of monarchy and liberty. He even sketched a proclamation which the king should address to the crowd assembled in the Champ-de-Mars. This speech, which was not delivered, might have changed the destinies of the monarchy. It might have preserved to Louis XVI his crown and surely his life. But the unique opportunity was lost.

On the eve of the festival the Archbishop of Toulouse wrote to La Marck: "The queen has told me that there are no means of inducing the king to speak tomorrow." The obstinacy with which Louis refused had nothing to do with any disapproval. In his speech to a deputation from the Assembly he said virtually all that it was proposed that he should say to the massed crowd. "And the most astonishing thing, it seemed to me," said the archbishop, "was that it was he who did it." But his total ignorance of the psychology of crowds rendered Louis deaf to the advice offered him. He had goodwill, but no understanding of his time. The gulf that separated the king from his advisers was a gulf that divided not men but centuries.

The festival of the Federation became the apotheosis of Lafayette. It aroused wild enthusiasm, although the elements seemed to have conspired to rob it of success. But in spite of a cold wind and driving rain, the spectators, with the constancy of the adepts of a new religion, passed a whole night on the Champ-de-Mars, singing and dancing round great fires. The soldiers were exhausted with cold and hunger. The women's dresses were soaked, the wind had carried away their hats, and their shoes sank in the mud. But nothing could extinguish their ardour. There were cheers for the sixty flags of the districts of Paris and for the eighty-three banners of the new departments as they were carried toward an open-air altar, to return next day to the provinces after being blessed.

There were cheers for the man who celebrated Mass on that solemn day, although to the initiated the Bishop of Autun had little of the odour of sanctity. The massed crowds, however, did not know that the man who was blessing their flags was equally sceptical in the matter of patriotism and in religion. As he approached the altar, with all eyes fixed on him, Talleyrand muttered to Lafayette: "Please don't make me laugh."

When the king took the oath to the constitution, "fifteen hundred thousand voices exclaimed 'I swear,' and that oath resounded to the farthest limits of France," we read in a contemporary account. But we also read: "All would have been glad if the king had come forward, crossed the circle, and taken that solemn oath in the presence of the people, who would have seen him from all sides." There is abundant evidence of this: "If the court had been better organized," wrote a deputy, "what advantage it might have taken of the absurd enthusiasm that filled most French heads!"

The recipient of all the popular acclamations was Lafayette. Seated on his horse in front of the altar—where Mirabeau would have had the king speak—he was in view of all, the hero of the popular imagination. When he pronounced the oath, the crowd who repeated it after him was carried away by enthusiasm and ready to sacrifice itself for him. His hands, his boots, even his saddle were kissed. At that moment he was a sort of sacred relic of the Revolution. Mirabeau saw with disdain this idolatry for a man whom he despised. Any worship that enslaved the soul and dimmed the lucidity of the mind was repugnant to him; he was disgusted by the transports of the crowd. In the evening, dining with Sieyès and other friends, he exclaimed: "With a people like this, if I should become a minister, stab me, for a year later you would be slaves."

9

"Four enemies are coming post-haste: taxes, bankruptcy, the army, winter," wrote Mirabeau at the beginning of August 1790. He saw no way out of the terrible position of the king and queen but a departure from Paris. On July 17, finding that the king had failed to secure any renewed popularity, he wrote to the court: "It is essential to go at least to Fontainebleau." But, he added, such a step should be taken, so to speak, legally, through the Assembly.

He was especially afraid of the growing demoralization of the army. He urged on the king the necessity of doing everything possible to attach the troops to himself. "I need not say that the king should review these regiments, on horseback and not in an armchair," he added pointedly; "that he should speak now and then to the officers and soldiers as well as to the National Guard, and above all should leave no opportunity for such orgies as that which served as a pretext for the events of October."

In a later note, dated August 13, ne added: "I did not mean that regiments must be collected and army corps formed at once. It would be most rash to attempt this, and probably impossible to carry it out. But there is not a moment to lose before settling in intention, *in petto*, the make-up of several corps of troops and choosing for each a general who deserves the full confidence of the Tuileries. Appoint at once an inspector general of the Swiss. What would be more natural than to give this important place to La Marck, the most faithful and most distinguished military leader you have, who will not leave you thereafter, unless on the scaffold."

In drafting this plan for armed preparation, Mirabeau asked La Marck to give him certain indications in writing. To his "very excellent note" he added the proposal concerning him: "I have said what your superstitious and rather silly delicacy has not allowed you to say." La Marck replied: "My superstitious and silly delicacy is in truth no more than the desire not to be employed further. Either there will be such disturbances that we shall have to draw the sword, and then I should have to choose; or disturbances will not come, and in that case I prefer not to have been employed."

But Mirabeau thought they would come. He wrote to the court: "Civil war is certain and perhaps necessary. Is it desired to accept it or to wage it, or is it possible and is it desired to prevent it? These are questions of supreme importance, and can be treated only in a rather long and free discussion, which is necessary in order that they may be thoroughly gone into and solved." He emphasized that the risk of a new interview was his and not the royal couple's. "I ask for this meeting, however difficult and dangerous it may be for me."

"The paper I am sending you, Monsieur le Comte," wrote the queen to Mercy in transmitting Mirabeau's note, "seems to me of a type and a style so extraordinary that I felt that you should become familiar with it before I speak to you about it. How can M. or any other thinking being imagine that the time should ever come, and especially at this moment, for us to provoke civil war? The project of making up in idea and *in petto* several corps of troops is absurd, if their heads are appointed in advance, and if they are not appointed they can do nothing." Her superficial and malicious intelligence, which excelled in seizing on slight slips and ridiculing them, led her to make light of the warnings of her secret adviser: "Frankly, it seems to me mad from one end to the other, and only the interests of M. de La Marck are well looked after."

The sinister phrase in which Mirabeau referred to La Marck's fidelity upset the queen. For a moment the terrible vision of the scaffold—so unlikely in that August of 1790—rose before her shocked eyes. But she dismissed it at once with a shrug of her shoulders and wrote disdainfully to Mercy that the phrase seemed to her "most out of place."

La Marck, commenting later on his friend's plans, noted: "The Swiss filled an important part in his system; he counted on those troops, and August 10, 1792, proved that in that matter he saw very clearly."

Knowing nothing of the queen's outburst, Mirabeau returned to the necessity of separating the Swiss troops from the rest of the army and giving them an inspector of their own. "What has just happened at Nancy," he wrote to the court, "and what is in preparation in Switzerland, prove that I had foreseen and calculated well, and what was foresight six weeks ago is insistently required in the existing circumstances."

He found it difficult to resign himself to the ungrateful part of a paid adviser whose warnings were never listened to. "I must wait," he wrote, "for a clap of thunder to end the deplorable lethargy." He tried in vain to persuade the king that he ought to choose "modern leaders of opinion" and give places to new men devoted to the monarchy. The ministers "will give places to their creatures," men of influence under the former regime. "And what is wanted is to give creatures not to ministers but to the king." He returned in vain to the necessity of a second interview. The queen categorically refused: "It is absolutely impossible to see M." Offended by the liberties he allowed himself, and repelled by his prophecies, she wrote to Mercy: "He must not expect it."

But in spite of the refusals he met with, and of the humiliating indifference shown to him, Mirabeau persisted in saying what he thought to be true and useful and in fighting for a cause without any help from those most concerned. It is a pitiable and tragic spectacle that is revealed by Mirabeau's notes. All the elements were supplied in them for the prevision of a fatal outcome. Everything was foretold, and not vaguely but clearly, and in striking phrases. And with the same precision with which the evil was diagnosed, the remedies were indicated, with the precautions to be taken and the mistakes to be avoided.

He carried on a lone struggle to serve the monarchy and to spare France the convulsions of anarchy. The tragedy of his lot was rendered the more poignant by the clearness with which he saw how vain were his efforts. "If fidelity consists sometimes, and more often than is commonly supposed, in being prepared to displease in order to serve, it consists also in braving the very perils that one has foreseen, perils that would have been evaded if one had been believed. So I shall continue to serve, even in the passive role to which they are condemning themselves, whatever repugnance I may have for this order of things. . . . But I shall always lament that so good a prince, and a queen so well endowed by nature, were of no service; even through the sacrifice of their consideration and their safety, to the restoration of their country; until, falling myself, and probably among the first, under fate's scythe, I become a memorable example of what is reserved for the men who are politically in advance of their contemporaries."

10

"Here, then, is this horrible secret revealed," declared the *lieutenant criminel* in charge of the Châtelet tribunal's investigation of the events of October 5 and 6, 1789. He was admitted on August 7, 1790, with a deputation, to the bar of the Assembly, to transmit to it, under sealed cover, the minutes of the inquiry. "What was our grief," he declared, "when we found that the depositions implicated two members of the National Assembly!" He named nobody, but the names were known. The official *Journal de Paris* had given those of Louis-Philippe-Joseph d'Orléans and Mirabeau the elder. The Châtelet had made a show of indignation at that indiscretion.

In the excited atmosphere Mirabeau, on whom all eyes were fixed, the Duc d'Orléans being absent from the sitting, calmly stood up to speak. He objected to the secrecy of the proceedings. "Certainly it would be fitting that after ten months of secret inquiry, after having employed ten months in spreading and multiplying suspicions, apprehensions, alarms, terrors against good or bad citizens, the tribunal, whose story will perhaps be necessary to the perfect comprehension of this affair, should cease to play a part and should return to a modest obscurity. But the right and the wish of the members inculpated is undoubtedly that everything should be known." He asked for the opening of the sealed packet and the communication of all the documents.

But the effervescence produced by the sensational speech of the *lieutenant criminel*, and fed by Mirabeau's enemies, was little reduced. He continued to be the butt of slander and provocation that aimed at destroying his coolness.

On August 18 the Assembly had to deal with a charge against one of the members of the right, the Abbé de Barmond, who was implicated in the flight of a prisoner from the Abbaye. Bonne Savardin, an officer on the retired list and the principal agent in a counter-revolutionary conspiracy, depending on support from abroad, had been arrested by order of the Comité des Recherches and brought before the Châtelet on a charge of high treason; during the investigation his friends had helped him to escape. He was caught at Châlons-sur-Marne in the carriage of the Abbé de Barmond, who was taking him and another of his accomplices, with false passports, to the frontier. The abbé, a former ecclesiastical counsellor of the *parlement* of Paris, was arrested by order of the Assembly and summoned to its bar. His counsel, Frondeville, who was allowed to defend him before the Assembly, expressed indignation at the arrest of his client "while the assassins of our princes have been going in freedom, for ten months, about this capital, and are, perhaps, sitting among us." Amid the tumult produced by this insinuation, Frondeville was called to the bar to be admonished. When at last he agreed to go down, he turned to Mirabeau and directly attacked him: "I am at the bar; come and join me. I accuse you."

"I know only one way, Monsieur," Mirabeau replied coldly, "of excusing you in the eyes of the Assembly, and if you wish I will undertake to get a hearing for your excuse."

"What will you say?" asked Frondeville, taken aback.

"I shall say," replied Mirabeau, "that as you are one of the proved false witnesses in the infamous proceedings at the Châtelet, and as I can probably get you hanged, in that trying situation one has the right to say anything."

Frondeville carried his aggressive defence of his client outside the Assembly. He had his pleading printed under the provocative title: *Speech That Had the Honour of Being Censured by the National Assembly*. A deputy called for Frondeville's arrest for insulting the Assembly. The right wing noisily interrupted; the left preserved a threatening silence. In this atmosphere of general tension a deputy of the right, M. de Faucigny, jumped up like a madman in the middle of the hall and shouted: "This has the air of an open war by the majority against the minority; there is only one way to end it, and that is to fall on these fellows with our swords." He made a wide gesture that included the left. The whole Assembly was on its feet. Shouts from every part demanded the immediate arrest of Faucigny. Frondeville was horrified at the scandal he had provoked. He ascended the tribune and, with tears in his eyes, said in a shaking voice: "Gentlemen, I am to blame, and I alone; I am ready to go to prison, but I implore you, let your justice fall upon me alone."

Amid a very inferno of noise Mirabeau demanded to speak from his place on the extreme left. From the other end of the hall, on the extreme right, the Abbé Maury, in his element in this atmosphere of oratorical violence, intervened: "I ask that before M. de Mirabeau is permitted to speak he shall be required to declare whether it is true that he has just said to one of his neighbours that the people should be summoned." There were vehement protests, ending in a sudden silence as Mirabeau went to the tribune.

"I shall not demean myself," he said, "by disposing of the charge that has just been made against me, unless the Assembly itself brings the charge and orders me to reply; in that case I think I shall have said all that is necessary in my justification if I give my accuser's name and my own."

The Abbé Maury started up under the sting of this contempt. Mirabeau asked for Frondeville's arrest for his own safety. "I have been concerned solely with this idea amid this hideous spectacle, the consequences of which have truly alarmed me, because we have so many defenders that our strength is at this moment our weakness."

The scene was brought to an end by a pitiful declaration from Faucigny that he had "lost his head." A decree drafted by Mirabeau closed the episode with a measure of clemency.

Nothing the right could do deceived the Assembly as to the complicity of the Abbé de Barmond. In vain did he declare that it was only out of pity for an unfortunate that he had sheltered Savardin and tried to place him in safety. The investigations of the Comité des Recherches confirmed the charges against the abbé. The Abbé Maury pleaded, with a reserve unusual in him, for the provisional liberation of Barmond. Mirabeau saw in this moderation a sort of silent invitation to a compromise, a deal, clemency for clemency. He would have nothing to do with such blackmail. He fulminated against the defence of an abuse of the right of asylum for a man accused of having "done his best to destroy the freedom of the people."

He passed at once to his own case, to put an end to the whispering campaign. "I, too, am accused, or rather, there are those who would like to see me accused." Amid furious interruptions from the right he shouted: "I appeal to the Comité des Rapports to hasten its work and to make public these terrible proceedings of the Châtelet, the divulging of which will put an end to all this insolence."

The coolness he showed in these stormy scenes cost him a great effort. "You are right in thinking, my friend, that this career is becoming more chancy every day," he wrote to Mauvillon at the beginning of August. "To begin with, I have never believed in a great revolution without bloodshed, and I no longer have any hope that the fermentation in the country, together with the movements abroad, will not lead to civil war; I do not even know whether that terrible crisis is not a necessary evil. And then, I personally have become the centre of interest of the ambitious, the factious, and the conspirators. The section of the popular party that is simply out for trouble, checkmated by me on various occasions, and beaten on the question of the right of peace and war, despairs of seeing me abandon monarchical principles, and, in consequence, has sworn to destroy me. The ministry, in its perfidy and cowardice, cannot forgive me, even in its own interest, for the service I have rendered to the nation. The throne has neither ideas nor a will of its own. The people, ignorant and anarchized, are driven hither and thither by all the political jugglers and by their own illusions. Certainly it is difficult to walk along a road so littered with traps. But I shall go ahead, in the consciousness of having been useful and of never having wanted anything else."

II

"I think they are very ill informed on foreign policy at Saint-Cloud," the Archbishop of Toulouse wrote to La Marck toward the end of July 1790. "And who could instruct them with a minister like M. de Montmorin? It would be very useful if Mirabeau, whose strong point, I think, is foreign policy, would give some sound and accurate ideas on this subject." Mirabeau's great knowledge of questions of foreign policy was generally recognized in the Assembly. He had travelled a great deal, unlike a good many of his colleagues, especially among the deputies of the *Tiers;* he had a thorough knowledge of several European countries, he spoke several languages, and he kept himself informed of recent political events abroad. Above all, since his youth he had been greatly interested in the questions of international policy and in the psychology of other nations. And he never lost sight of the repercussions of France's gigantic Revolution in other countries.

After the debate on the right of making war and peace, Mirabeau had suggested that the Assembly should occupy itself with the revision of existing treaties with foreign Powers. The Assembly elected a

diplomatic committee of six members, and Mirabeau was very naturally made its *rapporteur*.

The most important question with which the committee would have
to occupy itself was the family pact with the Spanish royal house. On
August 14 Mirabeau wrote to the court: "If you are condemned to a
passive role at home, why does the ministry want to drag you into activity abroad? What an abominable policy it is that aims directly at putting on Their Majesties the responsibility, inevitably entailed by a
perilous alliance, for a disastrous war in which there is not one chance
of success? How can it be dared to propose to the king to attempt for
Spain what he does not attempt for himself? I am amazed at all this
weakness united with all this audacity. I am too loyal, and too eager for
the restoration of order, not to maintain in the Foreign Affairs Committee that we concern ourselves only with our own affairs, and that
our one purpose must be to keep at peace with whoever is at peace
with us."

It was in this sense that he spoke in the Assembly on August 25, 1790,
as *rapporteur* of the diplomatic committee. It was necessary, he said,
to discover the best means of avoiding, without weakness, the scourge
of war. He recalled the unsettled state of French finances, and the un-
prepared state of the army and navy, and evoked the "political philosophy" in conformity with which Dupont wanted to modify the family
pact. He advanced two principles adopted by his committee: (1) All
treaties concluded in the past by the king must be observed by the nation until it has annulled them or modified them; (2) The king must be
asked to inform all the Powers that "since the unfailing desire for peace
and the renunciation of all conquest is the basis of our conduct, the
French nation regards as existing and obligatory in all treaties only
their purely defensive stipulations."

Always faithful to his idea of an agreement with England, "whose
great example has helped us to achieve freedom," he declared: "No, do
not suppose that a free and enlightened people will wish to profit by
our passing troubles to renew without justification the evils of war,
to attack our growing freedom, to stifle the happy development of the
principles it has transmitted to us; the supposition would be a sacrilege."
But his generous optimism did not lead him to neglect any precaution.
"In rendering homage to the philosophy of that people, our elder
brother in freedom, let us still listen to the counsels of prudence. We
can balance the number of English vessels only with the aid of those
of our ally; thus our interest obliges us to confirm our alliance with
Spain, and the only way to preserve it is faithfully to fulfil our treaties."

Mirabeau's speech met with a warm reception from the Assembly. The Spanish government was so pleased with the intervention of the former adversary of its state bank that it ordered the publication of a Spanish version of the speech. Mirabeau had ended by proposing an increase of the French fleet. The Assembly went beyond the figure he had proposed and demanded that the number of ships of the line be raised to forty-five, of which at least twelve should be armed in the Mediterranean ports.

At the end of the debate Mirabeau sent a memorandum to the court, apparently intended for transmission to Montmorin, in which he reviewed the European situation. In 1787, he wrote, "we were really paramount in Europe, and held the political balance in our hands. Prussia and England, without a fight, without an effort, without a victory, robbed us of that sceptre, which it would have been so easy for us to keep. . . . We are now isolated in the midst of our troubles, with only one ally, Spain. Far from abandoning ourselves to inaction and despair, we must redouble our activity and our courage, negotiate everywhere, and make all the Powers of Europe feel how important it is for them not to let France be crushed."

In a memorandum written a little later for the Comte de Mercy, Mirabeau wrote: "Just as in the peacefully constituted and peacefully organized nations the French Revolution rallies opinion round the legitimate authorities, so it endangers arbitrary and purely despotic governments. . . . It is the more important that shrewd princes should watch French affairs because they will then be more inclined to refrain from interfering in them. Burke has said that France offers nothing in politics but a great void. Burke has said a very stupid thing, for that void is a volcano and it would be impossible, without imprudence, to lose sight for a moment either of its subterranean movements or of its coming eruptions."

12

"Here, my dear Count, are two packets which you will give to no one but myself, whatever may happen," wrote Mirabeau to La Marck; "in case of death you will communicate them to anyone who takes sufficient interest in my memory to defend it." Far from desiring to want to hide from posterity his activities as a secret adviser, Mirabeau considered his memoranda addressed to the court as his justification before history. He wanted the public to know some day all that he had foreseen, all the wrongs his contemporaries had done to him, all that he had been unable to prevent. La Marck, who had been lifted by his great affection for Mirabeau out of the narrow frame of a courtier's destiny, and had gained from it a deeper sense of human values, understood the full significance of his friend's wish. "These packets, my dear Count, will have all my care," he wrote to him. "If I am still alive when you are lost to universal public affairs, my deep friendship for you and my belief in your superiority will assure to your memory all of which I am capable."

"I am very touched by your note," Mirabeau replied, "and I assure you that my courage is greatly revived by the idea that such a man as you will not permit me to be entirely misunderstood." And as if he had the same prophetic sense of his own fate as of his country's destinies, he concluded: "Either I shall soon produce a harvest, or I shall leave in your hands noble elements of apologia."

❧ XX ❦

The Royal Cattle

"I ASSURE you, Monsieur, that you will be doing a very great public service by coming to Versailles," Mirabeau had written in the autumn of 1789 to Reybaz. "Geneva, your friends, France, and, last and least, I myself, will all have the greatest need of you tomorrow morning."

Rarely did Mirabeau address himself to any man with such deference as to this modest Swiss pastor. He was trying to obtain his help at a time when he still had his Genevese collaborators with him and when his "workshop" was at full pressure. But Reybaz was not so easy to get as Dumont and Duroverai had been. He was austere, without ambition, self-confident and yet unassertive, and at the same time sufficiently well off to be able to live independently in Paris with his wife and daughter. He worked at journalism a little, wrote for the *Mercure de France*, and occupied himself with works on physics and mathematics. He declined Mirabeau's offers. At the foot of a letter from Dumont conveying a renewed invitation to visit Mirabeau, he put the note: "I decided not to go."

But nobody could resist Mirabeau, not even an austere Protestant pastor. After the departure of his Genevese collaborators, Mirabeau multiplied his appeals to Reybaz. He was careful to avoid the familiarity with which he had won so many other people. He remained ceremonious, grave, and deferential. He worked to win over the pastor's wife and daughter by lavishing the courtesies of which he had the secret. He put his carriage at their disposal; he sent them books and proofs of his speeches. He flattered Reybaz in the subtle and comprehensive manner against which not even the most sceptical can hold out. From May 1790 Reybaz was busy in Mirabeau's "workshop."

Mirabeau confided to him a particularly delicate task. The Abbé de Cournaud, professor of literature at the Collège de France, had recently proposed at the Jacobin Club the abolition of the celibacy of the clergy as a means of emptying the monasteries, of inducing the clergy to forget their fight for their properties, and of enabling them to obey "the laws of nature." Mirabeau wanted to bring the question before the Assembly. He wrote to Reybaz: "What I should like to show is that to permit priests to marry is, on the one hand, the only way of bringing them into the Revolution and of attaching them to it, and on the other hand, a good way of giving society estimable officers of morality."

Reybaz, interested in the subject and stimulated by assiduous praise, set to work with energy. But Robespierre forestalled Mirabeau's intervention in the Assembly. Toward the end of May he submitted a decree authorizing the marriage of priests. He met with such hostility that he was unable to gain a hearing. His motion, although suppressed, did him much harm in his electoral department. His brother warned him that he would lose the good opinion of the peasants if he renewed his proposal. The course of the debate in the Assembly made it impossible for Mirabeau to raise the subject again. Several months later, however, he delivered his speech in the 1789 Club.

2

In August 1790 the public debt was nearly two billion. On August 27 the president of the Assembly announced a memorandum from Necker on the means of liquidating the debt. Mirabeau was in the tribune. "I ask the Assembly to decide whether the reading of the minister's memorandum shall take place before or after I have spoken. For my part, eighteen months of activity among you have not accustomed me to ministerial initiative, and I must say that it would seem strange to me

that when a member of this Assembly is in the tribune he should be
required to make way for a minister's memorandum."

Mirabeau was heard before Necker. His intervention had been long
in preparation. Reybaz had drafted his speech, to which he attached
special importance. What he had to say was the fruit of deep thought
and of an inner conflict, for he had been a resolute opponent of paper
money. On this question he had parted from Clavière and dissociated
himself from the *Courrier de Provence*, in which Clavière was carrying
on a campaign in favour of the assignats.

The debate, outwardly financial, was in reality concerned with the
fate of the Revolution. The fall of the *ancien régime* had been the result of a financial deficit. The Revolution risked foundering in the abyss
of its debt. The sale of the ecclesiastical estates could not be carried
out because of the scarcity of money; the first issue of *assignats*, to the
amount of 400 million had proved insufficient for an operation on such
a scale. Men still remembered the financial debacle of John Law and
distrusted any kind of paper money. This time more substantial support must be provided for the currency than the customary financial
guarantees. The moral force of the Revolution had to be mobilized. Its
credit had to be used in order to make the creation of the assignats a
success. It was necessary also to carry through the sale of the Church
estates, and they had to be brought within reach of all by creating a
monetary medium accessible to all. The right well understood what
was at stake, and employed all its strength in opposition. The great
majority of the Assembly, ignorant of economic questions, hesitated
before the terrible responsibility it had to assume. And of this hesitation, of the doubts that troubled even the partisans of the new measure,
nothing must be allowed to become public; the measure must be voted
by acclamation so that the faith of the Assembly should spread even
to the half-hearted and the timid, enlisting their interest in the service
of the nation.

Mirabeau realized all that depended on his success in the Assembly.
He had left it to Reybaz to draft his speech, but the idea was his own.
He made no secret of the fact that what was at stake was not merely
a financial or economic measure: "If you had in your hands, gentlemen, a simple means, already tested, of multiplying the defenders of
the Revolution, of associating them through their interest with the
progress of your labours; if by any means you could inspire warmth
in favour of the constitution in those cold spirits who see in the revolutions of governments simply revolutions of fortune, and ask themselves
'What shall I lose? What shall I gain?'; if you could even change into

friends and supporters of the constitution its detractors and its enemies and that multitude of sufferers who look upon their fortune as buried beneath the ruins of the former government, and who accuse the new one of creating their distress; if, I say, there existed a means of repairing so many breaches, of conciliating so many interests, would you not consider that a sound policy should hasten to adopt it?" He urged the Assembly to consider the assignat currency from this point of view. "You would hesitate to adopt it as a measure of finance; embrace it as a sure and active instrument of the Revolution."

This speech, long, insistent, drafted with logic and clarity but in the rather dull style of Reybaz, into which Mirabeau infused the vitalizing rhythm of his eloquence, was immensely successful in the Assembly. Some historians of the French Revolution consider it as one of the most powerful and most effective delivered in that period. He carried the Assembly with him by his passion and inspired it with his faith. It voted unanimously that his speech should be printed.

Mirabeau wrote at once to Reybaz: "I send you all the compliments which the excellent speech you provided for me brought me." He only complained that the "gracious handwriting"—that of Reybaz's daughter—had proved rather small for him in the tribune. "I ask your permission," he concluded, "to come and correct the proofs with you. I also ask you to exercise at once the most absolute dictatorship over the speech wherever you are ready to grant naturalization to the few pages I have added."

As he expected, there were many objections and criticisms. Dupont de Nemours published anonymously a pamphlet, *Effect of the Assignats on the Price of Bread, by a Friend of the People*, in which he predicted that the superabundance of the assignats and their depreciation would send up the prices of all articles of consumption. Other important adversaries mobilized a whole arsenal of scientific arguments to combat his theory. Condorcet, in a good memorandum, deplored that Mirabeau, so penetrated until then with the "conservative" principles of society and so opposed to bankruptcy, had proposed a measure which was a concealed bankruptcy. He expected that the assignat would not circulate at all, that through the general mistrust it would be immobilized in the hands of the creditors of the state. But as between the lucid savant and the passionate orator, it was Mirabeau who was to be justified with his faith in the driving power of the Revolution, which was communicated to the assignats.

Lavoisier attacked Mirabeau with arguments drawn from incontestable economic experience. By the creation of fictitious money which

would double the circulation, France, possessing only two milliards
of real currency media, ran the risk of what in modern language is
called inflation. The assignat was already depreciated six per cent in
relation to gold and silver. The actual specie would disappear as soon
as it was feared to exchange it for depreciated assignats. A rise in prices
seemed to him inevitable, together with an immediate and disastrous
fall in the value of the assignat, plunging the country into the incalculable convulsions of an economic crisis. These forecasts were to be confirmed, but not immediately, and not by the sole play of economic fac-
tors. Lavoisier, like Condorcet, had counted without the miracle of
revolutionary faith. The assignat fell four per cent in value in 1790 and
nine per cent in 1791. It stood at seventy per cent in 1792, and crumbled
only when all Europe was at war with France, through the enormous
issues necessitated by the needs of the struggle. It played the part
which Mirabeau had foreseen in the sale of the national lands. At the
end of 1790 there was very vigorous buying. The Church estates were
absorbed in a few months. The lands were distributed among a very
large number of purchasers. The danger to which Mirabeau had referred of concentration in the hands of a few powerful capitalists had
been avoided. It was especially the middle class of the great towns that
filtered into the countryside. Attached to the soil by this ownership,
the revolutionary bourgeoisie was to become conservative and to form
the solid backbone of the future France.

3

After his adversary's oratorical triumph, Necker realized that his great
part in the destinies of France was ended. He sent in his resignation.
The royal couple did not try to keep him; they no longer feared commotion over his departure. Mirabeau recommended Clavière, who, he
said, was the actual author of the assignat, as Necker's successor: "An
upright accountant, difficult to deal with but abounding in ideas, not
unduly ambitious, a prodigious worker, capable of success if it is possible, and a victim of no consequence if he does not succeed; sufficiently well known to the Jacobins to be tolerated by them, and familiar
enough with them not to be devoted to them." This warm and psy-
chologically fair recommendation was without result. Clavière had to
wait for a graver hour for the realization of the dream he had cherished
for so many years.

Necker's departure would have passed entirely unnoticed if the municipality of a little town, Arcis-sur-Aube, had not shown too much

zeal and arrested him on his way to Switzerland. The Assembly reprimanded the municipality and permitted Necker to reach Coppet, where he passed the rest of his life commenting on his own past.

After his departure the battle for the assignat continued. An anonymous pamphlet, *Great Contradiction of M. de Mirabeau the Elder,* drew attention to Mirabeau's *volte-face.* Another had the sensational title *The Tribunes Sold to Mirabeau and to Charles Lameth; or France Betrayed.* A third was entitled *Mirabeau Overthrown, or the Proved Danger of the Assignats.* On the other hand, many petitions arrived in favour of the assignats. But the speakers of the right declared that often the signatures of these petitions were forged.

The Assembly was well aware of the secret purpose of the debate. The Triumvirate spoke in favour of the assignats; the Abbé Maury wanted to force Mirabeau into a duel, "man against man. I have no speech prepared," he said; "I ask of M. de Mirabeau to go to the tribune and speak there, and I will offer my objections, to which he will reply."

Mirabeau had long been prepared with his reply. He had sent to Reybaz all the pamphlets, indicating how one point and another should be dealt with. "Please find means of providing a noble reply to the charge made against me of having changed my views on paper money."

His second speech on the assignats, on September 27, 1790, was the longest he ever delivered. "The constitution will be overthrown, disaster inevitable, and France in dissolution, if the sale of the national properties does not take place without fail," he repeated. "Only this actual sale can save the common weal. Thus I include among the enemies of the state, I regard as a criminal toward the nation, anyone who tries to destroy this sacred basis of all our regenerative plans." To those who recalled that he had said in the past that the infamous term "paper money" should be banished from the language, and that he had described paper money as a circulating plague, he pointed out that he had said at the same time that a nation may be forced to have recourse to state notes, and that it will do so without serious injury if they represent a mortgage and are a medium of payment that may not be refused.

4

The end which Mirabeau pursued indefatigably was to consolidate the revolutionary conquests, to render the constitution more perfect and more capable of resisting future shocks. He proposed a whole plan of action to induce the Assembly to revise certain of its precipitate decrees, passed in moments of passion. "The National Assembly has reserved to itself the collection of its decrees on the constitution," he wrote to the court. "I had announced that I should profit by this occasion to make an open attack on all that part of its work which is causing the present ills of the kingdom. That meant entering into the breach and exposing myself, perhaps without auxiliaries, to great perils, but I cared little about making the Assembly recognize its own errors so long as I revealed them to Europe; so long as I gave a great example of respect for the constitution and of resistance to bad laws; and so long as I showed leadership for the good citizens who are seeking a way out of our misfortunes without finding it."

The Assembly agreed to collect and revise the articles of the constitution. Lafayette promised his aid to get Mirabeau appointed *rapporteur* of the committee of revision. Once more he failed to keep his word. "He has succeeded," complained Mirabeau, "in keeping me apart from or useless to my own work."

Mirabeau did not cease to pursue his other aim, of reconciling the royal couple with their time. "I have always said," he wrote to the court toward the end of September, "that the Revolution is completed but the constitution is not; that the various points on which it is impossible to go back have fortified rather than weakened the true royal authority; and that in a single year liberty has secured more sacrifices for the national prosperity than the royal authority could have done in several centuries."

At that time, when the art of guiding the masses was still a new art, he already assessed at its true value the influence of the national press in the spreading of enlightenment. "An assured means of success for the press," he wrote, "would be a newspaper sold at a very low price, and through that very fact with a very wide circulation, which, without carrying the suspicious imprimatur of the ministry, would nevertheless be its work." He sketched the programme of such a paper—"to prove especially that there can be no freedom without obedience to the law, no law without the force of public opinion, and no force of public opinion without confidence in the executive power. Also to trace the characters that distinguish patriotism from licence and the good citizen from the sedition-monger."

But a final appeasement could not be achieved without collaboration between the ministry and the Assembly, without a ministry proceeding from the heart of the Revolution and defending the throne. "There can be no more hesitation, the moment has come when the decree that makes it impossible to form a ministry within the Assembly must be openly attacked by the king and by all those who want to save monarchical rule and the kingdom," he wrote to the court. "The king will have on his side justice, the public interest, and the support of all enlightened men."

But the court was no more responsive to his advice than to his warnings. In face of its inertia Mirabeau fell once more into one of the crises of discouragement that succeeded each resumption of activity. His memoranda became less frequent, and he asked La Marck to explain to the Archbishop of Toulouse that the reason was "the strange behaviour of the court to me. It never profits by any of my advice, and considers that I am giving it nothing: every day it aggrandizes my enemy, it gives me no regular instruction, and it feigns to believe that I might destroy it. That is pitiable. It might be supposed that the house in which they sleep could be reduced to ashes without their being injured or even disturbed."

5

On August 31 the president of the Comité des Rapports, to which the disturbances of October 5 and 6, 1789, had been referred, asked permission to print its proceedings. "Twelve hundred galleys will take a long time to print," Mirabeau observed, "and yet the affair demands the utmost speed. I know that the attempt will be made in this publication to discover secret motives; but I am indifferent, since all will be known. I say I am indifferent, for I am not modest enough not to know that in the indictment of the Revolution I should be bound to have a place."

A thunder of applause greeted this proud declaration. But the Comte de Montlosier intervened: "If the proceedings are printed, those accused may escape."

"The escape of the witnesses," Mirabeau replied contemptuously, "is just as probable as that of the accused." The left cheered wildly. In the galleries there were also spontaneous demonstrations in favour of the speaker, who added: "And yet the accused are taking no steps to prevent the escape of the witnesses." The cheers resounded again.

The "indictment of the Revolution" had been awaited as a sensational event. Mirabeau knew the importance of the debate. He mobilized all the support he could count on in the Assembly. He knew that if he came victoriously through this test he would emerge with increased reputation. He was ambitious to become president of the Assembly. To waste no chance, he even agreed to a truce with Lafayette, who was once more trying to come to terms with him.

"I have not come to the tribune to defend myself," he said. "Ridiculous charges have been brought against me; not one has been proved, and if every one had been it would have established nothing against me; I do not for a moment regard myself as under an accusation. I am here so as not to miss a formal opportunity for clearing up the facts."

He mentioned the story of his having run along the ranks of the Flanders Regiment sword in hand, and the reports of statements supposed to have been made by him to M. de Virieu and to Mounier, and then proceeded: "I come to the third charge against me, that I advised M. d'Orléans not to leave for England." Mirabeau had no hesitation in speaking out. Lafayette had given his word that he would be present at the sitting, but he was not there. Mirabeau, angered by this defection, did not hesitate to attack him, for the first time in public. "Well, what conclusion is it proposed to draw? I did not give him this advice, for I have never spoken to him, but I am proud of having seen that it was given to him." He described Lafayette's imperious intervention and the effects of that precipitate departure, which left "without a rival the man to whom events had given a new dictatorship; the man who at that time possessed within the regime of freedom a police more active than that of the *ancien régime;* the man who, by forcing M. d'Orléans to leave, instead of having him judged and condemned, if he was guilty, by that act alone openly eluded the inviolability of the members of the Assembly."

He enumerated all the contradictions in the charge that he had been an accomplice of one of the chief inspirers of the excesses of October 5 and 6, 1789. After examining them, dissecting them, demolishing them, he summed up. "Thus nothing out of all that it would have been indispensable to prove has been proved," he continued, threateningly. "But I am forgetting that I have just been borrowing the language of an accused person, whereas I should use only that of an accuser."

Vehemently he exclaimed, pointing to the right: "The secret of those infernal proceedings is in the interest of those people whose evidence and whose calumnies have formed the texture of it; it is in the resources it has furnished to the enemies of the Revolution; it is in the heart of the judges, as will soon be graven in history by the most just and the most implacable vengeance."

These words were greeted with an explosion of enthusiasm. A member of the right, the Marquis de Ferrières, described the impression produced on the Assembly: "Mirabeau descended from the tribune amid the most lively and widespread applause, which continued until he reached his seat and long after he was seated. The nobles, the bishops, the witnesses, ashamed and embarrassed, seemed to have changed from accusers into accused. All remained in a dejected silence."

The Assembly decreed that there was no ground for any charge. Mirabeau had triumphed over the intrigues of his enemies. His success was so resounding that it went beyond his immediate purpose. In crushing his adversaries he imposed on them the esteem which they had grudged him though recognizing his talents. He was reconciled with the left, who had suspected his revolutionary ardour. The Triumvirate ceased campaigning against him.

6

Pitt declared to the French ambassador in June 1790 that his country desired peace, not only because that is always preferable for a wealthy trading nation, but because the country's financial affairs demanded it. Great Britain would do everything in the world, he said, to preserve the peace that "is so advantageous to us."

At the same time Great Britain was arming with redoubled vigour, profiting by the summer months to prepare for a conflict which she hoped to avoid. Pitt neglected nothing. The success achieved by Mirabeau in August 1790 when he had induced the Assembly to decree the arming of forty-five ships of the line was a matter of great concern to him. He knew that Spain would not give way so long as she could count on French help. The National Assembly was one of the new forces which he must bring into his calculations, and there was one man in the Assembly who seemed to him a power in himself. There was a British diplomat who boasted of his old friendship with Mirabeau. Toward the end of September or at the beginning of October 1790, Hugh Elliot was sent to Paris as a semi-official negotiator with unofficial power.

Scarcely six years had elapsed since Mirabeau had sought help from his old college friend. But during those six years he had gone far. In his friendships, however, and in his political convictions, nothing had changed. The British ambassador at Paris, Lord Gower, reported to his government that the interview between Elliot and Mirabeau had succeeded better than he had hoped, and that it had provided an easy means of maintaining friendly relations between British ministers and the dominant party in the Assembly.

Elliot reported to Pitt the friendliness he had found among the French patriots, and Pitt sent him minute instructions as to the policy to be followed in France. Great Britain must not be compromised by any step that might have the air of a request for French mediation, but Elliot was to try to induce the popular leaders to make representations to Spain to bring her to accept the British proposals and to keep the peace. Pitt thought it might even be possible for Elliot to secure the Assembly's agreement to give Spain no support in the event of her refusing the British conditions. But he must give no assurance, either directly or indirectly, that might go beyond the neutrality which Great Britain had always scrupulously observed in regard to France's internal dissensions.

Elliot had, however, nothing to offer to the official directors of French policy, no promise of recognition of the Revolution, no hope of an alliance. The French *émigrés* who were busy in London besmirching the leaders of the Revolution cannot have failed to give Mirabeau a reputation of venality; Elliot may have received oral instructions authorizing him to buy Mirabeau's support if necessary. But Elliot knew his old friend, or learned to know him now, better than that.

Several years later, when he met Mirabeau's most vicious slanderer, Gouverneur Morris, he declared to him that he had never known more than one man among the French who was truly capable, and that man was Mirabeau: "I knew him intimately. He was incorruptible." But Morris, though a little shaken by so definite an assurance, was not disarmed.

Mirabeau seemed to think also that a conciliatory attitude on the part of France would facilitate his old dream of an alliance with Great Britain. Elliot cannot have kept strictly to the latter part of Pitt's instructions. A meeting took place with the members of the diplomatic committee, to whom Elliot made a long statement, for, he wrote, nothing gets done in France without a regular oratorical debate. He spoke for an hour, explaining the British attitude, and suggesting that Spain wanted to embark on war "in concert with French *émigrés*." Lord Gower's dispatches seemed to insinuate that allusions had been made to a possibility of alliance. Elliot, very able and very anxious to succeed, replied to questions put to him so satisfactorily that he secured from the members of the committee a resolution that even if war came and Spain called for aid from France, there would be an inquiry into the causes of the conflict before such aid was granted. The committee informed Montmorin of its decision and asked him to make representations accordingly to Spain.

Elliot had won a complete success at Paris. But he had not been able to keep his mission secret as instructed by his government. The newspapers commented on his stay, though without giving its exact purpose. He saw many people; he dined several times with Mirabeau, and at La Marck's house with Louise de Ségur, the Duc de Biron, and the Marquise de Vauban.

On his return he tried to persuade Pitt of the firm establishment of the French Revolution. At the risk of diminishing his own merit as a negotiator, he tried also to convince Pitt that the party in power desired only peace and friendship with England.

Spain was conscious of her isolation. "I submit to your conditions," said Florida-Blanca, the Spanish prime minister, to the British envoy, Fitzherbert, "not because they are just but because I am forced. If France had given us aid, I should never have submitted, but alone we are no match for you. So, do what you want." On October 28, 1790, the treaty of the Escurial was signed, embodying the British claims in their entirety.

7

The royal couple had no intention of allying themselves with the popular party in order to save the monarchy, as Mirabeau suggested. At the beginning of October 1790 they began secret negotiations with the Baron de Breteuil, who had taken refuge in Switzerland. The Marquis d'Agoult, on his way back from Switzerland to France, had brought a memorandum from Breteuil in which the ex-minister urged the king to put an end "to the general mistrust with which the uncertainty of his course is filling all parties."

The queen still considered Breteuil, the author of the Austrian alliance, as a minister of the king, and his enforced dismissal as illegal and void. Breteuil and Agoult, who knew that it was necessary to secure the queen's assent before the king could be induced to take any step, arranged with the Bishop of Pamiers to have the memorandum brought before Marie Antoinette by Fersen, of whom it was public knowledge that he alone possessed the queen's confidence and her personal attachment. The plan set forth by Breteuil was for the royal couple "to leave Paris and retire to a safe place, and there to surround themselves by the loyal troops of General de Bouillé."

Both Mirabeau and La Marck were unaware of these secret negotiations. They were equally unaware that the queen had no intention of inducing Lafayette to form, as she had assured La Marck, an "open coalition" with Mirabeau, because she thought their hostility very useful to the royal projects; she seemed even deliberately to foster it. Nor had she any wish to appease the popular discontent of which Mirabeau held the spectre in front of her: she thought it even of advantage to royalty, as giving the moderates food for thought. Mirabeau's collaboration with the court proceeded in this atmosphere of insincerity.

8

Returning to the subject of a new ministry, Mirabeau wrote to the court: "Ministers may be taken either from among the Jacobins or from any other section. Jacobins in the ministry," he added with his extraordinary finesse, "will not be Jacobin ministers. For any man a great elevation is a crisis that heals the troubles he has and gives him others that he has not. Stationed at the helm, the wildest demagogue, gaining a closer view of the troubles of the kingdom, would recognize the insufficiency of the royal power. . . . But why not choose some ministers from the Jacobins and others from a different section of the popular party? Equality of power is a very strong instrument of understanding. The union would be a mutual corrective."

Mirabeau's proposal alarmed the court and horrified Marie Antoinette. La Marck himself no longer followed his friend: "I do not always agree entirely with Mirabeau, especially when he proposes to appoint ministers at the choice of the Jacobins," he wrote to Mercy. Mirabeau persisted, however. "I have to give advice even if I am sure it will not be followed," he wrote in one of his notes. But he felt more and more painfully that he was failing to hold the attention of the royal couple. He urged once more that he should be granted a second interview with the queen. He urged La Marck to support him, and La Marck replied that the queen's only reason for hesitating was the fear of being compromised. "If, however, you think every objection must be ignored it is not difficult to persuade her." In this troubled atmosphere La Marck himself lacked sincerity. He had not asked for the interview Mirabeau wanted.

The king had already been informed by the Marquis d'Agoult of the result of his inquiries of General de Bouillé. The general, a born soldier and a fervent royalist, was ready to enter into the project elaborated by Breteuil; he was content to appease his constitutionalist's conscience with the promise that the king would not seek to re-establish despotism. But Louis was incurably indecisive. The queen herself was hesitant; she was afraid, as she told her brother the Austrian emperor, of a precipitate move that might plunge them into new misfortunes.

Mirabeau had no knowledge of these negotiations, but he suddenly learned that the royal couple were also consulting Bergasse. Bergasse, as a young lawyer, had been briefed against Beaumarchais, and had

had a premature success. He imagined that fate had carried him to the height of celebrity. He thought he could become France's great legislator and hoped to dominate the Assembly by his eloquence. Disappointed by his lack of success, and frightened by the events of October 1789, he had resigned his seat. He was one of those vain and restless people who are prone to take refuge in an emotional mysticism. He was an impassioned disciple of Mesmer and had contributed by his writings to the diffusion of the theories of animal magnetism. Since his resignation he had salved his wounded pride by decrying the Assembly in the provinces. It was not true that he was the confidant and adviser of the court as Mirabeau imagined; he was one of the many people who offered the court advice that was scarcely listened to and never followed. A copy of a letter drafted by Bergasse for the king to write to the Assembly, a letter of which Louis had made no use, reached Mirabeau's hands. He fell into one of those violent tempers that shook him like a tempest. "I did not want to show any knowledge of the Bergasse story before talking to you about it," he wrote to La Marck, "for I shall not copy the stupidity of the royal cattle, and when I recognize a man's intelligence and uprightness and devotion I shall not decide on anything serious without consulting him, and I shall not keep on consulting him and never do what he says. So they mean to seek in the mesmeric tub a remedy for their troubles. Good God! what heads! what insanity!"

The phrase "the royal cattle" was too strong for La Marck. Mirabeau complained that he was unjust and cold. "I have not grown cold," replied La Marck; "there are things on which my judgment may differ from yours, but I do not think that makes me unjust. You advise them too much as if they had something of your character. Try to see them as they are." "This man," he complained to Mercy, "is sometimes very great and sometimes very little, perhaps very useful and also harmful. In a word, he is often above the rest and sometimes below them."

9

Mutiny had broken out at Brest in a squadron that had returned from the colonies. The municipality took steps that made the situation worse. The ministry showed itself incapable of repressing the disorders. The incident was brought before the Assembly and referred to the committees. Mirabeau informed the court that "the three committees sitting together have resolved to call on the Assembly to pray that the king will appoint a new ministry capable of getting the decrees of the National Assembly carried out." "The move against the ministers," wrote

La Marck to Mercy, "was made at Mirabeau's instance without informing me, in which he was at fault, and without informing the court, in which, in view of his position, he was yet more at fault."

Mirabeau defended himself from the suspicion of having pursued a personal aim: "If I had been thinking only of myself, I should have considered that anarchy would serve me better, would make me more necessary, than the establishment of any government." Once the step had been taken, whether at his instance or not, he tried to make the court realize its advantages.

At this time Mirabeau was ill. The doctors advised him to take the waters at Barèges. He could get away only for a few days, and returned in haste for the Assembly debate. From his bed, where, he said, he had just escaped from death, he dictated an important note to the court. "We count on the people's love for the monarch, but this means that it must be possible for the king's cause to be bound up with the people's cause, and not on any account with the interest of a few ministers. These ministers, who have allowed the royal authority to be weakened and destroyed in their hands, are an insuperable obstacle to the return of public confidence; in attacking them the Assembly is delivering the king rather than itself from them." He repeated that the king could not rule without collaborating with the dominant party, and that "a new ministry, formed at the instance of the majority and supported by it, would soon give him that advantage and would enable him to win back his influence."

Mirabeau got up from his bed to be present at the sitting of October 19, 1790, at which the *rapporteur* of the four committees entrusted with an inquiry into the events at Brest proposed that the president of the Assembly should "represent to His Majesty that the popular distrust of the existing ministers places the greatest obstacles in the way of the re-establishment of order, the administration of the laws, and the completion of the constitution."

There was a very lively discussion. Cazalès, in one of his best speeches, attacked the proposal. The *rapporteur* had declared at the outset that "a decree excludes the members of this Assembly from the ministry; it must be maintained; that is the palladium of liberty," and deputies of right and left united in resolute support of that attitude.

The proposal of the committees was rejected, however. Mirabeau saw in this vote the frustration of more than his own ambition. "It is evident," he wrote to the court, "that the king has lost where the ministers have gained. The popular party, which seemed to be returning to more moderate principles, will be further embittered by defeat and will redouble its excitement among the Jacobins, its precautions and efforts in the Assembly, and its demagogy in the provinces."

It was in a sense of discouragement that he attended the debate of October 21. At the end of the deliberations on the incidents at Brest it had been proposed that as soon as discipline had been restored the white ensign, which was still being flown from the ships, should be replaced by the national colours. But the right wing, after its triumph of the day before, showed "the most indiscreet and stupid mania." One of its deputies declared that the proposal was "a profanation of the glory and honour of the French flag." He exclaimed contemptuously: "Let the children have this new tricoloured toy."

This defiance of the Revolution outraged Mirabeau. He rushed to the tribune. "Everybody knows what terrible crises have arisen out of insults to national colours. Everybody knows of the fatal results on various occasions of the contempt which certain individuals have dared to show them; everybody knows with what mutual congratulations the whole nation received the monarch's command to the troops to wear these glorious colours, and wore them himself—that sign for the rallying of all the friends, all the children of liberty, all the defenders of the constitution; everybody knows that but a few months, a few weeks ago, anyone rash enough to show contempt for this token of patriotism would have paid for that crime with his head." The right interrupted his speech with violent hooting, but could not drown that great accusing voice. "Well, the trifling success of a fraudulent tactic in yesterday's sitting has lifted up the hearts of counter-revolutionaries; and in twenty-four hours, in a single night, all ideas have been so subverted, all principles have been so distorted, the mind of the people has been so misinterpreted, that you have heard it coolly said, to all intents and purposes, that 'we consider ourselves strong enough to hoist the white ensign, that is to say the flag of the counter-revolution, in place of the hateful colours of liberty.' "

The right wing, surprised by the violence of this attack, shouted its indignation, to which the left replied with a thunder of applause.

Once more Mirabeau was the mouthpiece of the Revolution, the voice of France, of the France of the morrow that would emerge victorious from all her trials, from anarchy, terror, reaction, the immortal France of the Rights of Man.

"Certainly, to anyone not in the secret," wrote La Marck later, "it would have been impossible to suppose that the man who spoke in those terms in the tribune was at the same time in correspondence with the court and busied with the reconstitution of the monarchy." The court, shocked by this speech, made no secret of its displeasure. Mirabeau had some trouble in justifying the vehemence of his speech, "which a violent attack had made very vigorous, that is to say, very oratorical." But to La Marck, who also heaped reproaches on him, he replied with perfect frankness: "Yesterday I was not in the least a demagogue; I was a great citizen and perhaps a clever orator. Are these stupid rascals, intoxicated with a purely fortuitous success, to make us a plain offer of counter-revolution, and is it to be supposed that I shall not thunder?"

10

A lion's jowl, with split upper lip, a flat nose, full cheeks covered with pockmarks, a powerful voice, and wide and vigorous gestures—Danton's face had, as a whole, a curious resemblance to that of Mirabeau. His ugliness was more vulgar, his voice more raucous, his laugh coarser, his gestures more brutal, his language more violent: he was known as the people's Mirabeau. On November 10, 1790, Danton appeared for the first time in the Assembly at the head of a deputation.

On October 27 all the sections of Paris had urged the mayor, Bailly, to send a deputation to the Assembly to demand the dismissal of the ministers as no longer possessing the confidence of the nation. Paris, conscious of her mission to safeguard the Revolution, was reproaching the Assembly for its timidity. Danton had been chosen as spokesman for the sections. This Parisian lawyer presented himself before the legislators as the incarnation of the revolutionary populace. He pronounced the case against the ministers as if he were preparing to ask for their capital punishment. The Archbishop of Bordeaux—Danton called him M. Champion—had "altered the text of decrees and chosen as royal commissioners declared enemies of the new order of things." M. de Saint-Priest—Danton, in the fashion of the morrow, called him M. Guignard—knew "no other patriotism than that which he learned from the policy of the Divan." Danton's language produced a violent tumult in the Assembly. Another son of the people, with the figure of a grenadier under his cassock, the Abbé Maury, rudely interrupted him. The two forces measured each other, in the service of two hostile causes, amid an indescribable uproar. Danton emerged victorious from the affray. "These three ministers," he roared, "must no longer arm against the people, even by the indulgence of the representatives of the people."

The Minister of Marine had already resigned after the debate on the events at Brest. A few days after Danton's intervention the ministers at whom he had aimed also resigned.

"Unfortunately the court is contributing to our embarrassment," wrote La Marck to Mercy. "Is it excusable, for instance, not to have been prepared in advance and ready at any moment to replace the present ministers at once? And is it not enough to make one despair when the court is caught at a loss, after having been warned so often on this important point?"

From the beginning of the crisis Mirabeau had feared Lafayette's influence on the formation of the new cabinet. He had warned the court that a Lafayette ministry would never have the required majority. This time the royal couple shared his mistrust. "The court," wrote La Marck to Mercy, "seems determined to make bad selections rather than accept those of Lafayette."

Mirabeau was thrown back into the tortuous path of intrigue. An abyss had opened between him and the Assembly, which in his eyes could not assure to the country a stable government or a more perfect constitution. Nothing was left of the enthusiasm with which he had welcomed the States General. But he was not one of those who abandon their post or withdraw into a contemptuous silence. The Assembly was still a powerful instrument in his hands, a field of action which he exploited for his own ends. For from now on he was alone, vigilant alike against counter-revolutionary intrigues and against the excesses of popular demagogy. He was out of his element in this secret work. But he remained faithful to the great principles by which he was guided: "No human effort," he repeated to the court, "will ever upset the bases of the constitution. The attempt may be made, but virtually the whole nation will support them, both in its own interest and in that of the monarch."

In the short time that had passed since the discussion on the incidents at Brest, events had shown La Marck how right Mirabeau was. "Unfortunately," he wrote to Mercy on November 9, 1790, "if the ferment that is being stirred up does not end, it will not be concerned only with the ministers. The public will not believe that they are resisting of their own accord; and as the king's weakness is generally realized, it will naturally be inferred that another hand, firmer and more powerful, is holding them back or directing them, and the results of such an opinion may become very grave. The queen has enemies enough for it to be sought to attribute the conduct of the king and his ministers to her influence. The formation of a national high court is about to be decreed."

Next day Danton demanded it from the Assembly. Direct threats against the queen began to be made.

"It is proposed that *the question of the regency and that of the king's divorce* be raised," wrote La Marck, underlining the words in his dismay. Mirabeau's passionate warnings against Lafayette were also confirmed. Barely a month had passed since Fersen, reflecting the queen's feeling, had been rejoicing in the success of her policy of neutralizing Lafayette and Mirabeau through their rivalry, when Lafayette suddenly faced the queen as a bitter enemy. "A few days ago," La Marck continued, "Lafayette had a long interview with the queen: he employed the most hateful means of disturbing her and went so far as to say that in order to obtain the divorce she would be called to account for adultery." It was from Lafayette that the queen first heard of the accusations of the revolutionary tribunal.

II

Party divisions were growing more bitter; differences of opinion led to personal quarrels. Incidents multiplied in the Assembly. On November 6 a Corsican deputation was admitted to the bar. It denounced as bad patriots and aristocrats two Corsican deputies, one of whom was the reactionary Abbé Peretti. The members of the right rushed to the bar and demanded that the Corsican deputation be driven out of the hall. The Abbé Maury and an opponent both entered the tribune, disputing the right of speech; the impetuous abbé seized his adversary in his strong arms and threw him down from the tribune. He lost all self-control and shouted to the "inculpated members" to "fight your own battle." The spirit of vendetta seemed to have entered the hall. The Corsican deputation proposed in self-defence that a letter written in Italian by the Abbé Peretti be read in translation. A member of the right shouted, to create an easy diversion: "The original!"

"Is in my hands," replied Mirabeau, rushing to the tribune. "I was greatly astonished when I heard a priest come to invoke individual vengeance as judge in the sanctuary of the laws." He read the incriminating letter, in which the Abbé Peretti declared that he could no longer keep silence "when the Assembly is out to destroy faith, piety, and religion." As he read this "apostolic correspondence," the deputies of the right massed round the tribune, excited and threatening. Mirabeau dominated the uproar. "I have said once in this tribune that our strength is our weakness. It would be too easy, indeed, to secure a striking vengeance for the insults offered me for me to be able to want it." Amid the applause from the hall and the galleries there were shouts of "Do you want to murder us?"

"If we have phalanxes at our disposal, and you have only libels at yours, it must be agreed that we are very patient," replied Mirabeau. "It would be too easy to get out of a difficulty by shouting and tumult." Suddenly the Abbé Peretti, infuriated, came up to the tribune and threw himself upon Mirabeau. A dagger glittered in his hand. Several of his colleagues had seen the murderous move, and one of them was quick enough to seize Peretti's wrist and disarm him.

❧ XXI ❦

Political Pharmacy

"MIRABEAU decorated his house like a fine lady's boudoir," wrote Dumont, shocked but a little envious. Arrived at eminence as a public man, Mirabeau denied himself nothing in his private life. He could not satisfy his passion for fine books. He bought part of Buffon's celebrated library. He busied himself with the arrangement of his books in the midst of the most important political affairs. He installed bookcases in the dining-room and filled them with superbly bound books and rare editions.

There was nothing conventional about the organization of his existence. He knew the value of free conversation and of the confidences exchanged round the table when servants were not present. "When the table was laid," wrote the Comte de Gorani, "we entered the dining-room; between the guests were placed dumb waiters with four tiers, covered with bottles, plates, glasses, and dinner services, so that each of us took what we wanted. When a course had been eaten, Mirabeau rang, and three valets quickly took away the empty dishes, and three others replaced them at once with the dishes that formed the next course." Mirabeau liked his food highly spiced. A lady related that the food was delicious but "so incendiary that I almost always spat blood when I dined with Mirabeau."

The luxury of his private life seemed a defiance of the good opinion of the masses who supported him. Mirabeau made no concession to his popularity. He made use of his title of count, his domestics wore livery though it had been officially suppressed, and his coat-of-arms appeared on his carriage.

His growing renown brought unexpected visitors to his house. One day Louise de Cabris appeared. As a woman who forgot nothing and forgave nothing, she had in no way put off her hatred. She had vehemently repudiated any relations with her elder brother, "a traitor to his God, his king, and his order." She had ostentatiously cultivated affectionate relations with her younger brother. In August 1789 she had taken refuge at Nice, the centre chosen by the first malcontents under the new regime. But the atmosphere of intrigue that surrounded her aroused the suspicion of the *émigrés*. They suspected her of being "an accomplice and spy of the Comte de Mirabeau." She was ostracized so pointedly that one day she was refused a box at the theatre. There was an attempt to force her to leave the town. She obstinately stayed there, screaming to everybody how she disagreed with her elder brother. She screamed it too loudly to be quite believed. Actually, concerned always for her own interest, she did not risk an open quarrel with so powerful a man.

Interest and perhaps curiosity brought her to see him while on a visit to Paris. One of Mirabeau's women friends met her at his table, together with Mme. du Saillant. The contrast between the two sisters was particularly striking. Caroline, stout and placid, with her clear complexion and fair hair tinged with auburn, and with her laughing grey-blue eyes, was the soul of easy good nature and careless gaiety. Louise, very dark, with a bilious complexion, was tense and defiant. She had become very stout, she had lost all her teeth, and her lined features increased her resemblance to her father. Incessant anxiety for her sick husband, added to money troubles, had robbed her of all feminine coquetry. Badly dressed and untidy, she retained nothing of her old beauty beyond her royal carriage and the imperious expression of her fiery eyes. At her brother's table she was like a ghost from his troubled past. Her presence bore witness to Mirabeau's power. But it was only a moment's truce in the hostility with which she pursued him. Mirabeau was not deceived. A woman friend noted the great dissimilarity between the two sisters; he whispered: "Mme. du Saillant is of the purest gold; Mme. de Cabris is a counter so perfectly gilded that it wants any amount of skill to detect the base metal."

2

Mirabeau was always, as he put it, "on the tripod." But in the midst of his feverish existence he nursed plans of retirement. One day he wrote to his old adversary Beaumarchais: "Like other people, I am getting very close to the age, and especially to the state of mind, in which I want to think only of my books and my garden; and I had cast my eyes on one of the national possessions, the Minimes, in the forest of Vincennes. I learn that you are thinking of it and even that you have made a bid for it; no doubt, if you want this charming place, you will pay much more for it than I could, because you are much more able to pay; that being so, I should feel it very disobliging to raise to your disadvantage the price of an object beyond my reach."

"I have long been seeking an opportunity of revenging myself on you; this you yourself offer, and I seize it with joy," Beaumarchais hastened to reply. "At the age of twelve, when about to go to my first Communion (does it make you laugh?), I was taken to the Minimes. A big picture of Judgment Day which was in the sacristy so fascinated me that I returned to it again and again. An old monk, a very religious man, took advantage of this to try to tear me from the world; he preached to me every time on the text of the picture, accompanying his sermon by a lunch. Since then I have always enjoyed seeing that close; and as soon as the estates of my poor tonsured friends were put up for sale I gave the order to outbid everyone else for this one. Many considerations united to make this acquisition very precious to me, but my vengeance is still more so, for I am no longer as good as I was in childhood. You would like my close; I give it up to you and abandon all my claims to it, only too glad to have *my enemy* at last within *four walls*. I alone can manage it now, after the fall of the bastilles. If in your wrath you are so generous as not to offer opposition at least to the salvation of my soul, reserve to me, Monsieur, the big picture of Judgment Day. You will be avenged on me as I am on you. If you need any information or even my assistance to facilitate your acquisition, speak, and I will do all you wish in the matter; for I am, Monsieur, the most implacable of all your enemies."

Thereafter the two former adversaries competed in generosity. Mirabeau promised the picture, and Beaumarchais replied with "the most sincere assurance of total forgetfulness of the past. Make a dining-room of my ancient sacristy, and I shall gladly accept a frugal lay repast." Mirabeau did not, however, buy the Minimes, but a property near Argenteuil, the Marais, formerly lived in by Helvétius, an elegant seventeenth-century building with a beautifully wooded park. The price was fifty thousand francs. Actually, save for a deposit on the furniture, it was never paid for.

This purchase revived all the slanders. Mirabeau took little notice of them amid his enjoyment, naïve or cynical, of his new prosperity. He collected not only books but rare prints and engraved stones. "I was surprised," wrote Dumont, "to see him open after dinner a casket containing several precious stones."

La Marck tried in vain to reason with him about his extravagance, for Mirabeau set out to convince La Marck that his expenditure was entirely reasonable: "The truth about this little bit of pedantry is that I have nothing in the world but my bookcase, which is already of considerable value; the fifty or sixty eminently beautiful and rare articles that may still be lacking will add ten times their intrinsic value; certain of the books are of more value to me than to most amateurs, and really my expenditure on these things is economic and productive."

La Marck replied sharply: "Yesterday, on leaving Montmorin, I met Duquesnoy, who tried to get me to give you facilities for the acquisition of that country house. So you have spoken to him about it, for I have not opened my mouth to anyone. I replied that it would be better for you to buy Versailles in six months than a shanty today. Talon came up and agreed with me, and spoke of the sumptuous books you have bought. Everybody has been talking to me about them. You would do well in the interests of both of us to give little ground for conjectures of this sort, of which a good many may be disagreeable for me."

Dumont also disapproved. One day he said to Clavière: "Mirabeau is very ill advised; anyone might think he is afraid of being thought a decent person." But Clavière replied: "He is necessary to us; he alone can manage the Jacobins and the court, and if he cost the nation a million, that million would not be badly employed."

3

La Marck was grieved at the indifference and coolness of the court to Mirabeau. He pleaded with the queen: "I have always said that the court would be more satisfied with Mirabeau if it offered him more means of being useful. But the king has done nothing to help Mirabeau to secure the revocation of the fatal decree that shut him off from power. The queen, too, has been inaccessible to all the appeals from her devoted servant."

As time passed the situation grew steadily worse. La Marck's letters to Mercy were a long series of laments at the approach to the abyss, of which he was an impotent witness. "The continuing ferment is the more disquieting since the queen is being more and more strongly attacked." Lafayette had lost some of his popularity and was no longer regarded by public opinion as irreplaceable, and the court did little to

profit by the eclipse of his influence. "The terror which the latest popular agitations have inspired in the king and queen has led them to submit
to him more than ever and to offer little opposition to the choice of
ministers he proposes."

One of the new ministers, Duport-Dutertre, Keeper of the Seals,
was a lawyer who in the past had helped Mirabeau in a private suit.
He was the first plain citizen to hold a portfolio in France, as the general's friends boasted. But it was a timorous though well-intentioned
ministry that Lafayette had chosen among his friends.

Montmorin was the only former minister retained. A little more
than a year had passed since he had sent a disdainful letter to Mirabeau
and refused to see him. Now he took the initiative in a reconciliation.
One morning La Marck was surprised by a visit from Talon, accompanied by Duquesnoy, deputy for Bar-le-Duc, a talented lawyer who
had entered the Assembly with very advanced ideas, but who was now
frightened by the wild revolutionary torrent. The two visitors described
themselves as "bearers of a message from M. de Montmorin," who
wanted to come to an understanding with Mirabeau. The emissaries
were particularly badly chosen. "I must be on my guard," wrote Mirabeau to the court when informing it of this move. But he yielded when
a second and a pressing invitation came from Montmorin.

The minister showed more tact in the interview with Mirabeau. "I
am asking you," he said, "for an act of confidence; first of all I must
merit it; thus I must remove all the suspicions that might keep you
on the defensive." He spoke to him of Lafayette. "He has deceived you;
but whom has he not deceived, either voluntarily or without knowing
or desiring it? Do you think that man is ambitious? His only ambition is
to be praised. Or desirous of power? He seeks the appearance of power
rather than the reality. Or faithful to friendship? He is a friend only
to himself. How, with such a character, could he have failed to deceive
you?"

It was a skilful opening and pleased the visitor. "Do you want to
know now what influence he has?" continued Montmorin. "He has
some on the court, but through fear. On the government, on the ministry, on the Council, he has none. He has never had any in that quarter,
for all he knew he knew through me." He, too, was abandoning the
man who was losing popular favour for the one to whom it was turning.

He came to the real purpose of the interview. "The terms I am on
with the queen do much to deprive me of success; and if that obstacle
became known my popularity would grow at her expense, a thing I
am far from desiring. What have I not done to gain her confidence?

I spoke out to her and she seemed touched by my zeal; three days later her household picked a quarrel with me on the subject of the Prince de Condé. I then had an interview with the queen and was ill treated. I want to be of service and can be only through the queen; I feel that she is the strongest element of the government."

Mirabeau was flattered, perhaps unconsciously, by this appeal for his protection. "I can be a useful intermediary," continued Montmorin, "between the nation and the monarch, and as I have never deceived any-one I can be trusted. We are clearly going to destruction, royalty, au-thority, the whole nation. What, then, must we do? Temporize, but govern; await a favouring wind, but prepare the sails."

These ideas were identical with Mirabeau's. To complete his con-quest, the minister employed the small coin ministers use for gaining confidence—confidences about persons. He criticized the Lameth brothers. "Only one of their sect deserves any consideration, Barnave. We must get him away from them or destroy him with them; I should prefer the former. I have a man in his circle, but I have not yet been able to make a money offer." He named the deputies on whom he could rely, among them the Bishop of Autun. His final weapon was skilful and direct flattery: "You are the only man who has been able to lose popularity through courage and regain it through prudence."

In asking Mirabeau to secure him the queen's confidence, Montmorin did not dream that he was signing his own death warrant. Some eighteen months after this conversation he was denounced as head of the alleged Austrian committee. Tracked down in the sanguinary days of August 1792, he paid for the alliance he had so coveted with the queen by death on the scaffold.

Mirabeau was delighted with the interview, which had lasted more than four hours. He had found the minister's views so entirely in con-formity with his own that he accepted his proposal with enthusiasm. "I was too sure that M. de Montmorin was sincere not to be so myself." He asked the queen for "secrecy even from the king, for fear that an indiscretion, by destroying the minister's confidence, might set an ob-stacle in the way of a coalition from which it is possible to draw a great advantage."

La Marck entirely agreed with Mirabeau. He urged the queen "not to lose the only resource that offers itself." He induced her to give a long interview to Montmorin, who showed the utmost gratitude and invited La Marck's advice with an eagerness which, said La Marck, "dis-turbed me far more than it flattered me."

But the atmosphere of dupery scarcely lifted. Montmorin was not given full confidence. La Marck, torn between his devotion to the queen and his friendship for Mirabeau, was not entirely sincere with him. It was not without a certain duplicity that he wrote to Mercy: "I am inclined to think that Montmorin will want to go further and to proceed more quickly than Mirabeau, who will calculate the chances more carefully and will never expose himself sufficiently to be as useful as he ought to be if he relied entirely on his talents and his courage and gave less thought to his apparent popularity."

<h2 style="text-align:center">4</h2>

The revolutionary spirit that breathed throughout France had incited the people of Avignon to rise against the papal authority and to demand annexation to France. Their petition to the Assembly was sent to the diplomatic committee for study. The left wing of the Assembly was in favour of annexation, the right against it; the moderates sought an indefinite adjournment of the question. Mirabeau wanted to avoid a rupture with Rome without discontenting the popular party. On November 20, 1790, he presented not a report, but an opinion from the committee. The committee considered that "in this question you should concern yourselves only with your greatest present advantage; and it has not found that it is to your interest at present to enter into possession of Avignon." He secured the dispatch of troops to Avignon to restore order and the adjournment of the debate.

The general ferment was particularly violent in the south, and Mirabeau was always attentive to events in Provence. He felt responsible for the destinies of the two towns that had elected him. There came a sudden clash at Aix. The nobles at Aix, obstinately feudal, collected in a club that wore the white cockade. They fraternized with the officers of the Lyon Regiment stationed in the town. At the end of a drinking bout the nobles and officers insulted the members of a hostile club. Shots were fired and blood flowed. To calm men's minds the municipality demanded the regiment's immediate withdrawal from the town. Some of the most turbulent of the aristocrats were arrested; among them Pascalis, who was known for his opposition to every reform of the institutions of Provence.

The regiment had scarcely left when the people, exasperated by recent excesses, rose, quickly overcame the National Guard, and were masters of the town. The mob broke open the prisons. It was drunk with the spirit of vengeance. Pascalis and two nobles were hanged from trees. "The Aix affair is even more terrible than is generally known, and two-thirds of the kingdom is almost in the same state," wrote Mirabeau to La Marck.

The rioting at Aix was discussed in the Assembly. Troops were to be sent to restore order. The Abbé Maury launched from the tribune a violent attack on the municipal officers as responsible for all that had happened.

"The crimes committed at Aix are too great, too deplorable, to need to be exaggerated," replied Mirabeau. He sought to exonerate the municipal officers, whose task, he said, was particularly difficult in a town "closer to the aristocratic meridian than to the democratic one."

At this moment André, deputy for the nobility at Aix, was elected president of the Assembly. He was known as the "two-edged knife" for his success in usually voting with the left but keeping on friendly terms with the right. He had declared himself a friend of Pascalis, and his election to the presidency was regarded by the Assembly as a reprobation of the rioting.

The two neighbouring towns infected each other. "Marseille is near to being lost for France and declaring herself a republic," wrote Mirabeau in alarm to La Marck. He felt obliged to intervene personally "to change the municipality and prevent the sack of the town." On the day of André's election he informed the Assembly of his intention to be away for a month. He wrote to the president to ask for a passport. He looked forward to playing again the glorious part he had once played in restoring order in his beloved Provence. But the announcement of his departure aroused a ferment. His adversaries on the right suspected him of intending to stir up the flames in Provence; Marat declared that "the infamous Riqueti" was fleeing to "the refugee conspirators at Turin"; his friends and supporters took alarm at his proposal. He suddenly appeared irreplaceable. The various sections of Paris sent deputations to beg him not to leave the capital. His popularity was so great that at the Jacobin Club Barnave found himself obliged to move a resolution to the same effect. Mirabeau, in yielding to these urgent representations, realized the full extent of his power over public opinion.

5

The civil constitution of the clergy, Talleyrand said later, "was perhaps the greatest political mistake made by the Assembly." Its repercussions appeared especially after the wide distribution of the *Exposition of Principles Concerning the Civil Constitution of the Clergy*, which was signed by twenty-nine bishops who were members of the Assembly and then by one hundred and ten others. It called for the express exception from the oath prescribed by the Assembly of "the objects dependent on the spiritual power," and for the Church's control of changes in the ecclesiastical hierarchy and in ecclesiastical discipline.

In the debate on November 27, 1790, Mirabeau denounced the *Exposition* as the work of those "who continue to meditate measures for overthrowing the constitution . . . while affecting to plead only the cause of God and to claim the rights of the spiritual power." He had taken no part in the work or the debates on the civil constitution of the clergy, as though he had felt what a source of trouble it would become. In speaking in the debate of November 27 he wanted above all to avoid the deepening of the gulf between the two parts of the nation. He knew that the majority of the Assembly were exasperated by the intrigues of the clergy and by the attitude of certain priests who were inciting the faithful to resistance; he knew that they were determined to eliminate that state within the state which was placing obstacles in the path of the Revolution. But he wanted to give the government time to negotiate with Rome, and he wanted to smooth the transition and especially to make the masses understand that the new measures constituted no threat to religion.

On the preceding evening the *rapporteur* of the three committees concerned had presented his report on the disturbances caused, particularly in Brittany, by the refusal of priests and bishops to take the prescribed oath. He had proposed a series of measures which included a week's grace to enable priests to take the oath; all who did not conform were to be deprived of their offices.

Mirabeau refuted the bishops' *Exposition* in a long argument, declaring: "No, gentlemen, they do not sincerely want order and justice; they want only to embroil and overthrow." He reproached the clergy with cloaking beneath religious arguments their political convictions and their desire to call a halt to the Revolution.

For the week's grace Mirabeau wanted to substitute an indefinite period. But his eloquence did not convert the Assembly to his moderate proposals: it served only to secure the adoption of the *rapporteur's* plan. "Mirabeau," wrote La Marck to Mercy, "proposed a fairly moderate decree, but preceded it with a very violent speech and so displeased almost everybody. He especially displeased the Tuileries, where they are tired of his incurable mania for courting popularity." La Marck even refrained from presenting himself to the queen, for he shared his friend's fall from favour.

The court's dissatisfaction, and his friend's, were not the only disagreeable results of Mirabeau's intervention. The decree of which he had unintentionally assured the triumph had graver consequences. For Louis XVI the Faith was the axis on which the whole world turned. His *valet de chambre* once heard him murmur, as he passed through the library of the Tuileries, "Those"—he pointed to the works of Voltaire and Rousseau—"are what have ruined France." He had long delayed giving his sanction to the decree on the civil constitution of the clergy; the Assembly now called for this sanction. He still hesitated, but Archbishop Boisgelin advised him to give it, assuring him that it was a sanction given under duress. The king submitted, but the divorce between the royal couple and revolutionary France was completed. The disastrous project of the flight from Paris took shape on the day of the signature of the decree. The king was waiting only for the arrival on the frontier of the troops asked for from the court of Vienna.

6

"Already all the French are auxiliaries of liberty; it remains only to make them all enemies of licence and auxiliaries of peace," said Mirabeau on November 20, 1790, in his inaugural speech to the Jacobins, who had just made him their president. (The office was held for a month.) The Society of Friends of the Constitution, which owed its popular designation to the Jacobin (Dominican) monastery in which it held its meetings, was playing a more and more important part in the political life of the country. Toward the end of 1790 it had a network of one hundred and fifty affiliated societies all over France. There were a thousand Paris members. Originally it was a deputies' club, and deputies still accounted for a third of the membership, which was recruited from every profession. In the great library, which the Dominicans had let to the club when its first meeting-place had become too small for it, writers like Laharpe, André Chénier, and Chamfort rubbed shoulders with financiers like Clavière and speculators like the Abbé d'Espagnac and rising politicians like Danton and Tallien; in the membership list famous names like those of Talma and David appear with those of printers and watchmakers; there were physicians like Mirabeau's friend Cabanis and journalists like Fréron and Desmoulins. The club held its meetings on days when the Assembly was not sitting; its president had to be a deputy. The vast low hall, with walls still covered with bookcases, pictures, and frescoes, often accommodated four or five hundred persons, who could contemplate on the walls the peaceful figure of Thomas Aquinas above the Fount of Knowledge, or the celebrated Jacobin motto, within a crown—"Live free or die."

At the end of 1790 the club was so powerful that it undertook the publication of a *Journal of the Friends of the Constitution*, edited by Choderlos de Laclos. In spite of the widening of its membership it preserved its eminently political character and its influence over the deputies. It prepared public opinion for coming debates and created an atmosphere round them. Desmoulins called the club's meetings "rehearsals for the Assembly." Mirabeau used his influence over the Jacobins in the interest of moderation, but his efforts were countered by a man who was gaining more and more influence over the Jacobins and who took part in every debate as an advocate of rigid revolutionary theory—Robespierre. "That man," said Mirabeau of him, "believes everything he says."

Faithful to the role he had assumed of advocate of the poorest and humblest, Robespierre protested against a decree of the Assembly which, according to him, excluded "passive" citizens (those without the franchise) from the National Guard. "The applause his admirable speech received," wrote Desmoulins, "so strong a censure of the morning's decree, seemed to alarm the president of the Jacobins. He ventured to call Robespierre to order, saying that it was not permitted to anyone to speak against a decree adopted." Mirabeau even reprimanded the "imprudent patriot." The members were indignant at this censure of their favourite orator. Failing to restore order, Mirabeau jumped on his chair and shouted: "Will all my colleagues come round me!" Robespierre's partisans, reported Desmoulins, were little impressed. But Charles de Lameth, with his arm still in a sling, answered Mirabeau's appeal and imposed silence.

Robespierre already had at his back the forces of the morrow, but the journal of the Jacobins seemed to follow Mirabeau. Choderlos de Laclos gave this formulation of his programme: "Equally far from the prejudices of the *ancien régime* and from the passions of the innovators, the motto of the members of the society is: Liberty and loyalty."

7

Mirabeau had no illusion left, no hope, not even sufficient self-confidence. Dumont, so critical toward him, brought out his extraordinary clear-sightedness: "It was with the same instinctive penetration that he fathomed the mind of the Assembly," he wrote, "and so often embarrassed his opponents by revealing their hidden motives, unmasking what they wanted to conceal from view; for him there existed, so to speak, no political enigma. He went straight to the most intimate secret, and his unaided sagacity was of more use to him than a multitude of spies in the enemy camp. I often thought his severe judgments were simply the result of hatred or jealousy; but in the event he was justified, and there was not an understanding man in the Assembly whose general conduct did not correspond to the idea he had of him. He began by distinguishing all the sides of a character; he had made for himself a language, difficult to understand, to express all his results; he had terms of his own for describing fractions of talents and qualities, vices and virtues, halves, quarters; and at a glance he seized on contradictions, real or apparent. No item of vanity, pretension, disguised ambition, crooked proceeding, escaped him; but he was equally able to see the good, the moral, the pure."

At the end of 1790 Mirabeau, utterly disillusioned, engaged in a lone struggle with the Assembly. On December 23 he emerged from his long silence with a memorandum to the court. The growing difficulties of the situation had induced it to consult him again. Mirabeau presented to the royal couple a comprehensive survey. He took twenty days to complete it. It was a plan of action for the future: "Survey the situation of France and the means of reconciling public liberty with the royal authority. . . . To form a systematic plan we need to know the real obstacles to be overcome, to determine the precise end at which we want to arrive, to determine the surest means of attaining it, and to assure the greatest exactitude in execution. Among the obstacles I count the king's indecision," he wrote with his uncompromising frankness, "the suspicions with which the queen is regarded, the frenzied demagogy of Paris, the state of feeling of the National Guard, and the irritability of the Assembly."

He combated in advance the objections of the court in its belief that it could rely on the part of the Assembly that was favourable to it. He spoke of "the incurable discredit into which the deputies of the nobility and the clergy have fallen." The surest means of "weakening the Assembly is to let it complete its system of taxation, which cannot, without a capacity it does not possess, be reconciled on one hand with the needs of the state and on the other with the blind instinct that makes the people imagine that the Revolution consists for them in paying nothing."

He warned the court against what it considered as its last resource, the general discontent: "There are no usable discontented elements that want both liberty and monarchical government." As for the dispossessed privileged classes, they were "almost as dangerous as the wildest demagogues." He warned the court above all against violent means that might bring about a general conflagration. He explained his views at length, patiently, reiterating his arguments, weighing his words, as though he felt the full merit of this clear-sightedness, so striking in the light of later events: "The Assembly must not be so ruined that popular disgust and unrest and anarchy become a torrent which no dyke can hold up. The great masses of men are difficult levers to move, but their force almost always deceives the hand that uses them.

"To attack the Revolution," he proceeded, "would be to overshoot the mark; for the movement that makes a great people give themselves better laws deserves support. . . . Both the spirit of the Revolution and many elements of its constitution must be accepted. . . . To work for a better constitution is the sole aim which prudence, honour, and the king's true interest, inseparable from that of the nation, permit him to adopt. In fact," he wrote, concluding this statement of his statesmanly wisdom, this virtual political testament, "I regard all the effects of the Revolution, and all that must be preserved of the constitution, as conquests so irrevocable that no upheaval, failing the dismemberment of the empire, could destroy them. . . . I do not even except an armed counter-revolution. The kingdom might be reconquered, but the conqueror would still have to come to terms with public opinion, would have to assure himself of the people's goodwill, would have to make good the destruction of the laws, and would have to leave the people to choose their administrators."

He justified to himself and to the court the struggle he was beginning against the Assembly: "It is because that result is well assured that the true friends of liberty can unite their efforts to attack the Assembly, and by that very act fulfil their duties as great citizens."

This point of view legitimized in his eyes the plan of campaign he elaborated against the Assembly. There must be a struggle "with it in prevision and popularity, destroying it by dissimulation and caresses rather than by open war, gradually ruining its credit by popular means and preparing patriotism itself to resist it." From the sphere of high political wisdom the project descended into the domain of intrigue. Mirabeau's advice and recommendations were dictated by his resentment. "I shall indicate certain means of setting traps for it, hindering its progress to show its powerlessness and weakness, to make it usurp all power more and more in order to make its tyranny feared."

Mirabeau felt that this network of intrigue was unworthy of him, for he remarked: "It has needed the last stage of the evils of the kingdom to induce me to indicate such means of my own accord; but what care

I for glory if the state must perish? If this were not a last resource with the salvation of a great people at stake, my character would lead me to reject all these means of dark intrigue and dissimulation, which I am forced to advise." He proposed to secure the support of a dozen deputies in the Assembly, who would be only half admitted into his confidence. He would give them support by buying the votes of those who, "having only their suffrage to offer, can be won over cheaply, or," he added cynically, "by simple promises."

"It is the last effort," he concluded. "If it is renounced, or if it fails, a funeral pall will cover the empire." At the moment when he completed his lengthy memorandum, did he know already that that last chance would not be seized? In any case, he added these words of hopelessness: "Where will the storm-tossed ship be carried? I do not know, but if I myself escape from the public shipwreck, I shall always say, with pride, in my retirement: 'I exposed myself to destruction to save them all; but they would not be saved.'"

8

"When I handed that document to the queen," wrote La Marck, "I myself read the last pages to her; they greatly impressed her." The king was then immersed in books dealing with the story of Charles I. But La Marck learned that he "had found great exaggeration in the picture drawn by Mirabeau of the dangers he was running." Such, added La Marck, was the king's apathy that even the works he was reading "gave him no impulse to rigorous action."

"Mirabeau's note is written in a very piquant manner," was all the Archbishop of Toulouse troubled to say. "Your note," Montmorin wrote to Mirabeau, "is excellent, and I am entirely in agreement with you throughout." This was not merely a polite formula. "The way he unreservedly accepted Mirabeau's plan," wrote La Marck, "did little to reassure me." He himself found the plan too vast and too complicated, but "in any case some good results should certainly be obtained." Later, after Mirabeau's death, and after his prophecies had been fulfilled, La Marck wrote in the preface to Mirabeau's correspondence with the court: "To many readers that vast project will appear impracticable, but it must be remembered that Mirabeau was to be the soul of the whole enterprise and to direct all the movements of the immense machine, and it is difficult to imagine what that astonishing man might not have been able to do if the collaborators he wanted to secure had really worked with him."

Mercy, though the incarnation of the diplomacy of the *ancien régime*, showed himself better able than even La Marck to judge the boldness of Mirabeau's ideas: "The plan seems to me to be perfect in theory," he wrote. But he saw its weak point at once, "its great practical difficulty, since it calls for co-operators with the energy of the one who directs their course."

Mirabeau himself was afraid of having frightened the court by his prophecies and by the boldness of his conceptions; he was afraid also of meeting with incredulity. He returned to the charge, repeating that the danger was growing daily: "The only salvation lies in a plan that combines statesmanship and intrigue, the courage of great citizens and the audacity of villains. We need a sort of political pharmacy in which the one leader, supplied equally well with health-giving simples and poisonous plants, mixes his medicines under the direction of his genius and with the patient's utter confidence." He added that he threw himself "at the feet of the queen to implore her not to break in our hands our last instrument of salvation. Woe to the rash person who should dare to tranquillize her!"

Mirabeau, who had seen Marie Antoinette only once, overestimated her capacity. La Marck, devoted as he was, knew her better. "The queen certainly has spirit and firmness that may suffice for great things," he wrote to Mercy, "but it must be admitted, and you will have been able to note it better than I, that whether in action or simply in conversation she does not always bring to bear the degree of sustained attention indispensable for thoroughly grasping what it is necessary to know in order to prevent mistakes and assure success."

The court began by collecting views on Mirabeau's plan. He, for his part, employed himself rallying all men of goodwill round the court. One day, at the beginning of February 1791, he sent this note by hand to Malouet: "I have long been more in agreement with you than you imagine; now I want to prove it to you." He proposed that they should meet next day at Montmorin's house. Malouet hurriedly wrote these words: "I shall be there."

In spite of their divergence of opinions, Malouet had a sort of involuntary esteem for Mirabeau. "For more than a year," he wrote, "Mirabeau had not had anything like the influence which it seemed that his oratorical gifts should assure him; the celebrity of his vices had exceeded that of his talents; but in the end he conquered the majority of the Assembly by an unprecedented mixture of good and bad principles, frequently approaching the soundest political ideas and fairly often abandoning them to attach himself still to the popular party. His interest, his ambition, and the accuracy of his views did not permit him to blind himself to the abyss that was opening beneath our feet. His patriotism did not go, as with many others, to absurd lengths; he loved liberty; he wanted it; but he was as convinced as I was that we were going astray."

Malouet at once responded to Mirabeau's appeal. Montmorin showed him a letter from the king requesting him to communicate Mirabeau's plan to the Abbé de Montesquieu and to Malouet and to send him their views before taking any action. Montmorin drew the memorandum from a deed-box in which it had been locked with other notes from Mirabeau to the court. By an indiscretion, perhaps deliberate, he had kept in the same folder with the notes a bond of the king's for two millions which was to be sent to Mirabeau in case of success. Malouet, disagreeably surprised, at once felt his confidence in Mirabeau's plan shaken. He questioned the minister as to the circumstances in which the money had been asked for and granted. "I should need," he said, "to be on my guard at tomorrow's meeting against the impression anything of this sort always makes on me. If there was nothing more than a money deal in Mirabeau's conversion, I should not feel it possible to boost his popularity. Already his expenditure has been commented on, and his house in the Chaussée-d'Antin. How could he escape from suspicions, investigations, denunciations from the Jacobins?"

But Montmorin, while taking credit for Mirabeau's rapprochement with the court, reassured him: "To begin with, what we gave him he did not demand. The baseness of the objections to the deal which you assume to exist do not exist. As for his expenditures, they can be quite well explained by the inheritance from his father." After allaying his suspicions, Montmorin urged Malouet to spend a day examining the plan, which he himself had been studying for six days after the king had kept it a week.

After thoroughly studying the plan, Malouet described it as "the last important attempt made to prevent the entire collapse of the monarchy." The meeting with Mirabeau that followed lasted from ten o'clock at night till two in the morning. Mirabeau was exhausted. His eyes were red and swollen. "He was horrible," said Malouet, "but never have I seen him more energetic or more eloquent."

Mirabeau said to him: "There is no longer time to calculate objections. If you find some in what I propose, do better, but act quickly, for we cannot live long. While we wait we shall die, of consumption or from violence. The more you insist on the evil that exists, the more urgent is its repair. Do you contest my means of carrying it out? Tell me of anyone who, with the same will as mine, is in a better position to act. All the sound part of the people, and even some of the mob, are with me. If I am suspected, if I am accused of selling out to the court, what do I care! Nobody will believe that I have sold my country's liberty, that I have prepared chains for it." Even Malouet's colourless transcription of this conversation retains Mirabeau's glowing tones when he exclaimed: "I will tell them, yes, I will tell them: 'You have seen me in your ranks fighting against tyranny, and that is what I am still combating; but the legal authority, the constitutional monarchy, the monarch's tutelary authority, these I have always reserved the right and the obligation to defend.'" And turning to Malouet he said: "Note well: I am the only one in that patriotic horde who can speak in that way without making a *volte-face*. I have never adopted their romanticism, or their metaphysic, or their useless crimes."

Malouet was overwhelmed in spite of himself. "The thundering voice, as though in the tribune, his animated gestures, the abundance and the precision of his ideas, electrified me as well. I shook off all my prejudices, all my doubts, and there I was sharing his emotion, praising his projects and his courage, enthusiastic about his methods."

Malouet and his friends were subjugated. They "counted their forces." They were ready to follow Mirabeau's directives. When they left late at night, they took with them "some hope of success." But Mirabeau was tired to death. The man with the Herculean figure was in danger of succumbing to his task. Malouet, concluding his account of the visit, wrote: "The interesting conversation would have continued till day came if we had not seen that he was exhausted with fatigue, covered with sweat, with a considerable amount of fever and unable to go on talking."

9

The battalion of the National Guards of his district, La Grange-Batelière, chose Mirabeau as their commandant, in place of a friend of Lafayette. On the day of his nomination, January 17, 1791, he wrote to the court with a mixture of playfulness and a strange humility: "May I do duty at the château [the Tuileries] like the other commandants?" The queen offered no encouragement. In vain did he actually mount guard at the Tuileries, to the great surprise of the British ambassador and the indignation of the Prussian, who wrote to his government: "The queen was on the point of suffering the humiliation of the Comte de Mirabeau guarding her person in the capacity of commandant of a battalion of the National Guard. She escaped that unpleasantness through the resignation of the Comte de Mirabeau two days after gaining that rank."

Mirabeau, rebuffed by the silence of the court, had in fact resigned on being appointed a member of the departmental administration of Paris. He aspired now to become *procureur-syndic* of the department; he would then, as Desmoulins, who supported him, wrote, have been "minister for Paris." His enemies disputed every inch of ground. In vain did Danton employ all his rough eloquence upon the thirty-six administrators of Paris to get Mirabeau appointed *procureur-syndic*. Mirabeau was beaten by a henchman of Lafayette. He contented himself with being elected a few days later, with Sieyès, a member of the Directory.

In these difficult days, in which his enemies were up in arms against him, La Marck's loyal friendship to him seems to have faltered. Mirabeau found him dissatisfied, bitter, suspicious. La Marck was in fact more and more worn out by a part that was far too much for him, and, as La Marck himself wrote, he was "disgusted, more and more every day, with this country, its men, its laws, and its manners." He remained only out of devotion to the queen.

10

"I was only three votes short for election as president [of the Assembly] at the first try," wrote Mirabeau to La Marck on January 3, 1791. "I shall carry it off, my good friend. Stir up the good aristocrats a bit; they nearly brought me in." Montmorin claimed to have been busy also with Mirabeau's candidature, "but with little to show as you see."

Toward the end of the month Mirabeau was ailing. "Although Mirabeau was born with a very vigorous temperament," wrote La Marck in his memoirs, "during all the time I knew him I never saw him in good health." The eye trouble grew worse. "His left eye became so inflamed that we feared he would lose it. He was subject to attacks of renal colic; in fact, infirmities succeeded each other without interruption." On January 28 Mirabeau informed his friend that he was blinder than ever and "trying remedies."

The presidential election was due next day. The Archbishop of Toulouse told La Marck that he had been working for Mirabeau's election; "I hope we shall have a hundred votes from the right." This time Mirabeau was elected unopposed. Unlike his predecessors, he made no speech on installation.

"He showed entirely new talents," recorded Dumont; "he introduced an orderliness and neatness of work of which no one had had any idea; he brushed away inessentials; with a single word he would clear up a question, with one word he would calm a tumult. He had the art of leadership and of fixing attention on himself even when, being unable to speak in the tribune, he seemed deprived of his finest prerogative."

It was during these glorious days of his presidency that there came a reminder of his past troubles. An unknown person informed him that a bill for eight hundred livres, long out of date, endorsed by Mirabeau, had been presented to him, and he had paid it, "only too pleased not to leave it too long in profane hands." Mirabeau replied to him at once that he had endorsed the bill "for a woman friend who had long shared my lot." He explained that the death of the bookseller Le Jay had involved him in a loss of one hundred and thirty thousand livres, and he added: "Certainly I ran wild in my youth, but there is not a man who has paid more scrupulously than I since I have had my fortune."

The fortnight of his presidency brought a series of triumphs for him. At its end the *Chronique de Paris* wrote: "He has restored to the post of president the dignity and nerve of which the disobediences and the insults of the right wing had deprived it."

During these days Mirabeau spent all of his strength and more. "My presidency," he wrote to Dumont, who had left for Geneva, "was the more of an ordeal because it was received with the greatest favour and imposed on me extravagant assiduity; it ended by exhausting me."

He had profoundly impressed the Assembly. His contemporaries never forgot the period of his presidency. Camille Desmoulins wrote: "One day, when the president's chair is relegated to the treasures of Saint-Denis, the Benedictine responsible for showing it to the curious will never say, 'This was the presidential chair of the National Assembly'; he will say, 'This was Mirabeau's chair.'"

⩺ XXII ⩹

The Obsequies of Achilles

"IF I believed in slow poisons," said Mirabeau to Dumont, "I should have no doubt that I had been poisoned. I feel myself wasting away, I feel myself being consumed by a slow fire." Dumont replied that his style of life would have killed any less robust man long ago.

Early in February Dumont left for Geneva. He was never again to see his friend. Mirabeau had a presentiment of it. "When we parted," wrote Dumont, "he embraced me with an emotion I had never seen in him." "It hurts me to death, my good friend," said Mirabeau, "it may be that we shall never see each other again. When I am no more, it will be realized what I was worth. The evils I averted will fall upon France from all quarters; that criminal faction that trembles before me will no longer have any restraint." He held the Assembly responsible: "They wanted to rule the king instead of ruling through him: a base faction will dominate them all and will cover France with horror." But though he saw the horrors and the streams of blood of the future, he did not disown either the past or the present. He meant to leave no doubt in his friend's mind: France could never return to the old order. He was concerned to make this clear and wrote to Dumont as soon as he had left: "Tell them, my friend, tell those of your compatriots who have in their hearts no reasons for disbelieving you, tell them, to the eternal shame of the impious who are calling down disasters upon us, and who may bring them on us, that our Revolution is made, saved, complete, irrevocable; and that, whatever may be the destiny of its authors, that of its enemies is to be crushed beneath the weight of the logic of facts and of the irresistible impulse given to the mind of man; tell them that none but narrow minds and arid souls will dare to form plans or aspirations to the contrary."

Defender alike of the Revolution and the monarchy, Mirabeau did not realize how irreconcilable were the two parts of that policy. His profession of faith in the Revolution, so often repeated in the notes to the court, ended by robbing him of the little credit he had with the queen. She wrote at the beginning of February 1791 to Mercy: "I think Mirabeau may be useful, though without trusting him in the slightest on any matter."

At that time Mirabeau, more and more alarmed at the effervescence of Paris, was occupied with the question of getting the royal family away from the capital. There could no longer be any question either of Fontainebleau or of any other open town. "The revolutionary spirit has made too much progress for it to be possible to leave the royal family exposed in that way to the risk of a simple act of violence." He proposed a fortified town on the eastern frontier, where fortresses and army were concentrated.

Without knowing it, Mirabeau was seconding Breteuil and Fersen when he suggested that General Bouillé surround the king with his best troops. He did not know that the plan of flight had already been drawn up. The court was also keeping all knowledge of Mirabeau's plans from the faithful royalists who were preparing its flight. The intendant of the civil list, La Porte, wrote to the king: "I will take the liberty to observe to Your Majesty that, whatever action you consider advisable on M. de Mirabeau's memorandum, it seems to me important to say nothing about it to those who are in charge of the other plan for leaving Paris." The king and queen were deceiving everybody. They were deceiving Montmorin as they were deceiving Mirabeau; they were even deceiving the faithful La Marck, who wrote: "By dint of returning to the charge with the king, we succeeded in inducing him to adopt Mirabeau's great plan in its entirety, and also the project of leaving Paris with the whole of the royal family."

By dint of persistence, La Marck also obtained the king's authorization for him to go to see Bouillé. Although he made the journey under the plausible pretext of accompanying his sister to Strasbourg, the news got abroad. Lafayette, who seems to have had informants everywhere, took alarm. He sent in advance to Bouillé, who was a relative of his, the news of La Marck's visit, and warned him against the "mysteries and intrigues" of Mirabeau and his friend, "hot-headed fellows both of them." He even sent him a confidential emissary to give him further information.

Whether in order to find out more about Mirabeau's plans or to conciliate him in view of his growing influence, Lafayette made new efforts to get into touch with him. "No doubt about it, the meeting should be agreed to," wrote La Marck to Mirabeau; "but at the same time it would occur to you that public attention should be attracted to this great man's advance." In accepting Lafayette's invitation to lunch Mirabeau pointed out to the friend of Lafayette who had brought it about that it was important to both of them that the meeting should be in the presence of confidential witnesses, and added: "La Marck is my intimate friend, and I must not and cannot have a secret from him."

Lafayette was so anxious to see Mirabeau that he met him at the house of their mutual friend. The interview revealed the extent to which their positions had changed. Mirabeau no longer needed an alliance with Lafayette. The general had missed his opportunity. Their paths were never again to run together. Bouillé wrote in his *Mémoires:* "A meeting between Mirabeau, Lafayette, and me, if it could have taken place with three persons so opposed in character and principles, might have saved the kingdom."

But at the moment when La Marck came to him, Bouillé was entirely ignorant of the part played by Mirabeau. La Marck thought he had a good introduction to Bouillé in a letter from the king, sealed with his private seal. But the royal pen gave this picture of Mirabeau and his collaborators: "Although these people are not estimable and I have paid a great deal to the first, I still think they can do me service. In Mirabeau's project you may find useful things; listen to it without being too much influenced and tell me what you think of it."

The reception which Bouillé gave La Marck after that recommendation was necessarily embarrassed and reserved. But as soon as he became acquainted with Mirabeau's plan his attitude changed. He was the only person whom the threads of both intrigues had reached. He knew the Breteuil plan, based on the intervention of foreign Powers. "Whatever happens," wrote Fersen to the King of Sweden, "the king will never be king without such foreign aid as will inspire respect even in those of his own party." Nobody judged the royalists more severely than this friend of the queen, for he added: "The king's party is composed entirely of incapable people, or people in such a state of fury and exasperation that they can be neither guided nor trusted in any way." Nothing could be done, he concluded, interpreting the mind of the royal couple, "without the aid of the neighbour Powers, Spain, Switzerland, and the Emperor, or without the assistance of the Northern Powers, to impress England, Prussia, and Holland."

But Bouillé was more perspicacious than the advisers who had imposed their ideas on the court. Unlike Fersen and the French *émigrés*, he had no wish to bring in foreign aid to restore the French throne. He preferred the Mirabeau plan, based on the forces within the country. After his first hesitation and reticence, he became communicative and confident. He considered Mirabeau as "the man who can most usefully serve the king, by working to change public opinion in Paris and the provinces." La Marck noted that he "showed lively indignation at Lafayette's conduct." Bouillé had himself been so discouraged about his personal position "that he was thinking of throwing up his command, in which he was scarcely obeyed, and leaving France to take service in Prussia or Sweden." He went to work with enthusiasm on the Mirabeau plan.

He wrote at once to the king to advise him "to have this plan put into effect and to cover Mirabeau with gold, giving him and promising him whatever he may ask."

Mirabeau quickly recovered courage when La Marck told him of Bouillé's action. "He was already preparing in his head the proclamation which the king would address to the nation as soon as he was at liberty," wrote La Marck. Mirabeau, he wrote, agreed with Bouillé that the king should speak publicly and as king. "A simple excursion to Compiègne, which might be changed into a longer journey if necessary, seemed to all of us the best course. If the king could be saved, it could be only by such means; but that unfortunate prince did not agree."

The truth was that the project of the disastrous flight that ended at Varennes was already decided on. It was even becoming known. Mirabeau said at that time to Cabanis, his friend and physician, speaking his real mind, although La Marck doubted it: "I have defended the monarchy to the end, I am even defending it now that I think it is lost, because its survival depended on the king and I still think it useful; but if he goes I shall ascend the tribune, have the throne declared vacant, and proclaim the Republic."

2

In the account books of Mme. Eloffe, *couturière-lingère* to the queen, appeared important items of purchases by Mesdames, the king's aunts. "Organdy blouses trimmed with marten and bordered with stones," black taffeta cloaks, nightdresses and nightcaps with maline frills, dresses and lace, "a very large quantity of ribbons of different colours," and, simply for trimmings, "tatted gold garlands" and flounces embroidered with spangles, to the sum of 1285 livres.

Mesdames were preparing for a long journey. They were doing it with an ostentation that aroused curiosity. On February 3, 1791, the municipality of Sèvres, informed of their preparations by the servants, warned the Jacobins. On that same day Mirabeau hastened to write to the court: "Mesdames' journey is not only dangerous for them but may be the cause of a thousand dangers for Their Majesties. The malevolent will interpret the departure of Mesdames as the certain presage of that of the king, and the factious will use it as the pretext for a new popular agitation. . . . In any case, the people of Paris will not look with indifference on a journey that takes away from the capital's consumption a million a year, and their disquiet will bring new storms." He added that it would be politic to prevent the departure of Mesdames. Failing that, he proposed that the king should write to the Assembly that he had not ventured to forbid the journey for fear of exceeding his powers and that he asked for a decree fixing his rights over the members of his family.

His advice met with the usual inattention from the king, and the alarm continued to spread. The women of the markets threatened to invade the château of Bellerive, the princesses' residence. The municipality sent a deputation to the king to express its anxiety. The king replied that when he was shown a decree of the Assembly forbidding travelling, he would prevent his aunts from leaving, but that until then they were free to leave the kingdom, like other citizens. A revolutionary journalist wrote: "*Salus populi suprema lex esto*. The public safety forbids Mesdames to take their persons and our millions to the Pope or elsewhere. Their persons we must guard as precious, for they help to guarantee us against the hostile intentions of their nephew M. d'Artois and their cousin Bourbon-Condé. . . . All that Mesdames take away belongs to us, even their chemises. Personally, I do not like our chemises going to Rome."

Desmoulins wrote: "It is false to say that the king's aunts enjoy the same rights as other citizens. Did the nation make them a present at birth of a million a year as Mesdames? No, Sire, your aunts have not the right to go and eat our millions in papal territory. Let them renounce their pensions. Let them restore to the coffers of the state all the gold they are taking away, and then let them go, if they choose, to Loretto or to Compostella."

On February 9 the tocsin sounded throughout Paris, and the thirty-six sections assembled and deliberated as to the means of preventing the princesses' departure. On the fourteenth the sections sent a deputation to the Assembly. "These sanctimonious women must be kept as hostages and a triple guard set on the rest of the family," wrote Marat on the same day in the *Ami du peuple*.

Mirabeau, as president of the Assembly, received a deputation from the municipality which asked for a law on the royal family's mode of existence. "You have just proposed to the constituent body," he said, "one of the biggest questions with which it has to deal." As an adviser who had not been listened to, he was embarrassed; as president he could not forestall the Assembly's decisions. He confined himself to sonorous, evasive, tactful phrases.

Without troubling about the excitement their journey was causing, Mesdames prepared to leave France. The department of Seine-et-Oise instructed the commandant-in-chief of the National Guard at Versailles, who was no other than Berthier, Napoleon's future chief of staff, to accompany the princesses. A detachment of *chasseurs* of Lorraine served as escort. They set out as they had travelled before the Revolution, with their habitual train of twenty people. Paris was in effervescence. Agitated women invaded the château of Bellerive, but they found only the vehicles that were to follow the princesses. The rumour spread that Monsieur was leaving. A crowd of women besieged the Luxembourg and compelled Monsieur to go under a good escort to the Tuileries and to swear to them that he would never abandon his brother. Suddenly the ladies had assumed great importance. The agitation spread from Paris to the provinces. The king sent a brief message to the Assembly, expressing his regret at his aunts' departure and repeating that it had been impossible for him to deprive them of the freedom which all French people possessed to go where they chose.

Mesdames were on their way, preceded by the noise their departure from Paris had made. The patriotic sentiments of the little town of Moret were very keen. The municipal officers examined the ladies' passports with particular care. They were still deliberating when the escort of *chasseurs* rode to the gates of the town and had them opened under threat of force. Mesdames continued their journey. The municipality addressed a complaint to the Assembly.

Suddenly Montmorin sent Mirabeau a note informing him that Mesdames had been arrested. The information soon reached the Assembly from the municipality of Arnay-le-Duc, which had carried out the arrest. Some declared the proceedings of the municipality illegal, others excused it, even if it was mistaken, on the ground of its high patriotic motives.

Mesdames had at once appealed to Paris. "They are sending Narbonne to you," wrote La Marck to Mirabeau. "Declare yourself their defendant. Then everything is easy for you, for so far there is no law against them."

Amid hostile shouts, Mirabeau demanded the reference of the affair to the executive power. He read the formula of reference: "The National Assembly, considering that no existing law of the kingdom prevents the free journey of Mesdames—" He interrupted himself to ask: "Is that so? Is there a law?" "There is one," replied a deputy. "I quote it; it is the safety of the people."

"The safety of the people," retorted Mirabeau contemptuously, "is not interested in whether Mesdames spend three or four more nights on the journey. All good citizens, no doubt, ought, in the circumstances that are weighing upon us, to remain at their post and show their attachment to the head of the nation. Mesdames have done an imprudent, an impolitic thing, but nothing illegal; thus there is nothing to deliberate about."

From the press the agitation passed to the crowd. In the evening the people invaded the gardens and courts of the Tuileries, shouting for the king to promise that his aunts' journey would be stopped. That evening Gorani dined with Mirabeau. "When we were at dessert," he recorded, "a messenger brought the news that more than twelve thousand men and women had been harangued by Robespierre and Marat and were agitating in the Tuileries for the recall of the king's aunts." Barnave had already tried to reason with the crowd, but without success. "Mirabeau did not lose a moment; we followed him, and when this man began to speak the agitators and their speakers said no more and order was restored."

Next day the passions unloosed in the streets continued to be voiced in the Assembly. There was a discussion on the decree proposed by Le Chapelier, *rapporteur* of the Committee on the Constitution, on the residence of public officials. The committee described the king as the first of the public officials and laid down the principle that so long as the Assembly was sitting he should reside in its neighbourhood. "It is proposed," exclaimed a royalist deputy, "to condemn the king to eternal imprisonment."

While the Assembly was in tumult, Mesdames, released thanks to Mirabeau, went peacefully on their way to Rome, apparently unconscious of all the disturbance they had caused. They continued to draw their requirements of finery from France. The account book of Mme. Eloffe registered in the course of the sanguinary month of August 1792 orders from Mesdames totalling more than two thousand livres for "head-dresses for blondes with Alençon butterfly basis."

Mirabeau wanted to avert the passing of a law that would prevent the king from leaving the capital and would interfere with his freedom of action. He wanted to gain time. "The law on residence is complete," he said, "but the law on the eligibility of public officials and the law on the regency have not yet been brought forward. I wish to see these plans as a whole; it is the only way of judging a complicated question."

The revolutionary journalists saw his intention. Fréron predicted that one day the whole court would cross the frontier and place itself under the protection of the emperor, and that the responsibility would fall upon Mirabeau.

Three days later the debate was sharper than ever. The Committee on the Constitution had been instructed to draft a law on the émigrés. The rapporteur himself, Le Chapelier, said that a law against the émigrés risked infringing the principles of the Constitution and the Rights of Man. Mirabeau asked permission "to read a page and a half of a letter addressed eight years ago to the most absolute despot in Europe." He read a passage from his letter to Frederick William II, and then proposed that the draft law on the émigrés should not be given a reading. The left noisily protested. Mirabeau had difficulty in making himself heard. When at last he succeeded he declared cuttingly that "it is not indignation but reflection that must make the laws," and that the draconic articles of the draft law "will certainly never enter into the decrees of the National Assembly of France." The draft law, he added, was impracticable.

While this stormy debate was proceeding, news reached the Assembly of a riot that had broken out in Paris. For some days the municipality had been carrying out repairs in the castle of Vincennes in order to use it to relieve congestion in the Paris prisons. The crowd saw in this work dark counter-revolutionary designs. The Faubourg Saint-Antoine, easily alarmed, started out for Vincennes, the men armed with picks and shovels. The castle was invaded, and the crowd began to demolish the keep, while the National Guard looked on passively. In the end Lafayette arrived with some disciplined battalions and succeeded in clearing the castle, not without some fighting. But when he returned at night to Paris, he found the gates of the Faubourg Saint-Antoine closed and had to secure a passage by threatening to bring guns against the gates. As he and his officers passed along the streets shots were fired at them.

On that same morning, February 28, royalists, warned the night before, crowded into the Tuileries. They were armed with swords, sabres, pistols, and poniards. The National Guard prepared to invade the royal apartments. The king took alarm at the threatening collision. He urged his partisans to disperse and not to ruin him by their mistaken zeal. They threw down their arms. A whole collection of them was found in the armouries. The National Guard broke them in the court of the Tuileries.

3

"You know the person with whom I have to deal," Marie Antoinette wrote later to Mercy. "At the moment when one thinks one has persuaded him, a single word or argument will change him without his noticing it; that is one reason why a thousand things cannot be attempted." The king's indecision seemed to serve her as an excuse for her own shortcomings. She avoided La Marck, who had felt obliged "to tell her the unvarnished truth." She did not even grant him an interview after his visit to Bouillé. He had to send her a written account of it and to warn her in writing that republican principles were growing stronger and would "inevitably entail the ruin of the royal power."

Only the police section of Mirabeau's plan had been put into execution. "Its influence begins to be felt in Paris," wrote La Marck to Mercy; "feeling toward the king is improving, and there is less talk of the queen." But that, he said, was not enough. "Louis XVI is incapable of reigning because of his apathy, of the resignation he takes for courage, and of his invincible repugnance to any hard thinking, which makes him break away from any conversation and any reflection on the dangerous situation in which his good-heartedness has placed him and his kingdom."

Such was the picture formed of the king by this most faithful observer. Mirabeau, too, seems to have realized that it was no longer possible to avert the fate of this sovereign who could not reign. His notes grew shorter and fewer, and came to a stop, without any explanation from him or any further request from the royal couple. His loose relations with the court ended without any open breach. The note on the results of the departure of Mesdames was the last he drew up.

4

"While the person of the monarch is entirely in Lafayette's hands, the government seems to be passing rapidly into the hands of Mirabeau," wrote the British ambassador on March 4. Mirabeau was at the height of his power. Lafayette realized this, and at the beginning of March he made fresh advances to Mirabeau.

At this time Mirabeau was overflowing with activity. His collaborators were preparing for him speeches on the duel, on the death penalty, and on the extradition of criminals. He was occupied especially with a problem which he regarded as of supreme importance, that of national education. But he was never to deliver the great speech he had prepared. On March 3 he spoke in the debate on a proposal to institute, under the supervision and with the aid of the state, life annuities for old people without resources. His speech was loudly applauded. But his plan was opposed by Robespierre and Buzot. The second phase of the Revolution was showing itself. Its representatives had already felt that philanthropy as a palliative of poverty was a hindrance to social progress.

5

Mirabeau's last acts were energetic interventions dictated by friendship. He asked Montmorin to give Condorcet the post of Treasury Commissioner. Montmorin considered that Condorcet "is no good for anything, and his republican principles are too much advertised," and he alluded to the charms of Mme. de Condorcet. But Mirabeau made a personal question of this nomination; he raged and chaffed until he got his way.

His last intervention was in favour of La Marck. La Marck owned important mines at Anzin in Hainaut and was afraid of losing his concession because of a strong current of public opinion in favour of the reservation of property in subterranean wealth exclusively to the owner of the surface land. He mobilized Pellenc, who prepared a vigorous intervention for Mirabeau. On February 17 La Marck warned Mirabeau: "The mines affair is down for tonight. Go to the Assembly and get this big question adjourned to a definite date, stating that you have been at work on it with an important speech. Pellenc is very well prepared, but is not ready for tonight."

This letter reached Mirabeau in the country, but he hurried back: "I am coming myself, even more seriously ill than when I came away, though I was done up." He secured the adjournment of the debate until March 21. La Marck appealed to all his friends in the Assembly. Mirabeau made the affair his own; he was almost jealous about it. La Marck may have feared that Mirabeau's vehemence would injure his cause, or he may have wished to reserve Mirabeau's vigorous intervention for later, but Mirabeau was almost offended at the idea. "I will not speak if you do not want me to, because in this matter I want only to serve you. But do not think either that the affair has no need of support or that there are many people on your side. . . . Let me know what you want; I will do it to the letter, all the more since I am only in Paris for the mines and minefields, but for which I should be among my trees."

He was not satisfied with the work of the "illustrious Pellenc"; he shortened it, added to it, recast it, read it and reread it several times; rarely had he taken so much trouble. In the course of the preliminary debate he gained a better idea of the difficulties: "If I do not take a hand in defending the true principles, without any doubt there will be no more mines in France and you will lose one of the main elements of your fortune. If I defend them, I shall floor the opposition." The *rapporteur* of the Committee of Agriculture and Commerce had laid down the principle that the mines were in the hands of the nation and at its disposal, that the owners of the surface should be preferred for the exploitation of the mines; and that the rights of past concessionnaires should be inspected.

The committee, Mirabeau objected, seemed to have envisaged this question only under its metaphysical aspect. "But abstractions which are the best method of reasoning are not the only elements, or the prime elements, of the art of governing. I claim that if the general interest and justice are the two foundations of property, neither the general interest nor equity demands that the mines should be accessories of the surface. I claim that the interior of the earth is not susceptible of partition; that the mines, through their irregular path, are still less so."

He was in agreement with the point of departure of the debate that the mines should be declared to be at the nation's disposal. But he insisted that it was impossible to rely for exploitation on the interest of the owners of the surface, "and to run all the risks of their idleness, their ignorance, or their lack of resources." He quoted the enormous expenditure required for the exploitation of mines, using as an example the Anzin Company, which belonged to La Marck. He drew a curious picture of the mining industry of his day. "It was after twenty-two years of work that the company reached the mine. The first seam was three hundred feet down and was valueless. To reach it it had been necessary to get past an underground torrent which covered the whole space for several leagues. The mine was reached by sounding; and it was necessary not to get rid of that mass of water, which was impossible, but to pass through it. An immense machine was built, a pit lined with timber. . . . Each timber-lined pit in the mines of Anzin, four hundred and sixty fathoms deep, cost four hundred thousand livres. There are twenty-five at Anzin and twelve in the mines of Fresnes and Vieux-Condé: this item alone cost fifteen millions. There are twelve fire-pumps at one hundred thousand livres each. The galleries and the other machines cost eight millions; six hundred horses are used; four thousand workers are employed. The expenditure on compensation granted according to the rules, and in pensions to sick workmen and to widows and children of workers, exceed one hundred thousand livres a year.

"What have the owners of the mines been given? A right of which nobody was making any use, a field more fertile in hopes than in successes, and often the opportunity of ruining themselves. . . . These men have been useful, they have fed our manufactures, increased our commerce, preserved our currency. Should they be despoiled? Could they be, without injustice? If they had had no concession they would have had a claim to one for their labours, their expenditures, and their services."

His eloquent speech, which was in tune with the physiocratic ideas of the period, had a great effect on the Assembly. But the question remained in suspense. Mirabeau occupied himself with Pellenc on a second speech which should clinch the matter.

He was still ill. He spent himself in the debate on the regency. Exhausted, obsessed by fears for the future, his nerves on edge, he sought relaxation in his usual style. For the evening of March 25, 1791, he invited to supper two dancers from the Opéra. But this time he paid for the excesses of the night with graver trouble than the ordinary depression of an imprudent voluptuary. He spent the following day in his home at Argenteuil. During the night he was seized with violent intestinal pains. On the twenty-seventh he could scarcely stand. Only with an enormous effort did he get up to go to Paris. He arrived at La Marck's house at nine in the morning. La Marck was struck by his worn face. Suddenly he fainted. La Marck tried to dissuade him from going to the Assembly, where the question of the mines was on the agenda, but Mirabeau would not hear of it. "My friend, those fellows are going to ruin you if I do not go." La Marck begged him to consider his health. "I am going to speak, you won't stop me," he repeated obstinately. But when he tried to get up his strength gave way.

He remembered his friend's old Tokay. He gulped down two glassfuls. After that he felt better. He would not let La Marck go with him. He did not want him even to be present at the Assembly. In the midst of nerving himself to an almost superhuman effort, he had the delicacy to try to spare his friend the painful suspense of an issue so vital to him. It was with that affectionate thought that Mirabeau left for what was to be, though he did not know it, his last speech in the Assembly. It was a strictly technical speech; he dwelt at length on points of detail, patiently took up the arguments of his adversaries, and calmly and surely reduced them to nothing. His brilliant oratorical career ended in a dull economic discussion. The great flame of his eloquence, which had so often fired the masses, flickered feebly through the arid material. But it sufficed to bring victory for a friend. La Marck kept the mines of Anzin, "among the finest in Europe."

Mirabeau left the sitting pallid and faint. He went unsteadily toward the Terrasse des Feuillants, where he had arranged to meet a young physician, Lachèze. A crowd pressed round him as usual. The physician had difficulty in keeping off the petitioners and the curious. "You are killing yourself," he said desperately. Mirabeau was determined to give La Marck the news of the success himself. He dragged himself to his house. It was three in the afternoon. His legs would carry him no farther. As he entered he threw himself on a sofa. "Your case is won," he said, "and I—I am dead."

But his immense will-power triumphed once more over his physical exhaustion. During a short respite from his sufferings, an interval between shooting pains and attacks of faintness, he resumed his indefatigable activity. He busied himself with schemes of which he confided the elaboration to Reybaz. It was as if his brain hurled defiance at his exhausted body. He wrote to his collaborator: "Here I am, keeping quiet to save my life, but with you only the head is busy, with me everything is. Happiness has spoilt you, were it not, indeed, that the masterpiece of living is to be happy and to make happy those around us. Misfortune has stung me, stimulated me, fired me, and," he added, and the phrase summed him up completely, "I am still burning though I am no more than ash."

6

"I need a rest," said Mirabeau to young Lachèze, "and if you are free for the day, give me the pleasure of your company in the country."

The days he regularly spent at the Marais were an unfailing remedy for depression and pain. He drank in the fresh air, his tired eyes bathed in the wide space, the spring breeze passed like clear water over his swollen eyelids. He had realized the dream he had dreamed so absurdly in his youth in the château of Mirabeau. A number of workers were busy about the house; he watched them at work, went among them loved and generous as a sovereign, distributing bread and meat and linen to their families. At the bottom of the garden there was being built, to his design, a temple of Liberty. He wanted to set up there the statue of what he called the first divinity of his heart. She was to have one hand on a column on which were to be engraved the words *Egalité des hommes*—Human Equality. Her other hand was to hold a sword within the book of the law. It was that unbeliever's profession of faith.

On that Sunday Mirabeau no longer felt the usual benefit from the Marais. He was suffering from too deep a fatigue, from ill health of too long standing. He had been tormented for some time by dull pain in the intestines. His stomach, once so strong, was subject to painful cramps. He suffered also from rheumatic pains in his arms and chest, sometimes vague and persistent, sometimes acute and spasmodic. His legs had swollen and were painfully heavy. He had occasional attacks of angina, which when they passed left him both exhausted and relieved, as though he had escaped from a great danger. "Though the most robust of men," his physician Cabanis wrote, "he had become susceptible to agitation from the slightest impressions; his muscles still remained those of a Hercules, but his nerves were almost those of a delicate and vapourish woman."

The change in his health was visible in his face, in his pallid complexion, in his heavy movements. His young physician Cabanis—a man with literary tastes and a passionate politician, almost republican in his views—watched him very closely, with a care heightened by friendship and admiration; he noted the change even in his friend's hair. It was naturally curly, but "in ill health and even when he was slightly upset the undulations," he noted, "were more or less effaced, and from root to tip the hair became of a softness that could be felt. Thus when I was asking about his health, my first questions to his valet turned on that phenomenon."

Mirabeau was himself aware of the change that was taking place. One day, when embracing the younger of his nieces, he said to her with a smile: "It is Death embracing the Spring."

But if sometimes he was alarmed at his condition, he acted as if he wanted to minimize it by paying no attention to it. On Monday he returned to Paris still in pain. A hot bath allayed the symptoms. Feeling better, and as if out of defiance, he went in the evening to the Théâtre Italien. Once more it was a woman who drew him there. Actresses of talent had always had a great attraction for him. Mlle. Morichelli, the prima donna of the Théâtre Italien, who was regarded as scarcely pretty but with great talent as a singer and actress, was the last woman who awakened the flame of passion in Mirabeau.

But the effort of will failed that evening. He found himself obliged to leave the theatre at the opening of the play. His pain had returned with violence. Leaning on the arm of Lachèze, he left his box and painfully descended the stairs. He was shivering. His breath was quick and gasping. His carriage was not in the street, and the young physician proposed that he should wait in a café. But in his condition Mirabeau did not like to be on view. He dragged himself home. "I found him almost suffocated," wrote Cabanis, "breathing with the greatest difficulty, his face swollen by the congestion of blood in the lung, the pulse intermittent and convulsive, the extremities cold; he was making a vain effort to suppress his groans."

Cabanis intervened at once with energy. He flattered himself that he had produced an almost miraculous improvement. "The cruellest and the most dangerous situation gave place to the most complete well-being." The improvement was maintained throughout the next day. With his natural optimism and his faculty of forgetting painful moments, Mirabeau fancied himself out of danger. He was full of admiration for Cabanis, whose brilliant intelligence may have been of more service than his medical experience. Always anxious to do his best for his friends, as flattered by their successes as if they had been his own, Mirabeau exclaimed: "Ah, yes, it is very sweet to owe one's life to one's friend." As soon as he was out of pain he thought of others; he thought of Mme. Helvétius, who was expecting Cabanis in the evening, and he insisted that he should go to see her, so that she should not be anxious at his absence. But Cabanis wanted to come back to pass the night with him. A grateful grasp of his hand: "Friend, I have not the courage to refuse you."

The improvement had been deceptive. During Wednesday the violent pains returned, with the same symptoms accentuated. The remedies were no longer effective. The patient struggled painfully for breath; his pulse was irregular, and he was suffering from angina.

The news of Mirabeau's illness spread through Paris, and his house was besieged by people asking about his condition. Groups formed in the street. People felt this news as a personal calamity. The king sent publicly twice during the day to inquire, and several times privately. Suddenly the Tuileries grasped the supreme importance of the man to whom it had grudged its confidence.

Lost in the crowd round Mirabeau's house, an old woman waited. It was the Marquise de Mirabeau. As soon as she learned that he was ill, she hurried to his house. But this was scarcely a tardy awakening of maternal solicitude. She was afraid of the influence of Mme. du Saillant and her daughters: she candidly admitted it. She remained more than six hours in a shed in the court of the house. She did not have herself announced. She watched the comings and goings. She heard the talk of the deeply disturbed crowd. But her mother's heart does not seem to have been capable any longer of sorrow. She waited apathetically, her eyes riveted on the door that was closed to her.

During the night Mirabeau grew worse. His physician stayed through the night, but Mirabeau let him sleep in spite of his sufferings. Spasms tore his chest, and his throat seemed to be in a vice. When Cabanis came down at dawn, he sent at once for a surgeon and for leeches. But neither bleeding nor mustard plasters nor leeches brought any relief. Every half-hour Cabanis gave the sick man six grains of musk as a sedative. He was himself alarmed—too late. Mme. du Saillant had wanted from the first to bring in the family doctor, but Mirabeau would not hear of it.

That morning, however, Mirabeau felt lost. He had not seen La Marck since his critical illness began. His faithful friend, knowing Mirabeau's need of rest and the extent to which he was disturbed by inquirers, had come several times a day to ask after the patient without attempting to see him. On Thursday morning, however, Mirabeau asked for him. As La Marck came in he noted the great change in his friend and the shadow of death over his face, and he burst into tears. Mirabeau was deeply moved. He had never seen this calm and distant man abandon himself unreservedly to emotion. From then on he continually asked for him.

Frochot nursed him with great devotion and much skill. "Nobody can move me so well as he does," said Mirabeau. "If I recover I shall write a good article on the art of sick-nursing. He is the one who has given me the chief ideas; he has also suggested the idea of some mechanical processes which it seems to me should be of advantage." When Frochot carefully raised his big head, which in his weakness had become so heavy, he said with a smile: "I wish I could leave it to you as a legacy."

He retained all his clearness of mind. He asked about everything that was happening in the Assembly. His dominant interest, foreign policy, still occupied his thoughts. He thought especially of the man who was one day to be the great adversary of revolutionary France. "That man Pitt," he said, "is the minister of preparations. He governs by means of what he threatens rather than what he does. If I had lived, I think I should have given him some trouble." His obstinacy also remained. Cabanis, alarmed at his responsibilities and yielding to pressure from Caroline and La Marck, sent for Dr. Petit. But Mirabeau would not be examined. Dr. Petit had to be content with an account given by his young colleague. Without having seen the patient, he approved, said Cabanis, his diagnosis and his treatment. The treatment consisted only of quinine together with "gentle laxatives."

Precious time had been lost, time beyond redress. On the strength of the list of symptoms given by Cabanis later, physicians diagnosed two affections, pericarditis of rheumatic origin, and formation of biliary calculi. Dumont, who on the strength of the same data, asked the opinion of different physicians in Geneva and in Edinburgh, was told by all of them that the treatment needed had not been given.

Mirabeau's weakness was extreme. He was given nothing to restore him except the quinine in stronger and stronger doses. The bulletins issued, for which there was such a demand that they had to be printed, mentioned this weakness. A young man wrote to Cabanis offering his blood for transfusion. The crowd continued to wait in the street, grave and silent, as though overwhelmed. Both ends of the street had been blocked to prevent the sound of vehicles from disturbing him.

On Thursday, when the serious state of the patient became evident, Duquesnoy wrote to La Marck: "You will be sure to have felt already the urgent and indispensable need for having our unfortunate friend's papers taken to your house." Montmorin also wrote in alarm to La Marck: "I am extremely alarmed and also afflicted. This contretemps is frightful. . . . If his condition continues to be so dangerous, do you not think that some precautions should be taken with regard to the papers? I am told that several persons might be compromised."

Mirabeau had a good idea of the personal alarms aroused by his condition. La Marck did not venture to mention the subject, but Mirabeau spoke to him about it: "My friend, I have in the house many papers that would compromise plenty of people, you and others, especially those whom I so wanted to rescue from the dangers that threatened them. It might be more prudent to destroy all these papers, but I confess that I cannot make up my mind to do so." He was especially preoccupied about his copies of his notes to the court. Far from wishing to hide that important part of his political activity, of which the general public of his day had no knowledge, he counted on events one day confirming his previsions and his judgments and revealing the full value of his efforts. "It is in these papers," he said, "that posterity will find, I hope, the best justification of my conduct in recent times; in them exists the honour of my memory. Could you not take away these papers and place them out of reach of our enemies? But promise me that one day these papers shall become known, and that your friendship shall avenge my memory by making them public." La Marck gave a solemn assurance to his friend, who, knowing that he could count on him, felt greatly relieved. La Marck sent for Pellenc at once. They collected all the papers and burned all those which they regarded as of minor importance. But in the haste of the sorting many papers were put into the fire whose destruction La Marck bitterly regretted later. At night La Marck took the papers to his house, taking precautions against being observed. But among the crowd of sympathizers in front of the house were secret agents who seemed to have accomplices within the house. The intendant of the civil list was able to tell the king at once that La Marck had been able to take away all the papers "that might interest Your Majesty."

That part of Mirabeau's career was rescued from oblivion. One day, when the storms which France suffered for so many years had passed over, La Marck faithfully carried out the promise he had given to the dying man.

7

Mirabeau's mind was at rest with regard to the future; but he was tormented by the present fate of those near to him. "I have debts," he said to Frochot, "and I do not know their exact amount; nor do I know what is the state of my fortune; I have many obligations, however, that weigh on my conscience and are near to my heart." Frochot spoke to La Marck, who hastened to reassure Mirabeau: "Go and tell him that if his estate is not sufficient to meet his legacies, I will take over those which his friendship cares to recommend to mine; let us give him a moment's more peace."

On the evening of the next day, Friday, Mirabeau had given up all hope and had sent for the notary to make his will. He was concerned especially for the fate of his son, the child to whom he had not been able to give his name. From the ashes of his past there rose also the pale features of the one woman whom he had loved with serene love and who had given him a period of happiness. More burning passions were eclipsed before the terrible reality of his end; only the memory of Henriette de Nehra persisted, poignant and sweet, the memory of a precious gift which he had not been able to keep. He had seen her only once since their separation. A few weeks before his illness, on his way to the Assembly, driving in the blue vis-à-vis that had become celebrated, he passed her in the street. He recognized her and made a sign that seemed strange to Henriette, and in which there was a mixture of pleasure and embarrassment. But he did not stop. At this hour, however, of the tragic close of his life, she was present in his mind, alongside the child of another woman, the Coco she had loved.

"I give and bequeath to the son of the Sieur Lucas, sculptor, known by the name of the little Coco," Mirabeau dictated to the notary, "the sum of twenty-four thousand livres, to be invested in an annuity on his life and for his profit by the kindness of my friend La Marck. I give and bequeath to Mme. de Haren de Nehra the sum of twenty thousand livres, to be invested for her profit and on her life by M. de La Marck." He made his nephew Saillant his heir and residuary legatee, subject to legacies to each of his sisters. He bequeathed to La Marck all his papers, letters, and manuscripts relative to public affairs. He also bequeathed to him his silver plate and his ring-cases with all their contents. He bequeathed to his dear Cabanis "papers on legislation, literature, and politics," a box surmounted by his portrait, and such books as he should choose from his library. He bequeathed to the young physician Lachèze "a ring to the value of fifty louis or a similar sum in coin at his choice," and he recommended La Marck "to secure a position for this good fellow." To his secretary Comps he bequeathed the sum of twenty thousand francs, and to Pellenc "a diamond worth one hundred louis or a like sum in coin at his choice." He asked to be buried in his house, the Marais, and desired that the ashes of his father and his grandmother should be taken thither.

But there were those whom he forgot. In this will, wrote the Marquise de Mirabeau, "there is no mention either of the Bailli de Mirabeau, or of Gabriel's wife . . . or of his nephew, or of Mme. de Cabris, or of me." She wrote also that the dying man had given Mme. du Saillant "a bundle of assignats as big as I am," and, violent and pugnacious as ever, she threatened to bring an action against his heirs.

Actually, Mirabeau's assets, as estimated by Frochot (who had been appointed executor with La Marck) in the statement he presented to the Assembly, scarcely covered half of his debts. Mirabeau had remained to the last in ignorance of the state of his fortune. After the first liquidation by the notary, the privileged debts totalled one hundred and sixteen thousand francs, while the rest totalled well over two hundred thousand francs. The bulk of his estate was represented by the proceeds of the sale of his library, of which Mirabeau had so well estimated the value: thanks to the competition of buyers from all over the world, it realized one hundred and forty thousand francs. La Marck, faithful to his promise, executed the last will of his friend and provided for his legacies. Dumont later quashed the slanders that had been published abroad. "If," he asked, "Spain and England had bought him, what became of the sums he received? Why did he die insolvent?"

8

The sun poured into the bedroom that looked over the court. The sick man had had his bed pushed close to the open window. He watched the trees in the little garden, where the first buds were swelling. He seemed to look caressingly on them. "If the good God is not there," he said to Frochot, "it is at least his cousin."

He spoke with a distinct, strong voice that surprised his doctor. He had passed a sleepless night, only becoming drowsy from time to time. His pain had diminished, and he was breathing more easily, but his heart was failing. Cabanis found his pulse "almost entirely gone." He no longer had any hope. But, crushed by his responsibilities, and remembering his exaggerated optimism on this Friday morning, he insisted on a visit from Dr. Petit. The sick man agreed at last to be examined. Dr. Petit arrived during the morning. "For a long time," said Cabanis, "the pulse has been imperceptible." Mirabeau's arms and hands were ice-cold. But an astonishing muscular force still persisted in his moribund frame. "I am going to speak frankly to a man who is supposed to like that best," said Mirabeau to the physician who had been called in too late. "I have also felt that one should only have a friend as doctor. There is my friend and my doctor. He has my entire and exclusive affection." This faculty of passionate and enthusiastic friendship, which had characterized Mirabeau throughout his life, did not disappear in the presence of death. Dr. Petit, attracted by this extraordinary patient, replied that the friend, in the true acceptation of the word, was even more the one who loved than the one who was loved, and on this principle he deserved to be regarded also as his friend. After the examination, Mirabeau asked him to tell him the whole truth as to his condition. "I think we shall save you," said Dr. Petit, "but I cannot guarantee it." Alone with Cabanis in the next room, he said: "The patient's condition is hopeless."

In spite of what his reason told him, a ray of hope still lived in Mirabeau. He examined, as if he were dealing with another person, what his disappearance would mean for public affairs. He measured the loss his country would suffer. For a moment he drowsed; then he awoke with a start: he seemed to hear cannon. "Are these already," he exclaimed, "the obsequies of Achilles?"

Suddenly the crowd saw the Bishop of Autun enter the house. "A worthy confessor," said someone cynically.

"It is not easy to reach you," said Talleyrand. "Half Paris is permanently outside your door. I have been, like the other half, three times a day to ask after you, and greatly regretted being unable to get past the crowd." The dying man and his visitor talked together for two hours. Mirabeau had passionately loved Talleyrand and had violently hated him. He had admired his intelligence and measured better than anyone else the abyss of his cupidity and his moral insensibility. But he knew that no one else could take up the task he had wanted to accomplish in foreign policy, a task which he regarded as sacred. Nothing transpired as to this long interview without witnesses, but from some allusions those nearest Mirabeau gathered that he had recommended to Talleyrand the plan of a close alliance with England. Talleyrand said later that in 1792 he tried in London "to reconcile Mirabeau and Pitt and to form between liberal England and revolutionary France an alliance which would have held the balance of the world." On leaving the sickroom Talleyrand took with him the sheets of a speech which Mirabeau had been unable to deliver.

"They say that conversation is bad for the sick," remarked Mirabeau; "not this one; one could live deliciously surrounded by one's friends and even die like that very agreeably."

Talleyrand may have been moved in spite of himself by the long talk of the dying man, and impressed by his calm detachment. But he reacted as he always reacted to emotion, with a witty phrase. He said: "Mirabeau has been dramatizing his death."

9

"My friend, I shall die today," said Mirabeau to Cabanis. The night of April 1–2 had been a very bad one. Cabanis had watched over him. His chest was more and more affected. He was in pain and had waited impatiently for the dawn of this day which was to be his last. He called his valet, who had been very unwell the night before. "How are you today?" he asked. "Ah, Monsieur, I wish you were in my place." Mirabeau replied after a moment: "No, no, I should not like you to be in mine."

He asked to be shaved—he was getting ready, he told Cabanis, "to enter pleasantly into the sleep from which one wakes no more." Slowly he bade farewell to everything around him. What perhaps cost him most was detaching himself from everyday reality. He had something to say to each of the servants who had tended him with the devotion he had always inspired in the humble. Legrain's wife had watched over him day and night. She was pregnant and suffering. "You have to look after your family; off you go—I want you to." But she refused to leave him.

He sent also for his secretary Comps, who was greatly attached to him. The two had had a long conversation during the night. He had been giving Comps advice and recommendations for his career. He had shown him the deep and minute interest he took in his future. The young man realized that that was a final farewell. He went up to his room in deep distress. He, too, had watched over the sick man for some days; he had refused to eat, and he remained alone in his room, dreading the approach of Mirabeau's death. He could not imagine an existence without the great man who had been his whole world. His own life seemed vain and worthless in face of the terrible loss the country was suffering. He knew nothing then of sores that heal, of irreparable losses that are survived.

At dawn there was a knock at his door. He thought it was an announcement of death. He jumped up, and without opening the door he shouted, wild with grief: "Yes, yes, in life and in death." He seized a knife and slashed at himself. The blood rushed from his wounds and he fainted. Mirabeau knew nothing of the drama proceeding above his head; or of the care bestowed on the young man, who returned to consciousness a few hours later.

The dying man's hands were ice-cold as his doctor held them. He could no longer speak. He asked for pen and paper. He wrote very plainly: "Sleep." His pains returned with violence. He wrote further: "Can a man leave his friend to die on the wheel, perhaps through several days?"

More and more agonizing pains followed the calm that had preceded the death struggle. Cabanis had sent for a narcotic, but the pharmacy was at a distance. The tortures Mirabeau was suffering wrung cries from him. "I am being deceived," he groaned to La Marck. And, recovering his voice in an explosion of wrath, he turned to Cabanis: "Were you not my doctor and my friend? Did you not promise to spare me the pains of such a death? Do you want me to take away with me regret at having trusted you?" He turned convulsively and looked up at the clear morning sky. La Marck was supporting him. It was half-past eight, Saturday, April 2, 1791.

Dr. Petit, standing by the bed, said: "He suffers no more."

10

In their revolt against the destiny that had robbed them of their great defender, the people felt the urge to accuse their enemies of bringing it about. The rumour of poisoning gained currency. On the Sunday morning placards were put up on the Palais-Royal, on the boulevards, and here and there all over Paris, charging the Lameth brothers and Barnave with having caused Mirabeau's death.

The public prosecutor of the first *arrondissement* of the department of Paris ordered an autopsy. The corpse yielded at once one of the secrets of Mirabeau's life. "His passion for women," his son wrote later, "was to some extent involuntary, or rather, entirely physical; the congenital result of a species of satyriasis tormented him all his life and showed itself still some hours after his death—a strange fact, assuredly, but certain."

La Marck wrote to the greatest surgeon of his day, Vicq d'Azyr: "The popular suspicions have made it a necessity; in a way it is an interrogation of Death on the crime it has committed. I hope you will be present; even the corpse of that great man can be judged only by men worthy of him."

The autopsy revealed traces of inflammation in the stomach, part of the liver, the right kidney, and the pericardium, which contained also a considerable quantity of thick yellowish matter. The autopsy also revealed lymphatic coagulations covering the whole of the outer surface of the heart. But according to the official opinion of the surgeons no trace of poison was revealed.

Mirabeau's son, who devoted his life to the memory of his father, clung obstinately to the theory of crime and collected all the evidence that seemed to confirm it. He quoted several surgeons who had been present at the autopsy and who declared that they had recognized undoubted traces of poison. Young Saillant also declared that he heard the word "erosion" pronounced by two young surgeons. Their professor had at once silenced them: "He was not poisoned, he cannot have been, understand that, you imprudent fellows! Do you want the king, the queen, the Assembly, and all of us massacred?"

On the day of the opening of the body the doctor summoned by La Marck went to the queen. Mme. Campan, who was present during the conversation, wrote: "This doctor assured her that the record of the state of the intestines was equally compatible with a death produced by violent remedies or one produced by poison. He said also that the experts had made a true report; but that it was more prudent to conclude that death was from natural causes, since, in the state of crisis in France, a person innocent of such a crime might be the victim of public vengeance."

Marie Antoinette, who had been so contemptuous in her behaviour to Mirabeau during his life, was strangely distressed by his death. Her woman's instinct told her how much she had lost. Mercy-Argenteau, who was always better aware of the queen's interests than she herself, wrote to La Marck: "Everything is going against us. There is no fighting against such bad luck."

II

When the Assembly met on Saturday it did not yet know its great loss. Its old president, Tronchet, rose to speak. The Assembly suspected what he had to say; someone shouted: "Ah, he is dead!" The president confirmed it, briefly and with emotion. There were tears on many faces, and men sobbed. Barrère proposed that all the members of the Assembly should attend the funeral. The president suggested a deputation, but there were shouts from all sides: "We will all go! All of us!"

A right-wing member of the clergy asked that the Assembly print the speech on inheritance which Mirabeau had been unable to deliver. This was the speech he had handed to Talleyrand. There was deep silence when the Bishop of Autun went to the tribune and said, in the cold and distant voice that seemed to belie the pathos of his words: "I went yesterday to see M. de Mirabeau; there were many people in the house, and I went with an even greater measure of sadness than that of the public regret. That spectacle of desolation filled one with the picture of death; it was everywhere—save in the spirit of the one in the most imminent danger. M. de Mirabeau was then still a public man, and it was still in that light that we might regard, as precious fragments, his last words wrested from the immense prey which Death was on the point of seizing." He concluded: "The author of this document is no more; I bring you his last work; and such was the union of his feeling and his thought, both equally devoted to the public cause, that in listening you are almost present at his last breath."

The speech on equality of inheritance in the direct line was, in point of fact, the work of Reybaz. But the main idea was Mirabeau's; it was he who had given Reybaz precise directives and had fired him, as Reybaz himself said, with the fever that consumed him. The subject had been particularly near to Mirabeau's heart.

Sunday's session was devoted almost entirely to the memory of Mirabeau. A deputation from the sections of Paris was brought to the bar; it presented the request that Mirabeau should be buried in the Champ-de-Mars, the field of the Federation, beneath the altar of the fatherland. The department of Paris sent a deputation in mourning to ask the Assembly "(1) that the new church of Sainte-Geneviève should be destined to receive the ashes of great men, dating from the epoch of our freedom; (2) that the National Assembly alone can judge to what men this honor should be awarded; (3) that Honoré Riqueti de Mirabeau be adjudged worthy of it."

The Assembly applauded. Robespierre eloquently supported the proposal. It was the homage of the second revolution to the man who had done his utmost to bar its way. Robespierre may have felt that the disappearance of his great rival opened vast possibilities for himself. Malouet had said that there were only two men belonging to the left of the Assembly who were capable of following a personal policy regardless of opinion: Mirabeau and Robespierre. From this third of April Robespierre seems to have drawn a new confidence in himself and an increased vigour, reflected in the wider horizon and the more incisive style of his interventions. His career began with the death of Mirabeau.

The Assembly decreed that the church of Sainte-Geneviève (the Panthéon) should be "destined to receive the ashes of great men," and that "Honoré Riqueti-Mirabeau is adjudged worthy to receive that honour. Above the pediment shall be graven these words: 'To her great men, their grateful country.'"

12

The people of Paris saw to it that the mourning for their great man should be rigorously observed. They had insisted on the closing of several shows during his illness; and, after his death, they called for the prohibition of all private rejoicings. One of the many sheets that told the story of Mirabeau's interment said: "The monarchists who had had the effrontery to hold a festival at Ruggieri's on the day of Mirabeau's death were driven out in disgrace by the people." At Argenteuil there was a ball. "A group of aristocrats," said another sheet, "gave themselves up to joy and to dancing on learning the news of the death of Mirabeau. The local chaplain of the Carmelites led this orgy. But he was seized by offended citizens, who wanted to hang him. The mayor saved him and sent him to the district of Saint-Germain."

There was a very brilliant ball in the Champs Elysées. The people were revolted at this indecency, broke into the salons, expelled the men dancers, and forced the women to take off the flowers and feathers they were wearing on their heads. The imprudent people went away on foot, pursued by hooting and insults from a threatening crowd. Mirabeau's death was the first great loss the people had suffered since they had won their freedom. They were determined that their grief should be respected.

At the Jacobin Club on the Sunday evening, a member proposed that the whole club should go to the funeral and that all the members should go into mourning for a week and on every anniversary of Mirabeau's death.

An immense procession started from the house of death. A detachment of cavalry led, followed by a deputation of sappers and gunners of the sixty battalions of the National Guard and from among the conquerors of the Bastille. At their side marched a deputation from the Invalides, made up of the most badly maimed soldiers. At the head of the National Guard, Lafayette, on horseback and surrounded by his staff, led the mourning for his great rival. The Hundred Swiss and the guards of the Hôtel de Ville preceded the band of the National Guard. "It was the first time in France," wrote Mme. de Staël, "that a man celebrated by his writings and his eloquence received honours which in the past had been accorded only to *grands seigneurs* or to warriors."

The clergy preceded the body. Mirabeau's coffin was to have been taken in a hearse, but the battalion of La Grange-Batalière claimed the honour of bearing it. Sixteen "citizen soldiers" carried it in relays along the interminable route. The flag of their battalion flew above the coffin, decorated with a civic crown.

Mirabeau's heart was carried in a leaden box covered with flowers. The Assembly followed the coffin, almost to a man. The few who were missing were noted. On the left there was only one, Pétion, who had refused to be present. Several members of the right were absent, but Cazalès, more intelligent than his colleagues, showed sincere and profound grief.

Almost all of the ministers were present, almost the whole of the Jacobin Club, the electors and deputies of the forty-eight sections, the staffs of the department and municipality of Paris, the judges of the tribunals, and deputations from all the patriotic clubs.

The procession was completed by a considerable detachment of infantry and cavalry. It extended over more than three miles, moving through streets packed with onlookers. More impressive than the bands was the silence of the crowd in its grief.

Night fell, but the dense, silent crowd patiently followed the procession. Midnight struck as the church of Sainte-Geneviève was reached. Mirabeau's body was laid by the side of that of Descartes.

13

On the morrow of his death, Mirabeau passed into legend. His tormented life ended in the apotheosis of his obsequies. But he had not left enough money to pay the funeral expenses. On the motion of Frochot, the Assembly paid them. It was the first national funeral.

Mirabeau had died at a turn in the road. Desmoulins, with his journalist's flair, realized it: "One of the talents of M. Mirabeau was such a knowledge of the moral tactics of his time that he did nothing that was not right and reasonable; his very death seems a fresh proof of it. It might have been supposed that the moment of his decease was of his own choosing. He left the world at the moment when, perhaps, his glory had reached the summit of the pyramid."

14

On November 13, 1792, during the debates on the proceedings against the king, the Minister of the Interior, who had been carrying out repairs at the Tuileries, was informed that a workman had discovered an iron chest in a wall of the château. "The king," wrote Mme. Campan, "had a prodigious quantity of papers and had the idea of having a hiding-place made very secretly in an interior corridor of his suite of rooms by a locksmith who had worked for him for more than ten years. This hiding-place would long have remained unknown but for the denunciation. The wall was painted to represent big stones, and the opening was thoroughly hidden in the brown grooves that formed the shaded part of these painted stones."

When the iron chest was opened, it was found to be filled with letters and memoranda. The papers were at once transmitted to the Assembly, and a committee of twelve members was placed in charge of their examination. There was nothing in Mirabeau's writing among these documents, but there were indications that revealed his relations with the court. The Comité d'Instruction Publique was requested to investigate and report on the measures to be taken with regard to Mirabeau's memory. The Convention ordered that his bust should be veiled until the report was presented.

Consternation reigned among his admirers. Manuel, who had indiscreetly taken possession of the police dossier containing the correspondence between Mirabeau and Sophie while he was at Vincennes, and who had published it a few months earlier with a laudatory preface, was one of the first to express indignation.

On 5 Frimaire of the year II—November 27, 1793—Marie-Joseph Chénier, who had composed an ode to Mirabeau on his death, presented the committee's report. "Mirabeau had only the orator's eloquence, he neglected the principal element, integrity, and it is for that reason that, exhumed by you, leaving his triumphal tomb, he appears today at your bar and comes to submit to judgment, his brow divested of the laurels of the tribune and of the brilliant aureole that guaranteed him immortality in the French Panthéon." A decree was passed in conformity with his conclusions: "The National Convention, having heard the report from its Comité d'Instruction Publique, and considering that there can be no great man without virtue, decrees that the body of Honoré-Gabriel Riqueti-Mirabeau shall be withdrawn from the French Panthéon. On the day when Mirabeau's body is withdrawn from the French Panthéon that of Marat shall be transferred thither."

Several months passed without Mirabeau's remains being disturbed. The storms over France accorded him a brief respite. But the Jacobins became active again. They demanded the carrying out of the decree. Yielding to them on November 25, 1794, the usher of the Convention came to the entrance to the Panthéon and there read the decree. Thereupon Mirabeau's coffin was carried out, and on the same day on which, according to the official account, "the impure remains of the royalist Mirabeau were thrown out by the side door," the ashes of Marat were transported with great ceremony to the Panthéon.

For a time Mirabeau's coffin remained in store. His body lay in a leaden coffin which was encased in a wooden one. The commissioners of the Panthéon section of Paris were astonished to find that the wooden coffin was relatively new. On opening it they found a parchment that provided the explanation. In September 1791 three devoted friends of Mirabeau, Vitry, "who loved that great man like a brother," his young secretary Comps, and Jean-Hippolyte Dudouit La Villette, who had the honour at his funeral of carrying the leaden vase that contained his heart, had made a pilgrimage to his tomb. They had found the coffin damaged, and, with the consent of La Marck, had ordered a new one to be made.

The commissioners charged with the mission of vengeance in the name of republican virtue transported Mirabeau's remains to the cemetery of Sainte-Catherine. They opened the outer coffin, broke the lead coffin, and threw what was left of the remains of a great man into a corner of the cemetery, carefully taking the lead coffin back into store.

The storms that had shaken Mirabeau's life had taken possession of his death. His great tormented body had been hurled from the pinnacle of glory into an abyss of execration. Nobody spoke up to defend his honour. Nobody attempted to recover his mortal remains from a remote corner of the cemetery.

All the convulsions which Mirabeau had foreseen overwhelmed the country. The king and the queen perished on the scaffold, whose shadow he had raised before their incredulous eyes. The Terror spilt rivers of blood. Many of his friends, many, too, of his enemies, knew the horror of the tumbrils. Other friends of his were dispersed to the farthest corners of the world, caught in the whirlwind that swept them into the arduous paths of exile.

The most faithful of his friends, La Marck, who resumed the name of Prinz von Arenberg, was charged by the emperor with the task of inducing Spain to show more activity in the war against France. Mirabeau's family, too, was destroyed or dispersed. His mother died in that same year, 1794, and so did his uncle the bailli. Caroline du Saillant was in prison with several members of her family. When she emerged after the Terror, her one concern was to collect the crumbs of her fortune and to borrow money to enable her numerous family to live.

One woman alone constituted herself the heir and guardian of a great tarnished glory. From the beginning of the Revolution the Comtesse de Mirabeau had taken refuge at Nice with her father, who was the representative there of the Comte d'Artois and the irreconcilable royalists. Summoned to return to France in the spring of 1792 on pain of death and confiscation of her property, she furnished a certificate that she was ill and "unable to leave her bed." This declaration covered the drama of a passion. In spite of her experiences, Emilie still had the sensuality and the imprudence of her youth. She was now pregnant; the father of her child was a lieutenant in a regiment in Nice, a member of a Sardinian family that had recently been ennobled—Focardi della Roccasparviera.

The Marquis de Marignane had changed no more than his daughter; he had kept his prejudices of rank and the obstinacy of his weak nature. He objected to this marriage with a count of such recent creation, swearing that he would rather see his daughter bear a bastard. But when Emilie brought a son into the world, he agreed to the marriage, which was celebrated on the eve of the war between France and Sardinia. Before long the Marquis de Marignane found himself obliged to accept a refuge and maintenance in the home of the Roccasparviera family which this despised son-in-law offered him.

When the Terror had passed, the Contessa della Rocca, wife of a Sardinian officer, was able in her quality of foreigner to claim the confiscated estates of the Marquis and Marquise de Marignane. In her new good fortune, she did not forget her former family. She wrote to Caroline: "I have married a very worthy and very excellent fellow, who covered himself with glory in this war. He made my father happy and we have owed him our existence during the three years, very nearly, that we have been united. I have a son on whom I am beginning to count, although that age is fragile, as I have learnt only too well at my expense. But this boy is very strong and seems to have an excellent constitution."

She generously helped Caroline from her recovered fortune and lent her considerable sums. But misfortune came again to her. The Conte della Rocca, who had returned seriously wounded from five years of war, died at the beginning of 1798 from the effects of a fall from a cab. "In the person of my second husband," wrote Emilie to Caroline, "I have lost happiness and the support of my existence, and of my father's."

This romantic interval in her life came to an end as completely as if it had never existed. Her grief seems to have opened the sources in her of a feminine sensitiveness of which she had herself been unaware. But it was not concerned with grief over the recently deceased. The widow installed herself in Paris. She had broken off all her relations with Provence and with Italy. She had left the father whose weakness had thrown such chains round her.

This woman who now lived only for her past resumed the name of Comtesse de Mirabeau. She joined her former sister-in-law, Mme. du Saillant. She chose as her home for the remainder of her days the former house of the Marquis de Mirabeau. In that house she chose the room that had been intended for the Comte de Mirabeau but had rarely been used by him. She owed everything to her second husband, happiness, shelter during the Terror, and even her present financial security. Of her first husband nothing remained but an abandoned memory, the reputation for venality, and the memory of an equivocal role and a gigantic fraud. There remained of him also the Vincennes correspondence that exalted his passionate love for another woman and placed herself on record in the odious part of a frigid wife, a frivolous and perfidious woman, and even an indifferent mother. But Emilie de Marignane, who had never loved Gabriel de Mirabeau in his lifetime, now devoted all her faculties for loving to the flouted shade of the dead.

She devoted herself to it to the exclusion of every other feeling. She even separated from her son, who, repudiated by his family, lived in the south of France under the indifferent guardianship of strangers. But she concerned herself with a boy of whom Caroline had taken charge. To this child of Mirabeau and another woman she devoted herself with maternal passion. It was to him and not to her own son, who died young in poverty and oblivion, that she bequeathed her fortune.

She occupied herself especially with the memory of the great departed. She had scarcely installed herself in Caroline's house when she urged her to take steps to exhume Mirabeau's remains and to obtain the return of the lead coffin. Her persistency gained her the consent of the Directory. But Mirabeau's remains could no longer be found. Emilie then devoted herself energetically to saving the shreds of his glory. It was she who made a cult of it with his young son, and it was in memory of her passionate interest that he devoted his life to his father's rehabilitation. "We saw her always occupied," he wrote, "with her Mirabeau. She never ceased to surround herself with his letters, his portraits, and his favourite songs, which she sang with a voice and an art still admirable."

A woman's posthumous love watched over his survival, a woman's belated loyalty perpetuated the pain of his death. Emilie de Mirabeau died, according to this son whom she had adopted, "in the room and in the very bed of Mirabeau, whose memory inspired her every day with more passionate regrets."

BIBLIOGRAPHY

Argenson, Marquis d'. *Mémoires*. Baudouin frères: Paris, 1825.

Arnaud, Raoul. *La vie turbulente de Camille Desmoulins*. Plon: Paris, 1928.

Arnaud-Bouteloup, Jeanne. *Le rôle politique de Marie-Antoinette*. Thèse pour le doctorat ès lettres. Orléans, 1924.

——. *Marie-Antoinette et l'art de son temps*. Imprimerie alsacienne: Strasbourg, 1924.

Aulard, F. A. *L'Eloquence parlementaire pendant la Révolution française*. Paris: 1882–86. 3 vols.

Barker, Sir Ernest. *Edmund Burke et la Révolution française*. Alcan, Les Presses Universitaires de France: Paris, 1940.

Barthou, Louis. *Mirabeau*. Heinemann: London, 1913.

Besenval, Baron Pierre-Victor de. *Mémoires*. Baudouin frères: Paris, 1821.

Blum, André. *La caricature révolutionnaire, 1789–1795*. Jouve: Paris, 1914.

Bradby, E. D. *The Life of Barnave*. Clarendon Press: Oxford, 1915. 2 vols.

Brissot [de Warville], Jacques Pierre. *Mémoires publiés avec étude critique et notes, par Cl. Perroud*. A. Picard et fils: Paris, 1912?. 2 vols.

Britsch, Amédée. "Philippe-Egalité avant la Révolution," *Revue des études historiques*, Paris, 1904.

Brougham, Lord Henry. *Historical Sketches of Statesmen who flourished in the time of George III, to which are added Remarks on the French Revolution*. Baudry's European Library: Paris, 1844.

Campan, Mme. *Mémoires sur la vie de Marie-Antoinette*. Firmin Didot frères: Paris, 1849.

Caste, Louis. *Mirabeau Lardanchet*. Lyon, 1942.

Chamfort, Sébastien Roch Nicolas. *Œuvres*. Chez le directeur de l'Imprimerie des Sciences ét Arts: rue Thérèse, Paris, L'an III de la République française.

——. *Œuvres. Précédées d'une étude sur sa vie et son esprit, par Arsène Houssaye*. V. Lecou: Paris, 1852.

Chapuisat, Edouard. *Necker*. Institut International d'Histoire de la Révolution française: Paris, 1938.

Cottin, Paul. *Mirabeau et Sophie de Monnier d'après leur correspondance inédite*. Plon: Paris, 1903.

Courrier de Provence, 1789, 1790, 1791.

Dard, Emile. *Le général Choderlos de Laclos*. Perrin: Paris, 1936.

———. *Le comte de Narbonne*. Plon: Paris, 1943.

Dumont, Etienne. *Souvenirs sur Mirabeau*. Paris, 1832.

Esmein, Adhémar. *Gouverneur Morris*. Hachette: Paris, 1906.

Faÿ, Bernard. *Benjamin Franklin*. Calmann-Lévy: Paris, 1929–31.

Focillon, Henri. *L'art et la Révolution*. Alcan, Les Presses Universitaires de France: Paris, 1940.

Funck-Brentano, Frantz. *L'affaire du collier*. Hachette: Paris, 1901.

Guillois, Antoine. *La marquise de Condorcet*. Ollendorf: Paris, 1897.

Guital, Georges. *Mirabeau et la Provence en 1789*. Paris and Aix, 1887.

Jaurès, Jean. *Histoire socialiste de la Révolution française*. Librairie de l'Humanité: Paris, 1922–24. 8 vols.

Jouvenel, Henri de. *La vie orageuse de Mirabeau*. Plon: Paris, 1928.

Kayser, Jacques. *La vie de La Fayette*. Gallimard: Paris, 1928.

Lacour-Gayet, George. *Talleyrand*. Payot: Paris, 1928–34. 4 vols.

Laprade, William Thomas. *England and the French Revolution, 1789–1797*. Johns Hopkins Press: Baltimore, 1909.

Le Forestier, R. *Les Illuminés de Bavière et la Franc-Maçonnerie allemande*. Hachette: Paris, 1914.

Loménie, Charles de. *Les Mirabeau*. E. Dentu: Paris, 1889–91. Vols. III, IV, and V.

Loménie, Louis Léonard de. *Les Mirabeau*. E. Dentu: Paris, 1879. Vols. I and II.

———. *Esquisses historiques et littéraires*. Calmann-Lévy: Paris, 1879.

———. *Beaumarchais et son temps*. Michel Levy frères: Paris, 1856.

———. *La comtesse de Rochefort et ses amis*. Michel Lévy frères: Paris, 1870.

Madelin, Louis. *Danton*. Hachette: Paris, 1914.

Marceau, A. *L'Allemagne et la Révolution française*. Editions Thaelmann: Paris, 1939.

Martin, Gaston. *La Franc-maçonnerie française et la préparation de la Révolution*. Les Presses Universitaires de France: Paris, 1926.

Mathiez, Albert. *Les grandes journées de la Constituante*. Hachette: Paris, 1913.

Maugras, Gaston. *Le duc de Lauzun et la cour de Marie-Antoinette*. Plon-Nourrit: Paris, 1907.

Mazé, Jules. *Louis XVI et Marie-Antoinette. Les journées révolutionnaires d'octobre 1789*. Hachette: Paris, 1939.

Meunier, Dauphin: *La comtesse de Mirabeau*. Perrin: Paris, 1908.

———. *Louise de Mirabeau, marquise de Cabris*. Emile-Paul frères: Paris, 1914.

Mirabeau, Honoré Gabriel Riqueti de. *Conseils à un jeune prince et lettre remise à Frédéric-Guillaume II, roi regnant de Prusse, le jour de son avenement au trône.* 1788.

———. *Correspondance entre le comte de Mirabeau et le comte de La Marck*, ed. by A. de Bacourt. V. Le Normant: Paris, 1851. 3 vols.

———. *Histoire secrète de la cour de Berlin, ouvrage posthume.* 1789.

———. *Lettres a Yet-Lie, avec une introduction et des notes de Dauphin Meunier.* Editions Montaigne: Paris, 1929.

———. *Lettres de Mirabeau à Chamfort.* Chez le directeur de la Décade philosophique, Paris, L'an V de la République française.

———. *Lettres inédites, mémoires, et entraits de mémoires écrits en 1781–1783.* Publiées par J. F. Vitry: Paris, 1806.

———. *Lettres originales de Mirabeau écrites du donjon de Vincennes, 1777–1780.* Recueillies par P. Manuel. J. B. Garnery: Paris, 1792. 4 vols.

———. *Mémoires biographiques, littéraires, et politiques écrits par lui-meme, par son père, son oncle, et son fils adoptif.* Delaunay: Paris, 1835.

———. *Travaux du comte de Mirabeau à la Constituante.* Paris, 1791. 6 vols.

Montlosier, Comte de. *Mémoires sur la Révolution française.* Paris, 1830. 2 vols.

Morley, John. *Edmund Burke.* Macmillan: London, 1867.

Mornet, Daniel. *Les origines intellectuelles de la Révolution française.* Armand Colin: Paris, 1933.

Neton, Albéric. *Sieyès.* Perrin: Paris, 1900.

Pingaud, Léonce. *Un agent secret sous la Révolution et l'Empire. Le comte d'Antraigues.* Plon: Paris, 1893.

Pons, Jean. *La Révolution française et l'avenement de la bourgeoisie.* Paris: 1938.

Ray, Jean. *La Révolution française et la pensée juridique: l'idée du règne de la loi.* Alcan, Les Presses Universitaires de France: Paris, 1940.

Reiset, Comte Gustave Armand Henri de (ed.). *Modes et usages au temps de Marie-Antoinette. Livre-journal de Madame Eloffe.* Firmin Didot: Paris, 1885.

Renouvin, Pierre. *L'Assemblée des Notables de 1787.* Paris, 1920.

Rivarol, Antoine. *Mémoires.* Paris, 1824.

Robiquet, Paul. *Théveneau de Morande.* Paris, 1882.

Rocquain, Félix. *L'esprit révolutionnaire avant la Révolution.* Plon: Paris, 1878.

Rousse, Edmond. *Mirabeau.* Hachette: Paris, 1891.

Schapiro, J. S. *Condorcet and the Rise of Liberation in France.* Harcourt, Brace: New York, 1934.

532 BIBLIOGRAPHY

Söderhjelm, Alma. *Fersen et Marie-Antoinette.* Editions Kra: Paris, 1930.

Sorel, Albert. *L'Europe et la Révolution française.* Plon-Nourrit: Paris, 1903.

———. "Les Mirabeau," in *Essais d'histoire et de critique.* Plon-Nourrit: Paris, 1913.

Staël-Holstein, Mme. de. *De l'Allemagne et des mœurs des Allemands.* Firmin Didot: Paris, 1856.

———. *Du caractère de M. Necker et de sa vie privée. Considérations sur les principaux événements de la Révolution française.* Firmin Didot: Paris, 1861.

Stern, Alfred. *La vie de Mirabeau.* Traduit de l'allemand. Emile Bouillon: Paris, 1896.

Stoker, John T. *William Pitt et la Révolution française.* Librairie de Recueil Sirey: Paris, 1935.

Szyster, Boruch. *La Révolution française et les Juifs.* Thèse pour le doctorat. Toulouse: 1929.

Thompson, J. M. *Robespierre.* Basil Blackwell: Oxford, 1935. 2 vols.

Van Doren, Carl. *Benjamin Franklin.* Viking Press: New York, 1938.

Van Leisen, Herbert. *Mirabeau et la Révolution royale.* B. Grasset: Paris, 1926.

Welschinger, Henri. *La mission secrète de Mirabeau à Berlin.* Plon: Paris, 1900.

Witte, Cornelis de. *La société française et la société anglaise au XVIIIe s.* Michel Lévy frères: Paris, 1864.

Index